Human–Computer Interaction

PEARSON
Education

We work with leading authors to develop the
strongest educational materials in computing,
bringing cutting-edge thinking and best learning
practice to a global market.

Under a range of well-known imprints, including
Prentice Hall, we craft high quality print and
electronic publications which help readers to
understand and apply their content, whether
studying or at work.

To find out more about the complete range of our
publishing, please visit us on the world wide web at:
www.pearsoned.co.uk

HUMAN–COMPUTER INTERACTION

Third Edition

Alan Dix, *Lancaster University*

Janet Finlay, *Leeds Metropolitan University*

Gregory D. Abowd, *Georgia Institute of Technology*

Russell Beale, *University of Birmingham*

Harlow, England • London • New York • Boston • San Francisco • Toronto • Sydney • Singapore • Hong Kong
Tokyo • Seoul • Taipei • New Delhi • Cape Town • Madrid • Mexico City • Amsterdam • Munich • Paris • Milan

Pearson Education Limited
Edinburgh Gate
Harlow
Essex CM20 2JE
England

and Associated Companies throughout the world

Visit us on the world wide web at:
www.pearsoned.co.uk

First published 1993
Second edition published 1998
Third edition published 2004

ISBN: 978-0-13-046109-4

British Library Cataloguing-in-Publication Data
A catalogue record for this book is available from the British Library

10   9   8
11

Typeset in 10/12^{1}/2pt Minion by 35
Printed and bound by Rotolito Lombarda, S.p.A., Milan, Italy

BRIEF CONTENTS

CONTENTS

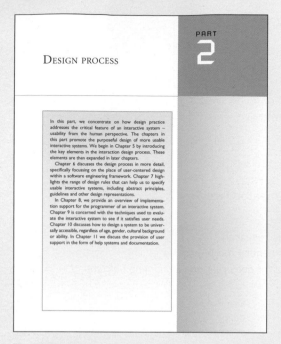

The part structure separates out introductory and more advanced material, with each part opener giving a simple description of what its constituent chapters cover

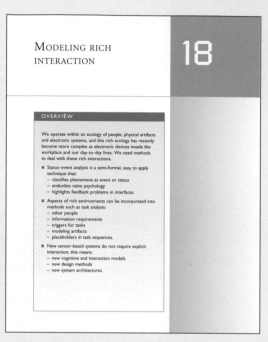

Bullet points at the start of each chapter highlight the core coverage

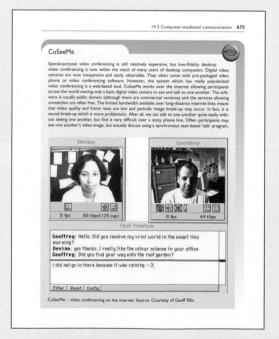

Boxed asides contain descriptions of particular tasks or technologies for additional interest, experimentation and discussion

Worked exercises within chapters provide step-by-step guidelines to demonstrate problem-solving techniques

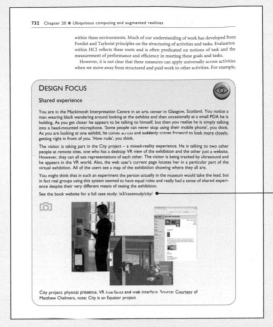

Frequent links to the book website for further information

Design Focus mini case studies highlight practical applications of HCI concepts

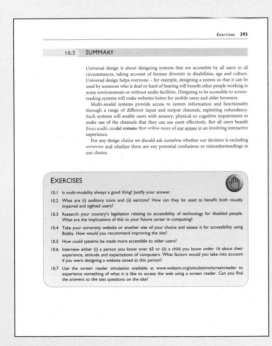

Chapter summaries reinforce student learning. Exercises at the end of chapters can be used by teachers or individuals to test understanding

Annotated further reading encourages readers to research topics in depth

FOREWORD

Human–computer interaction is a difficult endeavor with glorious rewards. Designing interactive computer systems to be effective, efficient, easy, and enjoyable to use is important, so that people and society may realize the benefits of computation-based devices. The subtle weave of constraints and their trade-offs – human, machine, algorithmic, task, social, aesthetic, and economic – generates the difficulty. The reward is the creation of digital libraries where scholars can find and turn the pages of virtual medieval manuscripts thousands of miles away; medical instruments that allow a surgical team to conceptualize, locate, and monitor a complex neuro-surgical operation; virtual worlds for entertainment and social interaction, responsive and efficient government services, from online license renewal to the analysis of parliamentary testimony; or smart telephones that know where they are and under-stand limited speech. Interaction designers create interaction in virtual worlds and embed interaction in physical worlds.

Human–computer interaction is a specialty in many fields, and is therefore multi-disciplinary, but it has an intrinsic relationship as a subfield to computer science. Most interactive computing systems are for some human purpose and interact with humans in human contexts. The notion that computer science is the study of algo-rithms has virtue as an attempt to bring foundational rigor, but can lead to ignoring constraints foundational to the design of successful interactive computer systems. A lesson repeatedly learned in engineering is that a major source of failure is the narrow optimization of a design that does not take sufficient account of contextual factors. Human users and their contexts are major components of the design problem that cannot be wished away simply because they are complex to address. In fact, that largest part of program code in most interactive systems deals with user interaction. Inadequate attention to users and task context not only leads to bad user interfaces, it puts entire systems at risk.

The problem is how to take into account the human and contextual part of a sys-tem with anything like the rigor with which other parts of the system are understood and designed – how to go beyond fuzzy platitudes like 'know the user' that are true, but do not give a method for doing or a test for having done. This is difficult to do, but inescapable, and, in fact, capable of progress. Over the years, the need to take into account human aspects of technical systems has led to the creation of new fields of study: applied psychology, industrial engineering, ergonomics, human factors, man–machine systems. Human–computer interaction is the latest of these, more complex in some ways because of the breadth of user populations and applications, the reach into cognitive and social constraints, and the emphasis on interaction. The experiences with other human-technical disciplines lead to a set of conclusions about how a discipline of human–computer interaction should be organized if it is to be successful.

First, design is where the action is. An effective discipline of human–computer interaction cannot be based largely on 'usability analysis', important though that may be. Usability analysis happens too late; there are too few degrees of freedom; and most importantly, it is not generative. Design thrives on understanding constraints, on insight into the design space, and on deep knowledge of the materials of the design, that is, the user, the task, and the machine. The classic landmark designs in human–computer interaction, such as the Xerox Star and the Apple Lisa/Macintosh, were not created from usability analysis (although usability analysis had important roles), but by generative principles for their designs by user interface designers who had control of the design and implementation.

Second, although the notion of 'user-centered design' gets much press, we should really be emphasizing 'task-centered design'. Understanding the purpose and context of a system is key to allocating functions between people and machines and to designing their interaction. It is only in deciding what a human–machine system should do and the constraints on this goal that the human and technical issues can be resolved. The need for task-centered design brings forward the need for methods of task analysis as a central part of system design.

Third, human–computer interaction needs to be structured to include both analytic and implementation methods together in the same discipline and taught together as part of the core. Practitioners of the discipline who can only evaluate, but not design and build are under a handicap. Builders who cannot reason analytically about the systems they build or who do not understand the human information processing or social contexts of their designs are under a handicap. Of course, there will be specialists in one or another part of human–computer interaction, but for there to be a successful field, there must be a common core.

Finally, what makes a discipline is a set of methods for doing something. A field must have results that can be taught and used by people other than their originators to do something. Historically, a field naturally evolves from a set of point results to a set of techniques to a set of facts, general abstractions, methods, and theories. In fact, for a field to be cumulative, there must be compaction of knowledge by crunching the results down into methods and theories; otherwise the field becomes fad-driven and a collection of an almost unteachably large set of weak results. The most useful methods and theories are generative theories: from some task analysis it is possible to compute some insightful property that constrains the design space of a system. In a formula: task analysis, approximation, and calculation. For example, we can predict that if a graphics system cannot update the display faster than 10 times/second then the illusion of animation will begin to break down. This constraint worked backwards has architectural implications for how to guarantee the needed display rate under variable computational load. It can be designed against.

This textbook, by Alan Dix, Janet Finlay, Gregory Abowd, and Russell Beale, represents how far human–computer interaction has come in developing and organizing technical results for the design and understanding of interactive systems. Remarkably, by the light of their text, it is pretty far, satisfying all the just-enumerated conclusions. This book makes an argument that by now there are many teachable results in human–computer interaction by weight alone! It makes an argument that these results form a cumulative discipline by its structure, with sections that organize the results systematically, characterizing human, machine, interaction, and the design process. There are analytic models, but also code implementation examples. It is no surprise that methods of task analysis play a prominent role in the text as do theories to help in the design of the interaction. Usability evaluation methods are integrated in their proper niche within the larger framework.

In short, the codification of the field of human–computer interaction in this text is now starting to look like other subfields of computer science. Students by studying the text can learn how to understand and build interactive systems. Human–computer interaction as represented by the text fits together with other parts of computer science. Moreover, human–computer interaction as presented is a challenge problem for advancing theory in cognitive science, design, business, or social-technical systems. Given where the field was just a few short years ago, the creation of this text is a monumental achievement. The way is open to reap the glorious rewards of interactive systems through a markedly less difficult endeavor, both for designer and for user.

Stuart K. Card
Palo Alto Research Center, Palo Alto, California

Preface to the third edition

It is ten years since the first edition of this book was published and much has changed. Ubiquitous computing and rich sensor-filled environments are finding their way out of the laboratory, not just into films and fiction, but also into our workplaces and homes. Now the computer really has broken its bounds of plastic and glass: we live in networked societies where personal computing devices from mobile phones to smart cards fill our pockets, and electronic devices surround us at home and at work. The web too has grown from a largely academic network into the hub of business and everyday lives. As the distinctions between physical and digital, work and leisure start to break down, human–computer interaction is also radically changing.

We have tried to capture some of the excitement of these changes in this revised edition, including issues of physical devices in Chapters 2 and 3, discussion of web interfaces in Chapter 21, ubiquitous computing in Chapters 4 and 20, and new models and paradigms for interaction in these new environments in Chapters 17 and 18. We have reflected aspects of the shift in use of technology from work to leisure in the analysis of user experience in Chapter 3, and in several of the boxed examples and case studies in the text. This new edition of *Human–Computer Interaction* is not just tracking these changes but looking ahead at emerging areas.

However, it is also rooted in strong principles and models that are not dependent on the passing technologies of the day. We are excited both by the challenges of the new and by the established foundations, as it is these foundations that will be the means by which today's students understand tomorrow's technology. So we make no apology for continuing the focus of previous editions on the theoretical and conceptual models that underpin our discipline. As the use of technology has changed, these models have expanded. In particular, the insular individual focus of early work is increasingly giving way to include the social and physical context. This is reflected in the expanded treatment of social and organizational analysis, including ethnography, in Chapter 13, and the analysis of artifacts in the physical environment in Chapter 18.

STRUCTURE

The structure of the new edition has been completely revised. This in part reflects the growth of the area: ten years ago HCI was as often as not a minority optional subject, and the original edition was written to capture the core material for a standard course. Today HCI is much expanded: some areas (like CSCW) are fully fledged disciplines in their own right, and HCI is studied from a range of perspectives and at different levels of detail. We have therefore separated basic material suitable for introductory courses into the first two parts, including a new chapter on interaction design, which adds new material on scenarios and navigation design and provides an overview suitable for a first course. In addition, we have included a new chapter on universal design, to reflect the growing emphasis on design that is inclusive of all, regardless of ability, age or cultural background. More advanced material focussing on different HCI models and theories is presented in Part 3, with extended coverage of social and contextual models and rich interaction. It is intended that these sections will be suitable for more advanced HCI courses at undergraduate and postgraduate level, as well as for researchers new to the field. Detailed coverage of the particular domains of web applications, ubiquitous computing and CSCW is given in Part 4.

  New to this edition is a full color plate section. Images flagged with a camera icon in the text can be found in color in the plate section.

WEBSITE AND SUPPORT MATERIALS

We have always believed that support materials are an essential part of a textbook of this kind. These are designed to supplement and enhance the printed book – physical and digital integration in practice. Since the first edition we have had exercises, mini-case studies and presentation slides for all chapters available electronically. For the second edition these were incorporated into a website including links and an online search facility that acts as an exhaustive index to the book and mini-encyclopedia of HCI. For visually disabled readers, access to a full online electronic text has also been available. The website is continuing to develop, and for the third edition provides all these features plus more, including WAP search, multi-choice questions, and extended case study material (see also color plate section). We will use the book website to bring you new exercises, information and other things, so do visit us at www.hcibook.com (also available via www.booksites.net/dix). Throughout the book you will find shorthand web references of the form /e3/a-page-url/. Just prepend http://www.hcibook.com to find further information. To assist users of the second edition, a mapping between the structures of the old and new editions is available on the web at: http://www.hcibook.com/e3/contents/map2e/

STYLISTIC CONVENTION

As with all books, we have had to make some global decisions regarding style and terminology. Specifically, in a book in which the central characters are 'the user' and 'the designer', it is difficult to avoid the singular pronoun. We therefore use the pronoun 'he' when discussing the user and 'she' when referring to the designer. In other cases we use 'she' as a generic term. This should not be taken to imply anything about the composition of any actual population.

Similarly, we have adopted the convention of referring to the field of 'Human–Computer Interaction' and the notion of 'human–computer interaction'. In many cases we will also use the abbreviation HCI.

ACKNOWLEDGEMENTS

In a book of this size, written by multiple authors, there will always be myriad people behind the scenes who have aided, supported and abetted our efforts. We would like to thank all those who provided information, pictures and software that have enhanced the quality of the final product. In particular, we are indebted to Wendy Mackay for the photograph of EVA; Wendy Hall and her colleagues at the University of Southampton for the screen shot of Microcosm; Saul Greenberg for the reactive keyboard; Alistair Edwards for Soundtrack; Christina Engelbart for the photographs of the early chord keyset and mouse; Geoff Ellis for the screen shot of Devina and himself using CuSeeMe; Steve Benford for images of the Internet Foyer; and Tony Renshaw who provided photographs of the eye tracking equipment. Thanks too to Simon Shum for information on design rationale, Robert Ward who gave us material on psycho-physiology, and Elizabeth Mynatt and Tom Rodden who worked with Gregory on material adapted in Chapter 20. Several of the boxed case studies are based on the work of multi-institution projects, and we are grateful to all those from the project teams of CASCO, thePooch SMART-ITS, TOWER, AVATAR-Conference and TEAM-HOS for boxes and case studies based on their work; and also to the EQUATOR project from which we drew material for the boxes on cultural probes, 'Ambient Wood' and 'City'. We would also like to thank all the reviewers and survey respondents whose feedback helped us to select our subject matter and improve our coverage; and our colleagues at our respective institutions and beyond who offered insight, encouragement and tolerance throughout the revision. We are indebted to all those who have contributed to the production process at Pearson Education and elsewhere, especially Keith Mansfield, Anita Atkinson, Lynette Miller, Sheila Chatten and Robert Chaundy.

Personal thanks must go to Fiona, Esther, Miriam, Rachel, Tina, Meghan, Aidan and Blaise, who have all endured 'The Book' well beyond the call of duty and over many years, and Bruno and 'the girls' who continue to make their own inimitable contribution.

Finally we all owe huge thanks to Fiona for her continued deep personal support and for tireless proofreading, checking of figures, and keeping us all moving. We would never have got beyond the first edition without her.

The efforts of all of these have meant that the book is better than it would otherwise have been. Where it could still be better, we take full responsibility.

Publisher's acknowledgements

We are grateful to the following for permission to reproduce copyright material:

Figure p. 2, Figures 3.14, 3.15, 3.16 and 5.13 and Exercise 8.4 screen shots reprinted by permission from Apple Computer, Inc.; Figure 2.11 reprinted by permission of Keith Cheverst; Figure 3.13 from The WebBook and Web Forager: An information workspace for the world-wide web in *CHI Conference Proceedings*, © 1996 ACM, Inc., reprinted by permission (Card, S. K., Robertson, G. G. and York, W. 1996); Figures 3.9, 3.19, 5.5, Chapter 14, Design Focus: Looking real – Avatar Conference screen shots, Figures 21.3, 21.10, 21.11 screen shot frames reprinted by permission from Microsoft Corporation; Tables 6.2 and 6.3 adapted from Usability engineering: our experience and evolution in *Handbook for Human–Computer Interaction* edited by M. Helander, Copyright 1988, with permission from Elsevier (Whiteside, J., Bennett, J. and Hotzblatt, K. 1988); Figure 7.1 adapted from The alternate reality kit – an animated environment for creating interactive simulations in *Proceedings of Workshop on Visual Languages*, © 1986 IEEE, reprinted by permission of IEEE (Smith, R. B. 1986); Figure 7.2 from Guidelines for designing user interface software in *MITRE Corporation Report MTR-9420*, reprinted by permission of The MITRE Corporation (Smith, S. L. and Mosier, J. N. 1986); Figure 7.3 reprinted by permission of Jenifer Tidwell; Figures 8.6 and 8.9 from *Xview Programming Manual*, Volume 7 of *The X Window System*, reprinted by permission of O'Reilly and Associates, Inc. (Heller, D. 1990); Figure 9.8 screen shot reprinted by permission of Dr. R. D. Ward; Figure 10.2 after Earcons and icons: their structure and common design principles in *Human-Computer Interaction*, 4(1), published and reprinted by permission of Lawrence Erlbaum Associates, Inc. (Blattner, M., Sumikawa, D. and Greenberg, R. 1989); Figure 10.5 reprinted by permission of Alistair D. N. Edwards; Figure 10.7 reprinted by permission of Saul Greenberg; Figure 11.2 screen shot reprinted by permission of Macromedia, Inc.; Table 12.1 adapted from *The Psychology of Human Computer Interaction*, published and reprinted by permission of Lawrence Erlbaum Associates, Inc. (Card, S. K., Moran, T. P. and Newell, A. 1983); Table 12.2 after Table in A comparison of input devices in elemental pointing and dragging tasks in *Reaching through technology – CHI'91 Conference Proceedings, Human Factors in Computing Systems*, April, edited by S. P. Robertson, G. M. Olson and J. S. Olson, © 1991 ACM, Inc., reprinted by permission (Mackenzie,

I. S., Sellen, A. and Buxton, W. 1991); Figure 14.1 from *Understanding Computers and Cognition: A New Foundation for Design*, published by Addison-Wesley, reprinted by permission of Pearson Education, Inc. (Winograd, T. and Flores, F. 1986); Figure 14.5 from *Theories of multi-party interaction. Technical report*, Social and Computer Sciences Research Group, University of Surrey and Queen Mary and Westfield Colleges, University of London, reprinted by permission of Nigel Gilbert (Hewitt, B., Gilbert, N., Jirotka, M. and Wilbur, S. 1990); Figure 14.6 from *Dialogue processes in computer-mediated communication: a study of letters in the com system. Technical report*, Linköping Studies in Arts and Sciences, reprinted by permission of Kerstin Severinson Eklundh (Eklundh, K. S. 1986); Chapter 14, Design Focus: Looking real – Avatar Conference, screen shots reprinted by permission of AVATAR-Conference project team; Figure 16.17 screen shot reprinted by permission of Harold Thimbleby; Figure 17.5 based on Verifying the behaviour of virtual world objects in *DSV-IS 2000 Interactive Systems: Design, Specification and Verification*. LNCS 1946, edited by P. Palanque and F. Paternò, published and reprinted by permission of Spinger-Verlag GmbH & Co. KG (Willans, J. S. and Harrison, M. D. 2001); Figure 18.4 icons reprinted by permission of Fabio Paternò; Chapter 19, p.675 CuSeeMe screen shot reprinted by permission of Geoff Ellis; Chapter 19, Design Focus: TOWER – workspace awareness, screen shots reprinted by permission of Wolfgang Prinz; Figure 20.1 reprinted by permission of Mitsubishi Electric Research Laboratories, Inc.; Figure 20.4 (right) reprinted by permission of Sony Computer Science Laboratories, Inc; Figure 20.9 from Cone trees. Animated 3d visualisation of hierarchical information in *Proceedings of the CH'91 Conference of Human Factors in Computing Systems*, © 1991 ACM, Inc., reprinted by permission (Robertson, G. G., Card, S. K., and Mackinlay, J. D. 1991); Figure 20.10 from Lifelines: visualising personal histories in *Proceedings of CH'96*, © 1996 ACM, Inc., reprinted by permission (Plaisant, C., Milash, B., Rose, A., Widoff, S. and Shneiderman, B. 1996); Figure 20.11 from Browsing anatomical image databases: a case study of the Visible Human in *CH'96 Conference Companion*, © 1996 ACM, Inc., reprinted by permission (North, C. and Korn, F. 1996); Figure 20.12 from Externalising abstract mathematical models in *Proceedings of CH'96*, © 1996 ACM, Inc., reprinted by permission (Tweedie, L., Spence, R., Dawkes, H. and Su, H. 1996); Figure 21.2 from The impact of Utility and Time on Distributed Information Retrieval in *People and Computers XII: Proceedings of HCI'97*, edited by H. Thimbleby, B. O'Conaill and P. Thomas, published and reprinted by permission of Spinger-Verlag GmbH & Co. KG (Johnson, C. W. 1997); Figure 21.4 screen shot reprinted by permission of the Departments of Electronics and Computer Science and History at the University of Southampton; Figure 21.6 Netscape browser window © 2002 Netscape Communications Corporation. Used with permission. Netscape has not authorized, sponsored, endorsed, or approved this publication and is not responsible for its content.

We are grateful to the following for permission to reproduce photographs:

Chapter 1, p. 50, Popperfoto.com; Chapter 2, p. 65, PCD Maltron Ltd; Figure 2.2 Electrolux; Figures 2.6 and 19.6 photos courtesy of Douglas Engelbart and Bootstrap Institute; Figure 2.8 (left) British Sky Broadcasting Limited; Figure 2.13 (bottom right) Sony (UK) Ltd; Chapter 2, Design Focus: Feeling the Road, BMW AG; Chapter 2, Design Focus: Smart-Its – making using sensors easy, Hans Gellersen; Figures 4.1 (right) and 20.2 (left) Palo Alto Research Center; Figure 4.2 and 20.3 (left) François Guimbretière; Figure 4.3 (bottom left) Franklin Electronic Publishers; Figure 5.2 (top plate and middle plate) Kingston Museum and Heritage Service, (bottom plate) V&A Images, The Victoria and Albert Museum, London; Chapter 5, Design Focus: Cultural probes, William W. Gaver, Anthony Boucher, Sarah Pennington and Brendan Walker, Equator IRC, Royal College of Art; Chapter 6, p. 245, from The 1984 Olympic Message System: a text of behavioural principle of system design in *Communications of the ACM*, 30(9), © 1987 ACM, Inc., reprinted by permission (Gould, J. D., Boies, S. J., Levy, S., Richards, J. T. and Schoonard, J. 1987); Figures 9.5 and 9.6 J. A. Renshaw; Figure 9.7 Dr. R. D. Ward; Figure 10.3 SensAble Technologies; Chapter 13, Design Focus: Tomorrow's hospital – using participatory design, Professor J. Artur Vale Serrano; Chapter 18, p. 650, Michael Beigl; Chapter 19, p. 678, Steve Benford, The Mixed Reality Laboratory, University of Nottingham; Chapter 19, Design Focus: SMS in action, Mark Rouncefield; Figure 20.2 (right) Ken Hinckley; Figure 20.3 (right) MIT Media Lab; Figure 20.4 (left) from Interacting with paper on the digital desk in *Communications of the ACM*, 36(7), © 1993 ACM, Inc., reprinted by permission (Wellner, P. 1993); Chapter 20, p. 726, Peter Phillips; Chapter 20, Design Focus: Ambient wood – augmenting the physical, Yvonne Rogers; Chapter 20, Design Focus: Shared experience, Matthew Chalmers.

We are grateful to the following for permission to reproduce text extracts:

Pearson Education, Inc. Publishing as Pearson Addison Wesley for an extract adapted from *Designing the User Interface: Strategies for Effective Human–Computer Interaction 3/e* by B. Shneiderman © 1998, Pearson Education, Inc; Perseus Books Group for an extract adapted from *The Design of Everyday Things* by D. Norman, 1998; and Wiley Publishing, Inc. for extracts adapted from 'Heuristic Evaluation' by Jakob Nielson and Robert L. Mack published in *Usability Inspection Methods* © 1994 Wiley Publishing, Inc.; IEEE for permission to base chapter 20 on 'The human experience' by Gregory Abowd, Elizabeth Mynatt and Tom Rodden which appeared in *IEEE Pervasive Computing Magazine*, Special Inaugural Issue on Reaching for Weiser's Vision, Vol. 1, Issue 1, pp. 48–58, Jan–March 2002. © 2002 IEEE.

In some instances we have been unable to trace the owners of copyright material, and we would appreciate any information that would enable us to do so.

INTRODUCTION

In the first edition of this book we wrote the following:

> This is the authors' second attempt at writing this introduction. Our first attempt fell victim to a design quirk coupled with an innocent, though weary and less than attentive, user. The word-processing package we originally used to write this introduction is menu based. Menu items are grouped to reflect their function. The 'save' and 'delete' options, both of which are correctly classified as file-level operations, are consequently adjacent items in the menu. With a cursor controlled by a trackball it is all too easy for the hand to slip, inadvertently selecting delete instead of save. Of course, the delete option, being well thought out, pops up a confirmation box allowing the user to cancel a mistaken command. Unfortunately, the save option produces a very similar confirmation box – it was only as we hit the 'Confirm' button that we noticed the word 'delete' at the top . . .

Happily this word processor no longer has a delete option in its menu, but unfortunately, similar problems to this are still an all too common occurrence. Errors such as these, resulting from poor design choices, happen every day. Perhaps they are not catastrophic: after all nobody's life is endangered nor is there environmental damage (unless the designer happens to be nearby or you break something in frustration!). However, when you lose several hours' work with no written notes or backup and a publisher's deadline already a week past, 'catastrophe' is certainly the word that springs to mind.

Why is it then that when computers are marketed as 'user friendly' and 'easy to use', simple mistakes like this can still occur? Did the designer of the word processor actually try to use it with the trackball, or was it just that she was so expert with the system that the mistake never arose? We hazard a guess that no one tried to use it when tired and under pressure. But these criticisms are not levied only on the designers of traditional computer software. More and more, our everyday lives involve programmed devices that do not sit on our desk, and these devices are just as unusable. Exactly how many VCR designers understand the universal difficulty people have trying to set their machines to record a television program? Do car radio designers actually think it is safe to use so many knobs and displays that the driver has to divert attention away from the road completely in order to tune the radio or adjust the volume?

Computers and related devices have to be designed with an understanding that people with specific tasks in mind will want to use them in a way that is seamless with respect to their everyday work. To do this, those who design these systems need to know how to think in terms of the eventual users' tasks and how to translate that knowledge into an executable system. But there is a problem with trying to teach the notion of designing computers for people. All designers *are* people and, most probably, they are users as well. Isn't it therefore intuitive to design for the user? Why does it need to be taught when we all know what a good interface looks like? As a result, the study of human–computer interaction (HCI) tends to come late in the designer's training, if at all. The scenario with which we started shows that this is a mistaken view; it is not at all intuitive or easy to design consistent, robust systems

---

DESIGN FOCUS

Things don't change

It would be nice to think that problems like those described at the start of the Introduction would never happen now. Think again! Look at the MacOS X 'dock' below. It is a fast launch point for applications; folders and files can be dragged there for instant access; and also, at the right-hand side, there sits the trash can. Imagine what happens as you try to drag a file into one of the folders. If your finger accidentally slips whilst the icon is over the trash can – oops!

Happily this is not quite as easy in reality as it looks in the screen shot, since the icons in the dock constantly move around as you try to drag a file into it. This is to make room for the file in case you want to place it in the dock. However, it means you have to concentrate very hard when dragging a file over the dock. We assume this is not a deliberate feature, but it does have the beneficial side effect that users are less likely to throw away a file by accident – whew!

In fact it is quite fun to watch a new user trying to throw away a file. The trash can keeps moving as if it didn't want the file in it. Experienced users evolve coping strategies. One user always drags files into the trash from the right-hand side as then the icons in the dock don't move around. So two lessons:

- designs don't always get better
- but at least users are clever.

Screen shot reprinted by permission from Apple Computer, Inc.

that will cope with all manner of user carelessness. The interface is not something that can be plugged in at the last minute; its design should be developed integrally with the rest of the system. It should not just present a 'pretty face', but should support the tasks that people actually want to do, and forgive the careless mistakes. We therefore need to consider how HCI fits into the design process.

Designing usable systems is not simply a matter of altruism towards the eventual user, or even marketing; it is increasingly a matter of law. National health and safety standards constrain employers to provide their workforce with usable computer systems: not just safe but *usable*. For example, EC Directive 90/270/EEC, which has been incorporated into member countries' legislation, requires employers to ensure the following when designing, selecting, commissioning or modifying software:

- that it is suitable for the task
- that it is easy to use and, where appropriate, adaptable to the user's knowledge and experience
- that it provides feedback on performance
- that it displays information in a format and at a pace that is adapted to the user
- that it conforms to the 'principles of software ergonomics'.

Designers and employers can no longer afford to ignore the user.

WHAT IS HCI?

The term *human–computer interaction* has only been in widespread use since the early 1980s, but has its roots in more established disciplines. Systematic study of human performance began in earnest at the beginning of the last century in factories, with an emphasis on manual tasks. The Second World War provided the impetus for studying the interaction between humans and machines, as each side strove to produce more effective weapons systems. This led to a wave of interest in the area among researchers, and the formation of the Ergonomics Research Society in 1949. Traditionally, ergonomists have been concerned primarily with the physical characteristics of machines and systems, and how these affect user performance. Human Factors incorporates these issues, and more cognitive issues as well. The terms are often used interchangeably, with Ergonomics being the preferred term in the United Kingdom and Human Factors in the English-speaking parts of North America. Both of these disciplines are concerned with user performance in the context of any system, whether computer, mechanical or manual. As computer use became more widespread, an increasing number of researchers specialized in studying the interaction between people and computers, concerning themselves with the physical, psychological and theoretical aspects of this process. This research originally went under the name *man–machine interaction*, but this became *human–computer interaction* in recognition of the particular interest in computers and the composition of the user population!

Another strand of research that has influenced the development of HCI is information science and technology. Again the former is an old discipline, pre-dating the introduction of technology, and is concerned with the management and manipulation of information within an organization. The introduction of technology has had a profound effect on the way that information can be stored, accessed and utilized and, consequently, a significant effect on the organization and work environment. Systems analysis has traditionally concerned itself with the influence of technology in the workplace, and fitting the technology to the requirements and constraints of the job. These issues are also the concern of HCI.

HCI draws on many disciplines, as we shall see, but it is in computer science and systems design that it must be accepted as a central concern. For all the other disciplines it can be a specialism, albeit one that provides crucial input; for systems design it is an essential part of the design process. From this perspective, HCI involves the design, implementation and evaluation of interactive systems in the context of the user's task and work.

However, when we talk about human–computer interaction, we do not necessarily envisage a single user with a desktop computer. By *user* we may mean an individual user, a group of users working together, or a sequence of users in an organization, each dealing with some part of the task or process. The user is whoever is trying to get the job done using the technology. By *computer* we mean any technology ranging from the general desktop computer to a large-scale computer system, a process control system or an embedded system. The system may include non-computerized parts, including other people. By *interaction* we mean any communication between a user and computer, be it direct or indirect. Direct interaction involves a dialog with feedback and control throughout performance of the task. Indirect interaction may involve batch processing or intelligent sensors controlling the environment. The important thing is that the user is interacting with the computer in order to accomplish something.

WHO IS INVOLVED IN HCI?

HCI is undoubtedly a multi-disciplinary subject. The ideal designer of an interactive system would have expertise in a range of topics: psychology and cognitive science to give her knowledge of the user's perceptual, cognitive and problem-solving skills; ergonomics for the user's physical capabilities; sociology to help her understand the wider context of the interaction; computer science and engineering to be able to build the necessary technology; business to be able to market it; graphic design to produce an effective interface presentation; technical writing to produce the manuals, and so it goes on. There is obviously too much expertise here to be held by one person (or indeed four!), perhaps even too much for the average design team. Indeed, although HCI is recognized as an interdisciplinary subject, in practice people tend to take a strong stance on one side or another. However, it is not possible to design effective interactive systems from one discipline in isolation. Input is needed from all sides. For example, a beautifully designed graphic display may be unusable if it ignores dialog constraints or the psychological limitations of the user.

In this book we want to encourage the multi-disciplinary view of HCI but we too have our 'stance', as computer scientists. We are interested in answering a particular question. How do principles and methods from each of these contributing disciplines in HCI help us to design better systems? In this we must be pragmatists rather than theorists: we want to know how to apply the theory to the problem rather than just acquire a deep understanding of the theory. Our goal, then, is to be multi-disciplinary but practical. We concentrate particularly on computer science, psychology and cognitive science as core subjects, and on their application to design; other disciplines are consulted to provide input where relevant.

THEORY AND HCI

Unfortunately for us, there is no general and unified theory of HCI that we can present. Indeed, it may be impossible ever to derive one; it is certainly out of our reach today. However, there is an underlying principle that forms the basis of our own views on HCI, and it is captured in our claim that people use computers to accomplish work. This outlines the three major issues of concern: the people, the computers and the tasks that are performed. The system must support the user's task, which gives us a fourth focus, usability: if the system forces the user to adopt an unacceptable mode of work then it is not usable.

There are, however, those who would dismiss our concentration on the task, saying that we do not even know enough about a theory of human tasks to support them in design. There is a good argument here (to which we return in Chapter 15). However, we can live with this confusion about what real tasks are because our understanding of tasks at the moment is sufficient to give us direction in design. The user's current tasks are studied and then supported by computers, which can in turn affect the nature of the original task and cause it to evolve. To illustrate, word processing has made it easy to manipulate paragraphs and reorder documents, allowing writers a completely new freedom that has affected writing styles. No longer is it vital to plan and construct text in an ordered fashion, since free-flowing prose can easily be restructured at a later date. This evolution of task in turn affects the design of the ideal system. However, we see this evolution as providing a motivating force behind the system development cycle, rather than a refutation of the whole idea of supportive design.

This word 'task' or the focus on accomplishing 'work' is also problematic when we think of areas such as domestic appliances, consumer electronics and e-commerce. There are three 'use' words that must all be true for a product to be successful; it must be:

useful – accomplish what is required: play music, cook dinner, format a document;

usable – do it easily and naturally, without danger of error, etc.;

used – make people want to use it, be attractive, engaging, fun, etc.

The last of these has not been a major factor until recently in HCI, but issues of motivation, enjoyment and experience are increasingly important. We are certainly even further from having a unified theory of experience than of task.

The question of whether HCI, or more importantly the design of interactive systems and the user interface in particular, is a science or a craft discipline is an interesting one. Does it involve artistic skill and fortuitous insight or reasoned methodical science? Here we can draw an analogy with architecture. The most impressive structures, the most beautiful buildings, the innovative and imaginative creations that provide aesthetic pleasure, all require inventive inspiration in design and a sense of artistry, and in this sense the discipline is a craft. However, these structures also have to be able to stand up to fulfill their purpose successfully, and to be able to do this the architect has to use science. So it is for HCI: beautiful and/or novel interfaces are artistically pleasing *and* capable of fulfilling the tasks required – a marriage of art and science into a successful whole. We want to reuse lessons learned from the past about how to achieve good results and avoid bad ones. For this we require both craft and science. Innovative ideas lead to more usable systems, but in order to maximize the potential benefit from the ideas, we need to understand not only that they work, but how and why they work. This scientific rationalization allows us to reuse related concepts in similar situations, in much the same way that architects can produce a bridge and know that it will stand, since it is based upon tried and tested principles.

The craft–science tension becomes even more difficult when we consider novel systems. Their increasing complexity means that our personal ideas of good and bad are no longer enough; for a complex system to be well designed we need to rely on something more than simply our intuition. Designers may be able to think about how one user would want to act, but how about groups? And what about new media? Our ideas of how best to share workloads or present video information are open to debate and question even in non-computing situations, and the incorporation of one version of good design into a computer system is quite likely to be unlike anyone else's version. Different people work in different ways, whilst different media color the nature of the interaction; both can dramatically change the very nature of the original task. In order to assist designers, it is unrealistic to assume that they can rely on artistic skill and perfect insight to develop usable systems. Instead we have to provide them with an understanding of the concepts involved, a scientific view of the reasons why certain things are successful whilst others are not, and then allow their creative nature to feed off this information: creative flow, underpinned with science; or maybe scientific method, accelerated by artistic insight. The truth is that HCI is required to be both a craft and a science in order to be successful.

HCI IN THE CURRICULUM

If HCI involves both craft and science then it must, in part at least, be taught. Imagination and skill may be qualities innate in the designer or developed through experience, but the underlying theory must be learned. In the past, when computers were used primarily by expert specialists, concentration on the interface was a luxury that was often relinquished. Now designers cannot afford to ignore the interface in favour of the functionality of their systems: the two are too closely intertwined. If the interface is poor, the functionality is obscured; if it is well designed, it will allow the system's functionality to support the user's task.

Increasingly, therefore, computer science educators cannot afford to ignore HCI. We would go as far as to claim that HCI should be integrated into every computer science or software engineering course, either as a recurring feature of other modules or, preferably, as a module itself. It should not be viewed as an 'optional extra' (although, of course, more advanced HCI options can complement a basic core course). This view is shared by the ACM SIGCHI curriculum development group, who propose a curriculum for such a core course [9]. The topics included in this book, although developed without reference to this curriculum, cover the main emphases of it, and include enough detail and coverage to support specialized options as well.

In courses other than computer science, HCI may well be an option specializing in a particular area, such as cognitive modeling or task analysis. Selected use of the relevant chapters of this book can also support such a course.

HCI must be taken seriously by designers and educators if the requirement for additional complexity in the system is to be matched by increased clarity and usability in the interface. In this book we demonstrate how this can be done in practice.

DESIGN FOCUS

Quick fixes

You should expect to spend both time and money on interface design, just as you would with other parts of a system. So in one sense there are no quick fixes. However, a few simple steps can make a dramatic improvement.

Think 'user'
Probably 90% of the value of any interface design technique is that it forces the designer to remember that someone (and in particular someone else) will use the system under construction.

Try it out
Of course, many designers will build a system that they find easy and pleasant to use, and they find it incomprehensible that anyone else could have trouble with it. Simply sitting someone down with an early version of an interface (without the designer prompting them at each step!) is enormously valuable. Professional usability laboratories will have video equipment, one-way mirrors and other sophisticated monitors, but a notebook and pencil and a home-video camera will suffice (more about evaluation in Chapter 9).

Involve the users
Where possible, the eventual users should be involved in the design process. They have vital knowledge and will soon find flaws. A mechanical syringe was once being developed and a prototype was demonstrated to hospital staff. Happily they quickly noticed the potentially fatal flaw in its interface.

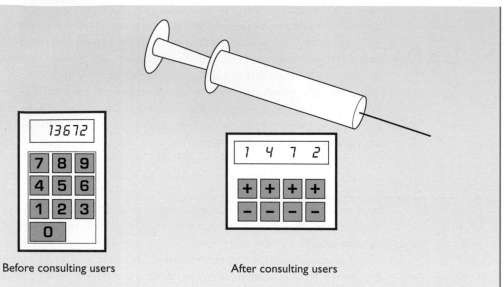

Before consulting users   After consulting users

Figure 0.1 Automatic syringe: setting the dose to 1372. The effect of one key slip before and after user involvement

The doses were entered via a numeric keypad: an accidental keypress and the dose could be out by a factor of 10! The production version had individual increment/decrement buttons for each digit (more about participatory design in Chapter 13).

Iterate

People are complicated, so you won't get it right first time. Programming an interface can be a very difficult and time-consuming business. So, the result becomes precious and the builder will want to defend it and minimize changes. Making early prototypes less precious and easier to throw away is crucial. Happily there are now many interface builder tools that aid this process. For example, mock-ups can be quickly constructed using HyperCard on the Apple Macintosh or Visual Basic on the PC. For visual and layout decisions, paper designs and simple models can be used (more about iterative design in Chapter 5).

FOUNDATIONS

In this part we introduce the fundamental components of an interactive system: the human user, the computer system itself and the nature of the interactive process. We then present a view of the history of interactive systems by looking at key interaction paradigms that have been significant.

Chapter 1 discusses the psychological and physiological attributes of the user, providing us with a basic overview of the capabilities and limitations that affect our ability to use computer systems. It is only when we have an understanding of the user at this level that we can understand what makes for successful designs. Chapter 2 considers the computer in a similar way. Input and output devices are described and explained and the effect that their individual characteristics have on the interaction highlighted. The computational power and memory of the computer is another important component in determining what can be achieved in the interaction, whilst due attention is also paid to paper output since this forms one of the major uses of computers and users' tasks today. Having approached interaction from both the human and the computer side, we then turn our attention to the dialog between them in Chapter 3, where we look at models of interaction. In Chapter 4 we take a historical perspective on the evolution of interactive systems and how they have increased the usability of computers in general.

THE HUMAN

OVERVIEW

- Humans are limited in their capacity to process information. This has important implications for design.

- Information is received and responses given via a number of input and output channels:
  - visual channel
  - auditory channel
  - haptic channel
  - movement.

- Information is stored in memory:
  - sensory memory
  - short-term (working) memory
  - long-term memory.

- Information is processed and applied:
  - reasoning
  - problem solving
  - skill acquisition
  - error.

- Emotion influences human capabilities.

- Users share common capabilities but are individuals with differences, which should not be ignored.

1.1 INTRODUCTION

This chapter is the first of four in which we introduce some of the 'foundations' of HCI. We start with the human, the central character in any discussion of interactive systems. The human, the *user*, is, after all, the one whom computer systems are designed to assist. The requirements of the user should therefore be our first priority.

In this chapter we will look at areas of human psychology coming under the general banner of *cognitive psychology*. This may seem a far cry from designing and building interactive computer systems, but it is not. In order to design something for someone, we need to understand their capabilities and limitations. We need to know if there are things that they will find difficult or, even, impossible. It will also help us to know what people find easy and how we can help them by encouraging these things. We will look at aspects of cognitive psychology which have a bearing on the use of computer systems: how humans perceive the world around them, how they store and process information and solve problems, and how they physically manipulate objects.

We have already said that we will restrict our study to those things that are relevant to HCI. One way to structure this discussion is to think of the user in a way that highlights these aspects. In other words, to think of a simplified *model* of what is actually going on. Many models have been proposed and it useful to consider one of the most influential in passing, to understand the context of the discussion that is to follow. In 1983, Card, Moran and Newell [56] described the *Model Human Processor*, which is a simplified view of the human processing involved in interacting with computer systems. The model comprises three subsystems: the perceptual system, handling sensory stimulus from the outside world, the motor system, which controls actions, and the cognitive system, which provides the processing needed to connect the two. Each of these subsystems has its own processor and memory, although obviously the complexity of these varies depending on the complexity of the tasks the subsystem has to perform. The model also includes a number of *principles of operation* which dictate the behavior of the systems under certain conditions.

We will use the analogy of the user as an information processing system, but in our model make the analogy closer to that of a conventional computer system. Information comes in, is stored and processed, and information is passed out. We will therefore discuss three components of this system: input–output, memory and processing. In the human, we are dealing with an intelligent information-processing system, and processing therefore includes problem solving, learning, and, consequently, making mistakes. This model is obviously a simplification of the real situation, since memory and processing are required at all levels, as we have seen in the Model Human Processor. However, it is convenient as a way of grasping how information is handled by the human system. The human, unlike the computer, is also influenced by external factors such as the social and organizational environment, and we need to be aware of these influences as well. We will ignore such factors for now and concentrate on the human's information processing capabilities only. We will return to social and organizational influences in Chapter 3 and, in more detail, in Chapter 13.

In this chapter, we will first look at the human's input–output channels, the senses and responders or effectors. This will involve some low-level processing. Secondly, we will consider human memory and how it works. We will then think about how humans perform complex problem solving, how they learn and acquire skills, and why they make mistakes. Finally, we will discuss how these things can help us in the design of computer systems.

1.2   INPUT–OUTPUT CHANNELS

A person's interaction with the outside world occurs through information being received and sent: input and output. In an interaction with a computer the user receives information that is output by the computer, and responds by providing input to the computer – the user's output becomes the computer's input and vice versa. Consequently the use of the terms input and output may lead to confusion so we shall blur the distinction somewhat and concentrate on the channels involved. This blurring is appropriate since, although a particular channel may have a primary role as input or output in the interaction, it is more than likely that it is also used in the other role. For example, sight may be used primarily in receiving information from the computer, but it can also be used to provide information to the computer, for example by fixating on a particular screen point when using an eyegaze system.

Input in the human occurs mainly through the senses and output through the motor control of the effectors. There are five major senses: sight, hearing, touch, taste and smell. Of these, the first three are the most important to HCI. Taste and smell do not currently play a significant role in HCI, and it is not clear whether they could be exploited at all in general computer systems, although they could have a role to play in more specialized systems (smells to give warning of malfunction, for example) or in augmented reality systems. However, vision, hearing and touch are central.

Similarly there are a number of effectors, including the limbs, fingers, eyes, head and vocal system. In the interaction with the computer, the fingers play the primary role, through typing or mouse control, with some use of voice, and eye, head and body position.

Imagine using a personal computer (PC) with a mouse and a keyboard. The application you are using has a graphical interface, with menus, icons and windows. In your interaction with this system you receive information primarily by sight, from what appears on the screen. However, you may also receive information by ear: for example, the computer may 'beep' at you if you make a mistake or to draw attention to something, or there may be a voice commentary in a multimedia presentation. Touch plays a part too in that you will feel the keys moving (also hearing the 'click') or the orientation of the mouse, which provides vital feedback about what you have done. You yourself send information to the computer using your hands, either by hitting keys or moving the mouse. Sight and hearing do not play a direct role in sending information in this example, although they may be used to receive information from a third source (for example, a book, or the words of another person) which is then transmitted to the computer.

In this section we will look at the main elements of such an interaction, first considering the role and limitations of the three primary senses and going on to consider motor control.

1.2.1 Vision

Human vision is a highly complex activity with a range of physical and perceptual limitations, yet it is the primary source of information for the average person. We can roughly divide visual perception into two stages: the physical reception of the stimulus from the outside world, and the processing and interpretation of that stimulus. On the one hand the physical properties of the eye and the visual system mean that there are certain things that cannot be seen by the human; on the other the interpretative capabilities of visual processing allow images to be constructed from incomplete information. We need to understand both stages as both influence what can and cannot be perceived visually by a human being, which in turn directly affects the way that we design computer systems. We will begin by looking at the eye as a physical receptor, and then go on to consider the processing involved in basic vision.

The human eye

Vision begins with light. The eye is a mechanism for receiving light and transforming it into electrical energy. Light is reflected from objects in the world and their image is focussed upside down on the back of the eye. The receptors in the eye transform it into electrical signals which are passed to the brain.

The eye has a number of important components (see Figure 1.1) which we will look at in more detail. The *cornea* and *lens* at the front of the eye focus the light into a sharp image on the back of the eye, the *retina*. The retina is light sensitive and contains two types of *photoreceptor*: *rods* and *cones*.

Rods are highly sensitive to light and therefore allow us to see under a low level of illumination. However, they are unable to resolve fine detail and are subject to light saturation. This is the reason for the temporary blindness we get when moving from a darkened room into sunlight: the rods have been active and are saturated by the sudden light. The cones do not operate either as they are suppressed by the rods. We are therefore temporarily unable to see at all. There are approximately 120 million rods per eye which are mainly situated towards the edges of the retina. Rods therefore dominate peripheral vision.

Cones are the second type of receptor in the eye. They are less sensitive to light than the rods and can therefore tolerate more light. There are three types of cone, each sensitive to a different wavelength of light. This allows color vision. The eye has approximately 6 million cones, mainly concentrated on the *fovea*, a small area of the retina on which images are fixated.

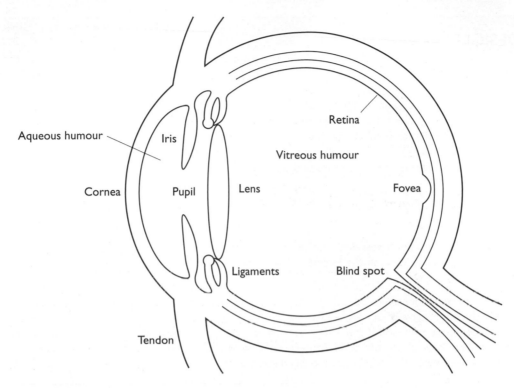

Figure 1.1   The human eye

Although the retina is mainly covered with photoreceptors there is one *blind spot* where the optic nerve enters the eye. The blind spot has no rods or cones, yet our visual system compensates for this so that in normal circumstances we are unaware of it.

The retina also has specialized nerve cells called *ganglion cells*. There are two types: X-cells, which are concentrated in the fovea and are responsible for the early detection of pattern; and Y-cells which are more widely distributed in the retina and are responsible for the early detection of movement. The distribution of these cells means that, while we may not be able to detect changes in pattern in peripheral vision, we can perceive movement.

Visual perception

Understanding the basic construction of the eye goes some way to explaining the physical mechanisms of vision but visual perception is more than this. The information received by the visual apparatus must be filtered and passed to processing elements which allow us to recognize coherent scenes, disambiguate relative distances and differentiate color. We will consider some of the capabilities and limitations of visual processing later, but first we will look a little more closely at how we perceive size and depth, brightness and color, each of which is crucial to the design of effective visual interfaces.

DESIGN FOCUS

Getting noticed

The extensive knowledge about the human visual system can be brought to bear in practical design. For example, our ability to read or distinguish falls off inversely as the distance from our point of focus increases. This is due to the fact that the cones are packed more densely towards the center of our visual field. You can see this in the following image. Fixate on the dot in the center. The letters on the left should all be equally readable, those on the right all equally harder.

This loss of discrimination sets limits on the amount that can be seen or read without moving one's eyes. A user concentrating on the middle of the screen cannot be expected to read help text on the bottom line.

However, although our ability to discriminate static text diminishes, the rods, which are concentrated more in the outer parts of our visual field, are very sensitive to changes; hence we see movement well at the edge of our vision. So if you want a user to see an error message at the bottom of the screen it had better be flashing! On the other hand clever moving icons, however impressive they are, will be distracting even when the user is not looking directly at them.

Perceiving size and depth　　Imagine you are standing on a hilltop. Beside you on the summit you can see rocks, sheep and a small tree. On the hillside is a farmhouse with outbuildings and farm vehicles. Someone is on the track, walking toward the summit. Below in the valley is a small market town.

Even in describing such a scene the notions of size and distance predominate. Our visual system is easily able to interpret the images which it receives to take account of these things. We can identify similar objects regardless of the fact that they appear to us to be of vastly different sizes. In fact, we can use this information to judge distances.

So how does the eye perceive size, depth and relative distances? To understand this we must consider how the image appears on the retina. As we noted in the previous section, reflected light from the object forms an upside-down image on the retina. The size of that image is specified as a *visual angle*. Figure 1.2 illustrates how the visual angle is calculated.

If we were to draw a line from the top of the object to a central point on the front of the eye and a second line from the bottom of the object to the same point, the visual angle of the object is the angle between these two lines. Visual angle is affected by both the size of the object and its distance from the eye. Therefore if two objects are at the same distance, the larger one will have the larger visual angle. Similarly, if two objects of the same size are placed at different distances from the eye, the

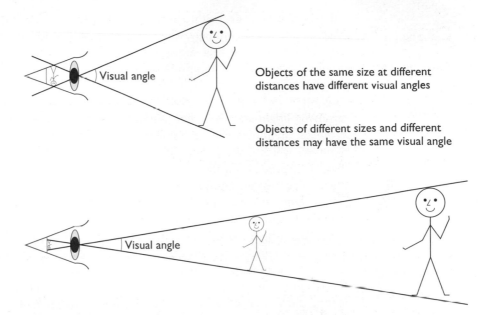

Objects of the same size at different distances have different visual angles

Objects of different sizes and different distances may have the same visual angle

Figure 1.2   Visual angle

furthest one will have the smaller visual angle. The visual angle indicates how much of the field of view is taken by the object. The visual angle measurement is given in either degrees or *minutes of arc*, where 1 degree is equivalent to 60 minutes of arc, and 1 minute of arc to 60 seconds of arc.

So how does an object's visual angle affect our perception of its size? First, if the visual angle of an object is too small we will be unable to perceive it at all. *Visual acuity* is the ability of a person to perceive fine detail. A number of measurements have been established to test visual acuity, most of which are included in standard eye tests. For example, a person with normal vision can detect a single line if it has a visual angle of 0.5 seconds of arc. Spaces between lines can be detected at 30 seconds to 1 minute of visual arc. These represent the limits of human visual acuity.

Assuming that we can perceive the object, does its visual angle affect our perception of its size? Given that the visual angle of an object is reduced as it gets further away, we might expect that we would perceive the object as smaller. In fact, our perception of an object's size remains constant even if its visual angle changes. So a person's height is perceived as constant even if they move further from you. This is the *law of size constancy*, and it indicates that our perception of size relies on factors other than the visual angle.

One of these factors is our perception of depth. If we return to the hilltop scene there are a number of *cues* which we can use to determine the relative positions and distances of the objects which we see. If objects overlap, the object which is partially covered is perceived to be in the background, and therefore further away. Similarly, the size and height of the object in our field of view provides a cue to its distance.

A third cue is familiarity: if we expect an object to be of a certain size then we can judge its distance accordingly. This has been exploited for humour in advertising: one advertisement for beer shows a man walking away from a bottle in the foreground. As he walks, he bumps into the bottle, which is in fact a giant one in the background!

Perceiving brightness   A second aspect of visual perception is the perception of *brightness*. Brightness is in fact a subjective reaction to levels of light. It is affected by *luminance* which is the amount of light emitted by an object. The luminance of an object is dependent on the amount of light falling on the object's surface and its reflective properties. Luminance is a physical characteristic and can be measured using a *photometer*. *Contrast* is related to luminance: it is a function of the luminance of an object and the luminance of its background.

Although brightness is a subjective response, it can be described in terms of the amount of luminance that gives a *just noticeable difference* in brightness. However, the visual system itself also compensates for changes in brightness. In dim lighting, the rods predominate vision. Since there are fewer rods on the fovea, objects in low lighting can be seen less easily when fixated upon, and are more visible in peripheral vision. In normal lighting, the cones take over.

Visual acuity increases with increased luminance. This may be an argument for using high display luminance. However, as luminance increases, *flicker* also increases. The eye will perceive a light switched on and off rapidly as constantly on. But if the speed of switching is less than 50 Hz then the light is perceived to flicker. In high luminance flicker can be perceived at over 50 Hz. Flicker is also more noticeable in peripheral vision. This means that the larger the display (and consequently the more peripheral vision that it occupies), the more it will appear to flicker.

Perceiving color   A third factor that we need to consider is perception of color. Color is usually regarded as being made up of three components: *hue*, *intensity* and *saturation*. Hue is determined by the spectral wavelength of the light. Blues have short wavelengths, greens medium and reds long. Approximately 150 different hues can be discriminated by the average person. Intensity is the brightness of the color, and saturation is the amount of whiteness in the color. By varying these two, we can perceive in the region of 7 million different colors. However, the number of colors that can be identified by an individual without training is far fewer (in the region of 10).

The eye perceives color because the cones are sensitive to light of different wavelengths. There are three different types of cone, each sensitive to a different color (blue, green and red). Color vision is best in the fovea, and worst at the periphery where rods predominate. It should also be noted that only 3–4% of the fovea is occupied by cones which are sensitive to blue light, making blue acuity lower.

Finally, we should remember that around 8% of males and 1% of females suffer from color blindness, most commonly being unable to discriminate between red and green.

The capabilities and limitations of visual processing

In considering the way in which we perceive images we have already encountered some of the capabilities and limitations of the human visual processing system. However, we have concentrated largely on low-level perception. Visual processing involves the transformation and interpretation of a complete image, from the light that is thrown onto the retina. As we have already noted, our expectations affect the way an image is perceived. For example, if we know that an object is a particular size, we will perceive it as that size no matter how far it is from us.

Visual processing compensates for the movement of the image on the retina which occurs as we move around and as the object which we see moves. Although the retinal image is moving, the image that we perceive is stable. Similarly, color and brightness of objects are perceived as constant, in spite of changes in luminance.

This ability to interpret and exploit our expectations can be used to resolve ambiguity. For example, consider the image shown in Figure 1.3. What do you perceive? Now consider Figure 1.4 and Figure 1.5. The context in which the object appears

Figure 1.3 An ambiguous shape?

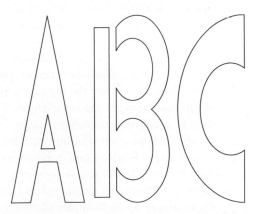

Figure 1.4 ABC

Figure 1.5   12 13 14

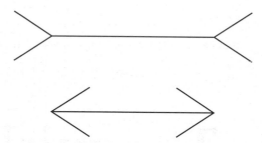

Figure 1.6   The Muller–Lyer illusion – which line is longer?

allows our expectations to clearly disambiguate the interpretation of the object, as either a B or a 13.

However, it can also create optical illusions. For example, consider Figure 1.6. Which line is longer? Most people when presented with this will say that the top line is longer than the bottom. In fact, the two lines are the same length. This may be due to a false application of the law of size constancy: the top line appears like a concave edge, the bottom like a convex edge. The former therefore seems further away than the latter and is therefore scaled to appear larger. A similar illusion is the Ponzo illusion (Figure 1.7). Here the top line appears longer, owing to the distance effect, although both lines are the same length. These illusions demonstrate that our perception of size is not completely reliable.

Another illusion created by our expectations compensating an image is the proof-reading illusion. Read the text in Figure 1.8 quickly. What does it say? Most people reading this rapidly will read it correctly, although closer inspection shows that the word 'the' is repeated in the second and third line.

These are just a few examples of how the visual system compensates, and sometimes overcompensates, to allow us to perceive the world around us.

Figure 1.7   The Ponzo illusion – are these the same size?

The quick brown fox jumps over the the lazy dog.

Figure 1.8   Is this text correct?

DESIGN FOCUS

Where's the middle?

Optical illusions highlight the differences between the way things are and the way we perceive them – and in interface design we need to be aware that we will not always perceive things exactly as they are. The way that objects are composed together will affect the way we perceive them, and we do not perceive geometric shapes exactly as they are drawn. For example, we tend to magnify horizontal lines and reduce vertical. So a square needs to be slightly increased in height to appear square and lines will appear thicker if horizontal rather than vertical.

Optical illusions also affect page symmetry. We tend to see the center of a page as being a little above the actual center – so if a page is arranged symmetrically around the actual center, we will see it as too low down. In graphic design this is known as the *optical center* – and bottom page margins tend to be increased by 50% to compensate.

Reading

So far we have concentrated on the perception of images in general. However, the perception and processing of text is a special case that is important to interface design, which invariably requires some textual display. We will therefore end this section by looking at *reading*. There are several stages in the reading process. First, the visual pattern of the word on the page is perceived. It is then decoded with reference to an internal representation of language. The final stages of language processing include syntactic and semantic analysis and operate on phrases or sentences.

We are most concerned with the first two stages of this process and how they influence interface design. During reading, the eye makes jerky movements called *saccades* followed by fixations. Perception occurs during the fixation periods, which account for approximately 94% of the time elapsed. The eye moves backwards over the text as well as forwards, in what are known as *regressions*. If the text is complex there will be more regressions.

Adults read approximately 250 words a minute. It is unlikely that words are scanned serially, character by character, since experiments have shown that words can be recognized as quickly as single characters. Instead, familiar words are recognized using word shape. This means that removing the word shape clues (for example, by capitalizing words) is detrimental to reading speed and accuracy.

The speed at which text can be read is a measure of its legibility. Experiments have shown that standard font sizes of 9 to 12 points are equally legible, given proportional spacing between lines [346]. Similarly line lengths of between 2.3 and 5.2 inches (58 and 132 mm) are equally legible. However, there is evidence that reading from a computer screen is slower than from a book [244]. This is thought to be due to a number of factors including a longer line length, fewer words to a page, orientation and the familiarity of the medium of the page. These factors can of course be reduced by careful design of textual interfaces.

A final word about the use of contrast in visual display: a negative contrast (dark characters on a light screen) provides higher luminance and, therefore, increased acuity, than a positive contrast. This will in turn increase legibility. However, it will also be more prone to flicker. Experimental evidence suggests that in practice negative contrast displays are preferred and result in more accurate performance [30].

1.2.2 Hearing

The sense of hearing is often considered secondary to sight, but we tend to underestimate the amount of information that we receive through our ears. Close your eyes for a moment and listen. What sounds can you hear? Where are they coming from? What is making them? As I sit at my desk I can hear cars passing on the road outside, machinery working on a site nearby, the drone of a plane overhead and bird song. But I can also tell *where* the sounds are coming from, and estimate how far away they are. So from the sounds I hear I can tell that a car is passing on a particular road near my house, and which direction it is traveling in. I know that building work is in progress in a particular location, and that a certain type of bird is perched in the tree in my garden.

The auditory system can convey a lot of information about our environment. But how does it work?

The human ear

Just as vision begins with light, hearing begins with vibrations in the air or *sound waves*. The ear receives these vibrations and transmits them, through various stages, to the auditory nerves. The ear comprises three sections, commonly known as the *outer ear*, *middle ear* and *inner ear*.

The outer ear is the visible part of the ear. It has two parts: the *pinna*, which is the structure that is attached to the sides of the head, and the *auditory canal*, along which sound waves are passed to the middle ear. The outer ear serves two purposes. First, it protects the sensitive middle ear from damage. The auditory canal contains wax which prevents dust, dirt and over-inquisitive insects reaching the middle ear. It also maintains the middle ear at a constant temperature. Secondly, the pinna and auditory canal serve to amplify some sounds.

The middle ear is a small cavity connected to the outer ear by the *tympanic membrane*, or ear drum, and to the inner ear by the *cochlea*. Within the cavity are the *ossicles*, the smallest bones in the body. Sound waves pass along the auditory canal and vibrate the ear drum which in turn vibrates the ossicles, which transmit the vibrations to the cochlea, and so into the inner ear. This 'relay' is required because, unlike the air-filled outer and middle ears, the inner ear is filled with a denser cochlean liquid. If passed directly from the air to the liquid, the transmission of the sound waves would be poor. By transmitting them via the ossicles the sound waves are concentrated and amplified.

The waves are passed into the liquid-filled cochlea in the inner ear. Within the cochlea are delicate hair cells or *cilia* that bend because of the vibrations in the cochlean liquid and release a chemical transmitter which causes impulses in the auditory nerve.

Processing sound

As we have seen, sound is changes or vibrations in air pressure. It has a number of characteristics which we can differentiate. *Pitch* is the frequency of the sound. A low frequency produces a low pitch, a high frequency, a high pitch. *Loudness* is proportional to the amplitude of the sound; the frequency remains constant. *Timbre* relates to the type of the sound: sounds may have the same pitch and loudness but be made by different instruments and so vary in timbre. We can also identify a sound's location, since the two ears receive slightly different sounds, owing to the time difference between the sound reaching the two ears and the reduction in intensity caused by the sound waves reflecting from the head.

The human ear can hear frequencies from about 20 Hz to 15 kHz. It can distinguish frequency changes of less than 1.5 Hz at low frequencies but is less accurate at high frequencies. Different frequencies trigger activity in neurons in different parts of the auditory system, and cause different rates of firing of nerve impulses.

The auditory system performs some filtering of the sounds received, allowing us to ignore background noise and concentrate on important information. We are selective in our hearing, as illustrated by the *cocktail party effect*, where we can pick out our name spoken across a crowded noisy room. However, if sounds are too loud, or frequencies too similar, we are unable to differentiate sound.

As we have seen, sound can convey a remarkable amount of information. It is rarely used to its potential in interface design, usually being confined to warning sounds and notifications. The exception is multimedia, which may include music, voice commentary and sound effects. However, the ear can differentiate quite subtle sound changes and can recognize familiar sounds without concentrating attention on the sound source. This suggests that sound could be used more extensively in interface design, to convey information about the system state, for example. This is discussed in more detail in Chapter 10.

Worked exercise   *Suggest ideas for an interface which uses the properties of sound effectively.*

Answer   You might approach this exercise by considering how sound could be added to an application with which you are familiar. Use your imagination. This is also a good subject for a literature survey (starting with the references in Chapter 10).

Speech sounds can obviously be used to convey information. This is useful not only for the visually impaired but also for any application where the user's attention has to be divided (for example, power plant control, flight control, etc.). Uses of non-speech sounds include the following:

■ Attention – to attract the user's attention to a critical situation or to the end of a process, for example.

■ Status information – continuous background sounds can be used to convey status information. For example, monitoring the progress of a process (without the need for visual attention).

■ Confirmation – a sound associated with an action to confirm that the action has been carried out. For example, associating a sound with deleting a file.

■ Navigation – using changing sound to indicate where the user is in a system. For example, what about sound to support navigation in hypertext?

1.2.3 Touch

The third and last of the senses that we will consider is touch or *haptic perception*. Although this sense is often viewed as less important than sight or hearing, imagine life without it. Touch provides us with vital information about our environment. It tells us when we touch something hot or cold, and can therefore act as a warning. It also provides us with feedback when we attempt to lift an object, for example. Consider the act of picking up a glass of water. If we could only see the glass and not feel when our hand made contact with it or feel its shape, the speed and accuracy of the action would be reduced. This is the experience of users of certain *virtual reality* games: they can see the computer-generated objects which they need to manipulate but they have no physical sensation of touching them. Watching such users can be an informative and amusing experience! Touch is therefore an important means of feedback, and this is no less so in using computer systems. Feeling buttons depress is an important part of the task of pressing the button. Also, we should be aware that, although for the average person, haptic perception is a secondary source of information, for those whose other senses are impaired, it may be vitally important. For such users, interfaces such as braille may be the primary source of information in the interaction. We should not therefore underestimate the importance of touch.

The apparatus of touch differs from that of sight and hearing in that it is not localized. We receive stimuli through the skin. The skin contains three types of sensory receptor: *thermoreceptors* respond to heat and cold, *nociceptors* respond to intense pressure, heat and pain, and *mechanoreceptors* respond to pressure. It is the last of these that we are concerned with in relation to human–computer interaction.

There are two kinds of mechanoreceptor, which respond to different types of pressure. *Rapidly adapting mechanoreceptors* respond to immediate pressure as the skin is indented. These receptors also react more quickly with increased pressure. However, they stop responding if continuous pressure is applied. *Slowly adapting mechanoreceptors* respond to continuously applied pressure.

Although the whole of the body contains such receptors, some areas have greater sensitivity or acuity than others. It is possible to measure the acuity of different areas of the body using the *two-point threshold test*. Take two pencils, held so their tips are about 12 mm apart. Touch the points to your thumb and see if you can feel two points. If you cannot, move the points a little further apart. When you can feel two points, measure the distance between them. The greater the distance, the lower the sensitivity. You can repeat this test on different parts of your body. You should find that the measure on the forearm is around 10 times that of the finger or thumb. The fingers and thumbs have the highest acuity.

A second aspect of haptic perception is *kinesthesis*: awareness of the position of the body and limbs. This is due to receptors in the joints. Again there are three types: rapidly adapting, which respond when a limb is moved in a particular direction; slowly adapting, which respond to both movement and static position; and positional receptors, which only respond when a limb is in a static position. This perception affects both comfort and performance. For example, for a touch typist, awareness of the relative positions of the fingers and feedback from the keyboard are very important.

Handling the goods

E-commerce has become very successful in some areas of sales, such as travel services, books and CDs, and food. However, in some retail areas, such as clothes shopping, e-commerce has been less successful. Why?

When buying train and airline tickets and, to some extent, books and food, the experience of shopping is less important than the convenience. So, as long as we know what we want, we are happy to shop online. With clothes, the experience of shopping is far more important. We need to be able to handle the goods, feel the texture of the material, check the weight to test quality. Even if we know that something will fit us we still want to be able to handle it before buying.

Research into haptic interaction (see Chapter 2 and Chapter 10) is looking at ways of solving this problem. By using special force feedback and tactile hardware, users are able to feel surfaces and shape. For example, a demonstration environment called TouchCity allows people to walk around a virtual shopping mall, pick up products and feel their texture and weight. A key problem with the commercial use of such an application, however, is that the haptic experience requires expensive hardware not yet available to the average e-shopper. However, in future, such immersive e-commerce experiences are likely to be the norm. (See www.novint.com/)

1.2.4 Movement

Before leaving this section on the human's input–output channels, we need to consider motor control and how the way we move affects our interaction with computers. A simple action such as hitting a button in response to a question involves a number of processing stages. The stimulus (of the question) is received through the sensory receptors and transmitted to the brain. The question is processed and a valid response generated. The brain then tells the appropriate muscles to respond. Each of these stages takes time, which can be roughly divided into reaction time and movement time.

Movement time is dependent largely on the physical characteristics of the subjects: their age and fitness, for example. Reaction time varies according to the sensory channel through which the stimulus is received. A person can react to an auditory signal in approximately 150 ms, to a visual signal in 200 ms and to pain in 700 ms. However, a combined signal will result in the quickest response. Factors such as skill or practice can reduce reaction time, and fatigue can increase it.

A second measure of motor skill is accuracy. One question that we should ask is whether speed of reaction results in reduced accuracy. This is dependent on the task and the user. In some cases, requiring increased reaction time reduces accuracy. This is the premise behind many arcade and video games where less skilled users fail at levels of play that require faster responses. However, for skilled operators this is not necessarily the case. Studies of keyboard operators have shown that, although the faster operators were up to twice as fast as the others, the slower ones made 10 times the errors.

Speed and accuracy of movement are important considerations in the design of interactive systems, primarily in terms of the time taken to move to a particular target on a screen. The target may be a button, a menu item or an icon, for example. The time taken to hit a target is a function of the size of the target and the distance that has to be moved. This is formalized in *Fitts' law* [135]. There are many variations of this formula, which have varying constants, but they are all very similar. One common form is

$$\text{Movement time} = a + b \log_2(\text{distance/size} + 1)$$

where a and b are empirically determined constants.

This affects the type of target we design. Since users will find it more difficult to manipulate small objects, targets should generally be as large as possible and the distance to be moved as small as possible. This has led to suggestions that pie-chart-shaped menus are preferable to lists since all options are equidistant. However, the trade-off is increased use of screen estate, so the choice may not be so simple. If lists are used, the most frequently used options can be placed closest to the user's start point (for example, at the top of the menu). The implications of Fitts' law in design are discussed in more detail in Chapter 12.

1.3   HUMAN MEMORY

Have you ever played the memory game? The idea is that each player has to recount a list of objects and add one more to the end. There are many variations but the objects are all loosely related: 'I went to the market and bought a lemon, some oranges, bacon . . .' or 'I went to the zoo and saw monkeys, and lions, and tigers . . .' and so on. As the list grows objects are missed out or recalled in the wrong order and so people are eliminated from the game. The winner is the person remaining at the end. Such games rely on our ability to store and retrieve information, even seemingly arbitrary items. This is the job of our memory system.

Indeed, much of our everyday activity relies on memory. As well as storing all our factual knowledge, our memory contains our knowledge of actions or procedures.

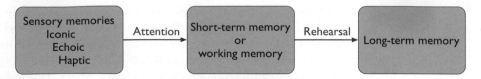

Figure 1.9   A model of the structure of memory

It allows us to repeat actions, to use language, and to use new information received via our senses. It also gives us our sense of identity, by preserving information from our past experiences.

But how does our memory work? How do we remember arbitrary lists such as those generated in the memory game? Why do some people remember more easily than others? And what happens when we forget?

In order to answer questions such as these, we need to understand some of the capabilities and limitations of human memory. Memory is the second part of our model of the human as an information-processing system. However, as we noted earlier, such a division is simplistic since, as we shall see, memory is associated with each level of processing. Bearing this in mind, we will consider the way in which memory is structured and the activities that take place within the system.

It is generally agreed that there are three types of memory or memory function: *sensory buffers*, *short-term memory* or *working memory*, and *long-term memory*. There is some disagreement as to whether these are three separate systems or different functions of the same system. We will not concern ourselves here with the details of this debate, which is discussed in detail by Baddeley [21], but will indicate the evidence used by both sides as we go along. For our purposes, it is sufficient to note three separate types of memory. These memories interact, with information being processed and passed between memory stores, as shown in Figure 1.9.

1.3.1 Sensory memory

The sensory memories act as buffers for stimuli received through the senses. A sensory memory exists for each sensory channel: *iconic memory* for visual stimuli, *echoic memory* for aural stimuli and *haptic memory* for touch. These memories are constantly overwritten by new information coming in on these channels.

We can demonstrate the existence of iconic memory by moving a finger in front of the eye. Can you see it in more than one place at once? This indicates a persistence of the image after the stimulus has been removed. A similar effect is noticed most vividly at firework displays where moving sparklers leave a persistent image. Information remains in iconic memory very briefly, in the order of 0.5 seconds.

Similarly, the existence of echoic memory is evidenced by our ability to ascertain the direction from which a sound originates. This is due to information being received by both ears. However, since this information is received at different times, we must store the stimulus in the meantime. Echoic memory allows brief 'play-back' of information. Have you ever had someone ask you a question when you are reading? You ask them to repeat the question, only to realize that you know what was asked after all. This experience, too, is evidence of the existence of echoic memory.

Information is passed from sensory memory into short-term memory by attention, thereby filtering the stimuli to only those which are of interest at a given time. Attention is the concentration of the mind on one out of a number of competing stimuli or thoughts. It is clear that we are able to focus our attention selectively, choosing to attend to one thing rather than another. This is due to the limited capacity of our sensory and mental processes. If we did not selectively attend to the stimuli coming into our senses, we would be overloaded. We can choose which stimuli to attend to, and this choice is governed to an extent by our *arousal*, our level of interest or need. This explains the cocktail party phenomenon mentioned earlier: we can attend to one conversation over the background noise, but we may choose to switch our attention to a conversation across the room if we hear our name mentioned. Information received by sensory memories is quickly passed into a more permanent memory store, or overwritten and lost.

1.3.2 Short-term memory

Short-term memory or working memory acts as a 'scratch-pad' for temporary recall of information. It is used to store information which is only required fleetingly. For example, calculate the multiplication 35×6 in your head. The chances are that you will have done this calculation in stages, perhaps 5×6 and then 30×6 and added the results; or you may have used the fact that $6 = 2 \times 3$ and calculated $2 \times 35 = 70$ followed by 3×70. To perform calculations such as this we need to store the intermediate stages for use later. Or consider reading. In order to comprehend this sentence you need to hold in your mind the beginning of the sentence as you read the rest. Both of these tasks use short-term memory.

Short-term memory can be accessed rapidly, in the order of 70 ms. However, it also decays rapidly, meaning that information can only be held there temporarily, in the order of 200 ms.

Short-term memory also has a limited capacity. There are two basic methods for measuring memory capacity. The first involves determining the length of a sequence which can be remembered in order. The second allows items to be freely recalled in any order. Using the first measure, the average person can remember 7 ± 2 digits. This was established in experiments by Miller [234]. Try it. Look at the following number sequence:

265397620853

Now write down as much of the sequence as you can remember. Did you get it all right? If not, how many digits could you remember? If you remembered between five and nine digits your *digit span* is average.

Now try the following sequence:

44 113 245 8920

Did you recall that more easily? Here the digits are grouped or *chunked*. A generalization of the 7 ± 2 rule is that we can remember 7 ± 2 *chunks* of information. Therefore chunking information can increase the short-term memory capacity. The limited capacity of short-term memory produces a subconscious desire to create chunks, and so optimize the use of the memory. The successful formation of a chunk is known as *closure*. This process can be generalized to account for the desire to complete or close tasks held in short-term memory. If a subject fails to do this or is prevented from doing so by interference, the subject is liable to lose track of what she is doing and make consequent errors.

DESIGN FOCUS

Cashing in

Closure gives you a nice 'done it' when we complete some part of a task. At this point our minds have a tendency to flush short-term memory in order to get on with the next job. Early automatic teller machines (ATMs) gave the customer money before returning their bank card. On receiving the money the customer would reach closure and hence often forget to take the card. Modern ATMs return the card first!

The sequence of chunks given above also makes use of pattern abstraction: it is written in the form of a UK telephone number which makes it easier to remember. We may even recognize the first sets of digits as the international code for the UK and the dialing code for Leeds – chunks of information. Patterns can be useful as aids to memory. For example, most people would have difficulty remembering the following sequence of chunks:

HEC ATR ANU PTH ETR EET

However, if you notice that by moving the last character to the first position, you get the statement 'the cat ran up the tree', the sequence is easy to recall.

In experiments where subjects were able to recall words freely, evidence shows that recall of the last words presented is better than recall of those in the middle [296]. This is known as the *recency effect*. However, if the subject is asked to perform another task between presentation and recall (for example, counting backwards) the recency effect is eliminated. The recall of the other words is unaffected. This suggests that short-term memory recall is damaged by interference of other information. However, the fact that this interference does not affect recall of earlier items provides some evidence for the existence of separate long-term and short-term memories. The early items are held in a long-term store which is unaffected by the recency effect.

Interference does not necessarily impair recall in short-term memory. Baddeley asked subjects to remember six-digit numbers and attend to sentence processing at the same time [21]. They were asked to answer questions on sentences, such as 'A precedes B: AB is true or false?'. Surprisingly, this did not result in interference, suggesting that in fact short-term memory is not a unitary system but is made up of a number of components, including a visual channel and an articulatory channel. The task of sentence processing used the visual channel, while the task of remembering digits used the articulatory channel, so interference only occurs if tasks utilize the same channel.

These findings led Baddeley to propose a model of working memory that incorporated a number of elements together with a central processing executive. This is illustrated in Figure 1.10.

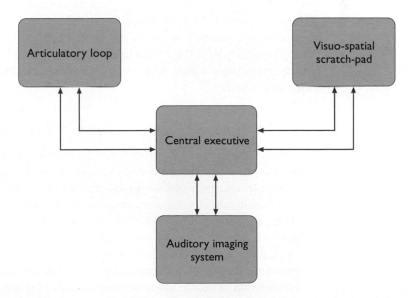

Figure 1.10   A more detailed model of short-term memory

DESIGN FOCUS

7 ± 2 revisited

When we looked at short-term memory, we noted the general rule that people can hold 7 ± 2 items or chunks of information in short-term memory. It is a principle that people tend to remember but it can be misapplied. For example, it is often suggested that this means that lists, menus and other groups of items should be designed to be no more than 7 items long. But use of menus and lists of course has little to do with short-term memory – they are available in the environment as cues and so do not need to be remembered.

On the other hand the 7 ± 2 rule would apply in command line interfaces. Imagine a scenario where a UNIX user looks up a command in the manual. Perhaps the command has a number of parameters of options, to be applied in a particular order, and it is going to be applied to several files that have long path names. The user then has to hold the command, its parameters and the file path names in short-term memory while he types them in. Here we could say that the task may cause problems if the number of items or chunks in the command line string is more than 7.

1.3.3 Long-term memory

If short-term memory is our working memory or 'scratch-pad', long-term memory is our main resource. Here we store factual information, experiential knowledge, procedural rules of behavior – in fact, everything that we 'know'. It differs from short-term memory in a number of significant ways. First, it has a huge, if not unlimited, capacity. Secondly, it has a relatively slow access time of approximately a tenth of a second. Thirdly, forgetting occurs more slowly in long-term memory, if at all. These distinctions provide further evidence of a memory structure with several parts.

Long-term memory is intended for the long-term storage of information. Information is placed there from working memory through rehearsal. Unlike working memory there is little decay: long-term recall after minutes is the same as that after hours or days.

Long-term memory structure

There are two types of long-term memory: *episodic memory* and *semantic memory*. Episodic memory represents our memory of events and experiences in a serial form. It is from this memory that we can reconstruct the actual events that took place at a given point in our lives. Semantic memory, on the other hand, is a structured record of facts, concepts and skills that we have acquired. The information in semantic memory is derived from that in our episodic memory, such that we can learn new facts or concepts from our experiences.

Semantic memory is structured in some way to allow access to information, representation of relationships between pieces of information, and inference. One model for the way in which semantic memory is structured is as a network. Items are

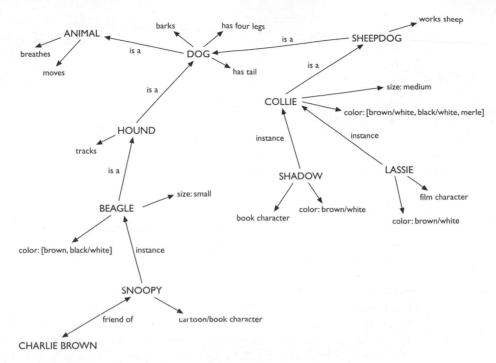

Figure 1.11   Long-term memory may store information in a semantic network

associated to each other in classes, and may inherit attributes from parent classes. This model is known as a *semantic network*. As an example, our knowledge about dogs may be stored in a network such as that shown in Figure 1.11.

Specific breed attributes may be stored with each given breed, yet general dog information is stored at a higher level. This allows us to generalize about specific cases. For instance, we may not have been told that the sheepdog Shadow has four legs and a tail, but we can infer this information from our general knowledge about sheepdogs and dogs in general. Note also that there are connections within the network which link into other domains of knowledge, for example cartoon characters. This illustrates how our knowledge is organized by association.

The viability of semantic networks as a model of memory organization has been demonstrated by Collins and Quillian [74]. Subjects were asked questions about different properties of related objects and their reaction times were measured. The types of question asked (taking examples from our own network) were 'Can a collie breathe?', 'Is a beagle a hound?' and 'Does a hound track?' In spite of the fact that the answers to such questions may seem obvious, subjects took longer to answer questions such as 'Can a collie breathe?' than ones such as 'Does a hound track?' The reason for this, it is suggested, is that in the former case subjects had to search further through the memory hierarchy to find the answer, since information is stored at its most abstract level.

A number of other memory structures have been proposed to explain how we represent and store different types of knowledge. Each of these represents a different

DOG

Fixed
- legs: 4

Default
- diet: carnivorous
- sound: bark

Variable
- size:
- color:

COLLIE

Fixed
- breed of: DOG
- type: sheepdog

Default
- size: 65 cm

Variable
- color:

Figure 1.12 A frame-based representation of knowledge

aspect of knowledge and, as such, the models can be viewed as complementary rather than mutually exclusive. Semantic networks represent the associations and relationships between single items in memory. However, they do not allow us to model the representation of more complex objects or events, which are perhaps composed of a number of items or activities. Structured representations such as *frames* and *scripts* organize information into data structures. *Slots* in these structures allow attribute values to be added. Frame slots may contain default, fixed or variable information. A frame is instantiated when the slots are filled with appropriate values. Frames and scripts can be linked together in networks to represent hierarchical structured knowledge.

Returning to the 'dog' domain, a frame-based representation of the knowledge may look something like Figure 1.12. The fixed slots are those for which the attribute value is set, default slots represent the usual attribute value, although this may be overridden in particular instantiations (for example, the Basenji does not bark), and variable slots can be filled with particular values in a given instance. Slots can also contain procedural knowledge. Actions or operations can be associated with a slot and performed, for example, whenever the value of the slot is changed.

Frames extend semantic nets to include structured, hierarchical information. They represent knowledge items in a way which makes explicit the relative importance of each piece of information.

Scripts attempt to model the representation of stereotypical knowledge about situations. Consider the following sentence:

> John took his dog to the surgery. After seeing the vet, he left.

From our knowledge of the activities of dog owners and vets, we may fill in a substantial amount of detail. The animal was ill. The vet examined and treated the animal. John paid for the treatment before leaving. We are less likely to assume the alternative reading of the sentence, that John took an instant dislike to the vet on sight and did not stay long enough to talk to him!

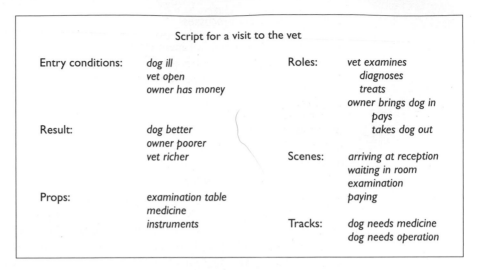

Figure 1.13 A script for visiting the vet

A script represents this default or stereotypical information, allowing us to interpret partial descriptions or cues fully. A script comprises a number of elements, which, like slots, can be filled with appropriate information:

Entry conditions   Conditions that must be satisfied for the script to be activated.

Result   Conditions that will be true after the script is terminated.

Props   Objects involved in the events described in the script.

Roles   Actions performed by particular participants.

Scenes   The sequences of events that occur.

Tracks   A variation on the general pattern representing an alternative scenario.

An example script for going to the vet is shown in Figure 1.13.

A final type of knowledge representation which we hold in memory is the representation of procedural knowledge, our knowledge of how to do something. A common model for this is the production system. Condition–action rules are stored in long-term memory. Information coming into short-term memory can match a condition in one of these rules and result in the action being executed. For example, a pair of production rules might be

```
IF dog is wagging tail
THEN pat dog

IF dog is growling
THEN run away
```

If we then meet a growling dog, the condition in the second rule is matched, and we respond by turning tail and running. (Not to be recommended by the way!)

Long-term memory processes

So much for the structure of memory, but what about the processes which it uses? There are three main activities related to long-term memory: storage or remembering of information, forgetting and information retrieval. We shall consider each of these in turn.

First, how does information get into long-term memory and how can we improve this process? Information from short-term memory is stored in long-term memory by rehearsal. The repeated exposure to a stimulus or the rehearsal of a piece of information transfers it into long-term memory.

This process can be optimized in a number of ways. Ebbinghaus performed numerous experiments on memory, using himself as a subject [117]. In these experiments he tested his ability to learn and repeat nonsense syllables, comparing his recall minutes, hours and days after the learning process. He discovered that the amount learned was directly proportional to the amount of time spent learning. This is known as the *total time hypothesis*. However, experiments by Baddeley and others suggest that learning time is most effective if it is distributed over time [22]. For example, in an experiment in which Post Office workers were taught to type, those whose training period was divided into weekly sessions of one hour performed better than those who spent two or four hours a week learning (although the former obviously took more weeks to complete their training). This is known as the *distribution of practice effect*.

However, repetition is not enough to learn information well. If information is not meaningful it is more difficult to remember. This is illustrated by the fact that it is more difficult to remember a set of words representing concepts than a set of words representing objects. Try it. First try to remember the words in list A and test yourself.

List A: Faith Age Cold Tenet Quiet Logic Idea Value Past Large

Now try list B.

List B: Boat Tree Cat Child Rug Plate Church Gun Flame Head

The second list was probably easier to remember than the first since you could visualize the objects in the second list.

Sentences are easier still to memorize. Bartlett performed experiments on remembering meaningful information (as opposed to meaningless such as Ebbinghaus used) [28]. In one such experiment he got subjects to learn a story about an unfamiliar culture and then retell it. He found that subjects would retell the story replacing unfamiliar words and concepts with words which were meaningful to them. Stories were effectively translated into the subject's own culture. This is related to the semantic structuring of long-term memory: if information is meaningful and familiar, it can be related to existing structures and more easily incorporated into memory.

Memorable or secure?

As online activities become more widespread, people are having to remember more and more access information, such as passwords and security checks. The average active internet user may have separate passwords and user names for several email accounts, mailing lists, e-shopping sites, e-banking, online auctions and more! Remembering these passwords is not easy.

From a security perspective it is important that passwords are random. Words and names are very easy to crack, hence the recommendation that passwords are frequently changed and constructed from random strings of letters and numbers. But in reality these are the hardest things for people to commit to memory. Hence many people will use the same password for all their online activities (rarely if ever changing it) and will choose a word or a name that is easy for them to remember, in spite of the obviously increased security risks. Security here is in conflict with memorability!

A solution to this is to construct a nonsense password out of letters or numbers that will have meaning to you but will not make up a word in a dictionary (e.g. initials of names, numbers from significant dates or postcodes, and so on). Then what is remembered is the meaningful rule for constructing the password, and not a meaningless string of alphanumeric characters.

So if structure, familiarity and concreteness help us in learning information, what causes us to lose this information, to forget? There are two main theories of forgetting: *decay* and *interference*. The first theory suggests that the information held in long-term memory may eventually be forgotten. Ebbinghaus concluded from his experiments with nonsense syllables that information in memory decayed logarithmically, that is that it was lost rapidly to begin with, and then more slowly. *Jost's law*, which follows from this, states that if two memory traces are equally strong at a given time the older one will be more durable.

The second theory is that information is lost from memory through interference. If we acquire new information it causes the loss of old information. This is termed *retroactive interference*. A common example of this is the fact that if you change telephone numbers, learning your new number makes it more difficult to remember your old number. This is because the new association masks the old. However, sometimes the old memory trace breaks through and interferes with new information. This is called *proactive inhibition*. An example of this is when you find yourself driving to your old house rather than your new one.

Forgetting is also affected by emotional factors. In experiments, subjects given emotive words and non-emotive words found the former harder to remember in the short term but easier in the long term. Indeed, this observation tallies with our experience of selective memory. We tend to remember positive information rather than negative (hence nostalgia for the 'good old days'), and highly emotive events rather than mundane.

It is debatable whether we ever actually forget anything or whether it just becomes increasingly difficult to access certain items from memory. This question is in some ways moot since it is impossible to prove that we *do* forget: appearing to have forgotten something may just be caused by not being able to retrieve it! However, there is evidence to suggest that we may not lose information completely from long-term memory. First, proactive inhibition demonstrates the recovery of old information even after it has been 'lost' by interference. Secondly, there is the 'tip of the tongue' experience, which indicates that some information is present but cannot be satisfactorily accessed. Thirdly, information may not be recalled but may be recognized, or may be recalled only with prompting.

This leads us to the third process of memory: information retrieval. Here we need to distinguish between two types of information retrieval, recall and recognition. In recall the information is reproduced from memory. In recognition, the presentation of the information provides the knowledge that the information has been seen before. Recognition is the less complex cognitive activity since the information is provided as a cue.

However, recall can be assisted by the provision of retrieval cues, which enable the subject quickly to access the information in memory. One such cue is the use of categories. In an experiment subjects were asked to recall lists of words, some of which were organized into categories and some of which were randomly organized. The words that were related to a category were easier to recall than the others [38]. Recall is even more successful if subjects are allowed to categorize their own lists of words during learning. For example, consider the following list of words:

child red plane dog friend blood cold tree big angry

Now make up a story that links the words using as vivid imagery as possible. Now try to recall as many of the words as you can. Did you find this easier than the previous experiment where the words were unrelated?

The use of vivid imagery is a common cue to help people remember information. It is known that people often visualize a scene that is described to them. They can then answer questions based on their visualization. Indeed, subjects given a description of a scene often embellish it with additional information. Consider the following description and imagine the scene:

The engines roared above the noise of the crowd. Even in the blistering heat people rose to their feet and waved their hands in excitement. The flag fell and they were off. Within seconds the car had pulled away from the pack and was careering round the bend at a desperate pace. Its wheels momentarily left the ground as it cornered. Coming down the straight the sun glinted on its shimmering paint. The driver gripped the wheel with fierce concentration. Sweat lay in fine drops on his brow.

Without looking back to the passage, what color is the car?

If you could answer that question you have visualized the scene, including the car's color. In fact, the color of the car is not mentioned in the description at all.

Improve your memory

Many people can perform astonishing feats of memory: recalling the sequence of cards in a pack (or multiple packs – up to six have been reported), or recounting π to 1000 decimal places, for example. There are also adverts to 'Improve Your Memory' (usually leading to success, or wealth, or other such inducement), and so the question arises: can you improve your memory abilities? The answer is yes; this exercise shows you one technique.

Look at the list below of numbers and associated words:

1	bun	6	sticks
2	shoe	7	heaven
3	tree	8	gate
4	door	9	wine
5	hive	10	hen

Notice that the words sound similar to the numbers. Now think about the words one at a time and visualize them, in as much detail as possible. For example, for '1', think of a large, sticky iced bun, the base spiralling round and round, with raisins in it, covered in sweet, white, gooey icing. Now do the rest, using as much visualization as you can muster: imagine how things would look, smell, taste, sound, and so on.

This is your reference list, and you need to know it off by heart.

Having learnt it, look at a pile of at least a dozen odd items collected together by a colleague. The task is to look at the collection of objects for only 30 seconds, and then list as many as possible without making a mistake or viewing the collection again. Most people can manage between five and eight items, if they do not know any memory-enhancing techniques like the following.

Mentally pick one (say, for example, a paper clip), and call it number one. Now visualize it interacting with the bun. It can get stuck into the icing on the top of the bun, and make your fingers all gooey and sticky when you try to remove it. If you ate the bun without noticing, you'd get a crunched tooth when you bit into it – imagine how that would feel. When you've really got a graphic scenario developed, move on to the next item, call it number two, and again visualize it interacting with the reference item, shoe. Continue down your list, until you have done 10 things.

This should take you about the 30 seconds allowed. Then hide the collection and try and recall the numbers in order, the associated reference word, and then the image associated with that word. You should find that you can recall the 10 associated items practically every time. The technique can be easily extended by extending your reference list.

1.4   THINKING: REASONING AND PROBLEM SOLVING

We have considered how information finds its way into and out of the human system and how it is stored. Finally, we come to look at how it is processed and manipulated. This is perhaps the area which is most complex and which separates humans from other information-processing systems, both artificial and natural. Although it is clear that animals receive and store information, there is little evidence to suggest that they can use it in quite the same way as humans. Similarly, artificial intelligence has produced machines which can see (albeit in a limited way) and store information. But their ability to use that information is limited to small domains.

Humans, on the other hand, are able to use information to reason and solve problems, and indeed do these activities when the information is partial or unavailable. Human thought is conscious and self-aware: while we may not always be able to identify the processes we use, we can identify the products of these processes, our thoughts. In addition, we are able to think about things of which we have no experience, and solve problems which we have never seen before. How is this done?

Thinking can require different amounts of knowledge. Some thinking activities are very directed and the knowledge required is constrained. Others require vast amounts of knowledge from different domains. For example, performing a subtraction calculation requires a relatively small amount of knowledge, from a constrained domain, whereas understanding newspaper headlines demands knowledge of politics, social structures, public figures and world events.

In this section we will consider two categories of thinking: reasoning and problem solving. In practice these are not distinct since the activity of solving a problem may well involve reasoning and vice versa. However, the distinction is a common one and is helpful in clarifying the processes involved.

1.4.1 Reasoning

Reasoning is the process by which we use the knowledge we have to draw conclusions or infer something new about the domain of interest. There are a number of different types of reasoning: *deductive*, *inductive* and *abductive*. We use each of these types of reasoning in everyday life, but they differ in significant ways.

Deductive reasoning

Deductive reasoning derives the logically necessary conclusion from the given premises. For example,

> If it is Friday then she will go to work
> It is Friday
> Therefore she will go to work.

It is important to note that this is the *logical* conclusion from the premises; it does not necessarily have to correspond to our notion of truth. So, for example,

> If it is raining then the ground is dry
> It is raining
> Therefore the ground is dry.

is a perfectly valid deduction, even though it conflicts with our knowledge of what is true in the world.

Deductive reasoning is therefore often misapplied. Given the premises

Some people are babies
Some babies cry

many people will infer that 'Some people cry'. This is in fact an invalid deduction since we are not told that all babies are people. It is therefore logically possible that the babies who cry are those who are not people.

It is at this point, where truth and validity clash, that human deduction is poorest. One explanation for this is that people bring their world knowledge into the reasoning process. There is good reason for this. It allows us to take short cuts which make dialog and interaction between people informative but efficient. We assume a certain amount of shared knowledge in our dealings with each other, which in turn allows us to interpret the inferences and deductions implied by others. If validity rather than truth was preferred, all premises would have to be made explicit.

Inductive reasoning

Induction is generalizing from cases we have seen to infer information about cases we have not seen. For example, if every elephant we have ever seen has a trunk, we infer that all elephants have trunks. Of course, this inference is unreliable and cannot be proved to be true; it can only be proved to be false. We can disprove the inference simply by producing an elephant without a trunk. However, we can never prove it true because, no matter how many elephants with trunks we have seen or are known to exist, the next one we see may be trunkless. The best that we can do is gather evidence to support our inductive inference.

In spite of its unreliability, induction is a useful process, which we use constantly in learning about our environment. We can never see all the elephants that have ever lived or will ever live, but we have certain knowledge about elephants which we are prepared to trust for all practical purposes, which has largely been inferred by induction. Even if we saw an elephant without a trunk, we would be unlikely to move from our position that 'All elephants have trunks', since we are better at using positive than negative evidence. This is illustrated in an experiment first devised by Wason [365]. You are presented with four cards as in Figure 1.14. Each card has a number on one side and a letter on the other. Which cards would you need to pick up to test the truth of the statement 'If a card has a vowel on one side it has an even number on the other'?

A common response to this (was it yours?) is to check the E and the 4. However, this uses only positive evidence. In fact, to test the truth of the statement we need to check negative evidence: if we can find a card which has an odd number on one side and a vowel on the other we have disproved the statement. We must therefore check E and 7. (It does not matter what is on the other side of the other cards: the statement does not say that all even numbers have vowels, just that all vowels have even numbers.)

| 4 | E | 7 | K |

Figure 1.14   Wason's cards

Filling the gaps

Look again at Wason's cards in Figure 1.14. In the text we say that you only need to check the E and the 7. This is correct, but only because we very carefully stated in the text that 'each card has a number on one side and a letter on the other'. If the problem were stated without that condition then the K would also need to be examined in case it has a vowel on the other side. In fact, when the problem is so stated, even the most careful subjects ignore this possibility. Why? Because the nature of the problem implicitly suggests that each card has a number on one side and a letter on the other.

This is similar to the embellishment of the story at the end of Section 1.3.3. In fact, we constantly fill in gaps in the evidence that reaches us through our senses. Although this can lead to errors in our reasoning it is also essential for us to function. In the real world we rarely have all the evidence necessary for logical deductions and at all levels of perception and reasoning we fill in details in order to allow higher levels of reasoning to work.

Abductive reasoning

The third type of reasoning is abduction. Abduction reasons from a fact to the action or state that caused it. This is the method we use to derive explanations for the events we observe. For example, suppose we know that Sam always drives too fast when she has been drinking. If we see Sam driving too fast we may infer that she has been drinking. Of course, this too is unreliable since there may be another reason why she is driving fast: she may have been called to an emergency, for example.

In spite of its unreliability, it is clear that people do infer explanations in this way, and hold onto them until they have evidence to support an alternative theory or explanation. This can lead to problems in using interactive systems. If an event always follows an action, the user will infer that the event is caused by the action unless evidence to the contrary is made available. If, in fact, the event and the action are unrelated, confusion and even error often result.

1.4.2 Problem solving

If reasoning is a means of inferring new information from what is already known, problem solving is the process of finding a solution to an unfamiliar task, using the knowledge we have. Human problem solving is characterized by the ability to adapt the information we have to deal with new situations. However, often solutions seem to be original and creative. There are a number of different views of how people solve problems. The earliest, dating back to the first half of the twentieth century, is the *Gestalt* view that problem solving involves both reuse of knowledge and insight. This has been largely superseded but the questions it was trying to address remain and its influence can be seen in later research. A second major theory, proposed in the 1970s by Newell and Simon, was the *problem space theory*, which takes the view that the mind is a limited information processor. Later variations on this drew on the earlier theory and attempted to reinterpret Gestalt theory in terms of information-processing theories. We will look briefly at each of these views.

Gestalt theory

Gestalt psychologists were answering the claim, made by behaviorists, that problem solving is a matter of reproducing known responses or trial and error. This explanation was considered by the Gestalt school to be insufficient to account for human problem-solving behavior. Instead, they claimed, problem solving is both *productive* and *reproductive*. Reproductive problem solving draws on previous experience as the behaviorists claimed, but productive problem solving involves insight and restructuring of the problem. Indeed, reproductive problem solving could be a hindrance to finding a solution, since a person may 'fixate' on the known aspects of the problem and so be unable to see novel interpretations that might lead to a solution.

Gestalt psychologists backed up their claims with experimental evidence. Kohler provided evidence of apparent insight being demonstrated by apes, which he observed joining sticks together in order to reach food outside their cages [202]. However, this was difficult to verify since the apes had once been wild and so could have been using previous knowledge.

Other experiments observed human problem-solving behavior. One well-known example of this is Maier's *pendulum problem* [224]. The problem was this: the subjects were in a room with two pieces of string hanging from the ceiling. Also in the room were other objects including pliers, poles and extensions. The task set was to tie the pieces of string together. However, they were too far apart to catch hold of both at once. Although various solutions were proposed by subjects, few chose to use the weight of the pliers as a pendulum to 'swing' the strings together. However, when the experimenter brushed against the string, setting it in motion, this solution presented itself to subjects. Maier interpreted this as an example of productive restructuring. The movement of the string had given insight and allowed the subjects to see the problem in a new way. The experiment also illustrates fixation: subjects were initially unable to see beyond their view of the role or use of a pair of pliers.

Although Gestalt theory is attractive in terms of its description of human problem solving, it does not provide sufficient evidence or structure to support its theories. It does not explain when restructuring occurs or what insight is, for example. However, the move away from behaviorist theories was helpful in paving the way for the information-processing theory that was to follow.

Problem space theory

Newell and Simon proposed that problem solving centers on the problem space. The problem space comprises *problem states*, and problem solving involves generating these states using legal state transition operators. The problem has an initial state and a goal state and people use the operators to move from the former to the latter. Such problem spaces may be huge, and so *heuristics* are employed to select appropriate operators to reach the goal. One such heuristic is *means–ends analysis*. In means–ends analysis the initial state is compared with the goal state and an operator chosen to reduce the difference between the two. For example, imagine you are reorganizing your office and you want to move your desk from the north wall of the room to the window. Your initial state is that the desk is at the north wall. The goal state is that the desk is by the window. The main difference between these two is the location of your desk. You have a number of operators which you can apply to moving things: you can carry them or push them or drag them, etc. However, you know that to carry something it must be light and that your desk is heavy. You therefore have a new subgoal: to make the desk light. Your operators for this may involve removing drawers, and so on.

An important feature of Newell and Simon's model is that it operates within the constraints of the human processing system, and so searching the problem space is limited by the capacity of short-term memory, and the speed at which information can be retrieved. Within the problem space framework, experience allows us to solve problems more easily since we can structure the problem space appropriately and choose operators efficiently.

Newell and Simon's theory, and their *General Problem Solver* model which is based on it, have largely been applied to problem solving in well-defined domains, for example solving puzzles. These problems may be unfamiliar but the knowledge that is required to solve them is present in the statement of the problem and the expected solution is clear. In real-world problems finding the knowledge required to solve the problem may be part of the problem, or specifying the goal may be difficult. Problems such as these require significant domain knowledge: for example, to solve a programming problem you need knowledge of the language and the domain in which the program operates. In this instance specifying the goal clearly may be a significant part of solving the problem.

However, the problem space framework provides a clear theory of problem solving, which can be extended, as we shall see when we look at skill acquisition in the next section, to deal with knowledge-intensive problem solving. First we will look briefly at the use of analogy in problem solving.

Worked exercise

Identify the goals and operators involved in the problem 'delete the second paragraph of the document' on a word processor. Now use a word processor to delete a paragraph and note your actions, goals and subgoals. How well did they match your earlier description?

Answer

Assume you have a document open and you are at some arbitrary position within it. You also need to decide which operators are available and what their preconditions and results are. Based on an imaginary word processor we assume the following operators (you may wish to use your own WP package):

Operator	Precondition	Result
delete_paragraph	Cursor at start of paragraph	Paragraph deleted
move_to_paragraph	Cursor anywhere in document	Cursor moves to start of next paragraph (except where there is no next paragraph when no effect)
move_to_start	Cursor anywhere in document	Cursor at start of document

Goal: *delete second paragraph in document*
Looking at the operators an obvious one to resolve this goal is delete_paragraph which has the precondition 'cursor at start of paragraph'. We therefore have a new subgoal: *move_to_paragraph*. The precondition is 'cursor anywhere in document' (which we can meet) but we want the second paragraph so we must initially be in the first.

We set up a new subgoal, move_to_start, with precondition 'cursor anywhere in document' and result 'cursor at start of document'. We can then apply *move_to_paragraph* and finally *delete_paragraph*.

We assume some knowledge here (that the second paragraph is the paragraph after the first one).

Analogy in problem solving

A third element of problem solving is the use of analogy. Here we are interested in how people solve novel problems. One suggestion is that this is done by mapping knowledge relating to a similar known domain to the new problem – called *analogical mapping*. Similarities between the known domain and the new one are noted and operators from the known domain are transferred to the new one.

This process has been investigated using analogous stories. Gick and Holyoak [149] gave subjects the following problem:

A doctor is treating a malignant tumor. In order to destroy it he needs to blast it with high-intensity rays. However, these will also destroy the healthy tissue surrounding the tumor. If he lessens the rays' intensity the tumor will remain. How does he destroy the tumor?

The solution to this problem is to fire low-intensity rays from different directions converging on the tumor. That way, the healthy tissue receives harmless low-intensity rays while the tumor receives the rays combined, making a high-intensity dose. The investigators found that only 10% of subjects reached this solution without help. However, this rose to 80% when they were given this analogous story and told that it may help them:

> A general is attacking a fortress. He can't send all his men in together as the roads are mined to explode if large numbers of men cross them. He therefore splits his men into small groups and sends them in on separate roads.

In spite of this, it seems that people often miss analogous information, unless it is semantically close to the problem domain. When subjects were not told to use the story, many failed to see the analogy. However, the number spotting the analogy rose when the story was made semantically close to the problem, for example a general using rays to destroy a castle.

The use of analogy is reminiscent of the Gestalt view of productive restructuring and insight. Old knowledge is used to solve a new problem.

1.4.3 Skill acquisition

All of the problem solving that we have considered so far has concentrated on handling unfamiliar problems. However, for much of the time, the problems that we face are not completely new. Instead, we gradually acquire skill in a particular domain area. But how is such skill acquired and what difference does it make to our problem-solving performance? We can gain insight into how skilled behavior works, and how skills are acquired, by considering the difference between novice and expert behavior in given domains.

Chess: of human and artificial intelligence

A few years ago, Deep Blue, a chess-playing computer, beat Gary Kasparov, the world's top Grand Master, in a full tournament. This was the long-awaited breakthrough for the artificial intelligence (AI) community, who have traditionally seen chess as the ultimate test of their art. However, despite the fact that computer chess programs can play at Grand Master level against human players, this does not mean they play in the same way. For each move played, Deep Blue investigated many millions of alternative moves and counter-moves. In contrast, a human chess player will only consider a few dozen. But, if the human player is good, these will usually be the right few dozen. The ability to spot patterns allows a human to address a problem with far less effort than a brute force approach. In chess, the number of moves is such that finally brute force, applied fast enough, has overcome human pattern-matching skill. In Go, which has far more possible moves, computer programs do not even reach a good club level of play. Many models of the mental processes have been heavily influenced by computation. It is worth remembering that although there are similarities, computer 'intelligence' is very different from that of humans.

A commonly studied domain is chess playing. It is particularly suitable since it lends itself easily to representation in terms of problem space theory. The initial state is the opening board position; the goal state is one player checkmating the other; operators to move states are legal moves of chess. It is therefore possible to examine skilled behavior within the context of the problem space theory of problem solving.

Studies of chess players by DeGroot, Chase and Simon, among others, produced some interesting observations [64, 65, 88, 89]. In all the experiments the behavior of chess masters was compared with less experienced chess players. The first observation was that players did not consider large numbers of moves in choosing their move, nor did they look ahead more than six moves (often far fewer). Masters considered no more alternatives than the less experienced, but they took less time to make a decision and produced better moves.

So what makes the difference between skilled and less skilled behavior in chess? It appears that chess masters remember board configurations and good moves associated with them. When given actual board positions to remember, masters are much better at reconstructing the board than the less experienced. However, when given random configurations (which were unfamiliar), the groups of players were equally bad at reconstructing the positions. It seems therefore that expert players 'chunk' the board configuration in order to hold it in short-term memory. Expert players use larger chunks than the less experienced and can therefore remember more detail.

This behavior is also seen among skilled computer programmers. They can also reconstruct programs more effectively than novices since they have the structures available to build appropriate chunks. They acquire plans representing code to solve particular problems. When that problem is encountered in a new domain or new program they will recall that particular plan and reuse it.

Another observed difference between skilled and less skilled problem solving is in the way that different problems are grouped. Novices tend to group problems according to superficial characteristics such as the objects or features common to both. Experts, on the other hand, demonstrate a deeper understanding of the problems and group them according to underlying conceptual similarities which may not be at all obvious from the problem descriptions.

Each of these differences stems from a better encoding of knowledge in the expert: information structures are fine tuned at a deep level to enable efficient and accurate retrieval. But how does this happen? How is skill such as this acquired? One model of skill acquisition is Anderson's *ACT** model [14]. ACT* identifies three basic levels of skill:

1. The learner uses general-purpose rules which interpret facts about a problem. This is slow and demanding on memory access.
2. The learner develops rules specific to the task.
3. The rules are tuned to speed up performance.

General mechanisms are provided to account for the transitions between these levels. For example, *proceduralization* is a mechanism to move from the first to the second. It removes the parts of the rule which demand memory access and replaces variables with specific values. *Generalization*, on the other hand, is a mechanism which moves from the second level to the third. It generalizes from the specific cases to general properties of those cases. Commonalities between rules are condensed to produce a general-purpose rule.

These are best illustrated by example. Imagine you are learning to cook. Initially you may have a general rule to tell you how long a dish needs to be in the oven, and a number of explicit representations of dishes in memory. You can instantiate the rule by retrieving information from memory.

```
IF cook[type, ingredients, time]
THEN
    cook for: time
cook[casserole, [chicken,carrots,potatoes], 2 hours]
cook[casserole, [beef,dumplings,carrots], 2 hours]
cook[cake, [flour,sugar,butter,eggs], 45 mins]
```

Gradually your knowledge becomes proceduralized and you have specific rules for each case:

```
IF type is casserole
AND ingredients are [chicken,carrots,potatoes]
THEN
    cook for: 2 hours
IF type is casserole
AND ingredients are [beef,dumplings,carrots]
THEN
    cook for: 2 hours
IF type is cake
AND ingredients are [flour,sugar,butter,eggs]
THEN
    cook for: 45 mins
```

Finally, you may generalize from these rules to produce general-purpose rules, which exploit their commonalities:

```
IF type is casserole
AND ingredients are ANYTHING
THEN
    cook for: 2 hours
```

The first stage uses knowledge extensively. The second stage relies upon known procedures. The third stage represents skilled behavior. Such behavior may in fact become automatic and as such be difficult to make explicit. For example, think of an activity at which you are skilled, perhaps driving a car or riding a bike. Try to describe to someone the exact procedure which you go through to do this. You will find this quite difficult. In fact experts tend to have to rehearse their actions mentally in order to identify exactly what they do. Such skilled behavior is efficient but may cause errors when the context of the activity changes.

1.4.4 Errors and mental models

Human capability for interpreting and manipulating information is quite impressive. However, we do make mistakes. Some are trivial, resulting in no more than temporary inconvenience or annoyance. Others may be more serious, requiring substantial effort to correct. Occasionally an error may have catastrophic effects, as we see when 'human error' results in a plane crash or nuclear plant leak.

Why do we make mistakes and can we avoid them? In order to answer the latter part of the question we must first look at what is going on when we make an error. There are several different types of error. As we saw in the last section some errors result from changes in the context of skilled behavior. If a pattern of behavior has become automatic and we change some aspect of it, the more familiar pattern may break through and cause an error. A familiar example of this is where we intend to stop at the shop on the way home from work but in fact drive past. Here, the activity of driving home is the more familiar and overrides the less familiar intention.

Other errors result from an incorrect understanding, or model, of a situation or system. People build their own theories to understand the causal behavior of systems. These have been termed *mental models*. They have a number of characteristics. Mental models are often partial: the person does not have a full understanding of the working of the whole system. They are unstable and are subject to change. They can be internally inconsistent, since the person may not have worked through the logical consequences of their beliefs. They are often unscientific and may be based on superstition rather than evidence. Often they are based on an incorrect interpretation of the evidence.

DESIGN FOCUS

Human error and false memories

In the second edition of this book, one of the authors added the following story:

> During the Second World War a new cockpit design was introduced for Spitfires. The pilots were trained and flew successfully during training, but would unaccountably bail out when engaged in dog fights. The new design had exchanged the positions of the gun trigger and ejector controls. In the heat of battle the old responses resurfaced and the pilots ejected. Human error, yes, but the designer's error, not the pilot's.

It is a good story, but after the book was published we got several emails saying 'Spitfires didn't have ejector seats'. It was Kai-Mikael Jää-Aro who was able to find what may have been the original to the story (and incidentally inform us what model of Spitfire was in our photo and who the pilot was!). He pointed us to and translated the story of Sierra 44, an S35E Draken reconnaissance aircraft.[1] The full story involves just about every perceptual and cognitive error imaginable, but the point that links to

---

1. Pej Kristoffersson, 1984. Sigurd 44 – Historien om hur man gör bort sig så att det märks by, *Flygrevyn* 2/1984, pp. 44–6.

the (false) Spitfire story is that in the Draken the red buttons for releasing the fuel 'drop' tanks and for the canopy release differed only in very small writing. In an emergency (burning fuel tanks) the pilot accidentally released the canopy and so ended up flying home cabriolet style.

There is a second story of human error here – the author's memory. When the book was written he could not recall where he had come across the story but was convinced it was to do with a Spitfire. It may be that he had been told the story by someone else who had got it mixed up, but it is as likely that he simply remembered the rough outline of the story and then 'reconstructed' the rest. In fact that is exactly how our memories work. Our brains do not bother to lay down every little detail, but when we 'remember' we rebuild what the incident 'must have been' using our world knowledge. This process is completely unconscious and can lead to what are known as *false memories*. This is particularly problematic in witness statements in criminal trials as early questioning by police or lawyers can unintentionally lead to witnesses being sure they have seen things that they have not. Numerous controlled psychological experiments have demonstrated this effect which furthermore is strongly influenced by biasing factors such as the race of supposed criminals.

To save his blushes we have not said here which author's failing memory was responsible for the Spitfire story, but you can read more on this story and also find who it was on the book website at: /e3/online/spitfire/

Courtesy of popperfoto.com

Assuming a person builds a mental model of the system being dealt with, errors may occur if the actual operation differs from the mental model. For example, on one occasion we were staying in a hotel in Germany, attending a conference. In the lobby of the hotel was a lift. Beside the lift door was a button. Our model of the system, based on previous experience of lifts, was that the button would call the lift. We pressed the button and the lobby light went out! In fact the button was a light switch and the lift button was on the inside rim of the lift, hidden from view.

Although both the light switch and the lift button were inconsistent with our mental models of these controls, we would probably have managed if they had been encountered separately. If there had been no button beside the lift we would have looked more closely and found the one on the inner rim. But since the light switch reflected our model of a lift button we looked no further. During our stay we observed many more new guests making the same error.

This illustrates the importance of a correct mental model and the dangers of ignoring conventions. There are certain conventions that we use to interpret the world and ideally designs should support these. If these are to be violated, explicit support must be given to enable us to form a correct mental model. A label on the button saying 'light switch' would have been sufficient.

1.5   EMOTION

So far in this chapter we have concentrated on human perceptual and cognitive abilities. But human experience is far more complex than this. Our emotional response to situations affects how we perform. For example, positive emotions enable us to think more creatively, to solve complex problems, whereas negative emotion pushes us into narrow, focussed thinking. A problem that may be easy to solve when we are relaxed, will become difficult if we are frustrated or afraid.

Psychologists have studied emotional response for decades and there are many theories as to what is happening when we feel an emotion and why such a response occurs. More than a century ago, William James proposed what has become known as the James–Lange theory (Lange was a contemporary of James whose theories were similar): that emotion was the interpretation of a physiological response, rather than the other way around. So while we may feel that we respond *to* an emotion, James contended that we respond physiologically to a stimulus and interpret that as emotion:

> Common sense says, we lose our fortune, are sorry and weep; we meet a bear, are frightened and run; we are insulted by a rival, are angry and strike. The hypothesis here . . . is that we feel sorry because we cry, angry because we strike, afraid because we tremble.
>
> (W. James, *Principles of Psychology*, page 449. Henry Holt, New York, 1890.)

Others, however, disagree. Cannon [54a], for example, argued that our physiological processes are in fact too slow to account for our emotional reactions, and that the physiological responses for some emotional states are too similar (e.g. anger and fear), yet they can be easily distinguished. Experience in studies with the use of drugs that stimulate broadly the same physiological responses as anger or fear seems to support this: participants reported physical symptoms but not the emotion, which suggests that emotional response is more than a recognition of physiological changes.

Schachter and Singer [312a] proposed a third interpretation: that emotion results from a person evaluating physical responses in the light of the whole situation. So whereas the same physiological response can result from a range of different situations, the emotion that is felt is based on a cognitive evaluation of the circumstance and will depend on what the person attributes this to. So the same physiological response of a pounding heart will be interpreted as excitement if we are in a competition and fear if we find ourselves under attack.

Whatever the exact process, what is clear is that emotion involves both physical and cognitive events. Our body responds biologically to an external stimulus and we interpret that in some way as a particular emotion. That biological response – known as *affect* – changes the way we deal with different situations, and this has an impact on the way we interact with computer systems. As Donald Norman says:

> Negative affect can make it harder to do even easy tasks; positive affect can make it easier to do difficult tasks.
>
> (D. A. Norman, Emotion and design: attractive things work better.
> *Interactions Magazine*, ix(4): 36–42, 2002.)

So what are the implications of this for design? It suggests that in situations of stress, people will be less able to cope with complex problem solving or managing difficult interfaces, whereas if people are relaxed they will be more forgiving of limitations in the design. This does not give us an excuse to design bad interfaces but does suggest that if we build interfaces that promote positive responses – for example by using aesthetics or reward – then they are likely be more successful.

1.6 INDIVIDUAL DIFFERENCES

In this chapter we have been discussing humans in general. We have made the assumption that everyone has similar capabilities and limitations and that we can therefore make generalizations. To an extent this is true: the psychological principles and properties that we have discussed apply to the majority of people. Notwithstanding this, we should remember that, although we share processes in common, humans, and therefore users, are not all the same. We should be aware of individual differences so that we can account for them as far as possible within our designs. These differences may be long term, such as sex, physical capabilities and intellectual capabilities. Others are shorter term and include the effect of stress or fatigue on the user. Still others change through time, such as age.

These differences should be taken into account in our designs. It is useful to consider, for any design decision, if there are likely to be users within the target group who will be adversely affected by our decision. At the extremes a decision may exclude a section of the user population. For example, the current emphasis on visual interfaces excludes those who are visually impaired, unless the design also makes use of the other sensory channels. On a more mundane level, designs should allow for users who are under pressure, feeling ill or distracted by other concerns: they should not push users to their perceptual or cognitive limits.

We will consider the issues of universal accessibility in more detail in Chapter 10.

1.7 PSYCHOLOGY AND THE DESIGN OF INTERACTIVE SYSTEMS

So far we have looked briefly at the way in which humans receive, process and store information, solve problems and acquire skill. But how can we apply what we have learned to designing interactive systems? Sometimes, straightforward conclusions can be drawn. For example, we can deduce that recognition is easier than recall and allow users to select commands from a set (such as a menu) rather than input them directly. However, in the majority of cases, application is not so obvious or simple. In fact, it may be dangerous, leading us to make generalizations which are not valid. In order to apply a psychological principle or result properly in design, we need to understand its context, both in terms of where it fits in the wider field of psychology and in terms of the details of the actual experiments, the measures used and the subjects involved, for example. This may appear daunting, particularly to the novice designer who wants to acknowledge the relevance of cognitive psychology but does not have the background to derive appropriate conclusions. Fortunately, principles and results from research in psychology have been distilled into guidelines for design, models to support design and techniques for evaluating design. Parts 2 and 3 of this book include discussion of a range of guidelines, models and techniques, based on cognitive psychology, which can be used to support the design process.

1.7.1 Guidelines

Throughout this chapter we have discussed the strengths and weaknesses of human cognitive and perceptual processes but, for the most part, we have avoided attempting to apply these directly to design. This is because such an attempt could only be partial and simplistic, and may give the impression that this is all psychology has to offer.

However, general design principles and guidelines can be and have been derived from the theories we have discussed. Some of these are relatively straightforward: for instance, recall is assisted by the provision of retrieval cues so interfaces should incorporate recognizable cues wherever possible. Others are more complex and context dependent. In Chapter 7 we discuss principles and guidelines further, many of which are derived from psychological theory. The interested reader is also referred to Gardiner and Christie [140] which illustrates how guidelines can be derived from psychological theory.

1.7.2 Models to support design

As well as guidelines and principles, psychological theory has led to the development of analytic and predictive models of user behavior. Some of these include a specific model of human problem solving, others of physical activity, and others attempt a more comprehensive view of cognition. Some predict how a typical computer user would behave in a given situation, others analyze why particular user behavior occurred. All are based on cognitive theory. We discuss these models in detail in Chapter 12.

1.7.3 Techniques for evaluation

In addition to providing us with a wealth of theoretical understanding of the human user, psychology also provides a range of empirical techniques which we can employ to evaluate our designs and our systems. In order to use these effectively we need to understand the scope and benefits of each method. Chapter 9 provides an overview of these techniques and an indication of the circumstances under which each should be used.

Worked exercise   *Produce a semantic network of the main information in this chapter.*

Answer   This network is potentially huge so it is probably unnecessary to devise the whole thing! Be selective. One helpful way to tackle the exercise is to approach it in both a top-down and a bottom-up manner. Top-down will give you a general overview of topics and how they relate; bottom-up can fill in the details of a particular field. These can then be

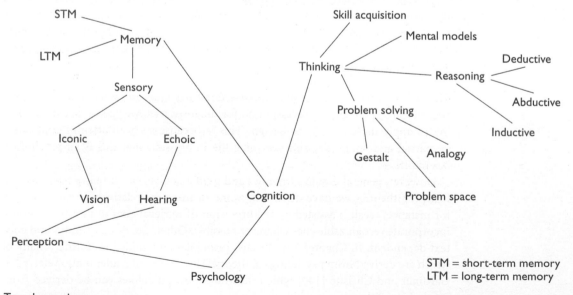

Top-down view

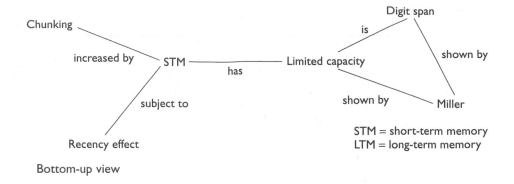

Bottom-up view

STM = short-term memory
LTM = long-term memory

'glued' together to build up the whole picture. You may be able to tackle this problem in a group, each taking one part of it. We will not provide the full network here but will give examples of the level of detail anticipated for the overview and the detailed versions. In the overview we have not included labels on the arcs for clarity.

1.8 SUMMARY

In this chapter we have considered the human as an information processor, receiving inputs from the world, storing, manipulating and using information, and reacting to the information received. Information is received through the senses, particularly, in the case of computer use, through sight, hearing and touch. It is stored in memory, either temporarily in sensory or working memory, or permanently in long-term memory. It can then be used in reasoning and problem solving. Recurrent familiar situations allow people to acquire skills in a particular domain, as their information structures become better defined. However, this can also lead to error, if the context changes.

Human perception and cognition are complex and sophisticated but they are not without their limitations. We have considered some of these limitations in this chapter. An understanding of the capabilities and limitations of the human as information processor can help us to design interactive systems which support the former and compensate for the latter. The principles, guidelines and models which can be derived from cognitive psychology and the techniques which it provides are invaluable tools for the designer of interactive systems.

EXERCISES

1.1 Devise experiments to test the properties of (i) short-term memory, (ii) long-term memory, using the experiments described in this chapter to help you. Try out your experiments on your friends. Are your results consistent with the properties described in this chapter?

1.2 Observe skilled and novice operators in a familiar domain, for example touch and 'hunt-and-peck' typists, expert and novice game players, or expert and novice users of a computer application. What differences can you discern between their behaviors?

1.3 From what you have learned about cognitive psychology devise appropriate guidelines for use by interface designers. You may find it helpful to group these under key headings, for example visual perception, memory, problem solving, etc., although some may overlap such groupings.

1.4 What are *mental models*, and why are they important in interface design?

1.5 What can a system designer do to minimize the memory load of the user?

1.6 Human short-term memory has a limited span. This is a series of experiments to determine what that span is. (You will need some other people to take part in these experiments with you – they do not need to be studying the course – try it with a group of friends.)

(a) *Kim's game*
Divide into groups. Each group gathers together an assortment of objects – pens, pencils, paper-clips, books, sticky notes, etc. The stranger the object, the better! You need a large number of them – at least 12 to 15. Place them in some compact arrangement on a table, so that all items are visible. Then, swap with another group for 30 seconds only and look at their pile. Return to your table, and on your own try to write down all the items in the other group's pile.

Compare your list with what they actually have in their pile. Compare the number of things you remembered with how the rest of your group did. Now think introspectively: what helped you remember certain things? Did you recognize things in their pile that you had in yours? Did that help? Do not pack the things away just yet.

Calculate the average score for your group. Compare that with the averages from the other group(s).

Questions: What conclusions can you draw from this experiment? What does this indicate about the capacity of short-term memory? What does it indicate that helps improve the capacity of short-term memory?

(b) *'I went to market...'*
In your group, one person starts off with 'I went to market and I bought a fish' (or some other produce, or whatever!). The next person continues 'I went to market and I bought a fish and I bought a bread roll as well'. The process continues, with each person adding some item to the list each time. Keep going around the group until you cannot remember the list accurately. Make a note of the first time someone gets it wrong, and then record the number of items that you can successfully remember. Some of you will find it hard to remember more than a few, others will fare much better. Do this a few more times with different lists, and then calculate your average score, and your group's average score.

Questions: What does this tell you about short-term memory? What do you do that helps you remember? What do you estimate is the typical capacity of human short-term memory? Is this a good test for short-term memory?

(c) *Improving your memory*
Try experiment 1.6(a) again, using the techniques on page 39.

Has your recall ability improved? Has your group's average improved? What does this show you about memory?

1.7 Locate one source (through the library or the web) that reports on empirical evidence on human limitations. Provide a full reference to the source. In one paragraph, summarize what the result of the research states in terms of a physical human limitation.

In a separate paragraph, write your thoughts on how you think this evidence on human capabilities impacts interactive system design.

RECOMMENDED READING

E. B. Goldstein, *Sensation and Perception*, 6th edition, Wadsworth, 2001.
A textbook covering human senses and perception in detail. Easy to read with many home experiments to illustrate the points made.

A. Baddeley, *Human Memory: Theory and Practice*, revised edition, Allyn & Bacon, 1997.
The latest and most complete of Baddeley's texts on memory. Provides up-to-date discussion on the different views of memory structure as well as a detailed survey of experimental work on memory.

M. W. Eysenck and M. T. Keane, *Cognitive Psychology: A Student's Handbook*, 4th edition, Psychology Press, 2000.
A comprehensive and readable textbook giving more detail on cognitive psychology, including memory, problem solving and skill acquisition.

S. K. Card, T. P. Moran and A. Newell, *The Psychology of Human–Computer Interaction*, Lawrence Erlbaum Associates, 1983.
A classic text looking at the human as an information processor in interaction with the computer. Develops and describes the Model Human Processor in detail.

A. Newell and H. Simon, *Human Problem Solving*, Prentice Hall, 1972.
Describes the problem space view of problem solving in more detail.

M. M. Gardiner and B. Christie, editors, *Applying Cognitive Psychology to User-Interface Design*, John Wiley, 1987.
A collection of essays on the implications of different aspects of cognitive psychology to interface design. Includes memory, thinking, language and skill acquisition. Provides detailed guidelines for applying psychological principles in design practice.

A. Monk, editor, *Fundamentals of Human Computer Interaction*, Academic Press, 1985.

A good collection of articles giving brief coverage of aspects of human psychology including perception, memory, thinking and reading. Also contains articles on experimental design which provide useful introductions.

ACT-R site. Website of resources and examples of the use of the cognitive architecture ACT-R, which is the latest development of Anderson's ACT model, http://act-r.psy.cmu.edu/

THE COMPUTER

2

OVERVIEW

A computer system comprises various elements, each of which affects the user of the system.

- Input devices for interactive use, allowing text entry, drawing and selection from the screen:
    - text entry: traditional keyboard, phone text entry, speech and handwriting
    - pointing: principally the mouse, but also touchpad, stylus and others
    - 3D interaction devices.

- Output display devices for interactive use:
    - different types of screen mostly using some form of bitmap display
    - large displays and situated displays for shared and public use
    - digital paper may be usable in the near future.

- Virtual reality systems and 3D visualization which have special interaction and display devices.

- Various devices in the physical world:
    - physical controls and dedicated displays
    - sound, smell and haptic feedback
    - sensors for nearly everything including movement, temperature, bio-signs.

- Paper output and input: the paperless office and the less-paper office:
    - different types of printers and their characteristics, character styles and fonts
    - scanners and optical character recognition.

- Memory:
    - short-term memory: RAM
    - long-term memory: magnetic and optical disks
    - capacity limitations related to document and video storage
    - access methods as they limit or help the user.

- Processing:
    - the effects when systems run too slow or too fast, the myth of the infinitely fast machine
    - limitations on processing speed
    - networks and their impact on system performance.

2.1 INTRODUCTION

In order to understand how humans interact with computers, we need to have an understanding of both parties in the interaction. The previous chapter explored aspects of human capabilities and behavior of which we need to be aware in the context of human–computer interaction; this chapter considers the computer and associated input–output devices and investigates how the technology influences the nature of the interaction and style of the interface.

We will concentrate principally on the traditional computer but we will also look at devices that take us beyond the closed world of keyboard, mouse and screen. As well as giving us lessons about more traditional systems, these are increasingly becoming important application areas in HCI.

Exercise: how many computers?

In a group or class do a quick survey:

■ How many computers do you have in your home?
■ How many computers do you normally carry with you in your pockets or bags?

Collate the answers and see who the techno-freaks are!

Discuss your answers.

After doing this look at /e3/online/how-many-computers/

When we interact with computers, what are we trying to achieve? Consider what happens when we interact with each other – we are either passing information to other people, or receiving information from them. Often, the information we receive is in response to the information that we have recently imparted to them, and we may then respond to that. Interaction is therefore a process of information transfer. Relating this to the electronic computer, the same principles hold: interaction is a process of information transfer, from the user to the computer and from the computer to the user.

The first part of this chapter concentrates on the transference of information from the user to the computer and back. We begin by considering a current typical computer interface and the devices it employs, largely variants of keyboard for text entry (Section 2.2), mouse for positioning (Section 2.3) and screen for displaying output (Section 2.4).

Then we move on to consider devices that go beyond the keyboard, mouse and screen: entering deeper into the electronic world with virtual reality and 3D interaction

(Section 2.5) and outside the electronic world looking at more physical interactions (Section 2.6).

In addition to direct input and output, information is passed to and fro via paper documents. This is dealt with in Section 2.7, which describes printers and scanners. Although not requiring the same degree of user interaction as a mouse or keyboard, these are an important means of input and output for many current applications.

We then consider the computer itself, its processor and memory devices and the networks that link them together. We note how the technology drives and empowers the interface. The details of computer processing should largely be irrelevant to the end-user, but the interface designer needs to be aware of the limitations of storage capacity and computational power; it is no good designing on paper a marvellous new interface, only to find it needs a Cray to run. Software designers often have high-end machines on which to develop applications, and it is easy to forget what a more typical configuration feels like.

Before looking at these devices and technology in detail we'll take a quick bird's-eye view of the way computer systems are changing.

2.1.1 A typical computer system

Consider a typical computer setup as shown in Figure 2.1. There is the computer 'box' itself, a keyboard, a mouse and a color screen. The screen layout is shown alongside it. If we examine the interface, we can see how its various characteristics are related to the devices used. The details of the interface itself, its underlying principles and design, are discussed in more depth in Chapter 3. As we shall see there are variants on these basic devices. Some of this variation is driven by different hardware configurations: desktop use, laptop computers, PDAs (personal digital assistants). Partly the diversity of devices reflects the fact that there are many different types of

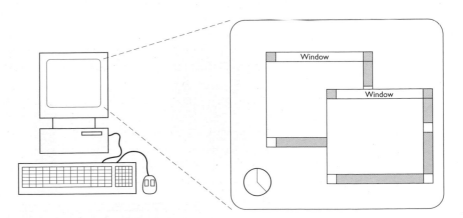

Figure 2.1   A typical computer system

data that may have to be entered into and obtained from a system, and there are also many different types of user, each with their own unique requirements.

2.1.2 Levels of interaction – batch processing

In the early days of computing, information was entered into the computer in a large mass – batch data entry. There was minimal interaction with the machine: the user would simply dump a pile of punched cards onto a reader, press the start button, and then return a few hours later. This still continues today although now with pre-prepared electronic files or possibly machine-read forms. It is clearly the most appropriate mode for certain kinds of application, for example printing pay checks or entering the results from a questionnaire.

With batch processing the interactions take place over hours or days. In contrast the typical desktop computer system has interactions taking seconds or fractions of a second (or with slow web pages sometimes minutes!). The field of Human–Computer Interaction largely grew due to this change in interactive pace. It is easy to assume that faster means better, but some of the paper-based technology discussed in Section 2.7 suggests that sometimes slower paced interaction may be better.

2.1.3 Richer interaction – everywhere, everywhen

Computers are coming out of the box! Information appliances are putting internet access or dedicated systems onto the fridge, microwave and washing machine: to automate shopping, give you email in your kitchen or simply call for maintenance when needed. We carry with us WAP phones and smartcards, have security systems that monitor us and web cams that show our homes to the world. Is Figure 2.1 really the typical computer system or is it really more like Figure 2.2?

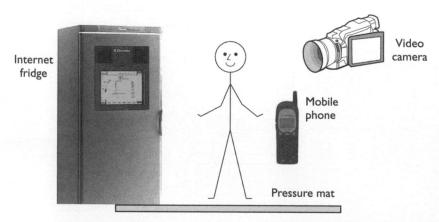

Figure 2.2   A typical computer system? Photo courtesy Electrolux

2.2   TEXT ENTRY DEVICES

Whether writing a book like this, producing an office memo, sending a thank you letter after your birthday, or simply sending an email to a friend, entering text is one of our main activities when using the computer. The most obvious means of text entry is the plain keyboard, but there are several variations on this: different keyboard layouts, 'chord' keyboards that use combinations of fingers to enter letters, and phone key pads. Handwriting and speech recognition offer more radical alternatives.

2.2.1 The alphanumeric keyboard

The keyboard is still one of the most common input devices in use today. It is used for entering textual data and commands. The vast majority of keyboards have a standardized layout, and are known by the first six letters of the top row of alphabetical keys, QWERTY. There are alternative designs which have some advantages over the QWERTY layout, but these have not been able to overcome the vast technological inertia of the QWERTY keyboard. These alternatives are of two forms: 26 key layouts and chord keyboards. A 26 key layout rearranges the order of the alphabetic keys, putting the most commonly used letters under the strongest fingers, or adopting simpler practices. In addition to QWERTY, we will discuss two 26 key layouts, alphabetic and DVORAK, and chord keyboards.

The QWERTY keyboard

The layout of the digits and letters on a QWERTY keyboard is fixed (see Figure 2.3), but non-alphanumeric keys vary between keyboards. For example, there is a difference between key assignments on British and American keyboards (in particular, above the 3 on the UK keyboard is the pound sign £, whilst on the US keyboard there is a dollar sign $). The standard layout is also subject to variation in the placement of brackets, backslashes and suchlike. In addition different national keyboards include accented letters and the traditional French layout places the main letters in different locations – the top line starts AZERTY.

Figure 2.3   The standard QWERTY keyboard

The QWERTY arrangement of keys is not optimal for typing, however. The reason for the layout of the keyboard in this fashion can be traced back to the days of mechanical typewriters. Hitting a key caused an arm to shoot towards the carriage, imprinting the letter on the head on the ribbon and hence onto the paper. If two arms flew towards the paper in quick succession from nearly the same angle, they would often jam – the solution to this was to set out the keys so that common combinations of consecutive letters were placed at different ends of the keyboard, which meant that the arms would usually move from alternate sides. One appealing story relating to the key layout is that it was also important for a salesman to be able to type the word 'typewriter' quickly in order to impress potential customers: the letters are all on the top row!

The electric typewriter and now the computer keyboard are not subject to the original mechanical constraints, but the QWERTY keyboard remains the dominant layout. The reason for this is social – the vast base of trained typists would be reluctant to relearn their craft, whilst the management is not prepared to accept an initial lowering of performance whilst the new skills are gained. There is also a large investment in current keyboards, which would all have to be either replaced at great cost, or phased out, with the subsequent requirement for people to be proficient on both keyboards. As whole populations have become keyboard users this technological inertia has probably become impossible to change.

How keyboards work

Current keyboards work by a keypress closing a connection, causing a character code to be sent to the computer. The connection is usually via a lead, but wireless systems also exist. One aspect of keyboards that is important to users is the 'feel' of the keys. Some keyboards require a very hard press to operate the key, much like a manual typewriter, whilst others are featherlight. The distance that the keys travel also affects the tactile nature of the keyboard. The keyboards that are currently used on most notebook computers are 'half-travel' keyboards, where the keys travel only a small distance before activating their connection; such a keyboard can feel dead to begin with, but such qualitative judgments often change as people become more used to using it. By making the actual keys thinner, and allowing them a much reduced travel, a lot of vertical space can be saved on the keyboard, thereby making the machine slimmer than would otherwise be possible.

Some keyboards are even made of touch-sensitive buttons, which require a light touch and practically no travel; they often appear as a sheet of plastic with the buttons printed on them. Such keyboards are often found on shop tills, though the keys are not QWERTY, but specific to the task. Being fully sealed, they have the advantage of being easily cleaned and resistant to dirty environments, but have little feel, and are not popular with trained touch-typists. Feedback is important even at this level of human–computer interaction! With the recent increase of repetitive strain injury (RSI) to users' fingers, and the increased responsibilities of employers in these circumstances, it may be that such designs will enjoy a resurgence in the near future. RSI in fingers is caused by the tendons that control the movement of the fingers becoming inflamed owing to overuse and making repeated unnatural movements.

There are a variety of specially shaped keyboards to relieve the strain of typing or to allow people to type with some injury (e.g. RSI) or disability. These may slope the keys towards the hands to improve the ergonomic position, be designed for single-handed use, or for no hands at all. Some use bespoke key layouts to reduce strain of finger movements. The keyboard illustrated is produced by PCD Maltron Ltd. for left-handed use. See www.maltron.com/

Source: www.maltron.com, reproduced courtesy of PCD Maltron Ltd.

Ease of learning – alphabetic keyboard

One of the most obvious layouts to be produced is the alphabetic keyboard, in which the letters are arranged alphabetically across the keyboard. It might be expected that such a layout would make it quicker for untrained typists to use, but this is not the case. Studies have shown that this keyboard is not faster for properly trained typists, as we may expect, since there is no inherent advantage to this layout. And even for novice or occasional users, the alphabetic layout appears to make very little difference to the speed of typing. These keyboards are used in some pocket electronic personal organizers, perhaps because the layout looks simpler to use than the QWERTY one. Also, it dissuades people from attempting to use their touch-typing skills on a very small keyboard and hence avoids criticisms of difficulty of use!

Ergonomics of use – DVORAK keyboard and split designs

The DVORAK keyboard uses a similar layout of keys to the QWERTY system, but assigns the letters to different keys. Based upon an analysis of typing, the keyboard is designed to help people reach faster typing speeds. It is biased towards right-handed people, in that 56% of keystrokes are made with the right hand. The layout of the keys also attempts to ensure that the majority of keystrokes alternate between hands, thereby increasing the potential speed. By keeping the most commonly used keys on the home, or middle, row, 70% of keystrokes are made without the typist having to stretch far, thereby reducing fatigue and increasing keying speed. The layout also aims to minimize the number of keystrokes made with the weak fingers. Many of these requirements are in conflict, and the DVORAK keyboard represents one possible solution. Experiments have shown that there is a speed improvement of between 10 and 15%, coupled with a reduction in user fatigue due to the increased ergonomic layout of the keyboard [230].

Other aspects of keyboard design have been altered apart from the layout of the keys. A number of more ergonomic designs have appeared, in which the basic tilted planar base of the keyboard is altered. Moderate designs curve the plane of the keyboard, making it concave, whilst more extreme ones split the keys into those for the left and right hand and curve both halves separately. Often in these the keys are also moved to bring them all within easy reach, to minimize movement between keys. Such designs are supposed to aid comfort and reduce RSI by minimizing effort, but have had practically no impact on the majority of systems sold.

2.2.2 Chord keyboards

Chord keyboards are significantly different from normal alphanumeric keyboards. Only a few keys, four or five, are used (see Figure 2.4) and letters are produced by pressing one or more of the keys at once. For example, in the *Microwriter*, the pattern of multiple keypresses is chosen to reflect the actual letter shape.

Such keyboards have a number of advantages. They are extremely compact: simply reducing the size of a conventional keyboard makes the keys too small and close together, with a correspondingly large increase in the difficulty of using it. The

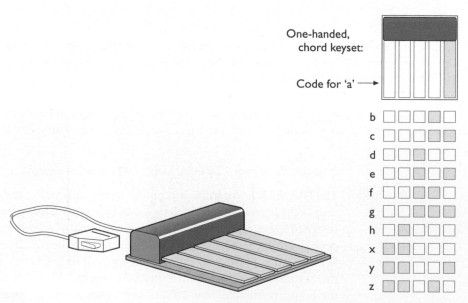

Figure 2.4 A very early chord keyboard (left) and its lettercodes (right)

learning time for the keyboard is supposed to be fairly short – of the order of a few hours – but social resistance is still high. Moreover, they are capable of fast typing speeds in the hands (or rather hand!) of a competent user. Chord keyboards can also be used where only one-handed operation is possible, in cramped and confined conditions.

Lack of familiarity means that these are unlikely ever to be a mainstream form of text entry, but they do have applications in niche areas. In particular, courtroom stenographers use a special form of two-handed chord keyboard and associated shorthand to enter text at full spoken speed. Also it may be that the compact size and one-handed operation will find a place in the growing wearables market.

DESIGN FOCUS

Numeric keypads

Alphanumeric keyboards (as the name suggests) include numbers as well as letters. In the QWERTY layout these are in a line across the top of the keyboard, but in most larger keyboards there is also a separate number pad to allow faster entry of digits. Number keypads occur in other contexts too, including calculators, telephones and ATM cash dispensers. Many people are unaware that there are two different layouts for numeric keypads: the calculator style that has '123' on the bottom and the telephone style that has '123' at the top.

It is a demonstration of the amazing adaptability of humans that we move between these two styles with such ease. However, if you need to include a numeric keypad in a device you must consider which is most appropriate for your potential users. For example, computer keyboards use calculator-style layout, as they are primarily used for entering numbers for calculations.

One of the authors was caught out by this once when he forgot the PIN number of his cash card. He half remembered the digits, but also his fingers knew where to type, so he 'practiced' on his calculator. Unfortunately ATMs use telephone-style layout!

| calculator | ATM | phone |

Typical key mapping:
1 – space, comma, etc. (varies)
2 – a b c
3 – d e f
4 – g h i
5 – j k l
6 – m n o
7 – p q r s
8 – t u v
9 – w x y z
0 – +, &, etc.

Figure 2.5   Mobile phone keypad. Source: Photograph by Alan Dix (Ericsson phone)

2.2.3 Phone pad and T9 entry

With mobile phones being used for SMS text messaging (see Chapter 19) and WAP (see Chapter 21), the phone keypad has become an important form of text input. Unfortunately a phone only has digits 0–9, not a full alphanumeric keyboard.

To overcome this for text input the numeric keys are usually pressed several times – Figure 2.5 shows a typical mapping of digits to letters. For example, the 3 key has 'def' on it. If you press the key once you get a 'd', if you press 3 twice you get an 'e', if you press it three times you get an 'f'. The main number-to-letter mapping is standard, but punctuation and accented letters differ between phones. Also there needs to be a way for the phone to distinguish, say, the 'dd' from 'e'. On some phones you need to pause for a short period between successive letters using the same key, for others you press an additional key (e.g. '#').

Most phones have at least two *modes* for the numeric buttons: one where the keys mean the digits (for example when entering a phone number) and one where they mean letters (for example when typing an SMS message). Some have additional modes to make entering accented characters easier. Also a special mode or setting is needed for capital letters although many phones use rules to reduce this, for example automatically capitalizing the initial letter in a message and letters following full stops, question marks and exclamation marks.

This is all very laborious and, as we will see in Chapter 19, experienced mobile phone users make use of a highly developed shorthand to reduce the number of keystrokes. If you watch a teenager or other experienced txt-er, you will see they often develop great typing speed holding the phone in one hand and using only their thumb. As these skills spread through society it may be that future devices use this as a means of small format text input. For those who never develop this physical dexterity some phones have tiny plug-in keyboards, or come with fold-out keyboards.

Another technical solution to the problem is the T9 algorithm. This uses a large dictionary to disambiguate words by simply typing the relevant letters once. For example, '3926753' becomes 'example' as there is only one word with letters that match (alternatives like 'ewbosld' that also match are not real words). Where there are ambiguities such as '26', which could be an 'am' or an 'an', the phone gives a series of options to choose from.

2.2.4 Handwriting recognition

Handwriting is a common and familiar activity, and is therefore attractive as a method of text entry. If we were able to write as we would when we use paper, but with the computer taking this form of input and converting it to text, we can see that it is an intuitive and simple way of interacting with the computer. However, there are a number of disadvantages with handwriting recognition. Current technology is still fairly inaccurate and so makes a significant number of mistakes in recognizing letters, though it has improved rapidly. Moreover, individual differences in hand-writing are enormous, and make the recognition process even more difficult. The most significant information in handwriting is not in the letter shape itself but in the stroke information – the way in which the letter is drawn. This means that devices which support handwriting recognition must capture the stroke information, not just the final character shape. Because of this, online recognition is far easier than reading handwritten text on paper. Further complications arise because letters within words are shaped and often drawn very differently depending on the actual word; the context can help determine the letter's identity, but is often unable to pro-vide enough information. Handwriting recognition is covered in more detail later in the book, in Chapter 10. More serious in many ways is the limitation on speed; it is difficult to write at more than 25 words a minute, which is no more than half the speed of a decent typist.

The different nature of handwriting means that we may find it more useful in situations where a keyboard-based approach would have its own problems. Such situations will invariably result in completely new systems being designed around the handwriting recognizer as the predominant mode of textual input, and these may bear very little resemblance to the typical system. Pen-based systems that use handwriting recognition are actively marketed in the mobile computing market, especially for smaller pocket organizers. Such machines are typically used for taking notes and jotting down and sketching ideas, as well as acting as a diary, address book and organizer. Using handwriting recognition has many advantages over using a keyboard. A pen-based system can be small and yet still accurate and easy to use, whereas small keys become very tiring, or even impossible, to use accurately. Also the pen-based approach does not have to be altered when we move from jotting down text to sketching diagrams; pen-based input is highly appropriate for this also.

Some organizer designs have dispensed with a keyboard completely. With such systems one must consider all sorts of other ways to interact with the system that are not character based. For example, we may decide to use *gesture recognition*, rather than commands, to tell the system what to do, for example drawing a line through a word in order to delete it. The important point is that a different input device that was initially considered simply as an alternative to the keyboard opens up a whole host of alternative interface designs and different possibilities for interaction.

Signature authentication

Handwriting recognition is difficult principally because of the great differences between different people's handwriting. These differences can be used to advantage in *signature authentication* where the purpose is to identify the user rather than read the signature. Again this is far easier when we have stroke information as people tend to produce signatures which *look* slightly different from one another in detail, but are formed in a similar fashion. Furthermore, a forger who has a copy of a person's signature may be able to copy the appearance of the signature, but will not be able to reproduce the pattern of strokes.

2.2.5　Speech recognition

Speech recognition is a promising area of text entry, but it has been promising for a number of years and is still only used in very limited situations. There is a natural enthusiasm for being able to talk to the machine and have it respond to commands, since this form of interaction is one with which we are very familiar. Successful recognition rates of over 97% have been reported, but since this represents one letter in error in approximately every 30, or one spelling mistake every six or so words, this is stoll unacceptible (*sic*)! Note also that this performance is usually quoted only for a restricted vocabulary of command words. Trying to extend such systems to the level of understanding natural language, with its inherent vagueness, imprecision and pauses, opens up many more problems that have not been satisfactorily solved even for keyboard-entered natural language. Moreover, since every person speaks differently, the system has to be trained and tuned to each new speaker, or its performance decreases. Strong accents, a cold or emotion can also cause recognition problems, as can background noise. This leads us on to the question of practicality within an office environment: not only may the background level of noise cause errors, but if everyone in an open-plan office were to talk to their machine, the level of noise would dramatically increase, with associated difficulties. Confidentiality would also be harder to maintain.

Despite its problems, speech technology has found niche markets: telephone information systems, access for the disabled, in hands-occupied situations (especially military) and for those suffering RSI. This is discussed in greater detail in Chapter 10, but we can see that it offers three possibilities. The first is as an alternative text entry device to replace the keyboard within an environment and using software originally designed for keyboard use. The second is to redesign a system, taking full advantage of the benefits of the technique whilst minimizing the potential problems. Finally, it can be used in areas where keyboard-based input is impractical or impossible. It is in the latter, more radical areas that speech technology is currently achieving success.

2.3   POSITIONING, POINTING AND DRAWING

Central to most modern computing systems is the ability to point at something on the screen and thereby manipulate it, or perform some function. There has been a long history of such devices, in particular in *computer-aided design* (CAD), where positioning and drawing are the major activities. Pointing devices allow the user to point, position and select items, either directly or by manipulating a pointer on the screen. Many pointing devices can also be used for free-hand drawing although the skill of drawing with a mouse is very different from using a pencil. The mouse is still most common for desktop computers, but is facing challenges as laptop and hand-held computing increase their market share. Indeed, these words are being typed on a laptop with a touchpad and no mouse.

2.3.1 The mouse

The mouse has become a major component of the majority of desktop computer systems sold today, and is the little box with the tail connecting it to the machine in our basic computer system picture (Figure 2.1). It is a small, palm-sized box housing a weighted ball – as the box is moved over the tabletop, the ball is rolled by the table and so rotates inside the housing. This rotation is detected by small rollers that are in contact with the ball, and these adjust the values of potentiometers. If you remove the ball occasionally to clear dust you may be able to see these rollers. The changing values of these potentiometers can be directly related to changes in position of the ball. The potentiometers are aligned in different directions so that they can detect both horizontal and vertical motion. The relative motion information is passed to the computer via a wire attached to the box, or in some cases using wireless or infrared, and moves a pointer on the screen, called the *cursor*. The whole arrangement tends to look rodent-like, with the box acting as the body and the wire as the tail; hence the term 'mouse'. In addition to detecting motion, the mouse has typically one, two or three buttons on top. These are used to indicate selection or to initiate action. Single-button mice tend to have similar functionality to multi-button mice, and achieve this by instituting different operations for a single and a double button click. A 'double-click' is when the button is pressed twice in rapid succession. Multi-button mice tend to allocate one operation to each particular button.

The mouse operates in a planar fashion, moving around the desktop, and is an indirect input device, since a transformation is required to map from the horizontal nature of the desktop to the vertical alignment of the screen. Left–right motion is directly mapped, whilst up–down on the screen is achieved by moving the mouse away–towards the user. The mouse only provides information on the relative movement of the ball within the housing: it can be physically lifted up from the desktop and replaced in a different position without moving the cursor. This offers the advantage that less physical space is required for the mouse, but suffers from being less intuitive for novice users. Since the mouse sits on the desk, moving it about is easy and users suffer little arm fatigue, although the indirect nature of the medium can lead to problems with hand–eye coordination. However, a major advantage of the mouse is that the cursor itself is small, and it can be easily manipulated without obscuring the display.

The mouse was developed around 1964 by Douglas C. Engelbart, and a photograph of the first prototype is shown in Figure 2.6. This used two wheels that slid across the desktop and transmitted x–y coordinates to the computer. The housing was carved in wood, and has been damaged, exposing one of the wheels. The original design actually offers a few advantages over today's more sleek versions: by tilting it so that only one wheel is in contact with the desk, pure vertical or horizontal motion can be obtained. Also, the problem of getting the cursor across the large screens that are often used today can be solved by flicking your wrist to get the horizontal wheel spinning. The mouse pointer then races across the screen with no further effort on your behalf, until you stop it at its destination by dropping the mouse down onto the desktop.

Figure 2.6 The first mouse. Photograph courtesy of Douglas Engelbart and Bootstrap Institute

Optical mice

Optical mice work differently from mechanical mice. A light-emitting diode emits a weak red light from the base of the mouse. This is reflected off a special pad with a metallic grid-like pattern upon which the mouse has to sit, and the fluctuations in reflected intensity as the mouse is moved over the gridlines are recorded by a sensor in the base of the mouse and translated into relative x, y motion. Some optical mice do not require special mats, just an appropriate surface, and use the natural texture of the surface to detect movement. The optical mouse is less susceptible to dust and dirt than the mechanical one in that its mechanism is less likely to become blocked up. However, for those that rely on a special mat, if the mat is not properly aligned, movement of the mouse may become erratic – especially difficult if you are working with someone and pass the mouse back and forth between you.

Although most mice are hand operated, not all are – there have been experiments with a device called the *footmouse*. As the name implies, it is a foot operated device, although more akin to an isometric joystick than a mouse. The cursor is moved by foot pressure on one side or the other of a pad. This allows one to dedicate hands to the keyboard. A rare device, the footmouse has not found common acceptance!

Interestingly foot pedals are used heavily in musical instruments including pianos, electric guitars, organs and drums and also in mechanical equipment including cars, cranes, sewing machines and industrial controls. So it is clear that in principle this is a good idea. Two things seem to have limited their use in computer equipment (except simulators and games). One is the practicality of having foot controls in the work environment: pedals under a desk may be operated accidentally, laptops with foot pedals would be plain awkward. The second issue is the kind of control being exercised. Pedals in physical interfaces are used predominantly to control one or more single-dimensional analog controls. It may be that in more specialized interfaces appropriate foot-operated controls could be more commonly and effectively used.

2.3.2 Touchpad

Touchpads are touch-sensitive tablets usually around 2–3 inches (50–75 mm) square. They were first used extensively in Apple Powerbook portable computers but are now used in many other notebook computers and can be obtained separately to replace the mouse on the desktop. They are operated by stroking a finger over their surface, rather like using a simulated trackball. The feel is very different from other input devices, but as with all devices users quickly get used to the action and become proficient.

Because they are small it may require several strokes to move the cursor across the screen. This can be improved by using acceleration settings in the software linking the trackpad movement to the screen movement. Rather than having a fixed ratio of pad distance to screen distance, this varies with the speed of movement. If the finger moves slowly over the pad then the pad movements map to small distances on the screen. If the finger is moving quickly the same distance on the touchpad moves the cursor a long distance. For example, on the trackpad being used when writing this section a very slow movement of the finger from one side of the trackpad to the other moves the cursor less than 10% of the width of the screen. However, if the finger is moved very rapidly from side to side, the cursor moves the whole width of the screen.

In fact, this form of acceleration setting is also used in other indirect positioning devices including the mouse. Fine settings of this sort of parameter makes a great difference to the 'feel' of the device.

2.3.3 Trackball and thumbwheel

The trackball is really just an upside-down mouse! A weighted ball faces upwards and is rotated inside a static housing, the motion being detected in the same way as for a mechanical mouse, and the relative motion of the ball moves the cursor. Because of this, the trackball requires no additional space in which to operate, and is therefore a very compact device. It is an indirect device, and requires separate buttons for selection. It is fairly accurate, but is hard to draw with, as long movements are difficult. Trackballs now appear in a wide variety of sizes, the most usual being about the same as a golf ball, with a number of larger and smaller devices available. The size and 'feel' of the trackball itself affords significant differences in the usability of the device: its weight, rolling resistance and texture all contribute to the overall effect.

Some of the smaller devices have been used in notebook and portable computers, but more commonly trackpads or nipples are used. They are often sold as alternatives to mice on desktop computers, especially for RSI sufferers. They are also heavily used in video games where their highly responsive behavior, including being able to spin the ball, is ideally suited to the demands of play.

Thumbwheels are different in that they have two orthogonal dials to control the cursor position. Such a device is very cheap, but slow, and it is difficult to manipulate the cursor in any way other than horizontally or vertically. This limitation can sometimes be a useful constraint in the right application. For instance, in CAD the designer is almost always concerned with exact verticals and horizontals, and a device that provides such constraints is very useful, which accounts for the appearance of thumbwheels in CAD systems. Another successful application for such a device has been in a drawing game such as Etch-a-Sketch in which straight lines can be created on a simple screen, since the predominance of straight lines in simple drawings means that the motion restrictions are an advantage rather than a handicap. However, if you were to try to write your signature using a thumbwheel, the limitations would be all too apparent. The appropriateness of the device depends on the task to be performed.

Although two-axis thumbwheels are not heavily used in mainstream applications, single thumbwheels are often included on a standard mouse in order to offer an alternative means to scroll documents. Normally scrolling requires you to grab the scroll bar with the mouse cursor and drag it down. For large documents it is hard to be accurate and in addition the mouse dragging is done holding a finger down which adds to hand strain. In contrast the small scroll wheel allows comparatively intuitive and fast scrolling, simply rotating the wheel to move the page.

2.3.4 Joystick and keyboard nipple

The joystick is an indirect input device, taking up very little space. Consisting of a small palm-sized box with a stick or shaped grip sticking up from it, the joystick is a simple device with which movements of the stick cause a corresponding movement of the screen cursor. There are two types of joystick: the *absolute* and the *isometric*. In the absolute joystick, movement is the important characteristic, since the position of the joystick in the base corresponds to the position of the cursor on the screen. In the isometric joystick, the pressure on the stick corresponds to the velocity of the cursor, and when released, the stick returns to its usual upright centered position. This type of joystick is also called the velocity-controlled joystick, for obvious reasons. The buttons are usually placed on the top of the stick, or on the front like a trigger. Joysticks are inexpensive and fairly robust, and for this reason they are often found in computer games. Another reason for their dominance of the games market is their relative familiarity to users, and their likeness to aircraft joysticks: aircraft are a favorite basis for games, leading to familiarity with the joystick that can be used for more obscure entertainment ideas.

A smaller device but with the same basic characteristics is used on many laptop computers to control the cursor. Some older systems had a variant of this called the keymouse, which was a single key. More commonly a small rubber nipple projects in the center of the keyboard and acts as a tiny isometric joystick. It is usually difficult for novices to use, but this seems to be related to fine adjustment of the speed settings. Like the joystick the nipple controls the rate of movement across the screen and is thus less direct than a mouse or stylus.

2.3.5 Touch-sensitive screens (touchscreens)

Touchscreens are another method of allowing the user to point and select objects on the screen, but they are much more direct than the mouse, as they detect the presence of the user's finger, or a stylus, on the screen itself. They work in one of a number of different ways: by the finger (or stylus) interrupting a matrix of light beams, or by capacitance changes on a grid overlaying the screen, or by ultrasonic reflections. Because the user indicates exactly which item is required by pointing to it, no mapping is required and therefore this is a direct device.

The touchscreen is very fast, and requires no specialized pointing device. It is especially good for selecting items from menus displayed on the screen. Because the screen acts as an input device as well as an output device, there is no separate hardware to become damaged or destroyed by dirt; this makes touchscreens suitable for use in hostile environments. They are also relatively intuitive to use and have been used successfully as an interface to information systems for the general public.

They suffer from a number of disadvantages, however. Using the finger to point is not always suitable, as it can leave greasy marks on the screen, and, being a fairly blunt instrument, it is quite inaccurate. This means that the selection of small regions is very difficult, as is accurate drawing. Moreover, lifting the arm to point to a vertical screen is very tiring, and also means that the screen has to be within about a meter of the user to enable it to be reached, which can make it too close for comfort. Research has shown that the optimal angle for a touchscreen is about 15 degrees up from the horizontal.

2.3.6 Stylus and light pen

For more accurate positioning (and to avoid greasy screens), systems with touch-sensitive surfaces often emply a stylus. Instead of pointing at the screen directly a small pen-like plastic stick is used to point and draw on the screen. This is particularly popular in PDAs, but they are also being used in some laptop computers.

An older technology that is used in the same way is the light pen. The pen is connected to the screen by a cable and, in operation, is held to the screen and detects a burst of light from the screen phosphor during the display scan. The light pen can therefore address individual pixels and so is much more accurate than the touchscreen.

Both stylus and light pen can be used for fine selection and drawing, but both can be tiring to use on upright displays and are harder to take up and put down when used together with a keyboard. Interestingly some users of PDAs with fold-out keyboards learn to hold the stylus held outwards between their fingers so that they can type whilst holding it. As it is unattached the stylus can easily get lost, but a closed pen can be used in emergencies.

Stylus, light pen and touchscreen are all very direct in that the relationship between the device and the thing selected is immediate. In contrast, mouse, touchpad, joystick and trackball all have to map movements on the desk to cursor movement on the screen.

However, the direct devices suffer from the problem that, in use, the act of pointing actually obscures the display, making it harder to use, especially if complex detailed selections or movements are required in rapid succession. This means that screen designs have to take into account where the user's hand will be. For example, you may want to place menus at the bottom of the screen rather than the top. Also you may want to offer alternative layouts for right-handed and left-handed users.

2.3.7 Digitizing tablet

The digitizing tablet is a more specialized device typically used for freehand drawing, but may also be used as a mouse substitute. Some highly accurate tablets, usually using a puck (a mouse-like device), are used in special applications such as digitizing information for maps.

The tablet provides positional information by measuring the position of some device on a special pad, or *tablet*, and can work in a number of ways. The *resistive tablet* detects point contact between two separated conducting sheets. It has advantages in that it can be operated without a specialized stylus – a pen or the user's finger is sufficient. The *magnetic tablet* detects current pulses in a magnetic field using a small loop coil housed in a special pen. There are also capacitative and electrostatic tablets that work in a similar way. The *sonic tablet* is similar to the above but requires no special surface. An ultrasonic pulse is emitted by a special pen which is detected by two or more microphones which then triangulate the pen position. This device can be adapted to provide 3D input, if required.

Digitizing tablets are capable of high resolution, and are available in a range of sizes. Sampling rates vary, affecting the resolution of cursor movement, which gets progressively finer as the sampling rate increases. The digitizing tablet can be used to detect relative motion *or* absolute motion, but is an indirect device since there is a mapping from the plane of operation of the tablet to the screen. It can also be used for text input; if supported by character recognition software, handwriting can be interpreted. Problems with digitizing tablets are that they require a large amount of desk space, and may be awkward to use if displaced to one side by the keyboard.

2.3.8 Eyegaze

Eyegaze systems allow you to control the computer by simply looking at it! Some systems require you to wear special glasses or a small head-mounted box, others are built into the screen or sit as a small box below the screen. A low-power laser is shone into the eye and is reflected off the retina. The reflection changes as the angle of the eye alters, and by tracking the reflected beam the eyegaze system can determine the direction in which the eye is looking. The system needs to be calibrated, typically by staring at a series of dots on the screen, but thereafter can be used to move the screen cursor or for other more specialized uses. Eyegaze is a very fast and accurate device, but the more accurate versions can be expensive. It is fine for selection but not for drawing since the eye does not move in smooth lines. Also in real applications it can be difficult to distinguish deliberately gazing at something and accidentally glancing at it.

Such systems have been used in military applications, notably for guiding air-to-air missiles to their targets, but are starting to find more peaceable uses, for disabled users and for workers in environments where it is impossible for them to use their hands. The rarity of the eyegaze is due partly to its novelty and partly to its expense, and it is usually found only in certain domain-specific applications. Within HCI it is particularly useful as part of evaluation as one is able to trace exactly where the user is looking [81]. As prices drop and the technology becomes less intrusive we may see more applications using eyegaze, especially in virtual reality and augmented reality areas (see Chapter 20).

2.3.9 Cursor keys and discrete positioning

All of the devices we have discussed are capable of giving near continuous 2D positioning, with varying degrees of accuracy. For many applications we are only

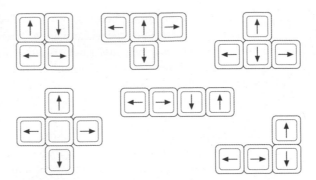

Figure 2.7 Various cursor key layouts

interested in positioning within a sequential list such as a menu or amongst 2D cells as in a spreadsheet. Even for moving within text discrete up/down left/right keys can sometimes be preferable to using a mouse.

Cursor keys are available on most keyboards. Four keys on the keyboard are used to control the cursor, one each for up, down, left and right. There is no standardized layout for the keys. Some layouts are shown in Figure 2.7, but the most common now is the inverted 'T'.

Cursor keys used to be more heavily used in character-based systems before windows and mice were the norm. However, when logging into remote machines such as web servers, the interface is often a virtual character-based terminal within a telnet window. In such applications it is common to find yourself in a 1970s world of text editors controlled sometimes using cursor keys and sometimes by more arcane combinations of control keys!

Small devices such as mobile phones, personal entertainment and television remote controls often require discrete control, either dedicated to a particular function such as volume, or for use as general menu selection. Figure 2.8 shows examples of these. The satellite TV remote control has dedicated '+/−' buttons for controlling volume and stepping between channels. It also has a central cursor pad that is used for on-screen menus. The mobile phone has a single central joystick-like device. This can be pushed left/right, up/down to navigate within the small 3×3 array of graphical icons as well as select from text menus.

2.4 DISPLAY DEVICES

The vast majority of interactive computer systems would be unthinkable without some sort of display screen, but many such systems do exist, though usually in specialized applications only. Thinking beyond the traditional, systems such as cars, hi-fis and security alarms all have different outputs from those expressible on a screen, but in the personal computer and workstation market, screens are pervasive.

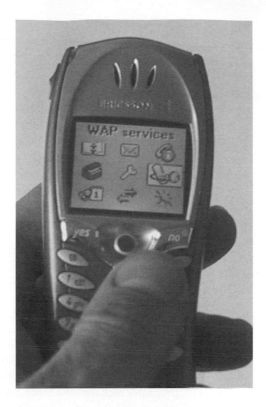

Figure 2.8 Satellite TV remote control and mobile phone. Source: Photograph left by Alan Dix with permission from British Sky Broadcasting Limited, photograph right by Alan Dix (Ericsson phone)

In this section, we discuss the standard computer display in detail, looking at the properties of bitmap screens, at different screen technologies, at large and situated displays, and at a new technology, 'digital paper'.

2.4.1 Bitmap displays – resolution and color

Virtually all computer displays are based on some sort of bitmap. That is the display is made of vast numbers of colored dots or pixels in a rectangular grid. These pixels may be limited to black and white (for example, the small display on many TV remote controls), in grayscale, or full color.

The color or, for monochrome screens, the intensity at each pixel is held by the computer's video card. One bit per pixel can store on/off information, and hence only black and white (the term 'bitmap' dates from such displays). More bits per pixel give rise to more color or intensity possibilities. For example, 8 bits/pixel give rise to $2^8 = 256$ possible colors *at any one time*. The set of colors make up what is called the *colormap*, and the colormap can be altered at any time to produce a different set of colors. The system is therefore capable of actually displaying many more than the number of colors in the colormap, but not simultaneously. Most desktop computers now use 24 or 32 bits per pixel which allows virtually unlimited colors, but devices such as mobile phones and PDAs are often still monochrome or have limited color range.

As well as the number of colors that can be displayed at each pixel, the other measure that is important is the resolution of the screen. Actually the word 'resolution' is used in a confused (and confusing!) way for screens. There are two numbers to consider:

■ the *total number* of pixels: in standard computer displays this is always in a 4:3 ratio, perhaps 1024 pixels across by 768 down, or 1600×1200; for PDAs this will be more in the order of a few hundred pixels in each direction.

■ the *density* of pixels: this is measured in pixels per inch. Unlike printers (see Section 2.7 below) this density varies little between 72 and 96 pixels per inch.

To add to the confusion, a monitor, liquid crystal display (LCD) screen or other display device will quote its maximum resolution, but the computer may actually give it less than this. For example, the screen may be a 1200×900 resolution with 96 pixels per inch, but the computer only sends it 800×600. In the case of a cathode ray tube (CRT) this typically will mean that the image is stretched over the screen surface giving a lower density of 64 pixels per inch. An LCD screen cannot change its pixel size so it would keep 96 pixels per inch and simply not use all its screen space, adding a black border instead. Some LCD projectors will try to stretch or reduce what they are given, but this may mean that one pixel gets stretched to two, or two pixels get 'squashed' into one, giving rise to display 'artifacts' such as thin lines disappearing, or uniform lines becoming alternately thick or thin.

Although horizontal and vertical lines can be drawn perfectly on bitmap screens, and lines at 45 degrees reproduce reasonably well, lines at any other angle and curves have 'jaggies', rough edges caused by the attempt to approximate the line with pixels.

When using a single color jaggies are inevitable. Similar effects are seen in bitmap fonts. The problem of jaggies can be reduced by using high-resolution screens, or by a technique known as *anti-aliasing*. Anti-aliasing softens the edges of line segments, blurring the discontinuity and making the jaggies less obvious.

Look at the two images in Figure 2.9 with your eyes slightly screwed up. See how the second anti-aliased line looks better. Of course, screen resolution is much higher, but the same principle holds true. The reason this works is because our brains are constantly 'improving' what we see in the world: processing and manipulating the raw sensations of the rods and cones in our eyes and turning them into something meaningful. Often our vision is blurred because of poor light, things being out of focus, or defects in our vision. Our brain compensates and tidies up blurred images. By deliberately blurring the image, anti-aliasing triggers this processing in our brain and we appear to see a smooth line at an angle.

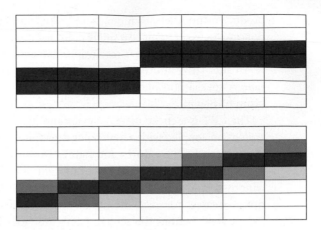

Figure 2.9 Magnified anti-aliased lines

2.4.2 Technologies

Cathode ray tube

The cathode ray tube is the television-like computer screen still most common as we write this, but rapidly being displaced by flat LCD screens. It works in a similar way to a standard television screen. A stream of electrons is emitted from an electron gun, which is then focussed and directed by magnetic fields. As the beam hits the phosphor-coated screen, the phosphor is excited by the electrons and glows (see Figure 2.10). The electron beam is scanned from left to right, and then flicked back to rescan the next line, from top to bottom. This is repeated, at about 30 Hz (that is, 30 times a second), per frame, although higher scan rates are sometimes used to reduce the flicker on the screen. Another way of reducing flicker is to use *interlacing*, in which the odd lines on the screen are all scanned first, followed by the even lines. Using a high-persistence phosphor, which glows for a longer time when excited, also reduces flicker, but causes image smearing especially if there is significant animation.

Black and white screens are able to display grayscale by varying the intensity of the electron beam; color is achieved using more complex means. Three electron guns are used, one each to hit red, green and blue phosphors. Combining these colors can

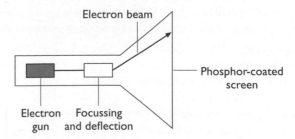

Figure 2.10 CRT screen

produce many others, including white, when they are all fully on. These three phosphor dots are focussed to make a single point using a *shadow mask*, which is imprecise and gives color screens a lower resolution than equivalent monochrome screens.

An alternative approach to producing color on the screen is to use *beam penetration*. A special phosphor glows a different color depending on the intensity of the beam hitting it.

The CRT is a cheap display device and has fast enough response times for rapid animation coupled with a high color capability. Note that animation does not necessarily mean little creatures and figures running about on the screen, but refers in a more general sense to the use of motion in displays: moving the cursor, opening windows, indicating processor-intensive calculations, or whatever. As screen resolution increases, however, the price rises. Because of the electron gun and focussing components behind the screen, CRTs are fairly bulky, though recent innovations have led to flatter displays in which the electron gun is not placed so that it fires directly at the screen, but fires parallel to the screen plane with the resulting beam bent through 90 degrees to hit the screen.

Health hazards of CRT displays

Most people who habitually use computers are aware that screens can often cause eyestrain and fatigue; this is usually due to flicker, poor legibility or low contrast. There have also been many concerns relating to the emission of radiation from screens. These can be categorized as follows:

■ X-rays which are largely absorbed by the screen (but not at the rear!)
■ ultraviolet and infrared radiation from phosphors in insignificant levels
■ radio frequency emissions, plus ultrasound (approximately 16 kHz)
■ electrostatic field which leaks out through the tube to the user. The intensity is dependent on distance and humidity. This can cause rashes in the user
■ electromagnetic fields (50 Hz to 0.5 MHz) which create induction currents in conductive materials, including the human body. Two types of effects are attributed to this: in the visual system, a high incidence of cataracts in visual display unit (VDU) operators, and concern over reproductive disorders (miscarriages and birth defects).

Research into the potentially harmful effect of these emissions is generally inconclusive, in that it is difficult to determine precisely what the causes of illness are, and many health scares have been the result of misinformed media opinion rather than scientific fact. However, users who are pregnant ought to take especial care and observe simple precautions. Generally, there are a number of common-sense things that can be done to relieve strain and minimize any risk. These include

■ not sitting too close to the screen
■ not using very small fonts
■ not looking at the screen for a long time without a break
■ working in well-lit surroundings
■ not placing the screen directly in front of a bright window.

Liquid crystal display

If you have used a personal organizer or notebook computer, you will have seen the light, flat plastic screens. These displays utilize liquid crystal technology and are smaller, lighter and consume far less power than traditional CRTs. These are also commonly referred to as flat-panel displays. They have no radiation problems associated with them, and are matrix addressable, which means that individual pixels can be accessed without the need for scanning.

Similar in principle to the digital watch, a thin layer of liquid crystal is sandwiched between two glass plates. The top plate is transparent and polarized, whilst the bottom plate is reflective. External light passes through the top plate and is polarized, which means that it only oscillates in one direction. This then passes through the crystal, reflects off the bottom plate and back to the eye, and so that cell looks white. When a voltage is applied to the crystal, via the conducting glass plates, the crystal twists. This causes it to turn the plane of polarization of the incoming light, rotating it so that it cannot return through the top plate, making the activated cell look black. The LCD requires refreshing at the usual rates, but the relatively slow response of the crystal means that flicker is not usually noticeable. The low intensity of the light emitted from the screen, coupled with the reduced flicker, means that the LCD is less tiring to use than standard CRT ones, with reduced eyestrain.

This different technology can be used to replace the standard screen on a desktop computer, and this is now common. However, the particular characteristics of compactness, light weight and low power consumption have meant that these screens have created a large niche in the computer market by monopolizing the notebook and portable computer systems side. The advent of these screens allowed small, light computers to be built, and created a large market that did not previously exist. Such computers, riding on the back of the technological wave, have opened up a different way of working for many people, who now have access to computers when away from the office, whether out on business or at home. Working in a different location on a smaller machine with different software obviously represents a different style of interaction and so once again we can see that differences in devices may alter the human–computer interaction considerably. The growing notebook computer market fed back into an investment in developing LCD screen technology, with supertwisted crystals increasing the viewing angle dramatically. Response times have also improved so that LCD screens are now used in personal DVD players and even in home television.

When the second edition of this book was being written the majority of LCD screens were black and white or grayscale, We wrote then 'it will be interesting to see whether color LCD screens supersede grayscale by the time the third edition of this book is prepared'. Of course, this is precisely the case. Our expectation is that by the time we produce the next edition LCD monitors will have taken over from CRT monitors completely.

Special displays

There are a number of other display technologies used in niche markets. The one you are most likely to see is the gas plasma display, which is used in large screens (see Section 2.4.3 below).

The random scan display, also known as the *directed beam refresh*, or *vector display*, works differently from the bitmap display, also known as raster scan, that we discussed in Section 2.4.1. Instead of scanning the whole screen sequentially and horizontally, the random scan draws the lines to be displayed directly. By updating the screen at at least 30 Hz to reduce flicker, the direct drawing of lines at any angle means that jaggies are not created, and higher resolutions are possible, up to 4096 × 4096 pixels. Color on such displays is achieved using beam penetration technology, and is generally of a poorer quality. Eyestrain and fatigue are still a problem, and these displays are more expensive than raster scan ones, so they are now only used in niche applications.

The *direct view storage tube* is used extensively as the display for an analog storage oscilloscope, which is probably the only place that these displays are used in any great numbers. They are similar in operation to the random scan CRT but the image is maintained by flood guns which have the advantage of producing a stable display with no flicker. The screen image can be incrementally updated but not selectively erased; removing items has to be done by redrawing the new image on a completely erased screen. The screens have a high resolution, typically about 4096 × 3120 pixels, but suffer from low contrast, low brightness and a difficulty in displaying color.

2.4.3 Large displays and situated displays

Displays are no longer just things you have on your desktop or laptop. In Chapter 19 we will discuss meeting room environments that often depend on large shared screens. You may have attended lectures where the slides are projected from a computer onto a large screen. In shops and garages large screen adverts assault us from all sides.

There are several types of large screen display. Some use gas plasma technology to create large flat bitmap displays. These behave just like a normal screen except they are big and usually have the HDTV (high definition television) wide screen format which has an aspect ratio of 16:9 instead of the 4:3 on traditional TV and monitors.

Where very large screen areas are required, several smaller screens, either LCD or CRT, can be placed together in a video wall. These can display separate images, or a single TV or computer image can be split up by software or hardware so that each screen displays a portion of the whole and the result is an enormous image. This is the technique often used in large concerts to display the artists or video images during the performance.

Possibly the large display you are most likely to have encountered is some sort of projector. There are two variants of these. In very large lecture theatres, especially older ones, you see projectors with large red, green and blue lenses. These each scan light across the screen to build a full color image. In smaller lecture theatres and in small meetings you are likely to see LCD projectors. Usually the size of a large book, these are like ordinary slide projectors except that where the slide would be there is a small LCD screen instead. The light from the projector passes through the tiny screen and is then focussed by the lens onto the screen.

The disadvantage of projected displays is that the presenter's shadow can often fall across the screen. Sometimes this is avoided in fixed lecture halls by using back projection. In a small room behind the screen of the lecture theatre there is a projector producing a right/left reversed image. The screen itself is a semi-frosted glass so that the image projected on the back can be seen in the lecture theatre. Because there are limits on how wide an angle the projector can manage without distortion, the size of the image is limited by the depth of the projection room behind, so these are less heavily used than front projection.

As well as for lectures and meetings, display screens can be used in various public places to offer information, link spaces or act as message areas. These are often called *situated displays* as they take their meaning from the location in which they are situated. These may be large screens where several people are expected to view or interact simultaneously, or they may be very small. Figure 2.11 shows an example of a small experimental situated display mounted by an office door to act as an electronic sticky note [70].

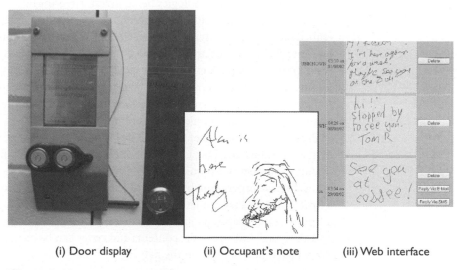

(i) Door display   (ii) Occupant's note   (iii) Web interface

Figure 2.11   Situated door display. Source: Courtesy of Keith Cheverst

DESIGN FOCUS

Hermes: a situated display

Office doors are often used as a noticeboard with messages from the occupant such as 'just gone out' or 'timetable for the week' and from visitors 'missed you, call when you get back'. The Hermes system is an electronic door display that offers some of the functions of sticky notes on a door [70]. Figure 2.11(i) shows an installed Hermes device fixed just beside the door, including the socket to use a Java iButton to authenticate the occupant. The occupant can leave messages that others can read (Figure 2.11(ii)) and people coming to the door can leave messages for the occupant. Electronic notes are smaller than paper ones, but because they are electronic they can be read remotely using a web interface (Figure 2.11(iii)), or added by SMS (see Chapter 19, Section 19.3.2).

The fact that it is situated – by a person's door – is very important. It establishes a context, 'Alan's door', and influences the way the system is used. For example, the idea of anonymous messages left on the door, where the visitor has had to be physically present, feels different from, say, anonymous emails.

See the book website for the full case study: /e3/casestudy/hermes/

2.4.4 Digital paper

A new form of 'display' that is still in its infancy is the various forms of digital paper. These are thin flexible materials that can be written to electronically, just like a computer screen, but which keep their contents even when removed from any electrical supply.

There are various technologies being investigated for this. One involves the whole surface being covered with tiny spheres, black one side, white the other. Electronics embedded into the material allow each tiny sphere to be rotated to make it black or white. When the electronic signal is removed the ball stays in its last orientation. A different technique has tiny tubes laid side by side. In each tube is light-absorbing liquid and a small reflective sphere. The sphere can be made to move to the top surface or away from it making the pixel white or black. Again the sphere stays in its last position once the electronic signal is removed.

Probably the first uses of these will be for large banners that can be reprogrammed or slowly animated. This is an ideal application, as it does not require very rapid updates and does not require the pixels to be small. As the technology matures, the aim is to have programmable sheets of paper that you attach to your computer to get a 'soft' printout that can later be changed. Perhaps one day you may be able to have a 'soft' book that appears just like a current book with soft pages that can be turned and skimmed, but where the contents and cover can be changed when you decide to download a new book from the net!

Virtual reality (VR) systems and various forms of 3D visualization are discussed in detail in Chapter 20. These require you to navigate and interact in a three-dimensional space. Sometimes these use the ordinary controls and displays of a desktop computer system, but there are also special devices used both to move and interact with 3D objects and to enable you to see a 3D environment.

2.5.1 Positioning in 3D space

Virtual reality systems present a 3D virtual world. Users need to navigate through these spaces and manipulate the virtual objects they find there. Navigation is not simply a matter of moving to a particular location, but also of choosing a particular orientation. In addition, when you grab an object in real space, you don't simply move it around, but also twist and turn it, for example when opening a door. Thus the move from mice to 3D devices usually involves a change from two degrees of freedom to six degrees of freedom, not just three.

Cockpit and virtual controls

Helicopter and aircraft pilots already have to navigate in real space. Many arcade games and also more serious applications use controls modeled on an aircraft cockpit to 'fly' through virtual space. However, helicopter pilots are very skilled and it takes a lot of practice for users to be able to work easily in such environments.

In many PC games and *desktop virtual reality* (where the output is shown on an ordinary computer screen), the controls are themselves virtual. This may be a simulated form of the cockpit controls or more prosaic up/down left/right buttons. The user manipulates these virtual controls using an ordinary mouse (or other 2D device). Note that this means there are two levels of indirection. It is a tribute to the flexibility of the human mind that people can not only use such systems but also rapidly become proficient.

The 3D mouse

There are a variety of devices that act as 3D versions of a mouse. Rather than just moving the mouse on a tabletop, you can pick it up, move it in three dimensions, rotate the mouse and tip it forward and backward. The 3D mouse has a full six degrees of freedom as its position can be tracked (three degrees), and also its up/down angle (called *pitch*), its left/right orientation (called *yaw*) and the amount it is twisted about its own axis (called *roll*) (see Figure 2.12). Various sensors are used to track the mouse position and orientation: magnetic coils, ultrasound or even mechanical joints where the mouse is mounted rather like an angle-poise lamp.

With the 3D mouse, and indeed most 3D positioning devices, users may experience strain from having to hold the mouse in the air for a long period. Putting the

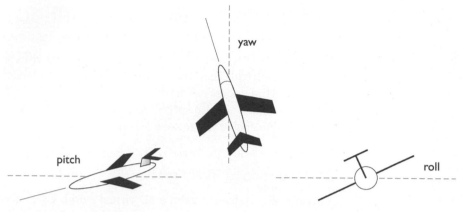

Figure 2.12 Pitch, yaw and roll

3D mouse down may even be treated as an action in the virtual environment, that is taking a nose dive.

Dataglove

One of the mainstays of high-end VR systems (see Chapter 20), the dataglove is a 3D input device. Consisting of a lycra glove with optical fibers laid along the fingers, it detects the joint angles of the fingers and thumb. As the fingers are bent, the fiber optic cable bends too; increasing bend causes more light to leak from the fiber, and the reduction in intensity is detected by the glove and related to the degree of bend in the joint. Attached to the top of the glove are two sensors that use ultrasound to determine 3D positional information as well as the angle of roll, that is the degree of wrist rotation. Such rich multi-dimensional input is currently a solution in search of a problem, in that most of the applications in use do not require such a comprehensive form of data input, whilst those that do cannot afford it. However, the availability of cheaper versions of the dataglove will encourage the development of more complex systems that are able to utilize the full power of the dataglove as an input device. There are a number of potential uses for this technology to assist disabled people, but cost remains the limiting factor at present.

The dataglove has the advantage that it is very easy to use, and is potentially very powerful and expressive (it can provide 10 joint angles, plus the 3D spatial information and degree of wrist rotation, 50 times a second). It suffers from extreme expense, and the fact that it is difficult to use in conjunction with a keyboard. However, such a limitation is shortsighted; one can imagine a keyboard drawn onto a desk, with software detecting hand positions and interpreting whether the virtual keys had been hit or not. The potential for the dataglove is vast; gesture recognition and sign language interpretation are two obvious areas that are the focus of active research, whilst less obvious applications are evolving all the time.

Virtual reality helmets

The helmets or goggles worn in some VR systems have two purposes: (i) they display the 3D world to each eye and (ii) they allow the user's head position to be tracked. We will discuss the former later when we consider output devices. The head tracking is used primarily to feed into the output side. As the user's head moves around the user ought to see different parts of the scene. However, some systems also use the user's head direction to determine the direction of movement within the space and even which objects to manipulate (rather like the eyegaze systems). You can think of this rather like leading a horse in reverse. If you want a horse to go in a particular direction, you use the reins to pull its head in the desired direction and the horse follows its head.

Whole-body tracking

Some VR systems aim to be immersive, that is to make the users feel as if they are really in the virtual world. In the real world it is possible (although not usually wise) to walk without looking in the direction you are going. If you are driving down the road and glance at something on the roadside you do not want the car to do a sudden 90-degree turn! Some VR systems therefore attempt to track different kinds of body movement. Some arcade games have a motorbike body on which you can lean into curves. More strangely, small trampolines have been wired up so that the user can control movement in virtual space by putting weight on different parts of the trampoline. The user can literally surf through virtual space. In the extreme the movement of the whole body may be tracked using devices similar to the dataglove, or using image-processing techniques. In the latter, white spots are stuck at various points of the user's body and the position of these tracked using two or more cameras, allowing the location of every joint to be mapped. Although the last of these sounds a little constraining for the fashion conscious it does point the way to less intrusive tracking techniques.

2.5.2 3D displays

Just as the 3D images used in VR have led to new forms of input device, they also require more sophisticated outputs. Desktop VR is delivered using a standard computer screen and a 3D impression is produced by using effects such as shadows, occlusion (where one object covers another) and perspective. This can be very effective and you can even view 3D images over the world wide web using a VRML (virtual reality markup language) enabled browser.

Seeing in 3D

Our eyes use many cues to perceive depth in the real world (see also Chapter 1). It is in fact quite remarkable as each eye sees only a flattened form of the world, like a photograph. One important effect is *stereoscopic vision* (or simply *stereo vision*).

Because each eye is looking at an object from a slightly different angle each sees a different image and our brain is able to use this to assess the relative distance of different objects. In desktop VR this stereoscopic effect is absent. However, various devices exist to deliver true stereoscopic images.

The start point of any stereoscopic device is the generation of images from different perspectives. As the computer is generating images for the virtual world anyway, this just means working out the right positions and angles corresponding to the typical distance between eyes on a human face. If this distance is too far from the natural one, the user will be presented with a giant's or gnat's eye view of the world!

Different techniques are then used to ensure that each eye sees the appropriate image. One method is to have two small screens fitted to a pair of goggles. A different image is then shown to each eye. These devices are currently still quite cumbersome and the popular image of VR is of a user with head encased in a helmet with something like a pair of inverted binoculars sticking out in front. However, smaller and lighter LCDs are now making it possible to reduce the devices towards the size and weight of ordinary spectacles.

An alternative method is to have a pair of special spectacles connected so that each eye can be blanked out by timed electrical signals. If this is synchronized with the frame rate of a computer monitor, each eye sees alternate images. Similar techniques use polarized filters in front of the monitor and spectacles with different polarized lenses. These techniques are both effectively using similar methods to the red–green 3D spectacles given away in some breakfast cereals. Indeed, these red–green spectacles have been used in experiments in wide-scale 3D television broadcasts. However, the quality of the 3D image from the polarized and blanked eye spectacles is substantially better.

The ideal would be to be able to look at a special 3D screen and see 3D images just as one does with a hologram – 3D television just like in all the best sci-fi movies! But there is no good solution to this yet. One method is to inscribe the screen with small vertical grooves forming hundreds of prisms. Each eye then sees only alternate dots on the screen allowing a stereo image at half the normal horizontal resolution. However, these screens have very narrow *viewing angles*, and are not ready yet for family viewing.

In fact, getting stereo images is not the whole story. Not only do our eyes see different things, but each eye also focusses on the current object of interest (small muscles change the shape of the lens in the pupil of the eye). The images presented to the eye are generated at some fixed focus, often with effectively infinite *depth of field*. This can be confusing and tiring. There has been some progress recently on using lasers to detect the focal depth of each eye and adjust the images correspondingly, similar to the technology used for eye tracking. However, this is not currently used extensively.

VR motion sickness

We all get annoyed when computers take a long time to change the screen, pop up a window, or play a digital movie. However, with VR the effects of poor display performance can be more serious. In real life when we move our head the image our eyes see changes accordingly. VR systems produce the same effect by using sensors in the goggles or helmet and then using the position of the head to determine the right image to show. If the system is slow in producing these images a lag develops between the user moving his head and the scene changing. If this delay is more than a hundred milliseconds or so the feeling becomes disorienting. The effect is very similar to that of being at sea. You stand on the deck looking out to sea, the boat gently rocking below you. Tiny channels in your ears detect the movement telling your brain that you are moving; your eyes see the horizon moving in one direction and the boat in another. Your brain gets confused and you get sick. Users of VR can experience similar nausea and few can stand it for more than a short while. In fact, keeping laboratories sanitary has been a major push in improving VR technology.

Simulators and VR caves

Because of the problems of delivering a full 3D environment via head-mounted displays, some virtual reality systems work by putting the user within an environment where the virtual world is displayed upon it. The most obvious examples of this are large flight simulators – you go inside a mock-up of an aircraft cockpit and the scenes you would see through the windows are projected onto the virtual windows. In motorbike or skiing simulators in video arcades large screens are positioned to fill the main part of your visual field. You can still look over your shoulder and see your friends, but while you are engaged in the game it surrounds you.

More general-purpose rooms called caves have large displays positioned all around the user, or several back projectors. In these systems the user can look all around and see the virtual world surrounding them.

2.6 PHYSICAL CONTROLS, SENSORS AND SPECIAL DEVICES

As we have discussed, computers are coming out of the box. The mouse keyboard and screen of the traditional computer system are not relevant or possible in applications that now employ computers such as interactive TV, in-car navigation systems or personal entertainment. These devices may have special displays, may use sound, touch and smell as well as visual displays, may have dedicated controls and may sense the environment or your own bio-signs.

2.6.1 Special displays

Apart from the CRT screen there are a number of visual outputs utilized in complex systems, especially in embedded systems. These can take the form of analog representations of numerical values, such as dials, gauges or lights to signify a certain system state. Flashing light-emitting diodes (LEDs) are used on the back of some computers to signify the processor state, whilst gauges and dials are found in process control systems. Once you start in this mode of thinking, you can contemplate numerous visual outputs that are unrelated to the screen. One visual display that has found a specialized niche is the head-up display that is used in aircraft. The pilot is fully occupied looking forward and finds it difficult to look around the cockpit to get information. There are many different things that need to be known, ranging from data from tactical systems to navigational information and aircraft status indicators. The head-up display projects a subset of this information into the pilot's line of vision so that the information is directly in front of her eyes. This obviates the need for large banks of information to be scanned with the corresponding lack of attention to what is happening outside, and makes the pilot's job easier. Less important information is usually presented on a smaller number of dials and gauges in the cockpit to avoid cluttering the head-up display, and these can be monitored less often, during times of low stress.

2.6.2 Sound output

Another mode of output that we should consider is that of auditory signals. Often designed to be used in conjunction with screen displays, auditory outputs are poorly understood: we do not yet know how to utilize sound in a sensible way to achieve maximum effect and information transference. We have discussed speech previously, but other sounds such as beeps, bongs, clanks, whistles and whirrs are all used to varying effect. As well as conveying system output, sounds offer an important level of feedback in interactive systems. Keyboards can be set to emit a click each time a key is pressed, and this appears to speed up interactive performance. Telephone keypads often sound different tones when the keys are pressed; a noise occurring signifies that the key has been successfully pressed, whilst the actual tone provides some information about the particular key that was pressed. The advantage of auditory feedback is evident when we consider a simple device such as a doorbell. If we press it and hear nothing, we are left undecided. Should we press it again, in case we did not do it right the first time, or did it ring but we did not hear it? And if we press it again but it actually did ring, will the people in the house think we are very rude, ringing insistently? We feel awkward and a little stressed. If we were using a computer system instead of a doorbell and were faced with a similar problem, we would not enjoy the interaction and would not perform as well. Yet it is a simple problem that could be easily rectified by a better initial design, using sound. Chapter 10 will discuss the use of the auditory channel in more detail.

2.6.3 Touch, feel and smell

Our other senses are used less in normal computer applications, but you may have played computer games where the joystick or artificial steering wheel vibrated, perhaps when a car was about to go off the track. In some VR applications, such as the use in medical domains to 'practice' surgical procedures, the *feel* of an instrument moving through different tissue types is very important. The devices used to emulate these procedures have *force feedback*, giving different amounts of resistance depending on the state of the virtual operation. These various forms of force, resistance and texture that influence our physical senses are called *haptic* devices.

Haptic devices are not limited to virtual environments, but are used in specialist interfaces in the real world too. Electronic braille displays either have pins that rise or fall to give different patterns, or may involve small vibration pins. Force feedback has been used in the design of in-car controls.

In fact, the car gives a very good example of the power of tactile feedback. If you drive over a small bump in the road the car is sent slightly off course; however, the chances are that you will correct yourself before you are consciously aware of the bump. Within your body you have reactions that push back slightly against pressure to keep your limbs where you 'want' them, or move your limbs out of the way when you brush against something unexpected. These responses occur in your lower brain and are very fast, not involving any conscious effort. So, haptic devices can access very fast responses, but these responses are not fully controlled. This can be used effectively in design, but of course also with caution.

Texture is more difficult as it depends on small changes between neighboring points on the skin. Also, most of our senses notice change rather than fixed stimuli, so we usually feel textures when we move our fingers over a surface, not just when resting on it. Technology for this is just beginning to become available

There is evidence that smell is one of the strongest cues to memory. Various historical recreations such as the Jorvik Centre in York, England, use smells to create a feeling of immersion in their static displays of past life. Some arcade games also generate smells, for example, burning rubber as your racing car skids on the track. These examples both use a fixed smell in a particular location. There have been several attempts to produce devices to allow smells to be recreated dynamically in response to games or even internet sites. The technical difficulty is that our noses do not have a small set of basic smells that are mixed (like salt/sweet/sour/bitter/savoury on our tongue), but instead there are thousands of different types of receptor responding to different chemicals in the air. The general pattern of devices to generate smells is to have a large repertoire of tiny scent-containing capsules that are released in varying amounts on demand – rather like a printer cartridge with hundreds of ink colors! So far there appears to be no mass market for these devices, but they may eventually develop from niche markets.

Smell is a complex multi-dimensional sense and has a peculiar ability to trigger memory, but cannot be changed rapidly. These qualities may prove valuable in areas where a general sense of location and awareness is desirable. For example, a project at the Massachusetts Institute of Technology explored the use of a small battery of scent generators which may be particularly valuable for *ambient displays* and background awareness [198, 161].

DESIGN FOCUS

Feeling the road

In the BMW 7 Series you will find a single haptic feedback control for many of the functions that would normally have dedicated controls. It uses technology developed by Immersion Corporation who are also behind the force feedback found in many medical and entertainment haptic devices. The iDrive control slides backwards and forwards and rotates to give access to various menus and lists of options. The haptic feedback allows the user to feel 'clicks' appropriate to the number of items in the various menu lists.

See: www.immersion.com/ and www.bmw.com/ Picture courtesy of BMW AG

2.6.4 Physical controls

Look at Figure 2.13. In it you can see the controls for a microwave, a washing machine and a personal MiniDisc player. See how they each use very different physical devices: the microwave has a flat plastic sheet with soft buttons, the washing machine large switches and knobs, and the MiniDisc has small buttons and an interesting multi-function end.

A desktop computer system has to serve many functions and so has generic keys and controls that can be used for a variety of purposes. In contrast, these dedicated control panels have been designed for a particular device and for a single use. This is why they differ so much.

Looking first at the microwave, it has a flat plastic control panel. The buttons on the panel are pressed and 'give' slightly. The choice of the smooth panel is probably partly for visual design – it looks streamlined! However, there are also good practical reasons. The microwave is used in the kitchen whilst cooking, with hands that may be greasy or have food on them. The smooth controls have no gaps where food can accumulate and clog buttons, so it can easily be kept clean and hygienic.

When using the washing machine you are handling dirty clothes, which may be grubby, but not to the same extent, so the smooth easy-clean panel is less important (although some washing machines do have smooth panels). It has several major

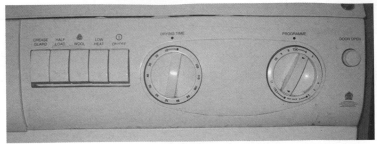

Figure 2.13 Physical controls on microwave, washing machine and MiniDisc. Source: Photograph bottom right by Alan Dix with permission from Sony (UK)

settings and the large buttons act both as control and display. Also the dials for dryer timer and the washing program act both as a means to set the desired time or program and to display the current state whilst the wash is in progress.

Finally, the MiniDisc controller needs to be small and unobtrusive. It has tiny buttons, but the end control is most interesting. It twists from side to side and also can be pulled and twisted. This means the same control can be used for two different purposes. This form of multi-function control is common in small devices.

We discussed the immediacy of haptic feedback and these lessons are also important at the level of creating physical devices; do keys, dials, etc., feel as if they have been pressed or turned? Getting the right level of resistance can make the device work naturally, give you feedback that you have done something, or let you know that you are controlling something. Where for some reason this is not possible, something has to be done to prevent the user getting confused, perhaps pressing buttons twice; for example, the smooth control panel of the microwave in Figure 2.13 offers no tactile feedback, but beeps for each keypress. We will discuss these design issues further when we look at user experience in Chapter 3 (Section 3.9).

Whereas texture is difficult to generate, it is easy to build into materials. This can make a difference to the ease of use of a device. For example, a touchpad is smooth, but a keyboard nipple is usually rubbery. If they were the other way round it would be hard to drag your finger across the touchpad or to operate the nipple without slipping. Texture can also be used to disambiguate. For example, most keyboards have a small raised dot on the 'home' keys for touch typists and some calculators and phones do the same on the '5' key. This is especially useful in applications when the eyes are elsewhere.

2.6.5 Environment and bio-sensing

In a public washroom there are often no controls for the wash basins, you simply put your hands underneath and (hope that) the water flows. Similarly when you open the door of a car, the courtesy light turns on. The washbasin is controlled by a small infrared sensor that is triggered when your hands are in the basin (although it is

DESIGN FOCUS

Smart-Its – making using sensors easy

Building systems with physical sensors is no easy task. You need a soldering iron, plenty of experience in electronics, and even more patience. Although some issues are unique to each sensor or project, many of the basic building blocks are similar – connecting simple microprocessors to memory and networks, connecting various standard sensors such as temperature, tilt, etc.

The Smart-Its project has made this job easier by creating a collection of components and an architecture for adding new sensors. There are a number of basic Smart-It boards – the photo on the left shows a microprocessor with wireless connectivity. Onto these boards are plugged a variety of modules – in the center is a sensor board including temperature and light, and on the right is a power controller.

See: www.smart-its.org/ Source: Courtesy of Hans Gellersen

sometimes hard to find the 'sweet spot' where this happens!). The courtesy lights are triggered by a small switch in the car door.

Although we are not always conscious of them, there are many sensors in our environment – controlling automatic doors, energy saving lights, etc. and devices monitoring our behavior such as security tags in shops. The vision of ubiquitous computing (see Chapters 4 and 20) suggests that our world will be filled with such devices. Certainly the gap between science fiction and day-to-day life is narrow; for example, in the film *Minority Report* (20th Century Fox) iris scanners identify each passer-by to feed them dedicated advertisements, but you can buy just such an iris scanner as a security add-on for your home computer.

There are many different sensors available to measure virtually anything: temperature, movement (ultrasound, infrared, etc.), location (GPS, global positioning, in mobile devices), weight (pressure sensors). In addition audio and video information can be analyzed to identify individuals and to detect what they are doing. This all sounds big brother like, but is also used in ordinary applications, such as the washbasin.

Sensors can also be used to capture physiological signs such as body temperature, unconscious reactions such as blink rate, or unconscious aspects of activities such as typing rate, vocabulary shifts (e.g. modal verbs). For example, in a speech-based game, Tsukahara and Ward use gaps in speech and prosody (patterns of rhythm, pitch and loudness in speech) to infer the user's emotional state and thus the nature of acceptable responses [350] and Allanson discusses a variety of physiological sensors to create 'electrophysiological interactive computer systems' [12].

2.7   PAPER: PRINTING AND SCANNING

Some years ago, a recurrent theme of information technology was the *paperless office*. In the paperless office, documents would be produced, dispatched, read and filed online. The only time electronic information would be committed to paper would be when it went out of the office to ordinary customers, or to other firms who were laggards in this technological race. This vision was fuelled by rocketing property prices, and the realization that the floor space for a wastepaper basket could cost thousands in rent each year. Some years on, many traditional paper files are now online, but the desire for the completely paperless office has faded. Offices still have wastepaper baskets, and extra floor space is needed for the special computer tables to house 14-inch color monitors.

In this section, we will look at some of the available technology that exists to get information to and from paper. We will look first at printing, the basic technology, and issues raised by it. We will then go on to discuss the movement from paper back into electronic media. Although the paperless office is no longer seen as the goal, the less-paper office is perhaps closer, now that the technologies for moving between media are better.

2.7.1 Printing

If anything, computer systems have made it easier to produce paper documents. It is so easy to run off many copies of a letter (or book), in order to get it looking 'just right'. Older printers had a fixed set of characters available on a printhead. These varied from the traditional line printer to golf-ball and daisy-wheel printers. To change a typeface or the size of type meant changing the printhead, and was an awkward, and frequently messy, job, but for many years the daisy-wheel printer was the only means of producing high-quality output at an affordable price. However, the drop in the price of laser printers coupled with the availability of other cheap high-quality printers means that daisy-wheels are fast becoming a rarity.

All of the popular printing technologies, like screens, build the image on the paper as a series of dots. This enables, in theory, any character set or graphic to be printed,

Common types of dot-based printers

Dot-matrix printers
These use an inked ribbon, like a typewriter, but instead of a single character-shaped head striking the paper, a line of *pins* is used, each of which can strike the ribbon and hence dot the paper. Horizontal resolution can be varied by altering the speed of the head across the paper, and vertical resolution can be improved by sending the head twice across the paper at a slightly different position. So, dot-matrix printers can produce fast draft-quality output or slower 'letter'-quality output. They are cheap to run, but could not compete with the quality of jet and laser printers for general office and home printing. They are now only used for bulk printing, or where carbon paper is required for payslips, check printing, etc.)

Ink-jet and bubble-jet printers
These operate by sending tiny blobs of ink from the printhead to the paper. The ink is squirted at pressure from an ink-jet, whereas bubble-jets use heat to create a bubble. Both are quite quiet in operation. The ink from the bubble-jet (being a bubble rather than a droplet) dries more quickly than the ink-jet and so is less likely to smear. Both approach laser quality, but the bubble-jet dots tend to be more accurately positioned and of a less broken shape.

Laser printer
This uses similar technology to a photocopier: 'dots' of electrostatic charge are deposited on a drum, which then picks up toner (black powder). This is then rolled onto the paper and cured by heat. The curing is why laser printed documents come out warm, and the electrostatic charge is why they smell of ozone! In addition, some toner can be highly toxic if inhaled, but this is more a problem for full-time maintenance workers than end-users changing the occasional toner cartridge.

Laser printers give nearly typeset-quality output, with top-end printers used by desktop publishing firms. Indeed, many books are nowadays produced using laser printers. The authors of this book have produced camera-ready copy for other books on 300 and 600 dpi laser printers, although this book required higher quality and the first edition was typeset at 1200 dpi onto special bromide paper.

limited only by the resolution of the dots. This resolution is measured in *dots per inch* (dpi). Imagine a sheet of graph paper, and building up an image by putting dots at the intersection of each line. The number of lines per inch in each direction is the resolution in dpi. For some mechanical printers this is slightly confused: the dots printed may be bigger than the gaps, neighboring printheads may not be able to print simultaneously and may be offset relative to one another (a diamond-shaped rather than rectangular grid). These differences do not make too much difference to the user, but mean that, given two printers at the same nominal resolution, the output of one looks better than that of the other, because it has managed the physical constraints better.

The most common types of dot-based printers are dot-matrix printers, ink-jet printers and laser printers. These are listed roughly in order of increasing resolution and quality, where dot-matrix printers typically have a resolution of 80–120 dpi rising to about 300–600 dpi for ink-jet printers and 600–2400 dpi for laser printers. By varying the quantity of ink and quality of paper, ink-jet printers can be used to print photo-quality prints from digital photographs.

Printing in the workplace

Although ink-jet and laser printers have the lion's share of the office and home printer market, there are many more specialist applications that require different technology.

Most shop tills use dot-matrix printing where the arrangement is often very clever, with one printhead serving several purposes. The till will usually print one till roll which stays within the machine, recording all transactions for audit purposes. An identical receipt is printed for the customer. In addition, many will print onto the customer's own check or produce a credit card slip for the customer to sign. Sometimes the multiple copies are produced using two or more layers of paper where the top layer receives the ink and the lower layers use pressure-sensitive paper – not possible using ink-jet or laser technology. Alternatively, a single printhead may move back and forth over several small paper rolls within the same machine, as well as moving over the slot for the customer's own check.

As any printer owner will tell you, office printers are troublesome, especially as they age. Different printing technology is therefore needed in harsh environments or where a low level of supervision is required. Thermal printers use special heat-sensitive paper that changes color when heated. The printhead simply heats the paper where it wants a dot. Often only one line of dots is produced per pass, in contrast to dot-matrix and ink-jet printers, which have several pins or jets in parallel. The image is then produced using several passes per line, achieving a resolution similar to a dot-matrix. Thermal paper is relatively expensive and not particularly nice to look at, but thermal printers are mechanically simple and require little maintenance (no ink or toner splashing about). Thermal printers are used in niche applications, for example industrial equipment, some portable printers, and fax machines (although many now use plain paper).

As well as resolution, printers vary in speed and cost. Typically, office-quality ink-jet or laser printers produce between four and eight pages per minute. Dot-matrix printers are more often rated in *characters per second* (cps), and typical speeds may be 200 cps for draft and 50 cps for letter-quality print. In practice, this means no more than a page or so per minute. These are maximum speeds for simple text, and printers may operate much more slowly for graphics.

Color ink-jet printers are substantially cheaper than even monochrome laser printers. However, the recurrent costs of consumables may easily dominate this initial cost. Both jet and laser printers have special-purpose parts (print cartridges, toner, print drums), which need to be replaced every few thousand sheets; and they must also use high-grade paper. It may be more difficult to find suitable grades of recycled paper for laser printers.

2.7.2 Fonts and page description languages

Some printers can act in a mode whereby any characters sent to them (encoded in ASCII, see Section 2.8.5) are printed, typewriter style, in a single font. Another case, simple in theory, is when you have a bitmap picture and want to print it. The dots to print are sent to the printer, and no further interpretation is needed. However, in practice, it is rarely so simple.

Many printed documents are far more complex – they incorporate text in many different fonts and many sizes, often italicized, emboldened and underlined. Within the text you will find line drawings, digitized photographs and pictures generated from 'paint' packages, including the ubiquitous 'clip art'. Sometimes the computer does all the work, converting the page image into a bitmap of the right size to be sent to the printer. Alternatively, a description of the page may be sent to the printer. At the simplest level, this will include commands to set the print position on the page, and change the font size.

More sophisticated printers can accept a *page description language*, the most common of which is PostScript. This is a form of programming language for printing. It includes some standard programming constructs, but also some special ones: paths for drawing lines and curves, sophisticated character and font handling and scaled bitmaps. The idea is that the description of a page is far smaller than the associated bitmap, reducing the time taken to send the page to the printer. A bitmap version of an A4 laser printer page at 300 dpi takes 8 Mbytes; to send this down a standard serial printer cable would take 10 minutes! However, a computer in the printer has to interpret the PostScript program to print the page; this is typically faster than 10 minutes, but is still the limiting factor for many print jobs.

Text is printed in a font with a particular size and shape. The size of a font is measured in points (pt). The point is a printer's measure and is about 1/72 of an inch. The *point size* of the font is related to its height: a 12 point font has about six lines per inch. The shape of a font is determined by its *font name*, for example Times Roman, Courier or Helvetica. Times Roman font is similar to the type of many newspapers, such as *The Times*, whereas Courier has a typewritten shape.

Courier is a fixed-pitch font
Times Roman is a variable-pitch serif font
Minion is also a variable-pitch serif font
Gill Sans is a variable-pitch sans-serif font
A mathematics font: αβξ±≠∈∀°⊥↑ℵ∂℘□□

Figure 2.14   Examples of different fonts

Some fonts, such as Courier, are *fixed pitch*, that is each character has the same width. The alternative is a variable-pitched font, such as Times Roman or Gill Sans, where some characters, such as the 'm', are wider than others, such as the 'i'. Another characteristic of fonts is whether they are *serif* or *sans-serif*. A serif font has fine, short cross-lines at the ends of the strokes, imitating those found on cut stone lettering. A sans-serif font has square-ended strokes. In addition, there are special fonts looking like Gothic lettering or cursive script, and fonts of Greek letters and special mathematical symbols.

This book is set in 10 point Minion font using PostScript. Minion is a variable-pitched serif font. Figure 2.14 shows examples of different fonts.

DESIGN FOCUS

Readability of text

There is a substantial body of knowledge about the readability of text, both on screen and on paper. An MSc student visited a local software company and, on being shown some of their systems, remarked on the fact that they were using upper case throughout their displays. At that stage she had only completed part of an HCI course but she had read Chapter 1 of this book and already knew that WORDS WRITTEN IN BLOCK CAPITALS take longer to read than those in lower case. Recall that this is largely because of the clues given by word shapes and is the principle behind 'look and say' methods of teaching children to read. The company immediately recognized the value of the advice and she instantly rose in their esteem!

However, as with many interface design guidelines there are caveats. Although lower-case words are easier to read, individual letters and nonsense words are clearer in upper case. For example, one writes flight numbers as 'BA793' rather than 'ba793'. This is particularly important when naming keys to press (for example, 'Press Q to quit') as keyboards have upper-case legends.

Font shapes can also make a difference; for printed text, serif fonts make it easier to run one's eye along a line of text. However, they usually reproduce less well on screen where the resolution is poorer.

2.7.3 Screen and page

A common requirement of word processors and desktop publishing software is that *what you see is what you get* (see also Chapters 4 and 17), which is often called by its acronym *WYSIWYG* (pronounced whizz-ee-wig). This means that the appearance of the document on the screen should be the same as its eventual appearance on the printed page. In so far as this means that, for example, centered text is displayed centered on the screen, this is reasonable. However, this should not cloud the fact that screen and paper are very different media.

A typical screen resolution is about 72 dpi compared with a laser printer at over 600 dpi. Some packages can show magnified versions of the document in order to help in this. Most screens use an additive color model using red, green and blue light, whereas printers use a subtractive color model with cyan, magenta, yellow and black inks, so conversions have to be made. In addition, the sizes and aspect ratios are very different. An A4 page is about 11 inches tall by 8 wide (297×210 mm), whereas a screen is often of similar dimensions, but wider than it is tall.

These differences cause problems when designing software. Should you try to make the screen image as close to the paper as possible, or should you try to make the best of each? One approach to this would be to print only what could be displayed, but that would waste the extra resolution of the printer. On the other hand, one can try to make the screen as much like paper as possible, which is the intention behind the standard use of black text on a white background, rotatable A4 displays, and tablet PCs. This is a laudable aim, but cannot get rid of all the problems.

A particular problem lies with fonts. Imagine we have a line of 'm's, each having a width of 0.15 inch (4 mm). If we print them on a 72 dpi screen, then we can make the screen character 10 or 11 dots wide, in which case the screen version will be narrower or wider than the printed version. Alternatively, we can print the screen version as near as possible to where the printed characters would lie, in which case the 'm's on the screen would have different spaces between them: 'mm mm mm mm m'. The latter looks horrible on the screen, so most software chooses the former approach. This means that text that aligns on screen may not do so on printing. Some systems use a uniform representation for screen and printer, using the same font descriptions and even, in the case of the Next operating system, PostScript for screen display as well as printer output (also PDF with MacOS X). However, this simply exports the problem from the application program to the operating system.

The differences between screen and printer mean that different forms of graphic design are needed for each. For example, headings and changes in emphasis are made using font style and size on paper, but using color, brightness and line boxes on screen. This is not usually a problem for the display of the user's own documents as the aim is to give the user as good an impression of the printed page as possible, given the limitations. However, if one is designing parallel paper and screen forms, then one has to trade off consistency between the two representations with clarity in each.

An overall similar layout, but with different forms of presentation for details, may be appropriate.

2.7.4 Scanners and optical character recognition

Printers take electronic documents and put them on paper – *scanners* reverse this process. They start by turning the image into a bitmap, but with the aid of *optical character recognition* can convert the page right back into text. The image to be converted may be printed, but may also be a photograph or hand-drawn picture.

There are two main kinds of scanner: flat-bed and hand-held. With a flat-bed scanner, the page is placed on a flat glass plate and the whole page is converted into a bitmap. A variant of the flat-bed is where sheets to be scanned are pulled through the machine, common in multi-function devices (printer/fax/copier). Many flat-bed scanners allow a small pile of sheets to be placed in a feed tray so that they can all be scanned without user intervention. Hand-held scanners are pulled over the image by hand. As the head passes over an area it is read in, yielding a bitmap strip. A roller at the ends ensures that the scanner knows how fast it is being pulled and thus how big the image is. The scanner is typically only 3 or 4 inches (80 or 100 mm) wide and may even be the size of a large pen (mainly used for scanning individual lines of text). This means at least two or three strips must be 'glued' together by software to make a whole page image, quite a difficult process as the strips will overlap and may not be completely parallel to one another, as well as suffering from problems of different brightness and contrast. However, for desktop publishing small images such as photographs are quite common, and as long as one direction is less than the width of the scanner, they can be read in one pass.

Scanners work by shining a beam of light at the page and then recording the intensity and color of the reflection. Like photocopiers, the color of the light that is shone means that some colors may appear darker than others on a monochrome scanner. For example, if the light is pure red, then a red image will reflect the light completely and thus not appear on the scanned image.

Like printers, scanners differ in resolution, commonly between 600 and 2400 dpi, and like printers the quoted resolution needs careful interpretation. Many have a lower resolution scanhead but digitally interpolate additional pixels – the same is true for some digital cameras. Monochrome scanners are typically only found in multi-function devices, but color scanners usually have monochrome modes for black and white or grayscale copying. Scanners will usually return up to 256 levels of gray or RGB (red, green, blue) color. If a pure monochrome image is required (for instance, from a printed page), then it can *threshold* the grayscale image; that is, turn all pixels darker than some particular value black, and the rest white.

Scanners are used extensively in *desktop publishing* (*DTP*) for reading in hand-drawn pictures and photographs. This means that cut and paste can be performed electronically rather than with real glue. In addition, the images can be rotated, scaled and otherwise transformed, using a variety of image manipulation software tools. Such tools are becoming increasingly powerful, allowing complex image transformations to be easily achieved; these range from color correction, through the merging of multiple images to the application of edge-detection and special effects filters. The use of multiple layers allows photomontage effects that would be impossible with traditional photographic or paper techniques. Even where a scanned image is simply going to be printed back out as part of a larger publication, some processing typically has to be performed to match the scanned colors with those produced during printing. For film photographs there are also special film scanners that can scan photographic negatives or color slides. Of course, if the photographs are digital no scanning is necessary.

Another application area is in document storage and retrieval systems, where paper documents are scanned and stored on computer rather than (or sometimes as well as) in a filing cabinet. The costs of maintaining paper records are enormous, and electronic storage can be cheaper, more reliable and more flexible. Storing a bitmap image is neither most useful (in terms of access methods), nor space efficient (as we will see later), so scanning may be combined with optical character recognition to obtain the text rather than the page image of the document.

Optical character recognition (OCR) is the process whereby the computer can 'read' the characters on the page. It is only comparatively recently that print could be reliably read, since the wide variety of typefaces and print sizes makes this more difficult than one would imagine – it is *not* simply a matter of matching a character shape to the image on the page. In fact, OCR is rather a misnomer nowadays as, although the document is optically scanned, the OCR software itself operates on the bitmap image. Current software can recognize 'unseen' fonts and can even produce output in word-processing formats, preserving super- and subscripts, centering, italics and so on.

Another important area is electronic publishing for multimedia and the world wide web. Whereas in desktop publishing the scanned image usually ends up (after editing) back on paper, in electronic publishing the scanned image is destined to be viewed on screen. These images may be used simply as digital photographs or may be made active, whereby clicking on some portion of the image causes pertinent information to be displayed (see Chapter 3 for more on the *point-and-click* style of interaction). One big problem when using electronic images is the plethora of formats for storing graphics (see Section 2.8.5). Another problem is the fact that different computers can display different numbers of colors and that the appearance of the same image on different monitors can be very different.

The importance of electronic publishing and also the ease of electronically manipulating images for printing have made the *digital camera* increasingly popular. Rather than capturing an image on film, a digital camera has a small light-sensitive chip that can directly record an image into memory.

Paper-based interaction

Paper is principally seen as an output medium. You type in some text, format it, print it and read it. The idea of the paperless office was to remove the paper from the write–read loop entirely, but it didn't fundamentally challenge its place in the cycle as an output medium. However, this view of paper as output has changed as OCR technology has improved and scanners become commonplace.

Workers at Xerox Palo Alto Research Center (also known as Xerox PARC) capitalized on this by using paper as a medium of interaction with computer systems [195]. A special identifying mark is printed onto forms and similar output. The printed forms may have check boxes or areas for writing numbers or (in block capitals!) words. The form can then be scanned back in. The system reads the identifying mark and thereby knows what sort of paper form it is dealing with. It doesn't have to use OCR on the printed text of the form as it printed it, but can detect the check boxes that have been filled in and even recognize the text that has been written. The identifying mark the researchers used is composed of backward and forward slashes, '\' and '/', and is called a *glyph*. An alternative would have been to use bar codes, but the slashes were found to fax and scan more reliably. The research version of this system was known as XAX, but it is now marketed as Xerox PaperWorks.

One application of this technology is mail order catalogs. The order form is printed with a glyph. When completed, forms can simply be collected into bundles and scanned in batches, generating orders automatically. If the customer faxes an order the fax-receiving software recognizes the glyph and the order is processed without ever being handled at the company end. Such a *paper user interface* may involve no screens or keyboards whatsoever.

Some types of paper now have identifying marks micro-printed like a form of textured watermark. This can be used both to identify the piece of paper (as the glyph does), and to identify the location on the paper. If this book were printed on such paper it would be possible to point at a word or diagram with a special pen-like device and have it work out what page you are on and where you are pointing and thus take you to appropriate web materials . . . perhaps the fourth edition . . .

It is paradoxical that Xerox PARC, where much of the driving work behind current 'mouse and window' computer interfaces began, has also developed this totally non-screen and non-mouse paradigm. However, the common principle behind each is the novel and appropriate use of different media for graceful interaction.

Worked exercise   *What input and output devices would you use for the following systems? For each, compare and contrast alternatives, and if appropriate indicate why the conventional keyboard, mouse and CRT screen may be less suitable.*

(a) portable word processor

(b) tourist information system

(c) tractor-mounted crop-spraying controller

(d) *air traffic control system*

(e) *worldwide personal communications system*

(f) *digital cartographic system.*

Answer   In the later exercise on basic architecture (see Section 2.8.6), we focus on 'typical' systems, whereas here the emphasis is on the diversity of different devices needed for specialized purposes. You can 'collect' devices – watch out for shop tills, bank tellers, taxi meters, lift buttons, domestic appliances, etc.

(a) Portable word processor

The determining factors are size, weight and battery power. However, remember the purpose: this is a word processor not an address book or even a data entry device.

(i)   LCD screen – low-power requirement

(ii) trackball or stylus for pointing

(iii) real keyboard – you can't word process without a reasonable keyboard and stylus handwriting recognition is not good enough

(iv) small, low-power bubble-jet printer – although not always necessary, this makes the package stand alone. It is probably not so necessary that the printer has a large battery capacity as printing can probably wait until a power point is found.

(b) Tourist information system

This is likely to be in a public place. Most users will only visit the system once, so the information and mode of interaction must be immediately obvious.

(i)   touchscreen only – easy and direct interaction for first-time users (see also Chapter 3)

(ii) NO mice or styluses – in a public place they wouldn't stay long!

(c) Tractor-mounted crop-spraying controller

A hostile environment with plenty of mud and chemicals. Requires numerical input for flow rates, etc., but probably no text

(i)   touch-sensitive keypad – ordinary keypads would get blocked up

(ii) small dedicated LED display (LCDs often can't be read in sunlight and large screens are fragile)

(iii) again no mice or styluses – they would get lost.

(d) Air traffic control system

The emphasis is on immediately available information and rapid interaction. The controller cannot afford to spend time searching for information; all frequently used information must be readily available.

(i)   several specialized displays – including overlays of electronic information on radar

(ii) light pen or stylus – high-precision direct interaction

(iii) keyboard – for occasional text input, but consider making it fold out of the way.

(e) Worldwide personal communications system

Basically a super mobile phone! If it is to be kept on hand all the time it must be very light and pocket sized. However, to be a 'communications' system one would imagine that it should also act as a personal address/telephone book, etc.

(i) standard telephone keypad – the most frequent use

(ii) small dedicated LCD display – low power, specialized functions

(iii) possibly stylus for interaction – it allows relatively rich interaction with the address book software, but little space

(iv) a 'docking' facility – the system itself will be too small for a full-sized keyboard(!), but you won't want to enter in all your addresses and telephone numbers by stylus!

(f) Digital cartographic system

This calls for very high-precision input and output facilities. It is similar to CAD in terms of the screen facilities and printing, but in addition will require specialized data capture.

(i) large high-resolution color VDU (20 inch or bigger) – these tend to be enormously big (from back to front). LCD screens, although promising far thinner displays in the long term, cannot at present be made large enough

(ii) digitizing tablet – for tracing data on existing paper maps. It could also double up as a pointing device for some interaction

(iii) possibly thumbwheels – for detailed pointing and positioning tasks

(iv) large-format printer – indeed very large: an A2 or A1 plotter at minimum.

2.8 MEMORY

Like human memory, we can think of the computer's memory as operating at different levels, with those that have the faster access typically having less capacity. By analogy with the human memory, we can group these into short-term and long-term memories (STM and LTM), but the analogy is rather weak – the capacity of the computer's STM is a lot more than seven items! The different levels of computer memory are more commonly called primary and secondary storage.

The details of computer memory are not in themselves of direct interest to the user interface designer. However, the limitations in capacity and access methods are important constraints on the sort of interface that can be designed. After some fairly basic information, we will put the raw memory capacity into perspective with the sort of information which can be stored, as well as again seeing how advances in technology offer more scope for the designer to produce more effective interfaces. In particular, we will see how the capacity of typical memory copes with video images as these are becoming important as part of multimedia applications (see Chapter 21).

2.8.1 RAM and short-term memory (STM)

At the lowest level of computer memory are the registers on the computer chip, but these have little impact on the user except in so far as they affect the general speed of the computer. Most currently active information is held in silicon-chip *random access memory (RAM)*. Different forms of RAM differ as to their precise access times, power consumption and characteristics. Typical access times are of the order of 10 nanoseconds, that is a hundred-millionth of a second, and information can be accessed at a rate of around 100 Mbytes (million bytes) per second. Typical storage in modern personal computers is between 64 and 256 Mbytes.

Most RAM is *volatile*, that is its contents are lost when the power is turned off. However, many computers have small amount of *non-volatile RAM*, which retains its contents, perhaps with the aid of a small battery. This may be used to store setup information in a large computer, but in a pocket organizer will be the whole memory. Non-volatile RAM is more expensive so is only used where necessary, but with many notebook computers using very low-power static RAM, the divide is shrinking. By strict analogy, non-volatile RAM ought to be classed as LTM, but the important thing we want to emphasize is the gulf between STM and LTM in a traditional computer system.

In PDAs the distinctions become more confused as the battery power means that the system is never completely off, so RAM memory effectively lasts for ever. Some also use flash memory, which is a form of silicon memory that sits between fixed content ROM (read-only memory) chips and normal RAM. Flash memory is relatively slow to write, but once written retains its content even with no power whatsoever. These are sometimes called silicon disks on PDAs. Digital cameras typically store photographs in some form of flash media and small flash-based devices are used to plug into a laptop or desktop's USB port to transfer data.

2.8.2 Disks and long-term memory (LTM)

For most computer users the LTM consists of *disks*, possibly with small tapes for *backup*. The existence of backups, and appropriate software to generate and retrieve them, is an important area for user security. However, we will deal mainly with those forms of storage that impact the interactive computer user.

There are two main kinds of technology used in disks: *magnetic disks* and *optical disks*. The most common storage media, floppy disks and hard (or fixed) disks, are coated with magnetic material, like that found on an audio tape, on which the information is stored. Typical capacities of floppy disks lie between 300 kbytes and 1.4 Mbytes, but as they are removable, you can have as many as you have room for on your desk. Hard disks may store from under 40 Mbytes to several gigabytes (Gbytes), that is several thousand million bytes. With disks there are two access times to consider, the time taken to find the right track on the disk, and the time to read the track. The former dominates random reads, and is typically of the order of 10 ms for hard disks. The transfer rate once the track is found is then very high, perhaps several hundred kilobytes per second. Various forms of large removable media are also available, fitting somewhere between floppy disks and removable hard disks, and are especially important for multimedia storage.

Optical disks use laser light to read and (sometimes) write the information on the disk. There are various high capacity specialist optical devices, but the most common is the *CD-ROM*, using the same technology as audio compact discs. CD-ROMs have a capacity of around 650 megabytes, but cannot be written to at all. They are useful for published material such as online reference books, multimedia and software distribution. Recordable CDs are a form of *WORM* device (write-once read-many) and are more flexible in that information can be written, but (as the name suggests) only once at any location – more like a piece of paper than a blackboard. They are obviously very useful for backups and for producing very secure audit information. Finally, there are fully rewritable optical disks, but the rewrite time is typically much slower than the read time, so they are still primarily for archival not dynamic storage. Many CD-ROM reader/writers can also read DVD format, originally developed for storing movies. Optical media are more robust than magnetic disks and so it is easier to use a *jukebox* arrangement, whereby many optical disks can be brought online automatically as required. This can give an online capacity of many hundreds of gigabytes. However, as magnetic disk capacities have grown faster than the fixed standard of CD-ROMs, some massive capacity stores are moving to large disk arrays.

2.8.3 Understanding speed and capacity

So what effect do the various capacities and speeds have on the user? Thinking of our typical personal computer system, we can summarize some typical capacities as in Table 2.1.

We think first of documents. This book is about 320,000 words, or about 2 Mbytes, so it would hardly make a dent in 256 Mbytes of RAM. (This size – 2 Mbytes – is unformatted and without illustrations; the actual size of the full data files is an order of magnitude bigger, but still well within the capacity of main memory.) To take a more popular work, the Bible would use about 4.5 Mbytes. This would still consume only 2% of main memory, and disappear on a hard disk. However, it might look tight on a smaller PDA. This makes the memory look not too bad, so long as you do not intend to put your entire library online. However, many word processors come with a dictionary and thesaurus, and there is no standard way to use the same one with several products. Together with help files and the program itself, it is not

Table 2.1 Typical capacities of different storage media

	STM small/fast	LTM large/slower
Media:	RAM	Hard disk
Capacity:	256 Mbytes	100 Gbytes
Access time:	10 ns	7 ms
Transfer rate:	100 Mbyte/s	30 Mbyte/s

unusual to find each application consuming tens or even hundreds of megabytes of disk space – it is not difficult to fill a few gigabytes of disk at all!

Similarly, although 256 Mbytes of RAM are enough to hold most (but not all) single programs, windowed systems will run several applications simultaneously, soon using up many megabytes. Operating systems handle this by *paging* unused bits of programs out of RAM onto disk, or even *swapping* the entire program onto disk. This makes little difference to the logical functioning of the program, but has a significant effect on interaction. If you select a window, and the relevant application happens to be currently swapped out onto the disk, it has to be swapped back in. The delay this causes can be considerable, and is both noticeable and annoying on many systems.

Technological change and storage capacity

Most of the changes in this book since the first and second editions have been additions where new developments have come along. However, this portion has had to be scrutinized line by line as the storage capacities of high-end machines when this book was first published in 1993 looked ridiculous as we revised it in 1997 and then again in 2003. One of our aims in this chapter was to give readers a concrete feel for the capacities and computational possibilities in standard computers. However, the pace of advances in this area means that it becomes out of date almost as fast as it is written! This is also a problem for design; it is easy to build a system that is sensible given a particular level of technology, but becomes meaningless later. The solution is either to issue ever more frequent updates and new versions, or to exercise a bit of foresight . . .

The delays due to swapping are a symptom of the *von Neumann bottleneck* between disk and main memory. There is plenty of information in the memory, but it is not where it is wanted, in the machine's RAM. The path between them is limited by the transfer rate of the disk and is too slow. Swapping due to the operating system may be difficult to avoid, but for an interactive system designer some of these problems can be avoided by thinking carefully about where information is stored and when it is transferred. For example, the program can be *lazy* about information transfer. Imagine the user wants to look at a document. Rather than reading in the whole thing before letting the user continue, just enough is read in for the first page to be displayed, and the rest is read during idle moments.

Returning to documents, if they are scanned as bitmaps (and not read using OCR), then the capacity of our system looks even less impressive. Say an 11×8 inch $(297 \times 210$ mm) page is scanned with an 8 bit grayscale (256 levels) setting at 1200 dpi. The image contains about one billion bits, that is about 128 Mbyte. So, our 100 Gbyte disk could store 800 pages – just OK for this book, but not for the Bible.

If we turn to video, things are even worse. Imagine we want to store moving video using 12 bits for each pixel (4 bits for each primary color giving 16 levels of brightness), each frame is 512×512 pixels, and we store at 25 frames per second.

This is by no means a high-quality image, but each frame requires approximately 400 kbytes giving 10 Mbytes per second. Our disk will manage about three hours of video – one good movie. Lowering our sights to still photographs, good digital cameras usually take 2 to 4 mega pixels at 24 bit color; that is 10 Mbytes of raw uncompressed image – you'd not get all your holiday snaps into main memory!

2.8.4 Compression

In fact, things are not quite so bad, since *compression* techniques can be used to reduce the amount of storage required for text, bitmaps and video. All of these things are highly redundant. Consider text for a moment. In English, we know that if we use the letter 'q' then 'u' is almost bound to follow. At the level of words, some words like 'the' and 'and' appear frequently in text in general, and for any particular work one can find other common terms (this book mentions 'user' and 'computer' rather frequently). Similarly, in a bitmap, if one bit is white, there is a good chance the next will be as well. Compression algorithms take advantage of this redundancy. For example, *Huffman encoding* gives short codes to frequent words [182], and *run-length encoding* represents long runs of the same value by length value pairs. Text can easily be reduced by a factor of five and bitmaps often compress to 1% of their original size.

For video, in addition to compressing each frame, we can take advantage of the fact that successive frames are often similar. We can compute the *difference* between successive frames and then store only this – compressed, of course. More sophisticated algorithms detect when the camera pans and use this information also. These differencing methods fail when the scene changes, and so the process periodically has to restart and send a new, complete (but compressed) image. For storage purposes this is not a problem, but when used for transmission over telephone lines or networks it can mean glitches in the video as the system catches up.

With these reductions it is certainly possible to store low-quality video at 64 kbyte/s; that is, we can store five hours of highly compressed video on our 1 Gbyte hard disk. However, it still makes the humble video cassette look very good value.

Probably the leading edge of video still and photographic compression is *fractal compression*. Fractals have been popularized by the images of the *Mandelbrot set* (that swirling pattern of computer-generated colors seen on many T-shirts and posters). Fractals refer to any image that contains parts which, when suitably scaled, are similar to the whole. If we look at an image, it is possible to find parts which are approximately self-similar, and these parts can be stored as a fractal with only a few numeric parameters. Fractal compression is especially good for textured features, which cause problems for other compression techniques. The *decompression* of the image can be performed to any degree of accuracy, from a very rough soft-focus image, to one *more* detailed than the original. The former is very useful as one can produce poor-quality output quickly, and better quality given more time. The latter is rather remarkable – the fractal compression actually fills in details that are not in the original. These details are not accurate, but look convincing!

2.8.5 Storage format and standards

The most common data types stored by interactive programs are text and bitmap images, with increasing use of video and audio, and this subsection looks at the ridiculous range of file storage standards. We will consider database retrieval in the next subsection.

The basic standard for text storage is the *ASCII* (American standard code for information interchange) character codes, which assign to each standard printable character and several control characters an internationally recognized 7 bit code (decimal values 0–127), which can therefore be stored in an 8 bit byte, or be transmitted as 8 bits including parity. Many systems extend the codes to the values 128–255, including line-drawing characters, mathematical symbols and international letters such as 'æ'. There is a 16 bit extension, the UNICODE standard, which has enough room for a much larger range of characters including the Japanese Kanji character set.

As we have already discussed, modern documents consist of more than just characters. The text is in different fonts and includes formatting information such as centering, page headers and footers. On the whole, the storage of formatted text is vendor specific, since virtually every application has its own file format. This is not helped by the fact that many suppliers attempt to keep their file formats secret, or update them frequently to stop others' products being compatible. With the exception of bare ASCII, the most common shared format is *rich text format* (*RTF*), which encodes formatting information including style sheets. However, even where an application will import or export RTF, it may represent a cut-down version of the full document style.

RTF regards the document as formatted text, that is it concentrates on the appearance. Documents can also be regarded as structured objects: this book has chapters containing sections, subsections . . . paragraphs, sentences, words and characters. There are *ISO standards* for document structure and interchange, which in theory could be used for transfer between packages and sites, but these are rarely used in practice. Just as the PostScript language is used to describe the printed page, *SGML* (*standard generalized markup language*) can be used to store structured text in a reasonably extensible way. You can define your own structures (the definition itself in SGML), and produce documents according to them. XML (extensible markup language), a lightweight version of SGML, is now used extensively for web-based applications.

For bitmap storage the range of formats is seemingly unending. The stored image needs to record the size of the image, the number of bits per pixel, possibly a color map, as well as the bits of the image itself. In addition, an icon may have a 'hot-spot' for use as a cursor. If you think of all the ways of encoding these features, or leaving them implicit, and then consider all the combinations of these different encodings, you can see why there are problems. And all this before we have even considered the effects of compression! There is, in fact, a whole software industry producing packages that convert from one format to another.

Given the range of storage standards (or rather lack of standards), there is no easy advice as to which is best, but if you are writing a new word processor and are about to decide how to store the document on disk, think, just for a moment, before defining yet another format.

2.8.6 Methods of access

Standard database access is by special key fields with an associated index. The user has to know the key before the system can find the information. A telephone directory is a good example of this. You can find out someone's telephone number if you know their name (the key), but you cannot find the name given the number. This is evident in the interface of many computer systems. So often, when you contact an organization, they can only help you if you give your customer number, or last order number. The usability of the system is seriously impaired by a shortsighted reliance on a single key and index. In fact, most database systems will allow multiple keys and indices, allowing you to find a record given partial information. So these problems are avoidable with only slight foresight.

There are valid reasons for not indexing on too many items. Adding extra indices adds to the size of the database, so one has to balance ease of use against storage cost. However, with ever-increasing disk sizes, this is not a good excuse for all but extreme examples. Unfortunately, brought up on lectures about algorithmic efficiency, it is easy for computer scientists to be stingy with storage. Another, more valid, reason for restricting the fields you index is privacy and security. For example, telephone companies will typically hold an online index that, given a telephone number, would return the name and address of the subscriber, but to protect the privacy of their customers, this information is not divulged to the general public.

It is often said that dictionaries are only useful for people who can spell. Bad spellers do not know what a word looks like so cannot look it up to find out. Not only in spelling packages, but in general, an application can help the user by matching badly spelt versions of keywords. One example of this is *do what I mean* (*DWIM*) used in several of Xerox PARC's experimental programming environments. If a command name is misspelt the system prompts the user with a close correct name. Menu-based systems make this less of an issue, but one can easily imagine doing the same with, say, file selection. Another important instance of this principle is *Soundex*, a way of indexing words, especially names. Given a key, Soundex finds those words which sound similar. For example, given McCloud, it would find MacCleod. These are all examples of *forgiving systems*, and in general one should aim to accommodate the user's mistakes. Again, there are exceptions to this: you do not want a bank's automated teller machine (ATM) to give money when the PIN number is *almost* correct!

Not all databases allow long passages of text to be stored in records, perhaps setting a maximum length for text strings, or demanding the length be fixed in advance. Where this is the case, the database seriously restricts interface applications where text forms an important part. At the other extreme, *free text retrieval* systems are centered on unformatted, unstructured text. These systems work by keeping an index of every word in every document, and so you can ask 'give me all documents with the words "human" and "computer" in them'. Programs, such as versions of the UNIX 'grep' command, give some of the same facilities by quickly scanning a list of files for a certain word, but are much slower. On the web, free text search is of course the standard way to find things using search engines.

Worked exercise   *What is the basic architecture of a computer system?*

Answer   In an HCI context, you should be assessing the architecture from the point of view of the user. The material for this question is scattered throughout the chapter. Look too at personal computer magazines, where adverts and articles will give you some idea of typical capabilities . . . and costs. They may also raise some questions: just what is the difference to the user between an 8 ms and a 10 ms disk drive?

The example answer below gives the general style, although more detail would be expected of a full answer. In particular, you need to develop a feel for capacities either as ball-park figures or in terms of typical capabilities (seconds of video, pages of text).

Example

The basic architecture of a computer system consists of the computer itself (with associated memory), input and output devices for user interaction and various forms of hard-copy devices. (Note, the 'computer science' answer regards output to the user and output to a printer as essentially equivalent. This is not an acceptable user-centered view.)

A typical configuration of user input–output devices would be a screen with a keyboard for typing text and a mouse for pointing and positioning. Depending on circumstance, different pointing devices may be used such as a stylus (for more direct interaction) or a touchpad (especially on portable computers).

The computer itself can be considered as composed of some processing element and memory. The memory is itself divided into short-term memory which is lost when the machine is turned off and permanent memory which persists.

2.9   PROCESSING AND NETWORKS

Computers that run interactive programs will process in the order of 100 million instructions per second. It sounds a lot and yet, like memory, it can soon be used up. Indeed, the first program written by one of the authors (some while ago) 'hung' and all attempts to debug it failed. Later calculation showed that the program would have taken more than the known age of the universe to complete! Failures need not be as spectacular as that to render a system unusable. Consider, for example, one drawing system known to the authors. To draw a line you press down the mouse button at one end, drag the mouse and then release the mouse button at the other end of the line – but not too quickly. You have to press down the button and then actually hold your hand steady for a moment, otherwise the line starts half way! For activities involving the user's hand–eye coordination, delays of even a fraction of a second can be disastrous.

Moore's law

Everyone knows that computers just get faster and faster. However, in 1965 Gordon Moore, co-founder of Intel, noticed a regularity. It seemed that the speed of processors, related closely to the number of transistors that could be squashed on a silicon wafer, was doubling every 18 months – exponential growth. One of the authors bought his first 'proper' computer in 1987; it was a blindingly fast 1.47 MHz IBM compatible (Macs were too expensive). By 2002 a system costing the same in real terms would have had a 1.5 GHz processor – 1000 times faster or 2^{10} in 15 years, that is 10×18 months.

There is a similar pattern for computer memory, except that the doubling time for magnetic storage seems to be closer to one year. For example, when the first edition of this book was written one of the authors had a 20 Mbyte hard disk; now, 11 years later, his disk is 30 Gbytes – around 2^{10} times more storage in just 10 years.

The effects of this are dramatic. If you took a young baby today and started recording a full audio video diary of every moment, day and night, of that child's life, by the time she was an old lady her whole life experience would fit into memory the size of a small grain of dust.

For more on Moore's law and life recording see: /e3/online/moores-law/

2.9.1 Effects of finite processor speed

As we can see, speed of processing can seriously affect the user interface. These effects must be taken into account when designing an interactive system. There are two sorts of faults due to processing speed: those when it is too slow, and those when it is too fast!

We saw one example of the former above. This was a *functional fault*, in that the program did the wrong thing. The system is supposed to draw lines from where the mouse button is depressed to where it is released. However, the program gets it wrong – after realizing the button is down, it does not check the position of the mouse fast enough, and so the user may have moved the mouse before the start position is registered. This is a fault at the implementation stage of the system rather than of the design. But to be fair, the programmer may not be given the right sort of information from lower levels of system software.

A second fault due to slow processing is where, in a sense, the program does the right thing, but the feedback is too slow, leading to strange effects at the interface. In order to avoid faults of the first kind, the system *buffers* the user input; that is, it remembers keypresses and mouse buttons and movement. Unfortunately, this leads to problems of its own. One example of this sort of problem is *cursor tracking*, which happens in character-based text editors. The user is trying to move backwards on the same line to correct an error, and so presses the cursor-left key. The cursor moves and when it is over the correct position, the user releases the key. Unfortunately, the system is behind in responding to the user, and so has a few more cursor-left keys to process – the cursor then overshoots. The user tries to correct this by pressing the cursor-right key, and again overshoots. There is typically no way for the user to tell whether the buffer is empty or not, except by interacting very slowly with the system and observing that the cursor has moved after every keypress.

A similar problem, *icon wars*, occurs on window systems. The user clicks the mouse on a menu or icon, and nothing happens; for some reason the machine is busy or slow. So the user clicks again, tries something else – then, suddenly, all the buffered mouse clicks are interpreted and the screen becomes a blur of flashing windows and menus. This time, it is not so much that the response is too slow – it is fast enough when it happens – but that the response is variable. The delays due to swapping programs in and out of main memory typically cause these problems.

Furthermore, a style of interaction that is optimal on one machine may not be so on a slower machine. In particular, mouse-based interfaces cannot tolerate delays between actions and feedback of more than a fraction of a second, otherwise the immediacy required for successful interaction is lost. If these responses cannot be met then a more old-fashioned, command-based interface may be required.

Whereas it is immediately obvious that slow responses can cause problems for the user, it is not so obvious why one should not always aim for a system to be as fast as possible. However, there are exceptions to this – the user must be able to read and understand the output of the system. For example, one of the authors was once given a demonstration disk for a spreadsheet. Unfortunately, the machine the demo was written on was clearly slower than the author's machine, not much, at worst half the speed, but different enough. The demo passed in a blur over the screen with nothing remaining on the screen long enough to read. Many high-resolution monitors suffer from a similar problem when they display text. Whereas older character-based terminals scrolled new text from the bottom of the screen or redrew from the top, bitmap screens often 'flash' up the new page, giving no indication of direction of movement. A final example is the rate of cursor flashing: the rate is often at a fixed

DESIGN FOCUS

The myth of the infinitely fast machine

The adverse effects of slow processing are made worse because the designers labor under the *myth of the infinitely fast machine* [93]. That is, they design and document their systems as if response will be immediate. Rather than blithely hoping that the eventual machine will be 'fast enough', the designer ought to plan explicitly for slow responses where these are possible. A good example, where buffering is clear and audible (if not visible) to the user, is telephones. Even if the user gets ahead of the telephone when entering a number, the tones can be heard as they are sent over the line. Now this is probably an accident of the design rather than deliberate policy, as there are so many other problems with telephones as interfaces. However, this type of serendipitous feedback should be emulated in other areas.

frequency, so varying the speed of the processor does not change the screen display. But a rate which is acceptable for a CRT screen is too fast for an LCD screen, which is more persistent, and the cursor may become invisible or a slight gray color.

In some ways the solution to these problems is easier: the designer can demand fixed delays (dependent on media and user preference) rather than just going as fast as the machine allows. To plan for the first problem, that of insufficient speed, the designer needs to understand the limitations of the computer system and take account of these at all stages in the design process.

2.9.2 Limitations on interactive performance

There are several factors that can limit the speed of an interactive system:

Computation bound This is rare for an interactive program, but possible, for example when using find/replace in a large document. The system should be designed so that long delays are not in the middle of interaction and so that the user gets some idea of how the job is progressing. For a very long process try to give an indication of duration *before* it starts; and during processing an indication of the stage that the process has reached is helpful. This can be achieved by having a counter or slowly filling bar on the screen that indicates the amount done, or by changing the cursor to indicate that processing is occurring. Many systems notice after they have been computing for some time and then say 'this may take some time: continue (Y/N)?'. Of course, by the time it says this the process may be nearly finished anyway!

Storage channel bound As we discussed in the previous section, the speed of memory access can interfere with interactive performance. We discussed one technique, laziness, for reducing this effect. In addition, if there is plenty of raw computation power and the system is held up solely by memory, it is possible to trade off memory against processing speed. For example, compressed data take less space to store, and is faster to read in and out, but must be compressed before storage and decompressed when retrieved. Thus faster memory access leads to increased processing time. If data is written more often than it is read, one can choose a technique that is expensive to compress but fairly simple to decompress. For many interactive systems the ability to browse quickly is very important, but users will accept delays when saving updated information.

Graphics bound For many modern interfaces, this is the most common bottleneck. It is easy to underestimate the time taken to perform what appear to be simple interface operations. Sometimes clever coding can reduce the time taken by common graphics operations, and there is tremendous variability in performance between programs running on the same hardware. Most computers include a special-purpose *graphics card* to handle many of the most common graphics operations. This is optimized for graphics operations and allows the main processor to do other work such as manipulating documents and other user data.

Network capacity   Most computers are linked by networks. At the simplest this can mean using shared files on a remote machine. When accessing such files it can be the speed of the network rather than that of the memory which limits performance. This is discussed in greater detail below.

2.9.3 Networked computing

Computer systems in use today are much more powerful than they were a few years ago, which means that the standard computer on the desktop is quite capable of high-performance interaction without recourse to outside help. However, it is often the case that we use computers not in their standalone mode of operation, but linked together in networks. This brings added benefits in allowing communication between different parties, provided they are connected into the same network, as well as allowing the desktop computer to access resources remote from itself. Such networks are inherently much more powerful than the individual computers that make up the network: increased computing power and memory are only part of the story, since the effects of allowing people much more extensive, faster and easier access to information are highly significant to individuals, groups and institutions.

One of the biggest changes since the first edition of this book has been the explosive growth of the internet and global connectivity. As well as fixed networks it is now normal to use a high bandwidth modem or wireless local area network (LAN) to connect into the internet and world wide web from home or hotel room anywhere in the world. The effects of this on society at large can only be speculated upon at present, but there are already major effects on computer purchases and perhaps the whole face of personal computation. As more and more people buy computers principally to connect to the internet the idea of the *network computer* has arisen – a small computer with no disks whose sole purpose is to connect up to networks.

The internet

The internet has its roots back in 1969 as DARPANET when the US Government's Department of Defense commissioned research into networking. The initial four mainframe computers grew to 23 in 1971 and the system had been renamed ARPANET. Growth has accelerated ever since: in 1984 there were over a thousand machines connected, in 1989 the 100,000 mark had been reached, and the latest estimates are in the millions. All the computers on the system, now known as the internet, speak a set of common languages (protocols); the two most important of these are *Transmission Control Protocol* (*TCP*) which moves data from A to B, and the *Internet Protocol* (*IP*) which specifies which B is being referred to so that the data goes to the correct place. Together these protocols are known as *TCP/IP*. Thus, at its most basic level, the internet is simply millions of computers connected together and talking to each other. Other protocols then build on these low-level capabilities to provide services such as electronic mail, in which participants send messages to each other; news, where articles of interest are posted to a special interest group and can be read by anyone subscribing to that group; and of course the world wide web.

Such networked systems have an effect on interactivity, over and above any additional access to distant peripherals or information sources. Networks sometimes operate over large distances, and the transmission of information may take some appreciable time, which affects the response time of the system and hence the nature of the interactivity. There may be a noticeable delay in response, and if the user is not informed of what is going on, he may assume that his command has been ignored, or lost, and may then repeat it. This lack of feedback is an important factor in the poor performance and frustration users feel when using such systems, and can be alleviated by more sensible use of the capabilities of the desktop machine to inform users of what is happening over the network.

Another effect is that the interaction between human and machine becomes an open loop, rather than a closed one. Many people may be interacting with the machine at once, and their actions may affect the response to your own. Many users accessing a single central machine will slow its response; database updates carried out by one user may mean that the same query by another user at slightly different times may produce different results. The networked computer system, by the very nature of its dispersal, distribution and multi-user access, has been transformed from a fully predictable, deterministic system, under the total control of the user, into a non-deterministic one, with an individual user being unaware of many important things that are happening to the system as a whole. Such systems pose a particular problem since ideals of consistency, informative feedback and predictable response are violated (see Chapter 7 for more on these principles). However, the additional power and flexibility offered by networked systems means that they are likely to be with us for a long time, and these issues need to be carefully addressed in their design.

Worked exercise   *How do you think new, fast, high-density memory devices and quick processors have influenced recent developments in HCI? Do they make systems any easier to use? Do they expand the range of applications of computer systems?*

Answer   Arguably it is not so much the increase in computer power as the decrease in the cost of that power which has had the most profound effect. Because 'ordinary' users have powerful machines on their desktops it has become possible to view that power as available for the interface rather than hoarded for number-crunching applications.

Modern graphical interaction consumes vast amounts of processing power and would have been completely impossible only a few years ago. There is an extent to which systems have to run faster to stay still, in that as screen size, resolution and color range increase, so does the necessary processing power to maintain the 'same' interaction. However, this extra processing is not really producing the same effect; screen quality is still a major block on effective interaction.

The increase in RAM means that larger programs can be written, effectively allowing the programmer 'elbow room'. This is used in two ways: to allow extra functionality and to support easier interaction. Whether the former really improves usability is debatable – unused functionality is a good marketing point, but is of no benefit to the user. The ease of use of a system is often determined by a host of small features, such as the appropriate choice of default options. These features make the interface seem 'simple', but make the program very complex . . . and large. Certainly the availability of elbow room, both in terms of memory and processing power, has made such features possible.

The increase in both short-term (RAM) and long-term (disks and optical storage) memory has also removed many of the arbitrary limits in systems: it is possible to edit documents of virtually unlimited size and to treat the computer (suitably backed up) as one's primary information repository.

Some whole new application areas have become possible because of advances in memory and processing. Most applications of multimedia including voice recognition and online storage and capture of video and audio, require enormous amounts of processing and/or memory. In particular, large magnetic and optical storage devices have been the key to electronic document storage whereby all paper documents are scanned and stored within a computer system. In some contexts such systems have completely replaced paper-based filing cabinets.

2.10 SUMMARY

In Sections 2.2 and 2.3, we described a range of input devices. These performed two main functions: text entry and pointing. The principal text entry device is the QWERTY keyboard, but we also discussed alternative keyboards, chord keyboards, the telephone keypad and speech input. Pointing devices included the mouse, touchpad, trackball and joystick, as well as a large array of less common alternatives including eyegaze systems.

Section 2.4 dealt mainly with the screen as a direct output device. We discussed several different technologies, in particular CRT and LCD screens and the common properties of all bitmap display devices. We considered some more recent display methods including large displays, situated displays and digital paper.

Section 2.5 looked at the devices used for manipulating and seeing virtual reality and 3D spaces. This included the dataglove, body tracking, head-mounted displays and cave environments.

In Section 2.6 we moved outside the computer entirely and looked at physical devices such as the special displays, knobs and switches of electronic appliances. We also briefly considered sound, touch and smell as outputs from computer systems and environmental and bio-sensing as inputs. These are topics that will be revisited later in the book.

Section 2.7 discussed various forms of printer and scanner. Typical office printers include ink-jet, bubble-jet and laser printers. In addition, dot-matrix and thermal printers are used in specialized equipment. We also discussed font styles and page description languages. Scanners are used to convert printed images and documents into electronic form. They are particularly valuable in desktop publishing and for electronic document storage systems.

In Section 2.8, we considered the typical capacities of computer memory, both of main RAM, likened to human short-term memory, and long-term memory stored on magnetic and optical disks. The storage capacities were compared with document sizes and video images. We saw that a typical hard disk could only hold about two minutes of moving video, but that compression techniques can increase the capacity dramatically. We also discussed storage standards – or rather the lack of them – including the ASCII character set and markup languages. The user ought to be able to access information in ways that are natural and tolerant of small slips. Techniques which can help this included multiple indices, free text databases, DWIM (do what I mean) and Soundex.

Section 2.9 showed how processing speed, whether too slow or too fast, can affect the user interface. In particular, we discussed the effects of buffering: cursor tracking and icon wars. Processing speed is limited by various factors: computation, memory access, graphics and network delays.

The lesson from this chapter is that the interface designer needs to be aware of the properties of the devices with which a system is built. This includes not only input and output devices, but all the factors that influence the behavior of the interface, since all of these influence the nature and style of the interaction.

EXERCISES

2.1   Individually or in a group find as many different examples as you can of physical controls and displays.

    (a) List them.
    (b) Try to group them, or classify them.
    (c) Discuss whether you believe the control or display is suitable for its purpose (Section 3.9.3 may also help).

Exercises 2.2 and 2.3 involve you examining a range of input and output devices in order to understand how they influence interaction.

2.2   A typical computer system comprises a QWERTY keyboard, a mouse and a color screen. There is usually some form of loudspeaker as well. You should know how the keyboard, mouse and screen work – if not, read up on it.

    What sort of input does the keyboard support? What sort of input does the mouse support? Are these adequate for all possible applications? If not, to which areas are they most suited? Do these areas map well onto the typical requirements for users of computer systems?

    If you were designing a keyboard for a modern computer, and you wanted to produce a faster, easier-to-use layout, what information would you need to know and how would that influence the design?

2.3   Pick a couple of computer input devices that you are aware of (joystick, light pen, touchscreen, trackball, eyegaze, dataglove, etc.) and note down how each has different attributes that support certain forms of interaction. You ought to know a little about all of these devices – if you don't, research them.

2.4 What is the myth of the infinitely fast machine?

2.5 Pick one of the following scenarios, and choose a suitable combination of input and output devices to best support the intended interaction. It may help to identify typical users or classes of user, and identify how the devices chosen support these people in their tasks. Explain the major problems that the input and output devices solve.

(a) *Environmental database*
A computer database is under development that will hold environmental information. This ranges from meteorological measurements through fish catches to descriptions of pollution, and will include topographical details and sketches and photographs. The data has to be accessed only by experts, but they want to be able to describe and retrieve any piece of data within a few seconds.

(b) *Word processor for blind people*
A word processor for blind users is needed, which can also be operated by sighted people. It has to support the standard set of word-processing tasks.

2.6 Describe Fitts' law (see Chapter 1). How does Fitts' law change for different physical selection devices, such as a three-button mouse, a touchpad, or a pen/stylus? (You'll need to do some research for this.)

RECOMMENDED READING

W. Buxton, There's more to interaction than meets the eye: some issues in manual input. In R. Baecker and W. Buxton, editors, *Readings in Human–Computer Interaction: A Multidisciplinary Approach*, Morgan Kaufmann, 1987.

D. J. Mayhew, *Principles and Guidelines in Software User Interface Design*, Chapter 12, Prentice Hall, 1992.
A look at input and output devices, complete with guidelines for using different devices.

A. Dix, Network-based interaction. In J. Jacko and A. Sears, editors, *Human–Computer Interaction Handbook*, Chapter 16, pp. 331–57, Lawrence Erlbaum, 2003.
Includes different kinds of network application and the effects of networks on interaction including rich media. Also look at all of Part II of Jacko and Sears, which includes chapters on input technology and on haptic interfaces.

THE INTERACTION

OVERVIEW

- Interaction models help us to understand what is going on in the interaction between user and system. They address the translations between what the user wants and what the system does.

- Ergonomics looks at the physical characteristics of the interaction and how these influence its effectiveness.

- The dialog between user and system is influenced by the style of the interface.

- The interaction takes place within a social and organizational context that affects both user and system.

3.1 INTRODUCTION

In the previous two chapters we have looked at the human and the computer respectively. However, in the context of this book, we are not concerned with them in isolation. We are interested in how the human user uses the computer as a tool to perform, simplify or support a task. In order to do this the user must communicate his requirements to the computer.

There are a number of ways in which the user can communicate with the system. At one extreme is batch input, in which the user provides all the information to the computer at once and leaves the machine to perform the task. This approach does involve an interaction between the user and computer but does not support many tasks well. At the other extreme are highly interactive input devices and paradigms, such as *direct manipulation* (see Chapter 4) and the applications of *virtual reality* (Chapter 20). Here the user is constantly providing instruction and receiving feedback. These are the types of interactive system we are considering.

In this chapter, we consider the communication between user and system: the *interaction*. We will look at some models of interaction that enable us to identify and evaluate components of the interaction, and at the physical, social and organizational issues that provide the context for it. We will also survey some of the different styles of interaction that are used and consider how well they support the user.

3.2 MODELS OF INTERACTION

In previous chapters we have seen the usefulness of models to help us to understand complex behavior and complex systems. Interaction involves at least two participants: the user and the system. Both are complex, as we have seen, and are very different from each other in the way that they communicate and view the domain and the task. The interface must therefore effectively translate between them to allow the interaction to be successful. This translation can fail at a number of points and for a number of reasons. The use of models of interaction can help us to understand exactly what is going on in the interaction and identify the likely root of difficulties. They also provide us with a framework to compare different interaction styles and to consider interaction problems.

We begin by considering the most influential model of interaction, Norman's *execution–evaluation cycle*; then we look at another model which extends the ideas of Norman's cycle. Both of these models describe the interaction in terms of the goals and actions of the user. We will therefore briefly discuss the terminology used and the assumptions inherent in the models, before describing the models themselves.

3.2.1 The terms of interaction

Traditionally, the purpose of an interactive system is to aid a user in accomplishing *goals* from some application *domain*. (Later in this book we will look at alternative interactions but this model holds for many work-oriented applications.) A domain defines an area of expertise and knowledge in some real-world activity. Some examples of domains are graphic design, authoring and process control in a factory. A domain consists of concepts that highlight its important aspects. In a graphic design domain, some of the important concepts are geometric shapes, a drawing surface and a drawing utensil. *Tasks* are operations to manipulate the concepts of a domain. A *goal* is the desired output from a performed task. For example, one task within the graphic design domain is the construction of a specific geometric shape with particular attributes on the drawing surface. A related goal would be to produce a solid red triangle centered on the canvas. An *intention* is a specific action required to meet the goal.

Task analysis involves the identification of the problem space (which we discussed in Chapter 1) for the user of an interactive system in terms of the domain, goals, intentions and tasks. We can use our knowledge of tasks and goals to assess the interactive system that is designed to support them. We discuss task analysis in detail in Chapter 15. The concepts used in the design of the system and the description of the user are separate, and so we can refer to them as distinct components, called the *System* and the *User*, respectively. The *System* and *User* are each described by means of a language that can express concepts relevant in the domain of the application. The *System*'s language we will refer to as the *core language* and the *User*'s language we will refer to as the *task language*. The core language describes computational attributes of the domain relevant to the *System* state, whereas the task language describes psychological attributes of the domain relevant to the *User* state.

The system is assumed to be some computerized application, in the context of this book, but the models apply equally to non-computer applications. It is also a common assumption that by distinguishing between user and system we are restricted to single-user applications. This is not the case. However, the emphasis is on the view of the interaction from a single user's perspective. From this point of view, other users, such as those in a multi-party conferencing system, form part of the system.

3.2.2 The execution–evaluation cycle

Norman's model of interaction is perhaps the most influential in Human–Computer Interaction, possibly because of its closeness to our intuitive understanding of the interaction between human user and computer [265]. The user formulates a plan of action, which is then executed at the computer interface. When the plan, or part of the plan, has been executed, the user observes the computer interface to evaluate the result of the executed plan, and to determine further actions.

The interactive cycle can be divided into two major phases: execution and evaluation. These can then be subdivided into further stages, seven in all. The stages in Norman's model of interaction are as follows:

1. Establishing the goal.
2. Forming the intention.
3. Specifying the action sequence.
4. Executing the action.
5. Perceiving the system state.
6. Interpreting the system state.
7. Evaluating the system state with respect to the goals and intentions.

Each stage is, of course, an activity of the user. First the user forms a goal. This is the user's notion of what needs to be done and is framed in terms of the domain, in the task language. It is liable to be imprecise and therefore needs to be translated into the more specific intention, and the actual actions that will reach the goal, before it can be executed by the user. The user perceives the new state of the system, after execution of the action sequence, and interprets it in terms of his expectations. If the system state reflects the user's goal then the computer has done what he wanted and the interaction has been successful; otherwise the user must formulate a new goal and repeat the cycle.

Norman uses a simple example of switching on a light to illustrate this cycle. Imagine you are sitting reading as evening falls. You decide you need more light; that is you establish the goal to get more light. From there you form an intention to switch on the desk lamp, and you specify the actions required, to reach over and press the lamp switch. If someone else is closer the intention may be different – you may ask them to switch on the light for you. Your goal is the same but the intention and actions are different. When you have executed the action you perceive the result, either the light is on or it isn't and you interpret this, based on your knowledge of the world. For example, if the light does not come on you may interpret this as indicating the bulb has blown or the lamp is not plugged into the mains, and you will formulate new goals to deal with this. If the light does come on, you will evaluate the new state according to the original goals – is there now enough light? If so, the cycle is complete. If not, you may formulate a new intention to switch on the main ceiling light as well.

Norman uses this model of interaction to demonstrate why some interfaces cause problems to their users. He describes these in terms of the *gulfs of execution* and the *gulfs of evaluation*. As we noted earlier, the user and the system do not use the same terms to describe the domain and goals – remember that we called the language of the system the *core language* and the language of the user the *task language*. The gulf of execution is the difference between the user's formulation of the actions to reach the goal and the actions allowed by the system. If the actions allowed by the system correspond to those intended by the user, the interaction will be effective. The interface should therefore aim to reduce this gulf.

The gulf of evaluation is the distance between the physical presentation of the system state and the expectation of the user. If the user can readily evaluate the presentation in terms of his goal, the gulf of evaluation is small. The more effort that is required on the part of the user to interpret the presentation, the less effective the interaction.

Human error – slips and mistakes

Human errors are often classified into *slips* and *mistakes*. We can distinguish these using Norman's gulf of execution.

If you understand a system well you may know exactly what to do to satisfy your goals – you have formulated the correct action. However, perhaps you mistype or you accidentally press the mouse button at the wrong time. These are called *slips*; you have formulated the right action, but fail to execute that action correctly.

However, if you don't know the system well you may not even formulate the right goal. For example, you may think that the magnifying glass icon is the 'find' function, but in fact it is to magnify the text. This is called a *mistake*.

If we discover that an interface is leading to errors it is important to understand whether they are slips or mistakes. Slips may be corrected by, for instance, better screen design, perhaps putting more space between buttons. However, mistakes need users to have a better understanding of the systems, so will require far more radical redesign or improved training, perhaps a totally different metaphor for use.

Norman's model is a useful means of understanding the interaction, in a way that is clear and intuitive. It allows other, more detailed, empirical and analytic work to be placed within a common framework. However, it only considers the system as far as the interface. It concentrates wholly on the user's view of the interaction. It does not attempt to deal with the system's communication through the interface. An extension of Norman's model, proposed by Abowd and Beale, addresses this problem [3]. This is described in the next section.

3.2.3 The interaction framework

The interaction framework attempts a more realistic description of interaction by including the system explicitly, and breaks it into four main components, as shown in Figure 3.1. The nodes represent the four major components in an interactive system – the *System*, the *User*, the *Input* and the *Output*. Each component has its own language. In addition to the *User*'s task language and the *System*'s core language, which we have already introduced, there are languages for both the *Input* and *Output* components. *Input* and *Output* together form the *Interface*.

As the interface sits between the *User* and the *System*, there are four steps in the interactive cycle, each corresponding to a translation from one component to another, as shown by the labeled arcs in Figure 3.2. The *User* begins the interactive cycle with the formulation of a goal and a task to achieve that goal. The only way the user can manipulate the machine is through the *Input*, and so the task must be articulated within the input language. The input language is translated into the core

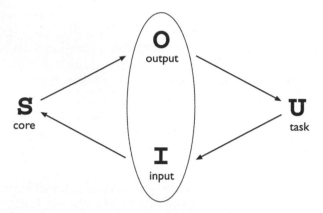

Figure 3.1   The general interaction framework

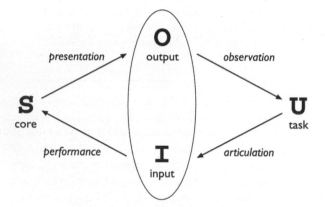

Figure 3.2   Translations between components

language as operations to be performed by the *System*. The *System* then transforms itself as described by the operations; the execution phase of the cycle is complete and the evaluation phase now begins. The *System* is in a new state, which must now be communicated to the *User*. The current values of system attributes are rendered as concepts or features of the *Output*. It is then up to the *User* to observe the *Output* and assess the results of the interaction relative to the original goal, ending the evaluation phase and, hence, the interactive cycle. There are four main translations involved in the interaction: articulation, performance, presentation and observation.

The *User*'s formulation of the desired task to achieve some goal needs to be *articulated* in the input language. The tasks are responses of the *User* and they need to be translated to stimuli for the *Input*. As pointed out above, this articulation is judged in terms of the coverage from tasks to input and the relative ease with which the translation can be accomplished. The task is phrased in terms of certain psychological attributes that highlight the important features of the domain for the *User*. If these psychological attributes map clearly onto the input language, then articulation of the task will be made much simpler. An example of a poor mapping, as pointed out by Norman, is a large room with overhead lighting controlled by a bank of switches. It is often desirable to control the lighting so that only one section of the room is lit. We are then faced with the puzzle of determining which switch controls which lights. The result is usually repeated trials and frustration. This arises from the difficulty of articulating a goal (for example, 'Turn on the lights in the front of the room') in an input language that consists of a linear row of switches, which may or may not be oriented to reflect the room layout.

Conversely, an example of a good mapping is in virtual reality systems, where input devices such as datagloves are specifically geared towards easing articulation by making the user's psychological notion of gesturing an act that can be directly realized at the interface. Direct manipulation interfaces, such as those found on common desktop operating systems like the Macintosh and Windows, make the articulation of some file handling commands easier. On the other hand, some tasks, such as repetitive file renaming or launching a program whose icon is not visible, are not at all easy to articulate with such an interface.

At the next stage, the responses of the *Input* are translated to stimuli for the *System*. Of interest in assessing this translation is whether the translated input language can reach as many states of the *System* as is possible using the *System* stimuli directly. For example, the remote control units for some compact disc players do not allow the user to turn the power off on the player unit; hence the off state of the player cannot be reached using the remote control's input language. On the panel of the compact disc player, however, there is usually a button that controls the power. The ease with which this translation from *Input* to *System* takes place is of less importance because the effort is not expended by the user. However, there can be a real effort expended by the designer and programmer. In this case, the ease of the translation is viewed in terms of the cost of implementation.

Once a state transition has occurred within the *System*, the execution phase of the interaction is complete and the evaluation phase begins. The new state of the *System* must be communicated to the *User*, and this begins by translating the *System* responses to the transition into stimuli for the *Output* component. This presentation translation must preserve the relevant system attributes from the domain in the limited expressiveness of the output devices. The ability to capture the domain concepts of the *System* within the *Output* is a question of expressiveness for this translation.

For example, while writing a paper with some word-processing package, it is necessary at times to see both the immediate surrounding text where one is currently composing, say, the current paragraph, and a wider context within the whole paper that cannot be easily displayed on one screen (for example, the current chapter).

Ultimately, the user must interpret the output to evaluate what has happened. The response from the *Output* is translated to stimuli for the *User* which trigger assessment. The observation translation will address the ease and coverage of this final translation. For example, it is difficult to tell the time accurately on an unmarked analog clock, especially if it is not oriented properly. It is difficult in a command line interface to determine the result of copying and moving files in a hierarchical file system. Developing a website using a markup language like HTML would be virtually impossible without being able to preview the output through a browser.

Assessing overall interaction

The interaction framework is presented as a means to judge the overall usability of an entire interactive system. In reality, all of the analysis that is suggested by the framework is dependent on the current task (or set of tasks) in which the *User* is engaged. This is not surprising since it is only in attempting to perform a particular task within some domain that we are able to determine if the tools we use are adequate. For example, different text editors are better at different things. For a particular editing task, one can choose the text editor best suited for interaction relative to the task. The best editor, if we are forced to choose only one, is the one that best suits the tasks most frequently performed. Therefore, it is not too disappointing that we cannot extend the interaction analysis beyond the scope of a particular task.

DESIGN FOCUS

Video recorder

A simple example of programming a VCR from a remote control shows that all four translations in the interaction cycle can affect the overall interaction. Ineffective interaction is indicated by the user not being sure the VCR is set to record properly. This could be because the user has pressed the keys on the remote control unit in the wrong order; this can be classified as an articulatory problem. Or maybe the VCR is able to record on any channel but the remote control lacks the ability to select channels, indicating a coverage problem for the performance translation. It may be the case that the VCR display panel does not indicate that the program has been set, a presentation problem. Or maybe the user does not interpret the feedback properly, an observational error. Any one or more of these deficiencies would give rise to ineffective interaction.

3.3   FRAMEWORKS AND HCI

As well as providing a means of discussing the details of a particular interaction, frameworks provide a basis for discussing other issues that relate to the interaction. The ACM SIGCHI Curriculum Development Group presents a framework similar to that presented here, and uses it to place different areas that relate to HCI [9].

In Figure 3.3 these aspects are shown as they relate to the interaction framework. In particular, the field of *ergonomics* addresses issues on the user side of the interface, covering both input and output, as well as the user's immediate context. Dialog design and interface styles can be placed particularly along the input branch of the framework, addressing both articulation and performance. However, dialog is most usually associated with the computer and so is biased to that side of the framework.

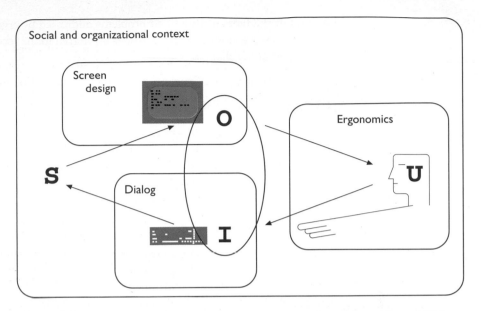

Figure 3.3   A framework for human–computer interaction. Adapted from ACM SIGCHI Curriculum Development Group [9]

Presentation and screen design relates to the output branch of the framework. The entire framework can be placed within a social and organizational context that also affects the interaction. Each of these areas has important implications for the design of interactive systems and the performance of the user. We will discuss these in brief in the following sections, with the exception of screen design which we will save until Chapter 5.

3.4   ERGONOMICS

Ergonomics (or human factors) is traditionally the study of the physical characteristics of the interaction: how the controls are designed, the physical environment in which the interaction takes place, and the layout and physical qualities of the screen. A primary focus is on user performance and how the interface enhances or detracts from this. In seeking to evaluate these aspects of the interaction, ergonomics will certainly also touch upon human psychology and system constraints. It is a large and established field, which is closely related to but distinct from HCI, and full coverage would demand a book in its own right. Here we consider a few of the issues addressed by ergonomics as an introduction to the field. We will briefly look at the arrangement of controls and displays, the physical environment, health issues and the use of color. These are by no means exhaustive and are intended only to give an indication of the types of issues and problems addressed by ergonomics. For more information on ergonomic issues the reader is referred to the recommended reading list at the end of the chapter.

3.4.1 Arrangement of controls and displays

In Chapter 1 we considered perceptual and cognitive issues that affect the way we present information on a screen and provide control mechanisms to the user. In addition to these cognitive aspects of design, physical aspects are also important. Sets of controls and parts of the display should be grouped logically to allow rapid access by the user (more on this in Chapter 5). This may not seem so important when we are considering a single user of a spreadsheet on a PC, but it becomes vital when we turn to safety-critical applications such as plant control, aviation and air traffic control. In each of these contexts, users are under pressure and are faced with a huge range of displays and controls. Here it is crucial that the physical layout of these be appropriate. Indeed, returning to the less critical PC application, inappropriate placement of controls and displays can lead to inefficiency and frustration. For example, on one particular electronic newsreader, used by one of the authors, the command key to read articles from a newsgroup (y) is directly beside the command key to unsubscribe from a newsgroup (u) on the keyboard. This poor design frequently leads to inadvertent removal of newsgroups. Although this is recoverable it wastes time and is annoying to the user. We saw similar examples in the Introduction to this book including the MacOS X dock. We can therefore see that appropriate layout is important in all applications.

We have already touched on the importance of grouping controls together logically (and keeping opposing controls separate). The exact organization that this will suggest will depend on the domain and the application, but possible organizations include the following:

functional controls and displays are organized so that those that are functionally related are placed together;

sequential controls and displays are organized to reflect the order of their use in a typical interaction (this may be especially appropriate in domains where a particular task sequence is enforced, such as aviation);

frequency controls and displays are organized according to how frequently they are used, with the most commonly used controls being the most easily accessible.

In addition to the organization of the controls and displays in relation to each other, the entire system interface must be arranged appropriately in relation to the user's position. So, for example, the user should be able to reach all controls necessary and view all displays without excessive body movement. Critical displays should be at eye level. Lighting should be arranged to avoid glare and reflection distorting displays. Controls should be spaced to provide adequate room for the user to manoeuvre.

DESIGN FOCUS

Industrial interfaces

The interfaces to office systems have changed dramatically since the 1980s. However, some care is needed in transferring the idioms of office-based systems into the industrial domain. Office information is primarily textual and slow varying, whereas industrial interfaces may require the rapid assimilation of multiple numeric displays, each of which is varying in response to the environment. Furthermore, the environmental conditions may rule out certain interaction styles (for example, the oil-soaked mouse). Consequently, industrial interfaces raise some additional design issues rarely encountered in the office.

Glass interfaces vs. dials and knobs

The traditional machine interface consists of dials and knobs directly wired or piped to the equipment. Increasingly, some or all of the controls are replaced with a glass interface, a computer screen through which the equipment is monitored and controlled. Many of the issues are similar for the two kinds of interface, but glass interfaces do have some special advantages and problems. For a complex system, a glass interface can be both cheaper and more flexible, and it is easy to show the same information in multiple forms (Figure 3.4). For example, a data value might be given both in a precise numeric field and also in a quick to assimilate graphical form. In addition, the same information can be shown on several screens. However, the information is not located in physical space and so vital clues to context are missing – it is easy to get lost navigating complex menu systems. Also, limited display resolution often means that an electronic representation of a dial is harder to read than its physical counterpart; in some circumstances both may be necessary, as is the case on the flight deck of a modern aircraft.

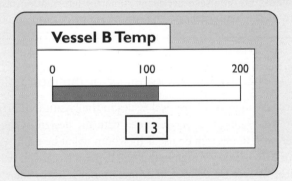

Figure 3.4   Multiple representations of the same information

Indirect manipulation

The phrase 'direct manipulation' dominates office system design (Figure 3.5). There are arguments about its meaning and appropriateness even there, but it is certainly dependent on the user being in primary control of the changes in the interface. The autonomous nature of industrial processes makes this an inappropriate model. In a direct manipulation system, the user interacts with an artificial world inside the computer (for example, the electronic desktop).

In contrast, an industrial interface is merely an intermediary between the operator and the real world. One implication of this indirectness is that the interface must provide feedback at two levels

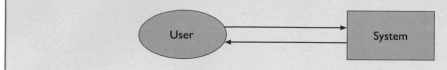

Figure 3.5   Office system – direct manipulation

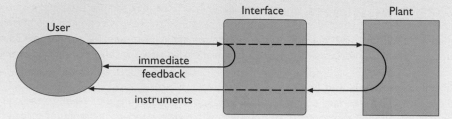

Figure 3.6   Indirect manipulation – two kinds of feedback

(Figure 3.6). At one level, the user must receive immediate feedback, generated by the interface, that keystrokes and other actions have been received. In addition, the user's actions will have some effect on the equipment controlled by the interface and adequate monitoring must be provided for this.

The indirectness also causes problems with simple monitoring tasks. Delays due to periodic sampling, slow communication and digital processing often mean that the data displayed are somewhat out of date. If the operator is not aware of these delays, diagnoses of system state may be wrong. These problems are compounded if the interface produces summary information displays. If the data comprising such a display are of different timeliness the result may be misleading.

3.4.2 The physical environment of the interaction

As well as addressing physical issues in the layout and arrangement of the machine interface, ergonomics is concerned with the design of the work environment itself. Where will the system be used? By whom will it be used? Will users be sitting, standing or moving about? Again, this will depend largely on the domain and will be more critical in specific control and operational settings than in general computer use. However, the physical environment in which the system is used may influence how well it is accepted and even the health and safety of its users. It should therefore be considered in all design.

The first consideration here is the size of the users. Obviously this is going to vary considerably. However, in any system the smallest user should be able to reach all the controls (this may include a user in a wheelchair), and the largest user should not be cramped in the environment.

In particular, all users should be comfortably able to see critical displays. For long periods of use, the user should be seated for comfort and stability. Seating should provide back support. If required to stand, the user should have room to move around in order to reach all the controls.

3.4.3 Health issues

Perhaps we do not immediately think of computer use as a hazardous activity but we should bear in mind possible consequences of our designs on the health and safety of users. Leaving aside the obvious safety risks of poorly designed safety-critical systems (aircraft crashing, nuclear plant leaks and worse), there are a number of factors that may affect the use of more general computers. Again these are factors in the physical environment that directly affect the quality of the interaction and the user's performance:

Physical position   As we noted in the previous section, users should be able to reach all controls comfortably and see all displays. Users should not be expected to stand for long periods and, if sitting, should be provided with back support. If a particular position for a part of the body is to be adopted for long periods (for example, in typing) support should be provided to allow rest.

Temperature   Although most users can adapt to slight changes in temperature without adverse effect, extremes of hot or cold will affect performance and, in excessive cases, health. Experimental studies show that performance deteriorates at high or low temperatures, with users being unable to concentrate efficiently.

Lighting   The lighting level will again depend on the work environment. However, adequate lighting should be provided to allow users to see the computer screen without discomfort or eyestrain. The light source should also be positioned to avoid glare affecting the display.

Noise   Excessive noise can be harmful to health, causing the user pain, and in acute cases, loss of hearing. Noise levels should be maintained at a comfortable level in the work environment. This does not necessarily mean no noise at all. Noise can be a stimulus to users and can provide needed confirmation of system activity.

Time   The time users spend using the system should also be controlled. As we saw in the previous chapter, it has been suggested that excessive use of CRT displays can be harmful to users, particularly pregnant women.

3.4.4 The use of color

In this section we have concentrated on the ergonomics of physical characteristics of systems, including the physical environment in which they are used. However, ergonomics has a close relationship to human psychology in that it is also concerned with the perceptual limitations of humans. For example, the use of color in displays is an ergonomics issue. As we saw in Chapter 1, the visual system has some limitations with regard to color, including the number of colors that are distinguishable and the relatively low blue acuity. We also saw that a relatively high proportion of the population suffers from a deficiency in color vision. Each of these psychological phenomena leads to ergonomic guidelines; some examples are discussed below.

Colors used in the display should be as distinct as possible and the distinction should not be affected by changes in contrast. Blue should not be used to display critical information. If color is used as an indicator it should not be the only cue: additional coding information should be included.

The colors used should also correspond to common conventions and user expectations. Red, green and yellow are colors frequently associated with stop, go and standby respectively. Therefore, red may be used to indicate emergency and alarms; green, normal activity; and yellow, standby and auxiliary function. These conventions should not be violated without very good cause.

However, we should remember that color conventions are culturally determined. For example, red is associated with danger and warnings in most western cultures, but in China it symbolizes happiness and good fortune. The color of mourning is black in some cultures and white in others. Awareness of the cultural associations of color is particularly important in designing systems and websites for a global market. We will return to these issues in more detail in Chapter 10.

3.4.5 Ergonomics and HCI

Ergonomics is a huge area, which is distinct from HCI but sits alongside it. Its contribution to HCI is in determining constraints on the way we design systems and suggesting detailed and specific guidelines and standards. Ergonomic factors are in general well established and understood and are therefore used as the basis for standardizing hardware designs. This issue is discussed further in Chapter 7.

3.5   INTERACTION STYLES

Interaction can be seen as a dialog between the computer and the user. The choice of interface style can have a profound effect on the nature of this dialog. Dialog design is discussed in detail in Chapter 16. Here we introduce the most common interface styles and note the different effects these have on the interaction. There are a number of common interface styles including

- command line interface
- menus
- natural language
- question/answer and query dialog
- form-fills and spreadsheets
- WIMP
- point and click
- three-dimensional interfaces.

As the WIMP interface is the most common and complex, we will discuss each of its elements in greater detail in Section 3.6.

```
sable.soc.staffs.ac.uk> javac HelloWorldApp
javac: invalid argument: HelloWorldApp
use: javac [-g][-O][-classpath path][-d dir] file.java...
sable.soc.staffs.ac.uk> javac HelloWorldApp.java
sable.soc.staffs.ac.uk> java HelloWorldApp
Hello world!!
sable.soc.staffs.ac.uk>
```

Figure 3.7   Command line interface

3.5.1 Command line interface

The command line interface (Figure 3.7) was the first interactive dialog style to be commonly used and, in spite of the availability of menu-driven interfaces, it is still widely used. It provides a means of expressing instructions to the computer directly, using function keys, single characters, abbreviations or whole-word commands. In some systems the command line is the only way of communicating with the system, especially for remote access using *telnet*. More commonly today it is supplementary to menu-based interfaces, providing accelerated access to the system's functionality for experienced users.

Command line interfaces are powerful in that they offer direct access to system functionality (as opposed to the hierarchical nature of menus), and can be combined to apply a number of tools to the same data. They are also flexible: the command often has a number of options or parameters that will vary its behavior in some way, and it can be applied to many objects at once, making it useful for repetitive tasks. However, this flexibility and power brings with it difficulty in use and learning. Commands must be remembered, as no cue is provided in the command line to indicate which command is needed. They are therefore better for expert users than for novices. This problem can be alleviated a little by using consistent and meaningful commands and abbreviations. The commands used should be terms within the vocabulary of the user rather than the technician. Unfortunately, commands are often obscure and vary across systems, causing confusion to the user and increasing the overhead of learning.

3.5.2 Menus

In a menu-driven interface, the set of options available to the user is displayed on the screen, and selected using the mouse, or numeric or alphabetic keys. Since the options are visible they are less demanding of the user, relying on recognition rather than recall. However, menu options still need to be meaningful and logically grouped to aid recognition. Often menus are hierarchically ordered and the option required is not available at the top layer of the hierarchy. The grouping

```
PAYMENT DETAILS                P3-7

please select payment method:
    1.  cash
    2.  check
    3.  credit card
    4.  invoice

    9.  abort transaction
```

Figure 3.8 Menu-driven interface

and naming of menu options then provides the only cue for the user to find the required option. Such systems either can be purely text based, with the menu options being presented as numbered choices (see Figure 3.8), or may have a graphical component in which the menu appears within a rectangular box and choices are made, perhaps by typing the initial letter of the desired selection, or by entering the associated number, or by moving around the menu with the arrow keys. This is a restricted form of a full WIMP system, described in more detail shortly.

3.5.3 Natural language

Perhaps the most attractive means of communicating with computers, at least at first glance, is by natural language. Users, unable to remember a command or lost in a hierarchy of menus, may long for the computer that is able to understand instructions expressed in everyday words! Natural language understanding, both of speech and written input, is the subject of much interest and research. Unfortunately, however, the ambiguity of natural language makes it very difficult for a machine to understand. Language is ambiguous at a number of levels. First, the syntax, or structure, of a phrase may not be clear. If we are given the sentence

```
The boy hit the dog with the stick
```

we cannot be sure whether the boy is using the stick to hit the dog or whether the dog is holding the stick when it is hit.

Even if a sentence's structure is clear, we may find ambiguity in the meaning of the words used. For example, the word 'pitch' may refer to a sports field, a throw, a waterproofing substance or even, colloquially, a territory. We often rely on the context and our general knowledge to sort out these ambiguities. This information is difficult to provide to the machine. To complicate matters more, the use of pronouns and relative terms adds further ambiguity.

Given these problems, it seems unlikely that a general natural language interface will be available for some time. However, systems can be built to understand restricted subsets of a language. For a known and constrained domain, the system can be provided with sufficient information to disambiguate terms. It is important in interfaces which use natural language in this restricted form that the user is aware of the limitations of the system and does not expect too much understanding.

The use of natural language in restricted domains is relatively successful, but it is debatable whether this can really be called natural language. The user still has to learn which phrases the computer understands and may become frustrated if too much is expected. However, it is also not clear how useful a general natural language interface would be. Language is by nature vague and imprecise: this gives it its flexibility and allows creativity in expression. Computers, on the other hand, require precise instructions. Given a free rein, would we be able to describe our requirements precisely enough to guarantee a particular response? And, if we could, would the language we used turn out to be a restricted subset of natural language anyway?

3.5.4 Question/answer and query dialog

Question and answer dialog is a simple mechanism for providing input to an application in a specific domain. The user is asked a series of questions (mainly with yes/no responses, multiple choice, or codes) and so is led through the interaction step by step. An example of this would be web questionnaires.

These interfaces are easy to learn and use, but are limited in functionality and power. As such, they are appropriate for restricted domains (particularly information systems) and for novice or casual users.

Query languages, on the other hand, are used to construct queries to retrieve information from a database. They use natural-language-style phrases, but in fact require specific syntax, as well as knowledge of the database structure. Queries usually require the user to specify an attribute or attributes for which to search the database, as well as the attributes of interest to be displayed. This is straightforward where there is a single attribute, but becomes complex when multiple attributes are involved, particularly if the user is interested in attribute A or attribute B, or attribute A and not attribute B, or where values of attributes are to be compared. Most query languages do not provide direct confirmation of what was requested, so that the only validation the user has is the result of the search. The effective use of query languages therefore requires some experience. A specialized example is the web search engine.

3.5.5 Form-fills and spreadsheets

Form-filling interfaces are used primarily for data entry but can also be useful in data retrieval applications. The user is presented with a display resembling a paper

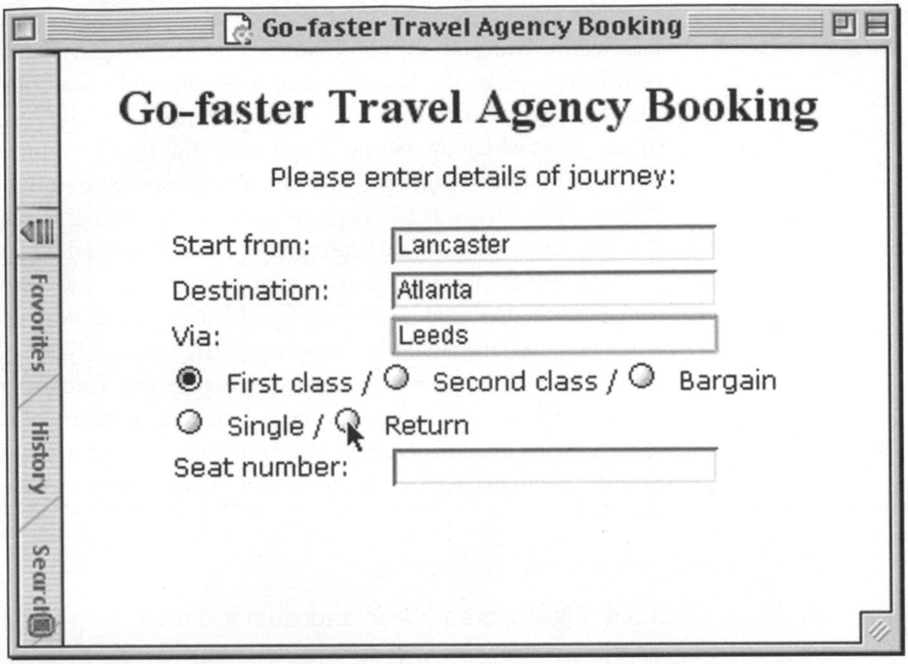

Figure 3.9   A typical form-filling interface. Screen shot frame reprinted by permission from Microsoft Corporation

form, with slots to fill in (see Figure 3.9). Often the form display is based upon an actual form with which the user is familiar, which makes the interface easier to use. The user works through the form, filling in appropriate values. The data are then entered into the application in the correct place. Most form-filling interfaces allow easy movement around the form and allow some fields to be left blank. They also require correction facilities, as users may change their minds or make a mistake about the value that belongs in each field. The dialog style is useful primarily for data entry applications and, as it is easy to learn and use, for novice users. However, assuming a design that allows flexible entry, form filling is also appropriate for expert users.

Spreadsheets are a sophisticated variation of form filling. The spreadsheet comprises a grid of cells, each of which can contain a value or a formula (see Figure 3.10). The formula can involve the values of other cells (for example, the total of all cells in this column). The user can enter and alter values and formulae in any order and the system will maintain consistency amongst the values displayed, ensuring that all formulae are obeyed. The user can therefore manipulate values to see the effects of changing different parameters. Spreadsheets are an attractive medium for interaction: the user is free to manipulate values at will and the distinction between input and output is blurred, making the interface more flexible and natural.

Pooches Pet Emporium					
Date	Description	Dog	Income	Outgoings	Balance
9/2/02	Fees – Mr C. Brown	Snoopy	96.37		96.37
10/2/02	Rubber bones			36.26	60.11
10/2/02	Fees – Mrs E. R. Windsor	7 corgis	1006.45		1066.56
12/2/02	Special order: 7 red carpets			47.28	992.28
16/2/02	Fees – Master T. Tin	Snowy	32.98		1025.26
17/2/02	Beefy Bruno's Bonemeal			243.47	781.79
21/2/02	Fees – Mr F. Flintstone	Dino	21.95		803.74
21/2/02	Special order: 1 Brontosaurus bone			6.47	797.27
28/2/02	Wages – Mr S. H. Ovelit			489.46	307.81

Figure 3.10   A typical spreadsheet

3.5.6 The WIMP interface

Currently many common environments for interactive computing are examples of the *WIMP* interface style, often simply called windowing systems. WIMP stands for windows, icons, menus and pointers (sometimes windows, icons, mice and pull-down menus), and is the default interface style for the majority of interactive computer systems in use today, especially in the PC and desktop workstation arena. Examples of WIMP interfaces include Microsoft Windows for IBM PC compatibles, MacOS for Apple Macintosh compatibles and various X Windows-based systems for UNIX.

Mixing styles

The UNIX windowing environments are interesting as the contents of many of the windows are often themselves simply command line or character-based programs (see Figure 3.11). In fact, this mixing of interface styles in the same system is quite common, especially where older *legacy systems* are used at the same time as more modern applications. It can be a problem if users attempt to use commands and methods suitable for one environment in another. On the Apple Macintosh, HyperCard uses a point-and-click style. However, HyperCard stack buttons look very like Macintosh folders. If you double click on them, as you would to open a folder, your two mouse clicks are treated as separate actions. The first click opens the stack (as you wanted), but the second is then interpreted in the context of the newly opened stack, behaving in an apparently arbitrary fashion! This is an example of the importance of *consistency* in the interface, an issue we shall return to in Chapter 7.

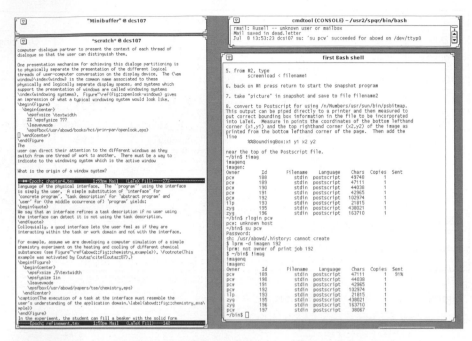

Figure 3.11   A typical UNIX windowing system – the OpenLook system.
Source: Sun Microsystems, Inc.

3.5.7 Point-and-click interfaces

In most multimedia systems and in web browsers, virtually all actions take only a single click of the mouse button. You may point at a city on a map and when you click a window opens, showing you tourist information about the city. You may point at a word in some text and when you click you see a definition of the word. You may point at a recognizable iconic button and when you click some action is performed.

This point-and-click interface style is obviously closely related to the WIMP style. It clearly overlaps in the use of buttons, but may also include other WIMP elements. However, the philosophy is simpler and more closely tied to ideas of *hypertext*. In addition, the point-and-click style is not tied to mouse-based interfaces, and is also extensively used in touchscreen information systems. In this case, it is often combined with a menu-driven interface.

The point-and-click style has been popularized by world wide web pages, which incorporate all the above types of point-and-click navigation: highlighted words, maps and iconic buttons.

3.5.8 Three-dimensional interfaces

There is an increasing use of three-dimensional effects in user interfaces. The most obvious example is virtual reality, but VR is only part of a range of 3D techniques available to the interface designer.

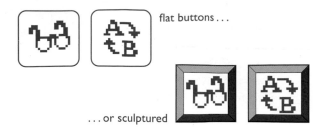

Figure 3.12 Buttons in 3D say 'press me'

The simplest technique is where ordinary WIMP elements, buttons, scroll bars, etc., are given a 3D appearance using shading, giving the appearance of being sculpted out of stone. By unstated convention, such interfaces have a light source at their top right. Where used judiciously, the raised areas are easily identifiable and can be used to highlight active areas (Figure 3.12). Unfortunately, some interfaces make indiscriminate use of sculptural effects, on every text area, border and menu, so all sense of differentiation is lost.

A more complex technique uses interfaces with 3D workspaces. The objects displayed in such systems are usually flat, but are displayed in perspective when at an angle to the viewer and shrink when they are 'further away'. Figure 3.13 shows one such system, WebBook [57]. Notice how size, light and occlusion provide a sense of

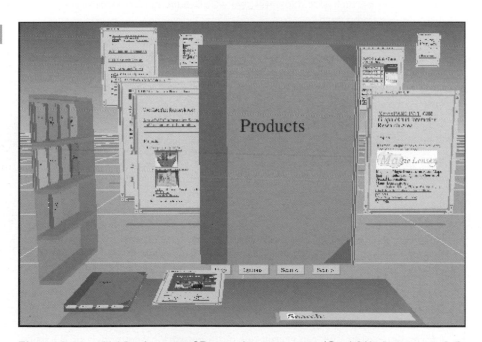

Figure 3.13 WebBook – using 3D to make more space (Card S.K., Robertson G.G. and York W. (1996). The WebBook and the Web Forager: An Information workspace for the World-Wide Web. *CHI96 Conference Proceedings*, 111–17. Copyright © 1996 ACM, Inc. Reprinted by permission)

distance. Notice also that as objects get further away they take up less screen space. Three-dimensional workspaces give you extra space, but in a more natural way than iconizing windows.

Finally, there are virtual reality and information visualization systems where the user can move about within a simulated 3D world. These are discussed in detail in Chapter 20.

These mechanisms overlap with other interaction styles, especially the use of sculptured elements in WIMP interfaces. However, there is a distinct interaction style for 3D interfaces in that they invite us to use our tacit abilities for the real world, and translate them into the electronic world. Novice users must learn that an oval area with a word or picture in it is a button to be pressed, but a 3D button says 'push me'. Further, more complete 3D environments invite one to move within the virtual environment, rather than watch as a spectator.

DESIGN FOCUS

Navigation in 3D and 2D

We live in a three-dimensional world. So clearly 3D interfaces are good . . . or are they? Actually, our 3D stereo vision only works well close to us and after that we rely on cruder measures such as 'this is in front of that'. We are good at moving obects around with our hands in three dimensions, rotating, turning them on their side. However, we walk around in two dimensions and do not fly. Not surprisingly, people find it hard to visualize and control movement in three dimensions.

Normally, we use gravity to give us a fixed direction in space. This is partly through the channels in the inner ear, but also largely through kinesthetic senses – feeling the weight of limbs. When we lose these senses it is easy to become disoriented and we can lose track of which direction is up: divers are trained to watch the direction their bubbles move and if buried in an avalanche you should spit and feel which direction the spittle flows.

Where humans have to navigate in three dimensions they need extra aids such as the artificial horizon in an airplane. Helicopters, where there are many degrees of freedom, are particularly difficult.

Even in the two-dimensional world of walking about we do not rely on neat Cartesian maps in our head. Instead we mostly use models of location such as 'down the road near the church' that rely on approximate topological understanding and landmarks. We also rely on properties of normal space, such as the ability to go backwards and the fact that things that are close can be reached quickly. When two-dimensional worlds are not like this, for example in a one-way traffic system or in a labyrinth, we have great difficulty [98].

When we design systems we should take into account how people navigate in the real world and use this to guide our navigation aids. For example, if we have a 3D interface or a virtual reality world we should normally show a ground plane and by default lock movement to be parallel to the ground. In information systems we can recruit our more network-based models of 2D space by giving landmarks and making it as easy to 'step back' as to go forwards (as with the web browser 'back' button).

See the book website for more about 3D vision: /e3/online/seeing-3D/

3.6   ELEMENTS OF THE WIMP INTERFACE

We have already noted the four key features of the WIMP interface that give it its name – windows, icons, pointers and menus – and we will now describe these in turn. There are also many additional interaction objects and techniques commonly used in WIMP interfaces, some designed for specific purposes and others more general. We will look at buttons, toolbars, palettes and dialog boxes. Most of these elements can be seen in Figure 3.14.

Together, these elements of the WIMP interfaces are called *widgets*, and they comprise the toolkit for interaction between user and system. In Chapter 8 we will describe windowing systems and interaction widgets more from the programmer's perspective. There we will discover that though most modern windowing systems provide the same set of basic widgets, the 'look and feel' – how widgets are physically displayed and how users can interact with them to access their functionality – of different windowing systems and toolkits can differ drastically.

3.6.1 Windows

Windows are areas of the screen that behave as if they were independent terminals in their own right. A window can usually contain text or graphics, and can be moved

Figure 3.14 Elements of the WIMP interface – Microsoft Word 5.1 on an Apple Macintosh. Screen shot reprinted by permission from Apple Computer, Inc.

or resized. More than one window can be on a screen at once, allowing separate tasks to be visible at the same time. Users can direct their attention to the different windows as they switch from one thread of work to another.

If one window overlaps the other, the back window is partially obscured, and then refreshed when exposed again. Overlapping windows can cause problems by obscuring vital information, so windows may also be *tiled*, when they adjoin but do not overlap each other. Alternatively, windows may be placed in a *cascading* fashion, where each new window is placed slightly to the left and below the previous window. In some systems this *layout policy* is fixed, in others it can be selected by the user.

Usually, windows have various things associated with them that increase their usefulness. *Scrollbars* are one such attachment, allowing the user to move the contents of the window up and down, or from side to side. This makes the window behave as if it were a real window onto a much larger world, where new information is brought into view by manipulating the scrollbars.

There is usually a title bar attached to the top of a window, identifying it to the user, and there may be special boxes in the corners of the window to aid resizing, closing, or making as large as possible. Each of these can be seen in Figure 3.15.

In addition, some systems allow windows within windows. For example, in Microsoft Office applications, such as Excel and Word, each application has its own window and then within this each document has a window. It is often possible to have different layout policies within the different application windows.

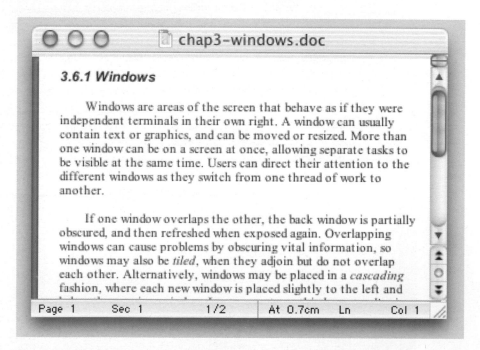

Figure 3.15 A typical window. Screen shot reprinted by permission from Apple Computer, Inc.

Figure 3.16   A variety of icons. Screen shot reprinted by permission from Apple Computer, Inc.

3.6.2 Icons

Windows can be closed and lost for ever, or they can be shrunk to some very reduced representation. A small picture is used to represent a closed window, and this representation is known as an *icon*. By allowing icons, many windows can be available on the screen at the same time, ready to be expanded to their full size by clicking on the icon. Shrinking a window to its icon is known as *iconifying* the window. When a user temporarily does not want to follow a particular thread of dialog, he can suspend that dialog by iconifying the window containing the dialog. The icon saves space on the screen and serves as a reminder to the user that he can subsequently resume the dialog by opening up the window. Figure 3.16 shows a few examples of some icons used in a typical windowing system (MacOS X).

Icons can also be used to represent other aspects of the system, such as a wastebasket for throwing unwanted files into, or various disks, programs or functions that are accessible to the user. Icons can take many forms: they can be realistic representations of the objects that they stand for, or they can be highly stylized. They can even be arbitrary symbols, but these can be difficult for users to interpret.

3.6.3 Pointers

The pointer is an important component of the WIMP interface, since the interaction style required by WIMP relies very much on pointing and selecting things such as icons. The mouse provides an input device capable of such tasks, although joysticks and trackballs are other alternatives, as we have previously seen in Chapter 2. The user is presented with a cursor on the screen that is controlled by the input device. A variety of pointer cursors are shown in Figure 3.17.

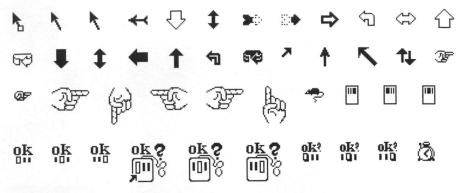

Figure 3.17　A variety of pointer cursors. Source: Sun Microsystems, Inc.

The different shapes of cursor are often used to distinguish *modes*, for example the normal pointer cursor may be an arrow, but change to cross-hairs when drawing a line. Cursors are also used to tell the user about system activity, for example a watch or hour-glass cursor may be displayed when the system is busy reading a file.

Pointer cursors are like icons, being small bitmap images, but in addition all cursors have a *hot-spot*, the location to which they point. For example, the three arrows at the start of Figure 3.17 each have a hot-spot at the top left, whereas the right-pointing hand on the second line has a hot-spot on its right. Sometimes the hot-spot is not clear from the appearance of the cursor, in which case users will find it hard to click on small targets. When designing your own cursors, make sure the image has an obvious hot-spot.

3.6.4 Menus

The last main feature of windowing systems is the *menu*, an interaction technique that is common across many non-windowing systems as well. A menu presents a choice of operations or services that can be performed by the system at a given time. In Chapter 1, we pointed out that our ability to recall information is inferior to our ability to recognize it from some visual cue. Menus provide information cues in the form of an ordered list of operations that can be scanned. This implies that the names used for the commands in the menu should be meaningful and informative.

The pointing device is used to indicate the desired option. As the pointer moves to the position of a menu item, the item is usually highlighted (by inverse video, or some similar strategy) to indicate that it is the potential candidate for selection. Selection usually requires some additional user action, such as pressing a button on the mouse that controls the pointer cursor on the screen or pressing some special key on the keyboard. Menus are inefficient when they have too many items, and so cascading menus are utilized, in which item selection opens up another menu adjacent to the item, allowing refinement of the selection. Several layers of cascading menus can be used.

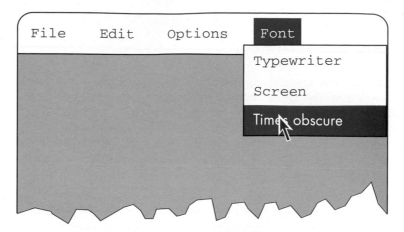

Figure 3.18   Pull-down menu

The main menu can be visible to the user all the time, as a *menu bar* and submenus can be pulled down or across from it upon request (Figure 3.18). Menu bars are often placed at the top of the screen (for example, MacOS) or at the top of each window (for example, Microsoft Windows). Alternatives include menu bars along one side of the screen, or even placed amongst the windows in the main 'desktop' area. Websites use a variety of menu bar locations, including top, bottom and either side of the screen. Alternatively, the main menu can be hidden and upon request it will pop up onto the screen. These *pop-up menus* are often used to present context-sensitive options, for example allowing one to examine properties of particular on-screen objects. In some systems they are also used to access more global actions when the mouse is depressed over the screen background.

Pull-down menus are dragged down from the title at the top of the screen, by moving the mouse pointer into the title bar area and pressing the button. Fall-down menus are similar, except that the menu automatically appears when the mouse pointer enters the title bar, without the user having to press the button. Some menus are pin-up menus, in that they can be 'pinned' to the screen, staying in place until explicitly asked to go away. Pop-up menus appear when a particular region of the screen, maybe designated by an icon, is selected, but they only stay as long as the mouse button is depressed.

Another approach to menu selection is to arrange the options in a circular fashion. The pointer appears in the center of the circle, and so there is the same distance to travel to any of the selections. This has the advantages that it is easier to select items, since they can each have a larger target area, and that the selection time for each item is the same, since the pointer is equidistant from them all. Compare this with a standard menu: remembering Fitts' law from Chapter 1, we can see that it will take longer to select items near the bottom of the menu than at the top. However, these *pie menus*, as they are known [54], take up more screen space and are therefore less common in interfaces.

Keyboard accelerators

Menus often offer *keyboard accelerators*, key combinations that have the same effect as selecting the menu item. This allows more expert users, familiar with the system, to manipulate things without moving off the keyboard, which is often faster. The accelerators are often displayed alongside the menu items so that frequent use makes them familiar. Unfortunately most systems do not allow you to use the accelerators while the menu is displayed. So, for example, the menu might say

> <u>F</u>ind   F3

However, when the user presses function key F3 nothing happens. F3 only works when the menu is *not* displayed – when the menu is there you must press 'F' instead! This is an example of an interface that is *dishonest* (see also Chapter 7).

The major problems with menus in general are deciding what items to include and how to group those items. Including too many items makes menus too long or creates too many of them, whereas grouping causes problems in that items that relate to the same topic need to come under the same heading, yet many items could be grouped under more than one heading. In pull-down menus the menu label should be chosen to reflect the function of the menu items, and items grouped within menus by function. These groupings should be consistent across applications so that the user can transfer learning to new applications. Menu items should be ordered in the menu according to importance and frequency of use, and opposite functionalities (such as 'save' and 'delete') should be kept apart to prevent accidental selection of the wrong function, with potentially disastrous consequences.

3.6.5 Buttons

Buttons are individual and isolated regions within a display that can be selected by the user to invoke specific operations. These regions are referred to as buttons because they are purposely made to resemble the push buttons you would find on a control panel. 'Pushing' the button invokes a command, the meaning of which is usually indicated by a textual label or a small icon. Buttons can also be used to toggle between two states, displaying status information such as whether the current font is italicized or not in a word processor, or selecting options on a web form. Such toggle buttons can be grouped together to allow a user to select one feature from a set of mutually exclusive options, such as the size in points of the current font. These are called *radio buttons*, since the collection functions much like the old-fashioned mechanical control buttons on car radios. If a set of options is not mutually exclusive, such as font characteristics like bold, italics and underlining, then a set of toggle buttons can be used to indicate the on/off status of the options. This type of collection of buttons is sometimes referred to as *check boxes*.

3.6.6 Toolbars

Many systems have a collection of small buttons, each with icons, placed at the top or side of the window and offering commonly used functions. The function of this *toolbar* is similar to a menu bar, but as the icons are smaller than the equivalent text more functions can be simultaneously displayed. Sometimes the content of the toolbar is fixed, but often users can *customize* it, either changing which functions are made available, or choosing which of several predefined toolbars is displayed.

DESIGN FOCUS

Learning toolbars

Although many applications now have toolbars, they are often underused because users simply do not know what the icons represent. Once learned the meaning is often relatively easy to remember, but most users do not want to spend time reading a manual, or even using online help to find out what each button does – they simply reach for the menu.

There is an obvious solution – put the icons on the menus in the same way that accelerator keys are written there. So in the 'Edit' menu one might find the option

Imagine now selecting this. As the mouse drags down through the menu selections, each highlights in turn. If the mouse is dragged down the extreme left, the effect will be very similar to selecting the icon from the toolbar, except that it will be incidental to selecting the menu item. In this way, the toolbar icon will be naturally learned from normal menu interaction.

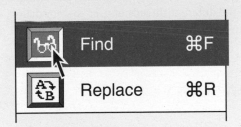

Selecting the menu option = selecting the icon

This trivial fix is based on accepted and tested knowledge of learning and has been described in more detail by one of the authors elsewhere [95]. Given its simplicity, this technique should clearly be used everywhere, but until recently was rare. However, it has now been taken up in the Office 97 suite and later Microsoft Office products, so perhaps will soon become standard.

3.6.7 Palettes

In many application programs, interaction can enter one of several *modes*. The defining characteristic of modes is that the interpretation of actions, such as keystrokes or gestures with the mouse, changes as the mode changes. For example, using the standard UNIX text editor vi, keystrokes can be interpreted either as operations to insert characters in the document (insert mode) or as operations to perform file manipulation (command mode). Problems occur if the user is not aware of the current mode. Palettes are a mechanism for making the set of possible modes and the active mode visible to the user. A palette is usually a collection of icons that are reminiscent of the purpose of the various modes. An example in a drawing package would be a collection of icons to indicate the pixel color or pattern that is used to fill in objects, much like an artist's palette for paint.

Some systems allow the user to create palettes from menus or toolbars. In the case of pull-down menus, the user may be able 'tear off' the menu, turning it into a palette showing the menu items. In the case of toolbars, he may be able to drag the toolbar away from its normal position and place it anywhere on the screen. Tear-off menus are usually those that are heavily graphical anyway, for example line-style or color selection in a drawing package.

3.6.8 Dialog boxes

Dialog boxes are information windows used by the system to bring the user's attention to some important information, possibly an error or a warning used to prevent a possible error. Alternatively, they are used to invoke a subdialog between user and system for a very specific task that will normally be embedded within some larger task. For example, most interactive applications result in the user creating some file that will have to be named and stored within the filing system. When the user or system wants to save the file, a dialog box can be used to allow the user to name the file and indicate where it is to be located within the filing system. When the save subdialog is complete, the dialog box will disappear. Just as windows are used to separate the different threads of user–system dialog, so too are dialog boxes used to factor out auxiliary task threads from the main task dialog.

3.7   INTERACTIVITY

When looking at an interface, it is easy to focus on the visually distinct parts (the buttons, menus, text areas) but the dynamics, the way they react to a user's actions, are less obvious. Dialog design, discussed in Chapter 16, is focussed almost entirely on the choice and specification of appropriate sequences of actions and corresponding changes in the interface state. However, it is typically not used at a fine level of detail and deliberately ignores the 'semantic' level of an interface: for example, the validation of numeric information in a forms-based system.

It is worth remembering that *interactivity* is the defining feature of an *interactive* system. This can be seen in many areas of HCI. For example, the recognition rate for *speech recognition* is too low to allow transcription from tape, but in an airline reservation system, so long as the system can reliably recognize *yes* and *no* it can reflect back its understanding of what you said and seek confirmation. Speech-based *input* is difficult, speech-based *interaction* easier. Also, in the area of information visualization the most exciting developments are all where users can interact with a visualization in real time, changing parameters and seeing the effect.

Interactivity is also crucial in determining the 'feel' of a WIMP environment. All WIMP systems appear to have virtually the same elements: windows, icons, menus, pointers, dialog boxes, buttons, etc. However, the precise behavior of these elements differs both within a single environment and between environments. For example, we have already discussed the different behavior of pull-down and fall-down menus. These look the same, but fall-down menus are more easily invoked by accident (and not surprisingly the windowing environments that use them have largely fallen into disuse!). In fact, menus are a major difference between the MacOS and Microsoft Windows environments: in MacOS you have to keep the mouse depressed through-out menu selection; in Windows you can click on the menu bar and a pull-down menu appears and remains there until an item is selected or it is cancelled. Similarly the detailed behavior of buttons is quite complex, as we shall see in Chapter 17.

In older computer systems, the order of interaction was largely determined by the machine. You did things when the computer was ready. In WIMP environments, the user takes the initiative, with many options and often many applications simultan-eously available. The exceptions to this are *pre-emptive* parts of the interface, where the system for various reasons wrests the initiative away from the user, perhaps because of a problem or because it needs information in order to continue.

The major example of this is *modal dialog boxes*. It is often the case that when a dialog box appears the application will not allow you to do anything else until the dialog box has been completed or cancelled. In some cases this may simply block the application, but you can perform tasks in other applications. In other cases you can do nothing at all until the dialog box has been completed. An especially annoying example is when the dialog box asks a question, perhaps simply for confirmation of an action, but the information you need to answer is hidden by the dialog box!

There are occasions when modal dialog boxes are necessary, for example when a major fault has been detected, or for certain kinds of instructional software. However, the general philosophy of modern systems suggests that one should mini-mize the use of pre-emptive elements, allowing the user maximum flexibility.

Interactivity is also critical in dealing with errors. We discussed slips and mistakes earlier in the chapter, and some ways to try to prevent these types of errors. The other way to deal with errors is to make sure that the user or the system is able to tell when errors have occurred. If users can *detect* errors then they can correct them. So, even if errors occur, the interaction as a whole succeeds. Several of the principles in Chapter 7 deal with issues that relate to this. This ability to detect and correct is important both at the small scale of button presses and keystrokes and also at the large scale. For example, if you have sent a client a letter and expect a reply, you can put in your diary a note on the day you expect a reply. If the other person forgets to reply or the letter gets lost in the post you know to send a reminder or ring when the due day passes.

3.8　THE CONTEXT OF THE INTERACTION

We have been considering the interaction between a user and a system, and how this is affected by interface design. This interaction does not occur within a vacuum. We have already noted some of the physical factors in the environment that can directly affect the quality of the interaction. This is part of the context in which the interaction takes place. But this still assumes a single user operating a single, albeit complex, machine. In reality, users work within a wider social and organizational context. This provides the wider context for the interaction, and may influence the activity and motivation of the user. In Chapter 13, we discuss some methods that can be used to gain a fuller understanding of this context, and, in Chapter 14, we consider in more detail the issues involved when more than one user attempts to work together on a system. Here we will confine our discussion to the influence social and organizational factors may have on the user's interaction with the system. These may not be factors over which the designer has control. However, it is important to be aware of such influences to understand the user and the work domain fully.

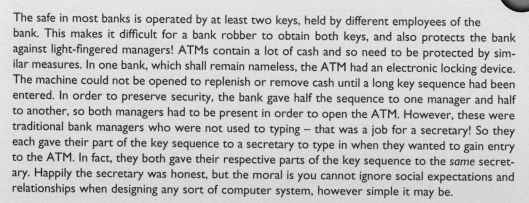

Bank managers don't type . . .

The safe in most banks is operated by at least two keys, held by different employees of the bank. This makes it difficult for a bank robber to obtain both keys, and also protects the bank against light-fingered managers! ATMs contain a lot of cash and so need to be protected by similar measures. In one bank, which shall remain nameless, the ATM had an electronic locking device. The machine could not be opened to replenish or remove cash until a long key sequence had been entered. In order to preserve security, the bank gave half the sequence to one manager and half to another, so both managers had to be present in order to open the ATM. However, these were traditional bank managers who were not used to typing – that was a job for a secretary! So they each gave their part of the key sequence to a secretary to type in when they wanted to gain entry to the ATM. In fact, they both gave their respective parts of the key sequence to the *same* secretary. Happily the secretary was honest, but the moral is you cannot ignore social expectations and relationships when designing any sort of computer system, however simple it may be.

The presence of other people in a work environment affects the performance of the worker in any task. In the case of peers, competition increases performance, at least for known tasks. Similarly the desire to impress management and superiors improves performance on these tasks. However, when it comes to acquisition of new skills, the presence of these groups can inhibit performance, owing to the fear of failure. Consequently, privacy is important to allow users the opportunity to experiment.

In order to perform well, users must be motivated. There are a number of possible sources of motivation, as well as those we have already mentioned, including fear, allegiance, ambition and self-satisfaction. The last of these is influenced by the user's perception of the quality of the work done, which leads to job satisfaction. If a system makes it difficult for the user to perform necessary tasks, or is frustrating to use, the user's job satisfaction, and consequently performance, will be reduced.

The user may also lose motivation if a system is introduced that does not match the actual requirements of the job to be done. Often systems are chosen and introduced by managers rather than the users themselves. In some cases the manager's perception of the job may be based upon observation of results and not on actual activity. The system introduced may therefore impose a way of working that is unsatisfactory to the users. If this happens there may be three results: the system will be rejected, the users will be resentful and unmotivated, or the user will adapt the intended interaction to his own requirements. This indicates the importance of involving actual users in the design process.

DESIGN FOCUS

Half the picture?

When systems are not designed to match the way people actually work, then users end up having to do 'work arounds'. Integrated student records systems are becoming popular in universities in the UK. They bring the benefits of integrating examination systems with enrolment and finance systems so all data can be maintained together and cross-checked. All very useful and time saving – in theory. However, one commonly used system only holds a single overall mark per module for each student, whereas many modules on UK courses have multiple elements of assessment. Knowing a student's mark on each part of the assessment is often useful to academics making decisions in examination boards as it provides a more detailed picture of performance. In many cases staff are therefore supplementing the official records system with their own unofficial spreadsheets to provide this information – making additional work for staff and increased opportunity for error.

On the other hand, the introduction of new technology may prove to be a motivation to users, particularly if it is well designed, integrated with the user's current work, and challenging. Providing adequate feedback is an important source of motivation for users. If no feedback is given during a session, the user may become bored, unmotivated or, worse, unsure of whether the actions performed have been successful. In general, an action should have an obvious effect to prevent this confusion and to allow early recovery in the case of error. Similarly, if system delays occur, feedback can be used to prevent frustration on the part of the user – the user is then aware of what is happening and is not left wondering if the system is still working.

3.9   EXPERIENCE, ENGAGEMENT AND FUN

Ask many in HCI about usability and they may use the words 'effective' and 'efficient'. Some may add 'satisfaction' as well. This view of usability seems to stem mainly from the Taylorist tradition of time and motion studies: if you can get the worker to pull the levers and turn the knobs in the right order then you can shave 10% off production costs.

However, users no longer see themselves as cogs in a machine. Increasingly, applications are focussed outside the closed work environment: on the home, leisure, entertainment, shopping. It is not sufficient that people can use a system, they must *want* to use it.

Even from a pure economic standpoint, your employees are likely to work better and more effectively if they enjoy what they are doing!

In this section we'll look at these more experiential aspects of interaction.

3.9.1 Understanding experience

Shopping is an interesting example to consider. Most internet stores allow you to buy things, but do you go shopping? Shopping is as much about going to the shops, feeling the clothes, being with friends. You can go shopping and never intend to spend money. Shopping is not about an efficient financial transaction, it is an experience.

But experience is a difficult thing to pin down; we understand the idea of a good experience, but how do we define it and even more difficult how do we design it?

Csikszentimihalyi [82] looked at extreme experiences such as climbing a rock face in order to understand that feeling of total engagement that can sometimes happen. He calls this *flow* and it is perhaps related to what some sportspeople refer to as being 'in the zone'. This sense of flow occurs when there is a balance between anxiety and boredom. If you do something that you know you can do it is not engaging; you may do it automatically while thinking of something else, or you may simply become bored. Alternatively, if you do something completely outside your abilities you may become anxious and, if you are half way up a rock face, afraid. Flow comes when you are teetering at the edge of your abilities, stretching yourself to or a little beyond your limits.

In education there is a similar phenomenon. The *zone of proximal development* is those things that you cannot quite do yourself, but you can do with some support, whether from teachers, fellow pupils, or electronic or physical materials. Learning is at its best in this zone. Notice again this touching of limits.

Of course, this does not fully capture the sense of experience, and there is an active subfield of HCI researchers striving to make sense of this, building on the work of psychologists and philosophers on the one hand and literary analysis, film making and drama on the other.

3.9.2 Designing experience

Some of the authors were involved in the design of virtual Christmas crackers. These are rather like electronic greetings cards, but are based on crackers. For those who have not come across them, Christmas crackers are small tubes of paper between 8 and 12 inches long (20–30 cm). Inside there are a small toy, a joke or motto and a paper hat. A small strip of card is threaded through, partly coated with gunpowder. When two people at a party pull the cracker, it bursts apart with a small bang from the gunpowder and the contents spill out.

The virtual cracker does not attempt to fully replicate each aspect of the physical characteristics and process of pulling the cracker, but instead seeks to reproduce the experience. To do this the original crackers experience was deconstructed and each aspect of the experience produced in a similar, but sometimes different, way in the new media. Table 3.1 shows the aspects of the experience deconstructed and reconstructed in the virtual cracker.

For example, the cracker contents are hidden inside; no one knows what toy or joke will be inside. Similarly, when you create a virtual cracker you normally cannot see the contents until the recipient has opened it. Even the recipient initially sees a page with just an image of the cracker; it is only after the recipient has clicked on the 'open' icon that the cracker slowly opens and you get to see the joke, web toy and mask.

The mask is also worth looking at. The first potential design was to have a picture of a face with a hat on it – well, it wouldn't rank highly on excitement! The essential feature of the paper hat is that you can dress up. An iconic hat hardly does that.

Table 3.1 The crackers experience [101]

	Real cracker	Virtual cracker
Surface elements		
Design	Cheap and cheerful	Simple page/graphics
Play	Plastic toy and joke	Web toy and joke
Dressing up	Paper hat	Mask to cut out
Experienced effects		
Shared	Offered to another	Sent by email, message
Co-experience	Pulled together	Sender can't see content until opened by recipient
Excitement	Cultural connotations	Recruited expectation
Hiddenness	Contents inside	First page – no contents
Suspense	Pulling cracker	Slow . . . page change
Surprise	Bang (when it works)	WAV file (when it works)

Instead the cracker has a link to a web page with a picture of a mask that you can print, cut out and wear. Even if you don't actually print it out, the fact that you could changes the experience – it is some dressing up you just happen not to have done yet.

A full description of the virtual crackers case study is on the book website at: /e3/casestudy/crackers/

3.9.3 Physical design and engagement

In Chapter 2 we talked about physical controls. Figure 2.13 showed controllers for a microwave, washing machine and personal MiniDisc player. We saw then how certain physical interfaces were suited for different contexts: smooth plastic controls for an easy clean microwave, multi-function knob for the MiniDisc.

Designers are faced with many constraints:

Ergonomic   You cannot physically push buttons if they are too small or too close.

Physical   The size or nature of the device may force certain positions or styles of control, for example, a dial like the one on the washing machine would not fit on the MiniDisc controller; high-voltage switches cannot be as small as low-voltage ones.

Legal and safety   Cooker controls must be far enough from the pans that you do not burn yourself, but also high enough to prevent small children turning them on.

Context and environment   The microwave's controls are smooth to make them easy to clean in the kitchen.

Aesthetic   The controls must look good.

Economic   It must not cost too much!

These constraints are themselves often contradictory and require trade-offs to be made. For example, even within the safety category front-mounted controls are better in that they can be turned on or off without putting your hands over the pans and hot steam, but back-mounted controls are further from children's grasp. The MiniDisc player is another example; it physically needs to be small, but this means there is not room for all the controls you want given the minimum size that can be manipulated. In the case of the cooker there is no obvious best solution and so different designs favor one or the other. In the case of the MiniDisc player the end knob is multi-function. This means the knob is ergonomically big enough to turn and physically small enough to fit, but at the cost of a more complex interaction style.

To add to this list of constraints there is another that makes a major impact on the ease of use and also the ability of the user to become engaged with the device, for it to become natural to use:

Fluidity   The extent to which the physical structure and manipulation of the device naturally relate to the logical functions it supports.

This is related closely to the idea of *affordances*, which we discuss in Section 5.7.2. The knob at the end of the MiniDisc controller affords turning – it is an obvious thing to do. However, this may not have mapped naturally onto the logical functions. Two of the press buttons are for cycling round the display options and for changing sound options. Imagine a design where turning the knob to clockwise cycled through the display options and turning it anti-clockwise cycled through the sound options. This would be a compact design satisfying all the ergonomic, physical and aesthetic constraints, but would not have led to as fluid an interaction. The physically opposite motions lead to logically distinct effects. However, the designers did a better job than this! The twist knob is used to move backwards and forwards through the tracks of the MiniDisc – that is, opposite physical movements produce opposite logical effects. Holding the knob out and twisting turns the volume up and down. Again, although the pull action is not a natural mapping, the twist maps very naturally onto controlling the sound level.

As well as being fluid in action, some controls portray by their physical appearance the underlying state they control. For example, the dial on the washing machine both sets the program and reflects the current stage in the washing cycle as it turns. A simple on/off switch also does this. However, it is also common to see the power on computers and hifi devices controlled by a push button – press for on, then press again for off. The button does not reflect the state at all. When the screen is on this is not a problem as the fact that there is something on the screen acts as a very immediate indicator of the state. But if the screen has a power save then you might accidentally turn the machine off thinking that you are turning it on! For this reason, this type of power button often has a light beside it to show you the power is on. A simple switch tells you that itself!

3.9.4 Managing value

If we want people to *want* to use a device or application we need to understand their personal values. Why should they want to use it? What value do they get from using it? Now when we say value here we don't mean monetary value, although that may be part of the story, but all the things that drive a person. For some people this may include being nice to colleagues, being ecologically friendly, being successful in their career. Whatever their personal values are, if we ask someone to do something or use something they are only likely to do it if the value to them exceeds the cost.

This is complicated by the fact that for many systems the costs such as purchase cost, download time of a free application, learning effort are incurred up front, whereas often the returns – faster work, enjoyment of use – are seen later. In economics, businesses use a measure called 'net present value' to calculate what a future gain is worth today; because money can be invested, £100 today is worth the same as perhaps £200 in five years' time. Future gain is discounted. For human decision making, future gains are typically discounted very highly; many of us are bad at saving for tomorrow or even keeping the best bits of our dinner until last. This means that not only must we understand people's value systems, but we must be able to offer

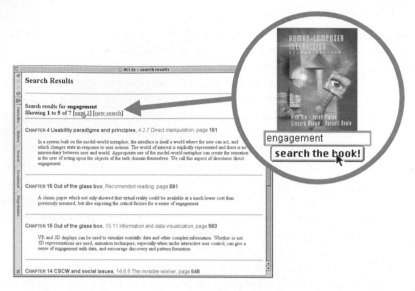

Figure 3.19 The web-based book search facility. Screen shot frame reprinted by permission from Microsoft Corporation

gains sooner as well as later, or at least produce a very good demonstration of potential future gains so that they have a *perceived* current value.

When we were preparing the website for the second edition of this book we thought very hard about how to give things that were of value to those who had the book, and also to those who hadn't. The latter is partly because we are all academics and researchers in the field and so want to contribute to the HCI community, but also of course we would like lots of people to buy the book. One option we thought of was to put the text online, which would be good for people without the book, but this would have less value to people who have the book (they might even be annoyed that those who hadn't paid should have access). The search mechanism was the result of this process (Figure 3.19). It gives value to those who have the book because it is a way of finding things. It is of value to those who don't because it acts as a sort of online encyclopedia of HCI. However, because it always gives the chapter and page number in the book it also says to those who haven't got the book: 'buy me'. See an extended case study about the design of the book search on the website at /e3/casestudy/search/

3.10 SUMMARY

In this chapter, we have looked at the interaction between human and computer, and, in particular, how we can ensure that the interaction is effective to allow the user to get the required job done. We have seen how we can use Norman's execution–evaluation model, and the interaction framework that extends it, to analyze the interaction in terms of how easy or difficult it is for the user to express what he wants and determine whether it has been done.

We have also looked at the role of ergonomics in interface design, in analyzing the physical characteristics of the interaction, and we have discussed a number of interface styles. We have considered how each of these factors can influence the effectiveness of the interaction.

Interactivity is at the heart of all modern interfaces and is important at many levels. Interaction between user and computer does not take place in a vacuum, but is affected by numerous social and organizational factors. These may be beyond the designer's control, but awareness of them can help to limit any negative effects on the interaction.

EXERCISES

3.1 Choose two of the interface styles (described in Section 3.5) that you have experience of using. Use the interaction framework to analyze the interaction involved in using these inter- face styles for a database selection task. Which of the distances is greatest in each case?

3.2 Find out all you can about natural language interfaces. Are there any successful systems? For what applications are these most appropriate?

3.3 What influence does the social environment in which you work have on your interaction with the computer? What effect does the organization (commercial or academic) to which you belong have on the interaction?

3.4 (a) Group the following functions under appropriate headings, assuming that they are to form the basis for a menu-driven word-processing system – the headings you choose will become the menu titles, with the functions appearing under the appropriate one. You can choose as many or as few menu headings as you wish. You may also alter the wordings of the functions slightly if you wish.

save, save as, new, delete, open mail, send mail, quit, undo, table, glossary, preferences, character style, format paragraph, lay out document, position on page, plain text, bold text, italic text, underline, open file, close file, open copy of file, increase point size, decrease point size, change font, add footnote, cut, copy, paste, clear, repaginate, add page break, insert graphic, insert index entry, print, print preview, page setup, view page, find word, change word, go to, go back, check spelling, view index, see table of contents, count words, renumber pages, repeat edit, show alternative document, help

(b) If possible, show someone else your headings, and ask them to group the functions under your headings. Compare their groupings with yours. You should find that there are areas of great similarity, and some differences. Discuss the similarities and discrepancies.

Why do some functions always seem to be grouped together?
Why do some groups of functions always get categorized correctly?
Why are some less easy to place under the 'correct' heading?
Why is this important?

3.5 Using your function groupings from Exercise 3.4, count the number of items in your menus.

(a) What is the average?
What is the disadvantage of putting all the functions on the screen at once?
What is the problem with using lots of menu headings?
What is the problem of using very few menu headings?

Consider the following: I can group my functions either into three menus, with lots of functions in each one, or into eight menus with fewer in each. Which will be easier to use? Why?

(b) *Optional experiment*
Design an experiment to test your answers. Perform the experiment and report on your results.

3.6 Describe (in words as well as graphically) the interaction framework introduced in *Human–Computer Interaction*. Show how it can be used to explain problems in the dialog between a user and a computer.

3.7 Describe briefly four different interaction styles used to accommodate the dialog between user and computer.

3.8 The typical computer screen has a WIMP setup (what does WIMP stand for?). Most common WIMP arrangements work on the basis of a desktop metaphor, in which common actions are likened to similar actions in the real world. For example, moving a file is achieved by selecting it and dragging it into a relevant folder or filing cabinet. The advantage of using a metaphor is that the user can identify with the environment presented on the screen. Having a metaphor allows users to predict the outcome of their actions more easily.

Note that the metaphor can break down, however. What is the real-world equivalent of formatting a disk? Is there a direct analogy for the concept of 'undo'? Think of some more examples yourself.

RECOMMENDED READING

D. A. Norman, *The Psychology of Everyday Things*, Basic Books, 1988. (Republished as *The Design of Everyday Things* by Penguin, 1991.)
A classic text, which discusses psychological issues in designing everyday objects and addresses why such objects are often so difficult to use. Discusses the execution–evaluation cycle. Very readable and entertaining. See also his more recent books *Turn Signals are the Facial Expressions of Automobiles* [267], *Things That Make Us Smart* [268] and *The Invisible Computer* [269].

R. W. Bailey, *Human Performance Engineering: A Guide for System Designers*, Prentice Hall, 1982.
Detailed coverage of human factors and ergonomics issues, with plenty of examples.

G. Salvendy, *Handbook of Human Factors and Ergonomics*, John Wiley, 1997.
Comprehensive collection of contributions from experts in human factors and ergonomics.

M. Helander, editor, *Handbook of Human–Computer Interaction. Part II: User Interface Design*, North-Holland, 1988.
Comprehensive coverage of interface styles.

J. Raskin, *The Humane Interface: New Directions for Designing Interactive Systems*, Addison Wesley, 2000.
Jef Raskin was one of the central designers of the original Mac user interface. This book gives a personal, deep and practical examination of many issues of interaction and its application in user interface design.

M. Blythe, A. Monk, K. Overbeeke and P. Wright, editors, *Funology: From Usability to Enjoyment*, Kluwer, 2003.
This is an edited book with chapters covering many areas of user experience. It includes an extensive review of theory from many disciplines from psychology to literary theory and chapters giving design frameworks based on these. The theoretical and design base is grounded by many examples and case studies including a detailed analysis of virtual crackers.

4

PARADIGMS

OVERVIEW

- Examples of effective strategies for building interactive systems provide paradigms for designing usable interactive systems.

- The evolution of these usability paradigms also provides a good perspective on the history of interactive computing.

- These paradigms range from the introduction of time-sharing computers, through the WIMP and web, to ubiquitous and context-aware computing.

4.1 INTRODUCTION

As we noted in Chapter 3, the primary objective of an interactive system is to allow the user to achieve particular goals in some application domain, that is, the interactive system must be usable. The designer of an interactive system, then, is posed with two open questions:

1. How can an interactive system be developed to ensure its usability?
2. How can the usability of an interactive system be demonstrated or measured?

One approach to answering these questions is by means of example, in which successful interactive systems are commonly believed to enhance usability and, therefore, serve as *paradigms* for the development of future products.

We believe that we now build interactive systems that are more usable than those built in the past. We also believe that there is considerable room for improvement in designing more usable systems in the future. As discussed in Chapter 2, the great advances in computer technology have increased the power of machines and enhanced the bandwidth of communication between humans and computers. The impact of technology alone, however, is not sufficient to enhance its usability. As our machines have become more powerful, the key to increased usability has come from the creative and considered application of the technology to accommodate and augment the power of the human. Paradigms for interaction have for the most part been dependent upon technological advances and their creative application to enhance interaction.

In this chapter, we investigate some of the principal historical advances in interactive designs. What is important to notice here is that the techniques and designs mentioned are recognized as major improvements in interaction, though it is sometimes hard to find a consensus for the reason behind the success. It is even harder to predict ahead what the new paradigms will be. Often new paradigms have arisen through exploratory designs that have then been seen, after the fact, to have created a new base point for future design.

We will discuss 15 different paradigms in this chapter. They do not provide mutually exclusive categories, as particular systems will often incorporate ideas from more than one of the following paradigms. In a way, this chapter serves as a history of interactive system development, though our emphasis is not so much on historical accuracy as on interactive innovation. We are concerned with the advances in interaction provided by each paradigm.

4.2 PARADIGMS FOR INTERACTION

4.2.1 Time sharing

In the 1940s and 1950s, the significant advances in computing consisted of new hardware technologies. Mechanical relays were replaced by vacuum electron tubes. Tubes were replaced by transistors, and transistors by integrated chips, all of which meant that the amount of sheer computing power was increasing by orders of magnitude. By the 1960s it was becoming apparent that the explosion of growth in computing power would be wasted if there was not an equivalent explosion of ideas about how to channel that power. One of the leading advocates of research into human-centered applications of computer technology was J. C. R. Licklider, who became the director of the Information Processing Techniques Office of the US Department of Defense's Advanced Research Projects Agency (ARPA). It was Licklider's goal to finance various research centers across the United States in order to encourage new ideas about how best to apply the burgeoning computing technology.

One of the major contributions to come out of this new emphasis in research was the concept of *time sharing*, in which a single computer could support multiple users. Previously, the human (or more accurately, the programmer) was restricted to batch sessions, in which complete jobs were submitted on punched cards or paper tape to an operator who would then run them individually on the computer. Time-sharing systems of the 1960s made programming a truly interactive venture and brought about a subculture of programmers known as 'hackers' – single-minded masters of detail who took pleasure in understanding complexity. Though the purpose of the first interactive time-sharing systems was simply to augment the programming capabilities of the early hackers, it marked a significant stage in computer applications for human use. Rather than rely on a model of interaction as a pre-planned activity that resulted in a complete set of instructions being laid out for the computer to follow, truly interactive exchange between programmer and computer was possible. The computer could now project itself as a dedicated partner with each individual user and the increased throughput of information between user and computer allowed the human to become a more reactive and spontaneous collaborator. Indeed, with the advent of time sharing, real human–computer interaction was now possible.

4.2.2 Video display units

As early as the mid-1950s researchers were experimenting with the possibility of presenting and manipulating information from a computer in the form of images on a video display unit (VDU). These display screens could provide a more suitable medium than a paper printout for presenting vast quantities of strategic information for rapid assimilation. The earliest applications of display screen images were developed in military applications, most notably the Semi-Automatic Ground Environment (SAGE) project of the US Air Force. It was not until 1962, however, when a young graduate student at the Massachusetts Institute of Technology (MIT), Ivan Sutherland, astonished the established computer science community with his *Sketchpad* program, that the capabilities of visual images were realized. As described in Howard Rheingold's history of computing book *Tools for Thought* [305]:

> Sketchpad allowed a computer operator to use the computer to create, very rapidly, sophisticated visual models on a display screen that resembled a television set. The visual patterns could be stored in the computer's memory like any other data, and could be manipulated by the computer's processor. . . . But Sketchpad was much more

than a tool for creating visual displays. It was a kind of simulation language that enabled computers to translate abstractions into perceptually concrete forms. And it was a model for totally new ways of operating computers; by changing something on the display screen, it was possible, via Sketchpad, to change something in the computer's memory.

Sketchpad demonstrated two important ideas. First, computers could be used for more than just data processing. They could extend the user's ability to abstract away from some levels of detail, visualizing and manipulating different representations of the same information. Those abstractions did not have to be limited to representations in terms of bit sequences deep within the recesses of computer memory. Rather, the abstractions could be made truly visual. To enhance human interaction, the information within the computer was made more amenable to human consumption. The computer was made to speak a more human language, instead of the human being forced to speak more like a computer. Secondly, Sutherland's efforts demonstrated how important the contribution of one creative mind (coupled with a dogged determination to see the idea through) could be to the entire history of computing.

4.2.3 Programming toolkits

Douglas Engelbart's ambition since the early 1950s was to use computer technology as a means of complementing human problem-solving activity. Engelbart's idea as a graduate student at the University of California at Berkeley was to use the computer to teach humans. This dream of naïve human users actually learning from a computer was a stark contrast to the prevailing attitude of his contemporaries that computers were a purposely complex technology that only the intellectually privileged were capable of manipulating. Engelbart's dedicated research team at the Stanford Research Institute in the 1960s worked towards achieving the manifesto set forth in an article published in 1963 [124]:

> By 'augmenting man's intellect' we mean increasing the capability of a man to approach a complex problem situation, gain comprehension to suit his particular needs, and to derive solutions to problems. . . . We refer to a way of life in an integrated domain where hunches, cut-and-try, intangibles, and the human 'feel for the situation' usefully coexist with powerful concepts, streamlined terminology and notation, sophisticated methods, and high-powered electronic aids.

Many of the ideas that Engelbart's team developed at the Augmentation Research Center – such as word processing and the mouse – only attained mass commercial success decades after their invention. A live demonstration of his oNLine System (NLS, also later known as NLS/Augment) was given in the autumn of 1968 at the Fall Joint Computer Conference in San Francisco before a captivated audience of computer sceptics. We are not so concerned here with the interaction techniques that were present in NLS, as many of those will be discussed later. What is important here is the method that Engelbart's team adopted in creating their very innovative and powerful interactive systems with the relatively impoverished technology of the 1960s.

Engelbart wrote of how humans attack complex intellectual problems like a carpenter who produces beautifully complicated pieces of woodwork with a good set of tools. The secret to producing computing equipment that aided human problem-solving ability was in providing the right *toolkit*. Taking this message to heart, his team of programmers concentrated on developing the set of programming tools they would require in order to build more complex interactive systems. The idea of building components of a computer system that will allow you to rebuild a more complex system is called bootstrapping and has been used to a great extent in all of computing. The power of programming toolkits is that small, well-understood components can be composed in fixed ways in order to create larger tools. Once these larger tools become understood, they can continue to be composed with other tools, and the process continues.

4.2.4 Personal computing

Programming toolkits provide a means for those with substantial computing skills to increase their productivity greatly. But Engelbart's vision was not exclusive to the computer literate. The decade of the 1970s saw the emergence of computing power aimed at the masses, computer literate or not. One of the first demonstrations that the powerful tools of the hacker could be made accessible to the computer novice was a graphics programming language for children called LOGO. The inventor, Seymour Papert, wanted to develop a language that was easy for children to use. He and his colleagues from MIT and elsewhere designed a computer-controlled mechanical turtle that dragged a pen along a surface to trace its path. A child could quite easily pretend they were 'inside' the turtle and direct it to trace out simple geometric shapes, such as a square or a circle. By typing in English phrases, such as `Go forward` or `Turn left`, the child/programmer could teach the turtle to draw more and more complicated figures. By adapting the graphical programming language to a model which children could understand and use, Papert demonstrated a valuable maxim for interactive system development – no matter how powerful a system may be, it will always be more powerful if it is easier to use.

Alan Kay was profoundly influenced by the work of both Engelbart and Papert. He realized that the power of a system such as NLS was only going to be successful if it was as accessible to novice users as was LOGO. In the early 1970s his view of the future of computing was embodied in small, powerful machines which were dedicated to single users, that is *personal computers*. Together with the founding team of researchers at the Xerox Palo Alto Research Center (PARC), Kay worked on incorporating a powerful and simple visually based programming environment, Smalltalk, for the personal computing hardware that was just becoming feasible. As technology progresses, it is now becoming more difficult to distinguish between what constitutes a personal computer, or workstation, and what constitutes a mainframe. Kay's vision in the mid-1970s of the ultimate handheld personal computer – he called it the Dynabook – outstrips even the technology we have available today [197].

4.2.5 Window systems and the WIMP interface

With the advent and immense commercial success of personal computing, the emphasis for increasing the usability of computing technology focussed on addressing the single user who engaged in a dialog with the computer in order to complete some work. Humans are able to think about more than one thing at a time, and in accomplishing some piece of work, they frequently interrupt their current train of thought to pursue some other related piece of work. A personal computer system which forces the user to progress in order through all of the tasks needed to achieve some objective, from beginning to end without any diversions, does not correspond to that standard working pattern. If the personal computer is to be an effective dialog partner, it must be as flexible in its ability to 'change the topic' as the human is.

But the ability to address the needs of a different user task is not the only requirement. Computer systems for the most part react to stimuli provided by the user, so they are quite amenable to a wandering dialog initiated by the user. As the user engages in more than one plan of activity over a stretch of time, it becomes difficult for him to maintain the status of the overlapping threads of activity. It is therefore necessary for the computer dialog partner to present the context of each thread of dialog so that the user can distinguish them.

One presentation mechanism for achieving this dialog partitioning is to separate physically the presentation of the different logical threads of user–computer conversation on the display device. The *window* is the common mechanism associated with these physically and logically separate display spaces. We discussed windowing systems in detail in Chapter 3.

Interaction based on windows, icons, menus and pointers – the WIMP interface – is now commonplace. These interaction devices first appeared in the commercial marketplace in April 1981, when Xerox Corporation introduced the 8010 Star Information System. But many of the interaction techniques underlying a windowing system were used in Engelbart's group in NLS and at Xerox PARC in the experimental precursor to Star, the Alto.

4.2.6 The metaphor

In developing the LOGO language to teach children, Papert used the metaphor of a turtle dragging its tail in the dirt. Children could quickly identify with the real-world phenomenon and that instant familiarity gave them an understanding of how they could create pictures. Metaphors are used quite successfully to teach new concepts in terms of ones which are already understood, as we saw when looking at analogy in Chapter 1. It is no surprise that this general teaching mechanism has been successful in introducing computer novices to relatively foreign interaction techniques. We have already seen how metaphors are used to describe the functionality of many interaction widgets, such as windows, menus, buttons and palettes. Tremendous commercial successes in computing have arisen directly from a judicious choice of metaphor. The Xerox Alto and Star were the first workstations based on the metaphor of the office desktop. The majority of the management tasks on a standard workstation have to do with file manipulation. Linking the set of tasks associated with file manipulation to the filing tasks in a typical office environment makes the actual computerized tasks easier to understand at first. The success of the desktop metaphor is unquestionable. Another good example in the personal computing domain is the widespread use of the spreadsheet metaphor for accounting and financial modeling.

Very few will debate the value of a good metaphor for increasing the initial familiarity between user and computer application. The danger of a metaphor is usually realized after the initial honeymoon period. When word processors were first introduced, they relied heavily on the typewriter metaphor. The keyboard of a computer closely resembles that of a standard typewriter, so it seems like a good metaphor from which to start. However, the behavior of a word processor is different from any typewriter. For example, the space key on a typewriter is passive, producing nothing on the piece of paper and just moving the guide further along the current line. For a typewriter, a space is not a character. However, for a word processor, the blank space *is* a character which must be inserted within a text just as any other character is inserted. So an experienced typist is not going to be able to predict correctly the behavior of pressing the spacebar on the keyboard by appealing to his experience with a typewriter. Whereas the typewriter metaphor is beneficial for providing a preliminary understanding of a word processor, the analogy is inadequate for promoting a full understanding of how the word processor works. In fact, the metaphor gets in the way of the user understanding the computer.

A similar problem arises with most metaphors. Although the desktop metaphor is initially appealing, it falls short in the computing world because there are no office equivalents for ejecting a floppy disk or printing a document. When designers try too hard to make the metaphor stick, the resulting system can be more confusing. Who thinks it is intuitive to drag the icon of a floppy disk to the wastebasket in order to eject it from the system? Ordinarily, the wastebasket is used to dispose of things that we never want to use again, which is why it works for deleting files. We must accept that some of the tasks we perform with a computer do not have real-world equivalents, or if they do, we cannot expect a single metaphor to account for all of them.

Another problem with a metaphor is the cultural bias that it portrays. With the growing internationalization of software, it should not be assumed that a metaphor will apply across national boundaries. A meaningless metaphor will only add another layer of complexity between the user and the system.

A more extreme example of metaphor occurs with *virtual reality* systems. In a VR system, the metaphor is not simply captured on a display screen. Rather, the user is also portrayed within the metaphor, literally creating an alternative, or virtual, reality. Any actions that the user performs are supposed to become more natural and so more movements of the user are interpreted, instead of just keypresses, button clicks and movements of an external pointing device. A VR system also needs to know the location and orientation of the user. Consequently, the user is often 'rigged' with special tracking devices so that the system can locate them and interpret their motion correctly.

4.2.7 Direct manipulation

In the early 1980s as the price of fast and high-quality graphics hardware was steadily decreasing, designers were beginning to see that their products were gaining popularity as their visual content increased. As long as the user–system dialog remained largely unidirectional – from user command to system command line prompt – computing was going to stay within the minority population of the hackers who revelled in the challenge of complexity. In a standard command line interface, the only way to get any feedback on the results of previous interaction is to know that you have to ask for it and to know how to ask for it. Rapid visual and audio *feedback* on a high-resolution display screen or through a high-quality sound system makes it possible to provide evaluative information for every executed user action.

Rapid feedback is just one feature of the interaction technique known as *direct manipulation*. Ben Shneiderman [320, 321] is attributed with coining this phrase in 1982 to describe the appeal of graphics-based interactive systems such as Sketchpad and the Xerox Alto and Star. He highlights the following features of a direct manipulation interface:

- visibility of the objects of interest
- incremental action at the interface with rapid feedback on all actions
- reversibility of all actions, so that users are encouraged to explore without severe penalties
- syntactic correctness of all actions, so that every user action is a legal operation
- replacement of complex command languages with actions to manipulate directly the visible objects (and, hence, the name direct manipulation).

The first real commercial success which demonstrated the inherent usability of direct manipulation interfaces for the general public was the Macintosh personal computer, introduced by Apple Computer, Inc. in 1984 after the relatively unsuccessful marketing attempt in the business community of the similar but more pricey Lisa computer. We discussed earlier how the desktop metaphor makes the computer domain of file management, usually described in terms of files and directories, easier to grasp by likening it to filing in the typical office environment, usually described in terms of documents and folders. The direct manipulation interface for the desktop metaphor requires that the documents and folders are made visible to the user as icons which represent the underlying files and directories. An operation such as moving a file from one directory to another is mirrored as an action on the visible document which is 'picked up and dragged' along the desktop from one folder to the next. In a command line interface to a filing system, it is normal that typographical errors in constructing the command line for a move operation would result in a syntactically incorrect command (for example, mistyping the file's name results in an error if you are fortunate enough not to spell accidentally the name of another file in the process). It is impossible to formulate a syntactically incorrect move operation with the pick-up-and-drag style of command. It is still possible for errors to occur at a deeper level, as the user might move a document to the wrong place, but it is relatively easy to detect and recover from those errors. While the document is dragged, continual visual feedback is provided, creating the illusion that the user is actually working in the world of the desktop and not just using the metaphor to help him understand.

Ed Hutchins, Jim Hollan and Donald Norman [187] provide a more psychological justification in terms of the *model-world metaphor* for the directness that the above example suggests. In Norman and Draper's collection of papers on user-centered design [270] they write:

> In a system built on the model-world metaphor, the interface is itself a world where the user can act, and which changes state in response to user actions. The world of interest is explicitly represented and there is no intermediary between user and world. Appropriate use of the model-world metaphor can create the sensation in the user of acting upon the objects of the task domain themselves. We call this aspect of directness *direct engagement*.

In the model-world metaphor, the role of the interface is not so much one of mediating between the user and the underlying system. From the user's perspective, the interface *is* the system.

A consequence of the direct manipulation paradigm is that there is no longer a clear distinction between input and output. In the interaction framework in Chapter 3 we talked about a user articulating input expressions in some input language and observing the system-generated output expressions in some output language. In a direct manipulation system, the output expressions are used to formulate subsequent input expressions. The document icon is an output expression in the desktop metaphor, but that icon is used by the user to articulate the move operation. This aggregation of input and output is reflected in the programming toolkits, as widgets are not considered as input or output objects exclusively. Rather, widgets embody both input and output languages, so we consider them as *interaction objects*.

Somewhat related to the visualization provided by direct manipulation is the *WYSIWYG* paradigm, which stands for 'what you see is what you get'. What you see on a display screen, for example when you are using a word processor, is not the actual document that you will be producing in the end. Rather, it is a representation or rendering of what that final document will look like. The implication with a WYSIWYG interface is that the difference between the representation and the final product is minimal, and the user is easily able to visualize the final product from the computer's representation. So, in the word-processing example, you would be able to see what the overall layout of your document would be from its image on screen, minimizing any guesswork on your part to format the final printed copy.

With WYSIWYG interfaces, it is the simplicity and immediacy of the mapping between representation and final product that matters. In terms of the interaction framework, the observation of an output expression is made simple so that assessment of goal achievement is straightforward. But WYSIWYG is not a panacea for usability. What you see is all you get! In the case of a word processor, it is difficult to achieve more sophisticated page design if you must always see the results of the layout on screen. For example, suppose you want to include a picture in a document you are writing. You design the picture and then place it in the current draft of your document, positioning it at the top of the page on which it is first referenced. As you make changes to the paper, the position of the picture will change. If you still want it to appear at the top of a page, you will no doubt have to make adjustments to the document. It would be easier if you only had to include the picture once, with a directive that it should be positioned at the top of the printed page, whether or not it appears that way on screen. You might sacrifice the WYSIWYG principle in order to make it easier to incorporate such floatable objects in your documents.

Worked exercise *Discuss the ways in which a full-page word processor is or is not a direct manipulation interface for editing a document using Shneiderman's criteria. What features of a modern word processor break the metaphor of composition with pen (or typewriter) and paper?*

Answer We will answer the first point by evaluating the word processor relative to the criteria for direct manipulation given by Shneiderman.

Visibility of the objects of interest
The most important objects of interest in a word processor are the words themselves. Indeed, the visibility of the text on a continual basis was one of the major usability advances in moving from line-oriented to display-oriented editors. Depending on the user's application, there may be other objects of interest in word processing that may or may not be visible. For example, are the margins for the text on screen similar to the ones which would eventually be printed? Is the spacing within a line and the line breaks similar? Are the different fonts and formatting characteristics of the text visible (without altering the spacing)? Expressed in this way, we can see the visibility criterion for direct manipulation as very similar to the criteria for a WYSIWYG interface.

Incremental action at the interface with rapid feedback on all actions
We expect from a word processor that characters appear in the text as we type them in at the keyboard, with little delay. If we are inserting text on a page, we might also expect that the format of the page adjust immediately to accommodate the new changes. Various word processors do this reformatting immediately, whereas with others changes in page breaks may take some time to be reflected. One of the other important actions which requires incremental and rapid feedback is movement of the window using the scroll button. If there is a significant delay between the input command to move the window down and the actual movement of the window on screen, it is quite possible that the user will 'overshoot' the target when using the scrollbar button.

Reversibility of all actions, so that users are encouraged to explore without severe penalties
Single-step undo commands in most word processors allow the user to recover from the last action performed. One problem with this is that the user must recognize the error before doing any other action. More sophisticated undo facilities allow the user to retrace back more than one command at a time. The kind of exploration this reversibility provides in a word processor is best evidenced with the ease of experimentation that is now available for formatting changes in a document (font types and sizes and margin changes). One problem with the ease of exploration is that emphasis may move to the look of a document rather than what the text actually says (style over content).

**Syntactic correctness of all actions, so that every user action is
a legal operation**

WYSIWYG word processors usually provide menus and buttons which the user uses
to articulate many commands. These interaction mechanisms serve to constrain the
input language to allow only legal input from the user. Document markup systems,
such as HTML and LaTeX, force the user to insert textual commands (which may be
erroneously entered by the user) to achieve desired formatting effects.

**Replacement of complex command languages with actions to manipulate
directly the visible objects**

The case for word processors is similar to that described above for syntactic correctness. In addition, operations on portions of text are achieved many times by allowing
the user to highlight the text directly with a mouse (or arrow keys). Subsequent action
on that text, such as moving it or copying it to somewhere else, can then be achieved
more directly by allowing the user to 'drag' the selected text via the mouse to its new
location.

To answer the second question concerning the drawback of the pen (or typewriter)
metaphor for word processing, we refer to the discussion on metaphors in Section
4.2.6. The example there compares the functionality of the space key in typewriting versus word processing. For a typewriter, the space key is passive; it merely moves the
insertion point one space to the right. In a word processor, the space key is active,
as it inserts a character (the space character) into the document. The functionality of
the typewriter space key is produced by the movement keys for the word processor
(typically an arrow key pointing right to move forward within one line). In fact, much of
the functionality that we have come to expect of a word processor is radically different
from that expected of a typewriter, so much so that the typewriter as a metaphor for
word processing is not all that instructive. In practice, modern typewriters have begun
to borrow from word processors when defining their functionality!

4.2.8 Language versus action

Whereas it is true that direct manipulation interfaces make some tasks easier to perform correctly, it is equally true that some tasks are more difficult, if not impossible.
Contrary to popular wisdom, it is not generally true that actions speak louder than
words. The image we projected for direct manipulation was of the interface as a
replacement for the underlying system as the world of interest to the user. Actions
performed at the interface replace any need to understand their meaning at any
deeper, system level. Another image is of the interface as the interlocutor or medi-
ator between the user and the system. The user gives the interface instructions and it
is then the responsibility of the interface to see that those instructions are carried out.
The user–system communication is by means of indirect language instead of direct
actions.

We can attach two meaningful interpretations to this language paradigm. The first
requires that the user understands how the underlying system functions and the

interface as interlocutor need not perform much translation. In fact, this interpretation of the language paradigm is similar to the kind of interaction which existed before direct manipulation interfaces were around. In a way, we have come full circle!

The second interpretation does not require the user to understand the underlying system's structure. The interface serves a more active role, as it must interpret between the intended operation as requested by the user and the possible system operations that must be invoked to satisfy that intent. Because it is more active, some people refer to the interface as an *agent* in these circumstances. We can see this kind of language paradigm at work in an information retrieval system. You may know what kind of information is in some internal system database, such as the UK highway code, but you would not know how that information is organized. If you had a question about speed limits on various roads, how would you ask? The answer in this case is that you would ask the question in whatever way it comes to mind, typing in a question such as, 'What are the speed limits on different roads?' You then leave it up to the interface agent to reinterpret your request as a legal query to the highway code database.

Whatever interpretation we attach to the language paradigm, it is clear that it has advantages and disadvantages when compared with the action paradigm implied by direct manipulation interfaces. In the action paradigm, it is often much easier to perform simple tasks without risk of certain classes of error. For example, recognizing and pointing to an object reduces the difficulty of identification and the possibility of misidentification. On the other hand, more complicated tasks are often rather tedious to perform in the action paradigm, as they require repeated execution of the same procedure with only minor modification. In the language paradigm, there is the possibility of describing a generic procedure once (for example, a looping construct which will perform a routine manipulation on all files in a directory) and then leaving it to be executed without further user intervention.

The action and language paradigms need not be completely separate. In the above example, we distinguished between the two paradigms by saying that we can describe generic and repeatable procedures in the language paradigm and not in the action paradigm. An interesting combination of the two occurs in *programming by example* when a user can perform some routine tasks in the action paradigm and the system records this as a generic procedure. In a sense, the system is interpreting the user's actions as a language script which it can then follow.

4.2.9 Hypertext

In 1945, Vannevar Bush, then the highest-ranking scientific administrator in the US war effort, published an article entitled 'As We May Think' in *The Atlantic Monthly*. Bush was in charge of over 6000 scientists who had greatly pushed back the frontiers of scientific knowledge during the Second World War. He recognized that a major drawback of these prolific research efforts was that it was becoming increasingly difficult to keep in touch with the growing body of scientific knowledge in the literature. In his opinion, the greatest advantages of this scientific revolution were to be gained by those individuals who were able to keep abreast of an ever-increasing flow of information. To that end, he described an innovative and futuristic information storage and retrieval apparatus – the *memex* – which was constructed with technology wholly existing in 1945 and aimed at increasing the human capacity to store and retrieve connected pieces of knowledge by mimicking our ability to create random associative links.

The memex was essentially a desk with the ability to produce and store a massive quantity of photographic copies of documented information. In addition to its huge storage capacity, the memex could keep track of links between parts of different documents. In this way, the stored information would resemble a vast interconnected mesh of data, similar to how many perceive information is stored in the human brain. In the context of scientific literature, where it is often very difficult to keep track of the origins and interrelations of the ever-growing body of research, a device which explicitly stored that information would be an invaluable asset.

We have already discussed some of the contributions of 'disciples' of Bush's vision – Douglas Engelbart and Alan Kay. One other follower was equally influenced by the ideas behind the memex, though his dreams have not yet materialized to the extent of Engelbart's and Kay's. Ted Nelson was another graduate student/dropout whose research agenda was forever transformed by the advent of the computer. An unsuccessful attempt to create a machine language equivalent of the memex on early 1960s computer hardware led Nelson on a lifelong quest to produce *Xanadu*, a potentially revolutionary worldwide publishing and information retrieval system based on the idea of interconnected, non-linear text and other media forms. A traditional paper is read from beginning to end, in a linear fashion. But within that text, there are often ideas or footnotes that urge the reader to digress into a richer topic. The linear format for information does not provide much support for this random and associated browsing task. What Bush's memex suggested was to preserve the non-linear browsing structure in the actual documentation. Nelson coined the phrase *hypertext* in the mid-1960s to reflect this non-linear text structure.

It was nearly two decades after Nelson coined the term that the first hypertext systems came into commercial use. In order to reflect the use of such non-linear and associative linking schemes for more than just the storage and retrieval of textual information, the term *hypermedia* (or *multimedia*) is used for non-linear storage of all forms of electronic media. We will discuss these systems in Part 4 of this book (see Chapter 21). Most of the riches won with the success of hypertext and hypermedia were not gained by Nelson, though his project Xanadu survives to this day.

4.2.10 Multi-modality

The majority of interactive systems still use the traditional keyboard and a pointing device, such as a mouse, for input and are restricted to a color display screen with some sound capabilities for output. Each of these input and output devices can be considered as communication channels for the system and they correspond to certain human communication channels, as we saw in Chapter 1. A *multi-modal* interactive system is a system that relies on the use of multiple human communication channels. Each different channel for the user is referred to as a modality of interaction. In this sense, all interactive systems can be considered multi-modal, for humans have always used their visual and haptic (touch) channels in manipulating a computer. In fact, we often use our audio channel to hear whether the computer is actually running properly.

However, genuine multi-modal systems rely to a greater extent on simultaneous use of multiple communication channels for both input and output. Humans quite naturally process information by simultaneous use of different channels. We point to someone and refer to them as 'you', and it is only by interpreting the simultaneous use of voice and touch that our directions are easily articulated and understood. Designers have wanted to mimic this flexibility in both articulation and observation by extending the input and output expressions an interactive system will support. So, for example, we can modify a gesture made with a pointing device by speaking, indicating what operation is to be performed on the selected object.

Multi-modal, multimedia and virtual reality systems form a large core of current research in interactive system design. These are discussed in more detail in Chapters 10, 20 and 21.

4.2.11 Computer-supported cooperative work

Another development in computing in the 1960s was the establishment of the first computer networks which allowed communication between separate machines. Personal computing was all about providing individuals with enough computing power so that they were liberated from dumb terminals which operated on a time-sharing system. It is interesting to note that as computer networks became widespread, individuals retained their powerful workstations but now wanted to reconnect themselves to the rest of the workstations in their immediate working environment, and even throughout the world! One result of this reconnection was the emergence of collaboration between individuals via the computer – called computer-supported cooperative work, or CSCW.

The main distinction between CSCW systems and interactive systems designed for a single user is that designers can no longer neglect the society within which any single user operates. CSCW systems are built to allow interaction between humans via the computer and so the needs of the many must be represented in the one product. A fine example of a CSCW system is electronic mail – *email* – yet another metaphor by which individuals at physically separate locations can communicate via electronic messages which work in a similar way to conventional postal systems. One user can compose a message and 'post' it to another user (specified by his electronic mail address). When the message arrives at the remote user's site, he is informed that a new message has arrived in his 'mailbox'. He can then read the message and respond as desired. Although email is modeled after conventional postal systems, its major advantage is that it is often much faster than the traditional system (jokingly referred to by email devotees as 'snail mail'). Communication turnarounds between sites across the world are in the order of minutes, as opposed to weeks.

Electronic mail is an instance of an asynchronous CSCW system because the participants in the electronic exchange do not have to be working at the same time in order for the mail to be delivered. The reason we use email is precisely because of its asynchronous characteristics. All we need to know is that the recipient will eventually receive the message. In contrast, it might be desirable for synchronous communication, which would require the simultaneous participation of sender and recipient, as in a phone conversation.

CSCW is a major emerging topic in current HCI research, and so we devote much more attention to it later in this book. CSCW systems built to support users working in groups are referred to as *groupware*. Chapter 19 discusses groupware systems in depth. In Chapter 14 the more general issues and theories arising from CSCW are discussed.

4.2.12 The world wide web

Probably the most significant recent development in interactive computing is the world wide web, often referred to as just the web, or WWW. The web is built on top of the internet, and offers an easy to use, predominantly graphical interface to information, hiding the underlying complexities of transmission protocols, addresses and remote access to data.

The internet (see Section 2.9) is simply a collection of computers, each linked by any sort of data connection, whether it be slow telephone line and modem or high-bandwidth optical connection. The computers of the internet all communicate using common data transmission protocols (*TCP/IP*) and addressing systems (*IP* addresses and *domain names*). This makes it possible for anyone to read anything from anywhere, in theory, if it conforms to the protocol. The web builds on this with its own layer of network protocol (http), a standard markup notation (such as HTML) for laying out pages of information and a global naming scheme (uniform resource locators or URLs). Web pages can contain text, color images, movies, sound and, most important, hypertext links to other web pages. Hypermedia documents can therefore be 'published' by anyone who has access to a computer connected to the internet.

The world wide web project was conceived in 1989 by Tim Berners-Lee, working at CERN, the European Particle Physics Laboratory at Geneva, as a means to enable the widespread distribution of scientific data generated at CERN and to share information between physicists worldwide. In 1991 the first text-based web browser was released. This was followed in early 1993 by several graphical web browsers, most significantly Mosaic developed by Marc Andreesen at the National Center for Supercomputer Applications (NCSA) at Champaign, Illinois. This was the defining moment at which the meteoric growth of the web began, rapidly growing to dominate internet traffic and change the public view of computing. Of all the 'heroes' of interactive computing named in this chapter, it is only Berners-Lee who has achieved widespread public fame.

Whilst the internet has been around since 1969, it did not become a major paradigm for interaction until the advent and ease of availability of well-designed graphical interfaces (browsers) for the web. These browsers allow users to access multimedia information easily, using only a mouse to point and click. This shift towards the integration of computation and communication is transparent to users; all they realize is that they can get the current version of published information practically instantly. In addition, the language used to create these multimedia documents is relatively simple, opening the opportunity of publishing information to any literate, and connected, person. However, there are important limitations of the web as a hypertext medium and in Chapter 21 we discuss some of the special design issues for the web. Interestingly, the web did not provide any technological breakthroughs; all the required functionality previously existed, such as transmission protocols, distributed file systems, hypertext and so on. The impact has been due to the ease of use of both the browsers and HTML, and the fact that *critical mass* (see Chapter 13) was established, first in academic circles, and then rapidly expanded into the leisure and business domains. The burgeoning interest led to service providers, those providing connections to the internet, to make it cheap to connect, and a whole new subculture was born.

Currently, the web is one of the major reasons that new users are connecting to the internet (probably even buying computers in the first place), and is rapidly becoming a major activity for people both at work and for leisure. It is much more a social phenomenon than anything else, with users attracted to the idea that computers are now boxes that connect them with interesting people and exciting places to go, rather than soulless cases that deny social contact. Computing often used to be seen as an anti-social activity; the web has challenged this by offering a 'global village' with free access to information and a virtual social environment. Web culture has emphasized liberality and (at least in principle) equality regardless of gender, race and disability. In practice, the demographics of web users are only now coming close to equal proportions in terms of gender, and, although internet use is increasing globally, the vast majority of websites are still hosted in the United States. Indeed, the web is now big business; corporate images and e-commerce may soon dominate the individual and often zany aspects of the web.

4.2.13 Agent-based interfaces

In the human world agents are people who work on someone's behalf: estate agents buy and sell property for their customers, literary agents find publishers for authors, travel agents book hotels and air tickets for tourists and secret agents obtain information (secretly) for their governments. Software agents likewise act on behalf of users within the electronic world. Examples include email agents which filter your mail for you and web crawlers which search the world wide web for documents you might find interesting. Agents can perform repetitive tasks, watch and respond to events when the user is not present and even learn from the user's own actions.

Some agents simply do what they are told. For example, many email systems allow you to specify filters, simple *if then* rules, which determine the action to perform on certain kinds of mail message:

If Sender: is bank manager
Then Urgency: is high

A major problem with such agents is developing a suitable language between human and agent which allows the user to express intentions. This is especially important when the agent is going to act in the user's absence. In this case, the user may not receive feedback of any mistake until long after the effects have become irreversible; hence the instructions have to be correct, and believed to be correct.

Other agents use artificial intelligence techniques to learn based on the user's actions. An early example of this was Eager [83]. Eager watches users while they work on simple HyperCard applications. When it notices that the user is repeating similar actions a small icon appears (a smiling cat!), suggesting the next action. The user is free either to accept the suggestion or to ignore it. When the user is satisfied that Eager knows what it is doing, it can be instructed to perform all the remaining actions in a sequence.

Eager is also an example of an agent, which has a clear *embodiment*, that is, there is a representation of Eager (the cat icon) in the interface. In contrast, consider Microsoft Excel which incorporates some intelligence in its sum (Σ) function. If the current cell is directly below a column of numbers, or if there is a series of numbers to the left of the current cell, the sum range defaults to be the appropriate cells. It is also clever about columns of numbers with subtotals so that they are not included twice in the overall total. As around 80% of all spreadsheet formulae are simple sums this is a very useful feature. However, the intelligence in this is not embodied, it is diffuse, somewhere in 'the system'. Although embodiment is not essential to an agent-based system it is one of the key features which enable users to determine where autonomy and intelligence may lie, and also which parts are stable [107].

We have already discussed the relationship between language and action paradigms in human–computer interaction. To some extent agent-based systems include aspects of both. Old command-based systems acted as intermediaries: you asked them to do something, they did what you wanted (if you were lucky), and then reported the results back to you. In contrast, direct manipulation emphasizes the user's own actions, possibly augmented by tools, on the electronic world. Agents act on the user's behalf, possibly, but not necessarily, instructed in a linguistic fashion. But unlike the original intermediary paradigm, an agent is typically acting within a world the user could also act upon. The difference is rather like that between a traditional shopkeeper who brings items to you as opposed to a shop assistant in a supermarket who helps you as you browse amongst the aisles. The latter does not prevent you from selecting your own items from the shelves, but aids you when asked.

In fact, the proponents of direct manipulation and agent-based systems do not see the paradigms as being quite as complementary as we have described them above. Although amicable, the positions on each side are quite entrenched.

4.2.14 Ubiquitous computing

Where does computing happen, and more importantly, where do we as users go to interact with a computer? The past 50 years of interactive computing show that we still think of computers as being confined to a box on a desk or in an office or lab. The actual form of the physical interface has been transformed from a noisy teletype terminal to a large, graphical display with a WIMP or natural language interface, but in all cases the user knows where the computer is and must walk over to it to begin interacting with it.

In the late 1980s, a group of researchers at Xerox PARC, led by Mark Weiser, initiated a research program with the goal of moving human–computer interaction away from the desktop and out into our everyday lives. Weiser observed:

> The most profound technologies are those that disappear. They weave themselves into the fabric of everyday life until they are indistinguishable from it.

These words have inspired a new generation of researchers in the area of *ubiquitous computing* [369, 370]. Another popular term for this emerging paradigm is *pervasive* computing, first coined by IBM. The intention is to create a computing infrastructure that permeates our physical environment so much that we do not notice the computer any longer. A good analogy for the vision of ubiquitous computing is the electric motor. When the electric motor was first introduced, it was large, loud and very noticeable. Today, the average household contains so many electric motors that we hardly ever notice them anymore. Their utility led to ubiquity and, hence, invisibility.

How long in the future will it be before we no longer notice the interactive computer? To some extent, this is already happening, since many everyday items, such as watches, microwaves or automobiles, contain many microprocessors that we don't directly notice. But, to a large extent, the vision of Weiser, in which the computer is hardly ever noticed, is a long way off.

To pursue the analogy with the electric motor a little further, one of the motor's characteristics is that it comes in many sizes. Each size is suited to a particular use. Weiser thought that it was also important to think of computing technology in different sizes. The original work at PARC looked at three different scales of computing: the yard, the foot and the inch. In the middle of the scale, a foot-sized computer is much like the personal computers we are familiar with today. Its size is suitable for every individual to have one, perhaps on their desk or perhaps in their bedroom or in their briefcase. A yard-sized computer, on the other hand, is so large that it would be suitable for wide open public spaces, and would be shared by a group of people. Perhaps there would be one of these in every home, or in a public hallway or auditorium. On the opposite side of the scale, an inch-sized computer would be a truly personal computing device that could fit in the palm of a hand. Everyone would have a number of these at their disposal, and they would be as prevalent and unremarkable as a pen or a pad of sticky notes.

There is an increasing number of examples of computing devices at these different scales. At the foot scale, laptop computers are, of course, everywhere, but more interesting examples of computing at this scale are commercially available *tablet computers* or research prototypes, such as an interactive storybook (see Figure 4.1). At the yard scale, there are various forms of high-resolution large screens and projected displays as we discussed in Chapter 2 (Section 2.4.3). These are still mainly used as output-only devices showing presentations or fixed messages, but there is

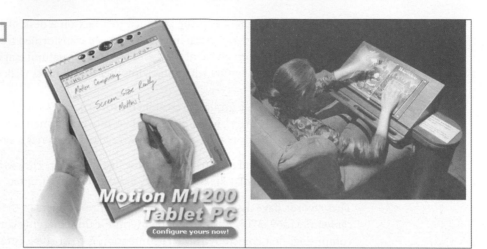

Figure 4.1 Examples of computing devices at the foot scale. On the left is a tablet computer – a Tablet PC from MotionComputing (Source: Motion Computing, Inc.). On the right is a research prototype, the Listen Reader, an interactive storybook developed at Palo Alto Research Center (picture courtesy Palo Alto Research Center)

Figure 4.2 The Stanford Interactive Mural, an example of a yard-scale interactive display surface created by tiling multiple lower-resolution projectors. Picture courtesy François Guimbretière

increasing use of more interactive shared public displays, such as the Stanford Interactive Mural shown in Figure 4.2. At the inch scale, there are many examples, from powerful, pocket-sized *personal organizers* or *personal digital assistants* (PDAs) to even smaller cellular phones or pagers, and many pocket electronic devices such as electronic dictionaries and translators (see Figure 4.3). There are even badges whose position can be automatically tracked.

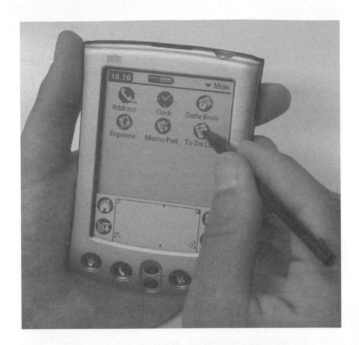

Figure 4.3 Example inch-scale devices. From left to right, a PDA, a mobile phone and pocket-sized electronic bible. Source: Top left photograph by Alan Dix (Palm Pilot Series V), bottom left photograph by Alan Dix with permission from Franklin Electronic Publishers, photograph right by Alan Dix (Ericsson phone)

This influx of diverse computing devices represents the *third wave of computing*, in which the ratio of computers to human drastically changes. In the first wave of computing, one large mainframe computer served many people. In the second wave, the PC revolution, computing devices roughly equalled the number of people using them. In the third wave, the devices far outnumber the people. It is precisely because of the large ratio of devices to people that Weiser and others note the importance of minimizing the attention demands of any single device.

Many different technologies are converging to make the dream of ubiquitous computing possible. These technologies include wireless networking, voice recognition, camera and vision systems, pen-based computing and positioning systems, to name a few. What all of these technologies provide is the ability to move the computer user away from a desktop, allow interaction in a number of modes (voice, gesture, handwriting) in addition to a keyboard, and make information about the user (through vision, speech recognition or positioning information) available to a computational device that may be far removed from the actual user.

Ubiquitous computing is not simply about nifty gadgets, it is what can be done with those gadgets. As Weiser pointed out, it is the applications that make ubiquitous computing revolutionary. In Chapter 20, we discuss some examples of the applications that ubiquitous computing makes possible, including the way this is becoming part of everyday life in places as diverse as the home, the car and even our own bodies. The vision of ubiquitous computing – first expressed by Weiser and grounded in experimental work done at Xerox PARC – is now starting to become reality.

4.2.15 Sensor-based and context-aware interaction

The yard-scale, foot-scale and inch-scale computers are all still clearly embodied devices with which we interact, whether or not we consider them 'computers'. There are an increasing number of proposed and existing technologies that embed computation even deeper, but unobtrusively, into day-to-day life. Weiser's dream was computers that 'permeate our physical environment so much that we do not notice the computers anymore', and the term ubiquitous computing encompasses a wide range from mobile devices to more pervasive environments.

We can consider the extreme situation in which the user is totally unaware of interaction taking place. Information can be gathered from sensors in the environment (pressure mats, ultrasonic movement detectors, weight sensors, video cameras), in our information world (web pages visited, times online, books purchased online), and even from our own bodies (heart rate, skin temperature, brain signals). This information is then used by systems that make inferences about our past patterns and current *context* in order to modify the explicit interfaces we deal with (e.g., modify default menu options) or to do things in the background (e.g., adjust the air conditioning).

We already encounter examples of this: lights that turn on when we enter a room, suggestions made for additional purchases at online bookstores, automatic doors and washbasins. For elderly and disabled people, assistive technologies already embody quite radical aspects of this. However, the vision of many is a world in which the whole environment is empowered to sense and even understand the context of activities within it.

Previous interactive computation has focussed on the user explicitly telling the computer exactly what to do and the computer doing what it is told. In *context-aware computing* the interaction is more implicit. The computer, or more accurately the sensor-enhanced environment, is using heuristics and other semi-intelligent means to predict what would be useful for the user. The data used for this inference and the inference itself are both fuzzy, probabilistic and uncertain. Automatically sensing context is, and will likely always remain, an imperfect activity, so it is important that the actions resulting from these 'intelligent' predictions be made with caution. Context-aware applications should follow the principles of *appropriate intelligence*:

1. Be right as often as possible, and useful when acting on these correct predictions.
2. Do not cause inordinate problems in the event of an action resulting from a wrong prediction.

The failure of 'intelligent' systems in the past resulted from following the first principle, but not the second. These new applications, which impinge so closely on our everyday lives, demand that the second principle of appropriate intelligence is upheld. (There is more on using intelligence in interfaces on the book website at /e3/online/intelligence/)

Arguably this is a more radical paradigm shift than any other since the introduction of interactive computing itself. Whereas ubiquitous computing challenges the idea of *where* computers are and how apparent they are to us, context-aware computing challenges *what it means to interact* with a computer. It is as if we have come full circle from the early days of computing. Large mainframes were placed in isolation from the principle users (programmers) and interaction was usually done through an intermediary operator. Half a century later, the implicit nature of interaction implied by sensing creates a human–computer relationship that becomes so seamless there is no conscious interaction at all.

This shift is so radical that one could even say it does not belong in this chapter about paradigms for interaction! In fact, this shift is so dramatic that it is unclear whether the basic models of interaction that have proved universal across technologies, for example Norman's execution–evaluation cycle (Chapter 3, Section 3.2.2), are applicable at all. We will return to this issue in Chapter 18.

4.3 SUMMARY

In this chapter, we have discussed paradigms that promote the usability of interactive systems. We have seen that the history of computing is full of examples of creative insight into how the interaction between humans and computers can be enhanced. While we expect never to replace the input of creativity in interactive system design, we still want to maximize the benefit of one good idea by repeating its benefit in many other designs. The problem with these paradigms is that they are rarely well defined. It is not always clear how they support a user in accomplishing some tasks. As a result, it is entirely possible that repeated use of some paradigm will not result in the design of a more usable system. The derivation of principles and theoretical models for interaction has often arisen out of a need to explain why a paradigm is successful and when it might not be. Principles can provide the repeatability that paradigms in themselves cannot provide. However, in defining these principles, it is all too easy to provide general and abstract definitions that are not very helpful to the designer. Therefore, the future of interactive system design relies on a complementary approach. The creativity that gives rise to new paradigms should be strengthened by the development of a theory that provides principles to support the paradigm in its repeated application. We will consider such principles and design rules in detail in Chapter 7 and more theoretical perspectives in Part 3.

EXERCISES

4.1. Choose one of the people mentioned in this chapter, or another important figure in the history of HCI, and create a web page biography on them. Try to get at least one picture of your subject, and find out about their life and work, with particular reference to their contribution to HCI.

4.2. Choose one paradigm of interaction and find three specific examples of it, not included in this chapter. Compare these three – can you identify any general principles of interaction that are embodied in each of your examples (see Chapter 7 for example principles)?

4.3. What new paradigms do you think may be significant in the future of interactive computing?

4.4. A truly ubiquitous computing experience would require the spread of computational capabilities literally everywhere. Another way to achieve ubiquity is to carry all of your computational needs with you everywhere, all the time. The field of *wearable computing* explores this interaction paradigm. How do you think the first-person emphasis of wearable computing compares with the third-person, or environmental, emphasis of ubiquitous computing? What impact would there be on context-aware computing if all of the sensors were attached to the individual instead of embedded in the environment?

RECOMMENDED READING

H. Rheingold, *Tools for Thought*, Prentice Hall, 1985.
An easy to read history of computing, with particular emphasis on developments in interactive systems. Much of the historical perspective of this chapter was influenced by this book.

T. Berners-Lee, *Weaving the Web: The Original Design and Ultimate Destiny of the World Wide Web*, Harper, 2000.
The history of the world wide web as told by its inventor Tim Berners-Lee makes interesting and enlightening reading.

M. M. Waldrop, *The Dream Machine: J.C.R. Licklider and the Revolution That Made Computing Personal*, Penguin, 2002.
A readable biography of Licklider and his pioneering work in making computing available to all.

T. Bardini, *Bootstrapping: Douglas Englebart, Coevolution and the Origins of Personal Computing (Writing Science)*, Stanford University Press, 2000.
Biography of another great pioneer of interactive computing, Doug Engelbart and his work at Stanford.

J. M. Nyce and P. Kahn, editors, and V. Bush, *From Memex to Hypertext: Vannevar Bush and the Mind's Machine*, Academic Press, 1992.
An edited collection of Bush's writing about Memex, together with essays from computing historians.

M. Weiser, Some computer science issues in ubiquitous computing, *Communications of the ACM*, Vol. 36, No. 7, pp. 75–84, July 1993.
Classic article on issues relating to ubiquitous computing, including hardware, interaction software, networks, applications and methods.

A. Dix, T. Rodden, N. Davies, J. Trevor, A. Friday and K. Palfreyman, Exploiting space and location as a design framework for interactive mobile systems, *ACM Transactions on Computer–Human Interaction (TOCHI)*, Vol. 7, No. 3, pp. 285–321, September 2000.
Explores the space of context sensitive designs focussed especially on location.

There are also a number of special journal issues on ubiquitous, sensor-based and context-aware computing in *ACM TOCHI*, *Human–Computer Interaction* and *Communications of the ACM* and dedicated journals such as *IEEE Pervasive* and *Personal Technologies Journal*.

Design process

In this part, we concentrate on how design practice addresses the critical feature of an interactive system – usability from the human perspective. The chapters in this part promote the purposeful design of more usable interactive systems. We begin in Chapter 5 by introducing the key elements in the interaction design process. These elements are then expanded in later chapters.

Chapter 6 discusses the design process in more detail, specifically focussing on the place of user-centered design within a software engineering framework. Chapter 7 highlights the range of design rules that can help us to specify usable interactive systems, including abstract principles, guidelines and other design representations

In Chapter 8, we provide an overview of implementation support for the programmer of an interactive system. Chapter 9 is concerned with the techniques used to evaluate the interactive system to see if it satisfies user needs. Chapter 10 discusses how to design a system to be universally accessible, regardless of age, gender, cultural background or ability. In Chapter 11 we discuss the provision of user support in the form of help systems and documentation.

INTERACTION DESIGN BASICS

5

OVERVIEW

Interaction design is about creating interventions in often complex situations using technology of many kinds including PC software, the web and physical devices.

- Design involves:
    - achieving goals within constraints and trade-off between these
    - understanding the raw materials: computer and human
    - accepting limitations of humans and of design.

- The design process has several stages and is iterative and never complete.

- Interaction starts with getting to know the users and their context:
    - finding out who they are and what they are like . . . probably not like you!
    - talking to them, watching them.

- Scenarios are rich design stories, which can be used and reused throughout design:
    - they help us see what users will want to do
    - they give a step-by-step walkthrough of users' interactions: including what they see, do and are thinking.

- Users need to find their way around a system. This involves:
    - helping users know where they are, where they have been and what they can do next
    - creating overall structures that are easy to understand and fit the users' needs
    - designing comprehensible screens and control panels.

- Complexity of design means we don't get it right first time:
    - so we need iteration and prototypes to try out and evaluate
    - but iteration can get trapped in *local maxima*, designs that have no simple improvements, but are not good
    - theory and models can help give good start points.

5.1   INTRODUCTION

Some of HCI is focussed on understanding: the academic study of the way people interact with technology. However, a large part of HCI is about doing things and making things – design.

In this chapter we will think about interaction design. Note that we are not just thinking about the design of interactive systems, but about the interaction itself. An office has just got a new electric stapler. It is connected to the mains electricity and is hard to move around, so when you want to staple papers together you go to the stapler. In the past when someone wanted to staple things they would take the stapler to their desk and keep it until someone else wanted it. You might write a letter, print it, staple it, write the next letter, staple it, and so on. Now you have to take the letters to be stapled across the office, so instead you write–print, write–print until you have a pile of things to staple and then take them across. The stapler influences the whole pattern of interaction.

So, interaction design is not just about the artifact that is produced, whether a physical device or a computer program, but about understanding and choosing how that is going to affect the way people work. Furthermore, the artifacts we give to people are not just these devices and programs, but also manuals, tutorials, online help systems. In some cases we may realize that no additional system is required at all, we may simply suggest a different way of using existing tools.

Because of this it may be better not to think of designing a system, or an artifact, but to think instead about *designing interventions*. The product of a design exercise is that we intervene to change the situation as it is; we hope, of course, changing it for the better!

In the next section we will ask 'what is design?' which sets the spirit for the rest of the chapter. Section 5.3 looks at the design process as a whole and this gives a framework for the following sections. Section 5.4 looks at aspects of the requirements-gathering phase of design focussed on getting to know and understand the user. This is followed in Section 5.5 by a look at scenarios, which are a way of recording existing situations and examining proposed designs. We then look at the details of designing the overall application structure in Section 5.6 and individual screen design in Section 5.7. Because design is never perfect first time (or ever!), most inter-action design involves several cycles of prototyping and evaluation. The chapter ends with an examination of the limits of this and why this emphasizes the importance of deep knowledge of more general theories and models of interaction.

This chapter also functions as an introduction to much of Part 2 and Part 3 of this book. In particular, Section 5.3 puts many of the succeeding chapters into the context of the overall design process. Many of the individual sections of this chapter give early views, or simple techniques, for issues and areas dealt with in detail later in the book.

| 5.2 | WHAT IS DESIGN? |

So what is design? A simple definition is:

achieving goals within constraints

This does not capture everything about design, but helps to focus us on certain things:

Goals   What is the purpose of the design we are intending to produce? Who is it for? Why do they want it? For example, if we are designing a wireless personal movie player, we may think about young affluent users wanting to watch the latest movies whilst on the move and download free copies, and perhaps wanting to share the experience with a few friends.

Constraints   What materials must we use? What standards must we adopt? How much can it cost? How much time do we have to develop it? Are there health and safety issues? In the case of the personal movie player: does it have to withstand rain? Must we use existing video standards to download movies? Do we need to build in copyright protection?

Of course, we cannot always achieve all our goals within the constraints. So perhaps one of the most important things about design is:

Trade-off   Choosing which goals or constraints can be relaxed so that others can be met. For example, we might find that an eye-mounted video display, a bit like those used in virtual reality, would give the most stable image whilst walking along. However, this would not allow you to show friends, and might be dangerous if you were watching a gripping part of the movie as you crossed the road.

Often the most exciting moments in design are when you get a radically different idea that allows you to satisfy several apparently contradictory constraints. However, the more common skill needed in design is to accept the conflict and choose the most appropriate trade-off. The temptation is to focus on one or other goal and optimize for this, then tweak the design to make it just satisfy the constraints and other goals. Instead, the best designs are where the designer understands the trade-offs and the factors affecting them. Paradoxically, if you focus on the trade-off itself the more radical solutions also become more apparent.

5.2.1 The golden rule of design

Part of the understanding we need is about the circumstances and context of the particular design problem. We will return to this later in the chapter. However, there are also more generic concepts to understand. The designs we produce may be different, but often the raw materials are the same. This leads us to the *golden rule of design*:

understand your materials

In the case of a physical design this is obvious. Look at a chair with a steel frame and one with a wooden frame. They are very different: often the steel frames are tubular or thin L or H section steel. In contrast wooden chairs have thicker solid legs. If you made a wooden chair using the design for a metal one it would break; if you made the metal one in the design for the wooden one it would be too heavy to move.

For Human–Computer Interaction the obvious materials are the human and the computer. That is we must:

- understand *computers*
  - limitations, capacities, tools, platforms
- understand *people*
  - psychological, social aspects, human error.

Of course, this is exactly the focus of Chapters 1 and 2. This is why they came first; we must understand the fundamental materials of human–computer interaction in order to design. In Chapters 3 and 4 we also looked at the nature of *interaction* itself. This is equally important in other design areas. For example, the way you fit seats and windows into an airplane's hull affects the safety and strength of the aircraft as a whole.

5.2.2 To err is human

It might sound demeaning to regard people as 'materials', possibly even dehumanizing. In fact, the opposite is the case: physical materials are treated better in most designs than people. This is particularly obvious when it comes to failures.

The news headlines: an aircrash claims a hundred lives; an industrial accident causes millions of pounds' worth of damage; the discovery of systematic mistreatment leads to thousands of patients being recalled to hospital. Some months later the public inquiries conclude: human error in the operation of technical instruments. The phrase 'human error' is taken to mean 'operator error', but more often than not the disaster is inherent in the design or installation of the human interface. Bad interfaces are slow or error-prone to use. Bad interfaces cost money and cost lives.

People make mistakes. This is not 'human error', an excuse to hide behind in accident reports, it is human nature. We are not infallible consistent creatures, but often make slips, errors and omissions. A concrete lintel breaks and a building collapses. Do the headlines read 'lintel error'? No. It is the nature of concrete lintels to break if they are put under stress and it is the responsibility of architect and engineer to ensure that a building only puts acceptable stress on the lintel. Similarly it is the nature of humans to make mistakes, and systems should be designed to reduce the likelihood of those mistakes and to minimize the consequences when mistakes happen.

Often when an aspect of an interface is obscure and unclear, the response is to add another line in the manual. People are remarkably adaptable and, unlike concrete lintels, can get 'stronger', but better training and documentation (although necessary) are not a panacea. Under stress, arcane or inconsistent interfaces will lead to errors.

If you design using a physical material, you need to understand how and where failures would occur and strengthen the construction, build in safety features or redundancy. Similarly, if you treat the human with as much consideration as a piece of steel or concrete, it is obvious that you need to understand the way human failures occur and build the rest of the interface accordingly.

5.2.3 The central message – the user

In this book you will find information on basic psychology, on particular technologies, on methods and models. However, there is one factor that outweighs all this knowledge. It is about attitude. Often it is said that the success of the various methods used in HCI lies not in how good they are, but in that they simply focus the mind of the designer on the user.

This is the core of interaction design: put the user first, keep the user in the center and remember the user at the end.

5.3   THE PROCESS OF DESIGN

Often HCI professionals complain that they are called in too late. A system has been designed and built, and only when it proves unusable do they think to ask how to do it right! In other companies usability is seen as equivalent to testing – checking whether people can use it and fixing problems, rather than making sure they can from the beginning. In the best companies, however, usability is designed in from the start.

In Chapter 6 we will look in detail at the software development process and how HCI fits within it. Here we'll take a simplified view of four main phases plus an iteration loop, focussed on the design of interaction (Figure 5.1).

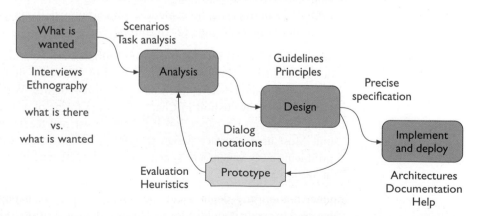

Figure 5.1   Interaction design process

Requirements – what is wanted   The first stage is establishing what exactly is needed. As a precursor to this it is usually necessary to find out what is currently happening. For example, how do people currently watch movies? What sort of personal appliances do they currently use?

There are a number of techniques used for this in HCI: interviewing people, videotaping them, looking at the documents and objects that they work with, observing them directly. We don't have a chapter dedicated to this, but aspects will be found in various places throughout the book. In particular, ethnography, a form of observation deriving from anthropology, has become very influential and is discussed in Chapter 13. We will look at some ways of addressing this stage in Section 5.4.

Analysis   The results of observation and interview need to be ordered in some way to bring out key issues and communicate with later stages of design. Chapter 15 and part of Chapter 18 deal with task models, which are a means to capture how people carry out the various tasks that are part of their work and life. In this chapter (Section 5.5), we will look at scenarios, rich stories of interaction, which can be used in conjunction with a method like task analysis or on their own to record and make vivid actual interaction. These techniques can be used both to represent the situation as it is and also the desired situation.

Design   Well, this is all about design, but there is a central stage when you move from what you want, to how to do it. There are numerous rules, guidelines and design principles that can be used to help with this and Chapter 7 discusses these in detail; whilst Chapter 10 looks at how to design taking into account many different kinds of user. We need to record our design choices in some way and there are various notations and methods to do this, including those used to record the existing situation. Chapters 16, 17 and 18 deal with ways of modeling and describing interaction. In this chapter, Section 5.6 will look at some simple notations for designing navigation within a system and some basic heuristics to guide the design of that navigation. Section 5.7 will look more closely at the layout of individual screens. It is at this stage also where input from theoretical work is most helpful, including cognitive models, organizational issues and understanding communication (Chapters 12, 13 and 14).

Iteration and prototyping   Humans are complex and we cannot expect to get designs right first time. We therefore need to evaluate a design to see how well it is working and where there can be improvements. We will discuss some techniques for evaluation in Chapter 9. Some forms of evaluation can be done using the design on paper, but it is hard to get real feedback without trying it out. Most user interface design therefore involves some form of prototyping, producing early versions of systems to try out with real users. We'll discuss this in Section 5.8.

Implementation and deployment   Finally, when we are happy with our design, we need to create it and deploy it. This will involve writing code, perhaps making hardware, writing documentation and manuals – everything that goes into a real system that can be given to others. Chapter 8 will deal with software architectures for user interfaces and there are details about implementing groupware in Chapter 19 and web interfaces in Chapter 21.

If you read all the chapters and look at all the techniques you might think 'help! how can I ever do all this?'. Of course the answer is you can't. Your time is limited – there is a trade-off between the length of the design period and the quality of the final design. This means one sometimes has to accept a design as final even if it is not perfect: it is often better to have a product that is acceptable but on time and to cost than it is to have one that has perfect interaction but is late and over budget.

It is easy to think that the goal, especially of the iterative stages, is to find usability problems and fix them. As you experience real designs, however, you soon find that the real problem is not to find faults – that is easy; nor to work out how to fix them – that may not be too difficult; instead the issue is: which usability problems is it worth fixing?

In fact, if you ever come across a system that seems to be perfect it is a badly designed system – badly designed not because the design is bad, but because too much effort will have been spent in the design process itself. Just as with all trade-offs, it may be possible to find radically different solutions that have a major effect but are cheap to implement. However, it is best not to plan assuming such bolts of inspiration will strike when wanted!

5.4   USER FOCUS

As we've already said, the start of any interaction design exercise must be the intended user or users. This is often stated as:

know your users

Because this sounds somewhat like a commandment it is sometimes even written 'know thy user' (and originally 'know the user' [162]). Note, too, a little indecision about user/users – much of traditional user interface design has focussed on a single user. We will discuss issues of collaboration extensively in Chapters 13 and 19, but even at this stage it is important to be aware that there is rarely one user of a system. This doesn't mean that every system is explicitly supporting collaboration like email does. However, almost every system has an impact beyond the person immediately using it.

Think about a stock control system. The warehouse manager queries the system to find out how many six-inch nails are in stock – just a single user? Why did he do this? Perhaps a salesperson has been asked to deliver 100,000 six-inch nails within a fortnight and wants to know if the company is able to fulfill the order in time. So the act of looking at the stock control system involves the warehouse manager, the salesperson and the client. The auditors want to produce a valuation of company assets including stock in hand, the assistant warehouse manager needs to update the stock levels while his boss is on holiday.

Over time many people are affected directly or indirectly by a system and these people are called *stakeholders* (see also Chapter 13). Obviously, tracing the tenuous links between people could go on for ever and you need to draw boundaries as to whom you should consider. This depends very much on the nature of the systems being designed, but largely requires plain common sense.

So, how do you get to know your users?

■ Who are they?

Of course, the first thing to find out is who your users are. Are they young or old, experienced computer users or novices? As we saw with the stock control system, it may not be obvious who the users are, so you may need to ask this question again as you find out more about the system and its context. This question becomes harder to answer if you are designing generic software, such as a word processor, as there are many different users with different purposes and characteristics. A similar problem arises with many websites where the potential visitors are far from homogenous. It may be tempting to try to think of a generic user with generic skills and generic goals; however, it is probably better, either instead or in addition, to think of several specific users.

■ Probably *not* like you!

When designing a system it is easy to design it as if *you* were the main user: you assume your own interests and abilities. So often you hear a designer say 'but it's obvious what to do'. It may be obvious for her! This is not helped by the fact that many software houses are primarily filled with male developers. Although individuals differ a lot there is a tendency for women to have better empathetic skills.

■ Talk to them.

It is hard to get yourself inside someone else's head, so the best thing is usually to ask them. This can take many forms: structured interviews about their job or life, open-ended discussions, or bringing the potential users fully into the design process. The last of these is called *participatory design* (see Chapter 13, Section 13.3.4). By involving users throughout the design process it is possible to get a deep knowledge of their work context and needs. The obvious effect of this is that it produces better designs. However, there is a second motivational effect, perhaps at least as important as the quality of the design. By being involved, users come to 'own' the design and become champions for it once deployed. Recall that a system must be not only useful and usable, but also *used*.

People may also be able to tell you about how things *really* happen, not just how the organization says they *should* happen. To encourage users to tell you this, you will need to win their trust, since often the actual practices run counter to corporate policy. However it is typically these ad hoc methods that make organizations work, not the official story!

Figure 5.2   Eadweard Muybridge's time-lapse photography. Source for top plate and middle plate: Kingston Museum and Heritage Service; source for bottom plate: V&A Images, The Victoria and Albert Museum, London

■ Watch them.

Although what people tell you is of the utmost importance, it is not the whole story.

When black-belt judo players are asked how they throw an opponent, their explanations do not match what they actually do. Think about walking – how do your legs and arms move? It is harder than you would think! Although people have run since the earliest times, it was only with Eadweard Muybridge's pioneering time-lapse photography in the 1870s that the way people actually walk, run and move became clear (see Figure 5.2). This is even more problematic with intellectual activities as it is notoriously difficult to introspect.

A professional in any field is very practiced and can *do* things in the domain. An academic in the same field may not be able to do things, but she knows *about* the things in the domain. These are different kinds of knowledge and skill. Sometimes people know both, but not necessarily so. The best sports trainers may not be the best athletes, the best painters may not be the best art critics.

Because of this it is important to watch what people do as well as hear what they say. This may involve sitting and taking notes of how they spend a day, watching particular activities, using a video camera or tape recorder. It can be done in an informal manner or using developed methods such as ethnography or contextual inquiry, which we will discuss in Chapter 13.

Sometimes users can be involved in this; for example, asking them to keep a diary or having a 15-minute buzzer and asking them to write down what they are doing when the buzzer sounds. Although this sounds just like asking the users what they do, the structured format helps them give a more accurate answer.

Another way to find out what people are doing is to look at the artifacts they are using and creating. Look at a typical desk in an office. There are papers, letters, files, perhaps a stapler, a computer, sticky notes . . . Some of these carry information, but if they were only important for the information in them they could equally well be

DESIGN FOCUS

Cultural probes

Traditional ethnography has involved watching people and being present. There is always a disruptive effect when someone is watching, but in, say, an office, after a while the ethnographer becomes 'part of the wallpaper' and most activities carry on as normal. However, in some environments, for example the home or with psychiatric patients, it is hard to go and watch people for long periods if at all. Cultural probes have been used as one way to gather rich views of an area without intrusion. These were originally developed as prompts for design [146], but have also been adopted as an added method for ethnography [170].

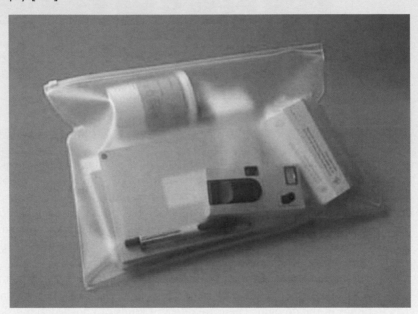

Source: Photograph courtesy of William W. Gaver

Cultural probes are small packs of items designed to provoke and record comments in various ways. They are given to people to take away and to open and use in their own environment. For example, one probe pack for the domestic environment includes a glass with a paper sleeve. You use the glass to listen to things and then write down what you hear. The same probe pack contains a repackaged disposable camera and a small solid-state voice recorder. When the packs are returned, the notes, recordings, photos, etc., are used as a means of understanding what is significant and important for the people in the environment and as a means of enculturing designers.

For more see /e3/online/cultural-probes/ and www.crd.rca.ac.uk/equator/domestic_probes.html

in the filing cabinet and just taken out when needed. The sticky note on the edge of Brian's screen saying 'book table' is not just information that he needs to book a restaurant table. The fact that it is on his screen is reminding him that something needs to be done. In Chapter 18 we will look at the role of artifacts in detail.

Betty is 37 years old. She has been Warehouse Manager for five years and has worked for Simpkins Brothers Engineering for 12 years. She didn't go to university, but has studied in her evenings for a business diploma. She has two children aged 15 and 7 and does not like to work late. She did part of an introductory in-house computer course some years ago, but it was interrupted when she was promoted and could no longer afford to take the time. Her vision is perfect, but her right-hand movement is slightly restricted following an industrial accident three years ago. She is enthusiastic about her work and is happy to delegate responsibility and take suggestions from her staff. However, she does feel threatened by the introduction of yet another new computer system (the third in her time at SBE).

Figure 5.3   Persona – a rich description of Betty the Warehouse Manager

In all these observational methods one should not just stop at the observation, but go back and discuss the observations with the users. Even if they were not previously aware of what they were doing, they are likely to be able to explain when shown. The observations tell you *what* they do, they will tell you *why*.

■ Use your imagination.

Even if you would like to involve many users throughout your design exercise this will not always be possible. It may be too costly, it may be hard to get time with them (e.g. hospital consultant), it may be that there are just too many (e.g. the web). However, even if you cannot involve actual users you can at least try to imagine their experiences.

Now this is very dangerous! It would be easy to think, 'if I were a warehouse manager I would do this'. The issue is not what *you* would do in the user's shoes but what *they* would do. This requires almost a kind of method acting. Imagine being a warehouse manager. What does the word 'undo' in the menu mean to him?

One method that has been quite successful in helping design teams produce user-focussed designs is the *persona*. A persona is a rich picture of an imaginary person who represents your core user group. Figure 5.3 gives an example persona of Betty the warehouse manager. A design team will have several of these personae covering different types of intended users and different roles. The personae will themselves be based on studies of actual users, observation, etc. When a design solution is proposed the team can ask, 'how would Betty react to this?'. The detail is deliberately more than is strictly necessary, but this is essential. It is only by feeling that Betty is a real person that the team can start to imagine how she will behave.

5.5   SCENARIOS

Scenarios are stories for design: rich stories of interaction. They are perhaps the simplest design representation, but one of the most flexible and powerful. Some scenarios are quite short: 'the user intends to press the "save" button, but accidentally

> Brian would like to see the new film *Moments of Significance* and wants to invite Alison, but he knows she doesn't like 'arty' films. He decides to take a look at it to see if she would like it and so connects to one of the movie-sharing networks. He uses his work machine as it has a higher bandwidth connection, but feels a bit guilty. He knows he will be getting an illegal copy of the film, but decides it is OK as he is intending to go to the cinema to watch it. After it downloads to his machine he takes out his new personal movie player. He presses the 'menu' button and on the small LCD screen he scrolls using the arrow keys to 'bluetooth connect' and presses the 'select' button. On his computer the movie download program now has an icon showing that it has recognized a compatible device and he drags the icon of the film over the icon for the player. On the player the LCD screen says 'downloading now', with a per cent done indicator and small whirling icon.
>
> During lunchtime Brian takes out his movie player, plugs in his earphones and starts to watch. He uses the arrow keys to skip between portions of the film and decides that, yes, Alison would like it. Then he feels a tap on his shoulder. He turns round. It is Alison. He had been so absorbed he hadn't noticed her. 'What are you watching', she says. 'Here, listen', he says and flicks a small switch. The built-in directional speaker is loud enough for both Brian and Alison to hear, but not loud enough to disturb other people in the canteen. Alison recognizes the film from trailers, 'surprised this is out yet' she says. 'Well actually . . .', Brian confesses, 'you'd better come with me to see it and make an honest man of me'. 'I'll think about it', she replies.

Figure 5.4   Scenario for proposed movie player

presses the "quit" button so loses his work'. Others are focussed more on describing the situation or context.

Figure 5.4 gives an example of a scenario for the personal movie player. Like the persona it is perhaps more detailed than appears necessary, but the detail helps make the events seem real. The figure shows plain text, but scenarios can be augmented by sketches, simulated screen shots, etc. These sketches and pictures are called *storyboards* and are similar to the techniques used in film making to envisage plot-lines.

Where the design includes physical artifacts the scenarios can be used as a script to act out potential patterns of use. For example, we might imagine a digital Swiss army knife, which has a small LCD screen and uses the toothpick as a stylus. The knife connects to the internet via a wireless link through your phone and gives interesting tips from other Swiss army knife users. Try getting two together at a party – you will see this would appeal! It sounds like a great design idea – but wait, try acting out the use. If you have a Swiss army knife, use it, or use something penknife-sized if you don't. The tip on the LCD says, 'open the stone remover': a small LED glows near the right blade – you open it. 'Now push the blade into the rubber of the grommet', it says. You do this and then look for the next instruction. Look at the knife in your hand . . . oops, your thumb is covering where the screen would be. Perhaps a voice interface would be better.

You can see already how scenarios force you to think about the design in detail and notice potential problems before they happen. If you add more detail you can get to a blow-by-blow account of the user–system interactions and then ask 'what is the user intending now?'; 'what is the system doing now?'. This can help to verify that the design would make sense to the user and also that proposed implementation architectures would work.

In addition scenarios can be used to:

Communicate with others – other designers, clients or users. It is easy to misunderstand each other whilst discussing abstract ideas. Concrete examples of use are far easier to share.

Validate other models   A detailed scenario can be 'played' against various more formal representations such as task models (discussed in Chapter 15) or dialog and navigation models (Chapter 16 and below).

Express dynamics   Individual screen shots and pictures give you a sense of what a system would look like, but not how it behaves.

In the next section we will discuss ways of describing the patterns of interaction with a system. These are more complex and involve networks or hierarchies. In contrast scenarios are linear – they represent a single path amongst all the potential interactions.

This linearity has both positive and negative points:

Time is linear   Our lives are linear as we live in time and so we find it easier to understand simple linear narratives. We are natural storytellers and story listeners.

But no alternatives   Real interactions have choices, some made by people, some by systems. A simple scenario does not show these alternative paths. In particular, it is easy to miss the unintended things a person may do.

Scenarios are a resource that can be used and reused throughout the design process: helping us see what is wanted, suggesting how users will deal with the potential design, checking that proposed implementations will work, and generating test cases for final evaluation.

For more examples of scenarios see: /e3/online/scenario/

5.6   NAVIGATION DESIGN

As we stressed, the object of design is not just a computer system or device, but the socio-technical intervention as a whole. However, as design progresses we come to a point where we do need to consider these most tangible outputs of design.

Imagine yourself using a word processor. You will be doing this in some particular social and physical setting, for a purpose. But now we are focussing on the computer system itself. You interact at several levels:

Widgets   The appropriate choice of widgets and wording in menus and buttons will help you know how to use them for a particular selection or action.

Screens or windows   You need to find things on the screen, understand the logical grouping of buttons.

Table 5.1 Levels of interaction

PC application	Website	Physical device
Widgets	Form elements, tags and links	Buttons, dials, lights, displays
Screen design	Page design	Physical layout
Navigation design	Site structure	Main modes of device
Other apps and operating system	The web, browser, external links	The real world!

Navigation within the application   You need to be able to understand what will happen when a button is pressed, to understand where you are in the interaction.

Environment   The word processor has to read documents from disk, perhaps some are on remote networks. You swap between applications, perhaps cut and paste.

You can see similar levels in other types of application and device, as Table 5.1 shows. There are differences; for example, in the web we have less control of how people enter a site and on a physical device we have the same layout of buttons and displays no matter what the internal state (although we may treat them differently).

We discussed graphical user interface widgets in Chapter 3 and in the next section we will look at details of screen design. In this section we will look mainly at navigation design, that is the main screens or modes within a system and how they interconnect. We will also briefly consider how this interacts with the wider environment.

Just in case you haven't already got the idea, the place to start when considering the structure of an application is to think about actual use:

■ who is going to use the application?
■ how do they think about it?
■ what will they do with it?

This can then drive the second task – thinking about structure. Individual screens or the layout of devices will have their own structure, but this is for the next section. Here we will consider two main kinds of issue:

■ local structure
  – looking from one screen or page out
■ global structure
  – structure of site, movement between screens.

5.6.1 Local structure

Much of interaction involves goal-seeking behavior. Users have some idea of what they are after and a partial model of the system. In an ideal world if users had perfect knowledge of what they wanted and how the system worked they could simply take the shortest path to what they want, pressing all the right buttons and links. However, in a world of partial knowledge users meander through the system. The important thing is not so much that they take the most efficient route, but that at each point in the interaction they can make some assessment of whether they are getting closer to their (often partially formed) goal.

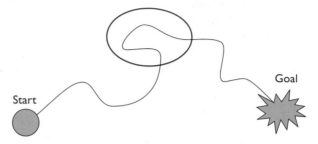

To do this goal seeking, each state of the system or each screen needs to give the user enough knowledge of what to do to get closer to their goal. In Chapter 7 we will look at various design rules, some of which address this issue. To get you started, here are four things to look for when looking at a single web page, screen or state of a device.

- knowing where you are
- knowing what you can do
- knowing where you are going – or what will happen
- knowing where you've been – or what you've done.

The screen, web page or device displays should make clear *where you are* in terms of the interaction or state of the system. Some websites show 'bread crumbs' at the top of the screen, the path of titles showing where the page is in the site (Figure 5.5). Similarly, in the scenario in Figure 5.4, the personal movie player says 'downloading now', so Brian knows that it is in the middle of downloading a movie from the PC.

It is also important to know *what you can do* – what can be pressed or clicked to go somewhere or do something. Some web pages are particularly bad in that it is unclear which images are pure decoration and which are links to take you somewhere.

On the web the standard underlined links make it clear which text is clickable and which is not. However, in order to improve the appearance of the page many sites change the color of links and may remove the underline too. This is especially confusing if underline is then used as simple emphasis on words that are not links! The

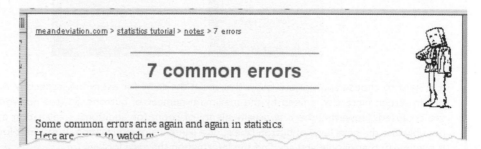

Figure 5.5 Breadcrumbs. Screen shot frame reprinted by permission from Microsoft Corporation

trade-off between appearance and ease of use may mean that this is the right thing to do, but you should take care before confusing the user needlessly.

Chic design is also a problem in physical devices. One of the authors was once in a really high-class hotel and found he could not locate the flush in the toilet. Only after much fumbling did he discover that one of the tiles could be pressed. The 'active' tile was level with the rest of the tiled wall – a very clean design, but not very usable!

You then need to know *where you are going* when you click a button or *what will happen*. Of course you can try clicking the button to see. In the case of a website or information system this may mean you then have to use some sort of 'back' mechanism to return, but that is all; however, in an application or device the action of clicking the button may already have caused some effect. If the system has an easy means to undo or reverse actions this is not so bad, but it is better if users do not have to use this 'try it and see' interaction. Where response times are slow this is particularly annoying.

Remember too that icons are typically not self-explanatory and should always be accompanied by labels or at the very least tooltips or some similar technique. A picture paints a thousand words, but typically only when explained first using fifteen hundred!

DESIGN FOCUS

Beware the big button trap

Public information systems often have touchscreens and so have large buttons. Watch someone using one of these and see how often they go to the wrong screen and have to use 'back' or 'home' to try again. If you look more closely you will find that each button has only one or two words on it giving the title of the next screen, and possibly some sort of icon. Quite rightly, the button label will be in a large font as users may have poor eyesight.

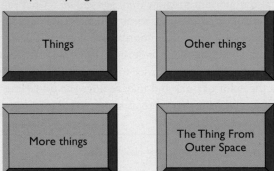

It is hard to choose appropriate labels that mean the same for everyone, especially when the breadth of the screen hierarchy is fixed by the maximum number of buttons. So it is no wonder that people get confused. However, there is usually plenty of room for additional explanation in a smaller font, possibly just the next level of button labels, or a sentence of explanation. It may not look as pretty, but it may mean that people actually find the information they are looking for.

Special care has to be taken if the same command or button press means something different in different contexts. These different contexts that change the interpretation of commands are called *modes*. Many older text editors would interpret pressing 'x' to mean 'enter me into the text' in a normal typing mode, but 'exit' in a special command mode. If modes are clearly visible or audible this is less of a problem and in Chapter 3 (Section 3.6.7) we saw how palettes are one way to achieve this. In general, modes are less of a problem in windowed systems where the mode is made apparent by the current window (if you remember which it is). However, physical devices may have minimal displays and may be operated without visual attention.

Finally, if you have just done some major action you also want some sort of confirmation of *what you've done*. If you are faultless and have perfect knowledge, of course you will be sure that you have hit the right key and know exactly what

DESIGN FOCUS

Modes

Alan's mobile phone has a lock feature to prevent accidental use. To remove the lock he has to press the 'C' (cancel) button which then asks for an additional 'yes' to confirm removing the lock. So, in 'locked' mode, 'C' followed by 'yes' means 'turn off lock' and these are the most frequent actions when Alan takes the phone from his pocket.

However, Alan is forgetful and sometimes puts the phone in his pocket unlocked. This leads to occasional embarrassing phone calls and also to another problem.

The 'yes' button is quite big and so this is often pressed while in his pocket. This puts the phone into 'dial recent numbers' mode with a list of recent calls on screen. In this mode, pressing 'C' gives a prompt 'delete number' and pressing 'yes' then deletes the number from the phone's address book. Unhappily, this often means he takes the phone from his pocket, automatically presses 'C', 'yes' only to see as he looks down to the handset the fatal words 'number deleted'. Of course there is no undo!

will happen. Remember, too, that to know what will happen, you would need to know everything about the internal state of the system and things outside, like the contents of files, networked devices, etc., that could affect it. In other words, if you were omniscient you could do it. For lesser mortals the system needs to give some *feedback* to say what has happened.

In an information system, there is a related but slightly different issue, which is to know *where you have been*. This helps you to feel in control and understand your navigation of the information space. The feeling of disorientation when you do not have sufficient means to know where you are and where you have been has been called 'lost in hyperspace'. Most web browsers offer a history system and also a 'back' button that keeps a list of recently visited pages.

5.6.2 Global structure – hierarchical organization

We will now look at the overall structure of an application. This is the way the various screens, pages or device states link to one another.

One way to organize a system is in some form of hierarchy. This is typically organized along functional boundaries (that is, different kinds of things), but may be organized by roles, user type, or some more esoteric breakdown such as modules in an educational system.

The hierarchy links screens, pages or states in logical groupings. For example, Figure 5.6 gives a high-level breakdown of some sort of messaging system. This sort of hierarchy can be used purely to help during design, but can also be used to structure the actual system. For example, this may reflect the menu structure of a PC application or the site structure on the web.

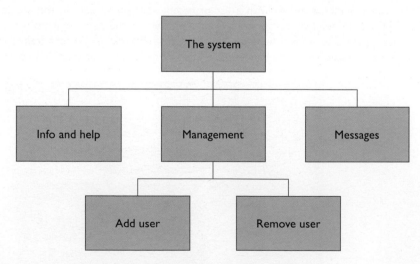

Figure 5.6 Application functional hierarchy

Any sort of information structuring is difficult, but there is evidence that people find hierarchies simpler than most. One of the difficulties with organizing information or system functionality is that different people have different internal structures for their knowledge, and may use different vocabulary. This is one of the places where a detailed knowledge of the intended users is essential: it is no good creating a hierarchy that the designers understand, but not the users . . . and all too commonly this is exactly what happens.

However much you think you have got the wording and categories right, because there are different users it is inevitable that not everyone will understand it perfectly. This is where clear guidance as suggested in Section 5.6.1 (knowing where you are going – or what will happen) is essential, as well as the means to allow users to change their mind if they make the wrong decisions.

There is also evidence that deep hierarchies are difficult to navigate, so it is better to have broad top-level categories, or to present several levels of menu on one screen or web page. Miller's magic number of 7 ± 2 for working memory capacity (see Chapter 1, Section 1.3.2) is often misused in this context. Many guidelines suggest that menu breadth, that is the number of choices available at each level in the menu, should be around seven. However, Miller's result applies only to working memory, not visual search. In fact, optimal breadth can be quite large, perhaps 60 or more items for a web index page if the items are organized in such a way that the eye can easily find the right one [206]. (See /e3/online/menu-breadth/ for more on optimal menu breadth.) Of course, to organize the items on the page requires further classification. However, here the critical thing is the naturalness of the classification, which itself may depend on the user's purpose. For example, if the user wants to look up information on a particular city, an alphabetical list of all city names would be fast, but for other purposes a list by region would be more appropriate.

5.6.3 Global structure – dialog

In a pure information system or static website it may be sufficient to have a fully hierarchical structure, perhaps with next/previous links between items in the same group. However, for any system that involves doing things, constantly drilling down from one part of the hierarchy to another is very frustrating. Usually there are ways of getting more quickly from place to place. For example, in a stock control system there may be a way of going from a stock item to all orders outstanding on that item and then from an order to the purchase record for the customer who placed the order. These would each be in a very different part of a hierarchical view of the application, yet directly accessible from one another.

As well as these cross-links in hierarchies, when you get down to detailed interactions, such as editing or deleting a record, there is obviously a flow of screens and commands that is not about hierarchy. In HCI the word 'dialog' is used to refer to this pattern of interactions between the user and a system.

Consider the following fragment from a marriage service:

Minister:	Do you *name* take this woman…
Man:	I do
Minister:	Do you *name* take this man…
Woman:	I do
Minister:	I now pronounce you man and wife

Notice this describes the general flow of the service, but has blanks for the names of the bride and groom. So it gives the pattern of the interaction between the parties, but is instantiated differently for each service. Human–computer dialog is just the same; there are overall patterns of movement between main states of a device or windows in a PC application, but the details differ each time it is run.

Recall that scenarios gave just one path through the system. To describe a full system we need to take into account different paths through a system and loops where the system returns to the same screen. There are various ways to do this, and in Chapter 16 we will expand on the wedding example and look at several different types of dialog model.

A simple way is to use a network diagram showing the principal states or screens linked together with arrows. This can:

■ show what leads to what
■ show what happens when
■ include branches and loops
■ be more task oriented than a hierarchy.

Figure 5.7 shows a network diagram illustrating the main screens for adding or deleting a user from the messaging system in Figure 5.6. The arrows show the general flow between the states. We can see that from the main screen we can get to either the 'remove user' screen or the 'add user' screen. This is presumably by selecting buttons or links, but the way these are shown we leave to detailed screen design. We can also see that from the 'add user' screen the system always returns to the main screen, but after the 'remove user' screen there is a further confirmation screen.

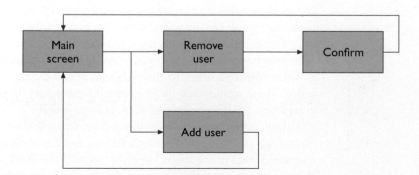

Figure 5.7 Network of screens/states

5.6.4 Wider still

Donne said 'No man is an Iland, intire of it selfe'. This is also true of the things we design. Each sits amongst other devices and applications and this in turn has to be reflected within our design.

This has several implications:

Style issues We should normally conform to platform standards, such as positions for menus on a PC application, to ensure consistency between applications. For example, on our proposed personal movie player we should make use of standard fast-forward, play and pause icons.

Functional issues On a PC application we need to be able to interact with files, read standard formats and be able to handle cut and paste.

Navigation issues We may need to support linkages between applications, for example allowing the embedding of data from one application in another, or, in a mail system, being able to double click an attachment icon and have the right application launched for the attachment.

On the web we have the added difficulty that other sites and applications may include links that bypass our 'home page' and other pages and go direct into the heart of our site or web application. Also, when we link to other sites, we have no control over them or the way their content may change over time.

5.7   SCREEN DESIGN AND LAYOUT

We have talked about the different elements that make up interactive applications, but not about how we put them together. A single screen image often has to present information clearly and also act as the locus for interacting with the system. This is a complex area, involving some of the psychological understanding from Chapter 1 as well as aspects of graphical design.

The basic principles at the screen level reflect those in other areas of interaction design:

Ask   What is the user doing?

Think   What information is required? What comparisons may the user need to make? In what order are things likely to be needed?

Design   Form follows function: let the required interactions drive the layout.

5.7.1 Tools for layout

We have a number of visual tools available to help us suggest to the user appropriate ways to read and interact with a screen or device.

```
Billing details:              Delivery details:
  Name:                         Name:
  Address: ...                  Address: ...
  Credit card no:               Delivery time:
─────────────────────────────────────────────────────
Order details:
  item                        quantity cost/item    cost
  size 10 screws (boxes)         7      3.71       25.97
     ... ...                      ...      ...        ...
```

Figure 5.8   Grouping related items in an order screen

Grouping and structure

If things logically belong together, then we should normally physically group them together. This may involve multiple levels of structure. For example, in Figure 5.8 we can see a potential design for an ordering screen. Notice how the details for billing and delivery are grouped together spatially; also note how they are separated from the list of items actually ordered by a line as well as spatially. This reflects the following logical structure:

```
Order:
    Administrative information
        Billing details
        Delivery details
    Order information
        Order line 1
        Order line 2
        ...
```

Order of groups and items

If we look at Figure 5.8 again we can see that the screen seems to naturally suggest reading or filling in the billing details first, followed by the delivery details, followed by the individual order items. Is this the right order?

In general we need to think: what is the natural order for the user? This should normally match the order on screen. For data entry forms or dialog boxes we should also set up the order in which the tab key moves between fields.

Occasionally we may also want to force a particular order; for example we may want to be sure that we do not forget the credit card details!

Decoration

Again looking at Figure 5.8, we can see how the design uses boxes and a separating line to make the grouping clear. Other decorative features like font style, and text or background colors can be used to emphasize groupings. Look at the microwave control

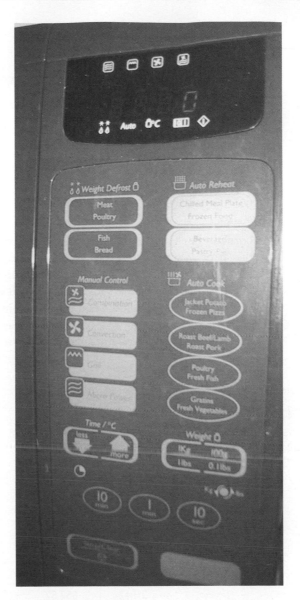

Figure 5.9 Microwave control panel

panel in Figure 5.9. See how the buttons differ in using the foreground and background colors (green and gold) so that groups are associated with one another. See also how the buttons are laid out to separate them into groups of similar function.

Alignment

Alignment of lists is also very important. For users who read text from left to right, lists of text items should normally be aligned to the left. Numbers, however, should

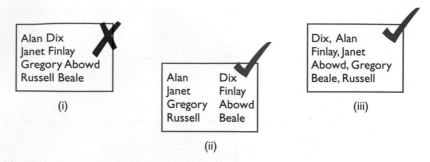

Figure 5.10   Looking up surnames

normally be aligned to the right (for integers) or at the decimal point. This is because the shape of the column then gives an indication of magnitude – a sort of mini-histogram. Items like names are particularly difficult. Consider list (i) in Figure 5.10. It is clearly hard to look someone up if you only know their surname. To make it easy, such lists should be laid out in columns as in (ii), or have forename and surname reversed as in (iii). (The dates in Figure 5.13, Section 5.7.3, pose similar problems, as the years do not align, even when the folder is sorted by date.)

DESIGN FOCUS

Alignment and layout matter

Look quickly at these two columns of numbers and try to find the biggest number in each column.

532.56	627.865
179.3	1.005763
256.317	382.583
15	2502.56
73.948	432.935
1035	2.0175
3.142	652.87
497.6256	56.34

Multiple column lists require more care. Text columns have to be wide enough for the largest item, which means you can get large gaps between columns. Figure 5.11 shows an example of this (i), and you can see how hard this makes it for your eye to scan across the rows. There are several visual ways to deal with this including: (ii) 'leaders' – lines of dots linking the columns; and (iii) using soft tone grays or colors behind rows or columns. This is also a time when it may be worth breaking other

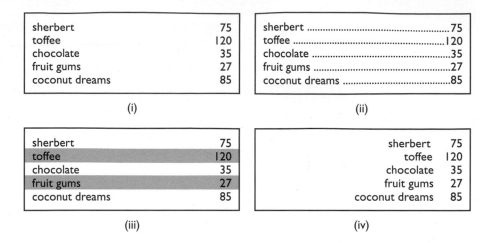

Figure 5.11 Managing multiple columns

alignment rules, perhaps right aligning some text items as in (iv). This last alternative might be a good solution if you were frequently scanning the numbers and only occasionally scanning the names of items, but not if you needed frequently to look up names (which anyway are not sorted in this figure!). You can also see that this is an example of a design trade-off – good alignment for individual columns versus ability to see relationship across rows.

White space

In typography the space between the letters is called the counter. In painting this is also important and artists may focus as much on the space between the foreground elements such as figures and buildings as on the elements themselves. Often the shape of the counter is the most important part of the composition of a painting and in calligraphy and typography the balance of a word is determined by giving an even weight to the counters. If one ignores the 'content' of a screen and instead concentrates on the counter – the space between the elements – one can get an overall feel for the layout. If elements that are supposed to be related look separate when you focus on the counter, then something is wrong. Screwing up your eyes so that the screen becomes slightly blurred is another good technique for taking your attention away from the content and looking instead at the broad structure.

Space can be used in several ways. Some of these are shown in Figure 5.12. The colored areas represent continuous areas of text or graphics. In (i) we can see space used to separate blocks as you often see in gaps between paragraphs or space between sections in a report. Space can also be used to create more complex structures. In (ii) there are clearly four main areas: ABC, D, E and F. Within one of these are three further areas, A, B and C, which themselves are grouped as A on its own, followed by B and C together. In Figure 5.12 (iii), we can see space used to highlight. This is a technique used frequently in magazines to highlight a quote or graphic.

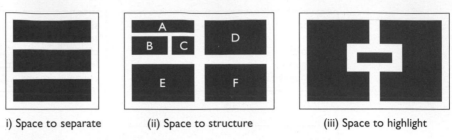

i) Space to separate   (ii) Space to structure   (iii) Space to highlight

Figure 5.12   Using white space in layout

5.7.2 User action and control

Entering information

Some of the most complicated and difficult screen layouts are found in forms-based interfaces and dialog boxes. In each case the screen consists not only of information presented to the user, but also of places for the user to enter information or select options. Actually, many of the same layout issues for data presentation also apply to fields for data entry. Alignment is still important. It is especially common to see the text entry boxes aligned in a jagged fashion because the field names are of different lengths. This is an occasion where right-justified text for the field labels may be best or, alternatively, in a graphical interface a smaller font can be used for field labels and the labels placed just above and to the left of the field they refer to.

For both presenting and entering information a clear logical layout is important. The task analysis techniques in Chapter 15 can help in determining how to group screen items and also the order in which users are likely to want to read them or fill them in. Knowing also that users are likely to read from left to right and top to bottom (depending on their native language!) means that a screen can be designed so that users encounter items in an appropriate order for the task at hand.

Knowing what to do

Some elements of a screen are passive, simply giving you information; others are active, expecting you to fill them in, or do something to them. It is often not even clear which elements are active, let alone what the effect is likely to be when you interact with them!

This is one of the reasons for platform and company style guides. If everyone designs buttons to look the same and menus to look the same, then users will be able to recognize them when they see them. However, this is not sufficient in itself. It is important that the labels and icons on menus are also clear. Again, standards can help for common actions such as save, delete or print. For more system-specific actions, one needs to follow broader principles. For example, a button says 'bold': does this represent the current *state* of a system or the *action* that will be performed if the button is pressed?

Affordances

These are especially difficult problems in multimedia applications where one may deliberately adopt a non-standard and avant-garde style. How are users supposed to know where to click? The psychological idea of *affordance* says that things may suggest by their shape and other attributes what you can do to them: a handle affords pulling or lifting; a button affords pushing. These affordances can be used when designing novel interaction elements. One can either mimic real-world objects directly, or try to emulate the critical aspects of those objects. What you must not do is depict a real-world object in a context where its normal affordances do not work!

Note also that affordances are not intrinsic, but depend on the background and culture of users. Most computer-literate users will click on an icon. This is not because they go around pushing pictures in art galleries, but because they have learned that this is an affordance of such objects in a computer domain. Similarly, such experienced users may well double click if a single click has no effect, yet novices would not even think of double clicking – after all, double clicking on most real buttons turns them off again!

5.7.3 Appropriate appearance

Presenting information

The way of presenting information on screen depends on the kind of information: text, numbers, maps, tables; on the technology available to present it: character display, line drawing, graphics, virtual reality; and, most important of all, on the purpose for which it is being used. Consider the window in Figure 5.13. The file listing is alphabetic, which is fine if we want to look up the details of a particular file, but makes it very difficult to find recently updated files. Of course, if the list were ordered by date then it would be difficult to find a particular file. Different purposes require different representations. For more complex numerical data, we may be considering scatter graphs, histograms or 3D surfaces; for hierarchical structures, we may consider outlines or organization diagrams. But, no matter how complex the data, the principle of matching presentation to purpose remains.

The issue of presentation has been around for many years, long before computers, interactive systems or HCI! Probably the best source for this issue is Tufte's book [351]. It is targeted principally at static presentations of information, as in books, but most design principles transfer directly.

We have an advantage when presenting information in an interactive system in that it is easy to allow the user to choose among several representations, thus making it possible to achieve different goals. For example, with Macintosh folder windows (as in Figure 5.13) the user can click on a column heading and the file list is reordered, so one can look at the files by, say, name or date. This is not an excuse for ignoring the user's purpose, but means that we can plan for a range of possible uses.

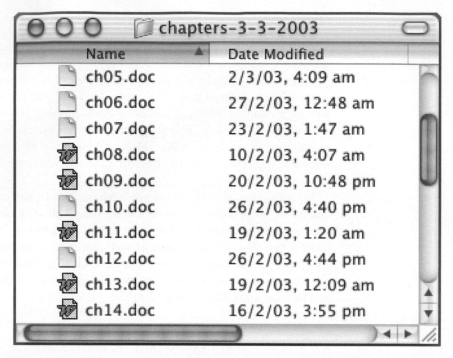

Figure 5.13 Alphabetic file listing. Screen shot reprinted by permission from Apple Computer, Inc.

Aesthetics and utility

Remember that a pretty interface is not necessarily a good interface. Ideally, as with any well-designed item, an interface should be aesthetically pleasing. Indeed, good graphic design and attractive displays can increase users' satisfaction and thus improve productivity.

However, beauty and utility may sometimes be at odds. For example, an industrial control panel will often be built up of the individual controls of several subsystems, some designed by different teams, some bought in. The resulting inconsistency in appearance may look a mess and suggest tidying up. Certainly some of this inconsistency may cause problems. For example, there may be a mix of telephone-style and calculator-style numeric keypads. Under stress it would be easy to mis-key when swapping between these. However, the diversity of controls can also help the operator keep track of which controls refer to which subsystem – any redesign must preserve this advantage.

The conflict between aesthetics and utility can also be seen in many 'well-designed' posters and multimedia systems. In particular, the backdrop behind text must have low contrast in order to leave the text readable; this is often not the case and graphic designers may include excessively complex and strong backgrounds because they look good. The results are impressive, perhaps even award winning, but completely unusable!

On a more positive note, careful application of aesthetic concepts can also aid comprehensibility. An example of this is the idea of the counter and use of space that we discussed earlier. In consumer devices these aesthetic considerations may often be the key differentiator between products, for example, the sleek curves of a car. This is not missed by designers of electronic goods: devices are designed to be good to touch and feel as well as look at and this is certainly one of the drivers for the futuristic shapes of the Apple iMac family.

THE COUNTER

Making a mess of it: color and 3D

One of the worst features in many interfaces is their appalling use of color. This is partly because many monitors only support a limited range of primary colors and partly because, as with the overuse of different fonts in word processors, the designer got carried away. Aside from issues of good taste, an overuse of color can be distracting and, remembering from Chapter 1 that a significant proportion of the population is color blind, may mean that parts of the text are literally invisible to some users. In general, color should be used sparingly and not relied upon to give information, but rather to reinforce other attributes.

The increasing use of 3D effects in interfaces has posed a whole new set of problems for text and numerical information. Whilst excellent for presenting physical information and certain sorts of graphs, text presented in perspective can be very difficult to read and the all too common 3D pie chart is all but useless. We will discuss ways to make 3D actually useful for visualization in Chapter 20.

DESIGN FOCUS

Checking screen colors

Even non-color-blind users will find it hard to read text where the intensity of the text and background are similar. A good trick is to adjust the color balance on your monitor so that it is reduced to grays, or to print screens on a black and white printer. If your screen is unreadable in grayscale then it is probably difficult to read in full color.

Localization / internationalization

If you are working in a different country, you might see a document being word processed where the text of the document and the file names are in the local language, but all the menus and instructions are still in English. The process of making software suitable for different languages and cultures is called *localization* or *internationalization*.

It is clear that words have to change and many interface construction toolkits make this easy by using *resources*. When the program uses names of menu items, error messages and other text, it does not use the text directly, but instead uses a resource identifier, usually simply a number. A simple database is constructed separately that binds these identifiers to particular words and phrases. A different resource database is constructed for each language, and so the program can be customized to use in a particular country by simply choosing the appropriate resource database.

However, changing the language is only the simplest part of internationalization. Much of the explicit guidance on alignment and layout is dependent on a left-to-right, top-to-bottom language such as English and most European languages. This obviously changes completely for other types of language. Furthermore, many icons and images are only meaningful within a restricted cultural context. Despite the apparent international hegemony of Anglo-American culture, one cannot simply assume that its symbols and norms will be universally understood. A good example of this is the use of ticks ✓ and crosses ✗. In Anglo-American culture these represent opposites, positive and negative, whereas in most of Europe the two are interchangeable.

5.8   ITERATION AND PROTOTYPING

Because human situations are complex and designers are not infallible it is likely that our first design will not be perfect! For this reason, almost all interaction design includes some form of iteration of ideas. This often starts early on with paper designs and storyboards being demonstrated to colleagues and potential users. Later in the design process one might use mockups of physical devices or tools such as Shockwave or Visual Basic to create prototype versions of software.

Any of these prototypes, whether paper-based or running software, can then be evaluated to see whether they are acceptable and where there is room for improvement. This sort of evaluation, intended to improve designs, is called *formative* evaluation. This is in contrast to *summative* evaluation, which is performed at the end to verify whether the product is good enough. Chapter 9 considers evaluation in detail. One approach is to get an expert to use a set of guidelines, for example the 'knowing where you are' list above, and look screen by screen to see if there are any violations. The other main approach is to involve real users either in a controlled experimental setting, or 'in the wild' – a real-use environment.

The result of evaluating the system will usually be a list of faults or problems and this is followed by a redesign exercise, which is then prototyped, evaluated . . . Figure 5.14 shows this process. The end point is when there are no more problems that can economically be fixed.

So iteration and prototyping are the universally accepted 'best practice' approach for interaction design. However, there are some major pitfalls of prototyping, rarely acknowledged in the literature.

Prototyping is an example of what is known as a *hill-climbing* approach. Imagine you are standing somewhere in the open countryside. You walk uphill and keep going uphill as steeply as possible. Eventually you will find yourself at a hill top. This

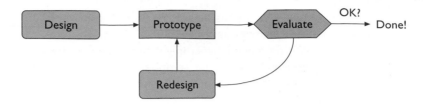

Figure 5.14   Role of prototyping

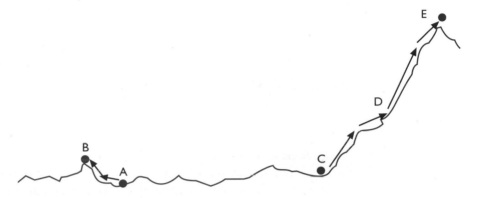

Figure 5.15   Moving little by little . . . but to where?

is exactly how iterative prototyping works: you start somewhere, evaluate it to see how to make it better, change it to make it better and then keep on doing this until it can't get any better.

However, hill climbing doesn't always work. Imagine you start somewhere near Cambridge, UK. If you keep moving uphill (and it is very difficult to work out which direction that is because it is very flat!), then eventually you would end up at the top of the Gog Magog hills, the nearest thing around . . . all of 300 feet. However, if you started somewhere else you might end up at the top of the Matterhorn. Hill-climbing methods always have the potential to leave you somewhere that is the best in the immediate area, but very poor compared with more distant places. Figure 5.15 shows this schematically: if you start at A you get trapped at the *local maximum* at B, but if you start at C you move up through D to the *global maximum* at E.

This problem of getting trapped at local maxima is also possible with interfaces. If you start with a bad design concept you may end at something that is simply a tidied up version of that bad idea!

From this we can see that there are two things you need in order for prototyping methods to work:

1. To understand what is wrong and how to improve.
2. A good start point.

The first is obvious; you cannot iterate the design unless you know what must be done to improve it. The second, however, is needed to avoid local maxima. If you wanted to climb as high as you could, you would probably book a plane to the Himalayas, not Cambridgeshire.

A really good designer might guess a good initial design based on experience and judgment. However, the complexity of interaction design problems means that this insight is hard. Another approach, very common in graphical design, is to have several initial design ideas and drop them one by one as they are developed further. This is a bit like parachuting 10 people at random points of the earth. One of them is perhaps likely to end up near a high mountain.

One of the things that theoretical methods and models, as found in Part 3 of this book, can do is to help us with both (1) and (2).

5.9   SUMMARY

We have seen that design in HCI is not just about creating devices or software, but instead is about the whole interaction between people, software and their environment. Because of this it is good to see the product of design not just as the obvious artifacts but as the whole intervention that changes the existing situation to a new one.

In Section 5.2, design was defined as 'achieving goals within constraints'. In the case of interaction design the goals are about improving some aspect of work, home or leisure using technology. The constraints remind us that the final design will inevitably involve trade-offs between different design issues and furthermore should never be 'perfect' as cost and timeliness should prevent indefinite tinkering. To achieve good design we must understand our materials and in the case of interaction design these materials include not just the computers and technical devices, but also humans. If we treated humans in design with only as much care as physical materials it is clear that 'human error' after accidents would be regarded as 'design error' – a good designer understands the natural limitations of ordinary people.

Section 5.3 gave a bird's-eye view of the design process, which gives a context for much of the rest of this book.

The process starts with understanding the situation as it is and the requirements for change. Section 5.4 provided some simple techniques for dealing with this: getting to know your users, who they are, remembering that they are different from you, but trying to imagine what it is like for them. You can talk to users, but you should also observe them in other ways, as we are all bad at articulating what we do. One way to help retain a user focus in design is to use personae – detailed word pictures of imaginary but typical users.

Section 5.5 introduced scenarios and rich stories about design, which can help us explore the design space and to discuss potential designs with other designers and potential users. Both scenarios and personae need to be vivid and to include rich contextual details – not just a record of user actions on the system!

The details of potential designs need to be worked out and in Section 5.6 we looked at the overall navigation design of the system. We started by looking at local structure, the way one screen, page or state of an application relates to those it immediately links to. The users need to know where they are, what they can do, what will happen when they do things, and what has happened in the past. This can aid users as they goal seek, or move closer towards their goals without having to necessarily understand completely the whole route there. The global structure of the application is also important. We saw how hierarchy diagrams can give a logical view of an application, which can be used to design menu or site structures. In contrast, the user dialog focusses on the flow of user and system actions. One way to do this is using network diagrams of screens or states of the system and how they link to one another. Any designed system must also relate to its environment: other applications, other websites, other physical devices.

In Section 5.7 we looked at screen design and layout. We saw that there were various visual tools that could help us to ensure that the physical structure of our screen emphasized the logical structure of the user interaction. These tools included physical grouping, ordering of items, decoration such as fonts, lines and color, alignment and the use of white space. These are important both for appropriate display of information and to lay out controls and data entry fields for ease of use. It is also important that controls have appropriate affordances – that is have visual and tactile attributes that suggest their use. Information presented on screen, whether individual items, tabular or graphical, should be appropriate to the user's purpose and this may mean allowing interactions to change the layout, for example re-sort tables by different columns. Aesthetics are also important, but may conflict with utility. Depending on the context you may need to make different trade-offs between these. Good graphical design is an area and a skill all of its own, but some features such as bad use of color and 3D effects are bad for both aesthetics and usability!

Finally, in Section 5.8, we saw that iteration is an essential part of virtually any interaction design process because we cannot get things right first time. However, iterative methods may get trapped in local maxima. To make iterative processes work, we need either extensive personal experience or theoretical understanding to help us get better initial designs.

EXERCISES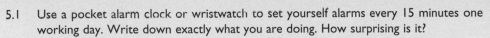

5.1 Use a pocket alarm clock or wristwatch to set yourself alarms every 15 minutes one working day. Write down exactly what you are doing. How surprising is it?

Exercises 5.2, 5.3, 5.4 and 5.5 are based around a nuclear reactor scenario on the book website at: /e3/scenario/nuclear/ You will need to read the scenario in order to answer these exercises.

5.2 Comment on the user of color in the Alarm Control, Emergency Shutdown and Emergency Confirm panels (Figure CS.2 – for figures, see the web scenario).

5.3 Comment on the use of layout and other elements in the control panels (Figures CS.1, CS.2 and CS.3), including the way in which various visual elements support or hinder logical grouping and sequence.

5.4 Working through the accident scenario, explain why the various problems arise.

5.5 Suggest potential ways of improving the interface to avoid a similar problem recurring.

RECOMMENDED READING

J. Preece, Y. Rogers and H. Sharp, *Interaction Design: Beyond Human–Computer Interaction*, John Wiley, 2002.
A general textbook on interaction design with especially strong focus on evaluation.

J. Carroll, editor, *Interacting with Computers*, Vol. 13, No. 1, special issue on 'Scenario-based system development', 2000.
Contributions from several authors on using scenarios in design.

J. Carroll, *Making Use: Scenario-Based Design of Human–Computer Interactions*, MIT Press, 2000.
John Carroll's own book dedicated solely to using scenarios in design.

J. McGrenere and W. Ho, Affordances: clarifying and evolving a concept, *Proceedings of Graphics Interface 2000*, pp. 179–86, 2000.
This paper reviews all the major work on affordances from Gibson's original definition and focusses especially on Norman's popularization of the word which has been the way many encounter it. It also reviews the work of Bill Gaver, who is probably the first person to use affordance as a concept within HCI.

E. Tufte, *Envisioning Information*, Graphics Press, Cheshire, USA, 1990, and
E. Tufte, *The Visual Display of Quantitative Information*, Graphics Press, Cheshire, USA, 1997.
Tufte's books are the 'must read' for graphical presentation, packed with examples and pictures – from timetables to Napoleon's disastrous Russian campaign.

HCI IN THE SOFTWARE PROCESS

6

OVERVIEW

- Software engineering provides a means of understanding the structure of the design process, and that process can be assessed for its effectiveness in interactive system design.

- Usability engineering promotes the use of explicit criteria to judge the success of a product in terms of its usability.

- Iterative design practices work to incorporate crucial customer feedback early in the design process to inform critical decisions which affect usability.

- Design involves making many decisions among numerous alternatives. Design rationale provides an explicit means of recording those design decisions and the context in which the decisions were made.

6.1   INTRODUCTION

In Chapter 4 we concentrated on identifying aspects of usable interactive systems by means of concrete examples of successful paradigms. The design goal is to provide reliable techniques for the repeated design of successful and usable interactive systems. It is therefore necessary that we go beyond the exercise of identifying paradigms and examine the process of interactive system design. In the previous chapter we introduced some of the elements of a user-centered design process. Here we expand on that process, placing the design of interactive systems within the established frameworks of software development.

Within computer science there is already a large subdiscipline that addresses the management and technical issues of the development of software systems – called *software engineering*. One of the cornerstones of software engineering is the *software life cycle*, which describes the activities that take place from the initial concept formation for a software system up until its eventual phasing out and replacement. This is not intended to be a software engineering textbook, so it is not our major concern here to discuss in depth all of the issues associated with software engineering and the myriad life-cycle models.

The important point that we would like to draw out is that issues from HCI affecting the usability of interactive systems are relevant within all the activities of the software life cycle. Therefore, software engineering for interactive system design is not simply a matter of adding one more activity that slots in nicely with the existing activities in the life cycle. Rather, it involves techniques that span the entire life cycle.

We will begin this chapter by providing an introduction to some of the important concepts of software engineering, in Section 6.2. Specifically, we will describe the major activities within the traditional software life cycle and discuss the issues raised by the special needs of interactive systems. We will then describe some specific approaches to interactive system design, which are used to promote product usability throughout the life cycle. In Section 6.3, we will discuss a particular methodology called *usability engineering* in which explicit usability requirements are used as goals for the design process. In Section 6.4, we consider iterative design practices that involve prototyping and participative evaluation. We conclude this chapter with a discussion of *design rationale*. Design is a decision-making activity and it is important to keep track of the decisions that have been made and the context in which they were made. Various design rationale techniques, presented in Section 6.5, are used to support this critical activity.

6.2   THE SOFTWARE LIFE CYCLE

One of the claims for software development is that it should be considered as an engineering discipline, in a way similar to how electrical engineering is considered for hardware development. One of the distinguishing characteristics of any engineering discipline is that it entails the structured application of scientific techniques to the development of some product. A fundamental feature of software engineering, therefore, is that it provides the structure for applying techniques to develop software systems. The software life cycle is an attempt to identify the activities that occur in software development. These activities must then be ordered in time in any development project and appropriate techniques must be adopted to carry them through.

In the development of a software product, we consider two main parties: the customer who requires the use of the product and the designer who must provide the product. Typically, the customer and the designer are groups of people and some people can be both customer and designer. It is often important to distinguish between the customer who is the client of the designing company and the customer who is the eventual user of the system. These two roles of customer can be played by different people. The group of people who negotiate the features of the intended system with the designer may never be actual users of the system. This is often particularly true of web applications. In this chapter, we will use the term 'customer' to refer to the group of people who interact with the design team and we will refer to those who will interact with the designed system as the user or end-user.

6.2.1 Activities in the life cycle

A more detailed description of the life cycle activities is depicted in Figure 6.1. The graphical representation is reminiscent of a waterfall, in which each activity naturally leads into the next. The analogy of the waterfall is not completely faithful to the real relationship between these activities, but it provides a good starting point for discussing the logical flow of activity. We describe the activities of this waterfall model of the software life cycle next.[1]

Requirements specification

In requirements specification, the designer and customer try to capture a description of *what* the eventual system will be expected to provide. This is in contrast to determining *how* the system will provide the expected services, which is the concern of later activities. Requirements specification involves eliciting information from the customer about the work environment, or domain, in which the final product will function. Aspects of the work domain include not only the particular functions that the software product must perform but also details about the environment in which it must operate, such as the people whom it will potentially affect and the new product's relationship to any other products which it is updating or replacing.

Requirements specification begins at the start of product development. Though the requirements are from the customer's perspective, if they are to be met by the

---

1 Some authors distinguish between the software development process and the software life cycle, the waterfall model being used to describe the former and not the latter. The main distinction for our purposes is that operation and maintenance of the product is not part of the development process.

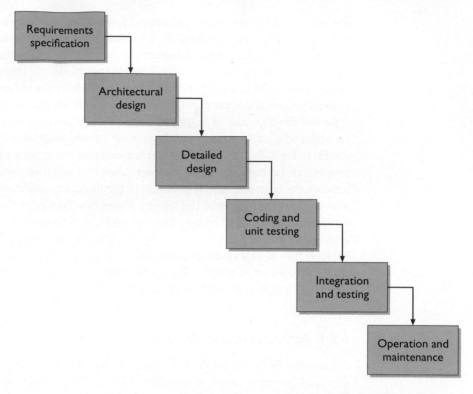

Figure 6.1   The activities in the waterfall model of the software life cycle

software product they must be formulated in a language suitable for implementation. Requirements are usually initially expressed in the native language of the customer. The executable languages for software are less natural and are more closely related to a mathematical language in which each term in the language has a precise interpretation, or semantics. The transformation from the expressive but relatively ambiguous natural language of requirements to the more precise but less expressive executable languages is one key to successful development. In Chapter 15 we discuss task analysis techniques, which are used to express work domain requirements in a form that is both expressive and precise.

Architectural design

As we mentioned, the requirements specification concentrates on what the system is supposed to do. The next activities concentrate on *how* the system provides the services expected from it. The first activity is a high-level decomposition of the system into components that can either be brought in from existing software products or be developed from scratch independently. An architectural design performs this decomposition. It is not only concerned with the functional decomposition of the system, determining which components provide which services. It must also describe the interdependencies between separate components and the sharing of resources that will arise between components.

There are many structured techniques that are used to assist a designer in deriving an architectural description from information in the requirements specification (such as CORE, MASCOT and HOOD). Details of these techniques are outside the scope of this book, but can be found in any good software engineering textbook. What we will mention here is that the majority of these techniques are adequate for capturing the *functional requirements* of the system – the services the system must provide in the work domain – but do not provide an immediate way to capture other *non-functional requirements* – features of the system that are not directly related to the actual services provided but relate to the manner in which those services must be provided. Some classic examples of non-functional requirements are the efficiency, reliability, timing and safety features of the system. Interactive features of the system, such as those that will be described by the principles in Chapter 7, also form a large class of non-functional requirements.

Detailed design

The architectural design provides a decomposition of the system description that allows for isolated development of separate components which will later be integrated. For those components that are not already available for immediate integration, the designer must provide a sufficiently detailed description so that they may be implemented in some programming language. The detailed design is a *refinement* of the component description provided by the architectural design. The behavior implied by the higher-level description must be preserved in the more detailed description.

Typically, there will be more than one possible refinement of the architectural component that will satisfy the behavioral constraints. Choosing the best refinement is often a matter of trying to satisfy as many of the non-functional requirements of the system as possible. Thus the language used for the detailed design must allow some analysis of the design in order to assess its properties. It is also important to keep track of the design options considered, the eventual decisions that were made and the reasons why, as we will discuss in Section 6.5 on design rationale.

Coding and unit testing

The detailed design for a component of the system should be in such a form that it is possible to implement it in some executable programming language. After coding, the component can be tested to verify that it performs correctly, according to some test criteria that were determined in earlier activities. Research on this activity within the life cycle has concentrated on two areas. There is plenty of research that is geared towards the automation of this coding activity directly from a low-level detailed design. Most of the work in *formal methods* operates under the hypothesis that, in theory, the transformation from the detailed design to the implementation is from one mathematical representation to another and so should be able to be entirely automated. Other, more practical work concentrates on the automatic generation of tests from output of earlier activities which can be performed on a piece of code to verify that it behaves correctly.

Integration and testing

Once enough components have been implemented and individually tested, they must be integrated as described in the architectural design. Further testing is done to ensure correct behavior and acceptable use of any shared resources. It is also possible at this time to perform some acceptance testing with the customers to ensure that the system meets their requirements. It is only after acceptance of the integrated system that the product is finally released to the customer.

It may also be necessary to certify the final system according to requirements imposed by some outside authority, such as an aircraft certification board. As of 1993, a European health and safety act requires that all employers provide their staff with usable systems. The international standards authority, ISO, has also produced a standard (ISO 9241) to define the usability of office environment workstations. Coupled together, the health and safety regulations and ISO 9241 provide impetus for designers to take seriously the HCI implications of their design.

Maintenance

After product release, all work on the system is considered under the category of maintenance, until such time as a new version of the product demands a total redesign or the product is phased out entirely. Consequently, the majority of the lifetime of a product is spent in the maintenance activity. Maintenance involves the correction of errors in the system which are discovered after release and the revision of the system services to satisfy requirements that were not realized during previous development. Therefore, maintenance provides feedback to all of the other activities in the life cycle, as shown in Figure 6.2.

6.2.2 Validation and verification

Throughout the life cycle, the design must be checked to ensure that it both satisfies the high-level requirements agreed with the customer and is also complete and internally consistent. These checks are referred to as *validation* and *verification*, respectively. Boehm [36a] provides a useful distinction between the two, characterizing validation as designing 'the right thing' and verification as designing 'the thing right'. Various languages are used throughout design, ranging from informal natural language to very precise and formal mathematical languages. Validation and verification exercises are difficult enough when carried out within one language; they become much more difficult, if not impossible, when attempted between languages.

Verification of a design will most often occur within a single life-cycle activity or between two adjacent activities. For example, in the detailed design of a component

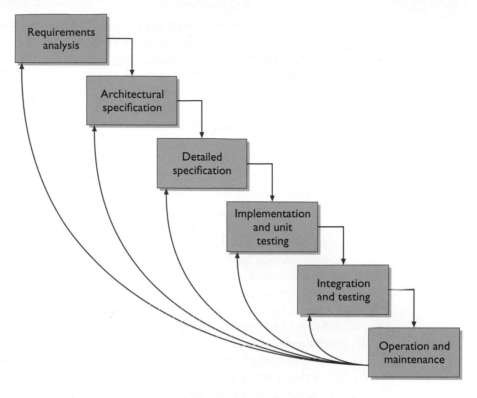

Figure 6.2 Feedback from maintenance activity to other design activities

of a payroll accounting system, the designer will be concerned with the correctness of the algorithm to compute taxes deducted from an employee's gross income. The architectural design will have provided a general specification of the information input to this component and the information it should output. The detailed description will introduce more information in refining the general specification. The detailed design may also have to change the representations for the information and will almost certainly break up a single high-level operation into several low-level operations that can eventually be implemented. In introducing these changes to information and operations, the designer must show that the refined description is a legal one within its language (internal consistency) and that it describes all of the *specified* behavior of the high-level description (completeness) in a provably correct way (relative consistency).

Validation of a design demonstrates that within the various activities the customer's requirements are satisfied. Validation is a much more subjective exercise than verification, mainly because the disparity between the language of the requirements and the language of the design forbids any objective form of proof. In interactive system design, the validation against HCI requirements is often referred to as evaluation and can be performed by the designer in isolation or in cooperation with the customer. We discuss evaluation in depth in Chapter 9.

An important question, which applies to both verification and validation, asks exactly what constitutes a proof. We have repeatedly mentioned the language used in any design activity and the basis for the semantics of that language. Languages with a mathematical foundation allow reasoning and proof in the objective sense. An argument based entirely within some mathematical language can be accepted or refuted based upon universally accepted measures. A proof can be entirely justified by the rules of the mathematical language, in which case it is considered a formal proof. More common is a rigorous proof, which is represented within some mathematical language but which relies on the understanding of the reader to accept its correctness without appeal to the full details of the argument, which could be provided but usually are not. The difference between formality and rigour is in the amount of detail the prover leaves out while still maintaining acceptance of the proof.

Proofs that are for verification of a design can frequently occur within one language or between two languages which both have a precise mathematical semantics. Time constraints for a design project and the perceived economic implications of the separate components usually dictate which proofs are carried out in full formality and which are done only rigorously (if at all). As research in this area matures and automated tools provide assistance for the mechanical aspects of proof, the cost of proof should decrease.

Validation proofs are much trickier, as they almost always involve a transformation between languages. Furthermore, the origin of customer requirements arises in the inherent ambiguity of the real world and not the mathematical world. This precludes the possibility of objective proof, rigorous or formal. Instead, there will always be a leap from the informal situations of the real world to any formal and structured development process. We refer to this inevitable disparity as the *formality gap*, depicted in Figure 6.3.

The formality gap means that validation will always rely to some extent on subjective means of proof. We can increase our confidence in the subjective proof by effective use of real-world experts in performing certain validation chores. These experts will not necessarily have design expertise, so they may not understand the

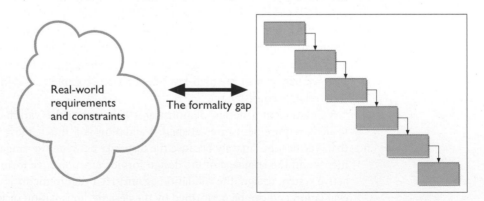

Figure 6.3   The formality gap between the real world and structured design

design notations used. Therefore, it is important that the design notations narrow the formality gap, making clear the claims that the expert can then validate. For interactive systems, the expert will have knowledge from a cognitive or psychological domain, so the design specification must be readily interpretable from a psychological perspective in order to validate it against interactive requirements of the system. We will discuss design techniques and notations that narrow the formality gap for validation of interactive properties of systems in Part 3.

6.2.3 Management and contractual issues

The life cycle described above concentrated on the more technical features of software development. In a technical discussion, managerial issues of design, such as time constraints and economic forces, are not as important. The different activities of the life cycle are logically related to each other. We can see that requirements for a system precede the high-level architectural design which precedes the detailed design, and so on. In reality, it is quite possible that some detailed design is attempted before all of the architectural design. In management, a much wider perspective must be adopted which takes into account the marketability of a system, its training needs, the availability of skilled personnel or possible subcontractors, and other topics outside the activities for the development of the isolated system.

As an example, we will take the development of a new aircraft on which there will be many software subsystems. The aircraft company will usually go through a concept evaluation period of up to 10 years before making any decision about actual product development. Once it has been decided to build a certain type of aircraft, loosely specified in the case of commercial aircraft in terms of passenger capacity and flight range, more explicit design activity follows. This includes joint analysis for both the specification of the aircraft and determination of training needs. It is only after the architectural specification of the aircraft is complete that the separate systems to be developed are identified. Some of these systems will be software systems, such as the flight management system or the training simulator, and these will be designed according to the life cycle described earlier. Typically, this will take four to five years. The separate aircraft systems are then integrated for ground and flight testing and certification before the aircraft is delivered to any customer airlines. The operating lifetime of an aircraft model is expected to be in the range of 20–40 years, during which time maintenance must be provided. The total lifetime of an aircraft from conception to phasing out is up to 55 years, only 4–5 years (excluding maintenance) of which contain the software life cycle which we are discussing in this chapter.

In managing the development process, the temporal relationship between the various activities is more important, as are the intermediate deliverables which represent the technical content, as the designer must demonstrate to the customer that progress is being made. A useful distinction, taken from McDermid [232], is that the technical perspective of the life cycle is described in *stages* of activity, whereas the managerial perspective is described in temporally bound *phases*. A phase is usually defined in terms of the documentation taken as input to the phase and the documentation delivered as output from the phase. So the requirements phase will take any marketing or conceptual development information, identifying potential customers, as input and produce a requirements specification that must be agreed upon between customer and designer.

This brings up another important issue from the management perspective. As the design activity proceeds, the customer and the designer must sign off on various documents, indicating their satisfaction with progress to date. These signed documents can carry a varying degree of contractual obligation between customer and designer. A signed requirements specification indicates both that the customer agrees to limit demands of the eventual product to those listed in the specification and also that the designer agrees to meet all of the requirements listed. From a technical perspective, it is easy to acknowledge that it is difficult, if not impossible, to determine all of the requirements before embarking on any other design activity. A satisfactory requirements specification may not be known until after the product has been in operation! From a management perspective, it is unacceptable to both designer and customer to delay the requirements specification that long.

So contractual obligation is a necessary consequence of managing software development, but it has negative implications on the design process as well. It is very difficult in the design of an interactive system to determine a priori what requirements to impose on the system to maximize its usability. Having to fix on some requirements too early will result either in general requirements that are very little guide for the designer or in specific requirements that compromise the flexibility of design without guaranteeing any benefits.

6.2.4 Interactive systems and the software life cycle

The traditional software engineering life cycles arose out of a need in the 1960s and 1970s to provide structure to the development of large software systems. In those days, the majority of large systems produced were concerned with data-processing applications in business. These systems were not highly interactive; rather, they were batch-processing systems. Consequently, issues concerning usability from an end-user's perspective were not all that important. With the advent of personal computing in the late 1970s and its huge commercial success and acceptance, most modern systems developed today are much more interactive, and it is vital to the success of any product that it be easy to operate for someone who is not expected to know much about how the system was designed. The modern user has a great amount of skill in the work that he performs without necessarily having that much skill in software development.

The life cycle for development we described above presents the process of design in a somewhat pipeline order. In reality, even for batch-processing systems, the actual design process is *iterative*, work in one design activity affecting work in any other activity both before or after it in the life cycle. We can represent this iterative relationship as in Figure 6.4, but that does not greatly enhance any understanding of the design process for interactive systems. You may ask whether it is worth the

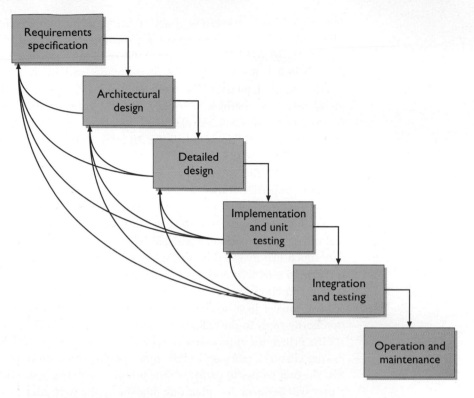

Figure 6.4   Representing iteration in the waterfall model

intellectual effort to understand the interactive system design process. Is there really much design effort spent on the interactive aspects of a system to warrant our attention? A classic survey in 1978 by Sutton and Sprague at IBM resulted in an estimate that 50% of the designer's time was spent on designing code for the user interface [338]. A more recent and convincing survey by Myers and Rosson has confirmed that that finding holds true for the 1990s [247]. So it is definitely worth the effort to provide structure and techniques to understand, structure and improve the interactive design process! In this section, we will address features of interactive system design which are not treated properly by the traditional software life cycle.

The traditional software life cycle suits a principled approach to design; that is, if we know what it is we want to produce from the beginning, then we can structure our approach to design in order to attain the goal. We have already mentioned how, in practice, designers do not find out all of the requirements for a system before they begin. Figure 6.4 depicts how discovery in later activities can be reflected in iterations back to earlier stages. This is an admission that the requirements capture activity is not executed properly. The more serious claim we are making here is that all of the requirements for an interactive system *cannot* be determined from the start, and there are many convincing arguments to support this position. The result is that systems must be built and the interaction with users observed and evaluated in order to determine how to make them more usable.

Our models of the psychology and sociology of the human and human cognition, whether in isolation or in a group, are incomplete and do not allow us to predict how to design for maximum usability. There is much research on models of human users that allow prediction of their performance with interactive systems, which we will discuss in Chapter 12. These models, however, either rely on too much detail of the system to be useful at very early and abstract stages of design (see the section in Chapter 12 on the keystroke-level model) or they only apply to goal-oriented planned activity and not highly interactive WIMP systems (refer to the discussion at the end of Chapter 12).

This dearth of predictive psychological theory means that in order to test certain usability properties of their designs, designers must observe how actual users interact with the developed product and measure their performance. In order for the results of those observations to be worthwhile, the experiments must be as close to a real interaction situation as possible. That means the experimental system must be very much like it would be in the final product whose requirements the designer is trying to establish! As John Carroll has pointed out, the very detail of the actual system can crucially affect its usability, so it is not worthwhile to experiment on crude estimates of it, as that will provide observations whose conclusions will not necessarily apply to the real system [59].

One principled approach to interactive system design, which will be important in later chapters, relies on a clear understanding early on in the design of the tasks that the user wishes to perform. One problem with this assumption is that the tasks a user will perform are often only known by the user after he is familiar with the system on which he performs them. The chicken-and-egg puzzle applies to tasks and the artifacts on which he performs those tasks. For example, before the advent of word processors, an author would not have considered the use of a contracting and expanding outlining facility to experiment easily and quickly with the structure of a paper while it was being typed. A typewriter simply did not provide the ability to perform such a task, so how would a designer know to support such a task in designing the first word processor?

Also, some of the tasks a user performs with a system were never explicitly intended as tasks by its designer. Take the example of a graphics drawing package that separates the constructed picture into separate layers. One layer is used to build graphical pictures which are entire objects – a circle or a square, for instance – and can be manipulated as those objects and retain their object identity. The other layer is used to paint pictures which are just a collection of pixels. The user can switch between the layers in order to create very complex pictures which are part object, part painted scene. But because of the complex interplay between overlapping images between the two layers, it is also possible to hide certain parts of the picture when in one layer and reveal them in the other layer. Such a facility will allow the user to do simple simulations, such as showing the effect of shadowing when switching a light on and off. It is very doubtful that the designers were thinking explicitly of supporting such simulation or animation tasks when they were designing these graphics systems, which were meant to build complex, but static, pictures.

A final point about the traditional software life cycle is that it does not promote the use of notations and techniques that support the user's perspective of the interactive system. We discussed earlier the purpose of validation and the formality gap. It is very difficult for an expert on human cognition to predict the cognitive demands that an abstract design would require of the intended user if the notation for the design does not reflect the kind of information the user must recall in order to interact. The same holds for assessing the timing behavior of an abstract design that does not explicitly mention the timing characteristics of the operations to be invoked or their relative ordering. Though no structured development process will entirely eliminate the formality gap, the particular notations used can go a long way towards making validation of non-functional requirements feasible with expert assistance.

In the remaining sections of this chapter, we will describe various approaches to augment the design process to suit better the design of interactive systems. These approaches are categorized under the banner of *user-centered design*.

6.3   USABILITY ENGINEERING

One approach to user-centered design has been the introduction of explicit *usability engineering* goals into the design process, as suggested by Whiteside and colleagues at IBM and Digital Equipment Corporation [377] and by Nielsen at Bellcore [260, 261]. Engineering depends on interpretation against a shared background of meaning, agreed goals and an understanding of how satisfactory completion will be judged. The emphasis for usability engineering is in knowing exactly what criteria will be used to judge a product for its usability.

The ultimate test of a product's usability is based on measurements of users' experience with it. Therefore, since a user's direct experience with an interactive system is at the physical interface, focus on the actual user interface is understandable. The danger with this limited focus is that much of the work that is accomplished in interaction involves more than just the surface features of the systems used to perform that work. In reality, the whole functional architecture of the system and the cognitive capacity of the users should be observed in order to arrive at meaningful measures. But it is not at all simple to derive measurements of activity beyond the physical actions in the world, and so usability engineering is limited in its application.

In relation to the software life cycle, one of the important features of usability engineering is the inclusion of a usability specification, forming part of the requirements specification, that concentrates on features of the user–system interaction which contribute to the usability of the product. Various attributes of the system are suggested as gauges for testing the usability. For each attribute, six items are defined to form the usability specification of that attribute. Table 6.1 provides an example of a usability specification for the design of a control panel for a video cassette recorder (VCR), based on the technique presented by Whiteside, Bennett and Holtzblatt [377].

Table 6.1 Sample usability specification for undo with a VCR

Attribute:	Backward recoverability
Measuring concept:	Undo an erroneous programming sequence
Measuring method:	Number of explicit user actions to undo current program
Now level:	No current product allows such an undo
Worst case:	As many actions as it takes to program in mistake
Planned level:	A maximum of two explicit user actions
Best case:	One explicit cancel action

In this example, we choose the principle of recoverability, described fully in Chapter 7, as the particular usability attribute of interest. Recoverability refers to the ability to reach a desired goal after recognition of some error in previous interaction. The recovery procedure can be in either a backward or forward sense. Current VCR design has resulted in interactive systems that are notoriously difficult to use; the redesign of a VCR provides a good case study for usability engineering. In designing a new VCR control panel, the designer wants to take into account how a user might recover from a mistake he discovers while trying to program the VCR to record some television program in his absence. One approach that the designer decides to follow is to allow the user the ability to undo the programming sequence, reverting the state of the VCR to what it was before the programming task began.

The backward recoverability attribute is defined in terms of a *measuring concept*, which makes the abstract attribute more concrete by describing it in terms of the actual product. So in this case, we realize backward recoverability as the ability to undo an erroneous programming sequence. The *measuring method* states how the attribute will be measured, in this case by the number of explicit user actions required to perform the undo, regardless of where the user is in the programming sequence.

The remaining four entries in the usability specification then provide the agreed criteria for judging the success of the product based on the measuring method. The *now level* indicates the value for the measurement with the existing system, whether it is computer based or not. The *worst case* value is the lowest acceptable measurement for the task, providing a clear distinction between what will be acceptable and what will be unacceptable in the final product. The *planned level* is the target for the design and the *best case* is the level which is agreed to be the best possible measurement given the current state of development tools and technology.

In the example, the designers can look at their previous VCR products and those of their competitors to determine a suitable now level. In this case, it is determined that no current model allows an undo which returns the state of the VCR to what it was before the programming task. For example, if a VCR allows you three separate recording programs, once you begin entering a new program in the number 1 program slot, the VCR forgets the previous contents of that slot and so you cannot recover it unless you remember what it was and then reprogram it.

Table 6.2 Criteria by which measuring method can be determined (adapted from Whiteside, Bennett and Holtzblatt [377], Copyright 1988, reprinted with permission from Elsevier)

1.	Time to complete a task
2.	Per cent of task completed
3.	Per cent of task completed per unit time
4.	Ratio of successes to failures
5.	Time spent in errors
6.	Per cent or number of errors
7.	Per cent or number of competitors better than it
8.	Number of commands used
9.	Frequency of help and documentation use
10.	Per cent of favorable/unfavorable user comments
11.	Number of repetitions of failed commands
12.	Number of runs of successes and of failures
13.	Number of times interface misleads the user
14.	Number of good and bad features recalled by users
15.	Number of available commands not invoked
16.	Number of regressive behaviors
17.	Number of users preferring your system
18.	Number of times users need to work around a problem
19.	Number of times the user is disrupted from a work task
20.	Number of times user loses control of the system
21.	Number of times user expresses frustration or satisfaction

Determining the worst case value depends on a number of things. Usually, it should be no lower than the now level. The new product should provide some improvement on the current state of affairs, and so it seems that at least some of the usability attributes should provide worst case values that are better than the now level. Otherwise, why would the customer bother with the new system (unless it can be shown to provide the same usability at a fraction of the cost)? The designers in the example have determined that the minimal acceptable undo facility would require the user to perform as many actions as he had done to program in the mistake. This is a clear improvement over the now level, since it at least provides for the possibility of undo. One way to provide such a capability would be by including an undo button on the control panel, which would effectively reverse the previous non-undo action. The designers figure that they should allow for the user to do a complete restoration of the VCR state in a maximum of two explicit user actions, though they recognize that the best case, at least in terms of the number of explicit actions, would require only one.

Tables 6.2 and 6.3, adapted from Whiteside, Bennett and Holtzblatt [377], provide a list of measurement criteria which can be used to determine the measuring method for a usability attribute and the possible ways to set the worst/best case and planned/now level targets. Measurements such as those promoted by usability engineering are also called *usability metrics*.

Table 6.3 Possible ways to set measurement levels in a usability specification (adapted from Whiteside, Bennett and Holtzblatt [377], Copyright 1988, reprinted with permission from Elsevier)

Set levels with respect to information on:

1. an existing system or previous version
2. competitive systems
3. carrying out the task without use of a computer system
4. an absolute scale
5. your own prototype
6. user's own earlier performance
7. each component of a system separately
8. a successive split of the difference between best and worst values observed in user tests

Table 6.4 Examples of usability metrics from ISO 9241

Usability objective	Effectiveness measures	Efficiency measures	Satisfaction measures
Suitability for the task	Percentage of goals achieved	Time to complete a task	Rating scale for satisfaction
Appropriate for trained users	Number of power features used	Relative efficiency compared with an expert user	Rating scale for satisfaction with power features
Learnability	Percentage of functions learned	Time to learn criterion	Rating scale for ease of learning
Error tolerance	Percentage of errors corrected successfully	Time spent on correcting errors	Rating scale for error handling

The ISO standard 9241, described earlier, also recommends the use of usability specifications as a means of requirements specification. Table 6.4 gives examples of usability metrics categorized by their contribution towards the three categories of usability: effectiveness, efficiency and satisfaction.

6.3.1 Problems with usability engineering

The major feature of usability engineering is the assertion of explicit usability metrics early on in the design process which can be used to judge a system once it is delivered. There is a very solid argument which points out that it is only through empirical approaches such as the use of usability metrics that we can reliably build more usable systems. Although the ultimate yardstick for determining usability may be by observing and measuring user performance, that does not mean that these measurements are the best way to produce a predictive design process for usability.

The problem with usability metrics is that they rely on measurements of very specific user actions in very specific situations. When the designer knows what the actions and situation will be, then she can set goals for measured observations. However, at early stages of design, designers do not have this information. Take our example usability specification for the VCR. In setting the acceptable and unacceptable levels for backward recovery, there is an assumption that a button will be available to invoke the undo. In fact, the designer was already making an implicit assumption that the user would be making errors in the programming of the VCR. Why not address the origin of the programming errors, then maybe undo would not be necessary?

We should recognize another inherent limitation for usability engineering, that is it provides a means of satisfying usability specifications and not necessarily usability. The designer is still forced to understand why a particular usability metric enhances usability for real people. Again, in the VCR example, the designer assumed that fewer explicit actions make the undo operation easier. Is that kind of assumption warranted?

6.4   ITERATIVE DESIGN AND PROTOTYPING

A point we raised earlier is that requirements for an interactive system cannot be completely specified from the beginning of the life cycle. The only way to be sure about some features of the potential design is to build them and test them out on real users. The design can then be modified to correct any false assumptions that were revealed in the testing. This is the essence of *iterative design*, a purposeful design process which tries to overcome the inherent problems of incomplete requirements specification by cycling through several designs, incrementally improving upon the final product with each pass.

The problems with the design process, which lead to an iterative design philosophy, are not unique to the usability features of the intended system. The problem holds for requirements specification in general, and so it is a general software engineering problem, together with technical and managerial issues.

On the technical side, iterative design is described by the use of *prototypes*, artifacts that simulate or animate some but not all features of the intended system. There are three main approaches to prototyping:

Throw-away   The prototype is built and tested. The design knowledge gained from this exercise is used to build the final product, but the actual prototype is discarded. Figure 6.5 depicts the procedure in using throw-away prototypes to arrive at a final requirements specification in order for the rest of the design process to proceed.

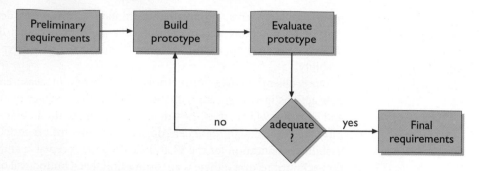

Figure 6.5 Throw-away prototyping within requirements specification

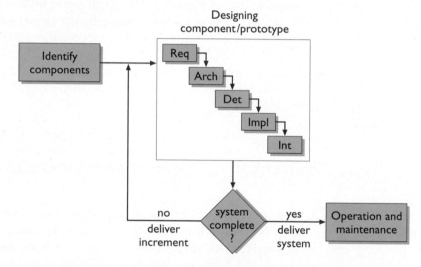

Figure 6.6 Incremental prototyping within the life cycle

Incremental   The final product is built as separate components, one at a time. There is one overall design for the final system, but it is partitioned into independent and smaller components. The final product is then released as a series of products, each subsequent release including one more component. This is depicted in Figure 6.6.

Evolutionary   Here the prototype is not discarded and serves as the basis for the next iteration of design. In this case, the actual system is seen as evolving from a very limited initial version to its final release, as depicted in Figure 6.7. Evolutionary prototyping also fits in well with the modifications which must be made to the system that arise during the operation and maintenance activity in the life cycle.

Prototypes differ according to the amount of functionality and performance they provide relative to the final product. An *animation* of requirements can involve no

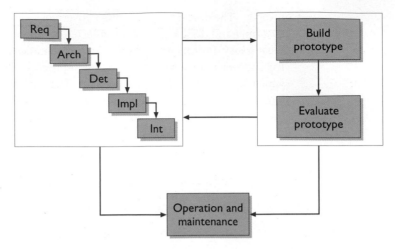

Figure 6.7   Evolutionary prototyping throughout the life cycle

real functionality, or limited functionality to simulate only a small aspect of the interactive behavior for evaluative purposes. At the other extreme, full functionality can be provided at the expense of other performance characteristics, such as speed or error tolerance. Regardless of the level of functionality, the importance of a prototype lies in its projected realism. The prototype of an interactive system is used to test requirements by evaluating their impact with real users. An honest appraisal of the requirements of the final system can only be trusted if the evaluation conditions are similar to those anticipated for the actual operation. But providing realism is costly, so there must be support for a designer/programmer to create a realistic prototype quickly and efficiently.

On the management side, there are several potential problems, as pointed out by Sommerville [327]:

Time   Building prototypes takes time and, if it is a throw-away prototype, it can be seen as precious time taken away from the real design task. So the value of prototyping is only appreciated if it is fast, hence the use of the term *rapid prototyping*. However, rapid development and manipulation of a prototype should not be mistaken for rushed evaluation which might lead to erroneous results and invalidate the only advantage of using a prototype in the first place.

Planning   Most project managers do not have the experience necessary for adequately planning and costing a design process which involves prototyping.

Non-functional features   Often the most important features of a system will be non-functional ones, such as safety and reliability, and these are precisely the kinds of features which are sacrificed in developing a prototype. For evaluating usability features of a prototype, response time – yet another feature often compromised in a prototype – could be critical to product acceptance. This problem is similar to the technical issue of prototype realism.

Contracts The design process is often governed by contractual agreements between customer and designer which are affected by many of these managerial and technical issues. Prototypes and other implementations cannot form the basis for a legal contract, and so an iterative design process will still require documentation which serves as the binding agreement. There must be an effective way of translating the results derived from prototyping into adequate documentation. A rapid prototyping process might be amenable to quick changes, but that does not also apply to the design process.

6.4.1 Techniques for prototyping

Here we will describe some of the techniques that are available for producing rapid prototypes.

Storyboards

Probably the simplest notion of a prototype is the *storyboard*, which is a graphical depiction of the outward appearance of the intended system, without any accompanying system functionality. Storyboards do not require much in terms of computing power to construct; in fact, they can be mocked up without the aid of any computing resource. The origins of storyboards are in the film industry, where a series of panels roughly depicts snapshots from an intended film sequence in order to get the idea across about the eventual scene. Similarly, for interactive system design, the storyboards provide snapshots of the interface at particular points in the interaction. Evaluating customer or user impressions of the storyboards can determine relatively quickly if the design is heading in the right direction.

Modern graphical drawing packages now make it possible to create storyboards with the aid of a computer instead of by hand. Though the graphic design achievable on screen may not be as sophisticated as that possible by a professional graphic designer, it is more realistic because the final system will have to be displayed on a screen. Also, it is possible to provide crude but effective *animation* by automated sequencing through a series of snapshots. Animation illustrates the dynamic aspects of the intended user–system interaction, which may not be possible with traditional paper-based storyboards. If not animated, storyboards usually include annotations and scripts indicating how the interaction will occur.

Limited functionality simulations

More functionality must be built into the prototype to demonstrate the work that the application will accomplish. Storyboards and animation techniques are not sufficient for this purpose, as they cannot portray adequately the interactive aspects of the system. To do this, some portion of the functionality must be *simulated* by the design team.

Programming support for simulations means a designer can rapidly build graphical and textual interaction objects and attach some behavior to those objects, which mimics the system's functionality. Once this simulation is built, it can be evaluated and changed rapidly to reflect the results of the evaluation study with various users.

For example, we might want to build a prototype for the VCR with undo described earlier using only a workstation display, keyboard and mouse. We could draw a picture of the VCR with its control panel using a graphics drawing package, but then we would want to allow a subject to use the mouse to position a finger cursor over one of the buttons to 'press' it and actuate some behavior of the VCR. In this way, we could simulate the programming task and experiment with different options for undoing.

DESIGN FOCUS

Prototyping in practice

IBM supplied the computerized information and messaging booths for the 1984 Olympics in Los Angeles. These booths were to be used by the many thousands of residents in the Olympic village who would have to use them with no prior training (extensive instructions in several hundred languages being impractical). IBM sampled several variants on the kiosk design of the telephone-based system, using what they called the hallway and storefront methodology [152]. The final system was intended to be a walk-up-and-use system, so it was important to get comments from people with no knowledge of the process. Early versions of the kiosk were displayed as storyboards on a mock kiosk design in the front hallway of the Yorktown Research Lab. Passers-by were encouraged to browse at the display much as they would a storefront in the window. As casual comments were made and the kiosk was modified according to those comments, more and more active evaluation was elicited. This procedure helped to determine the ultimate positioning of display screens and telephones for the final design.

An Olympic Message System Kiosk (Gould J. D., Boies S. J., Levy S., Richards J. T. and Schoonard J. (1987). The 1984 Olympic Message System: a test of behavioral principles of system design. *Communications of the ACM*, **30**(9), 758–69. Copyright © 1987 ACM, Inc. Reprinted by permission)

There are now plenty of prototyping tools available which allow the rapid development of such simulation prototypes. These simulation tools are meant to provide a quick development process for a very wide range of small but highly interactive applications. A well-known and successful prototyping tool is *HyperCard*, a simulation environment for the Macintosh line of Apple computers. HyperCard is similar to the animation tools described above in that the user can create a graphical depiction of some system, say the VCR, with common graphical tools. The graphical images are placed on cards, and links between cards can be created which control the sequencing from one card to the next for animation effects. What HyperCard provides beyond this type of animation is the ability to describe more sophisticated interactive behavior by attaching a *script*, written in the HyperTalk programming language, to any object. So for the VCR, we could attach a script to any control panel button to highlight it or make an audible noise when the user clicks the mouse cursor over it. Then some functionality could be associated to that button by reflecting some change in the VCR display window. Similar functionality is provided through tools such as Macromedia Flash and Director.

Most of the simulations produced are intended to be throw-away prototypes because of their relatively inefficient implementation. They are not intended to support full-blown systems development and they are unsatisfactory in that role. However, as more designers recognize the utility of prototyping and iterative design, they are beginning to demand ways of incorporating the prototypes into the final delivered systems – more along the lines of evolutionary prototyping. A good example of this is in the avionics industry, where it has long been recognized that iterative development via rapid prototyping and evaluation is essential for the design of flight deck instrumentation and controls. Workstation technology provides sufficient graphics capabilities to enable a designer to produce very realistic gauges, which can be assessed and critiqued by actual pilots. With the advent of the glass cockpit – in which traditional mechanical gauges are replaced by gauges represented on video displays – there is no longer a technology gap between the prototype designs of flight deck instruments and the actual instruments in flight. Therefore, it is a reasonable request by these designers that they be able to reuse the functionality of the prototypes in the actual flight simulators and cockpits, and this demand is starting to be met by commercial prototyping systems which produce efficient code for use in such safety-critical applications.

One technique for simulation, which does not require very much computer-supported functionality, is the *Wizard of Oz* technique. With this technique, the designers can develop a limited functionality prototype and enhance its functionality in evaluation by providing the missing functionality through human intervention. A participant in the evaluation of a new accounting system may not have any computer training but is familiar with accounting procedures. He is asked to sit down in front of the prototype accounting system and to perform some task, say to check the accounts receivable against some newly arrived payments. The naïve computer user will not know the specific language of the system, but you do not want him to worry about that. Instead, he is given instructions to type whatever seems the most natural commands to the system. One of the designers – the wizard in this scenario – is situated in another room, out of sight of the subject, but she is able to receive the subject's input commands and translate them into commands that will work on the prototype. By intervening between the user and system, the wizard is able to increase the perceived functionality of the system so that evaluation can concentrate on how the subject would react to the complete system. Examination of how the wizard had to interpret the subject's input can provide advice as to how the prototype must be enhanced in its later versions.

High-level programming support

HyperTalk was an example of a special-purpose high-level programming language which makes it easy for the designer to program certain features of an interactive system at the expense of other system features like speed of response or space efficiency. HyperTalk and many similar languages allow the programmer to attach functional behavior to the specific interactions that the user will be able to do, such as position and click on the mouse over a button on the screen. Previously, the difficulty of interactive programming was that it was so implementation dependent that the programmer would have to know quite a bit of intimate detail of the hardware system in order to control even the simplest of interactive behavior. These high-level programming languages allow the programmer to abstract away from the hardware specifics and think in terms that are closer to the way the input and output devices are perceived as interaction devices.

Though not usually considered together with such simulation environments, a *user interface management system* – or UIMS (pronounced 'you-imz') – can be considered to provide such high-level programming support. The frequent conceptual model put forth for interactive system design is to separate the application functionality from its presentation. It is then possible to program the underlying functionality of the system and to program the behavior of the user interface separately. The job of a UIMS, then, is to allow the programmer to connect the behavior at the interface with the underlying functionality. In Chapter 8 we will discuss in more detail the advantages and disadvantages of such a conceptual model and concentrate on the programming implementation support provided by a UIMS. What is of interest here is that the separation implied by a UIMS allows the independent development of the features of the interface apart from the underlying functionality. If the underlying system is already developed, then various prototypes of its interface can be quickly constructed and evaluated to determine the optimal one.

6.4.2 Warning about iterative design

Though we have presented the process of iterative design as not only beneficial but also necessary for good interactive system design, it is important to recognize some of its drawbacks, in addition to the very real management issues we have already raised. The ideal model of iterative design, in which a rapid prototype is designed, evaluated and modified until the best possible design is achieved in the given project time, is appealing. But there are two problems.

First, it is often the case that design decisions made at the very beginning of the prototyping process are wrong and, in practice, design inertia can be so great as never to overcome an initial bad decision. So, whereas iterative design is, in theory, amenable to great changes through iterations, it can be the case that the initial prototype has bad features that will not be amended. We will examine this problem through a real example of a clock on a microwave oven.[2] The clock has a numeric display of four digits. Thus the display is capable of showing values in the range from 00:00 to 99:99. The functional model of time for the actual clock is only 12 hours, so quite a few of the possible clock displays do not correspond to possible times (for example, 63:00, 85:49), even though some of them are legal four-digit time designations. That poses no problem, as long as both the designer and the ultimate users of the clock both share the knowledge of the discrepancy between possible clock displays and legal times. Such would not be the case for someone assuming a 24-hour time format, in which case the displays 00:30 and 13:45 would represent valid times in their model but not in the microwave's model. In this particular example, the subjects tested during the evaluation must have all shared the 12-hour time model, and the mismatch with the other users (with a 24-hour model) was only discovered after the product was being shipped. At this point, the only impact of iterative design was a change to the documentation alerting the reader to the 12-hour format, as it was too late to perform any hardware change.

The second problem is slightly more subtle, and serious. If, in the process of evaluation, a potential usability problem is diagnosed, it is important to understand the reason for the problem and not just detect the symptom. In the clock example, the designers could have noticed that some subjects with a 24-hour time model were having difficulty setting the time. Say they were trying to set the time for 14:45, but they were not being allowed to do that. If the designers did not know the subject's goals, they might not detect the 24/12 hour discrepancy. They would instead notice that the users were having trouble setting the time and so they might change the buttons used to set the time instead of other possible changes, such as an analog time dial, or displaying AM or PM on the clock dial to make the 12-hour model more obvious, or to change to a 24-hour clock.

The moral for iterative design is that it should be used in conjunction with other, more principled approaches to interactive system design. These principled approaches are the subject of Part 3 of this book.

6.5   DESIGN RATIONALE

In designing any computer system, many decisions are made as the product goes from a set of vague customer requirements to a deliverable entity. Often it is difficult to recreate the reasons, or rationale, behind various design decisions. *Design*

---

2 This example has been provided by Harold Thimbleby.

rationale is the information that explains why a computer system is the way it is, including its structural or architectural description and its functional or behavioral description. In this sense, design rationale does not fit squarely into the software life cycle described in this chapter as just another phase or box. Rather, design rationale relates to an activity of both reflection (doing design rationale) and documentation (creating a design rationale) that occurs throughout the entire life cycle.

It is beneficial to have access to the design rationale for several reasons:

- In an explicit form, a design rationale provides a communication mechanism among the members of a design team so that during later stages of design and/or maintenance it is possible to understand what critical decisions were made, what alternatives were investigated (and, possibly, in what order) and the reason why one alternative was chosen over the others. This can help avoid incorrect assumptions later.
- Accumulated knowledge in the form of design rationales for a set of products can be reused to transfer what has worked in one situation to another situation which has similar needs. The design rationale can capture the context of a design decision in order that a different design team can determine if a similar rationale is appropriate for their product.
- The effort required to produce a design rationale forces the designer to deliberate more carefully about design decisions. The process of deliberation can be assisted by the design rationale technique by suggesting how arguments justifying or discarding a particular design option are formed.

In the area of HCI, design rationale has been particularly important, again for several reasons:

- There is usually no single best design alternative. More often, the designer is faced with a set of trade-offs between different alternatives. For example, a graphical interface may involve a set of actions that the user can invoke by use of the mouse and the designer must decide whether to present each action as a 'button' on the screen, which is always visible, or hide all of the actions in a menu which must be explicitly invoked before an action can be chosen. The former option maximizes the operation visibility (see Chapter 7) but the latter option takes up less screen space. It would be up to the designer to determine which criterion for evaluating the options was more important and then communicating that information in a design rationale.
- Even if an optimal solution did exist for a given design decision, the space of alternatives is so vast that it is unlikely a designer would discover it. In this case, it is important that the designer indicates all alternatives that have been investigated. Then later on it can be determined if she has not considered the best solution or had thought about it and discarded it for some reason. In project management, this kind of accountability for design is good.
- The usability of an interactive system is very dependent on the context of its use. The flashiest graphical interface is of no use if the end-user does not have access to a high-quality graphics display or a pointing device. Capturing the context in

which a design decision is made will help later when new products are designed. If the context remains the same, then the old rationale can be adopted without revision. If the context has changed somehow, the old rationale can be re-examined to see if any rejected alternatives are now more favorable or if any new alternatives are now possible.

Lee and Lai [209] explain that various proponents of design rationale have different interpretations of what it actually is. We will make use of their classification to describe various design rationale techniques in this section. The first set of techniques concentrates on providing a historical record of design decisions and is very much tailored for use during actual design discussions. These techniques are referred to as process-oriented design rationale because they are meant to be integrated in the actual design process itself. The next category is not so concerned with historical or process-oriented information but rather with the structure of the space of all design alternatives, which can be reconstructed by post hoc consideration of the design activity. The structure-oriented approach does not capture historical information. Instead, it captures the complete story of the moment, as an analysis of the design space which has been considered so far. The final category of design rationale concentrates on capturing the claims about the psychology of the user that are implied by an interactive system and the tasks that are performed on them.

There are some issues that distinguish the various techniques in terms of their usability within design itself. We can use these issues to sketch an informal rationale for design rationale. One issue is the degree to which the technique impinges on the design process. Does the use of a particular design rationale technique alter the decision process, or does it just passively serve to document it? Another issue is the cost of using the technique, both in terms of creating the design rationale and in terms of accessing it once created. A related issue is the amount of computational power the design rationale provides and the level to which this is supported by automated tools. A design rationale for a complex system can be very large and the exploration of the design space changes over time. The kind of information stored in a given design rationale will affect how that vast amount of information can be effectively managed and browsed.

6.5.1 Process-oriented design rationale

Much of the work on design rationale is based on Rittel's *issue-based information system*, or *IBIS*, a style for representing design and planning dialog developed in the 1970s [308]. In IBIS (pronounced 'ibbiss'), a hierarchical structure to a design rationale is created. A root *issue* is identified which represents the main problem or question that the argument is addressing. Various *positions* are put forth as potential resolutions for the root issue, and these are depicted as descendants in the IBIS hierarchy directly connected to the root issue. Each position is then supported or refuted by *arguments*, which modify the relationship between issue and position. The hierarchy grows as secondary issues are raised which modify the root issue in some way. Each of these secondary issues is in turn expanded by positions and arguments, further sub-issues, and so on.

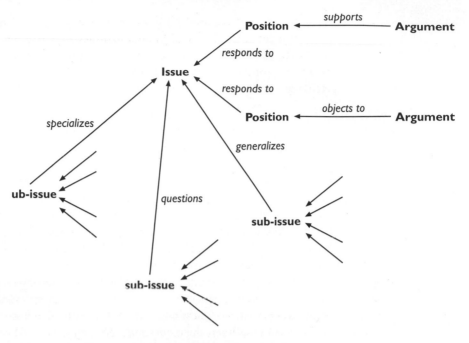

Figure 6.8   The structure of a gIBIS design rationale

A graphical version of IBIS has been defined by Conklin and Yakemovic [77], called *gIBIS* (pronounced 'gibbiss'), which makes the structure of the design rationale more apparent visually in the form of a directed graph which can be directly edited by the creator of the design rationale. Figure 6.8 gives a representation of the gIBIS vocabulary. Issues, positions and arguments are nodes in the graph and the connections between them are labeled to clarify the relationship between adjacent nodes. So, for example, an issue can suggest further sub-issues, or a position can respond to an issue or an argument can support a position. The gIBIS structure can be supported by a hypertext tool to allow a designer to create and browse various parts of the design rationale.

There have been other versions of the IBIS notation, both graphical and textual, besides gIBIS. Most versions retain the distinction between issues, positions and arguments. Some add further nodes, such as Potts and Bruns's [297] addition of design artifacts which represent the intermediate products of a design that lead to the final product and are associated with the various alternatives discussed in the design rationale. Some add a richer vocabulary to modify the relationships between the node elements, such as McCall's Procedural Hierarchy of Issues (PHI) [231], which expands the variety of inter-issue relationships. Interesting work at the University of Colorado has attempted to link PHI argumentation to computer-aided design (CAD) tools to allow critique of design (in their example, the design of a kitchen) as it occurs. When the CAD violates some known design rule, the designer is warned and can then browse a PHI argument to see the rationale for the design rule.

The use of IBIS and any of its descendants is process oriented, as we described above. It is intended for use during design meetings as a means of recording and structuring the issues deliberated and the decisions made. It is also intended to preserve the order of deliberation and decision making for a particular product, placing less stress on the generalization of design knowledge for use between different products. This can be contrasted with the structure-oriented technique discussed next.

6.5.2 Design space analysis

MacLean and colleagues [222] have proposed a more deliberative approach to design rationale which emphasizes a post hoc structuring of the space of design alternatives that have been considered in a design project. Their approach, embodied in the Questions, Options and Criteria (QOC) notation, is characterized as *design space analysis* (see Figure 6.9).

The design space is initially structured by a set of questions representing the major issues of the design. Since design space analysis is structure oriented, it is not so important that the questions recorded are the actual questions asked during design meetings. Rather, these questions represent an agreed characterization of the

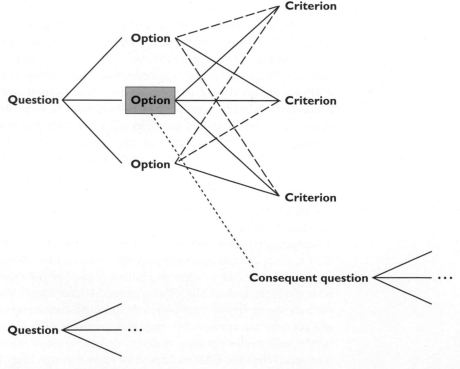

Figure 6.9   The QOC notation

issues raised based on reflection and understanding of the actual design activities. Questions in a design space analysis are therefore similar to issues in IBIS except in the way they are captured. Options provide alternative solutions to the question. They are assessed according to some criteria in order to determine the most favorable option. In Figure 6.9 an option which is favorably assessed in terms of a criterion is linked with a solid line, whereas negative links have a dashed line. The most favorable option is boxed in the diagram.

The key to an effective design space analysis using the QOC notation is deciding the right questions to use to structure the space and the correct criteria to judge the options. The initial questions raised must be sufficiently general that they cover a large enough portion of the possible design space, but specific enough that a range of options can be clearly identified. It can be difficult to decide the right set of criteria with which to assess the options. The QOC technique advocates the use of general criteria, like the usability principles we shall discuss in Chapter 7, which are expressed more explicitly in a given analysis. In the example of the action buttons versus the menu of actions described earlier, we could contextualize the general principle of operation visibility as the criterion that all possible actions are displayed at all times. It can be very difficult to decide from a design space analysis which option is most favorable. The positive and negative links in the QOC notation do not provide all of the context for a trade-off decision. There is no provision for indicating, for example, that one criterion is more important than any of the others and the most favorable option must be positively linked.

Another structure-oriented technique, called Decision Representation Language (DRL), developed by Lee and Lai, structures the design space in a similar fashion to QOC, though its language is somewhat larger and it has a formal semantics. The questions, options and criteria in DRL are given the names: decision problem, alternatives and goals. QOC assessments are represented in DRL by a more complex language for relating goals to alternatives. The sparse language in QOC used to assess an option relative to a criterion (positive or negative assessment only) is probably insufficient, but there is a trade-off involved in adopting a more complex vocabulary which may prove too difficult to use in practice. The advantage of the formal semantics of DRL is that the design rationale can be used as a computational mechanism to help manage the large volume of information. For example, DRL can track the dependencies between different decision problems, so that subsequent changes to the design rationale for one decision problem can be automatically propagated to other dependent problems.

Design space analysis directly addresses the claim that no design activity can hope to uncover all design possibilities, so the best we can hope to achieve is to document the small part of the design space that has been investigated. An advantage of the post hoc technique is that it can abstract away from the particulars of a design meeting and therefore represent the design knowledge in such a way that it can be of use in the design of other products. The major disadvantage is the increased overhead such an analysis warrants. More time must be taken away from the design activity to do this separate documentation task. When time is scarce, these kinds of overhead costs are the first to be trimmed.

6.5.3 Psychological design rationale

The final category of design rationale tries to make explicit the psychological claims of usability inherent in any interactive system in order better to suit a product for the tasks users have. This psychological design rationale has been introduced by Carroll and Rosson [62], and before we describe the application of the technique it is important to understand some of its theoretical background.

People use computers to accomplish some tasks in their particular work domain, as we have seen before. When designing a new interactive system, the designers take into account the tasks that users currently perform and any new ones that they may want to perform. This task identification serves as part of the requirements for the new system, and can be done through empirical observation of how people perform their work currently and presented through informal language or a more formal task analysis language (see Chapter 15). When the new system is implemented, or becomes an *artifact*, further observation reveals that in addition to the required tasks it was built to support, it also supports users in tasks that the designer never intended. Once designers understand these new tasks, and the associated problems that arise between them and the previously known tasks, the new task definitions can serve as requirements for future artifacts.

Carroll refers to this real-life phenomenon as the *task–artifact cycle*. He provides a good example of this cycle through the evolution of the electronic spreadsheet. When the first electronic spreadsheet, *VisiCalc*, was marketed in the late 1970s, it was presented simply as an automated means of supporting tabular calculation, a task commonly used in the accounting world. Within little over a decade of its introduction, the application of spreadsheets had far outstripped its original intent within accounting. Spreadsheets were being used for all kinds of financial analysis, 'what-if' simulations, report formatting and even as a general programming language paradigm! As the set of tasks expands, new spreadsheet products have flooded the marketplace trying to satisfy the growing customer base. Another good example of the task–artifact cycle in action is with word processing, which was originally introduced to provide more automated support for tasks previously achieved with a typewriter and now provides users with the ability to carry out various authoring tasks that they never dreamed possible with a conventional typewriter. And today, the tasks for the spreadsheet and the word processor are intermingled in the same artifact.

The purpose of psychological design rationale is to support this natural task–artifact cycle of design activity. The main emphasis is not to capture the designer's intention in building the artifact. Rather, psychological design rationale aims to make explicit the consequences of a design for the user, given an understanding of what tasks he intends to perform. Previously, these psychological consequences were left implicit in the design, though designers would make informal claims about their systems (for example, that it is more 'natural' for the user, or easier to learn).

The first step in the psychological design rationale is to identify the tasks that the proposed system will address and to characterize those tasks by questions that the user tries to answer in accomplishing them. For instance, Carroll gives an example of designing a system to help programmers learn the Smalltalk object-oriented programming language environment. The main task the system is to support is learning how Smalltalk works. In learning about the programming environment, the programmer will perform tasks that help her answer the questions:

- What can I do: that is, what are the possible operations or functions that this programming environment allows?
- How does it work: that is, what do the various functions do?
- How can I do this: that is, once I know a particular operation I want to perform, how do I go about programming it?

For each question, a set of *scenarios* of user–system behavior is suggested to support the user in addressing the question. For example, to address the question 'What can I do?', the designers can describe a scenario whereby the novice programmer is first confronted with the learning environment and sees that she can invoke some demo programs to investigate how Smalltalk programs work. The initial system can then be implemented to provide the functionality suggested by the scenarios (for example, some demos would be made accessible and obvious to the user/programmer from the very beginning). Once this system is running, observation of its use and some designer reflection is used to produce the actual psychological design rationale for that version of the system. This is where the psychological claims are made explicit. For example, there is an assumption that the programmer knows that what she can see on the screen relates to what she can do (if she sees the list of programs under a heading 'Demos', she can click on one program name to see the associated demo). The psychological claim of this demo system is that the user learns by doing, which is a good thing. However, there may also be negative aspects that are equally important to mention. The demo may not be very interactive, in which case the user clicks on it to initiate it and then just sits back and watches a graphic display, never really learning how the demo application is constructed in Smalltalk. These negative aspects can be used to modify later versions of the system to allow more interactive demos, which represent realistic, yet simple, applications, whose behavior and structure the programmer can appreciate.

By forcing the designer to document the psychological design rationale, it is hoped that she will become more aware of the natural evolution of user tasks and the artifact, taking advantage of how consequences of one design can be used to improve later designs.

Worked exercise   *What is the distinction between a process-oriented and a structure-oriented design rationale technique? Would you classify psychological design rationale as process or structure oriented? Why?*

Answer   The distinction between a process- and structure-oriented design rationale resides in what information the design rationale attempts to capture. Process-oriented design rationale is interested in recording an historically accurate description of a design team making some decision on a particular issue for the design. In this sense, process-oriented design rationale becomes an activity concurrent with the rest of the design process. Structure-oriented design rationale is less interested in preserving the historical evolution of the design. Rather, it is more interested in providing the conclusions of the design activity, so it can be done in a post hoc and reflective manner after the fact.

The purpose of psychological design rationale is to support the task–artifact cycle. Here, the tasks that the users perform are changed by the systems on which they perform the tasks. A psychological design rationale proceeds by having the designers of the system record what they believe are the tasks that the system should support and then building the system to support the tasks. The designers suggest scenarios for the tasks which will be used to observe new users of the system. Observations of the users provide the information needed for the actual design rationale of that version of the system. The consequences of the design's assumptions about the important tasks are then gauged against the actual use in an attempt to justify the design or suggest improvements.

Psychological design rationale is mainly a process-oriented approach. The activity of a claims analysis is precisely about capturing what the designers assumed about the system at one point in time and how those assumptions compared with actual use. Therefore, the history of the psychological design rationale is important. The discipline involved in performing a psychological design rationale requires designers to perform the claims analysis during the actual design activity, and not as post hoc reconstruction.

6.6 SUMMARY

In this chapter, we have shown how software engineering and the design process relate to interactive system design. The software engineering life cycle aims to structure design in order to increase the reliability of the design process. For interactive system design, this would equate to a reliable and reproducible means of designing predictably usable systems. Because of the special needs of interactive systems, it is essential to augment the standard life cycle in order to address issues of HCI.

Usability engineering encourages incorporating explicit usability goals within the design process, providing a means by which the product's usability can be judged. Iterative design practices admit that principled design of interactive systems alone cannot maximize product usability, so the designer must be able to evaluate early prototypes and rapidly correct features of the prototype which detract from the product usability.

The design process is composed of a series of decisions, which pare down the vast set of potential systems to the one that is actually delivered to the customer. Design rationale, in its many forms, is aimed at allowing the designer to manage the information about the decision-making process, in terms of when and why design decisions were made and what consequences those decisions had for the user in accomplishing his work.

EXERCISES

6.1 (a) How can design rationale benefit interface design and why might it be rejected by design teams?

(b) Explain QOC design rationale using an example to illustrate.

6.2 Imagine you have been asked to produce a prototype for the diary system discussed in the worked exercise in Section 7.2.3. What would be an appropriate prototyping approach to enable you to test the design using the usability metrics specified, and why?

RECOMMENDED READING

J. A. McDermid, editor, *The Software Engineer's Reference Book*, Butterworth–Heinemann, 1992.

A very good general reference book for all topics in software engineering. In particular, we refer you to Chapter 15 on software life cycles and Chapter 40 on prototyping.

I. Sommerville, *Software Engineering*, 6th edition, Addison-Wesley, 2000.

This textbook is one of the few texts in software engineering that specifically treats issues of interface design.

X. Faulkner, *Usability Engineering*, Macmillan, 2000.

An excellent and accessible introduction to usability engineering covering, amongst other things, user requirements capture and usability metrics.

J. Whiteside, J. Bennett and K. Holtzblatt, Usability engineering: our experience and evolution. In M. Helander, editor, *Handbook for Human–Computer Interaction*, North-Holland, 1988.

The seminal work on usability engineering. More recent work on usability engineering has also been published by Jakob Nielsen [260, 261].

J. M. Carroll and T. P. Moran, editors, *Design Rationale: Concepts, Techniques and Use*, Lawrence Erlbaum, 1996.

Expanded from a double special journal issue, this provides comprehensive coverage of relevant work in the field.

7 DESIGN RULES

OVERVIEW

■ Designing for maximum usability is the goal of interactive systems design.

■ Abstract principles offer a way of understanding usability in a more general sense, especially if we can express them within some coherent catalog.

■ Design rules in the form of standards and guidelines provide direction for design, in both general and more concrete terms, in order to enhance the interactive properties of the system.

■ The essential characteristics of good design are often summarized through 'golden rules' or heuristics.

■ Design patterns provide a potentially generative approach to capturing and reusing design knowledge.

7.1 INTRODUCTION

One of the central problems that must be solved in a user-centered design process is how to provide designers with the ability to determine the usability consequences of their design decisions. We require *design rules*, which are rules a designer can follow in order to increase the usability of the eventual software product. We can classify these rules along two dimensions, based on the rule's authority and generality. By authority, we mean an indication of whether or not the rule must be followed in design or whether it is only suggested. By generality, we mean whether the rule can be applied to many design situations or whether it is focussed on a more limited application situation. Rules also vary in their level of abstraction, with some abstracting away from the detail of the design solution and others being quite specific. It is also important to determine the origins of a design rule. We will consider a number of different types of design rules. *Principles* are abstract design rules, with high generality and low authority. *Standards* are specific design rules, high in authority and limited in application, whereas *guidelines* tend to be lower in authority and more general in application.

Design rules for interactive systems can be supported by psychological, cognitive, ergonomic, sociological, economic or computational theory, which may or may not have roots in empirical evidence. Designers do not always have the relevant background in psychology, cognitive science, ergonomics, sociology, business or computer science necessary to understand the consequences of those theories in the instance of the design they are creating. The design rules are used to apply the theory in practice. Often a set of design rules will be in conflict with each other, meaning that strict adherence to all of them is impossible. The theory underlying the separate design rules can help the designer understand the trade-off for the design that would result in following or disregarding some of the rules. Usually, the more general a design rule is, the greater the likelihood that it will conflict with other rules and the greater the need for the designer to understand the theory behind it.

We can make another rough distinction between principles, standards and guidelines. Principles are derived from knowledge of the psychological, computational and sociological aspects of the problem domains and are largely independent of the technology; they depend to a much greater extent on a deeper understanding of the human element in the interaction. They can therefore be applied widely but are not so useful for specific design advice. Guidelines are less abstract and often more technology oriented, but as they are also general, it is important for a designer to know what theoretical evidence there is to support them. A designer will have less of a need to know the underlying theory for applying a standard. However, since standards carry a much higher level of authority, it is more important that the theory underlying them be correct or sound.

The previous chapter was about the process of design, and we need to consider when design rules can be of use within that process. Design rules are mechanisms for restricting the space of design options, preventing a designer from pursuing design options that would be likely to lead to an unusable system. Thus, design rules would be most effective if they could be adopted in the earliest stages of the life cycle, such as in requirements specification and architectural design, when the space of possible designs is still very large. We have already seen, for example, in Chapter 6, how abstract principles can be applied in usability engineering.

However, if the designer does not understand the assumptions underlying a design rule, it is quite possible that early application can prevent the best design choice. For example, a set of design rules might be specific to a particular hardware platform and inappropriate for other platforms (for example, color versus monochrome screens, one- versus two- or three-button mouse). Such bias in some design rules causes them to be applicable only in later stages of the life cycle.

We will first discuss abstract principles, then go on to consider in more depth some examples of standards and guidelines for user-centered design. Finally, we will consider some well-known heuristics or 'golden rules' which, it has been suggested, provide a succinct summary of the essence of good design. We end the chapter with a discussion of design patterns, a relatively new approach to capturing design knowledge in HCI.

7.2 PRINCIPLES TO SUPPORT USABILITY

The most abstract design rules are general principles, which can be applied to the design of an interactive system in order to promote its usability. In Chapter 4 we looked at the different paradigms that represent the development of interactive systems. Derivation of principles for interaction has usually arisen out of a need to explain why a paradigm is successful and when it might not be. Principles can provide the repeatability which paradigms in themselves cannot provide. In this section we present a collection of usability principles. Since it is too bold an objective to produce a comprehensive catalog of such principles, our emphasis will be on structuring the presentation of usability principles in such a way that the catalog can be easily extended as our knowledge increases.

The principles we present are first divided into three main categories:

Learnability – the ease with which new users can begin effective interaction and achieve maximal performance.

Flexibility – the multiplicity of ways in which the user and system exchange information.

Robustness – the level of support provided to the user in determining successful achievement and assessment of goals.

In the following, we will subdivide these main categories into more specific principles that support them. In most cases, we are able to situate these more specific principles within a single category, but we have made explicit those cases when a principle falls into two of the above categories.

Table 7.1 Summary of principles affecting learnability

Principle	Definition	Related principles
Predictability	Support for the user to determine the effect of future action based on past interaction history	Operation visibility
Synthesizability	Support for the user to assess the effect of past operations on the current state	Immediate/eventual honesty
Familiarity	The extent to which a user's knowledge and experience in other real-world or computer-based domains can be applied when interacting with a new system	Guessability, affordance
Generalizability	Support for the user to extend knowledge of specific interaction within and across applications to other similar situations	–
Consistency	Likeness in input–output behavior arising from similar situations or similar task objectives	–

7.2.1 Learnability

Learnability concerns the features of the interactive system that allow novice users to understand how to use it initially and then how to attain a maximal level of performance. Table 7.1 contains a summary of the specific principles that support learnability, which we will describe below.

Predictability

Except when interacting with some video games, a user does not take very well to surprises. Predictability of an interactive system means that the user's knowledge of the interaction history is sufficient to determine the result of his future interaction with it. There are many degrees to which predictability can be satisfied. The knowledge can be restricted to the presently perceivable information, so that the user need not remember anything other than what is currently observable. The knowledge requirement can be increased to the limit where the user is actually forced to remember what every previous keystroke was and what every previous screen display contained (and the order of each!) in order to determine the consequences of the next input action.

Predictability of an interactive system is distinguished from deterministic behavior of the computer system alone. Most computer systems are ultimately deterministic machines, so that given the state at any one point in time and the operation which is to be performed at that time, there is only one possible state that can result. Predictability is a user-centered concept; it is deterministic behavior from the perspective of the user. It is not enough for the behavior of the computer system to be determined completely from its state, as the user must be able to take advantage of the determinism.

For example, a common mathematical puzzle would be to present you with a sequence of three or more numbers and ask you what would be the next number in the sequence. The assumption in this puzzle (and one that can often be incorrect) is that there is a unique function or algorithm that produces the entire sequence of numbers and it is up you to figure it out. We know the function, but all you know are the results it provides from the first three calculations. The function is certainly deterministic; the test for you is a test of its predictability given the first three numbers in the sequence.

As another, possibly more pertinent, example, imagine you have created a complex picture using a mouse-driven graphical drawing package. You leave the picture for a few days and then go back to change it around a bit. You are allowed to select certain objects for editing by positioning the mouse over the object and clicking a mouse button to highlight it. Can you tell what the set of selectable objects is? Can you determine which area of the screen belongs to which of these objects, especially if some objects overlap? Does the visual image on the screen indicate what objects form a compound object that can only be selected as a group? Predictability of selection in this example depends on how much of the history of the creation of the visual image is necessary in order for you to determine what happens when you click on the mouse button.

This notion of predictability deals with the user's ability to determine the effect of operations on the system. Another form of predictability has to do with the user's ability to know which operations can be performed. *Operation visibility* refers to how the user is shown the availability of operations that can be performed next. If an operation can be performed, then there may be some perceivable indication of this to the user. This principle supports the superiority in humans of recognition over recall. Without it, the user will have to remember when he can perform the operation and when he cannot. Likewise, the user should understand from the interface if an operation he might like to invoke cannot be performed.

Synthesizability

Predictability focusses on the user's ability to determine the effect of future interactions. This assumes that the user has some mental model (see Chapter 1) of how the system behaves. Predictability says nothing about the way the user forms a model of the system's behavior. In building up some sort of predictive model of the system's behavior, it is important for the user to assess the consequences of previous interactions in order to formulate a model of the behavior of the system. Synthesis, therefore, is the ability of the user to assess the effect of past operations on the current state.

When an operation changes some aspect of the internal state, it is important that the change is seen by the user. The principle of *honesty* relates to the ability of the user interface to provide an observable and informative account of such change. In the best of circumstances, this notification can come *immediately*, requiring no further interaction initiated by the user. At the very least, the notification should appear *eventually*, after explicit user directives to make the change observable. A good example of the distinction between immediacy and eventuality can be seen in the comparison between command language interfaces and visual desktop interfaces for a file management system. You have moved a file from one directory to another. The principle of honesty implies that after moving the file to its new location in the file system you are then able to determine its new whereabouts. In a command language system, you would typically have to remember the destination directory and then ask to see the contents of that directory in order to verify that the file has been moved (in fact, you would also have to check that the file is no longer in its original directory to determine that it has been moved and not copied). In a visual desktop interface, a visual representation (or icon) of the file is dragged from its original directory and placed in its destination directory where it remains visible (assuming the destination folder is selected to reveal its contents). In this case, the user need not expend any more effort to assess the result of the move operation. The visual desktop is immediately honest.

The problem with eventual honesty is that the user must know to look for the change. In a situation in which the user is learning a new interactive system, it is likely that he will not know to look for change. In earlier versions of the Apple Macintosh Finder, performing the operation to create a new folder in another folder did not necessarily result in that new folder's icon being visible in the original folder. New users (and even some experienced users) would often think that they had not issued the new folder operations correctly and would ask for another new folder (and another, and another, . . .). They would not know to search through the entire open folder for the latest addition. Then several minutes (hours, days) later, they would notice that there were a number of empty and untitled folders lying around. The eventual (accidental) discovery of the change brought about by the new folder operation was then difficult to associate to that operation. Fortunately, this problem was addressed in Version 7 of the Finder.

As another example of the benefit of immediate over eventual honesty, let us examine a typical global search and replace function in a word processor. Imagine you have noticed in the past a tendency to repeat words in a document (for example, you type 'the the' without noticing the error). In an attempt to automate your proofreading, you decide to replace globally all occurrences of 'the the' with 'the'. The typical global search and replace function performs this substitution without revealing the changes made to you. Suddenly, a careless typing error is transformed into unacceptable grammar as the sentence

We will prove the theorem holds as a corollary of the following lemma.

is transformed to

We will prove theorem holds as a corollary of the following lemma.

Familiarity

New users of a system bring with them a wealth of experience across a wide number of application domains. This experience is obtained both through interaction in the real world and through interaction with other computer systems. For a new user, the familiarity of an interactive system measures the correlation between the user's existing knowledge and the knowledge required for effective interaction. For example, when word processors were originally introduced the analogy between the word processor and a typewriter was intended to make the new technology more immediately accessible to those who had little experience with the former but a lot of experience with the latter. Familiarity has to do with a user's first impression of the system. In this case, we are interested in how the system is first perceived and whether the user can determine how to initiate any interaction. An advantage of a metaphor, such as the typewriter metaphor for word processing described above, is precisely captured by familiarity. Jordan et al. refer to this familiarity as the *guessability* of the system [196].

Some psychologists argue that there are intrinsic properties, or *affordances*, of any visual object that suggest to us how they can be manipulated (see also Chapter 5, Section 5.7.2). The appearance of the object stimulates a familiarity with its behavior. For example, the shape of a door handle can suggest how it should be manipulated to open a door, and a key on a keyboard suggests to us that it can be pushed. In the design of a graphical user interface, it is implied that a soft button used in a form's interface suggests it should be pushed (though it does not suggest how it is to be pushed via the mouse). Effective use of the affordances that exist for interface objects can enhance the familiarity of the interactive system.

Generalizability

Users often try to extend their knowledge of specific interaction behavior to situations that are similar but previously unencountered. The generalizability of an interactive system supports this activity, leading to a more complete predictive model of the system for the user. We can apply generalization to situations in which the user wants to apply knowledge that helps achieve one particular goal to another situation where the goal is in some way similar. Generalizability can be seen as a form of consistency.

Generalization can occur within a single application or across a variety of applications. For example, in a graphical drawing package that draws a circle as a constrained form of ellipse, we would want the user to generalize that a square can be drawn as a constrained rectangle. A good example of generalizability across a variety of applications can be seen in multi-windowing systems that attempt to provide cut/paste/copy operations to all applications in the same way (with varying degrees of success). Generalizability within an application can be maximized by any conscientious designer. One of the main advantages of standards and programming style guides, which we will discuss in Sections 7.3 and 7.4, is that they increase generalizability across a wide variety of applications within the same environment.

Consistency

Consistency relates to the likeness in behavior arising from similar situations or similar task objectives. Consistency is probably the most widely mentioned principle in the literature on user interface design. 'Be consistent!' we are constantly urged. The user relies on a consistent interface. However, the difficulty of dealing with consistency is that it can take many forms. Consistency is not a single property of an interactive system that is either satisfied or not satisfied. Instead, consistency must be applied relative to something. Thus we have consistency in command naming, or consistency in command/argument invocation.

Another consequence of consistency having to be defined with respect to some other feature of the interaction is that many other principles can be 'reduced' to qualified instances of consistency. Hence, familiarity can be considered as consistency with respect to past real-world experience, and generalizability as consistency with respect to experience with the same system or set of applications on the same platform. Because of this pervasive quality of consistency, it might be argued that consistency should be a separate category of usability principles, on the same level as learnability, flexibility and robustness. Rather than do that, we will discuss different ways in which consistency can be manifested.

Consistency can be expressed in terms of the form of input expressions or output responses with respect to the meaning of actions in some conceptual model of the system. For example, before the introduction of explicit arrow keys, some word processors used the relative position of keys on the keyboard to indicate directionality for operations (for example, to move one character to the left, right, up or down). The conceptual model for display-based editing is a two-dimensional plane, so the user would think of certain classes of operations in terms of movements up, down, left or right in the plane of the display. Operations that required directional information, such as moving within the text or deleting some unit of text, could be articulated by using some set of keys on the keyboard that form a pattern consistent with up, down, left and right (for example, the keys e, x, s and d, respectively). For output responses, a good example of consistency can be found in a warnings system for an aircraft. Warnings to the pilot are classified into three categories, depending on whether the situation with the aircraft requires immediate recovery action, eventual but not immediate action, or no action at all (advisory) on the part of the crew. These warnings are signalled to the crew by means of a centralized warnings panel in which the categories are consistently color coded (red for immediate, amber for eventual and green for advisory).

Grudin has argued that because of the relative nature of consistency it can be a dangerous principle to follow [160]. A good example he gives is the development and evolution of the standard typewriter keyboard. When keyboards for typewriters were first made, the designers laid out the keys in alphabetical order. Then it was discovered that such an arrangement of keys was both inefficient from the machine's perspective (adjacent typewriter keys pressed in succession caused jams in the mechanism, so the likelihood of this occurrence had to be designed out) and tiring for the typist (a touch-typist would not have equal stress distributed over all fingers). The resulting QWERTY and DVORAK keyboards have since been adopted to combat the problems of the 'consistent' keyboard layout.[1]

---

1 See Chapter 2 for a discussion of different keyboards.

Table 7.2   Summary of principles affecting flexibility

Principle	Definition	Related principles
Dialog initiative	Allowing the user freedom from artificial constraints on the input dialog imposed by the system	System/user pre-emptiveness
Multi-threading	Ability of the system to support user interaction pertaining to more than one task at a time	Concurrent vs. interleaving, multi-modality
Task migratability	The ability to pass control for the execution of a given task so that it becomes either internalized by the user or the system or shared between them	–
Substitutivity	Allowing equivalent values of input and output to be arbitrarily substituted for each other	Representation multiplicity, equal opportunity
Customizability	Modifiability of the user interface by the user or the system	Adaptivity, adaptability

7.2.2 Flexibility

Flexibility refers to the multiplicity of ways in which the end-user and the system exchange information. We identify several principles that contribute to the flexibility of interaction, and these are summarized in Table 7.2.

Dialog initiative

When considering the interaction between user and system as a dialog between partners (see Chapter 16), it is important to consider which partner has the initiative in the conversation. The system can initiate all dialog, in which case the user simply responds to requests for information. We call this type of dialog *system pre-emptive*. For example, a modal dialog box prohibits the user from interacting with the system in any way that does not direct input to the box. Alternatively, the user may be entirely free to initiate any action towards the system, in which case the dialog is *user pre-emptive*. The system may control the dialog to the extent that it prohibits the user from initiating any other desired communication concerning the current task or some other task the user would like to perform. From the user's perspective, a system-driven interaction hinders flexibility whereas a user-driven interaction favours it.

In general, we want to maximize the user's ability to pre-empt the system and minimize the system's ability to pre-empt the user. Although a system pre-emptive dialog is not desirable in general, some situations may require it. In a cooperative editor (in which two people edit a document at the same time) it would be impolite for you to erase a paragraph of text that your partner is currently editing. For safety reasons, it may be necessary to prohibit the user from the 'freedom' to do potentially serious damage. A pilot about to land an aircraft in which the flaps have asymmetrically failed in their extended position[2] should not be allowed to abort the landing, as this failure will almost certainly result in a catastrophic accident.

On the other hand, a completely user pre-emptive dialog allows the user to offer any input action at any time for maximum flexibility. This is not an entirely desirable situation, since it increases the likelihood that the user will lose track of the tasks that have been initiated and not yet completed. However, if the designers have a good understanding of the sets of tasks the user is likely to perform with a system and how those tasks are related, they can minimize the likelihood that the user will be prevented from initiating some task at a time when he wishes to do so.

Multi-threading

A thread of a dialog is a coherent subset of that dialog. In the user–system dialog, we can consider a thread to be that part of the dialog that relates to a given user task. *Multi-threading* of the user–system dialog allows for interaction to support more than one task at a time. *Concurrent* multi-threading allows simultaneous communication of information pertaining to separate tasks. *Interleaved* multi-threading permits a temporal overlap between separate tasks, but stipulates that at any given instant the dialog is restricted to a single task.

Multi-modality of a dialog is related to multi-threading. Coutaz has characterized two dimensions of multi-modal systems [80]. First, we can consider how the separate modalities (or channels of communication) are combined to form a single input or output expression. Multiple channels may be available, but any one expression may be restricted to just one channel (keyboard or audio, for example). As an example, to open a window the user can choose between a double click on an icon, a keyboard shortcut, or saying 'open window'. Alternatively, a single expression can be formed by a mixing of channels. Examples of such fused modality are error warnings, which usually contain a textual message accompanied by an audible beep. On the input side, we could consider chord sequences of input with a keyboard and mouse (pressing the shift key while a mouse button is pressed, or saying 'drop' as you drag a file over the trash icon). We can also characterize a multi-modality dialog depending on whether it allows concurrent or interleaved use of multiple modes.

A windowing system naturally supports a multi-threaded dialog that is interleaved amongst a number of overlapping tasks. Each window can represent a different task, for example text editing in one window, file management in another, a telephone directory in another and electronic mail in yet another. A multi-modal dialog can allow for concurrent multi-threading. A very simple example can occur in the

---

2 Flaps increase the surface area and curvature of the aircraft's wing, providing the extra lift necessary for, among other things, a smooth touchdown. An asymmetric failure results in extreme instability and the aircraft will not fly level.

windowing system with an audible bell. You are editing a program when a beep indicates that a new electronic mail message has arrived. Even though at the level of the system the audible beep has been interleaved with your requests from the keyboard to perform edits, the overlap between the editing task and the mail message from your perspective is simultaneous.

Task migratability

Task migratability concerns the transfer of control for execution of tasks between system and user. It should be possible for the user or system to pass the control of a task over to the other or promote the task from a completely internalized one to a shared and cooperative venture. Hence, a task that is internal to one can become internal to the other or shared between the two partners.

Spell-checking a paper is a good example of the need for task migratability. Equipped with a dictionary, you are perfectly able to check your spelling by reading through the entire paper and correcting mistakes as you spot them. This mundane task is perfectly suited to automation, as the computer can check words against its own list of acceptable spellings. It is not desirable, however, to leave this task completely to the discretion of the computer, as most computerized dictionaries do not handle proper names correctly, nor can they distinguish between correct and unintentional duplications of words. In those cases, the task is handed over to the user. The spell-check is best performed in such a cooperative way.

In safety-critical applications, task migratability can decrease the likelihood of an accident. For example, on the flight deck of an aircraft, there are so many control tasks that must be performed that a pilot would be overwhelmed if he had to perform them all. Therefore, mundane control of the aircraft's position within its flight envelope is greatly automated. However, in the event of an emergency, it must be possible to transfer flying controls easily and seamlessly from the system to the pilot.

Substitutivity

Substitutivity requires that equivalent values can be substituted for each other. For example, in considering the form of an input expression to determine the margin for a letter, you may want to enter the value in either inches or centimeters. You may also want to input the value explicitly (say 1.5 inches) or you may want to enter a calculation which produces the right input value (you know the width of the text is 6.5 inches and the width of the paper is 8.5 inches and you want the left margin to be twice as large as the right margin, so you enter $^2/_3$ $(8.5 - 6.5)$ inches). This input substitutivity contributes towards flexibility by allowing the user to choose whichever form best suits the needs of the moment. By avoiding unnecessary calculations in the user's head, substitutivity can minimize user errors and cognitive effort.

We can also consider substitutivity with respect to output, or the system's rendering of state information. *Representation multiplicity* illustrates flexibility for state rendering. For example, the temperature of a physical object over a period of time can be presented as a digital thermometer if the actual numerical value is important or as a graph if it is only important to notice trends. It might even be desirable to make these representations simultaneously available to the user. Each representation provides a perspective on the internal state of the system. At a given time, the user is free to consider the representations that are most suitable for the current task.

Equal opportunity blurs the distinction between input and output at the interface. The user has the choice of what is input and what is output; in addition, output can be reused as input. Thimbleby describes this principle as, 'If you can see it, you can use it!' It is a common belief that input and output are separate. Many have stressed the significance of the link between input and output. Equal opportunity pushes that view to the extreme. For example, in spreadsheet programs, the user fills in some cells and the system automatically determines the values attributed to some other cells. Conversely, if the user enters values for those other cells, the system would compute the values for the first ones. In this example, it is not clear which cells are the inputs and which are the outputs. Furthermore, this distinction might not be clear or useful to the user. In a drawing package, the user may draw a line by direct manipulation and the system would compute the length of the line; or conversely, the user may specify the line coordinates and the system would draw the line. Both means of manipulating the line are equally important and must be made equally available. Note that equal opportunity implies that the system is not pre-emptive towards the user.

Customizability

Customizability is the modifiability of the user interface by the user or the system. From the system side, we are not concerned with modifications that would be attended to by a programmer actually changing the system and its interface during system maintenance. Rather, we are concerned with the automatic modification that the system would make based on its knowledge of the user. We distinguish between the user-initiated and system-initiated modification, referring to the former as *adaptability* and the latter as *adaptivity*.

Adaptability refers to the user's ability to adjust the form of input and output. This customization could be very limited, with the user only allowed to adjust the position of soft buttons on the screen or redefine command names. This type of modifiability, which is restricted to the surface of the interface, is referred to as lexical customization. The overall structure of the interaction is kept unchanged. The power given to the user can be increased by allowing the definition of macros to speed up the articulation of certain common tasks. In the extreme, the interface can provide the user with programming language capabilities, such as the UNIX shell or the script language Hypertalk in HyperCard. Thimbleby points out that in these cases it would be suitable to apply well-known principles of programming languages to the user's interface programming language.

Adaptivity is automatic customization of the user interface by the system. Decisions for adaptation can be based on user expertise or observed repetition of

Table 7.3 Summary of principles affecting robustness

Principle	Definition	Related principles
Observability	Ability of the user to evaluate the internal state of the system from its perceivable representation	Browsability, static/dynamic defaults, reachability, persistence, operation visibility
Recoverability	Ability of the user to take corrective action once an error has been recognized	Reachability, forward/ backward recovery, commensurate effort
Responsiveness	How the user perceives the rate of communication with the system	Stability
Task conformance	The degree to which the system services support all of the tasks the user wishes to perform and in the way that the user understands them	Task completeness, task adequacy

certain task sequences. The distinction between adaptivity and adaptability is that the user plays an explicit role in adaptability, whereas his role in an adaptive interface is more implicit. A system can be trained to recognize the behavior of an expert or novice and accordingly adjust its dialog control or help system automatically to match the needs of the current user. This is in contrast with a system that would require the user to classify himself as novice or expert at the beginning of a session. We discuss adaptive systems further in the context of user support in Chapter 11. Automatic macro construction is a form of programming by example, combining adaptability with adaptivity in a simple and useful way. Repetitive tasks can be detected by observing user behavior and macros can be automatically (or with user consent) constructed from this observation to perform repetitive tasks automatically.

7.2.3 Robustness

In a work or task domain, a user is engaged with a computer in order to achieve some set of goals. The robustness of that interaction covers features that support the successful achievement and assessment of the goals. Here, we describe principles that support robustness. A summary of these principles is presented in Table 7.3.

Observability

Observability allows the user to evaluate the internal state of the system by means of its perceivable representation at the interface. As we described in Chapter 3, evaluation allows the user to compare the current observed state with his intention within the task–action plan, possibly leading to a plan revision. Observability can be discussed through five other principles: browsability, defaults, reachability, persistence and operation visibility. Operation visibility was covered in Section 7.2.1 in relation to predictability. The remaining four are discussed next.

Browsability allows the user to explore the current internal state of the system via the limited view provided at the interface. Usually the complexity of the domain does not allow the interface to show all of the relevant domain concepts at once. Indeed, this is one reason why the notion of task is used, in order to constrain the domain information needed at one time to a subset connected with the user's current activity. While you may not be able to view an entire document's contents, you may be able to see all of an outline view of the document, if you are only interested in its overall structure. Even with a restriction of concepts relevant to the current task, it is probable that all of the information a user needs to continue work on that task is not immediately perceivable. Or perhaps the user is engaged in a multi-threaded dialog covering several tasks. There needs to be a way for the user to investigate, or browse, the internal state. This browsing itself should not have any side-effects on that state; that is, the browsing commands should be passive with respect to the domain-specific parts of the internal state.

The availability of *defaults* can assist the user by passive recall (for example, a suggested response to a question can be recognized as correct instead of recalled). It also reduces the number of physical actions necessary to input a value. Thus, providing default values is a kind of error prevention mechanism. There are two kinds of default values: static and dynamic. Static defaults do not evolve with the session. They are either defined within the system or acquired at initialization. On the other hand, dynamic defaults evolve during the session. They are computed by the system from previous user inputs; the system is then adapting default values.

Reachability refers to the possibility of navigation through the observable system states. There are various levels of reachability that can be given precise mathematical definitions (see Chapter 17), but the main notion is whether the user can navigate from any given state to any other state. Reachability in an interactive system affects the recoverability of the system, as we will discuss later. In addition, different levels of reachability can reflect the amount of flexibility in the system as well, though we did not make that explicit in the discussion on flexibility.

Persistence deals with the duration of the effect of a communication act and the ability of the user to make use of that effect. The effect of vocal communication does not persist except in the memory of the receiver. Visual communication, on the other hand, can remain as an object which the user can subsequently manipulate long after the act of presentation. If you are informed of a new email message by a beep at your terminal, you may know at that moment and for a short while later that you have received a new message. If you do not attend to that message immediately, you may forget about it. If, however, some persistent visual information informs you of the incoming message (say, the flag goes up on your electronic mailbox), then that will serve as a reminder that an unread message remains long after its initial receipt.[3]

---

3 Chapter 19 discusses notification mechanisms for email in more detail.

Recoverability

Users make mistakes from which they want to recover. Recoverability is the ability to reach a desired goal after recognition of some error in a previous interaction. There are two directions in which recovery can occur, forward or backward. *Forward error recovery* involves the acceptance of the current state and negotiation from that state towards the desired state. Forward error recovery may be the only possibility for recovery if the effects of interaction are not revocable (for example, in building a house of cards, you might sneeze whilst placing a card on the seventh level, but you cannot undo the effect of your misfortune except by rebuilding). *Backward error recovery* is an attempt to undo the effects of previous interaction in order to return to a prior state before proceeding. In a text editor, a mistyped keystroke might wipe out a large section of text which you would want to retrieve by an equally simple undo button.

Recovery can be initiated by the system or by the user. When performed by the system, recoverability is connected to the notions of fault tolerance, safety, reliability and dependability, all topics covered in software engineering. However, in software engineering this recoverability is considered only with respect to system functionality; it is not tied to user intent. When recovery is initiated by the user, it is important that it determines the intent of the user's recovery actions; that is, whether he desires forward (negotiation) or backward (using undo/redo actions) corrective action.

Recoverability is linked to reachability because we want to avoid blocking the user from getting to a desired state from some other undesired state (going down a blind alley).

In addition to providing the ability to recover, the procedure for recovery should reflect the work being done (or undone, as the case may be). The principle of *commensurate effort* states that if it is difficult to undo a given effect on the state, then it should have been difficult to do in the first place. Conversely, easily undone actions should be easily doable. For example, if it is difficult to recover files which have been deleted in an operating system, then it should be difficult to remove them, or at least it should require more effort by the user to delete the file than to, say, rename it.

Responsiveness

Responsiveness measures the rate of communication between the system and the user. Response time is generally defined as the duration of time needed by the system to express state changes to the user. In general, short durations and instantaneous response times are desirable. Instantaneous means that the user perceives system reactions as immediate. But even in situations in which an instantaneous response cannot be obtained, there must be some indication to the user that the system has received the request for action and is working on a response.

As significant as absolute response time is response time *stability*. Response time stability covers the invariance of the duration for identical or similar computational resources. For example, pull-down menus are expected to pop up instantaneously as soon as a mouse button is pressed. Variations in response time will impede anticipation exploited by motor skill.

Task conformance

Since the purpose of an interactive system is to allow a user to perform various tasks in achieving certain goals within a specific application domain, we can ask whether the system supports all of the tasks of interest and whether it supports these as the user wants. *Task completeness* addresses the coverage issue and *task adequacy* addresses the user's understanding of the tasks.

It is not sufficient that the computer system fully implements some set of computational services that were identified at early specification stages. It is essential that the system allows the user to achieve any of the desired tasks in a particular work domain as identified by a task analysis that precedes system specification (see Chapter 15 for a more complete discussion of task analysis techniques). Task completeness refers to the level to which the system services can be mapped onto all of the user tasks. However, it is quite possible that the provision of a new computer-based tool will suggest to a user some tasks that were not even conceivable before the tool. Therefore, it is also desirable that the system services be suitably general so that the user can define new tasks.

Discussion of task conformance has its roots in an attempt to understand the success of direct manipulation interfaces. We can view the direct manipulation interface as a separate world from that inside the system. Task completeness covers only one part of the conformance. This separate world is understood and operated upon by the user. With the intuition of the Hutchins, Hollan and Norman model-world metaphor discussed in Chapter 4, we require that the task, as represented by the world of the interface, matches the task as understood by the user and supported by the system. If the model-world metaphor satisfies the principle of task adequacy, then the user will be directly on his task plan, minimizing the effort required in the articulation and observation translations discussed in the interaction framework of Chapter 3.

Worked exercise   *Look at some of the principles outlined in this section, and use one or two to provide a usability specification (see Chapter 6, Section 6.3) for an electronic meetings diary or calendar. First identify some of the tasks that would be performed by a user trying to keep track of future meetings, and then complete the usability specification assuming that the electronic system will be replacing a paper-based system. What assumptions do you have to make about the user and the electronic diary in order to create a reasonable usability specification?*

Answer   This exercise could be easily extended to a small project which would involve the design of such an electronic diary or calendar. The purpose of this smaller usability engineering exercise is to show how usability goals can be formulated early on to drive the design activity. We will select two of the usability principles from this chapter, which will serve as attributes for separate usability specifications.

In the first example, we will consider the interaction principle of guessability, which concerns how easy it is for new users to perform tasks initially. The measuring concept will be how long it takes a new user, without any instruction on the new system, to enter his first appointment in the diary. A sample usability specification is given below.

Attribute:	Guessability
Measuring concept:	Ease of first use of system without training
Measuring method:	Time to create first entry in diary
Now level:	30 seconds on paper-based system
Worst case:	1 minute
Planned level:	45 seconds
Best case:	30 seconds (equivalent to now)

The values in this usability specification might seem a little surprising at first, since we are saying that the best case is only equivalent to the currently achievable now level. The point in this example is that the new system is replacing a very familiar paper and pencil system which requires very little training. The objective of this system is not so much to improve guessability but to preserve it. Earlier, we discussed that the worst case level should not usually be worse than the now level, but we are hoping for this product to improve overall functionality of the system. The user will be able to do more things with the electronic diary than he could with the conventional system. As a result, we worry less about improving its guessability. Perhaps we could have been more ambitious in setting the best case value by considering the potential for voice input or other exotic input techniques that would make entry faster than writing.

As another example, we want to support the task migratability of the system. A frequent sort of task for a diary is to schedule weekly meetings. The conventional system would require the user to make an explicit entry for the meeting each week – the task of the scheduling is the responsibility of the user. In the new system, we want to allow the user to push the responsibility of scheduling over to the system, so that the user need only indicate the desire to have a meeting scheduled for a certain time each week and the system will take care of entering the meeting at all of the appropriate times. The task of scheduling has thus migrated over to the system. The usability specification for this example follows.

Attribute:	Task migratability
Measuring concept:	Scheduling a weekly meeting
Measuring method:	Time it takes to enter a weekly meeting appointment
Now level:	(Time to schedule one appointment) $\times$ (Number of weeks)
Worst case:	Time to schedule two appointments
Planned level:	$1.5 \times$ (Time to schedule one appointment)
Best case:	Time to schedule one appointment

In this specification, we have indicated that the now level is equivalent to the time it takes to schedule each appointment separately. The worst, planned and best case levels are all targeted at some proportion of the time it takes to schedule just a single appointment – a dramatic improvement. The difference between the worst, planned and best case levels is the amount of overhead it will take to indicate that a single appointment is to be considered an example to be repeated at the weekly level.

What are the assumptions we have to make in order to arrive at such a usability specification? One of the problems with usability specifications, discussed earlier, is that they sometimes require quite specific information about the design. For example, had we set one of our measuring methods to count keystrokes or mouse clicks, we would have had to start making assumptions about the method of interaction that the system would allow. Had we tried to set a usability specification concerning the browsing of the diary, we would have had to start making assumptions about the layout of the calendar (monthly, weekly, daily) in order to make our estimates specific enough to measure. In the examples we have provided above, we have tried to stay as abstract as possible, so that the usability specifications could be of use as early in the design life cycle as possible. A consequence of this abstractness, particularly evident in the second example, is that we run the risk in the usability specification of setting goals that may be completely unrealistic, though well intentioned. If the usability specification were to be used as a contract with the customer, such speculation could spell real trouble for the designer.

7.3 STANDARDS

Standards for interactive system design are usually set by national or international bodies to ensure compliance with a set of design rules by a large community. Standards can apply specifically to either the hardware or the software used to build the interactive system. Smith [324] points out the differing characteristics between hardware and software, which affect the utility of design standards applied to them:

Underlying theory Standards for hardware are based on an understanding of physiology or ergonomics/human factors, the results of which are relatively well known, fixed and readily adaptable to design of the hardware. On the other hand, software standards are based on theories from psychology or cognitive science, which are less well formed, still evolving and not very easy to interpret in the language of software design. Consequently, standards for hardware can directly relate to a hardware specification and still reflect the underlying theory, whereas software standards would have to be more vaguely worded.

Change Hardware is more difficult and expensive to change than software, which is usually designed to be very flexible. Consequently, requirements changes for hardware do not occur as frequently as for software. Since standards are also relatively stable, they are more suitable for hardware than software.

Historically, for these reasons, a given standards institution, such as the British Standards Institution (BSI) or the International Organization for Standardization (ISO) or a national military agency, has had standards for hardware in place before any for software. For example, the UK Ministry of Defence has published an Interim Defence Standard 00–25 on *Human Factors for Designers of Equipment*, produced in 12 parts:

Part 1   Introduction
Part 2   Body Size
Part 3   Body Strength and Stamina
Part 4   Workplace Design
Part 5   Stresses and Hazards
Part 6   Vision and Lighting

Part 7   Visual Displays
Part 8   Auditory Information
Part 9   Voice Communication
Part 10 Controls
Part 11 Design for Maintainability
Part 12 Systems

Only the last of these is concerned with the software design process. The international standard ISO 9241, entitled *Ergonomic Requirements for Office Work with Visual Display Terminals (VDT)s*, has 17 parts. Seven of these are concerned with hardware issues – requirements for visual display, keyboard layout, workstation layout, environment, display with reflections, display colors and non-keyboard input devices. Seven parts are devoted to software issues – general dialog principles, menu dialogs, presentation of information, user guidance, command dialogs, direct manipulation dialogs and form-filling dialogs. However, standards covering software issues are now being produced, for example, the draft standard ISO 14915 covers software ergonomics for multimedia user interfaces.

Figure 7.1 provides examples of the language of standards for displays. Note the increasing generality and vagueness of the language as we progress from the hardware issues in a UK defence standard for pilot cockpit controls and instrumentation through a German standard for user interface design of display workstations to a US military standard for display contents.

11.3 *Arrangement of displays*
11.3.1 Vertical Grouping. The engine display parameters shall be arranged so that the primary or most important display for a particular engine and airplane (thrust, torque, RPM, etc.) be located at the top of the display group if a vertical grouping is provided. The next most important display parameter shall be positioned under the primary display progressing down the panel with the least important at the bottom.

(a) A typical example of a military standard

5.1 *Subdivision of the display area*
In consideration of a simple, fast and accurate visual acquisition, the display area shall be divided into different sub-areas.
Such a division should be:

■ Input area
■ Output area
■ Area for operational indications (such as status and alarms)

(b) From German standard DIN 66 234 Part 3 (1984), adapted from Smith [324]

5.15.3.2.1 *Standardization*
The content of displays within a system shall be presented in a consistent manner.

(c) From US military standard MIL-STD-1472C, revised (1983), adapted from Smith [324]

Figure 7.1   Sample design standards for displays. Adapted from Smith [324].
Copyright © 1986 IEEE

One component of the ISO standard 9241, pertaining to usability specification, applies equally to both hardware and software design. In the beginning of that document, the following definition of usability is given:

Usability   The effectiveness, efficiency and satisfaction with which specified users achieve specified goals in particular environments.

Effectiveness   The accuracy and completeness with which specified users can achieve specified goals in particular environments.

Efficiency   The resources expended in relation to the accuracy and completeness of goals achieved.

Satisfaction   The comfort and acceptability of the work system to its users and other people affected by its use.

The importance of such a definition in the standard is as a means of describing explicit measurements for usability. Such metrics can support usability engineering, as we saw in Chapter 6.

The strength of a standard lies in its ability to force large communities to abide – the so-called authority we have referred to earlier. It should be noted that such authority does not necessarily follow from the publication of a standard by a national or international body. In fact, many standards applying to software design are put forth as suggestive measures, rather than obligatory. The authority of a standard (or a guideline, for that matter) can only be determined from its use in practice. Some software products become de facto standards long before any formal standards document is published (for example, the X windowing system).

There is a much longer history of standards in safety-critical domains, such as nuclear power plants or aircraft design, where the consequences of poor design outweigh the expense of principled design. It is only as the perceived costs of unusable software in less safety-critical domains have become less acceptable that there has been a greater effort in developing standards for promoting usability.

7.4   GUIDELINES

We have observed that the incompleteness of theories underlying the design of interactive software makes it difficult to produce authoritative and specific standards. As a result, the majority of design rules for interactive systems are suggestive and more general guidelines. Our concern in examining the wealth of available guidelines is in determining their applicability to the various stages of design. The more abstract the guideline, the more it resembles the principles that we outlined in Section 7.2, which would be most suited to requirements specification. The more specific the guideline, the more suited it is to detailed design. The guidelines can also be automated to some extent, providing a direct means for translating detailed design specifications into actual implementation. There are a vast amount of published guidelines for interactive system design (they are frequently referred to as guidelines for user interface design). We will present only a few examples here to demonstrate the content of guidelines in that vast literature.

Several books and technical reports contain huge catalogs of guidelines. A classic example was a very general list compiled by Smith and Mosier in 1986 at the Mitre Corporation and sponsored by the Electronic Systems Division of the US Air Force [325]. The basic categories of the Smith and Mosier guidelines are:

1. Data Entry
2. Data Display
3. Sequence Control
4. User Guidance
5. Data Transmission
6. Data Protection

Each of these categories is further broken down into more specific subcategories which contain the particular guidelines. Figure 7.2 provides an example of the information contained in the Smith and Mosier guidelines. A striking feature of this compendium of guidelines is the extensive cross-referencing within the catalog, and citation to published work that supports each guideline. The Mitre Corporation has taken advantage of this structure and implemented the Smith and Mosier guidelines on a hypertext system, which provides rapid traversal of the network of guidelines to investigate the cross-references and citations.

---

1. **Data Entry**

1.1 *Position Designation*

1.1–1 **Distinctive Cursor**
For position designation on an electronic display, provide a movable cursor with distinctive visual features (shape, blink, etc.).

Exception   When position designation involves only selection among displayed alternatives, highlighting selected items might be used instead of a separately displayed cursor.

Comment   When choosing a cursor shape, consider the general content of the display. For instance, an underscore cursor would be difficult to see on a display of underscored text, or on a graphical display containing many other lines.

Comment   If the cursor is changed to denote different functions (e.g. to signal deletion rather than entry), then each different cursor should be distinguishable from the others.

Comment   If multiple cursors are used on the same display (e.g. one for alphanumeric entry and one for line drawing), then each cursor should be distinguishable from the others.

Reference   Whitfield, Ball and Bird, 1983

See also   1.1–17   Distinctive multiple cursors
4.0–9   Distinctive cursor

Figure 7.2   Sample guideline from Smith and Mosier [325], courtesy of The MITRE Corporation

Table 7.4 Comparison of dialog styles mentioned in guidelines

Smith and Mosier [325]	Mayhew [230]
Question and answer	Question and answer
Form filling	Fill-in forms
Menu selection	Menus
Function keys	Function keys
Command language	Command language
Query language	–
Natural language	Natural language
Graphic selection	Direct manipulation

A more recent, equally comprehensive catalog of general guidelines has been compiled by Mayhew [230]. Though this catalog is only in book form, and so limits the possibility of quick cross-referencing, this is one of the best sources for the experimental results which back the specific guidelines.

A major concern for all of the general guidelines is the subject of *dialog styles*, which in the context of these guidelines pertains to the means by which the user communicates input to the system, including how the system presents the communication device. Smith and Mosier identify eight different dialog styles and Mayhew identifies seven (see Table 7.4 for a comparison). The only real difference is the absence of query languages in Mayhew's list, but we can consider a query language as a special case of a command language. These interface styles have been described in more detail in Chapter 3.

Most guidelines are applicable for the implementation of any one of these dialog styles in isolation. It is also important to consider the possibility of mixing dialog styles in one application. In contrasting the action and language paradigms in Chapter 4, we concluded that it is not always the case that one paradigm wins over the other for all tasks in an application and, therefore, an application may want to mix the two paradigms. This equates to a mixing of dialog styles – a direct manipulation dialog being suitable for the action paradigm and a command language being suitable for the language paradigm. Mayhew provides guidelines and a technique for deciding how to mix dialog styles.

In moving from abstract guidelines to more specific and automated ones, it is necessary to introduce assumptions about the computer platform on which the interactive system is designed. So, for example, in Apple's *Human Interface Guidelines: the Apple Desktop Interface*, there is a clear distinction between the abstract guidelines (or principles), independent of the specific Macintosh hardware and software, and the concrete guidelines, which assume them. The abstract guidelines provide the so-called philosophy of programming that Apple would like designers to adopt in programming applications for the Macintosh. The more concrete guidelines are then seen as more concrete manifestations of that philosophy.

As an example, one abstract principle espoused in the Apple guidelines is *consistency*:

Effective applications are both consistent within themselves and consistent with one another.

We discussed consistency in Section 7.2 under the larger usability category of learnability, and the meaning in this context is similar. A more concrete directive that Apple provides is the 'noun–verb' ordering guideline: the user first selects an object (the noun) from the visible set on the Desktop and then selects an operation (the verb) to be applied to the object. For the sake of consistency, this ordering guideline is to be followed for all operation invocation involving the explicit and separate indication of an operation and the object or arguments of that operation.

Another less straightforward example from the Apple guidelines refers to user control:

The user, not the computer, initiates and controls all actions.

We considered issues of dialog initiative in Section 7.2 under the general usability category of flexibility. As we mentioned there, the issue of dialog initiative involves a trade-off between user freedom and system protection. In general, single-user computer systems operate in strict abidance of this guideline for user control; the user is allowed to initiate any dialog at all with the computer, whether or not it will have the intended result. Part of the success of direct manipulation interfaces lies in their ability to constrain user interaction to actions which are both syntactically correct (for example, preventing errors due to slips in typing) and will probably correspond to the intended user tasks.

Other popular graphical user interface (GUI) systems have published guidelines that describe how to adhere to abstract principles for usability in the narrower context of a specific programming environment. These guidelines are often referred to as *style guides* to reflect that they are not hard and fast rules, but suggested conventions for programming in that environment. Some examples are the OpenLook and the Open Software Foundation (OSF) Motif graphical user interfaces, both of which have published style guides [337, 275]. Programming in the style of these GUIs involves the use of toolkits which provide high-level widgets, as we have mentioned earlier in this book and will discuss in more detail in Chapter 8. More importantly, each of these GUIs has its own *look and feel*, which describes their expected behavior. The style guides are intended to help a programmer capture the elements of the look and feel of a GUI in her own programming. Therefore, style guides for the look and feel of a GUI promote the consistency within and between applications on the same computer platform.

We discussed menus in Chapter 3 as one of the major elements of the WIMP interface. As one example of a guideline for the design of menus, the OpenLook style guide suggests the following for grouping items in the same menu:

Use white space between long groups of controls on menus or in short groups when screen real estate is not an issue.

The justification for such a guideline is that the more options (or controls, as the term is used in the quoted guideline) on a menu, the longer it will take a user to locate and point to a desired item. As we discussed in Chapter 1, humans chunk related information in the learning process and this can be used to increase the efficiency of searching. Grouping of related items in a menu can supplement this chunking procedure. But be warned! Remember the scenario described in the Introduction to this book, in which we fell victim to closely grouped menu items which had drastically different effects in our word processor. Saving and deleting files might be considered logically similar since they both deal with operations on the file level. But simple slips made in pointing (which are all too easy with trackball devices) can change an intended save operation into an unintended and dangerous delete.

Worked exercise   *Look up and report back guidelines for the use of color. Be able to state the empirical psychological evidence that supports the guidelines. Do the guidelines conflict with any other known guidelines? Which principles of interaction do they support?*

Answer   There are many examples of guidelines for the use of color in the literature. Here are three good sources:

- C. Marlin Brown, *Human–Computer Interface Design Guidelines*, Ablex, 1988.
- Deborah J. Mayhew, *Principles and Guidelines in Software User Interface Design*, Prentice Hall, 1992.
- Sun Microsystems, Inc., *OpenLook Graphical User Interface Application Style Guidelines*, Addison-Wesley, 1990.

Taking an example from Mayhew, we have the following design guideline for the use of color as an informational cue for the user (for example, to inform the user that a string of text is a warning or error message):

Do not use color without some other redundant cue.

Mayhew provides three reasons which empirically support this guideline:

1. Color may not be available on all machines on which the system is to be implemented. Therefore, if use of color is the only means to convey some important information to the user, then that information will be lost in a monochrome (no color) system. Redundant color coding will allow for portability across different computing platforms.
2. Empirical evidence shows that 8% of the (general) male population and 0.4% of the female population has some color deficiency, so they cannot accurately recognize or distinguish between various colors. Again, if color is the only means for conveying some information, this significant portion of the user population will be slighted.
3. It has been shown that redundant color coding enhances user performance

This guideline supports several of the principles discussed in this chapter:

Substitutivity   The system is able to substitute color-coded information and other means (for example, text, sound) to represent some important information. We could turn the argument around and suggest that the user be able to provide color input (by selecting from a palette menu) or other forms of input to provide relevant information to the system.

Observability This principle is all about the system being able to provide the user with enough information about its internal state to assist his task. Relying strictly on color-coded information, as pointed out above, could reduce the observability of a system for some users.

Synthesis If a change in color is used to indicate the changing status of some system entity (perhaps a change in temperature above a threshold value is signalled by an icon becoming red), those who cannot detect the change in color would be deprived of this information. Synthesis is about supporting the user's ability to detect such significant changes, especially when they are a result of previous user actions.

There is no evidence of existing guidelines that this particular guideline for color violates.

Another example of a color guideline (found in all three of the above references) is the demand to consider cultural information in the selection of particular colors. For example, Mayhew states that western cultures tend to interpret green to mean go or safe; red to mean stop, on, hot or emergency; and blue to mean cold or off. Using color to suggest these kinds of meanings is in support of the familiarity principle within learnability. However, in other cultures different meanings may be associated with these colors, as we saw in Chapter 3, and consistent use of color (another guideline) might lead to confusion. Hence, strict adherence to this guideline would suggest a violation of the consistency of color application guideline. However, if consistency is applied relative to the meaning of the color (as opposed to its actual color), this guideline would not have to conflict.

7.5   GOLDEN RULES AND HEURISTICS

So far we have considered a range of abstract principles and detailed guidelines, which can be used to help designers produce more usable systems. But all of these rules require a certain amount of commitment on the part of the designer, either to track down appropriate guidelines or to interpret principles. Is there a simpler way?

A number of advocates of user-centered design have presented sets of 'golden rules' or heuristics. While these are inevitably 'broad-brush' design rules, which may not be always be applicable to every situation, they do provide a useful checklist or summary of the essence of design advice. It is clear that any designer following even these simple rules will produce a better system than one who ignores them.

There are many sets of heuristics, but the most well used are Nielsen's ten heuristics, Shneiderman's eight golden rules and Norman's seven principles. Nielsen's heuristics are intended to be used in evaluation and will therefore be discussed in Chapter 9. We will consider the other two sets here.

7.5.1 Shneiderman's Eight Golden Rules of Interface Design

Shneiderman's eight golden rules provide a convenient and succinct summary of the key principles of interface design. They are intended to be used during design but can also be applied, like Nielsen's heuristics, to the evaluation of systems. Notice how they relate to the abstract principles discussed earlier.

1. *Strive for consistency* in action sequences, layout, terminology, command use and so on.
2. *Enable frequent users to use shortcuts*, such as abbreviations, special key sequences and macros, to perform regular, familiar actions more quickly.
3. *Offer informative feedback* for every user action, at a level appropriate to the magnitude of the action.
4. *Design dialogs to yield closure* so that the user knows when they have completed a task.
5. *Offer error prevention and simple error handling* so that, ideally, users are prevented from making mistakes and, if they do, they are offered clear and informative instructions to enable them to recover.
6. *Permit easy reversal of actions* in order to relieve anxiety and encourage exploration, since the user knows that he can always return to the previous state.
7. *Support internal locus of control* so that the user is in control of the system, which responds to his actions.
8. *Reduce short-term memory load* by keeping displays simple, consolidating multiple page displays and providing time for learning action sequences.

These rules provide a useful shorthand for the more detailed sets of principles described earlier. Like those principles, they are not applicable to every eventuality and need to be interpreted for each new situation. However, they are broadly useful and their application will only help most design projects.

7.5.2 Norman's Seven Principles for Transforming Difficult Tasks into Simple Ones

In Chapter 3 we discussed Norman's execution–evaluation cycle, in which he elaborates the seven stages of action. Later, in his classic book *The Design of Everyday Things*, he summarizes user-centered design using the following seven principles:

1. *Use both knowledge in the world and knowledge in the head.* People work better when the knowledge they need to do a task is available externally – either explicitly or through the constraints imposed by the environment. But experts also need to be able to internalize regular tasks to increase their efficiency. So systems should provide the necessary knowledge within the environment and their operation should be transparent to support the user in building an appropriate mental model of what is going on.
2. *Simplify the structure of tasks.* Tasks need to be simple in order to avoid complex problem solving and excessive memory load. There are a number of ways to simplify the structure of tasks. One is to provide mental aids to help the user keep track of stages in a more complex task. Another is to use technology to provide the user with more information about the task and better feedback. A third approach is to automate the task or part of it, as long as this does not detract from the user's experience. The final approach to simplification is to change the nature

of the task so that it becomes something more simple. In all of this, it is important not to take control away from the user.

3. *Make things visible*: bridge the gulfs of execution and evaluation. The interface should make clear what the system can do and how this is achieved, and should enable the user to see clearly the effect of their actions on the system.

4. *Get the mappings right*. User intentions should map clearly onto system controls. User actions should map clearly onto system events. So it should be clear what does what and by how much. Controls, sliders and dials should reflect the task – so a small movement has a small effect and a large movement a large effect.

5. *Exploit the power of constraints*, both natural and artificial. Constraints are things in the world that make it impossible to do anything but the correct action in the correct way. A simple example is a jigsaw puzzle, where the pieces only fit together in one way. Here the physical constraints of the design guide the user to complete the task.

6. *Design for error*. To err is human, so anticipate the errors the user could make and design recovery into the system.

7. *When all else fails, standardize*. If there are no natural mappings then arbitrary mappings should be standardized so that users only have to learn them once. It is this standardization principle that enables drivers to get into a new car and drive it with very little difficulty – key controls are standardized. Occasionally one might switch on the indicator lights instead of the windscreen wipers, but the critical controls (accelerator, brake, clutch, steering) are always the same.

Norman's seven principles provide a useful summary of his user-centered design philosophy but the reader is encouraged to read the complete text of *The Design of Everyday Things* to gain the full picture.

7.6 HCI PATTERNS

As we observed in Chapter 4, one way to approach design is to learn from examples that have proven to be successful in the past: to reuse the knowledge of what made a system – or paradigm – successful. Patterns are an approach to capturing and reusing this knowledge – of abstracting the essential details of successful design so that these can be applied again and again in new situations.

Patterns originated in architecture, where they have been used successfully, and they are also used widely in software development to capture solutions to common programming problems. More recently they have been used in interface and web design.

A pattern is an invariant solution to a recurrent problem within a specific context. Patterns address the problems that designers face by providing a 'solution statement'. This is best illustrated by example. Alexander, who initiated the pattern concept, proposes a pattern for house building called 'Light on Two Sides of Every Room'. The problem being addressed here is that

> When they have a choice, people will always gravitate to those rooms which have light on two sides, and leave the rooms which are lit only from one side unused and empty.

The proposed solution is to provide natural light from two sides of every room:

Locate each room so that it has outdoor space outside it on at least two sides, and then place windows in these outdoor walls so that natural light falls into every room from more than one direction [9a, pattern 159].

Note that the solution says nothing about where these windows should be located or at what angle they should be to each other. A room with windows on opposite walls, or at right angles, or with a window and a skylight would all fulfill the pattern. Patterns capture only the invariant properties of good design – the common elements that hold between all instances of the solution. The specific implementation of the pattern will depend on the circumstance and the designer's creativity.

There are many examples of HCI patterns, and the interested reader is referred to pattern collections and languages such as [345, 37, 356] and the Pattern Gallery, which illustrates some of the various forms used in HCI patterns [132]. A well-known example, 'go back to a safe place', adapted from Tidwell's Common Ground collection, is given as an illustration (Figure 7.3). This is quite a low-level interface pattern, but patterns can also address high-level issues such as organizational structures or cooperative groups. As you can see, the pattern states the problem and the solution but also includes a rationale, explaining where the pattern has come from and in what context it applies, and examples to illustrate the pattern.

The pattern also has references to other patterns, indicating both the context in which it can be applied (the top references) and the patterns that may be needed to complete it (the bottom references). This connects the patterns together into a *language*. Patterns in isolation have limited use, but by traversing the hierarchy, through these references, the user is assisted in generating a complete design.

Patterns and pattern languages are characterized by a number of features, which, taken as a whole, distinguish them from other design rules:

■ They capture design practice and embody knowledge about successful solutions: they come from practice rather than psychological theory.
■ They capture the essential common properties of good design: they do not tell the designer *how* to do something but what needs to be done and why.
■ They represent design knowledge at varying levels, ranging from social and organizational issues through conceptual design to detailed widget design.
■ They are not neutral but embody values within their rationale. Alexander's language clearly expresses his values about architecture. HCI patterns can express values about what is humane in interface design.
■ The concept of a pattern language is generative and can therefore assist in the development of complete designs.
■ They are generally intuitive and readable and can therefore be used for communication between all stakeholders.

Patterns are a relatively recent addition to HCI representations, in which there are still many research issues to resolve. For instance, it is not clear how patterns can best be identified or how languages should be structured to reflect the temporal concerns of interaction. However, the recent publication of a complete pattern language for web design [356], aimed at commercial designers, may mark a turning point and see a more widespread adoption of the approach in interface design.

... <u>NAVIGABLE SPACES</u> or <u>STEP BY STEP</u> and a <u>CONTROL PANEL</u> are in place, which require the user to be able to move through the steps page by page.

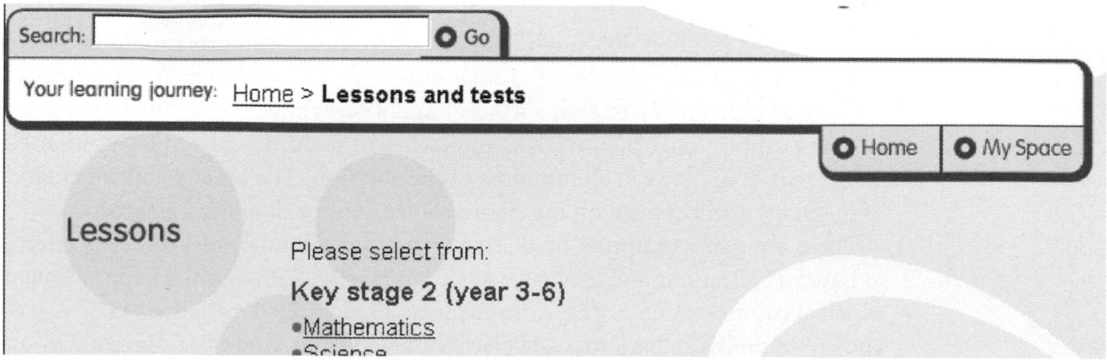

Search:	◉ Go

Your learning journey: <u>Home</u> > **Lessons and tests**

◉ Home | ◉ My Space

Lessons

Please select from:

Key stage 2 (year 3-6)

- Mathematics
- Science

From (<u>www.learn.co.uk</u>). An example of a toolbar that provides the option to return home and keeps track of the learning journey, providing the option to link back to a safe place.

❖ ❖ ❖

It is easy to get lost in the tangle of links in a website.

People don't use the web like a TV or magazine. They use the web to find what they are looking for and then stop. They may select a wrong link and not be able to find their way back to something relevant. They do not always keep track of where they've been. They may forget where they have been if they are interrupted when using the site.

You are more likely to explore a website if you are sure that you can easily get out of an undesired state or space; that assurance engenders a feeling of security. Backtracking out of a long navigation path can be very tedious.

Therefore:
Always include a way back to a place that acts as a 'vantage point' from where you can reorientate yourself.

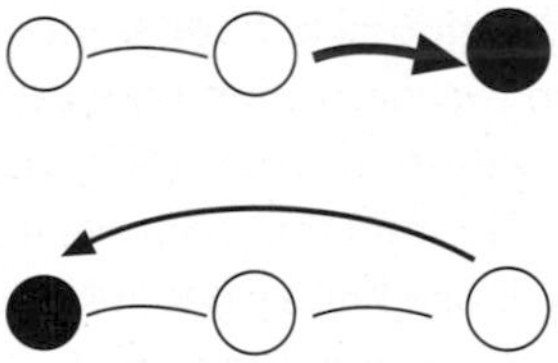

This pattern can be used in conjunction with <u>GO BACK ONE STEP</u> and <u>CONTINUE TO NEXT STEP</u>.

Figure 7.3 An example pattern 'go back to a safe place' adapted from Tidwell's Common Ground collection. Courtesy of Jenifer Tidwell

7.7 SUMMARY

We have seen how design rules can be used to provide direction for the design process, although the more general and interesting the design rule is for promoting usability, the further away it is from the actual language of design.

We have considered abstract principles, standards and guidelines, golden rules and heuristics, and patterns, and have looked at examples of each. The most abstract design rules are principles, which represent generic knowledge about good design practice. Standards and guidelines are more specific. Standards have the highest authority, being set by national or international bodies to ensure compliance by a large community. Guidelines are less authoritative but offer specific contextual advice, which can inform detailed design. Heuristics and 'golden rules' are succinct collections of design principles and advice that are easily assimilated by any designer. Patterns capture design practice and attempt to provide a generative structure to support the design process.

EXERCISES

7.1   What was the problem with the synthesis example comparing a command language interface with a visual interface? Can you suggest a fix to make a visual interface really immediately honest?

7.2   It has been suggested in this chapter that consistency could be considered a major category of interactive principles, on the same level as learnability, flexibility and robustness. If this was the case, which principles discussed in this chapter would appear in support of consistency?

7.3   Find as much information as you can on ISO standards that relate to usability. (**Hint:** Many standards are discussed in terms of ergonomics.) How many different standards and draft standards can you find?

7.4   Can you think of any instances in which the 'noun–verb' guideline for operations, as suggested in the Apple human interface guidelines for the Desktop Interface, would be violated? Suggest other abstract guidelines or principles besides consistency which support your example. (**Hint:** Think about moving files around on the Desktop.)

7.5   Can you think of any instances in which the user control guideline suggested by Apple is not followed? (**Hint:** Think about the use of dialog boxes.)

7.6   Find a book on guidelines. List the guidelines that are provided and classify them in terms of the activity in the software life cycle to which they would most likely apply.

7.7   (a) Distinguish between principles, guidelines and standards, using examples of each to illustrate.
       (b) Why is context important in selecting and applying guidelines and principles for interface design? Illustrate your answer with examples.

7.8   (a) Why are there few effective HCI standards?
       (b) How do 'golden rules' and heuristics help interface designers take account of cognitive psychology? Illustrate your answer with examples.

7.9   Using the web design pattern language in *The Design of Sites* [356] produce a design for an e-commerce site for a small retail business. How well does the language support the design process?

RECOMMENDED READING

H. Thimbleby, Design of interactive systems. In J. A. McDermid, editor, *The Software Engineer's Reference Book*, Chapter 57, Butterworth–Heinemann, 1992.
Thimbleby provides a very insightful list of general principles which apply to interactive systems. Some of the principles we have described in this chapter come from Thimbleby's work, though we have concentrated more on providing an overall organizational framework for the principles.

T. Stewart, Ergonomics user interface standards: are they more trouble than they are worth?, *Ergonomics*, Vol. 43, No. 7, pp. 1030–44, July 2000.
A review of the development of user interface standards, which considers the history of the endeavour, its successes and failures.

D. J. Mayhew, *Principles and Guidelines in Software User Interface Design*, Prentice Hall, 1992.
A comprehensive catalog of general interactive system guidelines which provides much of the experimental evidence to support specific guidelines.

B. Shneiderman, *Designing the User Interface*, 3rd edition, Addison-Wesley, 1998.
The source of Eight Golden Rules.

D. Norman, *The Design of Everyday Things*, MIT Press, 1998.
Classic exposition of design, including the seven principles.

D. Van Duyne, J. Landay and J. Hong, *The Design of Sites: Patterns, Principles and Processes for Crafting a Customer-centred Web Experience*, Addison-Wesley, 2003.
The first substantial and widely applicable HCI complete pattern language (for web design) presented accessibly for use in design teams.

The HCI Service, *HCI Tools & Methods Handbook*, 1991.
This booklet was produced under the United Kingdom Department of Trade and Industry (DTI) *Usability Now!* program. It contains a list of books on guidelines as well as a summary of the available user-centered design techniques as they can be applied to the software life cycle. The booklet and other information about the program is available from the HCI Service, PO Box 31, Loughborough, Leicestershire LE11 1QU, United Kingdom.

IMPLEMENTATION SUPPORT

8

OVERVIEW

- Programming tools for interactive systems provide a means of effectively translating abstract designs and usability principles into an executable form. These tools provide different levels of services for the programmer.

- Windowing systems are a central environment for both the programmer and user of an interactive system, allowing a single workstation to support separate user–system threads of action simultaneously.

- Interaction toolkits abstract away from the physical separation of input and output devices, allowing the programmer to describe behaviors of objects at a level similar to how the user perceives them.

- User interface management systems are the final level of programming support tools, allowing the designer and programmer to control the relationship between the presentation objects of a toolkit with their functional semantics in the actual application.

8.1   INTRODUCTION

In this chapter, we will discuss the programming support that is provided for the implementation of an interactive system. We have spent much effort up to this point considering design and analysis of interactive systems from a relatively abstract perspective. We did this because it was not necessary to consider the specific details of the devices used in the interaction. Furthermore, consideration of that detail was an obstacle to understanding the interaction from the user's perspective. But we cannot forever ignore the specifics of the device. It is now time to devote some attention to understanding just how the task of coding the interactive application is structured.

The detailed specification gives the programmer instructions as to what the interactive application must do and the programmer must translate that into machine executable instructions to say how that will be achieved on the available hardware devices. The objective of the programmer then is to translate down to the level of the software that runs the hardware devices. At its crudest level, this software provides the ability to do things like read events from various input devices and write primitive graphics commands to a display. Whereas it is possible in that crude language to produce highly interactive systems, the job is very tedious and highly error prone, amenable to computer hackers who relish the intricacy and challenge but not necessarily those whose main concern is the design of very usable interactive systems.

The programming support tools which we describe in this chapter aim to move that executable language up from the crudely expressive level to a higher level in which the programmer can code more directly in terms of the interaction objects of the application. The emphasis here is on how building levels of abstraction on top of the essential hardware and software services allows the programmer to build the system in terms of its desired *interaction techniques*, a term we use to indicate the intimate relationship between input and output. Though there is a fundamental separation between input and output devices in the hardware devices and at the lowest software level, the distinction can be removed at the programming level with the right abstractions and hiding of detail.

In the remainder of this chapter, we will address the various layers which constitute the move from the low-level hardware up to the more abstract programming concepts for interaction. We begin in Section 8.2 with the elements of a windowing system, which provide for device independence and resource sharing at the programming level. Programming in a window system frees the programmer from some of the worry about the input and output primitives of the machines the application will run on, and allows her to program the application under the assumption that it will receive a stream of event requests from the window manager. In Section 8.3 we describe the two fundamental ways this stream of events can be processed to link the interface with the application functionality: by means of a read–evaluation control loop internal to the application program or by a centralized notification-based technique external to it. In Section 8.4, we describe the use of toolkits as mechanisms to link input and output at the programming level. In Section 8.5, we discuss the large class of development tools lumped under the categories of user interface management systems, or UIMS, and user interface development systems, UIDS.

8.2 ELEMENTS OF WINDOWING SYSTEMS

In earlier chapters, we have discussed the elements of the WIMP interface but only with respect to how they enhance the interaction with the end-user. Here we will describe more details of windowing systems used to build the WIMP interface.

The first important feature of a windowing system is its ability to provide programmer independence from the specifics of the hardware devices. A typical workstation will involve some visual display screen, a keyboard and some pointing device, such as a mouse. Any variety of these hardware devices can be used in any interactive system and they are all different in terms of the data they communicate and the commands that are used to instruct them. It is imperative to be able to program an application that will run on a wide range of devices. To do this, the programmer wants to direct commands to an *abstract terminal*, which understands a more generic language and can be translated to the language of many other specific devices. Besides making the programming task easier, the abstract terminal makes portability of application programs possible. Only one translation program – or *device driver* – needs to be written for a particular hardware device and then any application program can access it.

A given windowing system will have a fixed generic language for the abstract terminal which is called its *imaging model*. The imaging models are sufficient to describe very arbitrary images. For efficiency reasons, specific primitives are used to handle text images, either as specific pixel images or as more generic font definitions.

Examples of imaging models

Pixels
The display screen is represented as a series of columns and rows of points – or pixels – which can be explicitly turned on or off, or given a color. This is a common imaging model for personal computers and is also used by the X windowing system.

Graphical kernel system (GKS)
An international standard which models the screen as a collection of connected segments, each of which is a macro of elementary graphics commands.

Programmer's hierarchical interface to graphics (PHIGS)
Another international standard, based on GKS but with an extension to model the screen as editable segments.

PostScript
A programming language developed by Adobe Corporation which models the screen as a collection of paths which serve as infinitely thin boundaries or stencils which can be filled in with various colors or textured patterns and images.

Though these imaging models were initially defined to provide abstract languages for output only, they can serve at least a limited role for input as well. So, for example, the pixel model can be used to interpret input from a mouse in terms of the pixel coordinate system. It would then be the job of the application to process the input event further once it knows where in the image it occurred. The other models above can provide even more expressiveness for the input language, because they can relate the input events to structures that are identifiable by the application program. Both PHIGS and PostScript have been augmented to include a more explicit model of input.

When we discussed the WIMP interface as an interaction paradigm in Chapter 4, we pointed out its ability to support several separate user tasks simultaneously. Windowing systems provide this capability by sharing the resources of a single hardware configuration with several copies of an abstract terminal. Each abstract terminal will behave as an independent *process* and the windowing system will coordinate the control of the concurrent processes. To ease the programming task again, this coordination of simultaneously active processes can be factored out of the individual applications, so that they can be programmed as if they were to operate in isolation. The window system must also provide a means of displaying the separate applications, and this is accomplished by dedicating a region of the display screen to each active abstract terminal. The coordination task then involves resolving display conflicts when the visible screen regions of two abstract terminals overlap.

In summary, we can see the role of a windowing system, depicted in Figure 8.1, as providing

independence from the specifics of programming separate hardware devices;

management of multiple, independent but simultaneously active applications.

Next, we discuss the possible architectures of a windowing system to achieve these two tasks.

8.2.1 Architectures of windowing systems

Bass and Coutaz [29] identify three possible architectures for the software to implement the roles of a windowing system. All of them assume that device drivers are separate from the application programs. The first option is to implement and replicate the management of the multiple processes within each of the separate applications. This is not a very satisfactory architecture because it forces each application to consider the difficult problems of resolving synchronization conflicts with the shared hardware devices. It also reduces the portability of the separate applications. The second option is to implement the management role within the kernel of the operating system, centralizing the management task by freeing it from the individual applications. Applications must still be developed with the specifics of the particular operating system in mind. The third option provides the most portability, as the management function is written as a separate application in its own right and

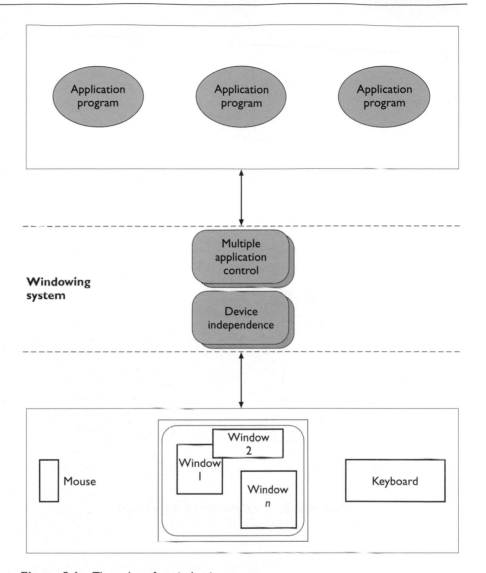

Figure 8.1   The roles of a windowing system

so can provide an interface to other application programs that is generic across all operating systems. This final option is referred to as the *client–server architecture*, and is depicted in Figure 8.2.

In practice, the divide among these proposed architectures is not so clear and any actual interactive application or set of applications operating within a window system may share features with any one of these three conceptual architectures. Therefore, it may have one component that is a separate application or process together with some built-in operating system support and hand-tuned application

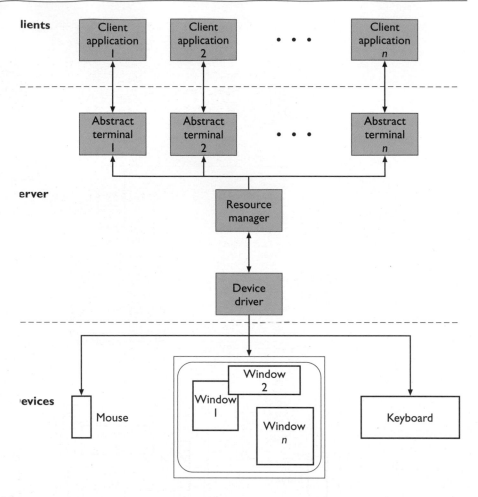

Figure 8.2 The client–server architecture

support to manage the shared resources. So applications built for a window system which is notionally based on the client–server model may not be as portable as one would think.

A classic example of a window system based on the client–server architecture is the industry-standard X Window System (Release 11), developed at the Massachusetts Institute of Technology (MIT) in the mid-1980s. Figure 8.3 shows the software architecture of X. X (or X11), as we mentioned earlier, is based on a pixel-based imaging model and assumes that there is some pointing mechanism available. What distinguishes X from other window systems, and the reason it has been adopted as a standard, is that X is based on a network protocol which clearly defines the server–client communication. The *X Protocol* can be implemented on different computers and operating systems, making X more device independent. It also means that client and server need not even be on the same system in order to communicate to

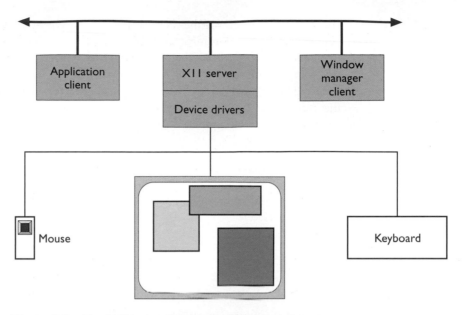

Figure 8.3   The X Window System (Release 11) architecture

the server. Each client of the X11 server is associated to an abstract terminal or main window. The X server performs the following tasks:

- allows (or denies) access to the display from multiple client applications;
- interprets requests from clients to perform screen operations or provide other information;
- demultiplexes the stream of physical input events from the user and passes them to the appropriate client;
- minimizes the traffic along the network by relieving the clients from having to keep track of certain display information, like fonts, in complex data structures that the clients can access by ID numbers.

A separate client – the *window manager* – enforces policies to resolve conflicting input and output requests to and from the other clients. There are several different window managers which can be used in X, and they adopt different policies. For example, the window manager would decide how the user can change the focus of his input from one application to another. One option is for the user to nominate one window as the active one to which all subsequent input is directed. The other option is for the active window to be implicitly nominated by the position of the pointing device. Whenever the pointer is in the display space of a window, all input is directed to it. Once the pointer is moved to a position inside another window, that window becomes active and receives subsequent input. Another example of window manager policy is whether visible screen images of the client windows can overlap or must be non-overlapping (called tiling). As with many other windowing systems, the client applications can define their own hierarchy of subwindows, each of which is constrained to the coordinate space of the parent window. This subdivision of the main client window allows the programmer to manage the input and output for a single application similar to the window manager.

To aid in the design of specific window managers, the X Consortium has produced the *Inter-Client Communication Conventions Manual (ICCCM)*, which provides conventions for various policy issues that are not included in the X definition. These policies include:

- rules for transferring data between clients;
- methods for selecting the active client for input focus;
- layout schemes for overlapping/tiled windows as screen regions.

8.3   PROGRAMMING THE APPLICATION

We now concentrate our attention on programming the actual interactive application, which would correspond to a client in the client–server architecture of Figure 8.2. Interactive applications are generally user driven in the sense that the action the application takes is determined by the input received from the user. We describe two programming paradigms which can be used to organize the flow of control within the application. The windowing system does not necessarily determine which of these two paradigms is to be followed.

The first programming paradigm is the *read–evaluation loop*, which is internal to the application program itself (see Figure 8.4). Programming on the Macintosh follows this paradigm. The server sends user inputs as structured events to the client application. As far as the server is concerned, the only importance of the event is the client to which it must be directed. The client application is programmed to read any event passed to it and determine all of the application-specific behavior that results as a response to it. The logical flow of the client application is indicated in the leftmost box of Figure 8.4. In pseudocode the read–evaluation loop would look like the following:

```
repeat
     read-event(myevent)
     case    myevent.type
             type_1 :
                     do type_1 processing
             type_2 :
                     do type_2 processing
                .
                .
                .
```

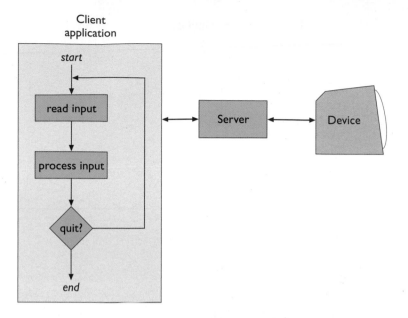

Client
application

Figure 8.4 The read–evaluate loop paradigm

```
          type_n :
                  do type_n processing
      end case
  end repeat
```

The application has complete control over the processing of events that it receives. The downside is that the programmer must execute this control over every possible event that the client will receive, which could prove a very cumbersome task. On the Macintosh, this process can be aided somewhat by programming tools, such as MacApp, which automate some of the tedium.

The other programming paradigm is *notification based*, in which the main control loop for the event processing does not reside within the application. Instead, a centralized *notifier* receives events from the window system and filters them to the application program in a way declared by the program (see Figure 8.5). The application program informs the notifier what events are of interest to it, and for each event declares one of its own procedures as a *callback* before turning control over to the notifier. When the notifier receives an event from the window system, it sees if that event was identified by the application program and, if so, passes the event and control over to the callback procedure that was registered for the event. After processing, the callback procedure returns control to the notifier, either telling it to continue receiving events or requesting termination.

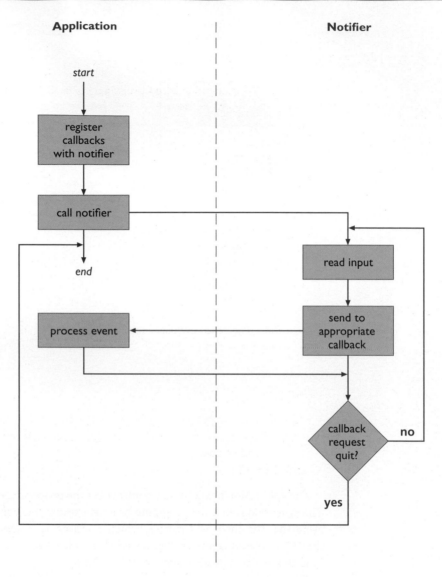

Figure 8.5 The notification-based programming paradigm

Control flow is centralized in the notifier, which relieves the application program of much of the tedium of processing every possible event passed to it by the window system. But this freedom from control does not come without a price. Suppose, for example, that the application program wanted to produce a pre-emptive dialog box, perhaps because it has detected an error and wants to obtain confirmation from the user before proceeding. The pre-emptive dialog effectively discards all subsequent user actions except for ones that it requires, say selection by the user inside a certain region of the screen. To do this in the read–evaluation paradigm is fairly

Example: a notification-based program

Figure 8.6 provides an example of notification-based programming in C using the XView toolkit (toolkits are described in the next section).

```
1.   /*
2.    * quit.c -- simple program to display a panel button that says
     "Quit".
3.    * Selecting the panel button exits the program.
4.    */
5.   # include <xview/xview.h>
6.   # include <xview/frame.h>
7.   # include <xview/panel.h>

8.   Frame frame;

9.   main  (argc, argv)
10.  int argc;
11.  char *argv[];
12.  {
13.      Panel panel;
14.      void quit();
15.
16.      xv_init(XV_INIT_ARGC_PTR_ARGV, &argc, argv, NULL);

17.      frame = (Frame) xv_create(NULL, FRAME,
18.          FRAME_LABEL,      argv[0],
19.          XV_WIDTH,         200,
20.          XV_HEIGHT,        100,
21.          NULL);

22.      panel = (Panel) xv_create(frame, PANEL, NULL);

23.      (void) xv_create(panel, PANEL_BUTTON,
24.              PANEL_LABEL_STRING,      "Quit",
25.              PANEL_NOTIFY_PROC,       quit,
26.              NULL);

27.      xv_main_loop(frame);
28.      exit(0);
29.  }

30.  void quit()
31.  {
32.      xv_destroy_safe(frame);
33.  }
```

Figure 8.6   A simple program to demonstrate notification-based programming. Example taken from Dan Heller [169], reproduced by permission of O'Reilly and Associates, Inc

The program produces a window, or frame, with one button, labeled `Quit`, which when selected by the pointer device causes the program to quit, destroying the window (see Figure 8.7 for the screen image produced by the sample program `quit.c`). Three objects are created in this program: the outermost frame, a panel within that frame and the button in the panel. The procedure `xv_create`, used on lines 17, 22 and 23 in the source code of Figure 8.6, is used by the application program to register the objects with the XView notifier. In the last instance on line 23, the application programmer informs the notifier of the callback procedure to be invoked when the object, a button, is selected. The application program then initiates the notifier by the procedure call `xv_main_loop`. When the notifier receives a select event for the button, control is passed to the procedure `quit` which destroys the outermost frame and requests termination.

Figure 8.7 Screen image produced by sample program `quit.c`

straightforward. Suppose the error condition occurred during the processing of an event of type `type_2`. Once the error condition is recognized, the application then begins another read–evaluation loop contained within that branch of the **case** statement. Within that loop, all non-relevant events can be received and discarded. The pseudocode example given earlier would be modified in the following way:

```
repeat
      read-event(myevent)
      case    myevent.type
              type_1 :
                      do type_1 processing
              type_2 :
                      . . .
                      if      (error-condition) then
                              repeat
                                      read-event(myevent2)
                                      case    myevent2.type
```

```
                                     type_1 :
                                        .
                                        .
                                        .
                                     type_n :
                        end case
                  until (end-condition2)
            end if
                 . . .
              .
              .
              .
            type_n :
                  do type_n processing
        end case
     until (end-condition)
```

In the notification-based paradigm, such a pre-emptive dialog would not be so simple, because the control flow is out of the hands of the application programmer. The callback procedures would all have to be modified to recognize the situations in which the pre-emptive dialog is needed and in those situations disregard all events which are passed to them by the notifier. Things would be improved, however, if the application programmer could in such situations access the notifier directly to request that previously acceptable events be ignored until further notice.

DESIGN FOCUS

Going with the grain

It is possible to use notification-based code to produce pre-emptive interface dialog such as a *modal dialog box*, but much more difficult than with an event-loop-based system. Similarly, it is possible to write event-loop-based code which is not pre-emptive, but again it is difficult to do so. If you are not careful, systems built using notification-based code will have lots of non-modal dialog boxes and vice versa. Each programming paradigm has a *grain*, a tendency to push you towards certain kinds of interface.

If you know that the interface you require fits more closely to one paradigm or another then it is worth selecting the programming paradigm to make your life easier! Often, however, you do not have a choice. In this case you have to be very careful to decide what kind of interface dialog you want *before* you (or someone else) start coding. Where the desired interface fits the grain of the paradigm you don't have to worry. Where the desired behavior runs against the grain you must be careful, both in coding and testing as these are the areas where things will go wrong.

Of course, if you don't *explicitly* decide what behavior you want or you specify it unclearly, then it is likely that the resulting system will simply run with the grain, whether or not that makes a good interface.

8.4 USING TOOLKITS

As we discussed in Chapter 4, a key feature of WIMP interfaces from the user's perspective is that input and output behaviors are intrinsically linked to independent entities on the display screen. This creates the illusion that the entities on the screen are the objects of interest – interaction objects we have called them – and that is necessary for the action world of a direct manipulation interface. A classic example is the mouse as a pointing device. The input coming from the hardware device is separate from the output of the mouse cursor on the display screen. However, since the visual movement of the screen cursor is linked with the physical movement of the mouse device, the user feels as if he is actually moving the visual cursor. Even though input and output are actually separate, the illusion causes the user to treat them as one; indeed, both the visual cursor and the physical device are referred to simply as 'the mouse'. In situations where this link is broken, it is easy to see the user's frustration.

In Figure 8.8, we show an example of how input and output are combined for interaction with a button object. As the user moves the mouse cursor over the button, it changes to a finger to suggest that the user can push it. Pressing the mouse button down causes the button to be highlighted and might even make an audible click like the keys on some keyboards, providing immediate feedback that the button has been pushed. Releasing the mouse button unhighlights the button and moving the mouse off the button changes the cursor to its initial shape, indicating that the user is no longer over the active area of the button.

From the programmer's perspective, even at the level of a windowing system, input and output are still quite separate for everything except the mouse, and it takes quite a bit of effort in the application program to create the illusion of the interaction object such as the button we have just described. To aid the programmer in fusing input and output behaviors, another level of abstraction is placed on top of the window system – the *toolkit*. A toolkit provides the programmer with a set of ready-made interaction objects – alternatively called interaction techniques, gadgets or widgets – which she can use to create her application programs. The interaction

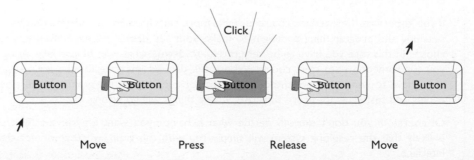

Figure 8.8 Example of behavior of a button interaction object

objects have a predefined behavior, such as that described for the button, that comes for free without any further programming effort. Toolkits exist for all windowing environments (for example, OSF/Motif and XView for the X Window system, the Macintosh Toolbox and the Software Development Toolkit for Microsoft Windows).

To provide flexibility, the interaction objects can be tailored to the specific situation in which they are invoked by the programmer. For example, the label on the button could be a parameter which the programmer can set when a particular button is created. More complex interaction objects can be built up from smaller, simpler ones. Ultimately, the entire application can be viewed as a collection of interaction objects whose combined behavior describes the semantics of the whole application.

The sample program quit.c in Figure 8.6 uses the XView toolkit. Programming with toolkits is suited to the notification-based programming paradigm. As we can see in the example, the button is created as a PANEL_BUTTON object (lines 23–26) and registers the appropriate callback routine for when the notifier receives a selection event for the button object. The button interaction object in the toolkit already has defined what actual user action is classified as the selection event, so the programmer need not worry about that when creating an instance of the button. The programmer can think of the event at a higher level of abstraction, that is as a selection event instead of as a release of the left mouse button.

In Chapter 7 we discussed the benefits of consistency and generalizability for an interactive system. One of the advantages of programming with toolkits is that they can enforce consistency in both input form and output form by providing similar behavior to a collection of widgets. For example, every button interaction object, within the same application program or between different ones, by default could have a behavior like the one described in Figure 8.8. All that is required is that the developers for the different applications use the same toolkit. This consistency of behavior for interaction objects is referred to as the *look and feel* of the toolkit. Style guides, which were described in the discussion on guidelines in Chapter 7, give additional hints to a programmer on how to preserve the look and feel of a given toolkit beyond that which is enforced by the default definition of the interaction objects.

Two features of interaction objects and toolkits make them amenable to an object-oriented approach to programming. First, they depend on being able to define a class of interaction objects which can then be invoked (or instantiated) many times within one application with only minor modifications to each instance. Secondly, building complex interaction objects is made easier by building up their definition based on existing simpler interaction objects. These notions of *instantiation* and *inheritance* are cornerstones of object-oriented programming. *Classes* are defined as templates for interaction objects. When an interaction object is created, it is declared as an instance of some predefined class. So, in the example quit.c program, frame is declared as an instance of the class FRAME (line 17), panel is declared as an instance of the class PANEL (line 22) and the button (no name) is declared as an instance of the class PANEL_BUTTON (line 23). Typically, a class template will provide default

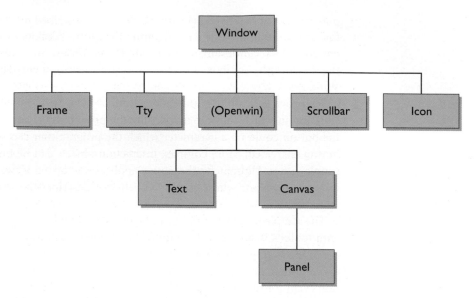

Figure 8.9 The single inheritance class hierarchy of the XView toolkit, after Heller [169], reproduced by permission of O'Reilly and Associates, Inc

values for various attributes. Some of those attributes can be altered in any one instance; they are sometimes distinguished as *instance attributes*.

In defining the classes of interaction objects themselves, new classes can be built which inherit features of one or other classes. In the simplest case, there is a strict *class hierarchy* in which each class inherits features of only one other class, its *parent class*. This simple form of inheritance is called *single inheritance* and is exhibited in the XView toolkit standard hierarchy for the window class in Figure 8.9. A more complicated class hierarchy would permit defining new classes which inherit from more than one parent class – called *multiple inheritance*.

DESIGN FOCUS

Java and AWT

The Java toolkit for developing windowed applications is called the Abstract Windowing Toolkit, AWT. It maps interface objects such as buttons, menus and dialog boxes onto corresponding Java classes. The programmer builds an interface either by using these classes directly or by *subclassing* them, that is specializing the behavior of the object in some way. This subclassing means that new interaction widgets can easily be added. The toolkit is notification based, but the mechanism has changed slightly between versions. In AWT 1.0 the programmer needs to subclass a button in order to specify its behavior when pressed. Since AWT 1.1 the programmer can use a method more like traditional callbacks, but based on registering special Java objects rather than functions.

We should point out that though most toolkits are structured in an object-oriented manner, that does not mean that the actual application programming language is object oriented. The example program `quit.c` was written in the C programming language, which is not an object-oriented language. It is best to think of object orientation as yet another programming paradigm which structures the way the programmer attacks the programming task without mandating a particular syntax or semantics for the programming language.

The programmer can tailor the behavior and appearance of an interaction object by setting the values of various instance attributes. These attributes must be set before the application program is compiled. In addition, some windowing systems allow various attributes of interaction objects to be altered without necessitating recompilation, though they may have to be set before the actual program is run. This tailorability is achieved via *resources* which can be accessed by the application program and change the compiled value of some attributes. For efficiency reasons, this tailorability is often limited to a small set of attributes for any given class.

Worked exercise *Scrolling is an effective means of browsing through a document in a window that is too small to show the whole document. Compare the different interactive behavior of the following two interaction objects to implement scrolling:*

- *A scrollbar is attached to the side of the window with arrows at the top and bottom. When the mouse is positioned over the arrow at the top of the screen (which points up), the window frame is moved upwards to reveal a part of the document above/before what is currently viewed. When the bottom arrow is selected, the frame moves down to reveal the document below/after the current view.*
- *The document is contained in a textual interaction object. Pressing the mouse button in the text object allows you to drag the document within the window boundaries. You drag up to browse down in the document and you drag down to browse up.*

The difference between the two situations can be characterized by noticing that, in the first case, the user is actually manipulating the window (moving it up or down to reveal the contents of the document), whereas, in the second case, the user is manipulating the document (pushing it up or down to reveal its contents through the windows). What usability principles would you use to justify one method over the other (also consider the case when you want to scroll from side to side as well as up and down)? What implementation considerations are important?

Answer There are many usability principles that can be brought to bear on an examination of scrolling principles. For example:

Observability The whole reason why scrolling is used is because there is too much information to present all at once. Providing a means of viewing document contents without changing the contents increases the observability of the system. Scrollbars also increase observability because they help to indicate the wider context of the information which is currently visible, typically by showing where the window of information fits within the whole document. However, observability does not address the particular design options put forth here.

Predictability   The value of a scrolling mechanism lies in the user being able to know where a particular scrolling action will lead in the document. The use of arrows on the scrollbar is to help the user predict the effect of the scrolling operation. If an arrow points up, the question is whether that indicates the direction the window is being moved (the first case) or the direction the actual text would have to move (the second case). The empirical question here is: to what object do users associate the arrow – the text or the text window? The arrow of the scrollbar is more closely connected to the boundary of a text window, so the more usual interpretation would be to have it indicate the direction of the window movement.

Synthesizability   You might think that it does not matter which object the user associates to the arrow. He will just have to learn the mapping and live with it. In this case, how easy is it to learn the mapping, that is can the user synthesize the meaning of the scrolling actions from changes made at the display? Usually, the movement of a box within the scrollbar itself will indicate the result of a scrolling operation.

Familiarity/guessability   It would be an interesting experiment to see whether there was a difference in the performance of new users for the different scrolling mechanisms. This might be the subject of a more extended exercise.

Task conformance   There are some implementation limitations for these scrolling mechanisms (see below). In light of these limitations, does the particular scrolling task prefer one over the other? In considering this principle, we need to know what kinds of scrolling activity will be necessary. Is the document a long text that will be browsed from end to end, or is it possibly a map or a picture which is only slightly larger than the actual screen so scrolling will only be done in small increments?

Some implementation considerations:

■ What scroll mechanisms does a toolkit provide? Is it easy to access the two options discussed above within the same toolkit?
■ In the case of the second scrolling option, are there enough keys on the mouse to allow this operation without interfering with other important mouse operations, such as arbitrarily moving the insertion point or selecting a portion of text or selecting a graphical item?
■ In the second option, the user places the mouse on a specific location within the window, and gestures to dictate the movement of the underlying document. What kind of behavior is expected when the mouse hits the boundary of the window? Is the scrolling limited in this case to steps bounded in size by the size of the window, so that scrolling between two distant points requires many separate smaller scrolling actions?

8.5   USER INTERFACE MANAGEMENT SYSTEMS

Despite the availability of toolkits and the valuable abstraction they provide programmers, there are still significant hurdles to overcome in the specification, design and implementation of interactive systems. Toolkits provide only a limited range of interaction objects, limiting the kinds of interactive behavior allowed between user and system. Toolkits are expensive to create and are still very difficult to use by non-programmers. Even experienced programmers will have difficulty using them to produce an interface that is predictably usable. There is a need for additional support for programmers in the design and use of toolkits to overcome their deficiencies. Also, none of the programming mechanisms we have discussed so far in this chapter is appropriate for non-expert programmers, so we still have a long way to go towards the goal of opening up interactive system implementation to those whose main concerns are with HCI and not programming.

The set of programming and design techniques which are supposed to add another level of services for interactive system design beyond the toolkit level are *user interface management systems*, or *UIMS* for short. The term UIMS is used quite widely in both industrial and academic circles and has come to represent a variety of topics. The main concerns of a UIMS, for our purposes, are:

- a conceptual architecture for the structure of an interactive system which concentrates on a separation between application semantics and presentation;
- techniques for implementing a separated application and presentation whilst preserving the intended connection between them;
- support techniques for managing, implementing and evaluating a run-time interactive environment.

We should acknowledge that some people feel that the term UIMS is inappropriate for all of the above tasks, preferring the term *user interface development systems*, or *UIDS*, to distinguish support tools which address many of the design activities that precede the management of the run-time system.

8.5.1 UIMS as a conceptual architecture

A major issue in this area of research is one of *separation* between the semantics of the application and the interface provided for the user to make use of that semantics. There are many good arguments to support this separation of concerns:

Portability   To allow the same application to be used on different systems it is best to consider its development separate from its device-dependent interface.

Reusability   Separation increases the likelihood that components can be reused in order to cut development costs.

Multiple interfaces   To enhance the interactive flexibility of an application, several different interfaces can be developed to access the same functionality.

Customization   The user interface can be customized by both the designer and the user to increase its effectiveness without having to alter the underlying application.

Once we allow for a separation between application and presentation, we must consider how those two partners communicate. This role of communication is referred to as *dialog control*. Conceptually, this provides us with the three major components of an interactive system: the application, the presentation and the dialog control. In terms of the actual implementation, this separation may not be so clear.

In Section 8.3, we described the two basic approaches to programming the application within an interactive system. In the read–evaluation loop, the control of the dialog is *internal* to the application. The application calls interface procedures when input or output is required. In notification-based programming, the dialog control resides *external* to the application. When the user performs some input action, the notifier then invokes the correct application procedure to handle the event. Most UIMS fall into this class of external dialog control systems, since they promote, to a greater extent, the separation between presentation and application. They do not, however, all use the technique of callbacks as was demonstrated in Section 8.4 for the use of toolkits.

The first acknowledged instance of a development system that supported this application–presentation separation was in 1968 with Newman's Reaction Handler. The term UIMS was coined by Kasik in 1982 [196a] after some preliminary research on how graphical input could be used to broaden the scope of HCI. The first conceptual architecture of what constituted a UIMS was formulated at a workshop in 1985 at Seeheim, Germany [285]. The logical components of a UIMS were identified as:

Presentation   The component responsible for the appearance of the interface, including what output and input is available to the user.

Dialog control   The component which regulates the communication between the presentation and the application.

Application interface   The view of the application semantics that is provided as the interface.

Figure 8.10 presents a graphical interpretation of the Seeheim model. We have included both application and user in Figure 8.10 to place the UIMS model more in the context of the interactive system (though you could argue that we have not provided enough of that context by mentioning only a single user and a single application). The application and the user are not explicit in the Seeheim model

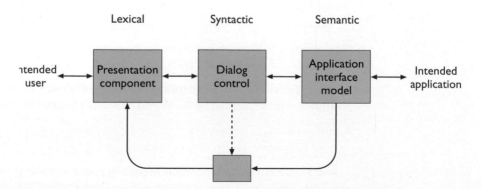

Figure 8.10   The Seeheim model of the logical components of a UIMS

because it was intended only to model the components of a UIMS and not the entire interactive system. By not making the application explicit in the model, external dialog control must have been assumed. From a programmer's perspective, the Seeheim model fits in nicely with the distinction between the classic lexical, syntactic and semantic layers of a computer system, familiar from compiler design.

One of the main problems with the Seeheim model is that, whereas it served well as a post hoc rationalization of how a UIMS was built up to 1985, it did not provide any real direction for how future UIMS should be structured. A case in point can be seen in the inclusion of the lowest box in Figure 8.10, which was intended to show that for efficiency reasons it would be possible to bypass an explicit dialog control component so that the application could provide greater application semantic feedback. There is no need for such a box in a conceptual architecture of the logical components. It is there because its creators did not separate logical concerns from implementation concerns.

Semantic feedback

One of the most ill-understood elements of the *Seeheim model* is the lower box: the *bypass* or *switch*. This is there to allow rapid semantic feedback. Examples of semantic feedback include freehand drawing and the highlighting of the trash bin on the Apple Macintosh when a file is dragged over it. As with all notions of levels in interface design, the definition of semantic feedback is not sharp, but it corresponds to those situations where it is impractical or impossible to use dialog-level abstractions to map application structures to screen representations.

The box represents the fact that in such circumstances the application component needs to address the presentation component directly, often to achieve suitable performance. It thus bypasses the dialog component. However, the box has an arrow from the dialog component which represents not a data flow, but control. Although the dialog does not mediate the presentation of information, it does control when and where the application is allowed to access the presentation; hence the alternative name of switch.

In graphical and WIMP-based systems the Seeheim components seem restrictive as single entities, and partly in response to this a later workshop developed the Arch–Slinky model [354]. This has more layers than the Seeheim model and, more importantly, recognizes that the mapping of these layers to components of a system may be more fluid than Seeheim suggests.

Another concern not addressed by the Seeheim model is how to build large and complex interactive systems from smaller components. We have seen that object-based toolkits are amenable to such a building blocks approach, and several other conceptual architectures for interactive system development have been proposed to take advantage of this. One of the earliest was the *model–view–controller* paradigm – MVC for short – suggested in the *Smalltalk* programming environment [233, 203, 212]. Smalltalk was one of the earliest successful object-oriented programming systems whose main feature was the ability to build new interactive systems based on

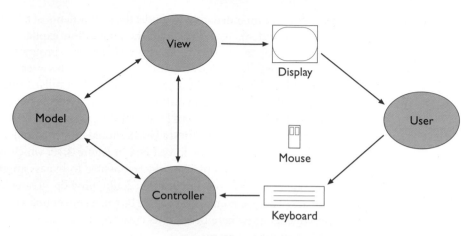

Figure 8.11   The model–view–controller triad in Smalltalk

existing ones. Within Smalltalk, the link between application semantics and presentation can be built up in units by means of the MVC triad. The model represents the application semantics; the view manages the graphical and/or textual output of the application; and the controller manages the input (see Figure 8.11).

The basic behavior of models, views and controllers has been embodied in general Smalltalk object classes, which can be inherited by instances and suitably modified. Smalltalk, like many other window toolkits, prescribes its own look and feel on input and output, so the generic view and controller classes (called `View` and `Controller`, respectively) do not need much modification after instantiation. Models, on the other hand, are very general because they must be used to portray any possible application semantics. A single model can be associated with several MVC triads, so that the same piece of application semantics can be represented by different input–output techniques. Each view–controller pair is associated to only one model.

Another so-called *multi-agent* architecture for interactive systems is the *presentation–abstraction–control* PAC model suggested by Coutaz [79]. PAC is based on a collection of triads also: with application semantics represented by the abstraction component; input and output combined in one presentation component; and an explicit control component to manage the dialog and correspondence between application and presentation (see Figure 8.12). There are three important differences between PAC and MVC. First, PAC groups input and output together, whereas MVC separates them. Secondly, PAC provides an explicit component whose duty it is to see that abstraction and presentation are kept consistent with each other, whereas MVC does not assign this important task to any one component, leaving it to the programmer/designer to determine where that chore resides. Finally, PAC is not linked to any programming environment, though it is certainly conducive to an object-oriented approach. It is probably because of this last difference that PAC could so easily isolate the control component; PAC is more of a conceptual architecture than MVC because it is less implementation dependent.

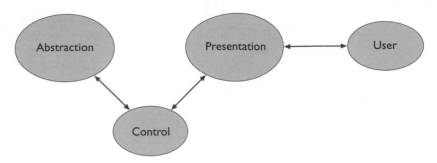

Figure 8.12   The presentation–abstraction–control model of Coutaz

8.5.2 Implementation considerations

We have made a point of distinguishing a conceptual architecture from any implementation considerations. It is, however, important to determine how components in a conceptual architecture can be realized. Implementations based on the Seeheim model must determine how the separate components of presentation, dialog controller and application interface are realized. Window systems and toolkits provide the separation between application and presentation. The use of callback procedures in notification-based programming is one way to implement the application interface as a notifier. In the standard X toolkit, these callbacks are directional as it is the duty of the application to register itself with the notifier. In MVC, callback procedures are also used for communication between a view or controller and its associated model, but this time it is the duty of the presentation (the view or controller) to register itself with the application (the model). Communication from the model to either view or controller, or between a view and a controller, occurs by the normal use of method calls used in object-oriented programming. Neither of these provides a means of separately managing the dialog.

Myers has outlined the various implementation techniques used to specify the dialog controller separately. Many of these will be discussed in Chapter 16 where we explicitly deal with dialog notations. Some of the techniques that have been used in dialog modeling in UIMS are listed here.

Menu networks   The communication between application and presentation is modeled as a network of menus and submenus. To control the dialog, the programmer must simply encode the levels of menus and the connections between one menu and the next submenu or an action. The menu is used to embody all possible user inputs at any one point in time. Links between menu items and the next displayed menu model the application response to previous input. A menu does not have to be a linear list of textual actions. The menu can be represented as graphical items or buttons that the user can select with a pointing device. Clicking on one button moves the dialog to the next screen of objects. In this way, a system like HyperCard can be considered a menu network.

Grammar notations   The dialog between application and presentation can be treated as a grammar of actions and responses, and, therefore, described by means of a formal context-free grammar notation, such as BNF (Backus–Naur form). These are good for describing command-based interfaces, but are not so good for more graphically-based interaction techniques. It is also not clear from a formal grammar what directionality is associated to each event in the grammar; that is, whether an event is initiated by the user or by the application. Therefore, it is difficult to model communication of values across the dialog controller, and that is necessary to maintain any semantic feedback from application to presentation.

State transition diagrams   State transition diagrams can be used as a graphical means of expressing dialog. Many variants on state transition diagrams will be discussed in Chapter 16. The difficulty with these notations lies in linking dialog events with corresponding presentation or application events. Also, it is not clear how communication between application and presentation is represented.

Event languages   Event languages are similar to grammar notations, except that they can be modified to express directionality and support some semantic feedback. Event languages are good for describing localized input–output behavior in terms of production rules. A production rule is activated when input is received and it results in some output responses. This control of the input–output relationship comes at a price. It is now more difficult to model the overall flow of the dialog.

Declarative languages   All of the above techniques (except for menu networks) are poor for describing the correspondence between application and presentation because they are unable to describe effectively how information flows between the two. They only view the dialog as a sequence of events that occur between two communicating partners. A declarative approach concentrates more on describing how presentation and application are related. This relationship can be modeled as a shared database of values that both presentation and application can access. Declarative languages, therefore, describe what should result from the communication between application and presentation, not how it should happen in terms of event sequencing.

Constraints   Constraints systems are a special subset of declarative languages. *Constraints* can be used to make explicit the connection between independent information of the presentation and the application. Implicit in the control component of the PAC model is this notion of constraint between values of the application and values of the presentation. Hill has proposed the *abstraction–link–view*, or ALV (pronounced 'AL-vee'), which makes the same distinctions as PAC [172]. However, Hill suggests an implementation of the communication between abstraction and view by means of the link component as a collection of two-way constraints between abstraction and view. Constraints embody dependencies between different values that must always be maintained. For instance, an intelligent piggy bank might display the value of its contents; there is the constraint that the value displayed to the outside observer of the piggy bank is the same as the value of money inside it. By using constraints, the link component is described separately from the abstraction and view. Hence, describing the link in terms of constraints is a way of achieving an independent description of the dialog controller.

Graphical specification   These techniques allow the dialog specification to be programmed graphically in terms of the presentation language itself. This technique can be referred to as *programming by demonstration* since the programmer is building up the interaction dialog directly in terms of the actual graphical interaction objects that the user will see, instead of indirectly by means of some textual specification language that must still be linked with the presentation objects. The major advantage of this graphical technique is that it opens up the dialog specification to the non-programmer, which is a very significant contribution.

Ultimately, the programmer would want access to a variety of these techniques in any one UIMS. For example, the Myers Garnet system combines a declarative constraints language with a graphical specification technique. There is an intriguing trend we should note as we proceed away from internal control of dialog in the application itself to external control in an independent dialog component to *presentation control* in the graphical specification languages. When the dialog is specified internal to the application, then it must know about presentation issues, which make the application less generic. External control is about specifying the dialog independent of the application or presentation. One of the problems with such an independent description is that the intended link between application and presentation is impossible to describe without some information about each, so a good deal of information of each must be represented, which may be both inefficient and cumbersome. Presentation control describes the dialog in the language in terms of the objects the user can see at the interface. Whereas this might provide a simple means of producing a dialog specification and be more amenable to non-programmers, it is also restrictive because the graphical language of a modern workstation is nowhere near as expressive as programming languages.

In summary, components of a UIMS which allow the description of the application separate from the presentation are advantageous from a software engineering perspective, but there has not yet been conclusive proof that they are as desirable in designing for usability. There is currently a struggle between difficult-to-use but powerful techniques for describing both the communication and the correspondence between application and presentation and simple-to-use but limited techniques. Programmers will probably always opt for powerful techniques that provide the most flexibility. Non-programmers will opt for simplicity despite the lack of expressiveness.

8.6   SUMMARY

In this chapter, we have concentrated on describing the programming support tools that are available for implementing interactive systems. We began with a description of windowing systems, which are the foundation of modern WIMP interfaces.

Window systems provide only the crudest level of abstraction for the programmer, allowing her to gain device independence and multiple application control. They do not, however, provide a means of separating the control of presentation and application dialog. We described two paradigms for interactive programming, and saw that these relate to two means of controlling that dialog – either internal to the application by means of a read–evaluation loop or external to the application by means of notification-based programming. Toolkits used with particular windowing systems add another level of abstraction by combining input and output behaviors to provide the programmer with access to interaction objects from which to build the components of the interactive system. Toolkits are amenable to external dialog control by means of callback procedures within the application. Other dialog control techniques are provided with yet another level of abstraction in interactive system development: user interface management systems. UIMS provide a conceptual architecture for dividing up the relationship between application and presentation, and various techniques were described to implement the logical components of a UIMS. An interesting additional means of dialog control can be seen to emerge in the use of graphical specification languages which move dialog control all the way across the spectrum to reside entirely within the presentation language. This presentation control opens up interactive programming to the non-expert programmer, but at the cost of a loss of expressiveness.

EXERCISES

8.1 In contrasting the read–evaluation loop and the notification-based paradigm for inter-active programs, construction of a pre-emptive dialog was discussed. How would a programmer describe a pre-emptive dialog by purely graphical means? (**Hint:** Refer to the discussion in Section 8.5 concerning the shift from external and independent dialog management to presentation control of the dialog.)

8.2 Look ahead to the example of the state transition diagram for font characteristics presented in Chapter 16 (Section 16.3.3). Compare different interaction objects that could implement this kind of dialog. Use examples from existing toolkits (pull-down menus or dialog boxes) or create a novel interaction object.

8.3 This exercise is based on the nuclear reactor scenario on the book website at: /e3/scenario/nuclear/

(a) In the Seeheim model: treating the Application Interface model and Application together, there are three main layers:
(i) presentation/lexical
(ii) dialog/syntactic
(iii) application/semantic.
For each of these three layers, list at least two different items of the description of the nuclear reactor control panel that are relevant to the level (that is, at least six items in total, two for each level).

(b) There are no items in the description that relate to the switch (rapid feedback) part of the Seeheim model. Why do you think this is?

8.4   A user has a word processor and a drawing package open. The word processor's window is uppermost. The user then clicks on the drawing window (see figure below). The drawing window pops to the front.

   Describe in detail the things that the window manager and applications perform during the processing of the mouse click in the above scenario. Explain any assumptions you make about the kind of window manager or application toolkits that are being used.

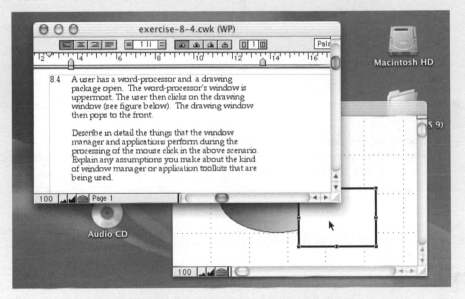

Screen shot reprinted by permission from Apple Computer, Inc.

8.5   A designer described the following interface for a save operation.

   The users initially see a screen with a box where they can type the file name (see Screen 1). The screen also has a 'list' button that they can use to obtain a listing of all the files in the current directory (folder). This list appears in a different window. When the user clicks the save button, the system presents a dialog box to ask the user to confirm the save (see Screen 2).

Screen 1

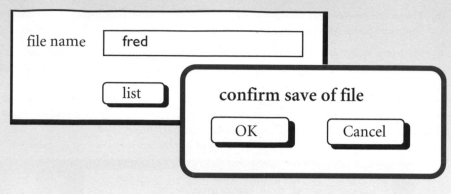

Screen 2

Two programmers independently coded the interface using two different window managers. Programmer A used an event-loop style of program whereas programmer B used a notifier (call-back) style.

(a) Sketch out the general structure of each program.
(b) Highlight any potential interface problems you expect from each programmer and how they could attempt to correct them.

RECOMMENDED READING

L. Bass and J. Coutaz, *Developing Software for the User Interface*, Addison-Wesley, 1991. This is dedicated to the issues we discuss in this chapter, along with general issues about software engineering for interactive systems. Full of programming examples and a detailed discussion of the Serpent UIMS.

B. A. Myers, *Creating User Interfaces by Demonstration*, Academic Press, 1988. Myers' work on the Peridot system is summarized in this book. Peridot was the precursor to the Garnet system. Readers interested in learning more about Garnet should consult the November 1990 issue of the journal *IEEE Computer* for an excellent introductory overview.

D. Olsen, *User Interface Management Systems: Models and Algorithms*, Morgan Kaufmann, 1992. Serious interactive system programmers who want to learn more details about the workings of a wide variety of UIMS should consult this book, written by a very respected member of the UIMS community.

D. Hix, Generations of user-interface management systems, *IEEE Software*, Vol. 7, No. 5, pp. 77–87, September 1990. A good introductory overview of the advances in UIMS technology and the future possibilities.

B. A. Myers, User-interface tools: introduction and survey, *IEEE Software*, Vol. 6, No. 1, pp. 47–61, January 1989.
As well as providing a review of user interface tools, this article provides a good set of references into the relevant literature.

G. F. Coulouris and H. W. Thimbleby, *HyperProgramming*, Addison-Wesley, 1993.
An introduction to programming HyperCard. Use of the programming facilities of HyperTalk allows one to prototype substantial parts of the functionality as well as the surface features of an interface.

P. H. Winston and S. Narasimhan, *On to Java*, 3rd edition, Addison-Wesley, 2001.
Java is another good way to get into user interface programming, as examples can easily be embedded into web pages as applets. This is a good first book on Java using the construction of an applet in AWT as its motivating example. For clear reference books on aspects of the language, look at the O'Reilly series.

C. Gram and G. Cockton, editors, *Design Principles for Interactive Software*, Chapman and Hall, 1996.
Produced by IFIP Working Group 2.7 (User Interface Engineering). This critically discusses several user interface architectures and looks at the way architecture can help or hinder the pursuit of principles similar to those in Chapter 7.

9

EVALUATION TECHNIQUES

OVERVIEW

■ Evaluation tests the usability, functionality and acceptability of an interactive system.

■ Evaluation may take place:
  – in the laboratory
  – in the field.

■ Some approaches are based on expert evaluation:
  – analytic methods
  – review methods
  – model-based methods.

■ Some approaches involve users:
  – experimental methods
  – observational methods
  – query methods.

■ An evaluation method must be chosen carefully and must be suitable for the job.

WHAT IS EVALUATION?

In previous chapters we have discussed a design process to support the design of usable interactive systems. However, even if such a process is used, we still need to assess our designs and test our systems to ensure that they actually behave as we expect and meet user requirements. This is the role of evaluation.

Evaluation should not be thought of as a single phase in the design process (still less as an activity tacked on the end of the process if time permits). Ideally, evaluation should occur throughout the design life cycle, with the results of the evaluation feeding back into modifications to the design. Clearly, it is not usually possible to perform extensive experimental testing continuously throughout the design, but analytic and informal techniques can and should be used. In this respect, there is a close link between evaluation and the principles and prototyping techniques we have already discussed – such techniques help to ensure that the design is assessed continually. This has the advantage that problems can be ironed out before considerable effort and resources have been expended on the implementation itself: it is much easier to change a design in the early stages of development than in the later stages. We can make a broad distinction between evaluation by the designer or a usability expert, without direct involvement by users, and evaluation that studies actual use of the system. The former is particularly useful for assessing early designs and prototypes; the latter normally requires a working prototype or implementation. However, this is a broad distinction and, in practice, the user may be involved in assessing early design ideas (for example, through focus groups), and expert-based analysis can be performed on completed systems, as a cheap and quick usability assessment. We will consider evaluation techniques under two broad headings: expert analysis and user participation.

Before looking at specific techniques, however, we will consider why we do evaluation and what we are trying to achieve.

GOALS OF EVALUATION

Evaluation has three main goals: to assess the extent and accessibility of the system's functionality, to assess users' experience of the interaction, and to identify any specific problems with the system.

The system's functionality is important in that it must accord with the user's requirements. In other words, the design of the system should enable users to perform their intended tasks more easily. This includes not only making the appropriate functionality available within the system, but making it clearly reachable by the user in terms of the actions that the user needs to take to perform the task. It also involves matching the use of the system to the user's expectations of the task. For example, if a filing clerk is used to retrieving a customer's file by the postal address, the same capability (at least) should be provided in the computerized file system. Evaluation at this level may also include measuring the user's performance with the system, to assess the effectiveness of the system in supporting the task.

In addition to evaluating the system design in terms of its functional capabilities, it is important to assess the user's experience of the interaction and its impact upon him. This includes considering aspects such as how easy the system is to learn, its usability and the user's satisfaction with it. It may also include his enjoyment and emotional response, particularly in the case of systems that are aimed at leisure or entertainment. It is important to identify areas of the design that overload the user in some way, perhaps by requiring an excessive amount of information to be remembered, for example. A fuller classification of principles that can be used as evaluation criteria is provided in Chapter 7. Much evaluation is aimed at measuring features such as these.

The final goal of evaluation is to identify specific problems with the design. These may be aspects of the design which, when used in their intended context, cause unexpected results, or confusion amongst users. This is, of course, related to both the functionality and usability of the design (depending on the cause of the problem). However, it is specifically concerned with identifying trouble-spots which can then be rectified.

9.3 EVALUATION THROUGH EXPERT ANALYSIS

As we have noted, evaluation should occur throughout the design process. In particular, the first evaluation of a system should ideally be performed before any implementation work has started. If the design itself can be evaluated, expensive mistakes can be avoided, since the design can be altered prior to any major resource commitments. Typically, the later in the design process that an error is discovered, the more costly it is to put right and, therefore, the less likely it is to be rectified. However, it can be expensive to carry out user testing at regular intervals during the design process, and it can be difficult to get an accurate assessment of the experience of interaction from incomplete designs and prototypes. Consequently, a number of methods have been proposed to evaluate interactive systems through expert analysis. These depend upon the designer, or a human factors expert, taking the design and assessing the impact that it will have upon a typical user. The basic intention is to identify any areas that are likely to cause difficulties because they violate known cognitive principles, or ignore accepted empirical results. These methods can be used at any stage in the development process from a design specification, through storyboards and prototypes, to full implementations, making them flexible evaluation approaches. They are also relatively cheap, since they do not require user involvement. However, they do not assess actual use of the system, only whether or not a system upholds accepted usability principles.

We will consider four approaches to expert analysis: cognitive walkthrough, heuristic evaluation, the use of models and use of previous work.

9.3.1 Cognitive walkthrough

Cognitive walkthrough was originally proposed and later revised by Polson and colleagues [294, 376] as an attempt to introduce psychological theory into the informal and subjective walkthrough technique.

The origin of the cognitive walkthrough approach to evaluation is the code walkthrough familiar in software engineering. Walkthroughs require a detailed review of a sequence of actions. In the code walkthrough, the sequence represents a segment of the program code that is stepped through by the reviewers to check certain characteristics (for example, that coding style is adhered to, conventions for spelling variables versus procedure calls, and to check that system-wide invariants are not violated). In the cognitive walkthrough, the sequence of actions refers to the steps that an interface will require a user to perform in order to accomplish some known task. The evaluators then 'step through' that action sequence to check it for potential usability problems. Usually, the main focus of the cognitive walkthrough is to establish how easy a system is to learn. More specifically, the focus is on learning through exploration. Experience shows that many users prefer to learn how to use a system by exploring its functionality hands on, and not after sufficient training or examination of a user's manual. So the checks that are made during the walkthrough ask questions that address this exploratory learning. To do this, the evaluators go through each step in the task and provide a 'story' about why that step is or is not good for a new user. To do a walkthrough (the term walkthrough from now on refers to the cognitive walkthrough, and not to any other kind of walkthrough), you need four things:

1. A specification or prototype of the system. It doesn't have to be complete, but it should be fairly detailed. Details such as the location and wording for a menu can make a big difference.
2. A description of the task the user is to perform on the system. This should be a representative task that most users will want to do.
3. A complete, written list of the actions needed to complete the task with the proposed system.
4. An indication of who the users are and what kind of experience and knowledge the evaluators can assume about them.

Given this information, the evaluators step through the action sequence (identified in item 3 above) to critique the system and tell a believable story about its usability. To do this, for each action, the evaluators try to answer the following four questions for each step in the action sequence.

1. **Is the effect of the action the same as the user's goal at that point?** Each user action will have a specific effect within the system. Is this effect the same as what the user is trying to achieve at this point? For example, if the effect of the action is to save a document, is 'saving a document' what the user wants to do?
2. **Will users see that the action is available?** Will users see the button or menu item, for example, that is used to produce the action? This is *not* asking whether they will recognize that the button is the one they want. This is merely asking whether

it is visible to them at the time when they will need to use it. Instances where the answer to this question might be 'no' are, for example, where a VCR remote control has a covered panel of buttons or where a menu item is hidden away in a submenu.

3. **Once users have found the correct action, will they know it is the one they need?** This complements the previous question. It is one thing for a button or menu item to be visible, but will the user recognize that it is the one he is looking for to complete his task? Where the previous question was about the visibility of the action, this one is about whether its meaning and effect is clear.

4. **After the action is taken, will users understand the feedback they get?** If you now assume that the user did manage to achieve the correct action, will he know that he has done so? Will the feedback given be sufficient confirmation of what has actually happened? This is the completion of the execution–evaluation interaction cycle (see Chapter 3). In order to determine if they have accomplished their goal, users need appropriate feedback.

It is vital to document the cognitive walkthrough to keep a record of what is good and what needs improvement in the design. It is therefore a good idea to produce some standard evaluation forms for the walkthrough. The cover form would list the information in items 1–4 in our first list above, as well as identifying the date and time of the walkthrough and the names of the evaluators. Then for each action (from item 3 on the cover form), a separate standard form is filled out that answers each of the four questions in our second list above. Any negative answer for any of the questions for any particular action should be documented on a separate usability problem report sheet. This problem report sheet should indicate the system being built (the version, if necessary), the date, the evaluators and a detailed description of the usability problem. It is also useful to indicate the severity of the problem, that is whether the evaluators think this problem will occur often, and how serious it will be for the users. This information will help the designers to decide priorities for correcting the design, since it is not always possible to fix every problem.

Example: programming a video recorder by remote control

We can illustrate how the walkthrough method works using a simple example. Imagine we are designing a remote control for a video recorder (VCR) and are interested in the task of programming the VCR to do timed recordings. Our initial design is shown in Figure 9.1. The picture on the left illustrates the handset in normal use, the picture on the right after the timed record button has been pressed. The VCR allows the user to program up to three timed recordings in different 'streams'. The next available stream number is automatically assigned. We want to know whether our design supports the user's task. We begin by identifying a representative task.

Program the video to time-record a program starting at 18.00 and finishing at 19.15 on channel 4 on 24 February 2005.

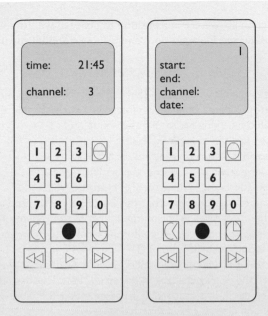

Figure 9.1   An initial remote control design

We will assume that the user is familiar with VCRs but not with this particular design.

The next step in the walkthrough is to identify the action sequence for this task. We specify this in terms of the user's action (UA) and the system's display or response (SD). The initial display is as the left-hand picture in Figure 9.1.

UA 1: Press the 'timed record' button
SD 1: Display moves to timer mode. Flashing cursor appears after 'start:'
UA 2: Press digits 1 8 0 0
SD 2: Each digit is displayed as typed and flashing cursor moves to next position
UA 3: Press the 'timed record' button
SD 3: Flashing cursor moves to 'end:'
UA 4: Press digits 1 9 1 5
SD 4: Each digit is displayed as typed and flashing cursor moves to next position
UA 5: Press the 'timed record' button
SD 5: Flashing cursor moves to 'channel:'
UA 6: Press digit 4
SD 6: Digit is displayed as typed and flashing cursor moves to next position
UA 7: Press the 'timed record' button
SD 7: Flashing cursor moves to 'date:'
UA 8: Press digits 2 4 0 2 0 5
SD 8: Each digit is displayed as typed and flashing cursor moves to next position
UA 9: Press the 'timed record' button
SD 9: Stream number in top right-hand corner of display flashes
UA 10: Press the 'transmit' button
SD 10: Details are transmitted to video player and display returns to normal mode

Having determined our action list we are in a position to proceed with the walkthrough. For each action (1–10) we must answer the four questions and tell a story about the usability of the system. Beginning with UA 1:

UA 1: Press the 'timed record' button

Question 1: Is the effect of the action the same as the user's goal at that point?

The timed record button initiates timer programming. It is reasonable to assume that a user familiar with VCRs would be trying to do this as his first goal.

Question 2: Will users see that the action is available?

The 'timed record' button is visible on the remote control.

Question 3: Once users have found the correct action, will they know it is the one they need?

It is not clear which button is the 'timed record' button. The icon of a clock (fourth button down on the right) is a possible candidate but this could be interpreted as a button to change the time. Other possible candidates might be the fourth button down on the left or the filled circle (associated with record). In fact, the icon of the clock is the correct choice but it is quite possible that the user would fail at this point. This identifies a potential usability problem.

Question 4: After the action is taken, will users understand the feedback they get?

Once the action is taken the display changes to the timed record mode and shows familiar headings (start, end, channel, date). It is reasonable to assume that the user would recognize these as indicating successful completion of the first action.

So we find we have a potential usability problem relating to the icon used on the 'timed record' button. We would now have to establish whether our target user group could correctly distinguish this icon from others on the remote.

The analysis proceeds in this fashion, with a walkthrough form completed for each action. We will leave the rest of the walkthrough for you to complete as an exercise. What other usability problems can you identify with this design?

9.3.2 Heuristic evaluation

A heuristic is a guideline or general principle or rule of thumb that can guide a design decision or be used to critique a decision that has already been made. *Heuristic evaluation*, developed by Jakob Nielsen and Rolf Molich, is a method for structuring the critique of a system using a set of relatively simple and general heuristics. Heuristic evaluation can be performed on a design specification so it is useful for evaluating early design. But it can also be used on prototypes, storyboards and fully functioning systems. It is therefore a flexible, relatively cheap approach. Hence it is often considered a *discount usability* technique.

The general idea behind heuristic evaluation is that several evaluators independently critique a system to come up with potential usability problems. It is important that there be several of these evaluators and that the evaluations be done independently. Nielsen's experience indicates that between three and five evaluators is sufficient, with five usually resulting in about 75% of the overall usability problems being discovered.

To aid the evaluators in discovering usability problems, a set of 10 heuristics are provided. The heuristics are related to *principles* and *guidelines* (see Chapter 7). These can be supplemented where required by heuristics that are specific to the particular domain. So, for example, if the system is for synchronous group communication, one might add 'awareness of other users' as a heuristic. Although Nielsen recommends the use of these 10 as providing the most effective coverage of the most common usability problems, other rules, such as those discussed in Chapter 7, could also be used.

Each evaluator assesses the system and notes violations of any of these heuristics that would indicate a potential usability problem. The evaluator also assesses the severity of each usability problem, based on four factors: how common is the problem, how easy is it for the user to overcome, will it be a one-off problem or a persistent one, and how seriously will the problem be perceived? These can be combined into an overall severity rating on a scale of 0–4:

0 = I don't agree that this is a usability problem at all
1 = Cosmetic problem only: need not be fixed unless extra time is available on project
2 = Minor usability problem: fixing this should be given low priority
3 = Major usability problem: important to fix, so should be given high priority
4 = Usability catastrophe: imperative to fix this before product can be released (Nielsen)

Nielsen's ten heuristics are:

1. **Visibility of system status** Always keep users informed about what is going on, through appropriate feedback within reasonable time. For example, if a system operation will take some time, give an indication of how long and how much is complete.
2. **Match between system and the real world** The system should speak the user's language, with words, phrases and concepts familiar to the user, rather than system-oriented terms. Follow real-world conventions, making information appear in natural and logical order.
3. **User control and freedom** Users often choose system functions by mistake and need a clearly marked 'emergency exit' to leave the unwanted state without having to go through an extended dialog. Support undo and redo.
4. **Consistency and standards** Users should not have to wonder whether words, situations or actions mean the same thing in different contexts. Follow platform conventions and accepted standards.
5. **Error prevention** Make it difficult to make errors. Even better than good error messages is a careful design that prevents a problem from occurring in the first place.
6. **Recognition rather than recall** Make objects, actions and options visible. The user should not have to remember information from one part of the dialog to another. Instructions for use of the system should be visible or easily retrievable whenever appropriate.
7. **Flexibility and efficiency of use** Allow users to tailor frequent actions. Accelerators – unseen by the novice user – may often speed up the interaction for the expert user to such an extent that the system can cater to both inexperienced and experienced users.

8. **Aesthetic and minimalist design** Dialogs should not contain information that is irrelevant or rarely needed. Every extra unit of information in a dialog competes with the relevant units of information and diminishes their relative visibility.

9. **Help users recognize, diagnose and recover from errors** Error messages should be expressed in plain language (no codes), precisely indicate the problem, and constructively suggest a solution.

10. **Help and documentation** Few systems can be used with no instructions so it may be necessary to provide help and documentation. Any such information should be easy to search, focussed on the user's task, list concrete steps to be carried out, and not be too large.

Once each evaluator has completed their separate assessment, all of the problems are collected and the mean severity ratings calculated. The design team will then determine the ones that are the most important and will receive attention first.

9.3.3 Model-based evaluation

A third expert-based approach is the use of models. Certain cognitive and design models provide a means of combining design specification and evaluation into the same framework. These are discussed in detail in Chapter 12. For example, the GOMS (goals, operators, methods and selection) model predicts user performance with a particular interface and can be used to filter particular design options. Similarly, lower-level modeling techniques such as the keystroke-level model provide predictions of the time users will take to perform low-level physical tasks.

Design methodologies, such as design rationale (see Chapter 6), also have a role to play in evaluation at the design stage. Design rationale provides a framework in which design options can be evaluated. By examining the criteria that are associated with each option in the design, and the evidence that is provided to support these criteria, informed judgments can be made in the design.

Dialog models can also be used to evaluate dialog sequences for problems, such as unreachable states, circular dialogs and complexity. Models such as state transition networks are useful for evaluating dialog designs prior to implementation. These are discussed in detail in Chapter 16.

9.3.4 Using previous studies in evaluation

Experimental psychology and human–computer interaction between them possess a wealth of experimental results and empirical evidence. Some of this is specific to a particular domain, but much deals with more generic issues and applies in a variety of situations. Examples of such issues are the usability of different menu types, the recall of command names, and the choice of icons.

A final approach to expert evaluation exploits this inheritance, using previous results as evidence to support (or refute) aspects of the design. It is expensive to repeat experiments continually and an expert review of relevant literature can avoid the need to do so. It should be noted that experimental results cannot be expected to hold arbitrarily across contexts. The reviewer must therefore select evidence carefully, noting the experimental design chosen, the population of participants used, the analyses performed and the assumptions made. For example, an experiment testing the usability of a particular style of help system using novice participants may not provide accurate evaluation of a help system designed for expert users. The review should therefore take account of both the similarities and the differences between the experimental context and the design under consideration. This is why this is an *expert* review: expertise in the area is required to ensure that correct assumptions are made.

9.4 EVALUATION THROUGH USER PARTICIPATION

The techniques we have considered so far concentrate on evaluating a design or system through analysis by the designer, or an expert evaluator, rather than testing with actual users. However, useful as these techniques are for filtering and refining the design, they are not a replacement for actual usability testing with the people for whom the system is intended: the users. In this section we will look at a number of different approaches to evaluation through user participation. These include empirical or experimental methods, observational methods, query techniques, and methods that use physiological monitoring, such as eye tracking and measures of heart rate and skin conductance.

User participation in evaluation tends to occur in the later stages of development when there is at least a working prototype of the system in place. This may range from a simulation of the system's interactive capabilities, without its underlying functionality (for example, the *Wizard of Oz* technique, which is discussed in Chapter 6, through a basic functional prototype to a fully implemented system. However, some of the methods discussed can also contribute to the earlier design stages, such as requirements capture, where observation and surveying users are important (see Chapter 13).

9.4.1 Styles of evaluation

Before we consider some of the techniques that are available for evaluation with users, we will distinguish between two distinct evaluation styles: those performed under laboratory conditions and those conducted in the work environment or 'in the field'.

Laboratory studies

In the first type of evaluation studies, users are taken out of their normal work environment to take part in controlled tests, often in a specialist usability laboratory (although the 'lab' may simply be a quiet room). This approach has a number of benefits and disadvantages.

A well-equipped usability laboratory may contain sophisticated audio/visual recording and analysis facilities, two-way mirrors, instrumented computers and the like, which cannot be replicated in the work environment. In addition, the participant operates in an interruption-free environment. However, the lack of context – for example, filing cabinets, wall calendars, books or interruptions – and the unnatural situation may mean that one accurately records a situation that never arises in the real world. It is especially difficult to observe several people cooperating on a task in a laboratory situation, as interpersonal communication is so heavily dependent on context (see Section 9.4.2).

There are, however, some situations where laboratory observation is the only option, for example, if the system is to be located in a dangerous or remote location, such as a space station. Also some very constrained single-user tasks may be adequately performed in a laboratory. Finally, and perhaps most commonly, we may deliberately want to manipulate the context in order to uncover problems or observe less used procedures, or we may want to compare alternative designs within a controlled context. For these types of evaluation, laboratory studies are appropriate.

Field studies

The second type of evaluation takes the designer or evaluator out into the user's work environment in order to observe the system in action. Again this approach has its pros and cons.

High levels of ambient noise, greater levels of movement and constant interruptions, such as phone calls, all make field observation difficult. However, the very 'open' nature of the situation means that you will observe interactions between systems and between individuals that would have been missed in a laboratory study. The context is retained and you are seeing the user in his 'natural environment'. In addition, some activities, such as those taking days or months, are impossible to study in the laboratory (though difficult even in the field).

On balance, field observation is to be preferred to laboratory studies as it allows us to study the interaction as it occurs in actual use. Even interruptions are important as these will expose behaviors such as saving and restoring state during a task. However, we should remember that even in field observations the participants are likely to be influenced by the presence of the analyst and/or recording equipment, so we always operate at a slight remove from the natural situation, a sort of Heisenberg uncertainty principle.

This is, of course, a generalization: there are circumstances, as we have noted, in which laboratory testing is necessary and desirable. In particular, controlled experiments can be useful for evaluation of specific interface features, and must normally be conducted under laboratory conditions. From an economic angle, we need to weigh the costs of establishing recording equipment in the field, and possibly disrupting the actual work situation, with the costs of taking one or more participants away from their jobs into the laboratory. This balance is not at all obvious and any study must weigh the loss of contextual information against the increased costs and difficulty of field studies.

9.4.2 Empirical methods: experimental evaluation

One of the most powerful methods of evaluating a design or an aspect of a design is to use a controlled experiment. This provides empirical evidence to support a particular claim or hypothesis. It can be used to study a wide range of different issues at different levels of detail.

Any experiment has the same basic form. The evaluator chooses a hypothesis to test, which can be determined by measuring some attribute of participant behavior. A number of experimental conditions are considered which differ only in the values of certain controlled variables. Any changes in the behavioral measures are attributed to the different conditions. Within this basic form there are a number of factors that are important to the overall reliability of the experiment, which must be considered carefully in experimental design. These include the participants chosen, the variables tested and manipulated, and the hypothesis tested.

Participants

The choice of participants is vital to the success of any experiment. In evaluation experiments, participants should be chosen to match the expected user population as closely as possible. Ideally, this will involve experimental testing with the actual users but this is not always possible. If participants are not actual users, they should be chosen to be of a similar age and level of education as the intended user group. Their experience with computers in general, and with systems related to that being tested, should be similar, as should their experience or knowledge of the task domain. It is no good testing an interface designed to be used by the general public on a participant set made up of computer science undergraduates: they are simply not representative of the intended user population.

A second issue relating to the participant set is the sample size chosen. Often this is something that is determined by pragmatic considerations: the availability of participants is limited or resources are scarce. However, the sample size must be large enough to be considered to be representative of the population, taking into account the design of the experiment and the statistical methods chosen.

Nielsen and Landauer [264] suggest that usability testing with a single participant will find about a third of the usability problems, and that there is little to be gained from testing with more than five. While this may be true of observational studies where the aim is simply to uncover usability issues, it is not possible to discover much about the extent of usability problems from such small numbers. Certainly, if the intention is to run a controlled experiment and perform statistical analysis on the results, at least twice this number is recommended.

Variables

Experiments manipulate and measure variables under controlled conditions, in order to test the hypothesis. There are two main types of variable: those that are 'manipulated' or changed (known as the independent variables) and those that are measured (the dependent variables).

Independent variables are those elements of the experiment that are manipulated to produce different conditions for comparison. Examples of independent variables in evaluation experiments are interface style, level of help, number of menu items and icon design. Each of these variables can be given a number of different values; each value that is used in an experiment is known as a *level* of the variable. So, for example, an experiment that wants to test whether search speed improves as the number of menu items decreases may consider menus with five, seven, and ten items. Here the independent variable, number of menu items, has three levels.

More complex experiments may have more than one independent variable. For example, in the above experiment, we may suspect that the speed of the user's response depends not only on the number of menu items but also on the choice of commands used on the menu. In this case there are two independent variables. If there were two sets of command names (that is, two levels), we would require six experimental conditions to investigate all the possibilities (three levels of menu size × two levels of command names).

Dependent variables, on the other hand, are the variables that can be measured in the experiment, their value is 'dependent' on the changes made to the independent variable. In the example given above, this would be the speed of menu selection. The dependent variable must be measurable in some way, it must be affected by the independent variable, and, as far as possible, unaffected by other factors. Common choices of dependent variable in evaluation experiments are the time taken to complete a task, the number of errors made, user preference and the quality of the user's performance. Obviously, some of these are easier to measure objectively than others. However, the more subjective measures can be applied against predetermined scales, and can be very important factors to consider.

Hypotheses

A hypothesis is a prediction of the outcome of an experiment. It is framed in terms of the independent and dependent variables, stating that a variation in the independent variable will cause a difference in the dependent variable. The aim of the experiment is to show that this prediction is correct. This is done by disproving the null hypothesis, which states that there is no difference in the dependent variable between the levels of the independent variable. The statistical measures described below produce values that can be compared with various levels of significance. If a result is significant it shows, at the given level of certainty, that the differences measured would not have occurred by chance (that is, that the null hypothesis is incorrect).

Experimental design

In order to produce reliable and generalizable results, an experiment must be carefully designed. We have already looked at a number of the factors that the experimenter must consider in the design, namely the participants, the independent and dependent variables, and the hypothesis. The first phase in experimental design then is to choose the hypothesis: to decide exactly what it is you are trying to demonstrate. In doing this you are likely to clarify the independent and dependent variables, in that you will have identified what you are going to manipulate and what change you expect. If your hypothesis does not clearly identify these variables then you need to rethink it. At this stage you should also consider your participants: how many are available and are they representative of the user group?

The next step is to decide on the *experimental method* that you will use. There are two main methods: *between-subjects* and *within-subjects*. In a between-subjects (or *randomized*) design, each participant is assigned to a different condition. There are at least two conditions: the experimental condition (in which the variable has been manipulated) and the control, which is identical to the experimental condition except for this manipulation. This control serves to ensure that it is the manipulation that is responsible for any differences that are measured. There may, of course, be more than two groups, depending on the number of independent variables and the number of levels that each variable can take.

The advantage of a between-subjects design is that any learning effect resulting from the user performing in one condition and then the other is controlled: each user performs under only one condition. The disadvantages are that a greater number of participants are required, and that significant variation between the groups can negate any results. Also, individual differences between users can bias the results. These problems can be handled by a careful selection of participants, ensuring that all are representative of the population and by matching participants between groups.

The second experimental design is within-subjects (or *repeated measures*). Here each user performs under each different condition. This design can suffer from transfer of learning effects, but this can be lessened if the order in which the conditions are tackled is varied between users, for example, group A do first condition followed by second and group B do second condition followed by first. Within-subjects is less costly than between-subjects, since fewer users are required, and it can be particularly effective where learning is involved. There is also less chance of effects from variation between participants.

The choice of experimental method will depend on the resources available, how far learning transfer is likely or can be controlled, and how representative the participant group is considered to be. A popular compromise, in cases where there is more than one independent variable, is to devise a mixed design where one variable is placed between-groups and one within-groups. So, returning to our example of the menu design, the participants would be split into two groups, one for each command set, but each group would perform in three conditions, corresponding to the three possible levels of the number of menu items.

Once we have determined the hypothesis we are trying to test, the variables we are studying, the participants at our disposal, and the design that is most appropriate, we have to decide how we are going to analyze the results we record. There are a number of statistical tests available, and the choice of test is vital to the success of the experiment. Different tests make different assumptions about the data and if an inappropriate test is chosen, the results can be invalid. The next subsection discusses the factors to consider in choosing a statistical test and surveys the most common statistical measures available.

Statistical measures

The first two rules of statistical analysis are to *look* at the data and to *save* the data. It is easy to carry out statistical tests blindly when a glance at a graph, histogram or table of results would be more instructive. In particular, looking at the data can expose *outliers*, single data items that are very different from the rest. Outliers are often the result of a transcription error or a freak event not connected to the experiment. For example, we notice that one participant took three times as long as everyone else to do a task. We investigate and discover that the participant had been suffering from flu on the day of the experiment. Clearly, if the participant's data were included it would bias the results.

Saving the data is important, as we may later want to try a different analysis method. It is all too common for an experimenter to take some averages or otherwise tabulate results, and then throw away the original data. At worst, the remaining statistics can be useless for statistical purposes, and, at best, we have lost the ability to trace back odd results to the original data, as, for example, we want to do for outliers.

Our choice of statistical analysis depends on the type of data and the questions we want to answer. It is worth having important results checked by an experienced statistician, but in many situations standard tests can be used.

Variables can be classified as either *discrete variables* or *continuous variables*. A discrete variable can only take a finite number of values or *levels*, for example, a screen color that can be red, green or blue. A continuous variable can take any value (although it may have an upper or lower limit), for example a person's height or the time taken to complete a task. A special case of continuous data is when they are *positive*, for example a response time cannot be negative. A continuous variable can be rendered discrete by clumping it into classes, for example we could divide heights into short (<5 ft (1.5 m)), medium (5–6 ft (1.5–1.8 m)) and tall (>6 ft (1.8 m)). In many interface experiments we will be testing one design against another. In these cases the independent variable is usually discrete.

The dependent variable is the measured one and subject to random experimental variation. In the case when this variable is continuous, the random variation may take a special form. If the form of the data follows a known *distribution* then special and more powerful statistical tests can be used. Such tests are called *parametric tests* and the most common of these are used when the variation follows the *normal distribution*. This means that if we plot a histogram of the random errors, they will

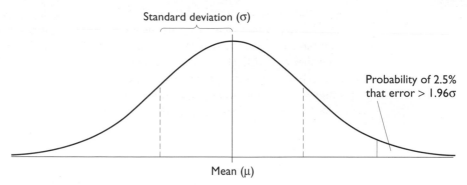

Figure 9.2 Histogram of normally distributed errors

form the well-known bell-shaped graph (Figure 9.2). Happily, many of these tests are fairly *robust*, that is they give reasonable results even when the data are not precisely normal. This means that you need not worry too much about checking normality during early analysis.

There are ways of checking whether data are really normal, but for these the reader should consult a statistics book, or a professional statistician. However, as a general rule, if data can be seen as the sum or average of many small *independent* effects they are likely to be normal. For example, the time taken to complete a *complex* task is the sum of the times of all the minor tasks of which it is composed. On the other hand, a subjective rating of the usability of an interface will not be normal. Occasionally data can be *transformed* to become approximately normal. The most common is the log-transformation, which is used for positive data with near-zero values. As a log-transformation has little effect when the data are clustered well away from zero, many experimenters habitually log-transform. However, this practice makes the results more difficult to interpret and is not recommended.

When we cannot assume that data are normally distributed, we must often resort to *non-parametric* tests. These are statistical tests that make no assumptions about the particular distribution and are usually based purely on the ranking of the data. That is, each item of a data set (for example, 57, 32, 61, 49) is reduced to its rank (3, 1, 4, 2), before analysis begins. Because non-parametric tests make fewer assumptions about the data than parametric tests, and are more resistant to outliers, there is less danger of getting spurious results. However, they are less *powerful* than the corresponding parametric tests. This means that, given the same set of data, a parametric test might detect a difference that the non-parametric test would miss.

A third sort of test is the contingency table, where we classify data by several discrete attributes and then count the number of data items with each attribute combination.

Table 9.1 lists some of the standard tests categorized by the form of independent and dependent variables (discrete/continuous/normal). Normality is not an issue

Table 9.1 Choosing a statistical technique

Independent variable	Dependent variable	
Parametric		
Two valued	Normal	Student's *t* test on difference of means
Discrete	Normal	ANOVA (ANalysis Of VAriance)
Continuous	Normal	Linear (or non-linear) regression factor analysis
Non-parametric		
Two valued	Continuous	Wilcoxon (or Mann–Whitney) rank-sum test
Discrete	Continuous	Rank-sum versions of ANOVA
Continuous	Continuous	Spearman's rank correlation
Contingency tests		
Two valued	Discrete	No special test, see next entry
Discrete	Discrete	Contingency table and chi-squared test
Continuous	Discrete	(Rare) Group independent variable and then as above

for the independent variable, but a special case is when it is discrete with only two values, for example comparing two systems. We cannot describe all the techniques here; for this you should use a standard statistics text, such as one of those recommended in the reading list. The table is only intended to guide you in your choice of test.

An extensive and accurate analysis is no use if it answers the wrong question. Examples of questions one might ask about the data are as follows:

Is there a difference? For example, is one system better than another? Techniques that address this are called *hypothesis testing*. The answers to this question are not simply yes/no, but of the form: 'we are 99% certain that selection from menus of five items is faster than that from menus of seven items'.

How big is the difference? For example, 'selection from five items is 260 ms faster than from seven items'. This is called *point estimation*, often obtained by averages.

How accurate is the estimate? For example, 'selection is faster by 260 ± 30 ms'. Statistical answers to this are in the form of either measures of variation such as the *standard deviation* of the estimate, or *confidence intervals*. Again, the answers one obtains are probabilistic: 'we are 95% certain that the difference in response time is between 230 and 290 ms'.

The experimental design issues we have discussed have been principally addressed at the first question. However, most of the statistical techniques listed above, both parametric and non-parametric, give some answer to one or both of the other questions.

Example of non-parametric statistics

We will not see an example of the use of non-parametric statistics later, so we will go through a small example here. Imagine we had the following data for response times under two conditions:

condition A: 33, 42, 25, 79, 52
condition B: 87, 65, 92, 93, 91, 55

We gather the data together and sort them into order: 25, 33, 42, . . . , 92, 93. We then substitute for each value its rank in the list: 25 becomes 1, 33 becomes 2, etc. The transformed data are then

condition A: 2, 3, 1, 7, 4
condition B: 8, 6, 10, 11, 9, 5

Tests are then carried out on the data. For example, to test whether there is any difference between the two conditions we can use the *Wilcoxon test*. To do this, we take each condition and calculate the sum of ranks, and subtract the least value it could have (that is, $1 + 2 + 3 + 4 + 5 = 15$ for condition A, $1 + 2 + 3 + 4 + 5 + 6 = 21$ for condition B), giving the statistic U:

	rank sum	least	U
condition A:	$(2 + 3 + 1 + 7 + 4)$	$- \quad 15 \quad =$	2
condition B:	$(8 + 6 + 10 + 11 + 9 + 5)$	$- \quad 21 \quad =$	28

In fact, the sum of these two U statistics, $2 + 28 = 30$, is the product of the number of data values in each condition 5×6. This will always happen and so one can always get away with calculating only one of the U. Finally, we then take the smaller of two U values and compare it with a set of *critical values* in a book of statistical tables, to see if it is unusually small. The table is laid out dependent on the number of data values in each condition (five and six). The critical value at the 5% level turns out to be 3. As the smallest statistic is smaller than this, we can *reject the null hypothesis* and conclude that there is likely to be a difference between the conditions. To be precise, it says that there is only a 1 in 20 (5%) chance that the data happened by chance. In fact the test is right – the authors constructed random data in the range 1–100 and then subtracted 10 from each of the values in condition A.

An example: evaluating icon designs

Imagine you are designing a new interface to a document-processing package, which is to use icons for presentation. You are considering two styles of icon design and you wish to know which design will be easier for users to remember. One set of icons uses naturalistic images (based on a paper document metaphor), the other uses abstract images (see Figure 9.3). How might you design an experiment to help you decide which style to use?

The first thing you need to do is form a hypothesis: what do you consider to be the likely outcome? In this case, you might expect the natural icons to be easier to recall since they are more familiar to users. We can therefore form the following hypothesis:

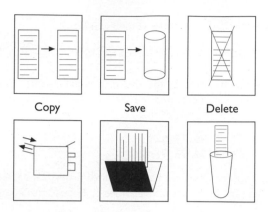

Copy   Save   Delete

Figure 9.3 Abstract and concrete icons for file operations

> Users will remember the natural icons more easily than the abstract ones.

The null hypothesis in this case is that there will be no difference between recall of the icon types.

This hypothesis clearly identifies the independent variable for our experiment: we are varying the style of icon. The independent variable has two levels: natural and abstract. However, when we come to consider the dependent variable, things are not so obvious. We have expressed our hypothesis in terms of users being able to remember *more easily*. How can we measure this? First we need to clarify exactly what we mean by the phrase *more easily*: are we concerned with the user's performance in terms of accurate recall or in terms of speed, for example, or are we looking at more subjective measures like user preference? In this example, we will assume that the speed at which a user can accurately select an icon is an indication of how easily it is remembered. Our dependent variables are therefore the number of mistakes in selection and the time taken to select an icon.

Of course, we need to control the experiment so that any differences we observe are clearly attributable to the independent variable, and so that our measurements of the dependent variables are comparable. To do this, we provide an interface that is identical in every way except for the icon design, and a selection task that can be repeated for each condition. The latter could be either a naturalistic task (such as producing a document) or a more artificial task in which the user has to select the appropriate icon to a given prompt. The second task has the advantage that it is more controlled (there is little variation between users as to how they will perform the task) and it can be varied to avoid transfer of learning. Before performing the selection task, the users will be allowed to learn the icons in controlled conditions: for example, they may be given a fixed amount of time to learn the icon meanings.

The next stage is to decide upon an experimental method. This may depend on the participants that are available, but in this case we will assume that we have sufficient participants from the intended user group. A between-subjects experiment would remove any learning effect for individual participants, but it would be more difficult

Table 9.2 Example experimental results – completion times

Participant number	Presentation order	(1) Natural (s)	(2) Abstract (s)	(3) Participant mean	(4) Natural (1)–(3)	(5) Abstract (2)–(3)
1	AN	656	702	679	−23	23
2	AN	259	339	299	−40	40
3	AN	612	658	635	−23	23
4	AN	609	645	627	−18	18
5	AN	1049	1129	1089	−40	40
6	NA	1135	1179	1157	−22	22
7	NA	542	604	573	−31	31
8	NA	495	551	523	−28	28
9	NA	905	893	899	6	−6
10	NA	715	803	759	−44	44
mean (μ)		698	750	724	−26	26
s.d. (σ)		265	259	262	14	14
			s.e.d. 117		s.e. 4.55	
Student's t			0.32 (n.s.)		5.78 ($p<1\%$, two tailed)	

to control for variation in learning style between participants. On balance, therefore, a within-subjects design is preferred, with order of presentation controlled.

So all that remains is to finalize the details of our experiment, given the constraints imposed by these choices. We devise two interfaces composed of blocks of icons, one for each condition. The user is presented with a task (say 'delete a document') and is required to select the appropriate icon. The selection task comprises a set of such presentations. In order to avoid learning effects from icon position, the placing of icons in the block can be randomly varied on each presentation. Each user performs the selection task under each condition. In order to avoid transfer of learning, the users are divided into two groups with each group taking a different starting condition. For each user, we measure the time taken to complete the task and the number of errors made.

Finally, we must analyze our results. Table 9.2 shows a possible set of results for ten participants.[1] The first five had the abstract icons presented first (order AN), and the last five had the natural icons presented first (order NA). Columns (1) and (2) in the table show the completion times for the task using natural and abstract icons respectively. As the times are the result of lots of presentations, we will assume that they are normally distributed. The main independent variable, the icon type, is two valued, suggesting we can use a simple difference of means with Student's t test (Table 9.1). In fact, because we have used a *within-subjects* design, there is another independent variable we have to take into account – the participant. This means we

---

1 Note that these are fabricated results for the purposes of exposition and this is a rather small sample set for real purposes.

have more than one discrete independent variable, and referring again to Table 9.1, we see that this implies we should use *analysis of variance (ANOVA)*. A full analysis of variance is quite complex, and is ideally done with the aid of a statistics package. However, this experiment is particularly simple, so we can use a simplified analysis.

Look at columns (2) and (3) of Table 9.2. The completion times range from less than 5 minutes (participant 2) to nearly 20 minutes (participant 6), showing a wide variation between individuals. This wide variation emphasizes the importance of the *within*-subjects design. To see how this affects the results, we will first try to analyze them ignoring the fact that each participant performed under each condition. At the end of the table, the mean and standard deviation have been calculated for each condition. These means can then be compared using Student's *t* test. The difference between the means is 52 seconds, but the *standard error of the difference* (s.e.d.) is 117. This is calculated as follows:

$$\text{s.e.d.} = \sqrt{\frac{\sigma_N^2}{n_N} + \frac{\sigma_A^2}{n_A}} = \sqrt{\frac{265^2}{10} + \frac{259^2}{10}} = 117.2$$

where σ_N and σ_A are the standard deviations (s.d.) of the two conditions, and n_N and n_A are the number of data items in each condition (10 in each). The s.e.d. is a measure of the expected variability of the difference between the means, and as we see the actual difference is well within this random variation. Testing the ratio 52/117 against tables of Student's *t* distribution indeed shows that this is not significant.

However, if we glance down the table, we see that in almost every case the time taken with the abstract icons is greater than the time taken for the natural icons. That is, the data seem to support our claim that natural icons are better than abstract ones, but the wide variation between individuals has hidden the effect.

A more sophisticated analysis, a special case of ANOVA, can expose the difference. Looking back at the table, column (3) shows, for each participant, the average of the time they took under the two conditions. This participant mean is then subtracted from the data for each condition, yielding columns (4) and (5). These columns show the effect of the icon design *once the differences between participants have been removed*. The two columns are redundant as they always add up to zero. They show that in all but one case (participant 9) the natural icons are faster than the abstract ones.

Even a non-parametric test would show this as a significant difference at the 5% level, but the use of a *t* test is more precise. We can take either column and see that the column average 26 is much greater than the standard error ($14.4/\sqrt{10}$). The ratio (mean/s.e.) is compared with the Student's *t* table (in statistical tables) using nine degrees of freedom (10 values minus 1 for the mean), and is indeed far greater than the 1% level (3.250); that is, the likelihood of getting our results by chance is less than 1 in 100. So, we reject the null hypothesis that there is no difference and conclude that natural icons are more easily remembered than abstract ones.

In fact, the last statement is not quite correct. What we have shown is that in this experiment natural icons are more *rapidly* remembered. Possibly, if we go on to analyze the errors, these may present a different story. If these error figures were quite large (say 15 errors or more per condition), then we may be able to assume these are normal and use ANOVA. If not, we can either use non-parametric tests, or make use of special tests based on the *binomial distribution*. We will not perform these analyses here. Possibly, looking at the errors we may find that the natural icons have *more* errors – it could well be that they are more rapidly, but less accurately, remembered. It is always worth keeping in mind the difference between the intended purpose of the experiment (to see which is better remembered) and the actual measurements (speed and accuracy).

Finally, one ought to look carefully at the experimental results to see whether there is any other effect that might confuse the results. The graphical presentation of results will help with this, possibly highlighting odd clumps in the data or other irregularities. In this experiment we may want to check to see if there has been any significant *transfer effect* between the first and second condition for each participant. The second set may be faster as the participants are more practiced, or possibly the second set may be slower as learning a second set of icons may be confusing. This will not matter if the effect is uniform – say they always are 15 seconds slower on the second test. But there may be systematic effects. For example, seeing the natural icons first might make it more difficult to learn the abstract ones, but not vice versa. If this were the case, our observed effect may be about the interference between the icon sets, rather than that one is better than the other.

Worked exercise   *Design an experiment to test whether adding color coding to an interface will improve accuracy. Identify your hypothesis, participant group, dependent and independent variables, experimental design, task and analysis approach.*

Answer   The following is only an example of the type of experiment that might be devised.

Participants   Taken from user population.

Hypothesis   Color coding will make selection more accurate.

IV   (Independent Variable) Color coding.

DV   (Dependent Variable) Accuracy measured as number of errors.

Design   Between-groups to ensure no transfer of learning (or within-groups with appropriate safeguards if participants are scarce).

Task   The interfaces are identical in each of the conditions, except that, in the second, color is added to indicate related menu items. Participants are presented with a screen of menu choices (ordered randomly) and verbally told what they have to select. Selection must be done within a strict time limit when the screen clears. Failure to select the correct item is deemed an error. Each presentation places items in new positions. Participants perform in one of the two conditions.

Analysis   *t* test.

Studies of groups of users

So far we have considered the experimental evaluation of single-user systems. Experiments to evaluate elements of group systems bring additional problems. Given the complexities of human–human communication and group working, it is hardly surprising that experimental studies of groups and of groupware are more difficult than the corresponding single-user experiments already considered. For the purpose of discussion, let us assume that we are evaluating a shared application with video connections between the participants and consider some of the problems we will encounter.

The participant groups   To organize, say, 10 experiments of a single-user system requires 10 participants. For an experiment involving groups of three, we will, of course, need 30 participants for the same number of experiments. In addition, experiments in group working are often longer than the single-user equivalents as we must allow time for the group to 'settle down' and some rapport to develop. This all means more disruption for participants and possibly more expense payments.

Arranging a mutually convenient slot when both participants and the equipment are available is no mean feat. Often the workstations being used in the experiment will be colleagues' personal systems, so we are trying to accommodate at least six people, not to mention the experimenters themselves.

Not surprisingly, many reports of group working involve only three or four groups. This is obviously a problem for statistical purposes, but not the primary obstacle.

The experimental task   Choosing a suitable task is also difficult. We may want to test a variety of different task types: creative, structured, information passing, and so on. Also, the tasks must encourage active cooperation, either because the task requires consensus, or because information and control is distributed among the participants. Obviously, the task also depends on the nature of the groupware system: if it has several available channels, we want to encourage broad use. For example, in the case of shared application with video, it should not be possible (or at least not easy) to perform the task without using the application, otherwise we are simply investigating video conferencing.

Creative tasks such as 'write a short report on . . .' or 'write a research proposal' are often effective, in that the participants must reach agreement, and can be asked to produce their final report using the shared application. Design tasks are also used. For instance, in one experiment, users of the York Conferencer system (see Figure 14.2 in Section 14.4) were asked to redesign a bank layout. A picture of the current layout was used as a background for the spatially arranged electronic pinboard, and the participants made use of this to arrange comments and suggestions close to the features they referred to.

Decision games, as used in management courses, are designed to test and train cooperative activity. They often rely for their success on group coordination, not individual ability. An example of this is the desert survival task, where the participants are told that they have crashed in the desert. They are given a list of items to rank in order of importance for their survival: knife, plastic sheet, etc. The participants must produce *one* list between them, a single knowledgeable participant cannot 'go it alone'. A computerized version of the game of Diplomacy has also been used (see Figure 14.5 in Section 14.4) as it includes aspects of conflict as well as cooperation.

Finally, time-critical simulated process control tasks force a higher pace of interaction as the participants control different parts of the model. An example of this is ARKola [147], a simulated bottling plant, which was used at Xerox PARC to investigate the importance of background noise in complex cooperative control tasks.

Often the chosen task will require extra implementation effort, and in the case of games this may be extensive. This is obviously a strong factor in the choice of a suitable task.

Data gathering Even in a single-user experiment we may well use several video cameras as well as direct logging of the application. In a group setting this is replicated for each participant. So for a three-person group, we are trying to synchronize the recording of six or more video sources and three keystroke logs. To compound matters, these may be spread over different offices, or even different sites. The technical problems are clearly enormous. Four-into-one video recording is possible, storing a different image in each quadrant of the screen, but even this is insufficient for the number of channels we would like.

One way round this is to focus on the participants individually, recording, for each one, the video images that are being relayed as part of the system (assuming there is a video connection) and the sounds that the participant hears. These can then be synchronized with the particular participant's keystrokes and additional video observations. Thus, we can recreate the situation as it appeared *to the participant*. From this recording, we may not be able to interpret the other participants' actions, but at least we have a complete record for one.

Given sufficient recording equipment, this can be repeated for each participant. Happily, the level of synchronization required between participants is not as great as that required for each one individually. One can simply start the recorders' clocks at the same time, but not worry about sub-second accuracy between participants. The important thing is that we can, as it were, relive the experience for each individual.

Analysis In true experimental tradition, we would like to see statistical differences between experimental conditions. We saw earlier that individual differences made this difficult in single-user experiments. If anything, group variation is more extreme. Given randomly mixed groups, one group will act in a democratic fashion; in another, a particular pair will dominate discussion; in a third, one of the participants will act as coordinator, filtering the others' contributions. The level of variation is such that even catastrophic failures under one condition and fabulous successes in another may not always lead to statistically significant results.

As an example of this, imagine we have some quantitative measure of quality of output. We will almost certainly have to use non-parametric tests, so imagine we have found that all the groups under one condition obtained higher scores than any group under the other condition. We would need at least four in each condition to obtain even 5% significance (one tailed). If our results were only slightly less good, say one of the generally better groups performed poorly, we would then require at least five in each condition.

Now this example only considered one condition, and assumed the best possible results. In general, we would expect that the spread between groups within conditions would be greater, and we may want to test more conditions at once. Our 10 groups will have to increase rapidly to stand any chance of statistically significant results. However, we saw above that even gathering 10 experimental groups is a significant problem.

There are three possible solutions to this problem. First, one can use within-group experiments, having each group work under several conditions. We have, of course, the normal problems of such analysis, transfer effects and the like, but we also have more chance of cancelling out the group effect. Secondly, we can look to a micro-analysis of features like gaps between utterances. Such measures are more likely to fit a standard distribution, and thus one can use more powerful parametric tests. In addition, they may be more robust to the large-scale social differences between groups.

The third solution is to opt for a more anecdotal analysis, looking for critical incidents – for example, interesting events or breakdowns – in the data. The concepts and methods for analyzing conversation in Chapter 14 can be used to drive such an analysis. The advantage of this approach is that instead of regarding group differences as a 'problem', they can be included in the analysis. That is, we can begin to look for the systematic ways in which different group structures interact with the communications media and applications they use.

Of course, experiments can be analyzed using both quantitative and qualitative methods. Indeed, any detailed anecdotal analysis of the logs will indicate fruitful measures for statistical analysis. However, if the number of experimental groups is limited, attempts at controlled experiments may not be productive, and may effectively 'waste' the groups used in the control. Given the high costs of group-working experiments, one must choose conditions that are likely to give interesting results, even if statistical analysis proves impossible.

Field studies with groups There are, of course, problems with taking groups of users and putting them in an experimental situation. If the groups are randomly mixed, then we are effectively examining the process of group formation, rather than that of a normal working group. Even where a pre-existent group is used, excluding people from their normal working environment can completely alter their working patterns. For a new system, there may be no 'normal' workplace and all we can do is produce an artificial environment. However, even with a new system we have the choice of producing a 'good' experiment or a naturalistic setting. The traditions of experimental psychology are at odds with those of more qualitative sociological analysis.

It can be argued that group work can only be studied in context. Moving out of the real situation will alter the very nature of the work that is studied. Alternative approaches from the social sciences, such as ethnography, have therefore become popular, particularly in relation to studying group interaction. Ethnography involves very detailed recording of the interactions between people, their environment and each other. The ethnographer attempts to remain outside the situation being studied and does not impose a particular viewpoint on what is observed. This is very different from the experimental perspective with its hypothesis testing. Ethnography is discussed in more detail in Chapter 13.

9.4.3 Observational techniques

A popular way to gather information about actual use of a system is to observe users interacting with it. Usually they are asked to complete a set of predetermined tasks, although, if observation is being carried out in their place of work, they may be observed going about their normal duties. The evaluator watches and records the users' actions (using a variety of techniques – see below). Simple observation is seldom sufficient to determine how well the system meets the users' requirements since it does not always give insight into the their decision processes or attitude. Consequently users are asked to elaborate their actions by 'thinking aloud'. In this section we consider some of the techniques used to evaluate systems by observing user behavior.

Think aloud and cooperative evaluation

Think aloud is a form of observation where the user is asked to talk through what he is doing as he is being observed; for example, describing what he believes is happening, why he takes an action, what he is trying to do.

Think aloud has the advantage of simplicity; it requires little expertise to perform (though can be tricky to analyze fully) and can provide useful insight into problems with an interface. It can also be employed to observe how the system is actually used. It can be used for evaluation throughout the design process, using paper or simulated mock-ups for the earlier stages. However, the information provided is often subjective and may be selective, depending on the tasks provided. The process of observation can alter the way that people perform tasks and so provide a biased view. The very act of describing what you are doing often changes the way you do it – like the joke about the centipede who was asked how he walked . . .

A variation on think aloud is known as *cooperative evaluation* [240] in which the user is encouraged to see himself as a collaborator in the evaluation and not simply as an experimental participant. As well as asking the user to think aloud at the beginning of the session, the evaluator can ask the user questions (typically of the 'why?' or 'what-if?' type) if his behavior is unclear, and the user can ask the evaluator for clarification if a problem arises. This more relaxed view of the think aloud process has a number of advantages:

- the process is less constrained and therefore easier to learn to use by the evaluator
- the user is encouraged to criticize the system
- the evaluator can clarify points of confusion at the time they occur and so maximize the effectiveness of the approach for identifying problem areas.

The usefulness of think aloud, cooperative evaluation and observation in general is largely dependent on the effectiveness of the recording method and subsequent analysis. The record of an evaluation session of this type is known as a *protocol*, and there are a number of methods from which to choose.

Protocol analysis

Methods for recording user actions include the following:

Paper and pencil   This is primitive, but cheap, and allows the analyst to note interpretations and extraneous events as they occur. However, it is hard to get detailed information, as it is limited by the analyst's writing speed. Coding schemes for frequent activities, developed during preliminary studies, can improve the rate of recording substantially, but can take some time to develop. A variation of paper and pencil is the use of a notebook computer for direct entry, but then one is limited to the analyst's typing speed, and one loses the flexibility of paper for writing styles, quick diagrams and spatial layout. If this is the only recording facility available then a specific note-taker, separate from the evaluator, is recommended.

Audio recording   This is useful if the user is actively 'thinking aloud'. However, it may be difficult to record sufficient information to identify exact actions in later analysis, and it can be difficult to match an audio recording to some other form of protocol (such as a handwritten script).

Video recording   This has the advantage that we can see *what* the participant is doing (*as long as* the participant stays within the range of the camera). Choosing suitable camera positions and viewing angles so that you get sufficient detail and yet keep the participant in view is difficult. Alternatively, one has to ask the participant not to move, which may not be appropriate for studying normal behavior! For single-user computer-based tasks, one typically uses two video cameras, one looking at the computer screen and one with a wider focus including the user's face and hands. The former camera may not be necessary if the computer system is being logged.

Computer logging   It is relatively easy to get a system automatically to record user actions at a keystroke level, particularly if this facility has been considered early in the design. It can be more difficult with proprietary software where source code is not available (although some software now provides built-in logging and playback facilities). Obviously, computer logging only tells us what the user is doing on the system, but this may be sufficient for some purposes. Keystroke data are also 'semantics free' in that they only tell us about the lowest-level actions, not why they were performed or how they are structured (although slight pauses and gaps can give clues). Direct logging has the advantages that it is cheap (except in terms of disk storage), unobtrusive and can be used for *longitudinal studies*, where we look at one or more users over periods of weeks or months. Technical problems with it are that the sheer volume of data can become unmanageable without automatic analysis, and that one often has to be careful to restore the state of the system (file contents, etc.) before replaying the logs.

User notebooks The participants themselves can be asked to keep logs of activity/ problems. This will obviously be at a very coarse level – at most, records every few minutes and, more likely, hourly or less. It also gives us 'interpreted' records, which have advantages and problems. The technique is especially useful in longit- udinal studies, and also where we want a log of unusual or infrequent tasks and problems.

In practice, one uses a mixture of recording methods as they complement one another. For instance, we may keep a paper note of special events and circum- stances, even when we have more sophisticated audio/visual recording. Similarly, we may use separate audio recording, even where a video recorder is used, as the quality of specialist audio recording is better than most built-in video micro- phones. In addition, we may use stereo audio recording, which helps us to locate out-of-screen noises. If one is using a collection of different sources, say audio, video (×2) and keystroke logging, there is considerable difficulty in synchronizing them during play-back. Most video recorders can superimpose an on-screen clock, which can help, but ideally one uses specialized equipment that can automatically synchronize the different sources, possibly merging several video displays onto a single screen. Unfortunately, this sort of equipment is often only available in spe- cialized laboratories.

With both audio and video recording, a major problem is *transcription*. Typing a transcript from a tape is not the same as taped dictation. The conversation will typically consist of part or broken sentences, mumbled words and inarticulated noises. In addition, the transcript will need annotating with the different voices (which may only be clear from context) and with non-verbal items such as pauses, emphases, equipment noises, phones ringing, etc. A good audio-typist will be accustomed to completing mumbled words and correcting ungrammatical sentences – typing *exactly* what is recorded may prove difficult. Some practitioners say that the use of typists is not good practice anyway as the analyst will miss many nuances that are lost in the written transcript. However, if you wish to pro- duce your own typed transcripts from tape, a course in touch-typing is highly recommended.

For video transcription, professional typists are not an option; there is no standard way of annotating video recordings, and the analyst must invent notations to suit the particular circumstances. The scale of this task is not to be underestimated. It is com- mon to talk to practitioners who have tens or hundreds of hours of video recording, but have only analyzed tiny fragments in detail. Of course, the fragments will have been chosen after more extensive perusal of the material, but it certainly removes any idea of comprehensive coverage.

Coding can be introduced to indicate particular events but it is sometimes difficult to determine a suitable coding scheme and to use this consistently, particularly if more than one person is doing the coding. A range of transcribers should therefore test coding schemes to ensure that they are being interpreted appropriately for a particular data set.

Automatic protocol analysis tools

Analyzing protocols, whether video, audio or system logs, is time consuming and tedious by hand. It is made harder if there is more than one stream of data to synchronize. One solution to this problem is to provide automatic analysis tools to support the task. These offer a means of editing and annotating video, audio and system logs and synchronizing these for detailed analysis.

EVA (*Experimental Video Annotator*) is a system that runs on a multimedia workstation with a direct link to a video recorder [220]. The evaluator can devise a set of buttons indicating different events. These may include timestamps and snapshots, as well as notes of expected events and errors. The buttons are used within a recording session by the evaluator to annotate the video with notes. During the session the user works at a workstation and is recorded, using video and perhaps audio and system logging as well. The evaluator uses the multimedia workstation running EVA. On the screen is the live video record and a view of the user's screen (see Figure 9.4). The evaluator can use the buttons to tag interesting events as they occur and can record additional notes using a text editor. After the session, the evaluator can ask to review the tagged segments and can then use these and standard video controls to search the information. Links can be made with other types of record such as audio and system logs. A system such as EVA alleviates the burden of video analysis but it is not without its problems. The act of tagging and annotating events can prevent the evaluator from actually concentrating on the events themselves. This may mean that events are missed or tagged late.

Commercial systems such as Observer Pro from Noldus have similar functionality to EVA; portable versions are now available for use in field studies (www.noldus.com).

Figure 9.4 EVA: an automatic protocol analysis tool. Source: Wendy Mackay

The *Workplace project* at Xerox PARC [348] also includes a system to aid protocol analysis. The main emphasis here is to support the analysis of synchronized information from different data streams, such as video, audio, notes and diagrams. Each data stream is viewed in an aligned display so that it is possible to compare the records of each for a given point in the interaction. The alignment may be based on timestamps or on an event or action and is implemented using hypertext links.

A third example is DRUM [223], which also provides video annotation and tagging facilities. DRUM is part of the MUSiC (Measuring the Usability of Systems in Context/Metrics for Usability Standards in Computing) toolkit, which supports a complete methodology for evaluation, based upon the application of usability metrics on analytic metrics, cognitive workload, performance and user satisfaction. DRUM is concerned particularly with measuring performance. The methodology provides a range of tools as well as DRUM, including manuals, questionnaires, analysis software and databases.

Systems such as these are extremely important as evaluation tools since they offer a means of handling the data that are collected in observational studies and allowing a more systematic approach to the analysis. The evaluator's task is facilitated and it is likely that more valuable observations will emerge as a result.

Post-task walkthroughs

Often data obtained via direct observation lack interpretation. We have the basic actions that were performed, but little knowledge as to why. Even where the participant has been encouraged to think aloud through the task, the information may be at the wrong level. For example, the participant may say 'and now I'm selecting the undo menu', but not tell us what was wrong to make undo necessary. In addition, a think aloud does not include information such as alternative, but not pursued, actions.

A walkthrough attempts to alleviate these problems, by reflecting the participants' actions back to them after the event. The transcript, whether written or recorded, is replayed to the participant who is invited to comment, or is directly questioned by the analyst. This may be done straightaway, when the participant may actually remember why certain actions were performed, or after an interval, when the answers are more likely to be the participant's post hoc interpretation. (In fact, interpretation is likely even in the former case.) The advantage of a delayed walkthrough is that the analyst has had time to frame suitable questions and focus on specific incidents. The disadvantage is a loss of freshness.

There are some circumstances when the participant cannot be expected to talk during the actual observation, for instance during a critical task, or when the task is too intensive. In these circumstances, the post-task walkthrough is the only way to obtain a subjective viewpoint on the user's behavior. There is also an argument that it is preferable to minimize non-task-related talk during direct observation in order to get as natural a performance as possible. Again this makes the walkthrough essential.

9.4.4 Query techniques

Another set of evaluation techniques relies on asking the user about the interface directly. Query techniques can be useful in eliciting detail of the user's view of a system. They embody the philosophy that states that the best way to find out how a system meets user requirements is to 'ask the user'. They can be used in evaluation and more widely to collect information about user requirements and tasks. The advantage of such methods is that they get the user's viewpoint directly and may reveal issues that have not been considered by the designer. In addition, they are relatively simple and cheap to administer. However, the information gained is necessarily subjective, and may be a 'rationalized' account of events rather than a wholly accurate one. Also, it may be difficult to get accurate feedback about alternative designs if the user has not experienced them, which limits the scope of the information that can be gleaned. However, the methods provide useful supplementary material to other methods. There are two main types of query technique: interviews and questionnaires.

Interviews

Interviewing users about their experience with an interactive system provides a direct and structured way of gathering information. Interviews have the advantages that the level of questioning can be varied to suit the context and that the evaluator can probe the user more deeply on interesting issues as they arise. An interview will usually follow a top-down approach, starting with a general question about a task and progressing to more leading questions (often of the form 'why?' or 'what if?') to elaborate aspects of the user's response.

Interviews can be effective for high-level evaluation, particularly in eliciting information about user preferences, impressions and attitudes. They may also reveal problems that have not been anticipated by the designer or that have not occurred under observation. When used in conjunction with observation they are a useful means of clarifying an event (compare the post-task walkthrough).

In order to be as effective as possible, the interview should be planned in advance, with a set of central questions prepared. Each interview is then structured around these questions. This helps to focus the purpose of the interview, which may, for instance, be to probe a particular aspect of the interaction. It also helps to ensure a base of consistency between the interviews of different users. That said, the evaluator may, of course, choose to adapt the interview form to each user in order to get the most benefit: the interview is not intended to be a controlled experimental technique.

Questionnaires

An alternative method of querying the user is to administer a questionnaire. This is clearly less flexible than the interview technique, since questions are fixed in advance, and it is likely that the questions will be less probing. However, it can be used to reach a wider participant group, it takes less time to administer, and it can be analyzed more rigorously. It can also be administered at various points in the design process, including during requirements capture, task analysis and evaluation, in order to get information on the user's needs, preferences and experience.

Given that the evaluator is not likely to be directly involved in the completion of the questionnaire, it is vital that it is well designed. The first thing that the evaluator must establish is the purpose of the questionnaire: what information is sought? It is also useful to decide at this stage how the questionnaire responses are to be analyzed. For example, do you want specific, measurable feedback on particular interface features, or do you want the user's impression of using the interface?

There are a number of styles of question that can be included in the questionnaire. These include the following:

General   These are questions that help to establish the background of the user and his place within the user population. They include questions about age, sex, occupation, place of residence, and so on. They may also include questions on previous experience with computers, which may be phrased as open-ended, multi-choice or scalar questions (see below).

Open-ended   These ask the user to provide his own unprompted opinion on a question, for example 'Can you suggest any improvements to the interface?'. They are useful for gathering general subjective information but are difficult to analyze in any rigorous way, or to compare, and can only be viewed as supplementary. They are also most likely to be missed out by time-conscious respondents! However, they may identify errors or make suggestions that have not been considered by the designer. A special case of this type is where the user is asked for factual information, for example how many commands were used.

Scalar   These ask the user to judge a specific statement on a numeric scale, usually corresponding to a measure of agreement or disagreement with the statement. For example,

> It is easy to recover from mistakes.
> Disagree   1   2   3   4   5   Agree

The granularity of the scale varies: a coarse scale (say, from 1 to 3) gives a clear indication of the meaning of the numbers (disagree, neutral and agree). However, it gives no room for varying levels of agreement, and users may therefore be tempted to give neutral responses to statements that they do not feel strongly about but with which they mildly disagree or agree. A very fine scale (say 1 to 10) suffers from the opposite problem: the numbers become difficult to interpret in a consistent way. One user will undoubtedly interpret the scale differently from another. A middle ground is therefore advisable. Scales of 1 to 5 or 1 to 7 have been used effectively. They are fine enough to allow users to differentiate adequately but still retain clarity in meaning. It can help to provide an indication of the meaning of intermediate scalar values. Odd-numbered scales are used most often but it is possible to use even-numbered scales (e.g. 1–6) if the 'neutral' option is not wanted. This does not allow for fence sitting – except decisively by selecting $3^{1}/_{2}$!).

Multi-choice   Here the respondent is offered a choice of explicit responses, and may be asked to select only one of these, or as many as apply. For example,

> How do you most often get help with the system (tick one)?
> Online manual   ❏
> Contextual help system   ❏
> Command prompt   ❏
> Ask a colleague   ❏
> Which types of software have you used (tick all that apply)?
> Word processor   ❏
> Database   ❏
> Spreadsheet   ❏
> Expert system   ❏
> Online help system   ❏
> Compiler   ❏

These are particularly useful for gathering information on a user's previous experience. A special case of this type is where the offered choices are 'yes' or 'no'.

Ranked   These place an ordering on items in a list and are useful to indicate a user's preferences. For example,

> Please rank the usefulness of these methods of issuing a command (1 most useful, 2 next, 0 if not used).
> Menu selection   ❏
> Command line   ❏
> Control key accelerator   ❏

These question types are all useful for different purposes, as we have noted. However, in order to reduce the burden of effort on the respondent, and so encourage a high response rate amongst users, it is best to use closed questions, such as scalar, ranked or multi-choice, as much as possible. These provide the user with alternative responses and so reduce the effort required. They also have the advantage of being easier to analyze. Responses can be analyzed in a number of ways, from determining simple percentages for each response, to looking at correlations and factor analysis. For more detail on available methods the reader is referred to the recommended reading list at the end of the chapter.

Whatever type of questionnaire is planned, it is wise to carry out a pilot study. This allows any problems with the questionnaire design to be ironed out before the questionnaire is distributed to potentially hundreds of users! The questionnaire should be tested on four or five users to see if the questions are comprehensible and the results are as expected and can be used in the manner intended. If users seem to be misunderstanding a particular question, it can then be rephrased (and retested) before the final version is sent out.

Distribution of questionnaires can also be problematic. It is important that the respondents are representative of the user population but you also need to ensure that you are able to reach as many potential respondents as possible. Return rate for questionnaires is quite low (often 25–30%) so many more need to be sent out to get a reasonable return. Questionnaires should ideally be distributed to a random subset of the user population. So, for example, if the population is all workers in a company, one may choose to send a questionnaire to every fourth person on an alphabetically ordered personnel list. However, questionnaires are now often distributed via the internet, either by email, where potential respondents can be selected randomly, or via a website, where the respondents are limited to those who visit the site and who may not be representative. In practice, questionnaire respondents are self-selecting anyway, in that only those who choose to respond are included in the study; if the questionnaire is designed to capture demographic information about each respondent then the level of representativeness (or otherwise) can be determined from the responses.

Worked exercise

You have been asked to compare user performance and preferences with two different learning systems, one using hypermedia (see Chapter 21), the other sequential lessons. Design a questionnaire to find out what the users think of the system. How would you go about comparing user performance with these two systems?

Answer   Assume that all users have used both systems.

Questionnaire
Consider the following questions in designing the questionnaire:

- what information is required?
- how is the questionnaire to be analyzed?

You are particularly interested in user preferences so questions should focus on different aspects of the systems and try to measure levels of satisfaction. The use of scales will make responses for each system easier to compare.

Table 9.3 shows an example questionnaire.

To test performance you would design an experiment where two groups of participants learn the same material using the two systems, and test how well they have learned (using a standard measurable test).

Participants   User group

IV   (Independent Variable) Style of learning system

DV   (Dependent Variable) Performance (measured as test score)

Design   Between-subjects design

Table 9.3 Questionnaire to compare two systems

PART I: Repeat for each system

Indicate your agreement or disagreement with the following statements. (I indicates complete disagreement and 5 complete agreement.)

The system tells me what to do at every point.

Disagree 1 2 3 4 5 Agree

It is easy to recover from mistakes.

Disagree 1 2 3 4 5 Agree

It is easy to get help when needed.

Disagree 1 2 3 4 5 Agree

I always know what the system is doing.

Disagree 1 2 3 4 5 Agree

I always know where I am in the training material.

Disagree 1 2 3 4 5 Agree

I have learned the material well using the system.

Disagree 1 2 3 4 5 Agree

I could have learned the material more effectively using a book.

Disagree 1 2 3 4 5 Agree

I always know how well I am doing.

Disagree 1 2 3 4 5 Agree

PART II: Comparing both systems:

Which system (choose 1) was most:

Helpful to use   A   B

Efficient to use   A   B

Enjoyable to use   A   B

Please add any comments you have about either system:

9.4.5 Evaluation through monitoring physiological responses

One of the problems with most evaluation techniques is that we are reliant on observation and the users telling us what they are doing and how they are feeling. What if we were able to measure these things directly? Interest has grown recently in the use of what is sometimes called objective usability testing, ways of monitoring physiological aspects of computer use. Potentially this will allow us not only to see more clearly exactly what users do when they interact with computers, but also to measure how they feel. The two areas receiving the most attention to date are eye tracking and physiological measurement.

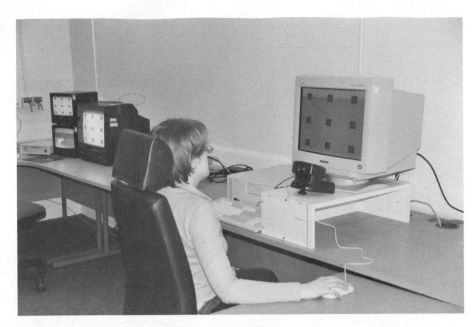

Figure 9.5 Eye-tracking equipment. Source: Courtesy of J. A. Renshaw

Eye tracking for usability evaluation

Eye tracking has been possible for many years, but recent improvements in hardware and software have made it more viable as an approach to measuring usability. The original eye trackers required highly invasive procedures where eye caps were attached to the cornea under anaesthetic. Clearly inappropriate for usability testing! Modern systems vary: some use a head-mounted camera to monitor the eye, but the most sophisticated do not involve any contact between the equipment and the participant, with the camera and light sources mounted in desk units (see Figures 9.5, 9.6) [112].

Furthermore, there have been rapid improvements in the software available both for the control of eye-tracking equipment and the analysis and visualization of the large volumes of data it produces.

Eye movements are believed to reflect the amount of cognitive processing a display requires and, therefore, how easy or difficult it is to process [150]. So measuring not only where people look, but also their patterns of eye movement, may tell us which areas of a screen they are finding easy or difficult to understand. Eye movement measurements are based on fixations, where the eye retains a stable position for a period of time, and saccades, where there is rapid ballistic eye movement from one point of interest to another. There are many possible measurements related to usability evaluation including:

Number of fixations The more fixations the less efficient the search strategy.

Fixation duration Longer fixations may indicate difficulty with a display.

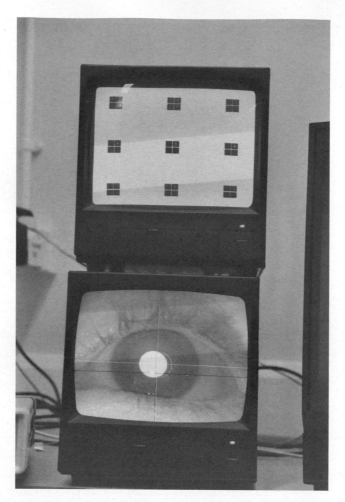

Figure 9.6   Calibrating the eye tracker. Source: Courtesy of J. A. Renshaw

Scan path   indicating areas of interest, search strategy and cognitive load. Moving straight to a target with a short fixation at the target is the optimal scan path but plotting scan paths and fixations can indicate what people look at, how often and for how long.

Eye tracking for usability is still very new and equipment is prohibitively expensive for everyday use. However, it is a promising technique for providing insights into what really attracts the eye in website design and where problem areas are in system use. More research is needed to interpret accurately the meaning of the various eye movement measurements, as well as to develop more accessible and robust equipment. But, given the potential for gathering new data measurements relatively unobtrusively, it is likely that eye tracking will become part of the standard equipment for usability laboratories in the coming few years.

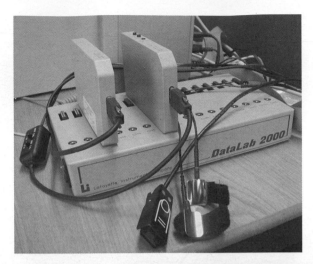

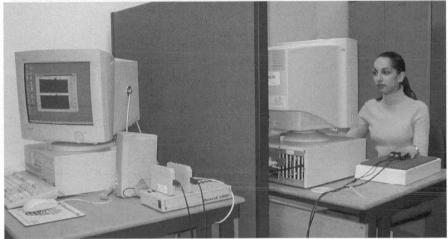

Figure 9.7 Data Lab Psychophysiology equipment showing some of the sensors (above) and a typical experimental arrangement (below) with sensors attached to the participant's fingers and the monitoring software displayed on the evaluator's machine. Source: Courtesy of Dr R. D. Ward

Physiological measurements

As we saw in Chapter 1, emotional response is closely tied to physiological changes. These include changes in heart rate, breathing and skin secretions. Measuring these physiological responses may therefore be useful in determining a user's emotional response to an interface [288, 363]. Could we determine which interaction events really cause a user stress or which promote relaxation?

Physiological measurement involves attaching various probes and sensors to the user (see Figure 9.7). These measure a number of factors:

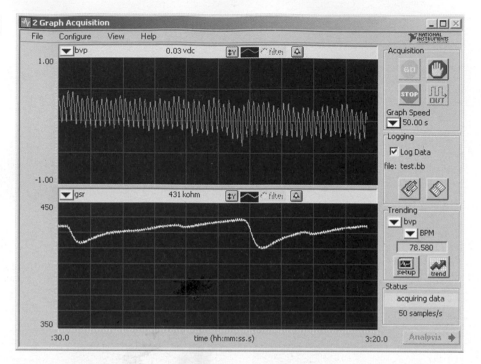

Figure 9.8 Output of monitoring pulse rate (above) and skin conductivity (below). Source: Screen shot courtesy of Dr R. D. Ward; frame source: National Instruments BioBench software

Heart activity, indicated by blood pressure, volume and pulse. These may respond to stress or anger.

Activity of the sweat glands, indicated by skin resistance or galvanic skin response (GSR). These are thought to indicate levels of arousal and mental effort.

Electrical activity in muscle, measured by the electromyogram (EMG). These appear to reflect involvement in a task.

Electrical activity in the brain, measured by the electroencephalogram (EEG). These are associated with decision making, attention and motivation.

Figure 9.8 illustrates the output obtained from such measurements.

One of the problems with applying these measurements to interaction events is that it is not clear what the relationship between these events and measurements might be. For example, if increased pulse rate is observed during an interactive task, does that indicate frustration with the interface or stress at being unable to complete the task? How will physiological changes differ in response to discrete events or to continuous interface use? Is it possible to map patterns of physiological measurement to specific emotional states?

These are still research questions but the approach is interesting, as it offers a potential means of objectively capturing information about the user's emotional state, which, as we saw in Chapter 1, impacts on our ability to solve problems and perform tasks.

9.5 CHOOSING AN EVALUATION METHOD

As we have seen in this chapter, a range of techniques is available for evaluating an interactive system at all stages in the design process. So how do we decide which methods are most appropriate for our needs? There are no hard and fast rules in this – each method has its particular strengths and weaknesses and each is useful if applied appropriately. However, there are a number of factors that should be taken into account when selecting evaluation techniques. These also provide a way of categorizing the different methods so that we can compare and choose between them. In this final section we will consider these factors.

9.5.1 Factors distinguishing evaluation techniques

We can identify at least eight factors that distinguish different evaluation techniques and therefore help us to make an appropriate choice. These are:

- the stage in the cycle at which the evaluation is carried out
- the style of evaluation
- the level of subjectivity or objectivity of the technique
- the type of measures provided
- the information provided
- the immediacy of the response
- the level of interference implied
- the resources required.

Design vs. implementation

The first factor to affect our choice of evaluation method is the stage in the design process at which evaluation is required. As we saw earlier in this chapter, it is desirable to include evaluation of some sort throughout the design process. The main distinction between evaluation of a design and evaluation of an implementation is that in the latter case a physical artifact exists. This may be anything from a paper mock-up to a full implementation, but it is something concrete that can be tested. Evaluation of a design, on the other hand, precedes this stage and seeks instead to provide information to feed the development of the physical artifact.

Roughly speaking, evaluation at the design stage needs to be quick and cheap so might involve design experts only and be analytic, whereas evaluation of the implementation needs to be more comprehensive, so brings in users as participants. There are, of course, exceptions to this: participatory design (see Chapter 13) involves users throughout the design process, and techniques such as cognitive walk-through are expert based and analytic but can be used to evaluate implementations as well as designs.

Early evaluation, whether of a design or an early prototype or mock-up, will bring the greatest pay-off since problems can be easily resolved at this stage. As more commitment is made to a particular design in the implementation, it becomes increasingly difficult for changes to be made, no matter what the evaluation suggests. Ironically, the most resources are often ploughed into late evaluations. This is less profitable and should be avoided, although obviously some evaluation with users is required with a complete, or almost complete, system, since some elements (such as system performance) will only be evident in the working system.

Laboratory vs. field studies

We have already discussed the pros and cons of these two styles of evaluation. Laboratory studies allow controlled experimentation and observation while losing something of the naturalness of the user's environment. Field studies retain the latter but do not allow control over user activity. Ideally the design process should include both styles of evaluation, probably with laboratory studies dominating the early stages and field studies conducted with the new implementation.

Subjective vs. objective

Evaluation techniques also vary according to their objectivity – some techniques rely heavily on the interpretation of the evaluator, others would provide similar information for anyone correctly carrying out the procedure. The more subjective techniques, such as cognitive walkthrough or think aloud, rely to a large extent on the knowledge and expertise of the evaluator, who must recognize problems and understand what the user is doing. They can be powerful if used correctly and will provide information that may not be available from more objective methods. However, the problem of evaluator bias should be recognized and avoided. One way to decrease the possibility of bias is to use more than one evaluator. Objective techniques, on the other hand, should produce repeatable results, which are not dependent on the persuasion of the particular evaluator. Controlled experiments are an example of an objective measure. These avoid bias and provide comparable results but may not reveal the unexpected problem or give detailed feedback on user experience. Ideally, both objective and subjective approaches should be used.

The extent to which the results are dependent on the subjective response of the user also varies. At one extreme is asking for the user's opinions, which is highly subjective; at the other is measuring physiological changes in the body, which are outside the user's control.

Qualitative vs. quantitative measures

The type of measurement provided by the evaluation technique is also an important consideration. There are two main types: *quantitative measurement* and *qualitative measurement*. The former is usually numeric and can be easily analyzed using statistical techniques. The latter is non-numeric and is therefore more difficult to analyze, but can provide important detail that cannot be determined from numbers. The type of measure is related to the subjectivity or objectivity of the technique, with subjective techniques tending to provide qualitative measures and objective techniques, quantitative measures. This is not a hard and fast rule, however. It is sometimes possible to quantify what is, in fact, qualitative information by mapping it onto a scale or similar measure. A common example of this is in questionnaires where qualitative information is being sought (for example, user preferences) but a quantitative scale is used. This is also common in experimental design where factors such as the quality of the user's performance are used as dependent variables, and measured on a quantitative scale.

Information provided

The level of information required from an evaluation may also vary. The information required by an evaluator at any stage of the design process may range from low-level information to enable a design decision to be made (for example, which font is most readable) to higher-level information, such as 'Is the system usable?'. Some evaluation techniques, such as controlled experiments, are excellent at providing low-level information – an experiment can be designed to measure a particular aspect of the interface. Higher-level information can be gathered using questionnaire and interview techniques, which provide a more general impression of the user's view of the system.

Immediacy of response

Another factor distinguishing evaluation techniques is the immediacy of the response they provide. Some methods, such as think aloud, record the user's behavior at the time of the interaction itself. Others, such as post-task walkthrough, rely on the user's recollection of events. Such recollection is liable to suffer from bias in recall and reconstruction, with users interpreting events according to their preconceptions. Recall may also be incomplete. However, immediate techniques can also be problematic, since the process of measurement can actually alter the way the user works.

Intrusiveness

Related to the immediacy of the response is the intrusiveness of the technique itself. Certain techniques, particularly those that produce immediate measurements, are obvious to the user during the interaction and therefore run the risk of influencing the way the user behaves. Sensitive activity on the part of the evaluator can help to reduce this but cannot remove it altogether. Most immediate evaluation techniques are intrusive, with the exception of automatic system logging. Unfortunately, this is limited in the information that it can provide and is difficult to interpret.

Resources

The final consideration when selecting an evaluation technique is the availability of resources. Resources to consider include equipment, time, money, participants, expertise of evaluator and context. Some decisions are forced by resource limitations: it is not possible to produce a video protocol without access to a video camera (and probably editing facilities as well). However, other decisions are not so clear cut. For example, time and money may be limited, forcing a choice between two possible evaluations. In these circumstances, the evaluator must decide which evaluation tactic will produce the most effective and useful information for the system under consideration. It may be possible to use results from other people's experiments to avoid having to conduct new experiments.

Some techniques are more reliant on evaluator expertise than others, for example the more formal analytic techniques. If evaluator expertise is limited, it may be more practical to use more simple heuristic methods than methods that require understanding of user goal structures and so on.

Finally, the context in which evaluation can occur will influence what can be done. For practical reasons it may not be possible to gain access to the intended users of a system (if it is a general system, for example). Or it may not be feasible to test the system in its intended environment (for example, a system for a space station or a defence system). In these circumstances simulations must be used.

9.5.2 A classification of evaluation techniques

Using the factors discussed in the previous section we can classify the evaluation techniques we have considered in this chapter. This allows us to identify the techniques that most closely fit our requirements. Table 9.4 shows the classification for

Table 9.4 Classification of analytic evaluation techniques

	Cognitive walkthrough	Heuristic evaluation	Review based	Model based
Stage	Throughout	Throughout	Design	Design
Style	Laboratory	Laboratory	Laboratory	Laboratory
Objective?	No	No	As source	No
Measure	Qualitative	Qualitative	As source	Qualitative
Information	Low level	High level	As source	Low level
Immediacy	N/A	N/A	As source	N/A
Intrusive?	No	No	No	No
Time	Medium	Low	Low–medium	Medium
Equipment	Low	Low	Low	Low
Expertise	High	Medium	Low	High

Table 9.5   Classification of experimental and query evaluation techniques

	Experiment	Interviews	Questionnaire
Stage	Throughout	Throughout	Throughout
Style	Laboratory	Lab/field	Lab/field
Objective?	Yes	No	No
Measure	Quantitative	Qualitative/ quantitative	Qualitative/ quantitative
Information	Low/high level	High level	High level
Immediacy	Yes	No	No
Intrusive?	Yes	No	No
Time	High	Low	Low
Equipment	Medium	Low	Low
Expertise	Medium	Low	Low

Table 9.6   Classification of observational evaluation techniques

	Think aloud[1]	Protocol analysis[2]	Post-task walkthrough
Stage	Implementation	Implementation	Implementation
Style	Lab/field	Lab/field	Lab/field
Objective?	No	No	No
Measure	Qualitative	Qualitative	Qualitative
Information	High/low level	High/low level	High/low level
Immediacy	Yes	Yes	No
Intrusive?	Yes	Yes[3]	No
Time	High	High	Medium
Equipment	Low	High	Low
Expertise	Medium	High	Medium

1 Assuming a simple paper and pencil record
2 Including video, audio and system recording
3 Except system logs

analytic techniques, Table 9.5 for experimental and query techniques, Table 9.6 for observational and Table 9.7 for monitoring techniques.

The classification is intended as a rough guide only – some of the techniques do not fit easily into such a classification since their use can vary considerably.

Table 9.7 Classification of monitoring evaluation techniques

	Eye tracking	Physiological measurement
Stage	Implementation	Implementation
Style	Lab	Lab
Objective?	Yes	Yes
Measure	Quantitative	Quantitative
Information	Low level	Low level
Immediacy	Yes	Yes
Intrusive?	No[1]	Yes
Time	Medium/high	Medium/high
Equipment	High	High
Expertise	High	High

1 If the equipment is not head mounted

9.6 SUMMARY

Evaluation is an integral part of the design process and should take place throughout the design life cycle. Its aim is to test the functionality and usability of the design and to identify and rectify any problems. It can also try to determine the user's attitude and response to the system. It can take place in a specialist laboratory or in the user's workplace, and may or may not involve active participation on the part of the user.

A design can be evaluated before any implementation work has started, to minimize the cost of early design errors. Most techniques for evaluation at this stage are analytic and involve using an expert to assess the design against cognitive and usability principles. Previous experimental results and modeling approaches can also provide insight at this stage. Once an artifact has been developed (whether a prototype or full system), experimental and observational techniques can be used to get both quantitative and qualitative results. Query techniques provide subjective information from the user. If more objective information is required, physiological monitoring can capture the user's physical responses to the system.

The choice of evaluation method is largely dependent on what is required of the evaluation. Evaluation methods vary in the stage at which they are commonly used and where they can be used. Some are more subjective than others and provide qualitative rather than quantitative measures. Some provide immediate information while others get feedback after the event. However, the more immediate methods also tend to intrude most seriously on the interaction. Finally, some require more resources in terms of time, equipment and expertise than others.

EXERCISES

9.1 In groups or pairs, use the cognitive walkthrough example, and what you know about user psychology (see Chapter 1), to discuss the design of a computer application of your choice (for example, a word processor or a drawing package). (**Hint:** Focus your discussion on one or two specific tasks within the application.)

9.2 What are the benefits and problems of using video in experimentation? If you have access to a video recorder, attempt to transcribe a piece of action and conversation (it does not have to be an experiment – a soap opera will do!). What problems did you encounter?

9.3 In Section 9.4.2, we saw that the observed results could be the result of interference. Can you think of alternative designs that may make this less likely? Remember that individual variation was very high, so you *must* retain a within-subjects design, but you may perform more tests on each participant.

9.4 Choose an appropriate evaluation method for each of the following situations. In each case identify:

(i) the participants
(ii) the technique used
(iii) representative tasks to be examined
(iv) measurements that would be appropriate
(v) an outline plan for carrying out the evaluation.

(a) You are at an early stage in the design of a spreadsheet package and you wish to test what type of icons will be easiest to learn.
(b) You have a prototype for a theatre booking system to be used by potential theatre-goers to reduce queues at the box office.
(c) You have designed and implemented a new game system and want to evaluate it before release.
(d) You have developed a group decision support system for a solicitor's office.
(e) You have been asked to develop a system to store and manage student exam results and would like to test two different designs prior to implementation or prototyping.

9.5 Complete the cognitive walkthrough example for the video remote control design.

9.6 In defining an experimental study, describe:

(a) how you as an experimenter would formulate the hypothesis to be supported or refuted by your study;
(b) how you would decide between a within-groups or between-groups experimental design with your subjects.

9.7 What are the factors governing the choice of an appropriate evaluation method for different interactive systems? Give brief details.

RECOMMENDED READING

C. Robson, *Experiment, Design and Statistics in Psychology*, 3rd edition, Penguin, 1994.
An accessible introduction to statistics and experimental design and analysis for the uninitiated, using worked examples throughout.

A. Monk, P. Wright, J. Haber and L. Davenport, *Improving your Human Computer Interface: A Practical Approach*, Prentice Hall, 1992.
An evaluator's guide to using the cooperative evaluation approach successfully.

M. Helander, editor, *Handbook of Human–Computer Interaction, Part V: Tools for Design and Evaluation*, North-Holland, 1988.
Reviews the major evaluation techniques.

C. Wharton, J. Rieman, C. Lewis and P. Polson, The cognitive walkthrough: a practitioner's guide. In J. Nielsen and R. L. Mack, editors, *Usability Inspection Methods*, John Wiley, 1994.
Describes the revised version of the cognitive walkthrough method of evaluation.

J. Nielsen, Heuristic evaluation. In J. Nielsen and R. L. Mack, editors, *Usability Inspection Methods*, John Wiley, 1994.
Covers the heuristic evaluation method in detail.

Interacting with Computers, Vol. 14, No. 2, special issue on emotion in interaction, February 2002.
A special journal issue containing several papers on the use of psychophysiology in studying emotional response to interaction.

A. T. Duchowski, *Eye Tracking Methodology: Theory and Practice*, Springer-Verlag, 2003.
A recent book providing a detailed introduction to eye-tracking theory, equipment and applications.

UNIVERSAL DESIGN

10

OVERVIEW

- Universal design is about designing systems so that they can be used by anyone in any circumstance.

- Multi-modal systems are those that use more than one human input channel in the interaction.

- These systems may, for example, use:
  - speech
  - non-speech sound
  - touch
  - handwriting
  - gestures.

- Universal design means designing for diversity, including:
  - people with sensory, physical or cognitive impairment
  - people of different ages
  - people from different cultures and backgrounds.

10.1 INTRODUCTION

We have already discussed the importance of designing for the user, considering human abilities and requirements. But is it possible to generalize about people and, if not, how do we address the issue of human diversity in our designs?

The discussion that we had on human psychology in Chapter 1 talked about general human abilities and, in reality, people are much more varied than the discussion suggests. People have different abilities and weaknesses; they come from different backgrounds and cultures; they have different interests, viewpoints and experiences; they are different ages and sizes. All of these things have an impact on the way in which an individual will use a particular computing application and, indeed, on whether or not they can use it at all. Given such diversity, we cannot assume a 'typical' user or design only for people like ourselves.

Universal design is the process of designing products so that they can be used by as many people as possible in as many situations as possible. In our case, this means particularly designing interactive systems that are usable by anyone, with any range of abilities, using any technology platform. This can be achieved by designing systems either to have built in redundancy or to be compatible with assistive technologies. An example of the former might be an interface that has both visual and audio access to commands; an example of the latter, a website that provides text alternatives for graphics, so that it can be read using a screen reader.

In this chapter, we will look at universal design in more detail. We will begin by examining seven principles of universal design. We will then look at multi-modal technology and how it can help to provide redundancy in interaction. Having identified some of the available technologies at our disposal, we will look in more detail at the particular areas of human diversity that we need to address.

10.2 UNIVERSAL DESIGN PRINCIPLES

We have defined universal design as 'the process of designing products so that they can be used by as many people as possible in as many situations as possible'. But what does that mean in practice? Is it possible to design anything so that anyone can use it – and if we could, how practical would it be? Wouldn't the cost be prohibitive? In reality, we may not be able to design everything to be accessible to everyone, and we certainly cannot ensure that everyone has the same experience of using a product, but we can work toward the aim of universal design and try to provide an *equivalent* experience.

Although it may seem like a huge task, universal design does not have to be complex or costly. In fact, if you are observant, you will see many examples of design that attempt to take account of user diversity. Next time you cross the road, look at the pavement. The curb may be lowered, to enable people who use wheelchairs to cross more easily. The paving near the curb may be of a different texture – with raised bumps or ridges – to enable people who cannot see to find the crossing point. Notice how many modern buildings have automatic doors that open on approach. Or lifts that offer both visual and auditory notification of the floor reached. And, whilst these designs make the crossing, the building and the lift more accessible to people who have disabilities, notice too how they also help other users. The parent with a child in a buggy, or the traveller with wheeled luggage, can cross the road more easily; the shopper with heavy bags, or the small child, can enter the building; and people are less likely to miss their floor because they weren't paying attention. Universal design is primarily about trying to ensure that you do not exclude anyone through the design choices you make but, by giving thought to these issues, you will invariably make your design better for everyone.

In the late 1990s a group at North Carolina State University in the USA proposed seven general principles of universal design [333]. These were intended to cover all areas of design and are equally applicable to the design of interactive systems. These principles give us a framework in which to develop universal designs.

Principle one is *equitable use*: the design is useful to people with a range of abilities and appealing to all. No user is excluded or stigmatized. Wherever possible, access should be the same for all; where identical use is not possible, equivalent use should be supported. Where appropriate, security, privacy and safety provision should be available to all.

Principle two is *flexibility in use*: the design allows for a range of ability and preference, through choice of methods of use and adaptivity to the user's pace, precision and custom.

Principle three is that the system be *simple and intuitive to use*, regardless of the knowledge, experience, language or level of concentration of the user. The design needs to support the user's expectations and accommodate different language and literacy skills. It should not be unnecessarily complex and should be organized to facilitate access to the most important areas. It should provide prompting and feedback as far as possible.

Principle four is *perceptible information*: the design should provide effective communication of information regardless of the environmental conditions or the user's abilities. Redundancy of presentation is important: information should be represented in different forms or modes (e.g. graphic, verbal, text, touch). Essential information should be emphasized and differentiated clearly from the peripheral content. Presentation should support the range of devices and techniques used to access information by people with different sensory abilities.

Principle five is *tolerance for error*: minimizing the impact and damage caused by mistakes or unintended behavior. Potentially dangerous situations should be removed or made hard to reach. Potential hazards should be shielded by warnings. Systems should fail safe from the user's perspective and users should be supported in tasks that require concentration.

Principle six is *low physical effort*: systems should be designed to be comfortable to use, minimizing physical effort and fatigue. The physical design of the system should allow the user to maintain a natural posture with reasonable operating effort. Repetitive or sustained actions should be avoided.

Principle seven requires *size and space for approach and use*: the placement of the system should be such that it can be reached and used by any user regardless of body size, posture or mobility. Important elements should be on the line of sight for both seated and standing users. All physical components should be comfortably reachable by seated or standing users. Systems should allow for variation in hand size and provide enough room for assistive devices to be used.

These seven principles give us a good starting point in considering universal design. They are not all equally applicable to all situations, of course. For example, principles six and seven would be vital in designing an information booth but less important in designing word-processing software. But they provide a useful checklist of considerations for designers, together with guidelines on how each principle can be achieved. It is interesting to note that these principles are closely related to the ones we met in Chapter 7, in the context of general user-centered design rules, indicating again that universal design is fundamentally good design for all.

10.3 MULTI-MODAL INTERACTION

As we have seen in the previous section, providing access to information through more than one mode of interaction is an important principle of universal design. Such design relies on *multi-modal interaction*.

As we saw in Chapter 1, there are five senses: sight, sound, touch, taste and smell.

Sight is the predominant sense for the majority of people, and most interactive systems consequently use the visual channel as their primary means of presentation, through graphics, text, video and animation.

However, sound is also an important channel, keeping us aware of our surroundings, monitoring people and events around us, reacting to sudden noises, providing clues and cues that switch our attention from one thing to another. It can also have an emotional effect on us, particularly in the case of music. Music is almost completely an auditory experience, yet is able to alter moods, conjure up visual images, evoke atmospheres or scenes in the mind of the listener.

Touch, too, provides important information: tactile feedback forms an intrinsic part of the operation of many common tools – cars, musical instruments, pens, anything that requires holding or moving. It can form a sensuous bond between individuals, communicating a wealth of non-verbal information.

Taste and smell are often less appreciated (until they are absent) but they also provide useful information in daily life: checking if food is bad, detecting early signs of fire, noticing that manure has been spread in a field, pleasure.

Examples of the use of sensory information are easy to come by (we looked at some in Chapter 1), but the important point is that our everyday interaction with each other and the world around us is multi-sensory, each sense providing different information that informs the whole. Since our interaction with the world is improved by multi-sensory input, it makes sense that interactive systems that utilize more than one sensory channel will also provide a richer interactive experience. In addition, such multi-sensory or multi-modal systems support the principle of redundancy required for universal design, enabling users to access the system using the mode of interaction that is most appropriate to their abilities.

The majority of interactive computer systems are predominantly visual in their interactive properties; often WIMP based, they usually make use of only rudimentary sounds while adding more and more visual information to the screen. As systems become more complex, the visual channel may be overloaded if too much information is presented all at once. This may lead to frustration or errors in use. By utilizing the other sensory channels, the visual channel can be relieved of the pressure of providing all the information required and so interaction should improve. The use of multiple sensory channels increases the *bandwidth* of the interaction between the human and the computer, and it also makes human–computer interaction more like the interaction between humans and their everyday environment, perhaps making the use of such systems more natural. However, it should always be remembered that multi-modal interaction is not just about enhancing the richness of the interaction, but also about redundancy. Redundant systems provide the *same* information through a range of channels, so, for example, information presented graphically is also captioned in readable text or speech, or a verbal narrative is provided with text captions. The aim is to provide at least an equivalent experience to all, regardless of their primary channel of interaction.

Usable sensory inputs

In computing, the visual channel is used as the predominant channel for communication, but if we are to use the other senses we have to consider their suitability and the nature of the information that they can convey.

The use of sound is an obvious area for further exploitation. There is little doubt that we use hearing a great deal in daily life, and so developing its application to the interface may be beneficial. Sound is already used, to a limited degree, in many interfaces: beeps are used as warnings and notification, recorded or synthesized speech and music are also used. Tactile feedback, as we have already seen, is also important in improving interactivity and so this represents another sense that we can utilize more effectively. However, taste and smell pose more serious problems for us. They are the least used of our senses, and are used more for receiving information than for communicating it. There are currently very few ways of implementing devices that can generate tastes and smells, and so these two areas are not supported. Whether this is a serious omission remains to be seen, but the tertiary nature of those senses tends to suggest that their incorporation, if it were possible, would focus on specialist applications, for example, in enhancing virtual reality systems.

Even if we do not use other senses in our systems, it is certainly worth thinking about the nature of these senses and what we gain from them as this will improve our understanding of the strengths and weaknesses of visual communication [96].

The next sections of this chapter will look at some of the alternative modes of human–computer communication, concentrating particularly on sound, touch, handwriting and gesture. We will consider how each mode can be used to create richer interaction and provide redundancy.

10.3.1 Sound in the interface

Sound is an important contributor to usability. There is experimental evidence to suggest that the addition of audio confirmation of modes, in the form of changes in keyclicks, reduces errors [237]. Video games offer further evidence, since experts tend to score less well when the sound is turned off than when it is on; they pick up vital clues and information from the sound while concentrating their visual attention on different things. The dual presentation of information through sound and vision supports universal design, by enabling access for users with visual and hearing impairments respectively. It also enables information to be accessed in poorly lit or noisy environments. Sound can convey transient information and does not take up screen space, making it potentially useful for mobile applications.

However, in spite of this, the auditory channel is comparatively little used in standard interfaces, and where it is used it is often peripheral to the interaction. Information provision is predominantly visual. There is a danger that this will over-load the visual channel, demanding that the user attend to too many things at once and select appropriate information from a mass of detail in the display. Reliance on visual information forces attention to remain focussed on the screen, and the per-sistence of visual information means that even detail that is quickly out of date may remain on display after it is required, cluttering the screen further. It also presents significant problems for people with visual impairment, whose access to applications can be severely restricted by solely visual output. More widespread effective use of sound in the interface would alleviate these problems. There are two types of sound that we could use: speech and non-speech.

Speech in the interface

Language is rich and complex. We learn speech naturally as children 'by example' – by listening to and mimicking the speech of those around us. This process seems so effortless that we often do not appreciate its complex structures, and it is not until we attempt to learn a new language later in life, or to make explicit the rules of the one we speak, that the difficulties inherent in language understanding become apparent. This complexity makes speech recognition and synthesis by computer very difficult.

Structure of speech   If we are fully to appreciate the problems involved with the computer-based recognition and generation of speech, we need first to understand the basic structure of speech. We will use English to illustrate but most other lan-guages have similar issues.

The English language is made up of 40 *phonemes*, which are the atomic elements of speech. Each phoneme represents a distinct sound, there being 24 consonants and 16 vowel sounds. Language is more than simple sounds, however. Emphasis, stress, pauses and pitch can all be used to alter the meaning and nature of an utterance, a common example being the rise in pitch at the end of a sentence to indicate a question in English. This alteration in tone and quality of the phonemes is termed *prosody* and is used, in addition to the actual words, to convey a great deal of meaning and emotion within a sentence. Prosodic information gives language its richness and texture, but is very difficult to quantify. Owing to the manner in which sound is produced in the vocal tract, mouth and nose of the speaker, the limitation in response speed means that phonemes sound differently when preceded by different phonemes. This is termed *co-articulation*, and the resulting differences in sound can be used to construct a set of *allophones*, which represent all the different sounds within the language. Ignoring prosodic information, the concatenation of allophones together should produce intelligible, articulate speech. However, depending on the analysis of language used, and the regional accent studied, there are between 120 and 130 allophones. These, in turn, can be formed into *morphemes*, which represent the smallest unit of language that has meaning. They are the basic building blocks of language rather than of speech. Morphemes can be either parts of words or whole words, and they are built into sentences using the rules of grammar of the language.

Even being able to decompose sentences into their basic parts does not mean that we can then understand them: the syntax (structure) only serves as a standard foundation upon which the semantics (meaning) is based. We are rarely aware of the complex structure of speech, and concentrate on extracting the meaning from the sentences we hear, rather than decomposing the sounds into their constituent parts.

Speech recognition   There have been many attempts at developing speech recognition systems, but, although commercial systems are now commonly and cheaply available, their success is still limited to single-user systems that require considerable training.

The complexity of language is one barrier to success, but there are other, more practical, problems also associated with the automatic recognition of the spoken word. Background noise can interfere with the input, masking or distorting the information, while speakers can introduce redundant or meaningless noises into the information stream by repeating themselves, pausing or using 'continuation' noises such as 'ummm' and 'errr' to fill in gaps in their usual speech. Variations between individuals also cause problems; people have unique voices, and systems that are successful are tuned to be sensitive to minute variations in tone and frequency of the speaker's voice – new speakers present different inflections to the system, which then fails to perform as well. A more serious problem is caused by regional accents, which vary considerably. This strong variation upsets the trained response of the recognition system. More serious still is the problem posed by different languages: everything from phonemes up can be different.

The phonetic typewriter

One early successful speech-based system is the *phonetic typewriter*. This uses a neural network that clusters similar sounds together (see Figure 10.1).

Designed to produce typed output from speech input in Finnish, it is trained on one particular speaker, and then generalizes to others. However, its performance with speakers other than the one on which it was trained is noticeably poorer, and it relies on a large dictionary of minute variations to supplement its general transcription mechanism. Without the dictionary, it achieves a significantly lower recognition rate.

One reason that the phonetic typewriter was able to achieve acceptable levels of recognition and transcription is that Finnish is a phonetic language, that is one which is spelt as it sounds. There are other phonetic languages, for example Welsh, but most languages do not have such a straightforward mapping between sound and text. Think of English words such as 'wait' and 'weight' or 'one' and 'won', for example.

Puzzle: How do you pronounce 'ghuti'? (Answer on the web pages!)

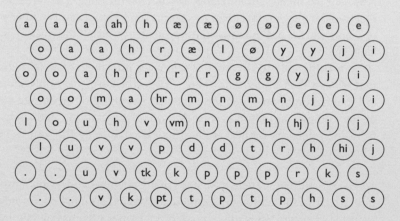

Figure 10.1   The phonetic typewriter

Speech recognition offers another mode of communication that may be used to supplement existing channels or be the primary one. When a user's hands are already occupied, such as in a factory, speech may prove to be the ideal input medium. Speech input does not require the use of a cumbersome keyboard and so in lightweight mobile situations there is a potential role for such systems. It also provides an alternative means of input for users with visual, physical and cognitive impairment as we will see later. Single-user, limited vocabulary systems can work satisfactorily, but the current success rate of recognition for general users and unconstrained language is still low.

Despite its limitations there are commercial systems employing speech recognition. Speech-based word processors are easily available and several computers use speech input as a marketing feature. Telephone-based systems also use speech, but they face a more difficult task as they must be speaker independent. At the simplest end, some systems ask you to speak an extension number, but, as tone dialing becomes universal, the advantage of this over typing the number is dubious! Other systems make more active use of voice, including information systems for airline bookings. These more sophisticated systems work because they are *interactive*: the system reflects back to the user its interpretation of the speech input, allowing the user to enter into a dialog to correct any errors. This is precisely what happens in normal conversation – we don't get it right all the time.

Speech synthesis   Complementary to speech recognition is speech synthesis. The notion of being able to converse naturally with a computer is an appealing one for many users, especially those who do not regard themselves as computer literate, since it reflects their natural, daily medium of expression and communication. However, there are as many problems in speech synthesis as there are in recognition. The most difficult problem is that we are highly sensitive to variations and intonation in speech, and are therefore intolerant of imperfections in synthesized speech. We are so used to hearing natural speech that we find it difficult to adjust to the monotonic, non-prosodic tones that synthesized speech can produce. In fact, most speech synthesizers can deliver a degree of prosody, but in order to decide what intonation to give to a word, the system must have an understanding of the domain. So an effective automatic reader would also need to be able to understand natural language, which is difficult. However, for 'canned' messages and responses, the prosody can be hand coded yielding much more acceptable speech.

Synthesized speech also brings other problems. Being transient, spoken output cannot be reviewed or browsed easily. It is intrusive, requiring either an increase in noise in the office environment or the use of headphones, either of which may be too large a price to pay for the benefits the system may offer.

However, there are some application areas in which speech synthesis has been successful. For users who are blind or partially sighted, synthesized speech offers an output medium which they can access. Screen readers are software packages that read the contents of a computer screen, using synthesized speech. Modern screen readers read more than simply the text on the screen. They read exactly what they find including icons, menus, punctuation and controls. They also read events, such as dialog boxes opening, so that they can be used with graphical interfaces.

Speech synthesis is also useful as a communication tool to assist people with physical disabilities that affect their speech. Here speech synthesis needs to produce output that is as natural as possible with as little input effort from the user as possible, perhaps using a simple switch. Human conversation is rapid and complex, making this a significant challenge. Most communication tools of this type use predefined messages, enabling the user to select a message appropriate to the context quickly and easily.

DESIGN FOCUS

Designing websites for screen readers

While screen readers provide users with visual impairments access to standard interfaces and software, web access can be more problematic. Screen readers can only read textual elements of web pages, so graphics and scripts cannot be interpreted. It is therefore important that web designers take account of these limitations and design sites to be accessible to people using screen readers. For example, HTML 'alt' tags should always be used for necessary graphics, and text alternative menus and navigation controls provided.

In addition, most read text across the page, so text arranged in columns can become garbled. For example, consider text arranged in two columns, such as the opening lines of these nursery rhymes:

Jack and Jill went up the hill   Mary had a little lamb
To fetch a pail of water   Its fleece was white as snow

With some screen readers, this text would be read as 'Jack and Jill went up the hill Mary had a little lamb To fetch a pail of water Its fleece was white as snow' – clearly nonsense. Where possible, text should make sense when read across a page.

Users of screen readers may also find it difficult to follow links embedded in text, particularly where there are several in a block of text. It can therefore be helpful to provide links to the main sections in a clear location where they will be read horizontally, such as at the top of the page.

If you want to experience something of what it is like to access the web using a screen reader, try the simulation produced by the Web Accessibility in Mind project, available at www.webaim.org/simulations/screenreader (accessed March 2003). Their site also contains a wealth of information about web accessibility.

Another useful resource to help you design accessible websites is the Web Accessibility Initiative's (WAI) checklist for accessibility. This is available on their website www.w3.org (accessed March 2003).

A tool that you can use to test your websites for accessibility is Bobby from Watchfire (bobby.cast.org, accessed March 2003). Bobby is a web-based accessibility evaluation tool that highlights problem areas of a given website and encourages accessible solutions. It provides suggestions for improvement using the guidelines provided by the WAI and the US Government's Section 508 legislation. Using Bobby, web designers can test their sites for accessibility and get advice for resolving any problems before the site goes live.

Used as a supplement to other output channels, speech can also enhance applications where the user's visual attention is focussed elsewhere, such as warnings in aircraft cockpits and, more recently, in cars. We will return to some of these applications later in the chapter.

Uninterpreted speech Speech does not have to be recognized by a computer to be useful in the interface. Fixed pre-recorded messages can be used to supplement or replace visual information. Recordings have natural human prosody and pronunciation, although quality is sometimes low. Segments of speech can be used together to construct messages, for example the announcements in many airports and railway stations.

Recordings of users' speech can also be very useful, especially in collaborative applications, for example many readers will have used voicemail systems. Also, recordings can be attached to other artifacts as *audio annotations* in order to communicate with others or to remind oneself at a later time. For example, audio annotations can be attached to Microsoft Word documents.

When recordings are replayed, they can be digitally speeded up. If you simply play an audio recording faster, the pitch rises – and human speech ends up sounding rather like Mickey Mouse. However, *digital signal-processing* techniques can accelerate a recording while keeping the same pitch. Speech can be played back at up to twice the normal rate without any loss of comprehensibility. This can be used in a telephone help desk where a pre-recorded message asks the enquirer to state his problem. The problem can then be replayed at an accelerated rate to the operator, reducing the operator time per enquiry. The utility of such methods needs careful analysis, however. The operator may often begin to act on a message while it is still playing, hence reducing any gain from faster playback. Furthermore, reduced interactivity may lead to more misunderstandings, and the enquirer's waiting time may be increased.

DESIGN FOCUS

Choosing the right kind of speech

If you include speech input in an interface you must decide what level of speech interaction you wish to support:

recording simply recording and replaying messages or annotations;

transcription turning speech into text as in a word processor;

control telling the computer what to do: for example, 'print this file'.

Each level has its own problems and advantages; for example, control only requires a limited vocabulary, but is more dangerous: 'I said print not delete ... !' However, the biggest problem arises if you try to mix these levels. In text we use quotes to make such distinctions, but they are hard in speech: 'insert the word "delete" before the word "before"'.

In fact, for general interface use, speech is best mixed with other modes of communication as happens in everyday life. For example, in a word processor you may use a tablet and pen to ring a word and then say 'move this word to here' as you tap the pen at the target location. This is exactly what you would do when talking through corrections to a document with someone.

Non-speech sound

We have considered the use of speech in the interface, but non-speech sounds can offer a number of advantages. As speech is serial, we have to listen to most of a sentence before we understand what is being said. Non-speech sounds can often be assimilated much more quickly. Speech is language dependent – a speech-based system requires translation for it to be used for another language group. The meaning of non-speech sounds can be learned regardless of language. Speech requires the user's attention. Non-speech sound can make use of the phenomenon of auditory adaptation: background sounds are ignored unless they change or cease. However, a disadvantage is that non-speech sounds have to be learned, whereas the meaning of a spoken message is obvious (at least to a user who is familiar with the language used).

Non-speech sound can be used in a number of ways in interactive systems. It is often used to provide transitory information, such as indications of network or system changes, or of errors. It can also be used to provide status information on background processes, since we are able to ignore continuous sounds but still respond to changes in those sounds. Users of early home computers with their noisy power supplies, and computer operators listening to the chatter of the printer and the spinning of disks and tape drives, both report that they are able to tell what stage a process is at by the characteristic sounds that are made.

Non-speech sound can also be used to provide a second representation of actions and objects in the interface to support the visual mode and provide confirmation for the user. It can be used for navigation round a system, either giving redundant supporting information to the sighted user or providing the primary source of information for the visually impaired. Experiments on auditory navigation [290] have demonstrated that auditory clues are adequate for a user to locate up to eight targets on a screen with reasonable speed and accuracy. This suggests that there is little reason for ignoring the role of sound in interfaces on the grounds that it may be too vague or inaccurate.

But what kind of non-speech sounds should we use in the interface? There are two alternatives: using sounds that occur naturally in the world and using more abstract generated sounds. We will consider an example of each type.

Auditory icons   Auditory icons [141] use natural sounds to represent different types of objects and actions in the interface. The SonicFinder [142] for the Macintosh was developed from these ideas, to enhance the interface through redundancy. Natural sounds are used because people recognize the source of a sound and its behavior rather than timbre and pitch [364]. For example, a noise will be identified as glass breaking or a hollow pipe being tapped. Such recognition is quite sophisticated: we can identify not only the source of a sound (e.g. tapping a pipe) but characteristics of the sound source (e.g. whether the pipe is hollow or solid).

In the SonicFinder, auditory icons are used to represent desktop objects and actions. So, for example, a folder is represented by a papery noise, and throwing something in the wastebasket by the sound of smashing. This helps the user to learn the sounds since they suggest familiar actions from everyday life. However, this advantage also creates a problem for auditory icons. Some objects and actions do not have obvious, naturally occurring sounds that identify them. In these cases a sound effect can be created to suggest the action or object but this moves away from the ideal of using familiar everyday sounds that require little learning. For example, copying has no immediate analog sound and in the SonicFinder it is indicated by the sound of pouring a liquid into a receptacle, with the pitch rising to indicate the progress of the copying.

SharedARK and ARKola

Natural sounds have been used to model environments such as a physics laboratory [145], called *SharedARK* (Shared Alternate Reality Kit) and a virtual manufacturing plant, *ARKola* [147]. In SharedARK, multiple users could perform physics experiments in a virtual laboratory. Sound was used in three different ways: as confirmation of actions, for status information and as aids to navigation. Confirmatory sounds use similar principles to the SonicFinder, providing redundant information that increases feedback. Process and state information sounds exist on two levels, global and local. Global sounds represent the state of the whole system and can be heard anywhere, while local sounds are specific to particular experiments and alter when the user changes from one experiment to another. Navigational information is provided by soundholders, which are auditory landmarks. They can be placed anywhere in the system and get louder as the user moves towards them, decreasing in volume when moving away. This allows the user to wander through an arena much greater than the size of the screen without getting lost and lets him return to specific areas very easily by returning to the soundholder.

In ARKola, a soft drinks factory was modeled, with two users attempting to optimize the factory's output, working remotely from each other and using an audio/video link. Input machines supplied raw materials while output machines capped the bottles and shipped them out. Each machine had an on/off switch and a rate control, with a sound that indicated its status; for example, the bottle dispenser made the sound of clinking glass, with a rhythm that indicated its operating speed. Splashing sounds indicated spilled liquids, while breaking glass showed that bottles were being lost. The users monitored the status of the plant by listening to the auditory clues, and were able to help each other more effectively, since they found it easier to monitor their own machines without having to spend time looking at them, and could hear when something had gone wrong with their partner's part of the system.

Non-speech sounds such as this can convey a lot of meaning very economically. A file arrives in a mailbox and, being a large file, it makes a weighty sound. If it is a text file it makes a rustling noise, whereas a compiled program may make a metallic clang. The sound can be muffled or clear, indicating whether the mailbox is hidden by other windows or not, while the direction of the sound would indicate the position of the mailbox icon on the screen. If the sound then echoes, as it would in a large, empty room, the system load is low. All this information can be presented in a second or so.

Worked exercise   *Think of a set of naturally occurring sounds to represent the operations in a standard drawing package (for example, draw, move, copy, delete, rotate).*

Answer   This can exercise the imagination! Are there natural analogies? For example, does the physical action, say, of drawing have a sound associated with it? The sound of a pencil on paper may be appropriate but is it identifiable? Similarly, a photocopier whirring could represent the copy operation, and tearing paper delete. Rotate and move are more difficult since the physical operation is not associated with a sound. Perhaps direction and movement can be indicated by sounds becoming nearer or more distant?

Earcons

An alternative to using natural sounds is to devise synthetic sounds. *Earcons* [36] use structured combinations of notes, called *motives*, to represent actions and objects (see Figure 10.2). These vary according to rhythm, pitch, timbre, scale and volume. There are two types of combination of earcon. *Compound earcons* combine different motives to build up a specific action, for example combining the motives for 'create' and 'file'. *Family earcons* represent compound earcons of similar types. As an example, operating system errors and syntax errors would be in the 'error' family. In this way, earcons can be hierarchically structured to represent menus. Earcons are easily grouped and refined owing to their compositional and hierarchical nature, but they require learning to associate with a specific task in the interface since there is an

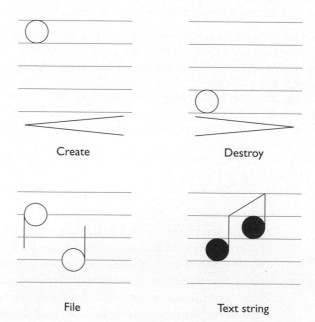

Figure 10.2 Earcons (after Blattner [36], reprinted by permission of Lawrence Erlbaum Associates, Inc.)

arbitrary mapping. Conversely, auditory icons have a semantic relationship with the function that they represent, but can suffer from there being no appropriate sound for some actions.

Earcons provide a structured approach to designing sound for the interface, but can users learn the sounds adequately, and what factors influence their use? Evidence suggests that people can learn to recognize earcons, and that the most important element in distinguishing different sounds is timbre, the characteristic quality of the sound produced by different instruments and voices [47]. Other factors such as pitch, rhythm and register should be used to supplement timbre in creating distinctive sets of musical earcons. Interestingly, the user's musical ability appears to have little effect on his ability to remember earcons: users were able to identify around 80% of earcons from hierarchically ordered sets of 30 or more, regardless of their musical background [45]. It is also possible to create compound earcons by playing sounds in parallel as well as serially. This obviously reduces the time taken to hear the sound but does not affect the user's accuracy [45].

10.3.2 Touch in the interface

We have already considered the importance of touch in our interaction with our environment, in Chapter 1. Touch is the only sense that can be used to both send and receive information. Although it is not yet widely used in interacting with computers, there is a significant research effort in this area and commercial applications are becoming available.

The use of touch in the interface is known as *haptic interaction*. Haptics is a generic term relating to touch, but it can be roughly divided into two areas: cutaneous perception, which is concerned with tactile sensations through the skin; and kinesthetics, which is the perception of movement and position. Both are useful in interaction but they require different technologies.

In Chapter 2, Section 2.6.3, we considered a number of examples of haptic devices, including some based on vibration against the skin (cutaneous) and others on resistance or force feedback (kinesthethic). They facilitate perception of properties such as shape, texture, resistance and temperature as well as comparative spatial properties such as size, height and position. This means haptics can provide information on the character of objects in the interface, as well as more realistic simulations of physical activities, either for entertainment or for training.

In this section, we will look in a little more detail at some of the different types of haptic devices and consider, in particular, the role of haptics in universal design. As we will see, touch can provide both a primary source of information for users with visual impairments and a richer multi-modal experience for sighted users.

One example of a tactile device is an electronic – or soft – braille display. Braille displays are made up of a number of cells (typically between 20 and 80), each containing six or eight electronically controlled pins that move up and down to produce braille representations of characters displayed on the screen. Whereas printed braille normally has six dots per cell, electronic braille typically has eight pins, with the extra two representing additional information about that cell, such as cursor position and character case.

Electronic braille displays benefit from two factors: a well-established tactile notation (braille) and a user group with expertise in using this notation. But can similar techniques be used to provide more generic tactile feedback, such as to display graphics? The problem with using raised pins for this type of display is the resolution required. Braille requires only six or eight pins; a graphical display would require many more, which raises the problem of fitting the necessary number of fast actuators (to move the pins) into a few cubic centimeters. This presents a serious engineering challenge.

The other main type of haptic device is the force feedback device, which provides kinesthetic information back to the user, allowing him to feel resistance, textures, friction and so on. One of the most commonly used examples is the PHANTOM range, from SensAble Technologies. The PHANTOM provides three-dimensional

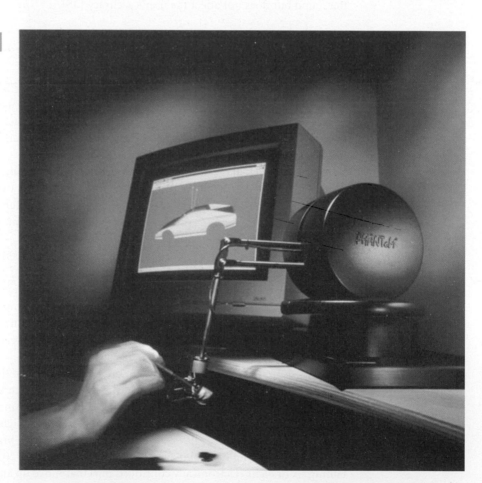

Figure 10.3 A PHANTOM Premium 1.5 haptic device. Source: Courtesy of SensAble Technologies

force feedback, allowing users to touch virtual objects. As well as offering the functionality of the mouse, in addition, the user's movement is monitored by optical sensors on the device, and these, together with models of the virtual objects, are used to calculate the forces applied back to the user. The user therefore can feel the outline and resistance of objects, their texture and position. This type of device has potential application for simulations and training situations where touch is important, such as medicine. It can also be used to provide a haptic 'image' of an interface, providing the user with information about the objects and their functionality based on how they feel. This offers another channel of information, which enhances the richness of the interaction and makes the design more universal.

At present, the hardware needed to support haptic interaction is prohibitively expensive for most users. But this is liable to change as the applications become more widespread and commercially viable.

10.3.3 Handwriting recognition

Like speech, we consider handwriting to be a very natural form of communication. The idea of being able to interpret handwritten input is very appealing, and handwriting appears to offer both textual and graphical input using the same tools. There are problems associated with the use of handwriting as an input medium, however, and in this section we shall consider these. We will first look at the mechanisms for capturing handwritten information, and then look at the problems of interpreting it.

Technology for handwriting recognition

The major piece of technology used to capture handwriting is the digitizing tablet, explained in more detail in Chapter 2. Free-flowing strokes made with a pen are transformed into a series of coordinates, approximately one every 1/50th of a second (or at the sampling rate of the digitizer). Rapid movements produce widely spaced dots, in comparison with slow movements: this introduces immediate errors into the information, since the detail of the stroke between dots is lost, as is the pressure information.

DESIGN FOCUS

Apple Newton

The Apple Newton was the first popular pen-based computer. Other systems, such as the GO Pen-Point computer, were available earlier, but did not achieve a significant breakthrough. One reason is that the Newton targeted the organizer market where miniature keyboards were difficult to use (and anyway managers don't use them!). Also this niche market did not demand large amounts of text input, and the graphical interface made it easy to do non-text-based tasks.

Handwriting recognition was acceptable for a number of reasons: the base algorithm achieved a reasonable level of writer-independent recognition; the algorithm was adaptive – it learned the characteristics of the owner during use; and it was word based, so that idiosyncrasies in connected writing could be learnt for common words. But, most important, it was *interactive*. After a word was written, the Newton printed its interpretation of the word; if it was wrong you could try again or correct it letter by letter. This gave the system a chance to learn and meant that errors were not fatal!

In fact, although it has survived, the Apple Newton, like many devices employing novel input techniques, did not achieve the level of success one might have envisaged. This may be because it arrived at the same time as portable computers became *really* portable, and perhaps because the Apple Newton was only suitable for large pockets (of both a sartorial and financial nature). Smaller organizers with both pen-based input and small keyboards are now available, and it remains to be seen whether these achieve the market breakthrough this technology promises.

Digitizing tablets have been refined by incorporating a thin screen on top to display the information, producing *electronic paper*. Advances in screen technology mean that such devices are small and portable enough to be realistically useful in handheld organizers such as the Apple Newton. Information written onto the digitizer can simply be redisplayed, or stored and redisplayed for further reference. However, while this has limited use in itself, systems are most useful when they are able to interpret the strokes received and produce text. It is this recognition that we will look at next.

Recognizing handwriting

The variation between the handwriting of individuals is large (see Figure 10.4); moreover, the handwriting of a single person varies from day to day, and evolves over the years.

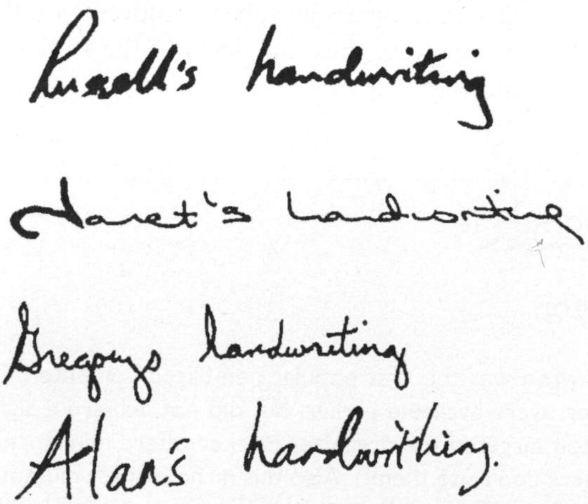

Figure 10.4   Handwriting varies considerably

These problems are reminiscent of those already discussed in speech recognition, and indeed the recognition problem is not dissimilar. The equivalent of co-articulation is also prevalent in handwriting, since different letters are written differently according to the preceding and successive ones. This causes problems for recognition systems, which work by trying to identify the lines that contain text, and then to segment the digitized image into separate characters. This is so difficult to achieve reliably that there are no systems in use today that are good at general cursive script recognition. However, when letters are individually written, with a small separation, the success of systems becomes more respectable, although they have to be trained to recognize the characteristics of the different users. If tested on an untrained person, success is limited again. Many of the solutions that are being attempted in speech recognition are also being tried in handwriting recognition systems, such as whole-word recognition, the use of context to disambiguate characters, and neural networks, which learn by example.

10.3.4 Gesture recognition

Gesture is a component of human–computer interaction that has become the subject of attention in multi-modal systems. Being able to control the computer with certain movements of the hand would be advantageous in many situations where there is no possibility of typing, or when other senses are fully occupied. It could also support communication for people who have hearing loss, if signing could be 'translated' into speech or vice versa. But, like speech, gesture is user dependent, subject to variation and co-articulation. The technology for capturing gestures is expensive, using either computer vision or a special dataglove (see Chapter 2). The dataglove provides easier access to highly accurate information, but is a relatively intrusive technology, requiring the user to wear the special Lycra glove. The interpretation of the sampled data is very difficult, since segmenting the gestures causes problems. A team from Toronto [131] has produced a gesture recognition system that translates hand movements into synthesized speech, using five neural networks working in parallel to learn and then interpret different parts of the inputs.

The Media Room at MIT uses a different approach in order to incorporate gestures into the interaction. The Media Room has one wall that acts as a large screen, with smaller touchscreens on either side of the user, who sits in a central chair. The user can navigate through information using the touchscreens, or by joystick, or by voice. Gestures are incorporated by using a position-sensing cube attached to a wristband worn by the user. The *put that there* system uses this gestural information coupled with speech recognition to allow the user to indicate what should be moved where by pointing at it. This is a much more natural form of interaction than having to specify verbally what it is that has to be moved and describing where it has to go, as well has having the advantage of conciseness. Such a short, simple verbal statement is much more easily interpreted by the speech recognition system than a long and complex one, with the resolution of ambiguity done by interpreting the other mode of interaction, the gesture. Each modality supports the other.

10.4 DESIGNING FOR DIVERSITY

We noted in Chapter 1 that, although we can make general observations about human capabilities, users in fact have different needs and limitations. Interfaces are usually designed to cater for the 'average' user, but unfortunately this may exclude people who are not 'average'. As we saw in the introduction to this chapter, people are diverse and there are many factors that must be taken into account if we are to come close to universal design.

In this section, we will consider briefly some of these factors and the particular challenges that each raises. We will consider three key areas: disability, age and culture.

10.4.1 Designing for users with disabilities

It is estimated that at least 10% of the population of every country has a disability that will affect interaction with computers. Employers and manufacturers of computing equipment have not only a moral responsibility to provide accessible products, but often also a legal responsibility. In many countries, legislation now demands that the workplace must be designed to be accessible or at least adaptable to all – the design of software and hardware should not unnecessarily restrict the job prospects of people with disabilities.

We will look briefly at sensory, physical and cognitive impairments and the issues they raise for interface design.

Visual impairment

The sensory impairment that has attracted the most attention from researchers, perhaps because it is potentially also one of the most debilitating as far as interaction is concerned, is visual impairment. The rise in the use of graphical interfaces reduces the possibilities for visually impaired users. In text-based interaction, screen readers using synthesized speech or braille output devices provided complete access to computers: input relied on touch-typing, with these mechanisms providing the output. However, today the standard interface is graphical. Screen readers and braille output are far more restricted in interpreting the graphical interface, as we saw in Section 10.3.1, meaning that access to computers, and therefore work involving computers, has been reduced rather than expanded for visually impaired people.

There are two key approaches to extending access: the use of sound and the use of touch. We have already considered these in Section 10.3 so we will summarize only briefly here.

A number of systems use sound to provide access to graphical interfaces for people with visual impairment. In Section 10.3.1 we looked at a range of approaches to the use of sound such as speech, earcons and auditory icons. All of these have been used in interfaces for blind users.

Soundtrack

Soundtrack is an early example of a word processor with an auditory interface, designed for users who are blind or partially sighted [118]. The visual items in the display have been given auditory analogs, made up of tones, with synthesized speech also being used. A two-row grid of four columns is Soundtrack's main screen (see Figure 10.5); each cell makes a different tone when the cursor is in it, and by using these tones the user can navigate around the system. The tones increase in pitch from left to right, while the two rows have different timbres. Clicking on a cell makes it speak its name, giving precise information that can reorient a user who is lost or confused. Double clicking on a cell reveals a submenu of items associated with the main screen item. Items in the submenu also have tones; moving down the menu causes the tone to fall whilst moving up makes it rise. A single click causes the cell to speak its name, as before, whilst double clicking executes the associated action.

Soundtrack allows text entry by speaking the words or characters as they are entered, with the user having control over the degree of feedback provided. It was found that users tended to count the different tones in order to locate their position on the screen, rather than just listen to the tones themselves, although one user with musical training did use the pitch.

Soundtrack provides an auditory solution to representing a visually based word processor, though the results are not extensible to visual interfaces in general. However, it does show that the human auditory system is capable of coping with the demands of highly interactive systems, and that the notion of auditory interfaces is a reasonable one.

File Menu	Edit Menu	Sound Menu	Format Menu
Alert	Dialog	Document1	Document2

Figure 10.5   The screen division in Soundtrack. Source: Courtesy of Alistair D. N. Edwards

Soundtrack (see the box above) was an early example of the use of non-speech sound to provide an auditory interface to a word processor. A major limitation of this application was the fact that it was a specialized system; it could not be used to augment commercially available software. Ideally, users with disabilities should have

DESIGN FOCUS

Mathematics for the blind

Solve the following equation: $3(x - 2) + 4 = 7 - 2(3 - x)$.

Did you do it in your head or use a piece of paper? When an equation is even slightly complex the instant response of a sighted person is to reach for paper and pencil. The paper acts as an *external memory*, allowing you to record and recall previous steps in a calculation. Blind children learning mathematics have to perform nearly all such calculations in their head, putting them at a severe disadvantage.

Mathtalk is a system developed as part of a European project to create a mathematics workstation for blind people [330]. It uses speech synthesis to speak formulae, and keyboard input to navigate and manipulate them. The first stage, simply speaking a formula out loud, is complex in itself. Given the spoken equation 'three *x* plus four equals seven', how do you know whether this is '$3x + 4 = 7$' or '$3(x + 4) = 7$'? To make it unambiguous one could say the latter as 'three open bracket *x* plus four close bracket equals seven', but this soon becomes very tedious. In fact, when reading mathematics people use several cues in their speech: longer and shorter gaps between terms, and prosody: rising and falling pitch (see Figure 10.6). The Mathtalk system includes a set of rules for generating such patterns suitable for most equations.

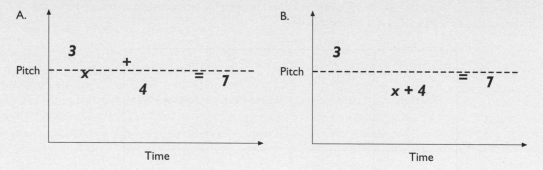

Figure 10.6   Pausing and pitch help distinguish between two expressions

Visual interaction with paper isn't just at the level of reading and writing whole equations. Recall from Chapter 1 that reading usually includes *regressions* where our eyes move backwards as well as forwards through text. Also, when seeing graphical material (remember that mathematics makes heavy use of brackets, symbols, superscripts, etc.), we rely on getting a quick feel for the material at a glance before examining it in detail. Both of these factors are crucial when reading an equation and so Mathtalk supports rapid keyboard-based navigation *within* each equation, and *algebra earcons*, short motives based on the rise and fall of the prosody of an equation.

Notice that Mathtalk uses *keyboard* input combined with speech output. Speech input is slow and error-prone compared with a keyboard. Braille output can also be used for mathematics, but only a small percentage of blind people read braille. Choosing the right input and output devices requires a deep knowledge of the user population and careful analysis of the intended tasks.

access to the same applications as anyone else. Outspoken is a Macintosh application that uses synthetic speech to make other Macintosh applications available to visually impaired users. A common problem with this and other screen readers and talking browsers (see Section 10.3.1) is the sheer amount of information represented. Browsing is difficult and all of the information must be held in the head of the user, putting a heavy load on memory.

A more recent development is the use of touch in the interface. As we saw in Section 10.3.2, there are two key approaches to this, both of which can be used to support people with visual impairment. Tactile interaction is already widely used in electronic braille displays, which represent what is on the screen through a dynamic braille output. It could also be used to provide more information about graphics and shape, if the engineering challenges of building higher resolution tactile devices can be overcome. Force feedback devices also have the potential to improve accessibility to users with visual impairment, since elements in the interface can be touched, and edges, textures and behavior used to indicate objects and actions. A limitation of this technology at present is that objects must be rendered using specialist software in order for the devices to calculate the appropriate force to apply back to the user. This again represents a move away from use of generic applications to specialist applications. However, it is likely that major applications will become 'haptic enabled' in the near future.

Hearing impairment

Compared with a visual disability where the impact on interacting with a graphical interface is immediately obvious, a hearing impairment may appear to have little impact on the use of an interface. After all, it is the visual not the auditory channel that is predominantly used. To an extent this is true, and computer technology can actually enhance communication opportunities for people with hearing loss. Email and instant messaging are great levellers and can be used equally by hearing and deaf users alike.

Gesture recognition has also been proposed to enable translation of signing to speech or text, again to improve communication particularly with non-signers.

However, the increase in multimedia and the use of sound in interfaces has, ironically, created some access difficulties for people with hearing problems. Many multimedia presentations contain auditory narrative. If this is not supplemented by textual captions, this information is lost to deaf users. Captioning audio content, where there is not already a graphical or textual version, also has the advantage of making audio files easier and more efficient to index and search, which in turn enhances the experience of all users – a sure sign of good universal design!

Physical impairment

Users with physical disabilities vary in the amount of control and movement that they have over their hands, but many find the precision required in mouse control difficult. Speech input and output is an option for those without speech difficulties.

An alternative is the eyegaze system (Chapter 2), which tracks eye movements to control the cursor, or a keyboard driver that can be attached to the user's head. If the user is unable to control head movement, gesture and movement tracking can be used to allow the user control. If the user has limited use of a keyboard, a predictive system, such as the Reactive keyboard [157], can help, by anticipating the commands that are being typed and offering them for execution. This can cut the typing requirement considerably. Predictions are based on what the user has typed in the current session or a previous one. The predictions therefore anticipate within the context in which the user is currently working (for example, operating system commands, programming text or free text). Figure 10.7 shows an interaction using the Reactive keyboard.

```
$   mail                                           ↑N
    cd news                                        ↑W
    cd news                                        ↑N
    cd rk/papers/ieee.computer                     ↑L
    cd rk/papers/ieee.computer

$   emacs paper.tex                                ↑L
    emacs paper.tex

$   rm paper.tex.CKP paper.tex.BAK                 ↑L
    rm paper.tex.CKP paper.tex.BAK

$   wc -w paper.tex                                ↑L
    wc -w paper.tex

$   readnews -n comp.sources.unix                  ↑N
    mail                                           ↑W
    mail                                           ↑N
    mail bdarragh%uncamult.bitnet@ucnet.ucalgary.c ↑L
    mail bdarragh%uncamult.bitnet@ucnet.ucalgary.c
```

User's dialog with the Reactive keyboard.
Only the last line in each group is actually executed.

Key	Description
↑C (control-C)	Accept the next predicted character
↑W	Accept the next predicted word
↑L	Accept the whole predicted line
↑N	Show the next alternative prediction
↑P	Show the previous alternative prediction

Reactive keyboard commands

Figure 10.7 An interaction using the Reactive keyboard. Source: Courtesy of Saul Greenberg

Speech impairment

For users with speech and hearing impairments, multimedia systems provide a number of tools for communication, including synthetic speech (see Section 10.3.1) and text-based communication and conferencing systems (see Chapter 19). Textual communication is slow, which can lower the effectiveness of the communication. Predictive algorithms have been used to anticipate the words used and fill them in, to reduce the amount of typing required. Conventions can help to provide context, which is lost from face-to-face communication, for example the 'smilie' :-), to indicate a joke. Facilities to allow turn-taking protocols to be established also help natural communication [256]. Speech synthesis also needs to be rapid to reflect natural conversational pace, so responses can be pre-programmed and selected using a single switch.

Dyslexia

Users with cognitive disabilities such as dyslexia can find textual information difficult. In severe cases, speech input and output can alleviate the need to read and write and allow more accurate input and output. In cases where the problem is less severe, spelling correction facilities can help users. However, these need to be designed carefully: often conventional spelling correction programs are useless for dyslexic users since the programs do not recognize their idiosyncratic word construction methods. As well as simple transpositions of characters, dyslexic users may spell phonetically, and correction programs must be able to deal with these errors.

Consistent navigation structure and clear signposting cues are also important to people with dyslexia. Color coding information can help in some cases and provision of graphical information to support textual can make the meaning of text easier to grasp.

Autism

Autism affects a person's ability to communicate and interact with people around them and to make sense of their environment. This manifests itself in a range of ways but is characterized by the *triad of impairments*:

1. Social interaction – problems in relating to others in a meaningful way or responding appropriately to social situations.
2. Communication – problems in understanding verbal and textual language including the use of gestures and expressions.
3. Imagination – problems with rigidity of thought processes, which may lead to repetitive behavior and inflexibility.

How might universal design of technology assist people with autism? There are two main areas of interest: communication and education.

Communication and social interaction are major areas of difficulty for people with autism. Computers, on the other hand, are often motivating, perhaps because they are relatively consistent, predictable and impersonal in their responses. The user is in control. Computer-mediated communication and virtual environments have been suggested as possible ways of enabling people with autism to communicate more easily with others, by giving the user control over the situation. Some people with autism have difficulties with language and may be helped by graphical representations of information and graphical input to produce text and speech. Again this is supported by providing redundancy in the design.

Computers may also have a role to play in education of children with autism, particularly by enabling them to experience (through virtual environments and games) social situations and learn appropriate responses. This can again provide a secure and consistent environment where the child is in control of his own learning. The use of computers to support people with autism in this way is still a new research area and it is likely that new software and tools will develop in the next few years.

10.4.2 Designing for different age groups

We have considered how people differ along a range of sensory, physical and cognitive abilities. However, there are other areas of diversity that impact upon the way we design interfaces. One of these is age. In particular, older people and children have specific needs when it comes to interactive technology.

Older people

The proportion of older people in the population is growing steadily. Contrary to popular stereotyping, there is no evidence that older people are averse to using new technologies, so this group represents a major and growing market for interactive applications. People are living longer, have more leisure time and disposable income, and older people have increased independence. These factors have all led to an increase in older users.

But the requirements of the older population may differ significantly from other population groups, and will vary considerably within the population group. The proportion of disabilities increases with age: more than half of people over 65 have some kind of disability. Just as in younger people with disabilities, technology can provide support for failing vision, hearing, speech and mobility. New communication tools, such as email and instant messaging, can provide social interaction in cases where lack of mobility or speech difficulties reduce face-to-face possibilities. Mobile technologies can be used to provide memory aids where there is age-related memory loss.

Some older users, while not averse to using technology, may lack familiarity with it and fear learning. They may find the terminology used in manuals and training books difficult to follow and alien (words like 'monitor' and 'boot', for example, may have a completely different meaning to an older person than a young person). Interests and concerns may also be different from younger users.

Once again, basic universal design principles are important here. Access to information must make use of redundancy and support the use of access technologies. Designs must be clear and simple and forgiving of errors. In addition, thought needs to be given to sympathetic and relevant training aimed at the user's current knowledge and skills.

In spite of the potential benefits of interactive technology to older people, very little attention has been paid to this area until recently. Researchers are now beginning to address issues such as how technology can best support older people, what the key design issues are, and how older people can be effectively included in the design process [46], and this area is likely to grow in importance in the future.

Children

Like older people, children have distinct needs when it comes to technology, and again, as a population, they are diverse. The requirements of a three year old will be quite different from those of a 12 year old, as will be the methods that can be used to uncover them. Children are, however, different from adults, and have their own goals and likes and dislikes. It is therefore important to involve them in the design of interactive systems that are for their use, though this in itself can be challenging as they may not share the designer's vocabulary or be able to verbalize what they think. Design approaches have therefore been developed specifically to include children actively as members of the design team. Alison Druin's Cooperative Inquiry approach [110] is based on contextual inquiry and participatory design, which we will consider in more detail in Chapter 13. Children are included in an *intergenera tional design team* that focusses on understanding and analyzing context. Team members, including children, use a range of sketching and note-taking techniques to record their observations. Paper prototyping, using art tools familiar to children, enables both adults and children to participate in building and refining prototype designs on an equal footing. The approach has been used effectively to develop a range of new technologies for children.

As well as their likes and dislikes, children's abilities will also be different from those of adults. Younger children may have difficulty using a keyboard for instance, and may not have well-developed hand–eye coordination. Pen-based interfaces can be a useful alternative input device [300]. Again, universal design principles guide us in designing interfaces that children can use. Interfaces that allow multiple modes of input, including touch or handwriting, may be easier for children than keyboard and mouse. Redundant displays, where information is presented through text, graphics and sound will also enhance their experience.

10.4.3 Designing for cultural differences

The final area of diversity we will consider is cultural difference. Cultural difference is often used synonymously with national differences but this is too simplistic. Whilst there are clearly important national cultural differences, such as those we saw in Chapter 5, other factors such as age, gender, race, sexuality, class, religion and political persuasion, may all influence an individual's response to a system. This is particularly the case when considering websites where often the explicit intention is to design for a particular culture or subculture.

Clearly, while all of these contribute to a person's cultural identity, they will not all always be relevant in the design of a given system. However, we can draw out some key factors that we need to consider carefully if we are to practice universal design. These include language, cultural symbols, gestures and use of color.

We encountered the problem of localization of software in Chapter 5. While toolkits, with different language resource databases, facilitate the translation of menu items, error messages and other text into the local language, this does not fully deal with the language issue. Layouts and designs may reflect a language read from left to right and top to bottom, which will be unworkable with languages that do not follow this pattern.

Similarly, symbols have different meanings in different cultures. As we saw in Chapter 5, ticks ✓ and crosses ✗ represent positive and negative respectively in some cultures, and are interchangeable in others. The rainbow is a symbol of covenant with God in Judeo–Christian religions, of diversity in the gay community and of hope and peace in the cooperative movement. We cannot assume that everyone will interpret symbols in the same way and should ensure that alternative meanings of symbols will not create problems or confusion for the user. The study of the meaning of symbols is known as *semiotics* and is a worthwhile diversion for the student of universal design.

Another area where diversity can cause misunderstanding is in the use of gesture. Recently, one of the authors was teaching a new class of international students and was disconcerted to see one sitting in the front row, smiling and shaking his head. After the lecture this student came and asked a question. Every time the author asked the student if he understood the explanation, he shook his head, so further explanation ensued, much to the frustration of the student! It was only after a few minutes that it became clear: the student was from India and his gestural convention was to shake his head in agreement, the opposite of the European interpretation of the gesture. Use of gesture is quite common in video and animation and care must be taken with differences such as this. As interactions begin to incorporate gesture in virtual reality and avatars, issues such as this will become even more significant.

Finally, colors are often used in interfaces to reflect 'universal' conventions, such as red for danger and green for go. But how universal are these conventions? In fact, red and green mean many different things in different countries. As well as danger, red represents life (India), happiness (China) and royalty (France). Green is a symbol of fertility (Egypt) and youth (China) as well as safety (Anglo-American). It is difficult to assume any universal interpretation of color but the intended significance of particular colors can be supported and clarified through redundancy – providing the same information in another form as well.

10.5   SUMMARY

Universal design is about designing systems that are accessible by all users in all circumstances, taking account of human diversity in disabilities, age and culture. Universal design helps everyone – for example, designing a system so that it can be used by someone who is deaf or hard of hearing will benefit other people working in noisy environments or without audio facilities. Designing to be accessible to screen-reading systems will make websites better for mobile users and older browsers.

Multi-modal systems provide access to system information and functionality through a range of different input and output channels, exploiting redundancy. Such systems will enable users with sensory, physical or cognitive impairments to make use of the channels that they can use most effectively. But all users benefit from multi-modal systems that utilize more of our senses in an involving interactive experience.

For any design choice we should ask ourselves whether our decision is excluding someone and whether there are any potential confusions or misunderstandings in our choice.

EXERCISES

10.1 Is multi-modality always a good thing? Justify your answer.

10.2 What are (i) auditory icons and (ii) earcons? How can they be used to benefit both visually impaired and sighted users?

10.3 Research your country's legislation relating to accessibility of technology for disabled people. What are the implications of this to your future career in computing?

10.4 Take your university website or another site of your choice and assess it for accessibility using Bobby. How would you recommend improving the site?

10.5 How could systems be made more accessible to older users?

10.6 Interview either (i) a person you know over 65 or (ii) a child you know under 16 about their experience, attitude and expectations of computers. What factors would you take into account if you were designing a website aimed at this person?

10.7 Use the screen reader simulation available at www.webaim.org/simulations/screenreader to experience something of what it is like to access the web using a screen reader. Can you find the answers to the test questions on the site?

RECOMMENDED READING

M. F. Story, J. L. Mueller and R. L. Mace, *The Universal Design File: Designing for People of All Ages and Abilities*, The Center for Universal Design, NC State University, USA, 1998. Available at: www.design.ncsu.edu/cud/pubs/center/books/ud_file/toc3b14.htm (last accessed March 2003).
A full discussion of universal design principles with examples to illustrate.

A. D. N. Edwards, editor, *Extra-ordinary Human–Computer Interaction*, Cambridge University Press, 1993.
A collection of papers representing research on interfaces for users with disabilities. The first of its kind.

The Web Accessibility Initiative: www.w3.org/WAI/
The World Wide Web Consortium's own project to make the web universally accessible. Contains extensive advice and guidelines.

I. Pitt and A. Edwards, *Design of Speech-based Devices: A Practical Guide*, Springer, 2002.
Covers the use of speech in the interface, including both the practical and theoretical issues.

J. Yunker, *Beyond Borders: Web Globalization Strategies*, New Riders Publishing, 2002.
A practical guide to internationalization of websites.

D. J. Moore and J. Taylor, Interactive multimedia systems for people with autism, *Journal of Educational Media*, Vol. 25, No. 3, pp. 169–77, 2001.
A useful review of the actual and potential uses of interactive media in the education of people with autism.

USER SUPPORT

OVERVIEW

- Users have different requirements for support at different times.

- User support should be:
  - available but unobtrusive
  - accurate and robust
  - consistent and flexible.

- User support comes in a number of styles:
  - command-based methods
  - context-sensitive help
  - tutorial help
  - online documentation
  - wizards and assistants
  - adaptive help.

- Design of user support must take account of:
  - presentation issues
  - implementation issues.

There is often an implicit assumption that if an interactive system is properly designed it will be completely intuitive to use and the user will require little or no help or training. This may be a grand ideal but it is far from true with even the best-designed systems currently available. It is even perhaps an unhelpful ideal: a computer is a complex piece of equipment – what other such equipment do we expect people to use without instruction or help? A more helpful approach is to assume that the user will require assistance at various times and design this help into the system.

The type of assistance users require varies and is dependent on many factors: their familiarity with the system, the job they are trying to do, and so on. There are four main types of assistance that users require:

■ quick reference
■ task-specific help
■ full explanation
■ tutorial.

Quick reference is used primarily as a reminder to the user of the details of tools he is basically familiar with and has used before. It may, for example, be used to find a particular command option, or to remind the user of the syntax of the command. Task-specific help is required when the user has encountered a problem in performing a particular task or when he is uncertain how to apply the tool to his particular problem. The help that is offered is directly related to what is being done. The more experienced or inquisitive user may require a full explanation of a tool or command to enable him to understand it more fully. This explanation will almost certainly include information that the user does not need at that time. The fourth type of support required by users is tutorial help. This is particularly aimed at new users of a tool and provides step-by-step instruction (perhaps by working through examples) of how to use the tool.

Each of these types of user support is complementary – they are required at different points in the user's experience with the system and fulfill distinct needs. Within these types of required support there will be numerous pieces of information that the user wants – definitions, examples, known errors and error recovery information, command options and accelerators, to name but a few. Some of these may be provided within the design of the interface itself but others must be included within the help or support system. We will look at appropriate ways of supporting these requirements. The different types of help required also imply the need for provision of different types of help system. In this chapter, we will look at a number of different types of user support system and will try to determine how to design a good user support system.

A distinction is often made between help systems and documentation. Help systems are problem oriented and specific, whereas documentation is system oriented and generic. This is an artificial distinction when considering the design of such systems since the same principles apply to both, and indeed there is a lot of overlap between the two. Instead of drawing a fixed line between the two, we will consider all types of user support in terms of the requirements they fulfill. We will also concentrate on online support, although much of what is said will be helpful in designing paper documentation and tutorials. Before we look in more detail at the different approaches to providing user support, we will think for a while about the general requirements that the ideal help system should have.

11.2   REQUIREMENTS OF USER SUPPORT

If we were to design the ideal help system, what would it look like? This is a difficult question to answer, but we can point to some features that we might like our help system to have. Not every help system will have all of these features, sometimes for good reason, but they are useful as benchmarks against which we can test the support tools we design. Then, if our system does not have these features, it will be by design and not by accident! Some of these terms have also been used in Chapter 7 in discussing principles for usability. The use of the terms here is more constrained but related.

11.2.1 Availability

The user needs to be able to access help at any time during his interaction with the system. In particular, he should not have to quit the application he is working on in order to open the help application. Ideally, it should run concurrently with any other application. This is obviously a problem for non-windowed systems if the help system is independent of the application that is running. However, in windowed systems there is no reason why a help facility should not be available constantly, at the press of a button.

11.2.2 Accuracy and completeness

It may seem obvious to state that the assistance provided should be accurate and complete. But in an age where applications are frequently updated, and different versions may be active at the same time, it is not a trivial problem. However, if the assistance provided proves not to match the actual behavior of the system the user will, at best, become disillusioned with the help facilities, and, at worst, get into difficulties. As well as providing an accurate reflection of the current state of the system, help should cover the *whole* system. This completeness is very important if the help provided is to be used effectively. The designer cannot predict the parts of the system the user will need help with, and must therefore assume that all parts must be supported. Finding no help available on a topic of interest is guaranteed to frustrate the user.

11.2.3 Consistency

As we have noted, users require different types of help for different purposes. This implies that a help system may incorporate a number of parts. The help provided by each of these must be consistent with all the others and within itself. Online help should also be consistent with paper documentation. It should be consistent in terms of content, terminology and style of presentation. This is also an issue where applications have internal user support – these should be consistent across the system. It is unhelpful if a command is described in one way here and in another there, or if the way in which help is accessed varies across applications. In fact, consistency itself can be thought of as a means of supporting the user since it reinforces learning of system usage.

11.2.4 Robustness

Help systems are often used by people who are in difficulty, perhaps because the system is behaving unexpectedly or has failed altogether. It is important then that the help system itself should be robust, both by correct error handling and predictable behavior. The user should be able to rely on being able to get assistance when required. For these reasons robustness is even more important for help systems than for any other part of the system.

11.2.5 Flexibility

Many help systems are rigid in that they will produce the same help message regardless of the expertise of the person seeking help or the context in which they are working. A flexible help system will allow each user to interact with it in a way appropriate to his needs. This will range from designing a modularized interactive help system, through context-sensitive help, to a full-blown adaptive help system, which will infer the user's expertise and task. We will look at context-sensitive and adaptive help in more detail later in the chapter. However, any help system can be designed to allow greater interactivity and flexibility in the level of help presented. For example, help systems built using hypertext principles allow the user to browse through the help, expanding topics as required. The top level provides a map of the subjects covered by the help and the user can get back to this level at any point. Although hypertext may not be appropriate for all help systems, the principle of flexible access is a useful one.

11.2.6 Unobtrusiveness

The final principle for help system design is unobtrusiveness. The help system should not prevent the user from continuing with normal work, nor should it interfere with the user's application. This is a problem at both ends of the spectrum. At one end the textual help system on a non-windowed interface may interrupt the user's work. A possible solution to this if no alternative is available is to use a split-screen presentation.

At the other end of the spectrum, an adaptive help system that can provide help actively on its own initiative, rather than at the request of the user, can intrude on the user and so become a hindrance rather than a help. It is important with these types of system that the 'suggest' option can be overridden by the user and switched off!

11.3 APPROACHES TO USER SUPPORT

As we noted in the previous section, there are a number of different approaches to providing help, each of which meets a particular need. These vary from simple captions to full adaptive help and tutoring systems. In this section we will concentrate on the styles of help provided rather than any particular help system (although we will use real help systems for illustration). We will then go on to look at adaptive help in more detail.

11.3.1 Command assistance

Perhaps the most basic approach to user support is to provide assistance at the command level – the user requests help on a particular command and is presented with a help screen or manual page describing it. This is the approach used in the UNIX *man* help system and the DOS *help* command, as well as through the search in Windows help.

This type of help is simple and efficient if the user knows what he wants to know about and is seeking either a reminder or more detailed information. However, it assumes that the user does know what he is looking for, which is often not the case. In any complex computer system there will be some commands that the user knows well and can use and some of which he is aware but uses rarely. Command assistance deals well with these. However, there will also be commands that the user does not know about but needs, and even commands that the user thinks exist but which do not. Command assistance cannot provide the user with help for these two groups of command.

11.3.2 Command prompts

In command line interfaces, command prompts provide help when the user encounters an error, usually in the form of correct usage prompts. Such prompts are useful if the error is a simple one, such as incorrect syntax, but again they assume knowledge of the command.

Another form of command prompting, which is not specifically intended to provide help but which supports the user to a limited degree, is the use of menus and selectable icons. These provide an aid to memory as well as making explicit what commands are available at a given time. However, they still assume a certain amount of knowledge about what the commands are for, so additional support is still required.

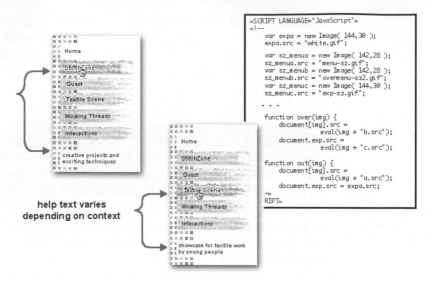

Figure 11.1 Context sensitive help on a web page using JavaScript rollovers

11.3.3 Context-sensitive help

Some help systems are context sensitive. These range from those that have specific knowledge of the particular user (which we will consider under adaptive help) to those that provide a simple help key or function that is interpreted according to the context in which it is called and will present help accordingly. Such systems are not necessarily particularly sophisticated. However, they do move away from placing the onus on the user to remember the command. They are often used in menu-based systems to provide help on menu options. The Microsoft Office *What's This?* option, tool-tips and some kinds of web page rollover are examples of this. When enabled, explanatory text is displayed when the cursor is over a screen widget (see Figure 11.1). The invocation of help is interpreted in terms of the context in which it is made.

11.3.4 Online tutorials

Online tutorials allow the user to work through the basics of an application within a test environment. The user can progress at his own speed and can repeat parts of the tutorial if needed. He will also get a feel for how the application works by experimenting with examples, albeit small ones, or by watching an automated demonstration of how to perform a task.

Most online tutorials have no intelligence: they know nothing about the user and his previous experience, nor about the domain nor even about teaching style. Intelligent tutoring systems, which use similar techniques to adaptive help systems (see Section 11.4), attempt to address this issue but, apart from tutoring programming applications, are impractical as tutorials for most applications. Online tutorials are therefore inflexible and often unforgiving. Some will fail to recognize the correct answer to a problem, simply because it is not formatted as expected.

An alternative to the traditional online tutorial is to allow the user to learn the system by exploring and experimenting with a version with limited functionality. This is the idea behind the *Training Wheels* interface proposed by Carroll and his colleagues at IBM [60]. The user is presented with a version of the full interface in which some of the functionality has been disabled. He can explore the rest of the system freely but if he attempts to use the blocked functionality he is told that it is unavailable. This approach allows the user freedom to investigate the system as he pleases but without risk. It was found that new users spent more time using this system than they did the full version, spent less time recovering from errors and gained a better understanding of the operation of the system.

11.3.5 Online documentation

Online documentation effectively makes the existing paper documentation available on computer. This makes the material available continually (assuming the machine is running!) in the same medium as the user's work and, potentially, to a large number of users concurrently. However, it can be argued that the type of (usually large) manuals that are appropriate as paper reference systems are less appropriate online. Paper is a familiar medium to most of us, and it is still the case that people prefer reading text on paper than on a computer screen. We have developed quite sophisticated browsing skills with a paper medium and books are designed to provide cues to aid this, such as indexing, contents and page numbering, as well as having physical cues such as position in the book. These features are not reproduced in most documentation systems. But paper manuals get lost easily, are constrained to one physical location, and are invariably somewhere else when you want them. Online documentation is one way of avoiding these problems.

Documentation is designed to provide a full description of the system's functionality and behavior in a systematic manner. It provides generic information that is not directed at any particular problem. The amount of information contained in manual pages is usually high, which can in itself create problems for the user – there is too much detail and this effectively 'masks' the information the user wants to find. Perhaps for this reason, online documentation is often used by more expert users as a resource or reference, sometimes to enable them to advise less experienced users. The experts may not know the information off the top of their head but they know where to find it and how to extract the details that are relevant to a given problem.

The use of hypertext can make online documentation more accessible to the inexperienced user (see Chapter 21 for more details of hypertext). Hypertext stores text in a network and connects related sections of text using selectable links. By clicking on a link, the user can go to a related subject instantly. Documentation structured using hypertext supports browsing and usually includes different media (for example, diagrams and visual examples). An example is the help system shown in Figure 11.2, and most Windows applications' help systems.

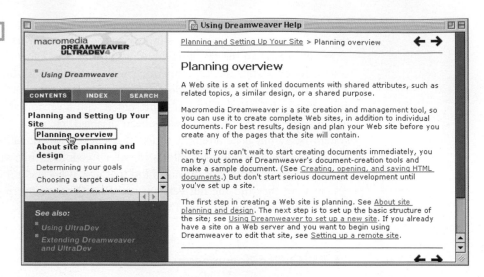

Figure 11.2 Screen shot of the online documentation for Macromedia's Dreamweaver Ultradev version 4.0. Courtesy of Macromedia, Inc.

However, this does suffer from a problem common to hypertext systems – navigation. The user can get lost within the hypertext and lose track of where he is and where he has been. A facility to return 'home' (to the top level) is usually provided but this may mean that the user wastes considerable time restarting his search.

An alternative approach which attempts to simplify online documentation and make it more accessible to novice and casual users is the *minimal manual* [58]. This simplifies the documentation by stripping out all but the bare essentials. The documentation that remains is focussed towards the user's tasks and emphasizes error recovery. Experiments with this manual showed that users learned to use the system 40% faster than with the full manual.

Simple guidelines for online documentation

- Use clear structure with headings to provide signposting.
- Organize information according to user tasks.
- Keep sentences short, to the point and jargon free. Use simple but unpatronizing language.
- Set out procedures in order and number steps. Highlight important steps.
- Use examples where possible.
- Support searching via an index, contents, glossary and free search.
- Include a list of error messages.
- Include Frequently Asked Questions (FAQ) with clear answers.

(Adapted from Hobbs and Moore [177]).

11.3.6 Wizards and assistants

A *wizard* is a task-specific tool that leads the user through the task, step by step, using information supplied by the user in response to questions along the way. They are distinct from demonstrations in that they allow the user actually to complete the task. For example, if the user wishes to format a resumé, the Microsoft Word resumé wizard will take him through a series of questions on the style and sections required, and ask him to enter some basic personal data. The wizard then creates a resumé matching the parameters submitted.

Wizards are common in modern applications and provide support for task completion. The user can perform quite complex tasks safely, quickly and accurately. This is particularly helpful in the case of infrequent tasks where the learning cost of doing the task manually may be prohibitive or where there are many steps that must be completed in a specific sequence. However, wizards can be unnecessarily constraining, they may not offer the user the options he wants, or they may request information that the user does not have. A well-designed wizard will allow the user to move back a step as well as forward, will provide a progress indicator showing how much of the task is completed and how many steps remain, and will offer sufficient information to allow the user to answer the questions.

Another more recent development in user support is the *assistant*. Assistants are software tools that monitor user behavior and offer suggestions or hints when they recognize familiar sequences. An early example of this is Eager (see also Chapter 4), a software agent that watches users as they work. When it notices the user repeating a sequence of actions, a cat icon appears, suggesting the next action. The user can accept or ignore the suggestion. Eager is unobtrusive and under user control at all times.

More recent examples of assistants have not been so successful. The Microsoft Office Assistant, 'Clippy', the infamous animated paper clip with the expressive eyebrows, was introduced in Office 97 but scrapped just a few years later with the introduction of XP. The official reason is that XP features make the need for the Office Assistant redundant, but the underlying reason is clear from Microsoft's own self-deprecating 'Clippy' homepage – the paper clip assistant was universally despised as irritating and unhelpful. So what went wrong? Remember the requirements for online help that we outlined at the beginning? One of these states that online assistance should be unobtrusive, and Clippy, with his long lists of suggestions, and continuous animations, was anything but. In addition, the suggestions made were often inappropriate – 'It looks like you're writing a letter' when you are in fact doing something completely different. Finally, the embodiment of the paper clip, though intended to be 'cute', was perceived by many frequent users as simply irritating.

Microsoft Office Assistant may have retired but he provides an important lesson in online user support. Help must be under the user's control and offers of help should be unobtrusive – it should not be up to the user to switch off the assistant or to close it down. The replacement Microsoft XP features such as *smart tags* have learned this lesson. Smart tags provide rapid access to actions associated with a particular task (for instance formatting a table) much as Office Assistant did. But smart tags are indicated by a small icon, which appears near the object of interest, then disappears when the user performs another action. It is up to the user to select the smart tag if it is of interest at that point, but the icon is small and unobtrusive enough to be ignored if not required. It is interesting that the tags are offered through a functional iconic representation – it seems that assistants with 'attitude' are out!

11.4 ADAPTIVE HELP SYSTEMS

In any large or complex computer system, users will be familiar with a subset of the available functionality, demonstrating expertise in some applications and having no experience with others, even to the point of being unaware of their existence. In addition, different users will have different needs and levels of understanding. Adaptive help systems attempt to address these problems by adapting the help that they provide to the individual user who is making the request and by actively suggesting alternative courses of action of which the user may not be aware.

Adaptive help is a special case of a general class of interactive systems, known as intelligent systems. These include domain-specific expert systems, intelligent tutoring systems and general adaptive interfaces. We will concentrate in this discussion on adaptive help systems, since they are most relevant here, and incorporate aspects of the others, but it should be noted that many of the techniques we will look at can be applied in these other systems. Since these represent a significant class of interactive system, we will cover the techniques in some detail.

Adaptive help systems operate by monitoring the activity of the user and constructing a model of him. This may include a model of his experience, preferences, mistakes, or a combination of some or all of these. Using this knowledge, together with knowledge of the domain in which the user is working, and, sometimes, general advisory or tutorial strategies, the adaptive help system will present help relevant to the user's current task and suited to his experience. That at least is the theory. In practice it is not as simple as it sounds. First, the knowledge requirements of such a system are considerable, and data on interaction are particularly difficult to interpret. Secondly, there is the issue of control and initiative within the interaction. Should the help system take an active role, removing some control from the user, and will the adaptivity confuse the user, if he perceives it as 'shifting ground'? Thirdly, what exactly should be adapted and what will be the result of the adaptivity? Finally, what is the scope of the modeling and adaptivity: does it extend beyond the application level and, if so, how does it deal with the variation in expertise of a single user across an entire system? We will consider some of the developments and solutions, concentrating, in particular, on the knowledge requirements.

DESIGN FOCUS

It's good to talk – help from real people

Although well-designed documentation and intelligent help systems are important, there is, perhaps, nothing like talking to a real person! As we noted in Section 11.3.5, expert users are often more likely to consult documentation, as there is a skill in knowing how it is organized. Studies of UNIX help found that novice users preferred not to look at *man* pages, instead they asked local experts who did look at the pages. This pattern of local experts has been found across all types of systems in many environments.

In web-based systems there are many ways of linking more static documentation with dynamic inter-personal support. There may be a link from the electronic to the personal: technical support sites often have some sort of email query form for when you cannot find what you want online. There may also be inter-personal to electronic links: a telephone support desk may email you a URL to guide you to suitable information.

Other users of a product can also be a source of help, and many product sites, especially open-source products, include some way for users to submit their tips or advice. For example, the online manual pages for the PHP web scripting language have for each function a series of user tips that you can add to yourself. There are important issues of community culture here as the tips are generally useful and do not include extraneous comments.

User community and manufacturers' technical support may be integrated. For example, Sun's Java developer support site includes a community area with online user forums and live chat with Sun staff, authors and other experts.

See www.php.net/ and http://developer.java.sun.com/developer/community/

11.4.1 Knowledge representation: user modeling

Every interactive system that is built incorporates some model of the user for whom it is intended. In many systems this model is the designer's view of the user and is implicit within the design. The designer has in mind a 'typical' user, and builds the interface accordingly. If the designer has done her homework this model can be quite effective. However, it does assume that all users are essentially the same and have the same requirements.

Other systems allow the user to provide a model of himself around which the system will be configured. Simple examples of this are browser or email preferences that can adjust certain parameters of the system to the requirements of the user. Such systems are called *adaptable*, since the user is able to adapt his own environment to suit his preferences. This increases the flexibility of the system but places the onus of the customization on the user. The result of this is that users have access only to the default system when they most need flexibility: that is, when they first start out. It is only later that they have the know-how to construct the necessary model.

The third approach to providing the system with a model of the user, and the one used in adaptive help systems, is to have the system construct and maintain a model of the user based on data gleaned from monitoring the user's interaction. This model can then be consulted when required. This automatic approach to user modeling also has the problem of the setup time required, during which time the user has a default system, but the onus to build the model is taken away from the user. Various suggestions have been made as to how to deal with the setup time, including getting the user to choose an initial default model, and building a model based on pre-use activity, such as game playing. The former is problematic in that again it makes the user decide on a model at a time when he may not have sufficient experience to do so effectively. The latter may not produce a model that is transferable to the actual domain. The most common approach is still to provide a basic start-up default model and concentrate on rapidly updating this for the actual user. The default model may be based on experimental or observational results gleaned in evaluation.

So how are user models constructed and maintained? There are a number of approaches. Some quantify user experience or classify users into stereotypes; some compare the user's behavior with some norm; others maintain a catalog of known errors and compare user actions to these.

Quantification

This is one of the most simple approaches to user modeling. The system recognizes a number of levels of expertise, which it will respond to in different ways. The user is placed on one of these levels, and moves between them, based on a quantitative measure of his expertise at that time. Different activities are given weightings, and the user is scored according to the weightings of the activities he takes part in. If the score exceeds a certain threshold, the user is moved to a different expertise level and the system adapts accordingly.

This approach is simple and measures the user at a coarse level of granularity. However, it is effective for simple adaptivity. For example, this method was used by Mason to adapt the presentation of command prompts to the user's level of experience [228]. The system used a set of rules, which dictated when a user's level of expertise changed. For example,

```
Move from Level 1 to Level 2
If
    the system has been used more than twice (0.25)
    commands x and y have been used effectively (0.20)
    help has not been accessed this session (0.25)
    the system has been used in the last 5 days
```

Such a model can only give a rough approximation of the user's expertise, but at the same time requires little analysis to extract the required information from the system logs. This approach can be used effectively in adaptive tutorials.

Stereotypes

Another approach to automatic user modeling is to work with stereotypes. Rather than attempting to build a truly individual model of the user, the system classifies the user as a member of a known category of users or stereotype. Stereotypes are based on user characteristics and may be simple, such as making a distinction between novice and expert users, or more complex, for example building a compound stereotype based on more than one piece of information. There are several ways of building stereotypes. One is to use information such as command use and errors to categorize different types of user and then to use rules to identify the stereotype to which the user belongs. An alternative method is to use a machine learning approach, such as neural networks, to learn examples of different types of user behavior (from actual logs) and then to classify users according to their closeness to the examples previously learned. Stereotypes are useful in that they represent the user at the level of granularity at which most adaptive help systems work, and do not attempt to produce a sophisticated model, which will not be fully utilized. After all, if the only information that is available about the user at any time is how he is interacting with the system, it is not possible to infer very much about the user himself. However, what can be inferred may be exactly what is required to provide the necessary level of help.

Overlay models

One of the most common techniques used is the overlay model. Here an idealized model, often of an expert user, is constructed and the individual user's behavior compared with it. The resulting user profile may represent either the commonality between the two models or the differences. An advantage of this style of modeling is that it allows a certain degree of diagnostic activity on the part of the system. Not only is the system aware of what the user is doing, but it also has a representation of optimal behavior. This provides a benchmark against which to measure the user's performance, and, if the user does not take the optimal course of action, gives an indication of the type of help or hint that is required.

A similar approach is used in error-based models where the system holds a record of known user errors and the user's actual behavior is compared with these. If this behavior matches an error in the catalog, then remedial action can be taken. Potential errors may be matched when partially executed and help given to enable the user to avoid the error, or recover more quickly. These types of modeling are also useful in intelligent tutoring systems where diagnostic information is required in order to decide how to proceed with the tutorial.

11.4.2 Knowledge representation: domain and task modeling

All adaptive help systems must have some knowledge of the system itself, in order to provide relevant and appropriate advice. This knowledge may include command use, common errors and common tasks. However, some help systems also attempt to build a model of the user's current task or plan. The motivation behind this is that the user is engaged in a particular problem-solving task and requires help at that level. Generic help, even adapted to the expertise and preference of the user, is not enough.

One common approach to this problem is to represent user tasks in terms of the command sequences that are required to execute them. As the user works, the commands used are compared with the stored task sequences and matched sequences are recovered. If the user's command sequence does not match a recognized task, help is offered. This approach was used in the PRIAM system [85].

Although an attractive idea, task recognition is problematic. In large domains it is unlikely that every possible method for reaching every possible user goal could be represented. Users may reasonably approach a task in a non-standard way, and inferring the user's intention from command usage is not a trivial problem. As we saw in Chapter 9, system logs do not always contain sufficient information for a human expert to ascertain what the user was trying to do. The problem is far greater for a computer.

Assistants and agents use task recognition at a basic level to monitor user behavior and provide hints and macros when a familiar or repeated sequence is noticed (see Section 11.3.6).

11.4.3 Knowledge representation: modeling advisory strategy

A third area of knowledge representation, which is sometimes included in adaptive help, is modeling advisory or tutorial strategies. Providing a help system with this type of information allows it not only to select appropriate advice for the user but also to use an appropriate method of giving advice.

As we have already seen, people require different types of help depending on their knowledge and circumstances. These include reminders, task-specific help and tutorial help. There is evidence to indicate that human experts follow different strategies when advising colleagues [293]. These include inferring the intention of the person seeking help and advising at that level or providing a number of solutions to the person's problem. Alternatively they may attempt to place the problem in a context and provide a 'sample solution' in that context.

Few adaptive help systems have attempted to model advisory strategy, and those that do provide a limited choice. Ideally, it would be useful if the help system had access to a number of alternative strategies and was able to choose an appropriate style of guidance in each case. However, this is very ambitious – too little is known about what makes a guidance strategy appropriate in which contexts. However, it is important that designers of adaptive help systems give some thought to advisory strategies, if only to make an informed choice about the strategy that is to be used.

The EuroHelp adaptive help system adopts a model of teacher–pupil, in which the system is envisaged as a teacher watching the user (pupil) work and offering advice and suggestions in an 'over-the-shoulder' fashion [126, 44]. In this case, instruction may be high to begin with but will become less obtrusive as the user finds his feet. The user is able to question the system at any point and responses are given in terms of the current context.

This mixed-initiative dialog is also used in the Activist/Passivist help system, which will accept requests from the user and actively offer suggestions and hints, particularly about areas of functionality that it infers the user is unfamiliar with [133].

11.4.4 Techniques for knowledge representation

All of the modeling approaches described rely heavily on techniques for knowledge representation from artificial intelligence. This is a whole subject in its own right and there is only room to outline the methods here (although some of the techniques are based on theories of memory and problem solving as discussed in Chapter 1). The interested reader is also referred to the text on artificial intelligence in the recommended reading list.

There are four main groups of techniques used in knowledge representation for adaptive help systems: rule based, frame based, network based and example based. Note that these general techniques are often combined to produce hybrid systems.

Rule-based techniques

Knowledge is represented as a set of rules and facts, which are interpreted using some inference mechanism. Predicate logic provides a powerful mechanism for representing declarative information, while production rules represent procedural information. Rule-based techniques can be used in relatively large domains and can represent actions to perform as well as knowledge for inference. A user model implemented using rule-based methods may include rules of the form

```
IF
    command is EDIT file I
AND
    last command is COMPILE file I
THEN
    task is DEBUG
    action is describe automatic debugger
```

Frame-based techniques

Frame-based systems are used to represent commonly occurring situations and default knowledge. A frame is a structure that contains labeled slots, representing related features. Each slot can be assigned a value or alternatively be given a default value. User input is matched against the frame values and a successful match may cause some action to be taken. They are useful in small domains. In user modeling the frame may represent the current profile of the user:

User
>   Expertise level: novice
>   Command: EDIT file1
>   Last command: COMPILE file1
>   Errors this session: 6
>   Action: describe automatic debugger

Network-based techniques

Networks represent knowledge about the user and system in terms of relationships between facts. One of the most common examples is the semantic network. The network is a hierarchy and children can inherit properties associated with their parents. This makes it a relatively efficient representation scheme and is useful for linking information clearly. Networks can also be used to link frame-based representations.

The compile example could be expanded within a semantic network:

CC is an instance of COMPILE
COMPILE is a command
COMPILE is related to DEBUG
COMPILE is related to EDIT
Automatic debugger facilitates DEBUG

Example-based techniques

Example-based techniques represent knowledge implicitly within a decision structure of a classification system. This may be a decision tree, in the case of an inductive learning approach such as ID3 [298], or links in a network in the case of neural networks. The decision structure is constructed automatically based on examples presented to the classifier. The classifiers effectively detect recurrent features within the examples and are able to use these to classify other input. An example may be a trace of user activity:

EDIT file1
COMPILE file1

This would be trained as an example of a particular task, for example DEBUG.

11.4.5 Problems with knowledge representation and modeling

Knowledge representation is the central issue in adaptive help systems, but it is not without its problems. Knowledge is often difficult to elicit, particularly if a domain expert is not available. This is particularly true of knowledge of user behavior, owing to its variability. It is especially difficult to ensure completeness and correctness of the knowledge base in these circumstances. Even if knowledge is available, the amount of knowledge required is substantial, making adaptive help an expensive option.

A second problem is interpreting the information appropriately. Although the knowledge base can be provided with detailed knowledge of the expected contexts and the domain in advance, during the interaction the only information that is available is the system log of the user's actions. As we saw in Chapter 9, interpreting system logs is very difficult because it is stripped of much context and there is no access to the user's intention or goal (except by inference). However, this data is not arbitrary and does contain recurrent patterns of activity, which can be used with care to infer task sequences and the like. However, it should be realized that these represent approximations only.

11.4.6 Other issues

Other issues that should be considered in designing an adaptive help system are initiative, effect and scope.

Initiative A major issue in adaptive help system design is that of initiative and control: should the user retain complete control over the system; should the system direct the interaction; or should a mixed dialog be supported? System activity can be intrusive to the user, particularly if badly handled. No user wants to be constantly told he is not performing a task in the most efficient manner! However, we know that there are normally large sections of system functionality of which the user is simply not aware. Without some form of system activity this problem will not be addressed. The solution seems to be to encourage mixed initiative in the interaction. The user should be able to question the system at any time, and the system can offer hints to the user. However, the latter should be offered sensitively and the user always allowed to continue as before if he wishes.

Effect Another issue that the designer should consider is the effect of the modeling and adaptivity: what exactly is going to be adapted and what information is needed to do this? All too often modeling systems use vast resources producing a detailed profile of the user, the bulk of which is never used. Modeling, whether of the user, the domain or strategies, should be directed towards the requirements of the help system. For example, if it is simply to offer different help to novices and experts, the system does not need details of task execution. Such considerations may reduce the overheads of adaptive help systems and make them more viable.

Scope Finally, the designer must consider the scope of the help: is it to be offered at an application level or system wide? The latter may be the ideal but is much more complex. If users are to be modeled at a system level, the model should take into account the levels of activity in which they are engaged and be able to distinguish actions at an application level. In many systems it would also have to cope with interleaving of activities and concurrent execution. Each of these makes the modeling activity more complex.

11.5 DESIGNING USER SUPPORT SYSTEMS

There are many ways of providing user support and it is up to the designer to decide which is most appropriate for any given system. However, there are a number of things which the designer should take into account. First, the design of user support should not be seen as an 'add-on' to system design. Ideally, the help system should be designed integrally with the rest of the system. If this is done, the help system will be relevant and consistent with the rest of the system. The same modeling and analytic techniques (for example, task analysis, see Chapter 15) used to design the system can guide the design of support material as well. Secondly, the designer should consider the content of the help and the context in which it will be used before the technology that will be required. Obviously, available technology is an important issue. However, concentrating on the task and the user will help to clarify the type of help required within the constraints of technical resources. Viewing the process in reverse may prevent the designer seeing beyond the technology she is familiar with. Bearing in mind the expected user requirements, the designer of help also needs to make decisions about how the help will be presented to the user and how this will be affected by implementation issues.

11.5.1 Presentation issues

How is help requested?

The first decision the designer must make is how the user will access help. There are a number of choices. Help may be a command, a button, a function which can be switched on or off, or a separate application. A command (usually) requires the user to specify a topic, and therefore assumes some knowledge, but may fit most consistently within the rest of the interface. A help button is readily accessible and does not interfere with existing applications, but may not always provide information specific to the user's needs. However, if the help button is a keyboard or mouse button, it can support context sensitivity, as we saw earlier. The help function is flexible since it can be activated when required and disabled when not. The separate application allows flexibility and multiple help styles but may interfere with the user's current application.

How is help displayed?

The second major decision that the designer must make is how the user will view the help. In a windowed system it may be presented in a new window. In other systems it may use the whole screen or part of the screen. Alternatively, help hints and prompts can be given in pop-up boxes or at the command line level. The presentation style that is appropriate depends largely on the level of help being offered and the space that it requires. Obviously, opening a manual page line by line is unhelpful, as is taking over the whole screen to give the user a hint. Some active help systems provide visual cues when they have a suggestion to make (for example, an icon may be highlighted) – this gives the user the option of taking the suggestion without forcing him to abandon or interrupt his work. Again this decision should take account of the rest of the design, and aim to provide consistency.

Effective presentation of help

Help screens and documentation should be designed in much the same way as an interface should be designed, taking into account the capabilities and task requirements of the user. No matter what technology is used to provide support, there are some principles for writing and presenting it effectively. Help and tutorial material should be written in clear, familiar language, avoiding jargon as much as possible. If paper manuals and tutorials exist, the terminology should be consistent between these and the online support material. Instructional material requires instructional language, and a help system should tell the user how to use the system rather than simply describing the system. It should not make assumptions about what the user knows in advance. For example, a help message on the use of windows might read

> To close the window, click on the box in the top right-hand corner of the window.

rather than

> Windows can be closed by clicking on the box in the top right-hand corner of the window.

An exception to this is in documentation where the intention is not only to instruct the user in how to use the system but to record a full description of the system's functionality. However, documentation should be presented so that information is readily accessible, and should present both instructional and descriptive information clearly. The physical layout of documentation can make a difference to its usability. Large blocks of text are difficult to read on screen, for example. This can be alleviated by breaking the documentation into clear logical sections, or by using technology such as hypertext to organize it. A useful style is to provide a summary of the key information prominently, with further information available if required. This can be done either by devising a hierarchical help system where each layer in the hierarchy provides increasing detail, or simply by using layout carefully. An index can be used as a summary of available topics but should be organized to reflect the functional relationships between the subjects rather than their alphabetic ordering. Consistency is also important here – each topic in the documentation should be described using the same format so that the user knows where to look for a particular type of information. Documentation and help may contain definitions, descriptions, examples, details of error messages, options and instructions. These should be clearly recognizable.

11.5.2 Implementation issues

Alongside the presentation issues the designer must make implementation decisions. Some of these may be forced by physical constraints, others by the choices made regarding the user's requirements for help. We have already considered how help may be requested and how it appears to the user. Obviously each of these decisions involves implementation questions: will help be an operating system command, a meta-command or an application? What physical constraints does the machine impose in terms of screen space, memory capacity and speed? Speed is a very important consideration, since an unacceptably slow response time is liable to make the system unusable no matter how well it has been designed. It is better to provide a simple help facility that responds quickly than a sophisticated, intelligent one that takes minutes to provide a solution.

Another issue the designer must decide is how the help data is to be structured: in a single file, a file hierarchy, a database? Again this will depend on the type of help that is required, but any structure should be flexible and extensible – systems are not static and new topics will inevitably need to be added to the help system. The data structure used will, to an extent, determine the type of search or navigation strategy that is provided. Will users be able to browse through the system or only request help on one topic at a time? The user may also want to make a hard copy of part of the help system to study later (this is particularly true of manuals and documentation). Will this facility be provided as part of the support system?

Finally, the designer should consider the authors of help material as well as its users. It is likely that, even if the designer writes the initial help texts, these will be extended by other authors at different times. Clear conventions and constraints on the presentation and implementation of help facilitate the addition of new material.

11.6   SUMMARY

This chapter has been concerned with user support in the form of help and documentation. No interactive system of any complexity is so intuitive that the user never requires help. Help should therefore be an integral part of the design. Users require different types of help, depending on the context and circumstances, and the user support facilities should support these. Different styles of help support different requirements and different types of user. We have considered several types of help system, including adaptive user support. It is important to select a support style and design user support with the user in mind, just as the design of the system is user centered. In particular, the presentation of help should take into account usability principles, and the language should be clear and instructional.

EXERCISES

11.1 Write a manual page for making a cup of coffee. Assume your user has no experience but will recognize a cup, a kettle, a spoon, etc. Swap your manual with a partner. Does your partner's manual give you sufficient instruction to make the cup of coffee? Discuss improvements with your partner and agree on a final version of the manual.

11.2 Find a computer application that you have never used before. Attempt to learn to use it using only the online support. Is there enough information to allow you to use the application effectively? Is the information easy to find? What improvements (if any) would you suggest?

11.3 What knowledge is needed to build an adaptive help system? Which do you think is most difficult to provide and why?

11.4 Look at as many online support systems as you can. Which do you find most useful and why? Try to assess them using the requirements discussed in Section 11.2.

11.5 Using your library facilities and the world wide web, investigate the benefits and limitations of adaptive help systems. What examples of adaptive and adaptable help are available and how useful are they?

11.6 What are the four main types of help that users may require? For each type, give an example of a situation in which it would be appropriate.

11.7 Which usability principles are especially important in the design of help systems, and why?

11.8 Describe some of the different approaches to providing user support systems, with examples.

11.9 Applications are often supported by an online version of the paper documentation; in some cases there is no paper documentation at all.

What are the advantages of online documentation? What are the disadvantages, and how can they be overcome?

11.10 Discuss the presentation issues involved in the design of effective and relevant help systems.

RECOMMENDED READING

R. C. Houghton, Online help systems: a conspectus, *Communications of the ACM*, Vol. 27, No. 2, February 1984.
A good review of non-adaptive help systems, most of which is still relevant today.

C. Turk and J. Kirkman, *Effective Writing*, 2nd edition, E. and F. N. Spon, 1989.
An excellent introduction to technical writing, including writing instructional material.

E. Rich and K. Knight, *Artificial Intelligence*, 2nd edition, McGraw-Hill, 1991.
A detailed text on artificial intelligence techniques. Readers should select appropriate sections on knowledge representation.

Clippy's home page: www.microsoft.com/Office/clippy/.
An interesting case study on how help can fail – and how failure can be turned to advantage. Accessed March 2003.

MODELS AND THEORIES

In all engineering disciplines, the designer recruits a selection of models to contribute to the design process. If we were building a new office block, for example, then we would use models of air circulation to design the ventilation system, structural models for the fabric and possibly social models for the detailed design of the office layout.

Models are used in other disciplines too. We may analyze the structure of a piece of music and decide that it is a rondo, or say that a poem is in sonnet form. Further, we may deliberately set out to write a sonnet, thus imposing the model upon the creative process. Craft is the art of design within constraint, and models help to formulate the constraints.

The chapters in Part 3 describe a range of models that can be used during the interface design process. Just as in the design of the office block several different types of model are required for different aspects of the building, so in interface design we would expect to use a whole selection of complementary methods.

Chapter 12 considers models with psychological or cognitive origins, where the emphasis is on formulating aspects of user behavior such as goal formation and problem solving. Chapter 13 discusses socio-technical models that attempt to describe the user within a social and organizational context, while Chapter 14 looks at models of collaboration and group interaction. Chapter 15 describes task analysis techniques for determining the relevant actions a user performs in some work domain. Chapter 16 is concerned with dialog description techniques used to specify and analyze the communication between user and system. Chapter 17 describes the use of general mathematical notations used in software engineering to specify and analyze abstract descriptions of interactive systems, and Chapter 18 extends these notations to model rich interactions.

12

COGNITIVE MODELS

OVERVIEW

Cognitive models represent users of interactive systems.

■ Hierarchical models represent a user's task and goal structure.

■ Linguistic models represent the user–system grammar.

■ Physical and device models represent human motor skills.

■ Cognitive architectures underlie all of these cognitive models.

12.1 INTRODUCTION

The techniques and models in this chapter all claim to have some representation of users as they interact with an interface; that is, they model some aspect of the user's understanding, knowledge, intentions or processing. The level of representation differs from technique to technique – from models of high-level goals and the results of problem-solving activities, to descriptions of motor-level activity, such as keystrokes and mouse clicks. The formalisms have largely been developed by psychologists, or computer scientists, whose interest is in understanding user behavior.

One way to classify the models is in respect to how well they describe features of the *competence* and *performance* of the user. Quoting from Simon [323]:

> Competence models tend to be ones that can predict legal behaviour sequences but generally do this without reference to whether they could actually be executed by users. In contrast, performance models not only describe what the necessary behaviour sequences are but usually describe both what the user needs to know and how this is employed in actual task execution.

Competence models, therefore, represent the kinds of behavior expected of a user, but they provide little help in analyzing that behavior to determine its demands on the user. Performance models provide analytical power mainly by focussing on routine behavior in very limited applications.

Another useful distinction between these models is whether they address the acquisition or formulation of a plan of activity or the execution of that plan. Referring back to the interaction framework presented in Chapter 3, this classification would mean that some models are concerned with understanding the *User* and his associated task language while others are concerned with the articulation translation between that task language and the *Input* language. The presentation of the cognitive models in this chapter follows this classification scheme, divided into the following categories:

■ hierarchical representation of the user's task and goal structure
■ linguistic and grammatical models
■ physical and device-level models.

The first category deals directly with the issue of formulation of goals and tasks. The second deals with the grammar of the articulation translation and how it is understood by the user. The third category again deals with articulation, but at the human motor level instead of at a higher level of human understanding.

Architectural assumptions about the user are needed in any of the cognitive models discussed here. Some of the more basic architectural assumptions were covered in Chapter 1, such as the distinction between long- and short-term memory. After discussing models in the three categories above, we will describe two additional cognitive architectures and how they are relevant for analyzing interactive system design.

Many of these nominally cognitive models have a rather computational flavor. This reflects the way that computational analogies are often used in cognitive psychology. The similarity between the language describing the user and that describing the computer has some advantages and some dangers. On the positive side it makes communication and analysis of the combined human–computer system easier. For instance, cognitive complexity theory (described later) produces models of both user goals and the system grammar, and can reason about their interaction. On the other hand, there is a danger that this will encourage a mechanistic view of the user.

12.2 GOAL AND TASK HIERARCHIES

Many models make use of a model of mental processing in which the user achieves goals by solving subgoals in a divide-and-conquer fashion. We will consider two models, *GOMS* and *CCT*, where this is a central feature. However, we will see similar features in other models, such as *TAG* (Section 12.3.2) and when we consider task analysis techniques (Chapter 15).

Imagine we want to produce a report on sales of introductory HCI textbooks. To achieve this goal we divide it into several subgoals, say gathering the data together, producing the tables and histograms, and writing the descriptive material. Concentrating on the data gathering, we decide to split this into further subgoals: find the names of all introductory HCI textbooks and then search the book sales database for these books. Similarly, each of the other subgoals is divided up into further subgoals, until some level of detail is found at which we decide to stop. We thus end up with a hierarchy of goals and subgoals. The example can be laid out to expose this structure:

```
produce report
    gather data
    .    find book names
    .    .   do keywords search of names database
                <<further subgoals>>
    .    .   sift through names and abstracts by hand
                <<further subgoals>>
    .    search sales database
                <<further subgoals>>
    layout tables and histograms
        <<further subgoals>>
    write description
        <<further subgoals>>
```

Various issues arise as one attempts such analyses of computer use.

Where do we stop? We can go on decomposing tasks until we get down to the individual hand and eye movements of the user, or we can stop at a more abstract level. Where do we start? In a similar way, we can start our analyses at different points in the hierarchy of goals. At the extreme we could extend our analysis to larger and larger goals: 'light hob' is a subgoal of 'boil peas' and so on to goals such as 'have my dinner', 'feed' and 'stay alive'.

These two questions are issues of *granularity*, and both of the methods described below leave this to some extent in the hands of the designer. Different design issues demand different levels of analysis. However, both methods operate at a relatively low level; neither would attempt to start with such an abstract goal as 'produce a report' which will involve real creativity and difficult problem solving. Instead they confine themselves to more routine learned behavior. This most abstract task is referred to as the *unit task*. The unit task does not require any problem-solving skills on the part of the user, though it frequently demands quite sophisticated problem-solving skills on the part of the designer to determine them.

What do we do when there are several ways of solving a problem, or if the solutions to two subgoals interact? Users will often have more than one way to achieve a goal and there must be some way of representing how they select between competing solutions.

Another important issue has to do with the treatment of error. Users are not perfect. A goal hierarchy may show how the perfect user would achieve a goal, but what can it say about difficulties the user may have along the way? In general, prediction of error behavior is poor amongst these hierarchical modeling techniques, though some (cognitive complexity theory (CCT), for example) can represent error behavior.

12.2.1 GOMS

The *GOMS* model of Card, Moran and Newell is an acronym for Goals, Operators, Methods and Selection [56]. A GOMS description consists of these four elements:

Goals   These are the user's goals, describing what the user wants to achieve. Further, in GOMS the goals are taken to represent a 'memory point' for the user, from which he can evaluate what should be done and to which he may return should any errors occur.

Operators   These are the lowest level of analysis. They are the basic actions that the user must perform in order to use the system. They may affect the system (for example, press the 'X' key) or only the user's mental state (for example, read the dialog box). There is still a degree of flexibility about the granularity of operators; we may take the command level 'issue the SELECT command' or be more primitive: 'move mouse to menu bar, press center mouse button . . .'.

Methods   As we have already noted, there are typically several ways in which a goal can be split into subgoals. For instance, in a certain window manager a currently selected window can be closed to an icon either by selecting the 'CLOSE' option from a pop-up menu, or by hitting the 'L7' function key. In GOMS these two goal decompositions are referred to as methods, so we have the CLOSE-METHOD and the L7-METHOD:

visit the web site – www.hcibook.com

**a constantly expanding
collection of resources
for students, teachers
and practitioners**

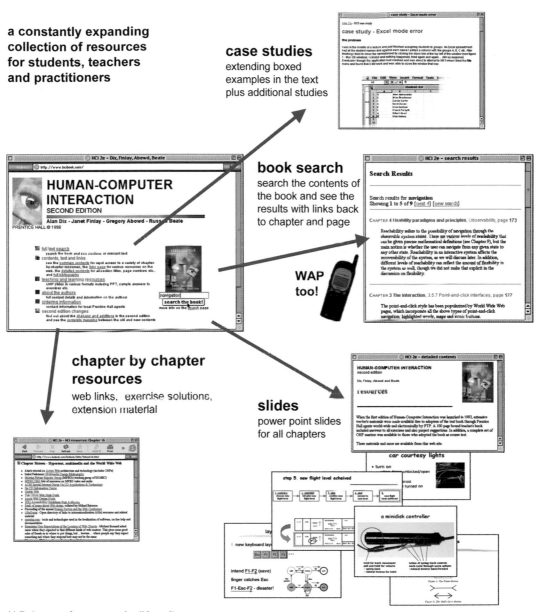

case studies
extending boxed
examples in the text
plus additional studies

book search
search the contents of
the book and see the
results with links back
to chapter and page

**WAP
too!**

**chapter by chapter
resources**

web links, exercise solutions,
extension material

slides
power point slides
for all chapters

N.B. images from second edition site

From DESIGN
FOCUS Smart-Its
– making using
sensors easy, p.96
Source: Courtesy
of Hans Gellersen

Figure 3.13
WebBook – using
3D to make more
space (Card, S.K.,
Robertson G.G. and
York W. (1996).
The WebBook and
the Web Forager:
An Information
workspace for the
World-Wide Web.
*CHI96 Conference
Proceedings*, 111–17.
Copyright © 1996
ACM, Inc.
Reprinted by
permission)

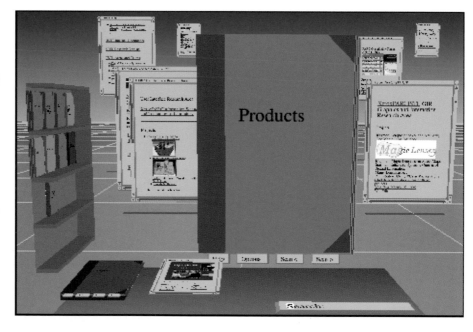

Figure 3.16
A variety of icons.
Screen shot
reprinted by
permission from
Apple Computer,
Inc.

Cracker from p.157

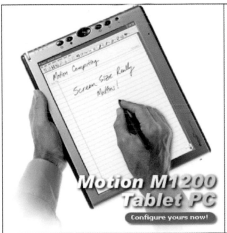

Figure 4.1 Examples of computing devices at the foot scale. On the left is a tablet computer – a Tablet PC from MotionComputing (Source: Motion Computing, Inc.). On the right is a research prototype, the Listen Reader, an interactive storybook developed at Palo Alto Research Center (picture courtesy Palo Alto Research Center)

Figure 4.2
The Stanford
Interactive Mural,
an example of a
yard-scale
interactive display
surface created by
tiling multiple
lower-resolution
projectors. Picture
courtesy François
Guimbretière

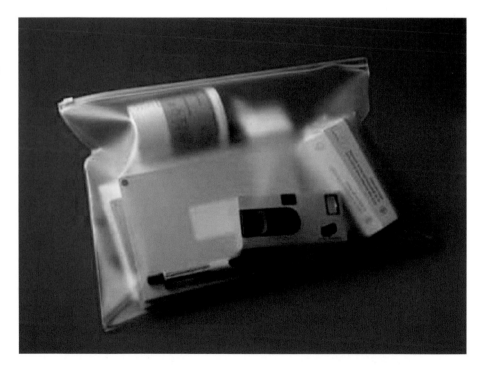

From DESIGN
FOCUS Cultural
probes, p.200.
Source: Photograph
courtesy of
William W. Gaver

Figure 9.5
Eye-tracking
equipment.
Source: Courtesy
of J. A. Renshaw

Figure 9.6
Calibrating the
eye tracker.
Source: Courtesy
of J. A. Renshaw

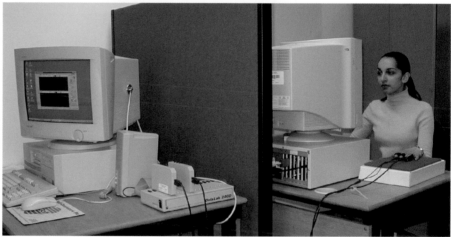

Figure 9.7 Data Lab Psychophysiology equipment showing some of the sensors (above) and a typical experimental arrangement (below) with sensors attached to the participant's fingers and the monitoring software displayed on the evaluator's machine. Source: Courtesy of Dr R. D. Ward

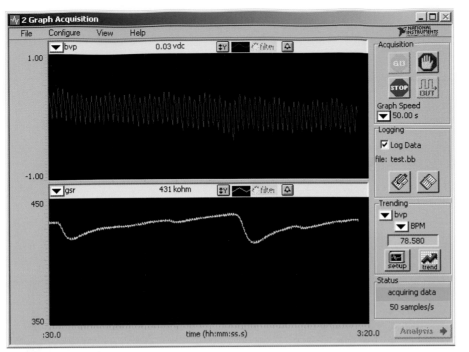

Figure 9.8
Output of monitoring pulse rate (above) and skin conductivity (below). Source: Screen shot courtesy of Dr R. D. Ward; frame source: National Instruments BioBench software

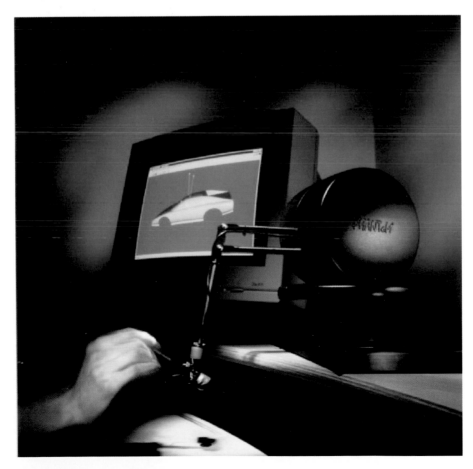

Figure 10.3
A PHANTOM Premium 1.5 haptic device. Source: Courtesy of SensAble Technologies

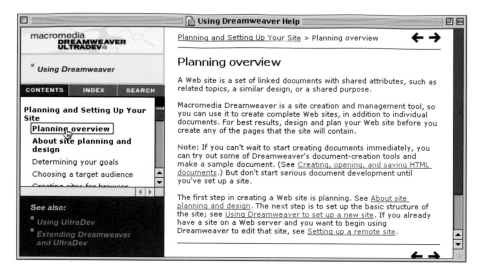

Figure 11.2 Screen shot of the online documentation for Macromedia's Dreamweaver Ultradev version 4.0. Courtesy of Macromedia, Inc.

From DESIGN FOCUS Looking real – Avatar Conference, p.481. Screen shot frame reprinted by permission from Microsoft Corporation. Screen shots courtesy of AVATAR-Conference project team

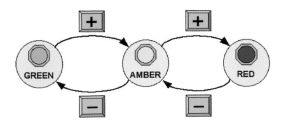

Figure 16.21
STN for alarm state

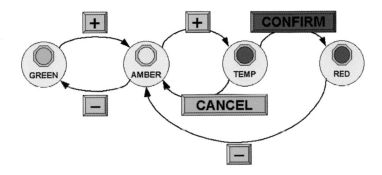

Figure 16.22
STN for revised
alarm state

MediaCup, p.650
Courtesy of
Michael Beigl,
University of
Karlsrühe

OnCue, p.651

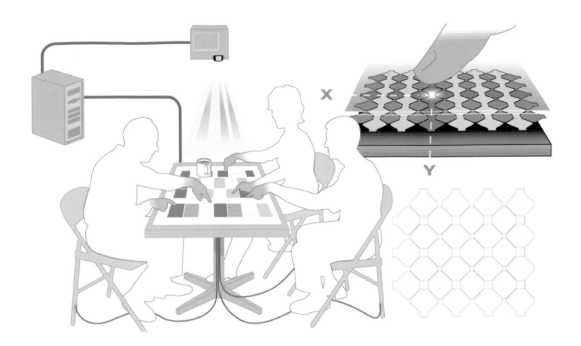

Figure 20.1 The DiamondTouch input technology from Mitsubishi Electric Research Lab (MERL) uses capacitive coupling through humans to provide a large-scale input surface for multiple simultaneous users. See www.merl.com/projects/DiamondTouch/ for more details. Source: Courtesy of Mitsubishi Electric Research Laboratories, Inc.

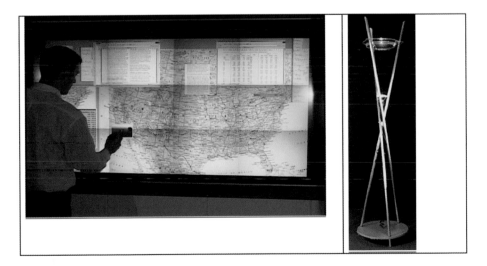

Figure 20.3 The figure on the left is the Stanford Interactive Mural, an example of a large-scale interactive display surface created by tiling multiple lower-resolution projectors. Picture courtesy François Guimbretière. The figure on the right is an example of an ambient display, the Water Lamp from Ishii's Tangible Media Group at the MIT Media Lab. Light shines upwards through a pan of water, which is actuated by digitally controlled solenoids that can tap the water and cause ripples. External information can be used to drive the tapping of the solenoids. Source: Courtesy of Hiroshi Ishii, MIT Media Lab. Photograph by Andrew Daly

Figure 20.4 On the left, the DigitalDesk prototype integrating physical and virtual desktop environments with the aid of projection and vision technology [374]. Source: © 1993 ACM, Inc. Reprinted by permission. On the right, the NaviCam system which recognized 2D glyphs on objects and then superimposed additional information over that object [303]. Source: Courtesy of Sony Computer Science Laboratories, Inc.

From DESIGN FOCUS Ambient Wood – augmenting the physical p.724. Photographs courtesy of Yvonne Rogers

From DESIGN FOCUS
Shared experience
p. 732. Source:
Courtesy of
Matthew Chalmers.
Note: City is an
Equator project

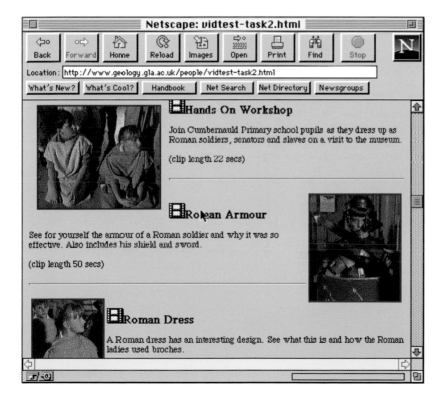

Figure 21.2
Hunterian Museum
– learning about the
Romans. Source
[194a] reprinted
with permission of
Springer-Verlag

Figure 21.3
Interacting with hypertext – Professor Alan's puzzle square. Screen shot frame reprinted by permission from Microsoft Corporation

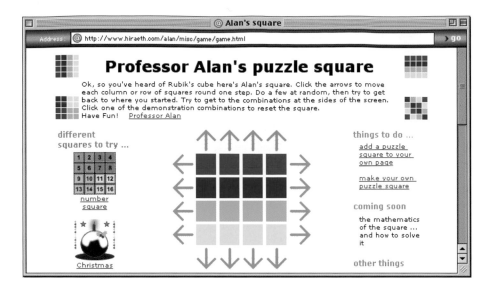

Figure 21.5
eClass – recording a lecture

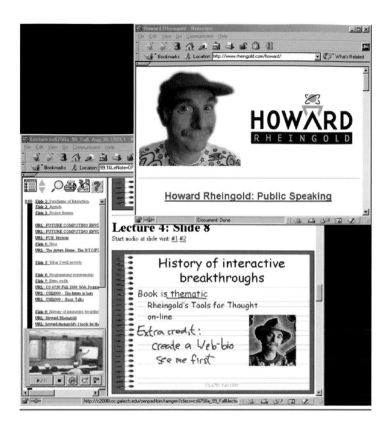

Figure 21.6
eClass – indexed playback on student's web browser. Source: Netscape browser window © 2002 Netscape Communications Corporation, used by permission

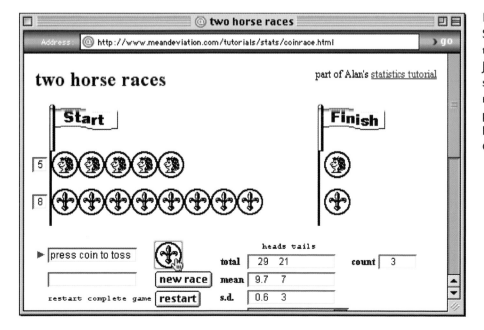

Figure 21.10
Simulated coin tossing using JavaScript. Screen shot frame reprinted by permission from Microsoft Corporation

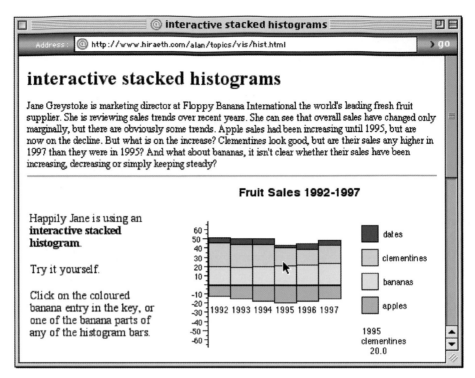

Figure 21.11 Dancing histograms using Java applet. Screen shot frame reprinted by permission from Microsoft Corporation

```
GOAL: ICONIZE-WINDOW
.      [select GOAL: USE-CLOSE-METHOD
.              .        MOVE-MOUSE-TO-WINDOW-HEADER
.              .        POP-UP-MENU
.              .        CLICK-OVER-CLOSE-OPTION
.            GOAL: USE-L7-METHOD
.              .        PRESS-L7-KEY]
```

The dots are used to indicate the hierarchical level of goals.

Selection   From the above snippet we see the use of the word `select` where the choice of methods arises. GOMS does not leave this as a random choice, but attempts to predict which methods will be used. This typically depends both on the particular user and on the state of the system and details about the goals. For instance, a user, Sam, never uses the `L7-METHOD`, except for one game, 'blocks', where the mouse needs to be used in the game until the very moment the key is pressed. GOMS captures this in a selection rule for Sam:

> User Sam:
>   Rule 1:   Use the `CLOSE-METHOD` unless another rule applies.
>   Rule 2:   If the application is 'blocks' use the `L7-METHOD`.

The goal hierarchies described in a GOMS analysis are almost wholly below the level of the unit task defined earlier. A typical GOMS analysis would therefore consist of a single high-level goal, which is then decomposed into a sequence of unit tasks, all of which can be further decomposed down to the level of basic operators:

```
GOAL: EDIT-MANUSCRIPT
.    GOAL: EDIT-UNIT-TASK repeat until no more unit tasks
```

The goal decomposition between the overall task and the unit tasks would involve detailed understanding of the user's problem-solving strategies and of the application domain. These are side-stepped entirely by the method as originally proposed. It would be possible to use the general notation in order to describe this subgoal structure (as for instance in the book report example above). This form of high-level goal description is adopted during *task analysis* which will be discussed in Chapter 15. In particular, the aim of *hierarchical task analysis* is to produce task decompositions, which would be similar (but in a different notation) to that in the book report example.

Analysis of the GOMS goal structure can yield measures of performance. The stacking depth of a goal structure can be used to estimate short-term memory requirements. The model of the users' mental processes implied by this is, of course, very idealized. Also, the selection rules can be tested for accuracy against user traces, and changed in response to discrepancies. In early experiments on the technique, the inventors were able to achieve on average a 90% correct prediction rate of user commands. Further, a very simple method of predicting times (basically assuming that each operator takes a constant time) was able to predict actual times with an error of 33%.

The original GOMS model has served as the basis for much of the cognitive modeling research in HCI. It was good for describing how experts perform routine tasks. Coupled with the physical device models discussed later, it can be used to predict the performance of these users in terms of execution times. It was never intended to provide the kind of information about the user's knowledge that could be compared across different tasks in order to predict things like training or transfer times.

DESIGN FOCUS

GOMS saves money

Some years ago the US telephone company NYNEX were intending to install a new computer system to support their operators. Before installation a detailed GOMS analysis was performed taking into account the cognitive and physical processes involved in dealing with a call. The particular technique was rather different from the original GOMS notation as described here. Because an operator performs several activities in parallel a PERT-style GOMS description was constructed [192, 154]. The PERT analysis was used to determine the critical path, and hence the time to complete a typical task. It was discovered that rather than speeding up operations, the new system would take longer to process each call. The new system was abandoned before installation, leading to a saving of many millions of dollars.

Worked exercise   *Create a GOMS description of the task of photocopying an article from a journal. Discuss the issue of closure (see Chapter 1) in terms of your GOMS description.*

Answer   One possible GOMS description of the goal hierarchy for this task is given below. Answers will vary depending on assumptions about the photocopier used as the model for the exercise. In this example, we will assume that the article is to be copied one page at a time and that a cover over the imaging surface of the copier has to be in place before the actual copy can be made.

```
GOAL: PHOTOCOPY-PAPER
.       GOAL: LOCATE-ARTICLE
.       GOAL: PHOTOCOPY-PAGE repeat until no more pages
.       .       GOAL: ORIENT-PAGE
.       .       .       OPEN-COVER
.       .       .       SELECT-PAGE
.       .       .       POSITION-PAGE
.       .       .       CLOSE-COVER
.       .       GOAL: PRESS-COPY-BUTTON
.       .       GOAL: VERIFY-COPY
.       .       .       LOCATE-OUT-TRAY
.       .       .       EXAMINE-COPY
.       GOAL: COLLECT-COPY
.       .       LOCATE-OUT-TRAY
```

```
.         .      REMOVE-COPY (outer goal satisfied!)
.    GOAL:  RETRIEVE-JOURNAL
.         .      OPEN-COVER
.         .      REMOVE-JOURNAL
.         .      CLOSE-COVER
```

The closure problem which appears in this example occurs when the copy of the article is removed from the photocopier out tray, satisfying the overall goal for the task. In the above description, however, the original journal article is still on the imaging surface of the photocopier, and the cover is closed. The user could easily forget to remove the journal. How could the photocopying procedure be revised to eliminate this problem? One answer is to force the goal RETRIEVE-JOURNAL to be satisfied before COLLECT-COPY.

12.2.2 Cognitive complexity theory

Cognitive complexity theory, introduced by Kieras and Polson [199], begins with the basic premises of goal decomposition from GOMS and enriches the model to provide more predictive power. CCT has two parallel descriptions: one of the user's goals and the other of the computer system (called the *device* in CCT). The description of the user's goals is based on a GOMS-like goal hierarchy, but is expressed primarily using *production rules*. We introduced production rules in Chapter 1 and we further describe their use in CCT below. For the system grammar, CCT uses *generalized transition networks*, a form of *state transition network*. This will not be described here, but state transition networks will be discussed in detail in Chapter 16.

The production rules are a sequence of rules:

if *condition* then *action*

where *condition* is a statement about the contents of working memory. If the condition is true then the production rule is said to fire. An *action* may consist of one or more elementary actions, which may be either changes to the working memory, or external actions such as keystrokes. The production rule 'program' is written in a LISP-like language.

As an example, we consider an editing task using the UNIX vi text editor. The task is to insert a space where one has been missed out in the text, for instance if we noticed that in the above paragraph we had written 'cognitivecomplexity theory'. This is a reasonably frequent typing error and so we assume that we have developed good procedures to perform the task. We consider a fragment of the associated CCT production rules.

```
(SELECT-INSERT-SPACE
IF (AND (TEST-GOAL perform unit task)
        (TEST-TEXT task is insert space)
        (NOT (TEST-GOAL insert space))
        (NOT (TEST-NOTE executing insert space)) )
```

```
THEN ( (ADD-GOAL insert space)
       (ADD-NOTE executing insert space)
       (LOOK-TEXT task is at %LINE %COL) ))
(INSERT-SPACE-DONE
IF (AND (TEST-GOAL perform unit task)
        (TEST-NOTE executing insert space)
        (NOT (TEST-GOAL insert space)) )
THEN ( (DELETE-NOTE executing insert space)
       (DELETE-GOAL perform unit task)
       (UNBIND %LINE %COL) ))
(INSERT-SPACE-1
IF (AND (TEST-GOAL insert space)
        (NOT (TEST-GOAL move cursor))
        (NOT (TEST-CURSOR %LINE %COL)) )
THEN ( (ADD-GOAL move cursor to %LINE %COL) ))
(INSERT-SPACE-2
IF (AND (TEST-GOAL insert space)
        (TEST-CURSOR %LINE %COL) )
THEN ( (DO-KEYSTROKE 'I')
       (DO-KEYSTROKE SPACE)
       (DO-KEYSTROKE ESC)
       (DELETE-GOAL insert space) ))
```

To see how these rules work, imagine that the user has just seen the typing mistake and thus the contents of working memory (w.m.) are

```
(GOAL perform unit task)
(TEXT task is insert space)
(TEXT task is at 5 23)
(CURSOR 8 7)
```

TEXT refers to the text of the manuscript that is being edited and CURSOR refers to the insertion cursor on the screen. Of course, these items are not actually located in working memory – they are external to the user – but we assume that knowledge from observing them is stored in the user's working memory.

The location (5,23) is the line and column of the typing mistake where the space is required. However, the current cursor position is at line 8 and column 7. This is of course acquired into the user's working memory by looking at the screen. Looking at the four rules above (SELECT-INSERT-SPACE, INSERT-SPACE-DONE, INSERT-SPACE-1 and INSERT-SPACE-2), only the first can fire. The condition for SELECT-INSERT-SPACE is:

```
(AND (TEST-GOAL perform unit task)
            true because (GOAL perform unit task) is in w.m.
     (TEST-TEXT task is insert space)
            true because (TEXT task is insert space) is in w.m.
```

```
(NOT (TEST-GOAL insert space))
        true because (GOAL insert space) is not in w.m.
(NOT (TEST-NOTE executing insert space)) )
        true because (NOTE executing insert space)
        is not in w.m.
```

So, the rule fires and its action is performed. This action has no external effect in terms of keystrokes, but adds extra information to working memory. The (LOOK-TEXT task is at %LINE %COL) looks for a corresponding entry and *binds* LINE and COL to 5 and 23 respectively. These are variables, somewhat as in a normal programming language, which are referred to again in other rules.

The contents of working memory after the firing of rule SELECT-INSERT-SPACE are as follows (note that the order of elements of working memory is arbitrary):

```
(GOAL perform unit task)
(TEXT task is insert space)
(TEXT task is at 5 23)
(NOTE executing insert space)
(GOAL insert space)
(LINE 5)
(COL 23)
(CURSOR 8 7)
```

At this point neither rule SELECT-INSERT-SPACE nor INSERT-SPACE-DONE will fire as the entry (GOAL insert space) will make their conditions false. As LINE is bound to 5 and COL is bound to 23, the condition (TEST-CURSOR %LINE %COL) will be false also, and hence only rule INSERT-SPACE-1 can fire.

After this rule's actions have been performed, the working memory will include the entry (GOAL move cursor to 5 23). The rules for moving the cursor are not included here, but would be quite extensive, moving up/down and right/left depending on the relative positions of the cursor and the target location. Eventually, assuming the cursor movement is successful, the cursor would be at (5,23) whence rule INSERT-SPACE-2 would be able to fire. This would perform the keystrokes: I, SPACE and ESC, which in vi puts the editor into insert mode, types the space and then leaves insert mode. The action also removes the insert space goal from working memory as this goal has been achieved.

Now the goal has been removed, the second rule INSERT-SPACE-DONE is free to fire, which 'tidies up' working memory. In particular, it 'unbinds' the variables LINE and COL, that is it removes the bindings for them from working memory.

Notice that the rules did not fire in the order they were written. Although they look somewhat like the if–then–else commands one would get in a standard programming language, they behave very differently. The rules are all active and at each moment any rule that has its conditions true may fire. Some rules may never fire; for instance, if the cursor is at the correct position the third rule would not fire. Furthermore, the same rule may fire repeatedly; for example, if we were to write out the production rules for moving the cursor, one rule may well be

```
(MOVE-UP
IF   (AND  (TEST-GOAL move-up)
           (TEST-CURSOR-BELOW %LINE) )
THEN  (  (       DO-KEYSTROKE 'K') ))
```

This rule is to type 'K' (the vi command to move the cursor up one line) while the cursor is below the desired line. It will, of course, be constantly refired until the cursor is at the correct line.

Notice that the keystrokes for actually inserting the space, once you are at the right position, have been *proceduralized*. That is, the user does not go through the subgoals 'enter insert mode', 'type space', 'leave insert mode'. For a complex insertion, it is quite likely that the user will perform exactly these goals. However, the act of inserting a single space is assumed to be so well rehearsed that it is stored as a single chunk. That is, the rules above represent *expert* knowledge of the vi editor.

Of course, novices may well do exactly the same keystrokes as the experts, but the way they store the knowledge will be different. To cope with this, CCT has a set of 'style' rules for novices. These limit the form of the conditions and actions in the production rules. Basically, novices are expected to test constantly all the rules in their working memory and to check for feedback from the system after every keystroke. Thus a set of 'novice' rules would not include the proceduralized form of insert space. Bovair, Kieras and Polson provide a list of many style rules which can be used to embody certain psychological assumptions about the user (novice/expert distinction is only one) in a CCT description [39].

The rules in CCT need not represent error-free performance. They can be used to explain error phenomena, though they cannot predict them. For instance, the rules above for inserting a space are 'buggy' – they do not check the editor's mode. Imagine you had just been typing the 'cognitive' in 'cognitivecomplexity theory' (with the space missing), you think for a few minutes and then look again at the screen and notice that the space is missing. The cursor is at the correct position for the space, so rule INSERT-SPACE-1 never gets fired and we go directly through the sequence: SELECT-INSERT-SPACE, INSERT-SPACE-2 then INSERT-SPACE-DONE. You type 'i', a space and then escape. However, the 'i' assumes that you are in vi's command mode, and is the command to move the editor into insert mode. If, however, after typing 'cognitive' you had not typed escape, to get you back into command mode, the whole sequence would be done in insert mode. The text would read: 'cognitiveI complexity theory'.

The CCT rules are closely related to GOMS-like goal hierarchies; the rules may be generated from such a hierarchy, or alternatively, we may analyze the production rules to obtain the goal tree:

```
GOAL: insert space
  .       GOAL: move cursor - if not at right position
  .       PRESS-KEY-I
  .       PRESS-SPACE
  .       PRESS-ESCAPE
```

The stacking depth of this goal hierarchy (as described for GOMS) is directly related to the number of (GOAL . . .) terms in working memory.

In fact, the CCT rules can represent more complex plans than the simple sequential hierarchies of GOMS. The continuous activity of all production rules makes it possible to represent concurrent plans. For example, one could have one set of production rules representing the goal of writing a book, and another set representing the goal of drinking tea. These rules could both be active simultaneously, thus allowing an author to drink tea whilst typing. Despite this apparent flexibility, CCT is not normally used in this way. It is not clear why this is, except that CCT, like GOMS, is aimed at low-level, *proceduralized* goals – that is, the *unit task*. It is reasonable that successive unit tasks be chosen from different activities: the author may delete a word, have a drink, do a word search, but each time a complete unit task would be performed – the author does not take a drink of tea in the middle of deleting a word.

We have seen how CCT rules may be informally analyzed to discuss issues of proceduralization and error behavior, and how we can relate them to GOMS-like goal hierarchies. However, the main aim of CCT is (as its name suggests) to be able to measure the complexity of an interface.

Basically, the more production rules in the CCT description the more difficult the interface is to learn. This claim rests on the assumption that the production rules represent reasonably accurately the way knowledge is stored and therefore that the time taken to learn an interface is roughly proportional to the number of rules you have to learn.

We have only discussed the user side of CCT here. If the cognitive user description is complemented by a description of the system, it is claimed that one can predict the difficulty of the mapping between the user's goals and the system model. The generalized transition networks that describe the system grammar themselves have a hierarchical structure. Thus both the description of the user and that of the system can be represented as hierarchies. These can then be compared to find mismatches and to produce a measure of dissonance.

There are various problems with CCT. As with many 'rich' description methods, the size of description for even a part of an interface can be enormous. Furthermore, there may be several ways of representing the same user behavior and interface behavior, yielding different measures of dissonance. To some extent this is catered for by the novice style rules, but there is no such set of rules for the system description.

Another problem is the particular choice of notations. Production rules are often suggested as a good model of the way people remember procedural knowledge, but there are obvious 'cludges' in the CCT description given above. In particular, the working memory entry (NOTE executing insert space) is there purely to allow the INSERT-SPACE-DONE rule to fire at the appropriate time. It is not at all clear that it has any real cognitive significance. One may also question whether the particular notation chosen for the system is critical to the method. One might choose to represent the system using any one of the dialog description notations in Chapter 16. Different notations would probably yield slightly different measures of dissonance.

However, one should regard CCT as an engineering tool giving one a rough measure of learnability and difficulty combined with a detailed description of user behavior.

This can then be used by analysts employing their professional expertise. Arguably, the strength of the central idea of CCT lies beyond the particular notations used.

12.2.3 Problems and extensions of goal hierarchies

The formation of a goal hierarchy is largely a post hoc technique and runs a very real risk of being defined by the computer dialog rather than the user. One way to rectify this is to produce a goal structure based on pre-existing manual procedures and thus obtain a natural hierarchy [201]. To be fair, GOMS defines its domain to be that of expert use, and thus the goal structures that are important are those which users develop out of their use of the system. However, such a natural hierarchy may be particularly useful as part of a CCT analysis, representing a very early state of knowledge.

On the positive side, the conceptual framework of goal hierarchies and user goal stacks can be used to express interface issues, not directly addressed by the notations above. For instance, we can use this to examine in more detail the closure problem with early automated teller machines (ATMs) mentioned in the Design Focus box in Chapter 1, Section 1.3.2. These early ATMs gave the customers the money before returning their cards. Unfortunately, this led to many customers leaving their cards behind. This was despite on-screen messages telling them to wait. This is referred to as a problem of *closure*. The user's principal goal is to get money; when that goal is satisfied, the user does not complete or close the various subtasks which still remain open:

```
GOAL: GET-MONEY
.  GOAL: USE-ATM
.  .   INSERT-CARD
.  .   ENTER-PIN
.  .   ENTER-AMOUNT
.  .   COLLECT-MONEY
        << outer goal now satisfied goal stack popped >>
.  .   COLLECT-CARD - subgoal operators missed
```

Banks (at least some of them) soon changed the dialog order so that the card was always retrieved before the money was dispensed. A general rule that can be applied to any goal hierarchy from this is that no higher-level goal should be satisfied until all subgoals have been satisfied. However, it is not always easy to predict when the user will consider a goal to have been satisfied. For instance, one of the authors has been known to collect his card and forget the money!

12.3 LINGUISTIC MODELS

The user's interaction with a computer is often viewed in terms of a language, so it is not surprising that several modeling formalisms have developed centered around this concept. Several of the dialog notations described in Chapter 16 are also based on linguistic ideas. Indeed, BNF grammars are frequently used to specify dialogs. The models here, although similar in form to dialog design notations, have been proposed with the intention of understanding the user's behavior and analyzing the cognitive difficulty of the interface.

12.3.1 BNF

Representative of the *linguistic approach* is Reisner's use of Backus–Naur Form (*BNF*) rules to describe the dialog grammar [301]. This views the dialog at a purely syntactic level, ignoring the semantics of the language. BNF has been used widely to specify the syntax of computer programming languages, and many system dialogs can be described easily using BNF rules. For example, imagine a graphics system that has a line-drawing function. To select the function the user must select the 'line' menu option. The line-drawing function allows the user to draw a polyline, that is a sequence of line arcs between points. The user selects the points by clicking the mouse button in the drawing area. The user double clicks to indicate the last point of the polyline.

```
draw-line       ::- select-line + choose-points
                    + last-point
select-line     ::= position-mouse + CLICK-MOUSE
choose-points   ::= choose-one
                    | choose-one + choose-points
choose-one      ::= position-mouse + CLICK-MOUSE
last-point      ::= position-mouse + DOUBLE-CLICK-MOUSE
position-mouse  ::= empty | MOVE-MOUSE + position-mouse
```

The names in the description are of two types: *non-terminals*, shown in lower case, and *terminals*, shown in upper case. Terminals represent the lowest level of user behavior, such as pressing a key, clicking a mouse button or moving the mouse. Non-terminals are higher-level abstractions. The non-terminals are defined in terms of other non-terminals and terminals by a definition of the form

```
name ::= expression
```

The '::=' symbol is read as 'is defined as'. Only non-terminals may appear on the left of a definition. The right-hand side is built up using two operators '+' (sequence) and '|' (choice). For example, the first rule says that the non-terminal draw-line is defined to be select-line followed by choose-points followed by last-point. All of these are non-terminals, that is they do not tell us what the basic user actions are. The second rule says that select-line is defined to be position-mouse (intended to be over the 'line' menu entry) followed by CLICK-MOUSE. This is our first terminal and represents the actual clicking of a mouse.

To see what position-mouse is, we look at the last rule. This tells us that there are two possibilities for position-mouse (separated by the '|' symbol). One option is that position-mouse is empty – a special symbol representing no action. That is, one option is not to move the mouse at all. The other option is to do a MOVE-MOUSE action followed by position-mouse. This rule is recursive, and this second position-mouse may itself either be empty or be a MOVE-MOUSE action followed by position-mouse, and so on. That is, position-mouse may be any number of MOVE-MOUSE actions whatsoever.

Similarly, choose-points is defined recursively, but this time it does not have the option of being empty. It may be *one or more* of the non-terminal choose-one which is itself defined to be (like select-line) position-mouse followed by CLICK-MOUSE.

The BNF description of an interface can be analyzed in various ways. One measure is to count the number of rules. The more rules an interface requires to use it, the more complicated it is. This measure is rather sensitive to the exact way the interface is described. For example, we could have replaced the rules for choose-points and choose-one with the single definition

```
choose-points ::= position-mouse + CLICK-MOUSE
               | position-mouse + CLICK-MOUSE + choose-points
```

A more robust measure also counts the number of '+' and '|' operators. This would, in effect, penalize the more complex single rule. Another problem arises with the rule for select-line. This is identical to the choose-one rule. However, the acts of selecting a menu option and choosing a point on a drawing surface are obviously so different that they must surely be separated. Decisions like this about the structure of a BNF description are less of a problem in practice than the corresponding problems we had with CCT.

In addition to these complexity measures for the language as a whole, we can use the BNF definition to work out how many basic actions are required for a particular task, and thus obtain a crude estimate of the difficulty of that task.

The BNF description above only represented the user's actions, not the user's perception of the system's responses. This input bias is surprisingly common amongst cognitive models, as we will discuss in Section 12.4. Reisner has developed extensions to the basic BNF descriptions, which attempt to deal with this by adding 'information-seeking actions' to the grammar.

12.3.2 Task–action grammar

Measures based upon BNF have been criticized as not 'cognitive' enough. They ignore the advantages of consistency both in the language's structure and in its use of command names and letters. *Task–action grammar* (*TAG*) [284] attempts to deal with some of these problems by including elements such as parametrized grammar rules to emphasize consistency and encoding the user's world knowledge (for example, up is the opposite of down).

To illustrate consistency, we consider the three UNIX commands: cp (for copying files), mv (for moving files) and ln (for linking files). Each of these has two possible forms. They either have two arguments, a source and destination filename, or have any number of source filenames followed by a destination directory:

```
copy ::=    'cp' + filename + filename
          | 'cp' + filenames + directory
move ::=    'mv' + filename + filename
          | 'mv' + filenames + directory
link ::=    'ln' + filename + filename
          | 'ln' + filenames + directory
```

Measures based upon BNF could not distinguish between these consistent commands and an inconsistent alternative – say if ln took its directory argument first. Task–action grammar was designed to reveal just this sort of consistency. Its description of the UNIX commands would be

```
file-op[Op] :=   command[Op] + filename + filename
               | command[Op] + filenames + directory
command[Op=copy] := 'cp'
command[Op=move] := 'mv'
command[Op=link] := 'ln'
```

This captures the consistency of the commands and closely resembles the original textual description. One would imagine that a measure of the complexity of the language based on the TAG description would be better at predicting actual learning and performance than a simple BNF one.

As well as handling consistency well, TAG has features for talking about 'world knowledge'. For example, imagine we have two command line interfaces for moving a mechanical turtle around the floor.

Command interface 1
```
movement[Direction]
       := command[Direction] + distance + RETURN
command[Direction=forward]    := 'go 395'
command[Direction=backward]   := 'go 013'
command[Direction=left]       := 'go 712'
command[Direction=right]      := 'go 956'
```

Command interface 2
```
movement[Direction]
       := command[Direction] + distance + RETURN
command[Direction=forward]    := 'FORWARD'
command[Direction=backward]   := 'BACKWARD'
command[Direction=left]       := 'LEFT'
command[Direction=right]      := 'RIGHT'
```

The first interface may not be as silly as it seems; the command 'go 395' could refer to the address of a machine-code routine, which performs the appropriate movement. However, it is absolutely clear that the second interface is preferable to the first. TAG includes a special form known-item, which is used to denote information that the user will already know, and thus not need to learn in order to use the system. Using this form, the TAG rules for the second interface are rewritten

Command interface 2

```
movement[Direction]
      := command[Direction] + distance + RETURN
command[Direction]:= known-item[Type=word,Direction]
*  command[Direction=forward]   := 'FORWARD'
*  command[Direction=backward]  := 'BACKWARD'
*  command[Direction=left]      := 'LEFT'
*  command[Direction=right]     := 'RIGHT'
```

The starred rules can be generated from the second rule using the user's world knowledge. They are included in any TAG description for completeness, but are not counted in any measure of complexity.

Sometimes it may not be clear what the appropriate command is, but once we know one, the rest become obvious. For example, consider a simple database displaying a list of records. We are expecting two commands, one to move up the list to the previous record, and another to move down the list to the next record. There are several options for the commands, for instance UP/DOWN, PREVIOUS/NEXT, possibly in upper or lower case, possibly also just the first letter of the relevant word. In addition, one might have mixed-up command sets such as UP/NEXT or N/previous. The fact that any of the former set of commands is easier to learn than the mixed-up commands is called *congruence*. TAG has a notation to describe the congruence of an interface. The notation F('next') is used to denote the feature set related to the word 'next'. That is, next/previous. With this notation a congruent grammar requires only one 'real' rule, such as

```
browse[Direction] := F('next') + return
*  browse[Direction=up]    := 'previous' + return
*  browse[Direction=down]  := 'next' + return
```

We have seen that the notation allows one to say that the commands RIGHT and LEFT are consistent for opposite actions. How do we know that the user regards the opposite of RIGHT to be LEFT rather than WRONG? Obviously, the inclusion of world knowledge depends upon the user of the system – the above certainly assumes that the user's language is English. The designer is responsible for the input of this world knowledge into the TAG description and its validity will depend on the professional judgment of the designer. However, TAG will make these assumptions clear and thus, by highlighting them, hold them up for inspection.

12.4 THE CHALLENGE OF DISPLAY-BASED SYSTEMS

Both goal hierarchical and grammar-based techniques were initially developed when most interactive systems were command line, or at most, keyboard and cursor based. There are significant worries, therefore, about how well these approaches can generalize to deal with more modern windowed and mouse-driven interfaces.

Both families of techniques largely ignore system output – what the user sees. The implicit assumption is that the users know exactly what they want to do and execute the appropriate command sequences blindly. There are exceptions to this. We have already mentioned how Reisner's BNF has been extended to include assertions about output. In addition, TAG has been extended to include information about how the display can affect the grammar rules [180].

Another problem for grammars is the lowest-level lexical structure. Pressing a cursor key is a reasonable *lexeme*, but moving a mouse one pixel is less sensible. In addition, pointer-based dialogs are more display oriented. Clicking a cursor at a particular point on the screen has a meaning dependent on the current screen contents. This problem can be partially resolved by regarding operations such as 'select region of text' or 'click on quit button' as the terminals of the grammar. If this approach is taken, the detailed mouse movements and parsing of mouse events in the context of display information (menus, etc.) are abstracted away.

Goal hierarchy methods have different problems, as more display-oriented systems encourage less structured methods for goal achievement. Instead of having well-defined plans, the user is seen as performing a more exploratory task, recognizing fruitful directions and backing out of others. Typically, even when this exploratory style is used at one level, we can see within it and around it more goal-oriented methods. So, for example, we might consider the high-level goal structure

```
WRITE_LETTER
.       FIND_SIMILAR_LETTER
.       COPY_IT
.       EDIT_COPY
```

However, the task of finding a similar letter would be exploratory, searching through folders, etc. Such recognition-based searching is extremely difficult to represent as a goal structure. Similarly, the actual editing would depend very much on non-planned activities: 'ah yes, I want to reuse that bit, but I'll have to change that'. If we then drop to a lower level again, goal hierarchies become more applicable. For instance, during the editing stage we might have the 'delete a word' subdialog:

```
DELETE_WORD
.       SELECT_WORD
.       .       MOVE_MOUSE_TO_WORD_START
.       .       DEPRESS_MOUSE_BUTTON
.       .       MOVE_MOUSE_TO_WORD_END
.       .       RELEASE_MOUSE_BUTTON
.       CLICK_ON_DELETE
.       .       MOVE_MOUSE_TO_DELETE_ICON
.       .       CLICK_MOUSE_BUTTON
```

Thus goal hierarchies can partially cope with display-oriented systems by an appropriate choice of level, but the problems do emphasize the rather prescriptive nature of the cognitive models underlying them.

These problems have been one of the factors behind the growing popularity of *situated action* [334] and *distributed cognition* [208, 185] in HCI (see also Chapter 14). Both approaches emphasize the way in which actions are contingent upon events and determined by context, rather than being pre-planned. At one extreme, protagonists of these approaches seem to deny any planned actions or long-term goals. On the other hand, traditional cognitive modelers are modeling *display-based cognition* using production rules and similar methods, which include sensory data within the models.

At a low level, chunked expert behavior is modeled effectively using hierarchical or linguistic models, and is where the *keystroke-level model* (discussed in Section 12.5.1 below) has proved effective. In contrast, it is clear that no amount of cognitive modeling can capture the activity during the writing of a poem. Between these two, cognitive models will have differing levels of success and utility. Certainly, models at all but the lowest levels must take into account the user's reactions to feedback from the system, otherwise they cannnot address the fundamental issue of *interactivity* at all.

12.5   PHYSICAL AND DEVICE MODELS

12.5.1 Keystroke-level model

Compared with the deep cognitive understanding required to describe problem-solving activities, the human motor system is well understood. *KLM* (*Keystroke-Level Model* [55]) uses this understanding as a basis for detailed predictions about user performance. It is aimed at unit tasks within interaction – the execution of simple command sequences, typically taking no more than 20 seconds. Examples of this would be using a search and replace feature, or changing the font of a word. It does not extend to complex actions such as producing a diagram. The assumption is that these more complex tasks would be split into subtasks (as in GOMS) before the user attempts to map them into physical actions. The task is split into two phases:

acquisition of the task, when the user builds a mental representation of the task;

execution of the task using the system's facilities.

KLM only gives predictions for the latter stage of activity. During the acquisition phase, the user will have decided how to accomplish the task using the primitives of the system, and thus, during the execution phase, there is no high-level mental activity – the user is effectively expert. KLM is related to the GOMS model, and can be thought of as a very low-level GOMS model where the method is given.

The model decomposes the execution phase into five different physical motor operators, a mental operator and a system response operator:

K   Keystroking, actually striking keys, including shifts and other modifier keys.

B   Pressing a mouse button.

P   Pointing, moving the mouse (or similar device) at a target.

H   Homing, switching the hand between mouse and keyboard.

D   Drawing lines using the mouse.

M   Mentally preparing for a physical action.

R   System response which may be ignored if the user does not have to wait for it, as in copy typing.

The execution of a task will involve interleaved occurrences of the various operators. For instance, imagine we are using a mouse-based editor. If we notice a single character error we will point at the error, delete the character and retype it, and then return to our previous typing point. This is decomposed as follows:

1. Move hand to mouse   H[mouse]
2. Position mouse after bad character   PB[LEFT]
3. Return to keyboard   H[keyboard]
4. Delete character   MK[DELETE]
5. Type correction   K[char]
6. Reposition insertion point   H[mouse]**MPB**[LEFT]

Notice that some operators have descriptions added to them, representing which device the hand homes to (for example, [mouse]) and what keys are hit (for example, LEFT – the left mouse button).

The model predicts the total time taken during the execution phase by adding the component times for each of the above activities. For example, if the time taken for one keystroke is t_K, then the total time doing keystrokes is

$$T_K = 2t_K$$

Similar calculations for the rest of the operators give a total time of

$$T_{execute} = T_K + T_B + T_P + T_H + T_D + T_M + T_R$$
$$= 2t_K + 2t_B + t_P + 3t_H + 0 + 2t_M + 0$$

In this example, the system response time was zero. However, if the user had to wait for the system then the appropriate time would be added. In many typing tasks, the user can type ahead anyway and thus there is no need to add response times. Where needed, the response time can be measured by observing the system.

The times for the other operators are obtained from empirical data. The keying time obviously depends on the typing skill of the user, and different times are thus used for different users. Pressing a mouse button is usually quicker than typing (especially for two-finger typists), and a more accurate time prediction can be made by separating out the button presses **B** from the rest of the keystrokes **K**. The pointing time can be calculated using Fitts' law (see Chapter 1), and thus depends on the size and position of the target.[1] Alternatively, a fixed time based on average within

---

1 The form of Fitts' law used with the original KLM is $K \log_2(D/S + 0.5)$, where D is the distance to the target and S is the target size. We will use this form for calculations in this subsection, but revert to the form $a + b \log_2(D/S + 1)$ in the next subsection when we consider Buxton's three-state model, as this form was used for these experiments.

Table 12.1   Times for various operators in the keystroke-level model (adapted from Card, Moran and Newell [56], published and reprinted by permission of Lawrence Erlbaum Associates, Inc.)

Operator	Remarks	Time (s)
K	Press key	
	good typist (90 wpm)	0.12
	poor typist (40 wpm)	0.28
	non-typist	1.20
B	Mouse button press	
	down or up	0.10
	click	0.20
P	Point with mouse	
	Fitts' law	$0.1 \log_2(D/S + 0.5)$
	average movement	1.10
H	Home hands to and from keyboard	0.40
D	Drawing – domain dependent	–
M	Mentally prepare	1.35
R	Response from system – measure	–

wpm = words per minute

screen pointing can be used. Drawing time depends on the number and length of the lines drawn, and is fairly domain specific, but one can easily use empirical data for more general drawing tasks. Finally, homing time and mental preparation time are assumed constant. Typical times are summarized in Table 12.1.

The mental operator is probably the most complex part of KLM. Remember that the user is assumed to have decided what to do, and how to do it. The mental preparation is thus just the slight pauses made as the user recalls what to do next. There are complicated heuristics for deciding where to put **M** operators, but they all boil down to the level of chunking (see Chapter 1 for a discussion of chunking). If the user types a word, or a well-known command name, this will be one chunk, and hence only require one mental operator. However, if a command name was an acronym which the user was recalling letter by letter, then we would place one **M** operator per letter.

The physical operator times all depend on the skills of the user. Also, the mental operator depends on the level of chunking, and hence the expertise of the user. You must therefore decide before using KLM predictions just what sort of user you are thinking about. You cannot even work out the operators and then fill in the times later, as different users may choose different methods and have different placings of **M** operators due to chunking. This sounds rather onerous, but the predictions made by KLM are only meant to be an approximation, and thus reasonable guesses about levels of expertise are enough.

Individual predictions may be interesting, but the power of KLM lies in comparison. Given several systems, we can work out the methods to perform key tasks, and then use KLM to tell us which system is fastest. This is considerably cheaper than conducting lengthy experiments (levels of individual variation would demand vast numbers of trials – see Chapter 9). Furthermore, the systems need not even exist. From a description of a proposed system, we can predict the times taken for tasks. As well as comparing systems, we can compare methods within a system. This can be useful in preparing training materials, as we can choose to teach the faster methods.

Using the keystroke-level model

As an example, we compare the two methods for iconizing a window given in Section 12.2.1. One used the 'L7' function key, and the other the 'CLOSE' option from the window's pop-up menu. The latter is obtained by moving to the window's title bar, depressing the left mouse button, dragging the mouse down the pop-up menu to the 'CLOSE' option, and then releasing the mouse button. We assume that the user's hand is on the mouse to begin with, and hence only the L7-METHOD will require a homing operator. The operators for the two methods are as follows:

L7-METHOD   **H**[to keyboard] **MK**[L7 function key]
CLOSE-METHOD   **P**[to menu bar] **B**[LEFT down] **MP**[to option] **B**[LEFT up]

The total times are thus

L7-METHOD   = 0.4 + 1.35 + 0.28
                 = 2.03 seconds

CLOSE-METHOD   = 1.1 + 0.1 + 1.35 + 1.1 + 0.1
                 = 3.75 seconds

The first calculation is quite straightforward, but the second needs a little unpacking. The button presses are separate down and then up actions and thus each is timed at only 0.1 of a second, rather than 0.2 for a click, or 0.28 for typing. We have also used the simplified average of 1.1 seconds for the pointing task. From these predictions, we can see that the L7-METHOD is far faster. In Section 12.2.1, Sam's selection rule was to use the L7-METHOD when playing blocks. To do so, he can go on playing the game using the mouse in his right hand whilst moving his left hand over the key. Thus the real time for Sam, from when he takes his attention from the game to when the command is given, is less: 2.03 seconds minus the homing time, that is 1.63 seconds. Given the method is so fast, why does Sam not use it all the time?

Perhaps the average estimates for pointing times have biased our estimate. We can be a little more precise about the CLOSE-METHOD timing if we use Fitts' law instead of the average 1.1 seconds. The mouse will typically be in the middle of a 25 line high window. The title bar is 1.25 lines high. Thus the distance to target ratio for the first pointing task is 10:1. The 'CLOSE' option is four items down on the pop-up menu; hence the ratio for the second pointing task is 4:1. Thus we can calculate the pointing times:

P[to menu bar]   = $0.1 \log_2(10.5)$ = 0.339
P[to option]   = $0.1 \log_2(4.5)$ = 0.217

With these revised timings, KLM predicts the CLOSE-METHOD will take 2.1 seconds. So Sam's selection rule is not quite as bad as it initially seemed!

Worked exercise   *Do a keystroke-level analysis for opening up an application in a visual desktop interface using a mouse as the pointing device, comparing at least two different methods for performing the task. Repeat the exercise using a trackball. Consider how the analysis would differ for various positions of the trackball relative to the keyboard and for other pointing devices.*

Answer   We provide a keystroke-level analysis for three different methods for launching an application on a visual desktop. These methods are analyzed for a conventional one-button mouse, a trackball mounted away from the keyboard and one mounted close to the keyboard. The main distinction between the two trackballs is that the second one does not require an explicit repositioning of the hands, that is there is no time required for homing the hands between the pointing device and the keyboard.

Method 1 Double clicking on application icon

Steps	Operator	Mouse	Trackball₁	Trackball₂
1. Move hand to mouse	**H**[mouse]	0.400	0.400	0.000
2. Mouse to icon	**P**[to icon]	0.664	1.113	1.113
3. Double click	**2B**[click]	0.400	0.400	0.400
4. Return to keyboard	**H**[kbd]	0.400	0.400	0.000
Total times		1.864	2.313	1.513

Method 2 Using an accelerator key

Steps	Operator	Mouse	Trackball₁	Trackball₂
1. Move hand to mouse	**H**[mouse]	0.400	0.400	0.000
2. Mouse to icon	**P**[to icon]	0.664	1.113	1.113
3. Click to select	**B**[click]	0.200	0.200	0.200
4. Pause	**M**	1.350	1.350	1.350
5. Return to keyboard	**H**[kbd]	0.400	0.400	0.000
6. Press accelerator	**K**	0.200	0.200	0.200
Total times		3.214	3.663	2.763

Method 3 Using a menu

Steps	Operator	Mouse	Trackball₁	Trackball₂
1. Move hand to mouse	**H**[mouse]	0.400	0.400	0.000
2. Mouse to icon	**P**[to icon]	0.664	1.113	1.113
3. Click to select	**B**[click]	0.200	0.200	0.200
4. Pause	**M**	1.350	1.350	1.350
5. Mouse to file menu	**P**	0.664	1.113	1.113
6. Pop-up menu	**B**[down]	0.100	0.100	0.100
7. Drag to open	**P**[drag]	0.713	1.248	1.248
8. Release mouse	**B**[up]	0.100	0.100	0.100
9. Return to keyboard	**H**[kbd]	0.400	0.400	0.000
Total times		4.591	6.024	5.224

Card, Moran and Newell empirically validated KLM against a range of systems, both keyboard and mouse based, and a wide selection of tasks. The predictions were found to be remarkably accurate (an error of about 20%). KLM is thus one of the few models capable of giving accurate quantitative predictions about performance. However, the range of applications is correspondingly small. It tells us a lot about the micro-interaction, but not about the larger-scale dialog.

We have seen that you have to be quite careful, as the approximations you make can radically change the results – KLM is a guide, not an oracle. We should also add a word of caution about the assumption that fastest is best. There are certainly situations where this is so, for example highly repetitive tasks such as telephony or data entry. However, even expert users will often not use the fastest method. For example, the expert may have a set of general-purpose, non-optimal methods, rather than a few task-specific methods.

12.5.2 Three-state model

In Chapter 2, we saw that a range of pointing devices exists in addition to the mouse. Often these devices are considered logically equivalent, if the same inputs are available *to the application*. That is, so long as you can select a point on the screen, they are all the same. However, these different devices – mouse, trackball, light pen – feel very different. Although the devices are similar from the application's viewpoint, they have very different sensory–motor characteristics.

Buxton has developed a simple model of input devices [53], the *three-state model*, which captures some of these crucial distinctions. He begins by looking at a mouse. If you move it with no buttons pushed, it normally moves the mouse cursor about. This tracking behavior is termed state 1. Depressing a button over an icon and then moving the mouse will often result in an object being dragged about. This he calls state 2 (see Figure 12.1).

If instead we consider a light pen with a button, it behaves just like a mouse when it is touching the screen. When its button is not depressed, it is in state 1, and when its button is down, state 2. However, the light pen has a third state, when the light pen is not touching the screen. In this state the system cannot track the light pen's position. This is called state 0 (see Figure 12.2).

A touchscreen is like the light pen with no button. While the user is not touching the screen, the system cannot track the finger – that is, state 0 again. When the user touches the screen, the system can begin to track – state 1. So a touchscreen is a state 0–1 device whereas a mouse is a state 1–2 device. As there is no difference between a state 0–2 and a state 0–1 device, there are only the three possibilities we have seen.

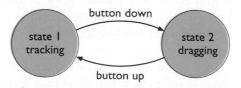

Figure 12.1   Mouse transitions: states 1 and 2

Figure 12.2 Light pen transitions: three states

The only additional complexity is if the device has several buttons, in which case we would have one state for each button: 2_{left}, 2_{middle}, 2_{right}.

One use of this classification is to look at different pointing tasks, such as icon selection or line drawing, and see what state 0–1–2 behavior they require. We can then see whether a particular device can support the required task. If we have to use an inadequate device, it is possible to use keyboard keys to add device states. For example, with a touchscreen, we may nominate the escape key to be the 'virtual' mouse button whilst the user's finger is on the screen. Although the mixing of keyboard and mouse keys is normally a bad habit, it is obviously necessary on occasions.

At first, the model appears to characterize the states of the device by the inputs available to the system. So, from this perspective, state 0 is clearly different from states 1 and 2. However, if we look at the state 1–2 transaction, we see that it is symmetric with respect to the two states. In principle, there is no reason why a program should not decide to do simple mouse tracking whilst in state 2 and drag things about in state 1. That is, there is no reason until you want to type something! The way we can tell state 1 from state 2 is by the activity of the *user*. State 2 requires a button to be pressed, whereas state 1 is one of relative relaxation (whilst still requiring hand–eye coordination for mouse movement). There is a similar difference in tension between state 0 and state 1.

It is well known that Fitts' law has different timing constants for different devices. Recall that Fitts' law says that the time taken to move to a target of size S at a distance D is:

$$a + b \log_2(D/S + 1)$$

The constants a and b depend on the particular pointing device used and the skill of the user with that device. However, the insight given by the three-state model is that these constants also depend on the device state. In addition to the timing, the final accuracy may be affected.

These observations are fairly obvious for state 0–1 devices. With a touchscreen, or light pen, a cursor will often appear under the finger or pen when it comes in contact with the screen. The accuracy with which you can move the cursor around will be far greater than the accuracy with which you can point in the first place. Also it is reasonable to expect that the Fitts' law constant will be different, although not so obvious which will be faster.

There is a similar difference between states 1 and 2. Because the user is holding a button down, the hand is in a state of tension and thus pointing accuracy and speed may be different. Experiments to calculate Fitts' law constants in states 1 and 2 have

Table 12.2 Fitts' law coefficients (after MacKenzie, Sellen and Buxton [221], © 1991 ACM, Inc. Reprinted by permission)

	Device	*a* (ms)	*b* (ms/bit)
Pointing (state 1)			
	Mouse	−107	223
	Trackball	75	300
Dragging (state 2)			
	Mouse	135	249
	Trackball	−349	688

shown that these differences do exist [221]. Table 12.2 shows the results obtained for a mouse and trackball.

We can recalculate the KLM prediction for the CLOSE-METHOD using these data. Recall that the method had two pointing operators, one to point to the window's title bar (with a distance to target size ratio of 10:1), the second to drag the selection down to 'CLOSE' on the pop-up menu (4:1). Thus the first pointing operator is state 1 and the second is state 2. The times are thus

Mouse
$$\mathbf{P}[\text{to menu bar}] = -107 + 223 \log_2(11) = 664 \text{ ms}$$
$$\mathbf{P}[\text{to option}] \quad = 135 + 249 \log_2(5) \quad = 713 \text{ ms}$$

Trackball
$$\mathbf{P}[\text{to menu bar}] = 75 + 300 \log_2(11) \quad = 1113 \text{ ms}$$
$$\mathbf{P}[\text{to option}] \quad = -349 + 688 \log_2(5) \quad = 1248 \text{ ms}$$

giving a further revised time for the CLOSE-METHOD of 2.93 seconds using a mouse and 3.91 seconds using a trackball.

12.6 COGNITIVE ARCHITECTURES

The formalisms we have seen so far have some implicit or explicit model of how the user performs the cognitive processing involved in carrying out a task. For instance, the concept of taking a problem and solving it by divide and conquer using subgoals is central to GOMS. CCT assumes the distinction between long- and short-term memory, with production rules being stored in long-term memory and 'matched' against the contents of short-term (or working) memory to determine which 'fire'. The values for various motor and mental operators in KLM were based on the Model Human Processor (MHP) architecture of Card, Moran and Newell [56]. Another common assumption, which we have not discussed in this chapter, is the distinction between linguistic levels – semantic, syntactic and lexical – as an architectural model of the user's understanding.

In Chapter 1, we discussed some of these architectural descriptions of the user as an information-processing machine. Our emphasis in this section will be to describe a couple more architectural models that are quite distinct from those described in Chapter 1 and assumed in the earlier parts of this chapter. Here we will see that the architectural assumptions are central to the description of the cognitive modeling that these approaches offer.

There are interesting differences of emphasis between these architectural models and the previous models. The hierarchical and linguistic notations tend to assume perfect dialog on the user's part. They may measure the complexity of that perfect dialog, but tend not to consider diversions from the optimal command sequences. However, for the architectural models in this section the prediction and understanding of error is central to their analyses.

12.6.1 The problem space model

Rational behavior is characterized as behavior that is intended to achieve a specific goal. This element of rationality is often used to distinguish between intelligent and machine-like behavior. In the field of artificial intelligence (AI), a system exhibiting rational behavior is referred to as a *knowledge-level* system. A knowledge-level system contains an *agent* behaving in an environment. The agent has knowledge about itself and its environment, including its own goals. It can perform certain actions and sense information about its changing environment. As the agent behaves in its environment, it changes the environment and its own knowledge. We can view the overall behavior of the knowledge-level system as a sequence of environment and agent states as they progress in time. The goal of the agent is characterized as a preference over all possible sequences of agent/environment states.

Contrast this rational behavior with another general computational model for a machine, which is not rational. In computer science, it is common to describe a problem as the search through a set of possible states, from some initial state to a desired state. The search proceeds by moving from one state to another possible state by means of operations or actions, the ultimate goal of which is to arrive at one of the desired states. This very general model of computation is used in the ordinary task of the programmer. Once she has identified a problem and a means of arriving at the solution to the problem (the algorithm), the programmer then represents the problem and algorithm in a programming language, which can be executed on a machine to reach the desired state. The architecture of the machine only allows the definition of the search or *problem space* and the actions that can occur to traverse that space. Termination is also assumed to happen once the desired state is reached. Notice that the machine does not have the ability to formulate the problem space and its solution, mainly because it has no idea of the goal. It is the job of the programmer to understand the goal and so define the machine to achieve it.

We can adapt the state-based computational model of a machine in order to realize the architecture of a knowledge-level system. The new computational model is the *problem space model*, based on the problem-solving work of Newell and Simon at Carnegie–Mellon University (see Chapter 1). A problem space consists of a set of states and a set of operations that can be performed on the states. Behavior in a problem space is a two-step process. First, the current operator is chosen based on the current state and then it is applied to the current state to achieve the new state. The problem space must represent rational behavior, and so it must characterize the goal of the agent. A problem space represents a goal by defining the desired states as a subset of all possible states. Once the initial state is set, the task within the problem space is to find a sequence of operations that form a path within the state space from the initial state to one of the desired states, whereupon successful termination occurs.

From the above description, we can highlight four different activities that occur within a problem space: goal formulation, operation selection, operation application and goal completion. The relationship between these problem space processes and knowledge-level activity is key. Perception that occurs at the knowledge level is performed by the goal formulation process, which creates the initial state based on observations of the external environment. Actions at the knowledge level are operations in the problem space which are selected and applied. The real knowledge about the agent and its environment and goals is derived from the state/operator information in the problem space. Because of the goal formulation process, the set of desired states indicates the knowledge-level goal within the problem space. The operation selection process selects the appropriate operation at a given point in time because it is deemed the most likely to transform the state in the problem space to one of the desired states; hence rational behavior is implied.

The cycle of activity within the problem space is as follows. Some change in the external environment, which is relevant to the goal of the agent, is sensed by the goal formulation process, which in turn defines the set of desired states for the agent and its initial state for the following task. The operation selection process suggests an operation that can act on that state and transform it 'closer' to a desired state. The operation application process executes the operation, changing the current state and surrounding environment. If the new state is a desired state, then the goal has been achieved and the goal completion process reverts the agent to inactive.

The real power of the problem space architecture is in recursion. The activity of any of the processes occurs only when the knowledge it needs to complete its chore is immediately available. For example, to decide which operation is most likely to lead to a desired state, the problem space will need to know things about its current state and that of the environment. If that information is not immediately available, then activity cannot continue. In that case, another problem space is invoked with the goal of finding out the information that was needed by the parent problem space. In this way, we can see the evolution of problems spaces as a stack-like structure, new spaces being invoked and placed on the problem space stack only to be popped off the stack once they achieve their goal.

Though the problem space model described briefly above is not directly implementable, it is the basis for at least one executable cognitive architecture, called Soar.

We shall not discuss the details of Soar's implementation here; instead we refer you to Laird, Newell and Rosenbloom [205]. An interesting application of the Soar implementation of problem spaces has been done by Young and colleagues on *programmable user models* (or *PUMs*) [386]. Given a designer's description of an intended procedure or task that is to be carried out with an interactive system, an analysis of that procedure produces the knowledge that would be necessary and available for any user attempting the task. That knowledge is encoded in the problem space architecture of Soar, producing a 'programmed' user model (the PUM) to accomplish the goal of performing the task. By executing the PUM, the stacking and unstacking of problem spaces needed to accomplish the goal can be analyzed to measure the cognitive load of the intended procedure. More importantly, if the PUM cannot achieve the goal because it cannot find some knowledge necessary to complete the task, this indicates to the designer that there is a problem with the intended design. In this way, erroneous behavior can be predicted before implementation.

12.6.2 Interacting cognitive subsystems

Barnard has proposed a very different cognitive architecture, called *interacting cognitive subsystems* (*ICS*) [24, 25, 27]. ICS provides a model of perception, cognition and action, but unlike other cognitive architectures, it is not intended to produce a description of the user in terms of sequences of actions that he performs. ICS provides a more holistic view of the user as an information-processing machine. The emphasis is on determining how easy particular procedures of action sequences become as they are made more automatic within the user.

ICS attempts to incorporate two separate psychological traditions within one cognitive architecture. On the one hand is the architectural and general-purpose information-processing approach of short-term memory research. On the other hand is the computational and representational approach characteristic of psycholinguistic research and AI problem-solving literature.

The architecture of ICS is built up by the coordinated activity of nine smaller subsystems: five peripheral subsystems are in contact with the physical world and four are central, dealing with mental processes. Each subsystem has the same generic structure. A subsystem is described in terms of its typed inputs and outputs along with a memory store for holding typed information. It has transformation functions for processing the input and producing the output and permanently stored information. Each of the nine subsystems is specialized for handling some aspect of external or internal processing. For example, one peripheral subsystem is the visual system for describing what is seen in the world. An example of a central subsystem is one for the processing of propositional information, capturing the attributes and identities of entities and their relationships with each other (a particular example is that propositional information represents '"knowing" that a particular word has four syllables, begins with "P" and refers to an area in central London' [27]).

ICS is another example of a general cognitive architecture that can be applied to interactive design. One of the features of ICS is its ability to explain how a user proceduralizes action. Remember in the discussion of CCT we distinguished between novice and expert use of an interactive system. Experts can perform complicated sequences of actions as if without a thought, whereas a novice user must contemplate each and every move (if you do not believe this distinction is accurate, observe users at an ATM and see if you can tell the expert from the novice). The expert recognizes the task situation and recalls a 'canned' procedure of actions which, from experience, results in the desired goal being achieved. They do not have to think beyond the recognition of the task and consequent invocation of the correct procedure. Such proceduralized behavior is much less prone to error. A good designer will aid the user in proceduralizing his interaction with the system and will attempt to design an interface that suggests to the user a task for which he already has a proceduralized response. It is for this reason that ICS has been suggested as a design tool that can act as an expert system to advise a designer in developing an interface.

12.7   SUMMARY

In this chapter, we have discussed a wide selection of cognitive models of the users of interactive systems. Cognitive models attempt to represent the users as they interact with a system, modeling aspects of their understanding, knowledge, intentions or processing. We divided cognitive models into three categories. The first described the hierarchical structuring of the user's task and goal structures. The GOMS model and CCT were examples of cognitive models in this category. The second category was concerned with linguistic and grammatical models, which emphasized the user's understanding of the user–system dialog. BNF and TAG were described as examples in this category. Most of these cognitive models have focussed on the execution activity of the user, neglecting his perceptive ability and how that might affect less planned and natural interaction strategies. The third category of cognitive models was based on the more solid understanding of the human motor system, applicable in situations where the user does no planning of behavior and executes actions automatically. KLM was used to provide rough measures of user performance in terms of execution times for basic sequences of actions. Buxton's three-state model for pointing devices allowed for a finer distinction between execution times than with KLM. We concluded this chapter with a discussion of cognitive architectures, the assumptions of which form the foundation for any cognitive models. In addition to the basic architectural distinction between long- and short-term memory, we discussed two other cognitive architectures – the problem space model and ICS – which apply different assumptions to the analysis of interactive systems.

EXERCISES

12.1 Recall the CCT description of the rule INSERT-SPACE-2 discussed in Section 12.2.2:

```
(INSERT-SPACE-2
IF  (AND (TEST-GOAL insert space)
                (TEST-CURSOR %LINE %COL) )
THEN    (       (DO-KEYSTROKE 'I')
                (DO-KEYSTROKE SPACE)
                (DO-KEYSTROKE ESC)
                (DELETE-GOAL insert space) ))
```

As we discussed, this is already proceduralized; that is, the rule is an expert rule. Write new 'novice' rules where the three keystrokes are not proceduralized. That is, you should have separate rules for each keystroke and suitable goals (such as GET-INTO-INSERT-MODE) to fire them.

12.2 One of the assumptions underlying the programmable user model approach is that it is possible to provide an algorithm to describe the user's behavior in interacting with a system. Taking this position to the extreme, choose some common task with a familiar interactive system (for example, creating a column of numbers in a spreadsheet and calculating their sum, or any other task you can think of) and describe the algorithm needed by the user to accomplish this task. Write the description in pseudocode. Does this exercise suggest any improvements in the system?

RECOMMENDED READING

S. K. Card, T. P. Moran and A. Newell, *The Psychology of Human Computer Interaction*, Lawrence Erlbaum, 1983.
A classic text in this field of cognitive models, in which the basic architectural assumptions of the Model Human Processor architecture are explained as well as the GOMS model and KLM.

S. Bovair, D. E. Kieras and P. G. Polson, The acquisition and performance of text-editing skill: a cognitive complexity analysis, *Human–Computer Interaction*, Vol. 5, No. 1, pp. 1–48, 1990.
This article provides a definitive description of CCT by means of an extended example. The authors also provide the definition of various style rules for writing CCT descriptions to distinguish, for example, between novice and expert users.

F. Schiele and T. Green, HCI formalisms and cognitive psychology: the case of task–action grammars. In M. D. Harrison and H. W. Thimbleby, editors, *Formal Methods in Human–Computer Interaction*, Chapter 2, Cambridge University Press, 1990.

A good description of TAG with several extended examples based on the Macintosh interface. The authors provide a good comparative analysis of TAG versus other cognitive modeling techniques.

A. Newell, G. Yost, J. E. Laird, P. S. Rosenbloom and E. Altmann, Formulating the problem-space computational model. In R. F. Rashid, editor, *CMU Computer Science: A 25th Anniversary Commemorative*, Chapter 11, ACM Press, 1991.
The description of the problem space cognitive architecture was informed by this article, which also contains references to essential work on the Soar platform.

J. Carroll, editor, *HCI Models, Theories, and Frameworks: Toward an Interdisciplinary Science*, Morgan Kaufmann, 2003.
See chapters by Scott MacKenzie on motor behavior models (Fitts' law and beyond), Bonnie John on information processing and skilled behavior (GOMS and related models) and Stephen Payne on cognitive and mental models.

13 SOCIO-ORGANIZATIONAL ISSUES AND STAKEHOLDER REQUIREMENTS

OVERVIEW

- There are several organizational issues that affect the acceptance of technology by users and that must therefore be considered in system design:
  - systems may not take into account conflict and power relationships
  - those who benefit may not do the work
  - not everyone may use systems.

- In addition to generic issues, designers must identify specific stakeholder requirements within their organizational context.

- Socio-technical models capture both human and technical requirements.

- Soft systems methodology takes a broader view of human and organizational issues.

- Participatory design includes the user directly in the design process.

- Ethnographic methods study users in context, attempting to take an unbiased perspective.

13.1   INTRODUCTION

As we saw in Chapter 3, technology does not exist in a vacuum. It is used within a specific context, and is influenced by many factors within that context. The different people affected by the introduction of a system are known as stakeholders and their needs can be both complex and conflicting. In addition, we need to understand how the introduction of the system might actually change the organizational and work practices that are currently in place and what the impact of this might be.

In this chapter we look in more detail at the socio-organizational context of use and discuss some of the generic issues that can affect the acceptance of technology in organizations. We then look at a number of approaches to modeling the socio-organizational context and the requirements of the stakeholders within it.

Requirements capture is an important part of all software engineering methodologies but often this activity focusses primarily on the functional requirements of the system – what the system must be able to do – with less emphasis on non-functional human issues such as usability and acceptability. Even where such matters are considered, they may reflect only the management's view of the user's needs rather than gathering information from the users themselves. Stakeholder requirements modeling redresses this balance by identifying the needs of all stakeholders, including the user and anyone else affected by the system, within the context in which it will be used.

We will begin this chapter by discussing some of the organizational issues that arise when new technological solutions are introduced. We then outline a number of models and methods that can be used to capture this broader view of stakeholder requirements, including socio-technical models, soft systems methodology, participatory design and the ethnographic approach.

13.2   ORGANIZATIONAL ISSUES

In this section, we shall look at some of the organizational issues that affect the acceptance and relevance of information and communication systems. These factors often sit 'outside' the system as such, and may involve individuals who never use it. Yet it is often these factors more than any other that determine the success or failure of computer systems. Many systems supporting work in organizations are supporting groups of workers, but this may be through specialist groupware systems (see Chapter 19) or through shared data or processes.

13.2.1 Cooperation or conflict?

The term 'computer-supported *cooperative* work' (CSCW) seems to assume that groups will be acting in a cooperative manner. This is obviously true to some extent;

even opposing football teams cooperate to the extent that they keep (largely) within the rules of the game, but their cooperation only goes so far. People in organizations and groups have conflicting goals, and systems that ignore this are likely to fail spectacularly.

Imagine that an organization is already highly computerized, the different departments all have their own systems and the board decides that an integrated information system is needed. The production manager can now look directly at stocks when planning the week's work, and the marketing department can consult the sales department's contact list to send out marketing questionnaires. All is rosy and the company will clearly run more efficiently – or will it?

The storekeeper always used to understate stock levels slightly in order to keep an emergency supply, or sometimes inflate the quoted levels when a delivery was due from a reliable supplier. Also, requests for stock information allowed the storekeeper to keep track of future demands and hence plan future orders. The storekeeper has now lost a sense of control and important sources of information. Members of the sales department are also unhappy: their contacts are their livelihood. The last thing they want is someone from marketing blundering in and spoiling a relationship with a customer built up over many years. Some of these people may resort to subverting the system, keeping 'sanitized' information online, but the real information in personal files. The system gradually loses respect as the data it holds is incorrect, morale in the organization suffers and productivity drops. The board gets worried and meets to consider upgrading the computer system!

Before installing a new computer system, whether explicitly 'cooperative' or not, one must identify the *stakeholders* who will be affected by it. These are not just the immediate users, but anyone whose jobs will be altered, who supplies or gains information from it, or whose power or influence within the organization will increase or decrease. It will frequently be the case that the formal 'client' who orders the system falls very low on the list of those affected. Be very wary of changes that take power, influence or control from some stakeholders without returning something tangible in their place.

13.2.2 Changing power structures

The identification of stakeholders will uncover information transfer and power relationships that cut across the organizational structure. Indeed, all organizations have these informal networks that support both social and functional contacts. However, the official lines of authority and information tend to flow up and down through line management. New communications media may challenge and disrupt these formal managerial structures.

The physical layout of an organization often reflects the formal hierarchy: each department is on a different floor, with sections working in the same area of an office. If someone from sales wants to talk to someone from marketing then one of them must walk to the other's office. Their respective supervisors can monitor the contact. Furthermore, the physical proximity of colleagues can foster a sense of departmental loyalty. An email system has no such barriers; it is as easy to 'chat' to someone in another department as in your own. This challenges the mediating and controlling role of the line managers.

Furthermore, in face-to-face conversation, the manager can easily exert influence over a subordinate: both know their relative positions and this is reflected in the patterns of conversation and in other non-verbal cues. Email messages lose much of this sense of presence and it is more difficult for a manager to exercise authority. The 'levelling' effect even makes it possible for subordinates to direct messages 'diagonally' across the hierarchy, to their manager's peers, or, even worse, to their manager's manager!

Many organizations are moving toward flatter management structures anyway, so from a strategic viewpoint these effects may be acceptable. But can the organization cope with a disaffected junior management during the transition? For other organizations the effects may be less welcome and the system dropped or heavily regulated. In one case, an email system was introduced and was agreed to be functioning well, but the management, feeling a loss of control and suspicion over their subordinates' communications, introduced logging so that all email messages could be monitored. The system quickly fell into disuse. Logging of email is becoming more widespread with employers using it to identify cases of system 'abuse' by employees. But such activity must be handled carefully: it is as likely to backfire on the management by reducing the productive use of email as it is to have the desired effect.

Technology can be an important vector of social change, but if violent reaction is to be avoided, the impact of the technology must be assessed before it is introduced. In the short term, solutions must be carefully matched to the existing social and organizational structures.

13.2.3 The invisible worker

The ability to work and collaborate at a distance can allow functional groups to be distributed over different sites. This can take the form of cross-functional neighbourhood centers, where workers from different departments do their jobs in electronic contact with their functional colleagues. Alternatively, distributed groupware can allow the true home-based teleworker to operate on similar terms to an office-based equivalent. The ecological and economic advantages of such working practices are now becoming well established, and it seems that communications and CSCW technology can overcome many of the traditional barriers.

In fact, a closer examination reveals that the barriers to such working are not technological but managerial. First of all, management style may make remote working all but impossible. If the approach in an organization is 'management by presence', that is you know someone is working because they are in the office, then there is no way a remote worker is going to be trusted. If, on the other hand, the style is 'management by objectives', that is you know your subordinates are working because they are doing their jobs and producing results, then remote working is not so problematical. Even where remote working is accepted, the lack of physical presence can be a problem. When the time comes for promotion, the present employee may seem more worthy than the distant one – not because of any object-ive criteria, but because presence increases perceived worth.

We can see that, again, social and managerial relationships completely dominate technological considerations. Many video-based groupware systems are intended to create a sense of engagement, of active participation and social presence. Whether this will be sufficient to overcome ingrained attitudes remains to be seen.

13.2.4 Who benefits?

One frequent reason for the failure of information systems is that the people who get the benefits from the system are not the same as those who do the work. One ex-ample, which we discuss in more detail in Chapter 19, is structured message systems such as Lens. In these systems the sender has to do work in putting information into fields appropriately, but it is the recipient who benefits. Another example is shared calendars. The beneficiary of the system is a manager who uses the system to arrange meeting times, but whose personal secretary does the work of keeping the calendar up to date. Subordinates are less likely to have secretarial support, yet must keep up the calendar with little perceived benefit. Of course, chaos results when a meeting is automatically arranged and the subordinates may have to rearrange commitments that have not been recorded on the system. The manager may force use by edict or the system may simply fall into disuse. Many such groupware systems are introduced on a 'see if it works' basis, and so the latter option is more likely.

The lesson is that information systems should aim for some level of *symmetry*. If you have to do work for the system, you should obtain some benefit from it. For the shared calendar, this might involve improving the personal user interface, so that there are definite advantages in using the online system to plan your time rather than using paper (it could even print out Filofax pages). In addition, if people use electronic organizers one could consider integrating these into the system.

13.2.5 Free rider problem

Even where there is no bias toward any particular people, a system may still not function symmetrically, which may be a problem, particularly with shared com-munication systems. One issue is the *free rider problem*. Take an electronic con-ferencing system. If there is plenty of discussion of relevant topics then there are obvious advantages to subscribing and reading the contributions. However, when considering writing a contribution, the effort of doing so may outweigh any benefits. The total benefit of the system for each user outweighs the costs, but for any particu-lar decision the balance is overturned.

To see this situation in a different context imagine an eccentric philanthropist who has gathered three strangers into a room. They are invited to throw money into a pot in the center. When they have done so, the philanthropist will double the money in the pot and then divide it up between them and send them on their way. Each stranger reasons 'If I put in three pennies, then our benefactor will double this to six. These will be distributed between three of us, so I will have only two returned to me.' Clearly, unless the strangers can come to some understanding none of them will put any money in the pot, and none will benefit.

A few free riders in a conference system are often not a problem, as the danger is more likely from too much activity. In addition, in electronic conferences the patterns of activity and silence may reflect other factors such as expertise. However, it is easy for the number of free riders gradually to increase and the system slide into disuse. It is hard to enforce equal use, except by restrictive schemes such as round-robin contributions (everyone contributes something however short). In the real world, such problems are often solved by social pressure, and the free rider reacts to the collective censure of the group. Increasing the *visibility* of participants' contributions might also help these social mechanisms. For example, one could display an activity meter showing the number of contributions from each subscriber. Of course, people may then choose not to subscribe in the first place!

13.2.6 Critical mass

Another issue related to the free rider problem is the need to develop a *critical mass*. When telephones were only in public places, their use as a form of pervasive interpersonal communication was limited. However, once a large number of people have telephones in their homes it becomes worthwhile paying to have a telephone installed. In cost/benefit terms, the early subscribers probably have a smaller benefit than the cost. Only when the number of subscribers increases beyond the critical mass does the benefit *for all* dominate the cost (see Figure 13.1). The situation for conferencing systems and email is, of course, very similar.

We can learn something from the lessons of the telephone system and other successful technologies (but remember, telephones took the best part of 100 years to become pervasive in affluent countries). The telephone was useful for subgroups before it became beneficial for all. Even when only a small proportion of the

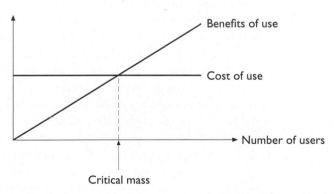

Figure 13.1 Cost/benefit of system use

population had personal telephones, they still formed a significant proportion of their social group, so these cliques of use could grow gradually over time.

The same is true of email. Even a group of two or three people in an organization can use email effectively between themselves. If an organization consists of widening circles of highly connected subgroups, then take-up can grow from the core to the wider group. Of course, the benefits increase as it becomes pervasive, but even a tiny user group ensures that the benefits outweigh the costs. Clearly, we must design any new system so that it has benefits even when its user population is small.

13.2.7 Automating processes – workflow and BPR

The major task in many organizations is moving pieces of paper around. An order is received by phone and an order form filled in by the sales executive. The order form is passed to accounts who check the credit rating and if all is okay it is passed on to stores who check availability and collect the order together at the picking line. When the order is dispatched, a delivery note is packed with the order and a copy is returned to accounts, who send an invoice to the customer.

Organizations have many such processes, and *workflow* systems aim to automate much of the process using electronic forms, which are forwarded to the relevant person based on pre-coded rules. Some workflow systems are built using special-purpose groupware, often based on a notation for describing the desired workflow. Coordinator (see Section 14.3.6) is an example of a workflow system where the rules are heavily influenced by speech act theory. In addition, workflow systems may be implemented using more general structured message systems, including Lotus Notes (see the Design Focus in this section).

The rigid form of a typical workflow system is an example of *global structuring* (see Chapter 19 for more details). The danger with any form of global structuring is that it may conflict with or inhibit more informal and less structured patterns of activity which also contribute to the organization's free running.

A more radical approach to organizational processes is found in *business process re-engineering* (*BPR*). Traditionally, organizations have been structured around functions: sales, accounts, stores, manufacturing. However, the purpose of an organization can be seen in terms of key business processes. The ordering/delivery process described above is a typical and important example. In BPR these processes are recorded and analyzed. Problems in the current process are noted and the whole process may be redesigned in order to make the path of the process more efficient. For example, instead of sending an order to the accounts department to approve, a list of customer credit limits could be given to the sales executives. They could then check the credit rating of the customer whilst on the phone and only forward the order to accounts if there are any unusual problems. Finally, and most radically, the whole structure of the organization may be modified to reflect and support the key processes more closely. Typically, this involves stripping layers of middle management. BPR as an issue engenders zealots and reactionaries in equal measure.

DESIGN FOCUS

Implementing workflow in Lotus Notes

Lotus Notes can be used to implement workflow systems in a straightforward manner. The sales executive fills in an electronic form which is automatically emailed to the accounts department. When it is approved the order form is automatically emailed to stores, and so on.

However, interruptions due to email can be disruptive and reduce efficiency. An alternative is actively not to mail items for action to people, but instead to make them available within their electronic environment. This is like the difference between having a form for approval pushed in front of you to sign compared with having a pile of order forms sitting in your in-tray. In the latter case you can organize your own work, but cannot forget to process the forms as they sit as a permanent reminder – an *environmental cue*.

Within the electronic world of Notes such environmental cues can be implemented using its views mechanism. Each database can have associated several views, lists of items in the database. The definition of the view specifies which fields of each item should be listed and also which items should be included in the list, based on various criteria. The simplest filtering criterion is the type of the message, but more complex criteria can include the state of various fields.

In the ordering process example, there can be a single database. When an order is received, the sales executive creates a new order item and fills in the details of the customer and required products. However, the sales executive does not have write permission for the 'approved' field. The accounts department has a view of the same database. This view lists only those orders which have completed customer details, but a blank 'approved' field. Thus all orders received appear in this listing until they have the 'approved' field completed, at which point they disappear from the view (but not the database). Similarly, the stores department has a view whose rule only shows orders with a completed 'approved' field. Thus the views act as a sort of to-do list.

In the first scenario, the workflow is *automated* and control rests in the system. In the second scenario, the workflow is *supported* leaving control to the users.

13.2.8 Evaluating the benefits

We have seen several problems that can arise from the mismatch between information systems and organizational and social factors. Let us assume that we have a system in place – and it has not fallen apart at the seams. Everyone seems happy with it and there are no secret resentments. Now it is time to count the cost – it was an expensive system to buy and install, but was it worth it?

This is an almost impossible question to answer. The benefits from cooperative systems, especially organization-wide systems such as email or electronic conferencing, are in terms of job satisfaction or more fluid information flow. Some, such as the *video wall* (see Chapter 19), are expected primarily to help social contact within the organization. It may be possible to measure contentment and job satisfaction using attitude questionnaires (see Chapter 9), but any hard economic benefit will be so diffuse as to be unquantifiable.

However, a similar argument could be (and has been) framed for computer use in general. The benefits are difficult to quantify, but, over time, it has become clear that the competitive edge of information technology is necessary for survival in the modern world. Perhaps the same will be said of cooperative systems in a few years.

13.3   CAPTURING REQUIREMENTS

As we have already seen, problems can arise when a system is introduced without a full understanding of all the people who will be affected by it. But how can we better understand and support complex organizational structures, workgroups and potentially conflicting stakeholder needs? We begin by capturing and analyzing requirements, but we need to do this within the work context, taking account of the complex mix of concerns felt by different stakeholders and the structures and processes operating in the workgroups.

In this section we consider several approaches: socio-technical modeling, soft systems methodology, participatory design, ethnographic methods and contextual inquiry. All are aimed at understanding the reality of work contexts and the perspectives of different stakeholders. All recognize that technology can be successfully deployed only if it is done with an understanding of the context of use, but each takes a slightly different approach to the problem. Before we look in more detail at these approaches we need to clarify what we mean when we talk about 'stakeholders'.

13.3.1 Who are the stakeholders?

Understanding stakeholders is key to many of the approaches to requirements capture, since in an organizational setting it is not simply the end-user who is affected by the introduction of new technology. Imagine that a new billing system is to be introduced by a local gas supplier. Who will be affected by this decision? Obviously, the people who are responsible for producing and sending out bills – they will be the ones using the system directly. But where do they get the information from to produce the bills? To whom do they send the bills? Who determines the level of charging and on what grounds? Who stands to make a profit from increased revenue? Who will suffer if customers choose to switch supplier due to the improved service? Meter readers, customers, managers, regulators, shareholders and competitors are all stakeholders in the system. We need approaches that will capture the complexity of their concerns, which may be in conflict with each other.

A stakeholder, therefore, can be defined as anyone who is affected by the success or failure of the system. It can be useful to distinguish different categories of stakeholder, and the following categorization from the CUSTOM approach (see [200]) is helpful for this:

Primary stakeholders are people who actually use the system – the end-users.

Secondary stakeholders are people who do not directly use the system, but receive output from it or provide input to it (for example, someone who receives a report produced by the system).

Tertiary stakeholders are people who do not fall into either of the first two categories but who are directly affected by the success or failure of the system (for example, a director whose profits increase or decrease depending on the success of the system).

Facilitating stakeholders are people who are involved with the design, development and maintenance of the system.

Classifying stakeholders – an airline booking system

An international airline is considering introducing a new booking system for use by associated travel agents to sell flights directly to the public. The stakeholders can be classified as follows:

- **Primary stakeholders:** travel agency staff, airline booking staff
- **Secondary stakeholders:** customers, airline management
- **Tertiary stakeholders:** competitors, civil aviation authorities, customers' traveling companions, airline shareholders
- **Facilitating stakeholders:** design team, IT department staff

---

The aim of the design team is to meet the needs of as many stakeholders as possible. However, the reality is that usually stakeholder needs are in conflict with each other. Sometimes this does not matter: a company is unlikely to be too concerned that its competitors' requirement to maintain advantage over it is under threat by the new system (though they need to be aware to monitor how effectively they are maintaining their advantage). However, sometimes it does matter. In the example above, the airline booking system must be usable by travel agency staff but must also fulfill the customer need to find an appropriate ticket at the right price. If it fails in this, the whole system will fail, as the customer will go elsewhere and business will be lost.

As a general rule, the priority of stakeholder needs diminishes as you go down the categories. So primary stakeholders usually take priority over the others. However, this is not always the case. Imagine designing the control panel of a hospital life support machine. The primary stakeholders will be medical staff monitoring a patient's condition. But who, in fact, has the greatest interest in this system working? Surely it is the patient, whose life is dependent on the system's success? In this case the tertiary stakeholder is of vital importance.

All of the approaches we are considering here are concerned with understanding stakeholders within their organizational context.

13.3.2 Socio-technical models

Early in the twentieth century, studies of work focussed on how humans needed to adapt to technical innovations. *Technological determinism*, the view that social change is primarily dictated by technology, with human and social factors being secondary concerns, was prevalent. The socio-technical systems view came about to counter this technology-centric position, by stressing that work systems were composed of both human and machine elements and that it was the interrelationship between these that should be central.

Socio-technical models for interactive systems are therefore concerned with technical, social, organizational and human aspects of design. They recognize the fact that technology is not developed in isolation but as part of a wider organizational environment. It is important to consider social and technical issues side by side so that human issues are not overruled by technical considerations.

The key focus of the socio-technical approach is to describe and document the impact of the introduction of a specific technology into an organization. Methods vary but most attempt to capture certain common elements:

- The problem being addressed: there is a need to understand why the technology is being proposed and what problem it is intended to solve.
- The stakeholders affected, including primary, secondary, tertiary and facilitating, together with their objectives, goals and tasks.
- The workgroups within the organization, both formal and informal.
- The changes or transformations that will be supported.
- The proposed technology and how it will work within the organization.
- External constraints and influences and performance measures.

Information is gathered using methods such as interviews, observation, focus groups and document analysis. The methods guide this information-gathering process and help the analyst to make sense of what is discovered. By attempting to understand these issues, socio-technical approaches aim to provide a detailed view of the role technology will play and the requirements of successful deployment.

We will compare two approaches to illustrate how this may work in practice.

CUSTOM methodology

CUSTOM is a socio-technical methodology designed to be practical to use in small organizations [200]. It is based on the User Skills and Task Match (USTM) approach, developed to allow design teams to understand and fully document user requirements [219]. CUSTOM focusses on establishing stakeholder requirements: all stakeholders are considered, not just the end-users.

It is applied at the initial stage of design when a *product opportunity* has been identified, so the emphasis is on capturing requirements. It is a forms-based methodology, providing a set of questions to apply at each of its stages.

There are six key stages to carry out in a CUSTOM analysis:

1. Describe the organizational context, including its primary goals, physical characteristics, political and economic background.
2. Identify and describe stakeholders. All stakeholders are named, categorized (as primary, secondary, tertiary or facilitating) and described with regard to personal issues, their role in the organization and their job. For example, CUSTOM addresses issues such as stakeholder motivation, disincentives, knowledge, skills, power and influence within the organization, daily tasks and so on.
3. Identify and describe work-groups. A work-group is any group of people who work together on a task, whether formally constituted or not. Again, work-groups are described in terms of their role within the organization and their characteristics.
4. Identify and describe task–object pairs. These are the tasks that must be performed, coupled with the objects that are used to perform them or to which they are applied.
5. Identify stakeholder needs. Stages 2–4 are described in terms of both the current system and the proposed system. Stakeholder needs are identified by considering the differences between the two. For example, if a stakeholder is identified as currently lacking a particular skill that is required in the proposed system then a need for training is identified.
6. Consolidate and check stakeholder requirements. Here the stakeholder needs list is checked against the criteria determined at earlier stages.

Stages 2 to 4 are described in terms of the current situation (before the new technology is introduced) and the proposed situation (after deployment). Stakeholders are asked to express their views not only of their current role and position but of their expectations in the light of the changes that will be made. In this way, stakeholder concerns and goals are elaborated. In addition, the impact of the technology on working practices is considered (Stage 3) and the transformations that will be supported by the system specified (Stage 4).

A shorter version of CUSTOM stakeholder analysis

CUSTOM questions investigate a range of stakeholder characteristics, such as the following:

- What does the stakeholder have to achieve and how is success measured?
- What are the stakeholder's sources of job satisfaction? What are the sources of dissatisfaction and stress?
- What knowledge and skills does the stakeholder have?
- What is the stakeholder's attitude toward work and computer technology?
- Are there any work-group attributes that will affect the acceptability of the product to the stakeholder?
- What are the characteristics of the stakeholder's task in terms of frequency, fragmentation and choice of actions?
- Does the stakeholder have to consider any particular issues relating to responsibility, security or privacy?
- What are the physical conditions in which the stakeholder is working?

The changes from the current position to the proposed position represent the issues that need to be addressed to ensure successful deployment, and these are made explicit during Stages 5 and 6.

CUSTOM provides a useful framework for considering stakeholder requirements and the use of forms and questions (a 'manual' for its use is available [200]) makes it relatively straightforward, if somewhat time consuming, to apply. For less complex situations, a shortened version of CUSTOM stakeholder analysis is available (see the boxed text above). This also provides a checklist for investigations for stages 2–4.

Open System Task Analysis (OSTA)

OSTA [116] is an alternative socio-technical approach, which attempts to describe what happens when a technical system is introduced into an organizational work environment. Like CUSTOM, OSTA specifies both social and technical aspects of the system. However, whereas in CUSTOM these aspects are framed in terms of stakeholder perspectives, in OSTA they are captured through a focus on tasks.

OSTA has eight main stages:

1. The primary task which the technology must support is identified in terms of users' goals.
2. Task inputs to the system are identified. These may have different sources and forms that may constrain the design.
3. The external environment into which the system will be introduced is described, including physical, economic and political aspects.
4. The transformation processes within the system are described in terms of actions performed on or with objects.
5. The social system is analyzed, considering existing work-groups and relationships within and external to the organization.
6. The technical system is described in terms of its configuration and integration with other systems.
7. Performance satisfaction criteria are established, indicating the social and technical requirements of the system.
8. The new technical system is specified.

OSTA uses notations familiar to designers, such as data flow diagrams and textual descriptions.

13.3.3 Soft systems methodology

The socio-technical models we have looked at focus on identifying requirements from both human and technical perspectives, but they assume a technological solution is being proposed. Soft systems methodology (SSM) arises from the same tradition but takes a view of the organization as a system of which technology and people are components. There is no assumption of a particular solution: the emphasis is rather on understanding the situation fully. SSM was developed by Checkland [66]

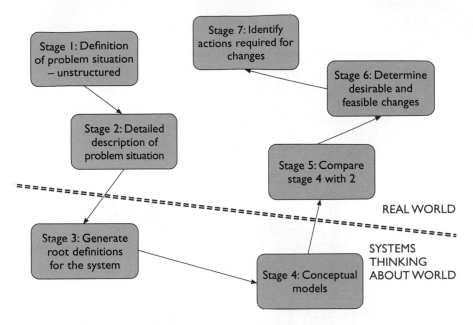

Figure 13.2 The seven stages of soft systems methodology. (Adapted from Checkland [66], p.163)

to help designers reach an understanding of the context of technological developments and the influences and concerns that exist within the system under consideration. SSM has seven stages (see Figure 13.2). A distinction is made between the 'real-world' stages (1–2, 5–7) and the systems stages (3–4).

We will outline the stages here but will focus on those that help capture requirements. The first stage of SSM is the recognition of the problem and initiation of analysis. This is followed by a detailed description of the problem situation: developing a *rich picture*. This will include all the stakeholders, the tasks they carry out and the groups they work in, the organizational structure and its processes and the issues raised by each stakeholder. Any knowledge elicitation techniques can be used to gather the information to build the rich picture, including observation (and video and audio recording), structured and unstructured interviews and questionnaires, and workshops incorporating such activities as role play, simulations and critical incident analysis. In general, less structured approaches are used initially to avoid artificially constraining the description. The rich picture can be in any style – there are no right or wrong answers – but it should be clear and informative to the designer. Certain conventions are widely accepted, however. Speech balloons are used to represent stakeholder issues; crossed swords represent conflicts within the system; and the eye represents external influences or observers. Figure 13.3 shows an example of a rich picture with all of these elements.

Rich pictures are in themselves useful tools to aid understanding of a situation. The rich picture is informal and relatively intuitive. It captures succinctly the potentially conflicting interests of the various stakeholders and the other influences on a

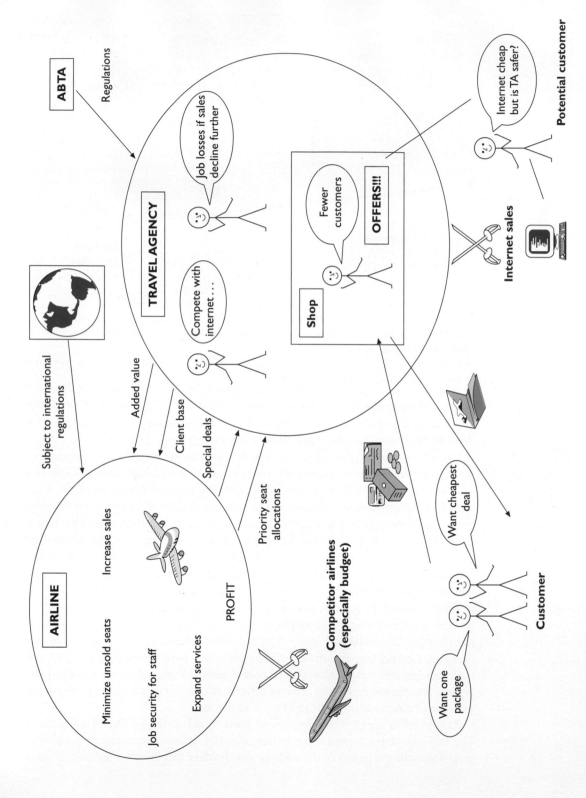

Figure 13.3 A rich picture of a travel agency

design situation. It provides an understandable summary of the designer's understanding that can be easily checked with stakeholders, and it can even be developed collaboratively with stakeholders as part of the consultation process – allowing all parties to contribute to the rich picture sketch. These benefits have led to a number of researchers in HCI proposing their use (outside the full SSM methodology) to inform the design process (see, for example, [239]).

At the next stage in SSM we move from the real world to the systems world and attempt to generate *root definitions* for the system, which define the essence of what the system is about. There may be several root definitions of a system, representing different stakeholder perspectives, for example. Root definitions are described in terms of specific elements, summarized using the acronym, CATWOE:

Clients – those who receive output or benefit from the system.

Actors – those who perform activities within the system.

Transformations – the changes that are effected by the system. This is a critical part of the root definition as it leads to the activities that need to be included in the next stage. These 'transform' the inputs of the system into the required outputs.

Weltanschauung – (from the German) meaning world view. This is how the system is perceived in a particular root definition.

Owner – those to whom the system belongs, to whom it is answerable and who can authorize changes to it.

Environment – the world in which the system operates and by which it is influenced.

Root definition for airline management: an airline booking system

Revisiting our earlier example, an international airline is considering introducing a new booking system for use by associated travel agents to sell flights directly to the public. That is, a system owned by the airline management; operated by associated travel agency staff; working in associated travel agency offices worldwide; operating within regulations specified by international civil aviation authorities and national contract legislation; to sell flights to and reserve seats for customers; and to generate a profit for the company.

- **Client:** customer
- **Actor:** travel agency staff
- **Transformation:** customer's intention and request to travel transformed into sale of seat on flight and profit for organization
- **Weltanschauung:** profits can be optimized by more efficient sales
- **Owner:** airline management
- **Environment:** Regulations of international civil aviation authorities and national contract legislation. Local agency policies worldwide

Once the root definitions have been developed, the *conceptual model* is devised. The conceptual model defines what the system has to do to fulfill the root definitions. It includes identifying the transformations and activities in the system and modeling them hierarchically in terms of what is achieved and how it is achieved. This process is iterative and is likely to take several cycles before it is complete and accurate.

Next we return to the real world with our systems descriptions and compare the actual system with the conceptual model, identifying discrepancies and thereby highlighting any necessary changes or potential problems. For example, a particular activity may have more processes in the real world than in the conceptual model, which may suggest that a reduction of processes for that activity is needed.

In the final stages, we determine which changes are necessary and beneficial to the system as a whole – changes may be structural, procedural or social, for example – and decide on the actions required to effect those changes.

SSM is a flexible approach, which supports detailed consideration of the design context. However, it takes practice to use effectively. There is no single right (or wrong) answer – the SSM is successful if it aids the designer's understanding of the wider system.

13.3.4 Participatory design

Participatory design is a philosophy that encompasses the whole design cycle. It is design in the workplace, where the user is involved not only as an experimental subject or as someone to be consulted when necessary but as a member of the design team. Users are therefore active collaborators in the design process, rather than passive participants whose involvement is entirely governed by the designer. The argument is that users are experts in the work context and a design can only be effective within that context if these experts are allowed to contribute actively to the design process. In addition, introduction of a new system is liable to change the work context and organizational processes, and will only be accepted if these changes are acceptable to the user. Participatory design therefore aims to refine system requirements iteratively through a design process in which the user is actively involved.

Participatory design has three specific characteristics. It aims to improve the work environment and task by the introduction of the design. This makes design and evaluation context or work oriented rather than system oriented. Secondly, it is characterized by collaboration: the user is included in the design team and can contribute to every stage of the design. Finally, the approach is iterative: the design is subject to evaluation and revision at each stage.

The participatory design process utilizes a range of methods to help convey information between the user and designer. They include

Brainstorming   This involves all participants in the design pooling ideas. This is informal and relatively unstructured although the process tends to involve 'on-the-fly' structuring of the ideas as they materialize. All information is recorded without judgment. The session provides a range of ideas from which to work. These can be filtered using other techniques.

Storyboarding   This has been discussed in more detail in Chapter 6. Storyboards can be used as a means of describing the user's day-to-day activities as well as the potential designs and the impact they will have.

Workshops   These can be used to fill in the missing knowledge of both user and designer and provide a more focussed view of the design. They may involve mutual enquiry in which both parties attempt to understand the context of the design from each other's point of view. The designer questions the user about the work environment in which the design is to be used, and the user can query the designer on the technology and capabilities that may be available. This establishes common ground between the user and designer and sets the foundation for the design that is to be produced. The use of role play can also allow both user and designer to step briefly into one another's shoes.

Pencil and paper exercises   These allow designs to be talked through and evaluated with very little commitment in terms of resources. Users can 'walk through' typical tasks using paper mock-ups of the system design. This is intended to show up discrepancies between the user's requirements and the actual design as proposed. Such exercises provide a simple and cheap technique for early assessment of models. PICTIVE [242] is one such approach to paper prototyping, which includes representative stakeholders in a video recorded design session. Each participant prepares 'homework' focussing on the requirements of the system from their particular perspective, which is then used to introduce and orientate the PICTIVE session. Materials such as sticky notes, highlighters, plastic labels, paper and scissors are used on a shared design surface to produce a low-tech prototype of the proposed system, which is finally tested by the group against the tasks identified.

Such methods are not exclusively used in participatory design, of course, and can be used more widely to promote clearer understanding between designer and stakeholders.

Participatory design originated in Scandinavia, where it is now promoted by law and in accepted work practices, but it has not been widely practiced, at least in its fullest form, elsewhere. This may be due to the time and cost involved in what is, by definition, a context-specific design, as well as the organizational implications of the shift of power and responsibility.

However, principles from the participatory design approach have been incorporated in a number of widely used methodologies. We outline one of them – to show how a participatory philosophy can be integrated into organizational and stakeholder analysis.

Effective Technical and Human Implementation of Computer-based Systems (ETHICS)

ETHICS [243] is a method developed by Enid Mumford within the socio-technical tradition, but it is distinct in its view of the role of stakeholders in the process. In the

DESIGN FOCUS

Tomorrow's hospital – using participatory design

The nurse walks around the ward to a patient's bedside. She takes her PDA from her pocket and enters the patient's name. Her PDA is connected via a wireless network to the central patient treatment database and the patient's information comes on screen including reminders of treatments needed. First is a blood pressure and heart rate check. She does these checks and enters the results. A mild painkiller is also prescribed. She gets the tablet, which is individually wrapped in a bar coded packet. Her PDA has a built-in bar code reader and she scans this across the tablet. The system registers the drug's use and removes it from the to-do list as she gives the patient the tablet with a glass of water.

A picture of tomorrow's hospital? In fact, this is exactly the day-to-day activity in Hospital da Trofa, just outside Porto, Portugal. There have been numerous attempts to use PDA-based systems in hospitals. But most have failed. So why is this one being used? The hospital is part of a European Commission funded project Team-HOS and the system was designed using a methodology that has a strong *participatory* focus [316]. From the beginning, nurses, doctors, pharmacologists and dieticians were involved in and in control of the design. It has benefited from their knowledge and experience, which is why it does the right things for the context. Furthermore, the pride with which the hospital staff describe the system shows that they really feel it is their system, not one imposed from above.

See the book website for an extended case study: /e3/casestudy/trofa/

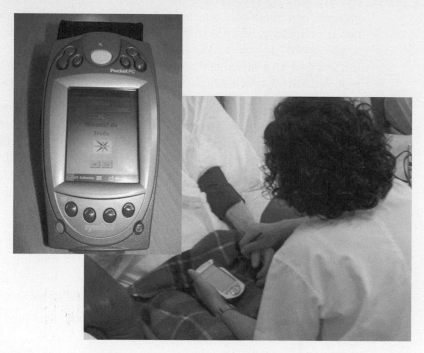

See: www.ieeta.pt/team-hos/ Source: Courtesy of Professor J. Artur Vale Serrano

ETHICS methodology, stakeholders are included as participants in the decision-making process. ETHICS considers the process of system development as one of managing change: conflicts will occur and must be negotiated to ensure acceptance and satisfaction with the system. If any party is excluded from the decision-making process then their knowledge and contribution is not utilized and they are more likely to be dissatisfied. However, participation is not always complete. Mumford recognizes three levels of participation:

Consultative – the weakest form of participation where participants are asked for their opinions but are not decision makers.

Representative – a representative of the participant group is involved in the decision-making process.

Consensus – all stakeholders are included in the decision-making process.

The usual practice is that design groups are set up to include representatives from each stakeholder group and these groups make the design decisions, overseen by a steering committee of management and employee representatives. The design groups then address the following issues and activities:

1. *Make the case for change.* Change for its own sake is inappropriate. If a case cannot be made for changing the current situation then the process ends and the system remains as it is.
2. *Identify system boundaries.* This focusses on the context of the current system and its interactions with other systems, in terms of business, existing technology, and internal and external organizational elements. How will the change impact upon each of these?
3. *Describe the existing system*, including a full analysis of inputs and outputs and the various other activities supported, such as operations, control and coordination.
4. *Define key objectives*, identifying the purpose and function of each area of the organization.
5. *Define key tasks*: what tasks need to be performed to meet these objectives?
6. *Define key information needs*, including those identified by analysis of the existing system and those highlighted by definition of key tasks.
7. *Diagnose efficiency needs*, those elements in the system that cause it to underperform or perform incorrectly. If these are internal they can be redesigned out of the new system; if they are external then the new system must be designed to cope with them.
8. *Diagnose job satisfaction needs*, with a view to increasing job satisfaction where it is low.
9. *Analyze likely future changes*, whether in technology, external constraints (such as legal requirements), economic climate or stakeholder attitudes. This is necessary to ensure that the system is flexible enough to cope with change.
10. *Specify and prioritize objectives based on efficiency*, job satisfaction and future needs. All stakeholders should be able to contribute here as it is a critical stage and conflicting priorities need to be negotiated. Objectives are grouped as either primary (must be met) or secondary (desirable to meet).

The final stages of the ETHICS approach focus on the actual design and evaluation of the system. Necessary organizational changes are designed alongside the technical system. These are then specified in detail, implemented and evaluated.

The ETHICS approach attempts to reach a solution that meets both user and task requirements by having specialist teams negotiate objectives and rank potential solutions. The emphasis is on reaching a solution that ranks highly on job satisfaction to ensure that the solution is acceptable.

It ensures participation at every stage through representative design teams, but can be expensive and time consuming to carry out. However, the benefits in terms of job satisfaction and higher productivity may balance out the initial investment.

13.3.5 Ethnographic methods

All of the approaches considered so far have included some level of consultation and observation of the stakeholders. However, the focus of this has been on gathering stakeholder perspectives rather than specifically studying actual work practice. It can be argued that work can only be understood and studied in context. This is consonant with the ideas of distributed cognition. Taking a worker away from the workplace changes the very nature of the worker's actions. Real action is *situated action*; it occurs in interaction with the materials and people of the workplace [334]. In extremis, it is claimed that an action can only be understood in the place, in the social situation, and at the *time* at which it occurred. Such a level of contextualization is obviously useless for design, and its advocates will in practice generalize from their observations, even if they ostensibly eschew such generalization.

Even if one does not wish to take such an extreme view, it is clear that studying workers in their own situations is extremely worthwhile.

Many branches of sociology and anthropology have long recognized that one cannot study people divorced from their social and cultural context. In particular, *ethnography* has become very influential, particularly in the study of group systems. We were introduced to ethnography briefly in Chapter 9 but here we will consider it in a little more detail, and discuss an approach to contextual requirements capture that reflects the ethnographic tradition but has been developed to be highly practical.

Ethnography is based on very detailed recording of the interactions between people and between people and their environment. It has a special focus on social relationships and how they affect the nature of work. The ethnographer does not enter actively into the situation, and does not see things from a particular person's viewpoint. However, an aim is to be encultured, to understand the situation from within its own cultural framework. Culture here means that of the particular workgroup or organization, rather than that of society as a whole. Ethnographers try to take an unbiased and open-ended view of the situation. They report and do not like to speculate, so it is often unclear how well their approach can contribute to the design of new systems.

Ethnography and participatory design

The ethnographic approach differs markedly from the approach of participatory design. In participatory design the workers come *out* of their work situation, either physically or mentally, and share the design task with the professional designers – effectively the workers become designers. The participatory designer enters into the subjective experience of the workplace. Ethnographic and other situated approaches take the analyst *into* the workplace, while retaining a level of objectivity. The advantage is that the analyst sees the whole group's perspective, rather than that of involved individuals, but the analyst, however much in tune with the workers, is still 'out there'. On the other hand, involving the workers in the design process in itself increases their motivation and acceptance whether or not the resulting design is 'optimal'.

We now look briefly at an approach that takes a pragmatic rather than purist ethnographic perspective, *contextual inquiry*.

Contextual inquiry

Contextual inquiry has much in common with the ethnographic tradition: it studies the user in context, trying to capture the reality of his work culture and practice. However, it is also an approach rooted in practice and it differs in a number of significant ways from pure ethnographic study: the intention is to understand and to interpret the data gathered, and rather than attempting to take an open-ended view, the investigator acknowledges and challenges her particular focus. In addition, the explicit aim is to design a new system, whereas in a pure ethnographic study, it would be open ended.

The model of contextual inquiry is of the investigator being apprenticed to the user to learn about his work. Interviews take place in the workplace so that the objects, artifacts and relationships of the work can be better understood. Examples of work are collected and both verbal and non-verbal communication is studied. The idea is to be as comprehensive in the data gathering as possible and to be concrete. Another central notion of contextual inquiry is that of partnership: the user is the expert in the workplace and is therefore encouraged to lead the investigation. However, the investigator is not a passive observer. Her objective is to gain a shared understanding of how the work happens and, to do so, she questions meaning and offers interpretations of what she observes. The aim is to draw out the implications of comments and actions and understand (rather than assume) what they really mean. In order to do this honestly and effectively the investigator must know her focus – her pre-existing beliefs and assumptions about the situation – and be prepared to challenge and adjust them in the face of new information.

Contextual inquiry focusses on a 2–3 hour interview with the user in the workplace. The idea is to capture and record as much detail as possible, including what the user says and does (step by step), how he communicates and coordinates with others, his feelings and responses to the situation, and a shared understanding of the meaning of actions and artifacts. In addition, objects, examples and artifacts of work are collected and annotated, and the physical work environment is sketched and annotated to show how it is used.

A number of models of the work are developed to capture what is important in the user's work situation:

- The sequence model elaborates the steps required to complete a specific task, as well as the triggers that initiate that sequence of steps.
- The physical model maps the physical work environment and how it impacts upon work practice, for example, an office plan showing where different work activities happen.
- The flow model shows the lines of coordination and communication between the user and other participants within and outside the workplace.
- The cultural model reflects the influences of work culture and policy and shows the scope of these influences. This may include official or unofficial codes of behavior, common expectations (which may or may not be explicit) and value systems.
- The artifact model describes the structure and use of a particular artifact within the work process.

Once the interview is complete, the data must be consolidated with those from other users and stakeholders. There is not space here to elaborate the whole process (see [35] for details) but interviews are transcribed and interpreted as soon as possible after the event by the design team. The team comes together to consider the interview data and to identify commonalities across stakeholders. Affinity diagrams are used to group related information by posting notes on the wall representing a particular comment or observation and grouping these into a hierarchy of related themes. The themes are not pre-determined but arise from the data as they are examined.

Each of the models above is also consolidated across users to provide a common view of the situation. The result is a representation of the required task sequences, artifacts and communication channels that must be supported in the new system as well as the physical and cultural constraints that must be taken into account.

13.4　SUMMARY

We have seen that organizational factors can make or break the deployment of information and communications technology. Any computer system may interfere with the existing authority and social relationships within an organization. There may be a mismatch between those who benefit, and those who do the work. Even where there is no in-built bias, the free rider may put in little personal effort, benefiting from the work of the rest of the group.

We need to identify stakeholders who will be affected directly or indirectly. In particular, junior and middle management may feel they lose control and authority by the introduction of electronic communications. Another example is teleworking, which is made easier by advances in telecommunications, but which makes the worker less visible to management. Even where a system is perceived to be useful, it is hard to quantify its benefits as they are diffused throughout the organization.

In this chapter, we have discussed a selection of socio-organizational approaches to capturing stakeholder requirements, including socio-technical models, soft systems methodology, participatory design and ethnographic approaches. Socio-technical models focus on representing both the human and technical sides of the system in parallel to reach a solution that is compatible with each. SSM models the organization, of which the user is part, as a system. Participatory design sees the user as active not only in using the technology but in designing it. Ethnography, on the other hand, views the user in context, attempting to collect an unbiased view of the user's work culture and practice.

EXERCISES

13.1 A group of universities has decided to collaborate to produce an information system to help potential students find appropriate courses. The system will be distributed free to schools and careers offices on CD-ROM and will provide information about course contents and requirements, university and local facilities, fees and admissions procedures. Identify the main stakeholders for this system, categorize them and describe them and their activities, currently and with regard to the proposed system, using the CUSTOM framework.

13.2 For the scenario proposed above:

(i) Produce a rich picture showing the problem situation (you can use any format that you find helpful).

(ii) Produce a root definition, using CATWOE, of the system from the viewpoint of the university.

What transformations or activities are required to make sure that the root definition is supported?

13.3 The example in Section 13.3.2 (soft systems methodology) provides a root definition for an airline booking system from the perspective of the airline owner. How would this change if it was presented from the perspective of the customer?

13.4 Find case studies of participatory design in action and use these to provide a critique of the approach. What are the benefits and weaknesses of participatory design and how might any weaknesses be addressed?

13.5 You are designing a new system to help people manage their 'to do' lists. Use the contextual inquiry approach to interview a colleague to see how they make use of such lists. Make sure you interview them in context – in their study or workplace for example. Produce sequence, flow, artifact, cultural and physical models of the activity.

RECOMMENDED READING

K. D. Eason, *Information Technology and Organizational Change*, Taylor and Francis, 1988.

Clear coverage of socio-technical and organizational issues in design.

P. B. Checkland, *Systems Thinking, Systems Practice: includes a 30 Year Retrospective*, John Wiley, 1999.

The classic text on soft systems methodology in detail, in a new edition with reflections on the development and use of the methodology.

J. Greenbaum and M. Kyng, *Design at Work: Cooperative Design of Computer Systems*, Lawrence Erlbaum, 1991.

An excellent collection of papers on participatory design philosophy and practice.

E. Mumford, *Effective Systems Design and Requirements Analysis: The ETHICS Approach*, Palgrave, 1995.

A book outlining the ETHICS approach by its developer.

H. Beyer and K. Holtzblatt, *Contextual Design: Defining Customer Centered Systems*, Morgan Kaufmann, 1998.

A full exposition of the contextual design methodology, of which contextual inquiry is a part.

COMMUNICATION AND COLLABORATION MODELS

OVERVIEW

All computer systems, single-user or multi-user, interact with the work-groups and organizations in which they are used.

- We need to understand normal human–human communication:
  - face-to-face communication involves eyes, face and body
  - conversation can be analyzed to establish its detailed structure.

- This can then be applied to text-based conversation, which has:
  - reduced feedback for confirmation
  - less context to disambiguate utterances
  - slower pace of interaction
  but is more easily reviewed.

- Group working is more complex than that of a single person:
  - it is influenced by the physical environment
  - experiments are more difficult to control and record
  - field studies must take into account the social situation.

14.1	INTRODUCTION

> No man is an *Iland*, intire of it selfe; every man is a peece of the *Continent*, a part of the *maine*.
>
> John Donne[1]

It is clear that groupware systems, such as email or conferencing systems, involve more than one person. However, to some extent all systems influence and are influenced by the groups and social situations in which they are placed. The field of computer-supported cooperative work (CSCW) encompasses both specific groupware systems and the effects of computers on cooperative working in general.

We begin this chapter by looking at human communication. Effective communication clearly underlies much collaborative work and many systems aim to support communication at a distance. Face-to-face communication is often seen as the ideal to which computer-mediated communication should aim. Section 14.2 describes some of its features, and shows how even video-based communications lose many of the subtle cues. Body language, tone of voice and eye contact are all crucial in enabling smooth conversation. We then look at a slightly higher level in Section 14.3, at the structure of conversation. In particular, we will see that typical utterances are ambiguous and dependent on the context in which they are spoken. This section concludes by looking at speech act theory and the Coordinator system which has been both influential and controversial in CSCW. Understanding spoken conversation gives some clues as to the effective design of text-based communication such as email systems or electronic conferencing. Section 14.4 discusses text-based communication in this context, including a discussion of the relative merits and features of linear text and hypertext systems.

In Section 14.5 we move away from computer-mediated communication and look at the wider issues of group working. Groups are dynamic both in composition and behavior, and effective group working is dependent on the work environment. Because of these and other factors, the study of group behavior, and therefore evaluating groupware, is far more complex than that of single-user systems.

14.2	FACE-TO-FACE COMMUNICATION

Face-to-face contact is the most primitive form of communication – primitive, that is, in terms of technology. If, on the other hand, we consider the style of communication, the interplay between different channels and productivity, we instead find that face-to-face is the most sophisticated communication mechanism available.

---

1 Devotions upon Emergent Occasions, XVII, 1624.

The first thing to note is that face-to-face communication involves not just speech and hearing, but also the subtle use of body language and eyegaze. We will discuss a range of these phenomena, and how they influence our use of computer-mediated communications. We will concentrate on two-person conversations as group dynamics are discussed later in Section 14.5. Also, we will principally compare face-to-face with video and audio channels and we will address the special problems of text-based communications in Section 14.4.

14.2.1 Transfer effects and personal space

When we come to use computer-mediated forms of communication, we carry forward all our expectations and social norms from face-to-face communication. People are very adaptable and can learn new norms to go with new media (for example, the use of 'over' for turn-taking when using a walkie-talkie). However, success with new media is often dependent on whether the participants can use their existing norms. Furthermore, the rules of face-to-face conversation are not conscious, so, when they are broken, we do not always recognize the true problem. We may just have a feeling of unease, or we may feel that our colleague has been rude.

An example of these problems concerns personal space. When we converse with one another we tend to stand with our heads a fairly constant distance apart. If people start to converse at opposite ends of a room, they will quickly move toward one another until they are a few feet apart. The exact distance depends somewhat on context; a high level of noise may make people come closer just to be heard. However, even in crowded rooms, conversants will dip their heads toward one another whilst speaking and then straighten up to restore their personal distance. Direction is also important. We can accept people closer to us if they are at our sides or behind than if we are facing them. Because of this, passengers on tube trains, forced to be close, will incline their faces at an angle to one another whilst talking.

Personal space also differs across cultures: North Americans get closer than Britons, and southern Europeans and Arabs closer still. This can cause considerable problems during cross-cultural meetings. Imagine a Briton, Eustace Warbuck-Smyth, and an American, Bud Sterton, conversing. After a few minutes Eustace is bent backwards over a table, trying to maintain his personal distance, whilst Bud stands almost knee to knee trying to get close enough. Eustace feels Bud is either rather aggressive, or possibly over-friendly. Bud, on the other hand, feels Eustace is rather distant and uninterested. Unless the situation gets extreme, or the participants are trained in non-verbal skills, they will be unaware of why they feel uncomfortable.

A similar problem can occur in a video conference. Imagine Eustace and Bud have monitors with cameras mounted above, so that their offices are connected. The zoom on each camera is adjustable and Bud's camera is set with a wide focus, whilst Eustace's is set with a high level of zoom. So, if Bud and Eustace are the same distance from their cameras and monitors, then Bud sees Eustace's whole face filling the screen, whereas Eustace sees Bud sat on his chair in the middle of his office. Eustace moves closer to the monitor to see Bud more clearly, while Bud pushes his chair back to get away from Eustace's 2 foot (60 cm) high face – *touché*. Of course, the problem gets worse if the cameras are positioned in different places relative to the monitors, or if the monitors are different sizes. Ideally, Bud ought to be able to adjust the zoom on Eustace's camera and vice versa. In fact, there is some evidence that the 'glass wall' afforded by the video screen makes the precise distance less important, which could have a positive effect during cross-cultural meetings. However, gross distortions, as described above, need to be avoided.

14.2.2 Eye contact and gaze

Long-term gazing into one another's eyes is usually reserved for lovers. However, normal conversation uses eye contact extensively, if not as intently. Our eyes tell us whether our colleague is listening or not; they can convey interest, confusion or boredom. Sporadic direct eye contact (both looking at one another's eyes) is important in establishing a sense of engagement and social presence. People who look away when you look at them may seem shifty and appear to be hiding something. Furthermore, relative frequency of eye contact and who 'gives way' from direct eye contact is closely linked to authority and power.

Naturally, all these clues are lost if we have no visual contact. However, the misleading clues via a video connection can be worse. In Chapter 19 (Section 19.3.4) we discuss the problems of obtaining effective eye contact with standard video equipment. If the camera is strapped to the top of the monitor (a common arrangement) both participants will look as if their eyes are slightly dropped. We will look at some technical solutions to this in Chapter 19.

Despite these problems with direct eye contact, many signals can be easily read through a video channel. You can see whether your colleague looks quizzical or bored, confused or excited. This involves not just the eyes, but the whole facial expression, and this is apparent even on poor-quality video or very small (pocket-TV-sized) monitors. Experiments have shown that remotely working participants experience a greater sense of social presence if video is used in addition to an audio link.

As well as having a role in establishing rapport between the participants, eyegaze is useful in establishing the focus of the conversation. If you say 'now where does this screw go?', there may be many screws, but your colleague can see which one you are looking at. Video connections are unlikely to show enough of your office for your colleague to be able to interpret such clues, but a focus that just catches the corner of the monitor and desk can help.

14.2.3 Gestures and body language

In a similar but more direct way, we use our hands to indicate items of interest. This may be conscious and deliberate as we point to the item, or may be a slight wave of the hand or alignment of the body. Again, a video connection may not be sufficient to allow our colleagues to read our movements. This can be a serious problem since our conversation is full of expressions such as 'let's move this one there', where the 'this' and 'there' are indicated by gestures (or eyegaze). This is called *deictic reference* (see Chapter 19, Sections 19.4 and 19.6 for more details).

Several groupware systems attempt to compensate for these losses. In Section 19.4.2, we discuss the idea of a group pointer, a mouse-controlled icon which can be used to point to things on a shared screen. Somewhat more esoteric, but more immediate, are the shared work surfaces (Section 19.4.3) which mix an image of the participants' hands with the electronic screen. The participants can then simply point at the relevant item on the screen, as they would face-to-face.

Of course, the group pointer, although used in remote groupware, is also used in synchronous co-located groupware such as meeting rooms. That is, even though the participants can converse face-to-face, they still need deictic aids. One reason for this is that their electronic screens, although logically shared (they can all see the same thing), are not physically shared (they are in different places). So, if Jemima points to her own screen, her colleagues do not know what she is pointing at.

Even when the participants are in the same room, the existence of electronic equipment can interfere with the body language used in normal face-to-face communication. The fact that attention is focused on keyboard and screen can reduce the opportunities for eye contact. Also, large monitors may block participants' views of one another's bodies, reducing their ability to interpret gestures and body position. Most computer-supported meeting rooms recess monitors into the desks to reduce these problems.

14.2.4 Back channels, confirmation and interruption

It is easy to think of conversation as a sequence of utterances: A says something, then B says something, then back to A. This process is called *turn-taking* and is one of the fundamental structures of conversation. However, each utterance is itself the result of intricate negotiation and interaction. Consider the following transcript:

Alison: Do you fancy that film ... er ... 'The Green' *um* ... it starts at eight.
Brian: Great!

Alison has asked Brian whether he wants to go to the cinema (or possibly to watch the television at home). She is a bit vague about the film, but Brian obviously does not mind! However, if we had listened to the conversation more closely and watched Alison and Brian we would have seen more exchanges. As Alison says 'that film *er* . . .', she looks at Brian. From the quizzical look on his face he obviously does not know which film she is talking about. She begins to expand 'The Green *um* . . .', and light dawns; she can see it in his eyes and he probably makes a small affirmative sound 'uh huh'.

The nods, grimaces, shrugs of the shoulder and small noises are called *back channels*. They feed information back from the listener to the speaker at a level below the turn-taking of the conversation. The existence of back channels means that the speaker can afford to be slightly vague, adding details until it is obvious that the listener understands. Imagine making no response as someone talks to you, no little 'yes'es, no nods or raised eyebrows. You could answer questions and speak in turn, but not use back channels. It is likely that your colleague would soon become very uncomfortable, possibly rambling on with ever more detailed explanations, looking for some sign of understanding:[2]

> Do you fancy that film…*er*…'The Green' *um*…the one with Charles Dermot in …you know with that song, *er* and the black cat on the poster…*uhh*

These back channel responses use a range of sensory channels. So, as we restrict the forms of communication we lose the back channels. Even video communications tend to use, at most, head and shoulder shots, so we lose some body movement and gestures. On the other hand, a larger view means reduced detail, so we lose information whatever focus we choose. Audio-only links (such as the telephone) have to rely on purely verbal back channel responses – the little 'yes'es. Surprisingly, despite the loss of many back channels, people still cope well with these restricted media, and communication is still reasonably effective. However, you may have had the experience, when speaking to someone on the telephone, of suddenly getting the feeling that they have gone away, or the line has gone dead. This is likely to be when you have received insufficient back channel responses (and perhaps you have been going on a bit). Transcontinental telephones are especially problematic as they are often only half duplex, that is the sound only goes in one direction at a time. So, while you are speaking, you can hear none of your partner's back channel responses.

Text-based communication, in electronic conferencing, usually has no back channels whatsoever. Any confirmation must be given explicitly in the listener's next utterance. This may confuse an analysis of text-based conversation as the utterances do not correspond simply to utterances in speech.

14.2.5 Turn-taking

As well as giving confirmation to the speaker that you understand, and indications when you do not, back channels can be used to interrupt politely. Starting to speak in the middle of someone's utterance can be rude, but one can say something like 'well uh' accompanied by a slight raising of the hands and a general tensing of the body and screwing of the eyes. This tells the speaker that you would like to interrupt, allowing a graceful transition. In this case, the listener *requested* the floor. *Turn-taking* is the process by which the roles of speaker and listener are exchanged. Back channels are often a crucial part of this process.

---

2 Don't try this as an experiment on your friends, or you may end up without any! Instead try it with a colleague who knows what is going on. Even when you both know not to expect back channel responses the experience can be disconcerting. Furthermore, you will both find it very difficult to refrain from back channel responses.

DESIGN FOCUS

Looking real – Avatar Conference

Avatars, artificial representations of people, are used in various forms of online communication. Often these are based on some form of cartoon image, but the Avatar Conference project has produced a virtual meeting environment with photo-realistic avatars. These are produced by photographing participants from several angles and then using the photographs to texture map an artificial figure. This is then rendered in a 3D virtual meeting room.

Participants can use internet phone or simple text chat and the latter has translation options to aid international meetings. The avatar for the current speaker moves its mouth and makes other animations, but is not synchronized with the actual speech. The aim is to make the participants more engaged in the online meeting.

The screen shots show two views of the conference application. One with the virtual meeting room central (left), the other with the currently displayed presentation materials central (right). People found the 3D avatars exciting and an initial 'hook' – this is very important, remember in the Introduction, the need for a system to be actually *used*.

However, the participant response after using the application for even a short time was in favor of the more presentation-centered rather than avatar-centered view. It may be that current avatars are not quite realistic enough to warrant the central position, or it may reflect the fact that in a real meeting the focus is on the presentation rather than on the other participants.

See: www.exodus.gr/Avatar_Conference/ and www.avatame.com/ Screen shot frame reprinted by permission from Microsoft Corporation. Screen shots courtesy of AVATAR-Conference project team

In other cases, the speaker may explicitly *offer* the floor to the other participant. This may be in the form of a direct question, 'what do you think?', or simply a very strong change of tone.

More often the speaker will offer the floor to the listener by leaving a small gap in speech. These gaps are typically no more than a fraction of a second; indeed gaps of even a few seconds give completely different signals and interrupt the flow of conversation. The gap is often at some point which may require clarification, or where the listener may want to comment. So, Alison may well have waited for half a second after saying 'Do you fancy that film', in case Brian were to respond 'Oh you mean the one with the black cat on the poster'. As he did not say anything, she continued with her turn.

The role of '*um*'s and '*ah*'s is very important. They can be used by either particip-ant during the gap to *claim* the turn. So, if Brian wanted to respond in the middle of the utterance, but had not yet framed his utterance, he might begin '*um* the one . . .'. As it was, Brian did not respond, so Alison starts '*er*' which says to Brian 'I'm going to continue, but I'm thinking'. Alternatively, Alison could have started to '*er*' as soon as she had said the word 'film'. This would have told Brian *not* to interrupt.

These turn-offering gaps are just the places where the speaker expects some back channel response even if no turn exchange takes place. A total lack of response will be taken, depending on the circumstances, as assent to the speaker, or perhaps as lack of understanding.

As we can see, turn-offering gaps form a central part in the eliciting of back channel responses and in negotiating turn-taking. They are obviously connected principally with the audio channel (although some gestures may be used to maintain or claim the floor). Half-duplex channels (such as intercontinental phone calls) are volume sensitive in order to track the speaker. Unfortunately, some of the '*um*'s and '*er*'s used to maintain or claim the floor may fall below the volume threshold and thus not be transmitted. This may lead to apparent rude interruptions or snub-bing of one party by the other.

An even more serious problem is encountered during long-distance, satellite-based communications due to the time lags. To transmit a signal, it must go up to the satellite and then back down to the earth. A geostationary satellite is at a height of approximately 100,000 km above the earth – a quarter of the distance to the moon. Radio waves will take about 700 milliseconds to go up to the satellite and back down again. This time, together with the processing delays on the ground and in the satellite, add up to about a 2 second lag. There is thus a 4 second gap between one participant doing or saying something and when the effects of that upon the other participant become evident.

We now imagine Alison and Brian talking via satellite. Alison pauses for half a second after the words 'that film', 2 seconds later Brian hears the end of the word 'film', after a few hundred milliseconds he notices the gap and begins to say 'Oh'; by this time Alison has waited $2^{1}/_{2}$ seconds, and the gap is getting embarrassing, so she continues 'The Green *um* . . . the one with Charles Dermot in'. Then, 2 seconds into this, that is over 4 seconds since she began to pause, she hears Brian try to cut in (how rude!), but he stops talking again when he hears her continuing.

The above scenario is *not* contrived. Tapes of video conferences show just this behavior, with a single speaker going on and on as all her attempts to pass on the floor fail. There is no obvious solution to this problem, except the technological one of using high-bandwidth land or sub-ocean lines, when these become available, rather than satellite.

CONVERSATION

We have looked at the low-level issues of speech and gesture during face-to-face conversation. We now turn to the structure of the conversation itself. Most analysis of conversation focusses on two-person conversations, but this can range from informal social chat over the telephone to formal courtroom cross-examination. As well as the discipline of *conversational analysis*, there are other sociological and psychological understandings of conversation. However, the techniques, as 'borrowed' and used to study computer-mediated conversation, would not always find favor with the purist from the discipline from which they originated!

There are three uses for theories of conversation in CSCW. First, they can be used to analyze transcripts, for example from an electronic conference. This can help us to understand how well the participants are coping with electronic communication. Secondly, they can be used as a guide for design decisions – an understanding of normal human–human conversation can help avoid blunders in the design of electronic media. Thirdly, and most controversially, they can be used to drive design – structuring the system around the theory.

We will concentrate mainly on the first goal, although this will have implications throughout for design. Only when we consider *speech act theory* and *Coordinator* in Section 14.3.6 will we see an example of a theory-driven system.

14.3.1 Basic conversational structure

Imagine we have a transcript of a conversation, recalling from Chapter 9 that the production of such a transcript is not a simple task. For example, a slightly different version of Alison and Brian's conversation may look like this:

> **Alison**: Do you fancy that film?
> **Brian**: The *uh* (*500 ms*) with the black cat – 'The Green whatsit'?
> **Alison**: Yeah, go at *uh*… (*looks at watch – 1.2 s*)…20 to?
> **Brian**: Sure.

This transcript is quite heavily annotated with the lengths of pauses and even Alison's action of looking at her watch. However, it certainly lacks the wealth of gesture and back channel activity that were present during the actual conversation. Transcripts may be less well documented, perhaps dropping the pause timings, or more detailed, adding more actions, where people were looking and some back channelling. Whilst thinking about the structure of conversation, the transcript above is sufficient.

As we have noted previously, the most basic conversational structure is *turn-taking*. On the whole we have an alternating pattern: Alison says something, then Brian, then Alison again. The speech within each turn is called an *utterance*. There can be exceptions to this turn-taking structure even within two-party conversation. For example, if there is a gap in the conversation, the same party may pick up the thread, even if she was the last speaker. However, such gaps are normally of short duration, enough to allow turn-claiming if required, but short enough to consider the speech a single utterance.

Often we can group the utterances of the conversation into pairs: a question and an answer, a statement and an agreement. The answer or response will normally follow directly after the question or statement and so these are called *adjacency pairs*. We can look at Alison and Brian's conversation above as two adjacency pairs, one after the other. First, Alison asks Brian whether he knows about the film and he responds. Second, she suggests a time to go and he agrees. We can codify this structure as: A-x, B-x, A-y, B-y, where the first letter denotes the speaker (Alison or Brian) and the second letter labels the adjacency pair.

The requirement of adjacency can be broken if the pair is interposed with other pairs for clarification, etc.:

Brian: Do you want some gateau?
Alison: Is it very fattening?
Brian: Yes, very.
Alison: And lots of chocolate?
Brian: Masses.
Alison: I'll have a big slice then.

This conversation can be denoted: B-x, A-y, B-y, A-z, B-z, A-x. Adjacency pair 'x' ('Do you want some gateau?'–'I'll have a big slice then') is split by two other pairs 'y' and 'z'. One would normally expect the interposed pairs to be relevant to the outer pair, seeking clarification or determining information needed for the response.

Some would say that the adjacency pair is not just a basic structure of conversation but *the* fundamental structure. It is clearly true that we normally respond to the most recent utterance. However, it is less clear whether a simple pairing up of utterances is always possible or useful.

For an example of this difficulty, let us look back to the transcript at the beginning of the section. We see that the pair structure is not completely clear. Alison's second utterance begins a new pair, 'go at 20 to?', but it began with 'yeah' responding to Brian's previous utterance. Indeed, Brian's first response 'the *uh* . . . with the black cat . . .' could be seen as a request for clarification. That is, we are now looking at the conversation as having a structure of A-x, B-y, A-yz, B-z, where Alison's second utterance serves as both a response to Brian's request for clarification ('y') and starts a new pair concerning the time ('z'). But in this case, what happens to the second half of the original 'x' pair? We are forced to regard it as implicit in one of Brian's utterances. Alison's 'go at 20 to?' clearly suggests that Brian has committed himself, so we assume that the tone of Brian's description of the film suggested acceptance. So, Brian's first utterance, like Alison's second, serves a dual purpose: A-x, B-xy, A-yz, B-z.

Despite these difficulties, we see that the search for adjacency pairs forces us to examine closely the structure of the conversation. Whether such structures are really part of the conversation, or imposed by us upon it, is less clear. Later we shall see far more complex conversational structures.

14.3.2 Context

Take a single utterance from a conversation, and it will usually be highly ambiguous if not meaningless: 'the *uh* with the black cat – "The Green whatsit"'. Each utterance and each fragment of conversation is heavily dependent on *context*, which must be used to *disambiguate* the utterance. We can identify two types of context within conversation:

internal context – dependence on earlier utterances. For example, when Brian says 'masses' in the last transcript, this is meaningful in the light of Alison's question 'and lots of chocolate?'. This in turn is interpreted in the context of Brian's original offer of gateau.

external context – dependence on the environment. For example, if Brian had said simply 'do you want one?', this could have meant a slice of gateau, or, if he had been holding a bottle, a glass of wine, or, if accompanied by a clenched fist, a punch on the nose.

Arguably, even a complete conversation is heavily context dependent – without knowing the situation and the social relations between the participants, how can we understand their words? Taking a more pragmatic approach, the importance of external context has implications for system design and for data collection. From a design perspective, we will look for groupware which both maximizes shared context and which makes the level of sharing clear.

Turning to data collection, we can see the importance of annotating transcripts with gestures, eyegaze and details of the environment. However, if one noted everything down, 90% would be irrelevant to the conversational level of analysis. Recording the interesting details without flooding the transcript is clearly a skilled job. If one has rich recordings, say from several video sources, then a simple verbal transcript may be sufficient as it will be possible to refer back to the video when interesting incidents are found in the written transcript.

When collecting data from groupware systems, it is also very important to have synchronized records of the participants' conversation (whether audio, video or text based) and their electronic workspaces. We need to know what the participants can see on their screens in order to interpret their remarks to one another. In the case where participants may have different views at the same time, we are likely to see *breakdowns* in the conversation, where one participant makes an utterance depending on his screen, whereas his colleague sees something different on her screen.

A specific form of context dependence is *deictic reference* (Section 14.2.3). When accompanied by a pointed finger, an expression like 'that post is leaning a bit' is clearly dependent on external context. However, there are very similar uses of internal context:

Brian: (*Points*) That post is leaning a bit.
Alison: That's the one you put in.

Brian's utterance uses external context, whereas Alison's very similar utterance uses internal context. Her 'that' refers to the post Brian was talking about, not the one he is pointing at. To see this, consider the similar fragment:

> **Brian:**   The corner post is leaning a bit.
> **Alison:**   That's the one you put in.

Real speech, probably more than the written word, is full of *indexicals*, words like 'that', 'this', 'he', 'she' and 'it'. Obviously when used in written text, like *this*, words such as *these* make use of purely internal context. In spoken speech any of the above words can be accompanied by gestures or eyegaze for external context, or simply used, as Alison did, to refer to previous things in the conversation. Some of the words tend to be more likely to be external ('that', 'this') than others ('he', 'she'), but you can easily think of cases of both forms of use. Furthermore, the attachment of pronouns and other indexicals to the things they denote may depend on the semantics of a sentence: 'Oh no! Eustace has hit Bud. He'll kill him, I know he will.' Does the speaker mean that Eustace will kill Bud, or vice versa? The answer depends on the speaker's knowledge of Eustace and Bud. If Bud is a 22 stone (138 kg) trucker and Eustace has trouble lifting cans of beans then we interpret the sentence one way. If, on the other hand, Eustace has a black belt in karate . . .

One consequence of the use of context in speech is the fragmentary nature of utterances. The example transcripts are, if anything, atypically grammatical. Although there is evidence of rules of grammar for the spoken word, these are very different, and much more relaxed, than the written equivalent.

14.3.3 Topics, focus and forms of utterance

Given that conversation is so dependent on context, it is important that the participants have a shared focus. We have addressed this in terms of the external focus – the objects that are visible to the participants – but it is also true of the internal focus of the conversation.

> **Alison:**   Oh, look at your roses . . .
> **Brian:**   Mmm, but I've had trouble with greenfly.
> **Alison:**   They're the symbol of the English summer.
> **Brian:**   Greenfly?
> **Alison:**   No roses silly!

Alison began the conversation with the *topic* of roses. Brian shifts to the related, but distinct, topic of greenfly. However, for some reason Alison has missed this shift in focus, so when she makes her second utterance, her focus and Brian's differ, leading to the *breakdown* in communication. The last two utterances are a recovery which re-establishes a shared *dialog focus*.

In general, we can go through a transcript annotating the utterances by the topics to which they refer. The identification of topics and assigning utterances to them is a somewhat subjective affair, and one may want to use several levels of topic categorization. Of course, those points where such a labeling is difficult are interesting in themselves. They may either represent potential points of breakdown (as above), or show where external context is needed to disambiguate the conversation. Also of interest is the way that the participants negotiate changes in dialog focus, either because they recognize a divergence, or because one party wants to shift the focus of the conversation.

This sort of analysis can be pursued for its own sake, but has a more pragmatic interest in the analysis of computer-mediated conversation and design of groupware. We want to know where breakdowns occur in order to see whether these are due to the electronic medium. We also want to understand the shifts in focus and the reliance on external context and compare these with the shared objects available through the computer system.

Another way of classifying utterances is by their relation to the task in hand. At one extreme the utterance may have no direct relevance at all, either a digression or purely social. Looking at the task-related conversation, the utterances can be classified into three kinds [335]:

substantive directly relevant to the development of the topic;

annotative points of clarification, elaborations, etc.;

procedural talking about the process of collaboration itself.

In addition, the procedural utterances may be related to the structure of collaboration itself, or may be about the technology supporting the collaboration. The latter is usually in response to a breakdown where the technology has intruded into the communication.

Alison and Brian are now discussing the best way to get to the cinema. Alison is using a whiteboard to draw a map.

1. **Alison**: You go along this road until you get to the river.
2. **Brian**: Do you stop before the river or after you cross it?
3. **Alison**: Before.
4. **Brian**: Draw the river in blue and the roads black…
5. **Alison**: So, you turn right beside the river.
6. **Brian**: Past the pub.
7. **Alison**: Yeah…Is there another black pen, this one's gone dry?

Alison's first utterance, turn 1, is substantive. Brian then interrupts with an annotative utterance, asking a question of clarification, which is answered by Alison at 3. Brian then makes a procedural point (perhaps prompted by his confusion at 2). In turns 5 and 6, the conversation again becomes substantive, but then the pen runs out, and utterance 7 is a procedural remark concerning the communication technology (pen and whiteboard).

The last form of utterance (procedural technological) is most interesting when analyzing transcripts of computer-mediated conversation as it represents points where the system became apparent to the participants. However, it is also interesting to compare the forms of conversation used in, say, an electronic conference with those in normal speech. For example, a hypertext-oriented conference will allow digressions without any danger of losing the flow of the conference, thus encouraging annotative and procedural utterances.

14.3.4 Breakdown and repair

We have already seen an example of *breakdown* in conversation. When Alison and Brian were talking about Brian's roses, they failed to maintain a shared focus. Brian tried to interpret Alison's utterance in terms of his focus and failed, or rather the meaning in that focus was unusual – greenfly are the symbol of the English summer? He then questioned Alison and the confusion was cleared. This correction after breakdown is called *repair*.

If we look at transcripts of computer-mediated conversations, and see many breakdowns, we should not be surprised: face-to-face and spoken conversations are full of it. We may see breakdowns at many levels. The divergence of topic focus is a quite high level of breakdown. It often becomes apparent when we find failures to identify the referent of an indexical or deictic reference. Alternatively, such a failure may be due to the speaker using an ambiguous indexical: 'Eustace has just hit Bud . . . he's bleeding' – that is, Eustace is bleeding, Bud was wearing a crash helmet.

At a lower level, we may see breakdown due to incorrectly read gestures or eye-gaze, and through missed or inappropriate back channel responses. For instance, in Section 14.2.5, we described the problems in turn-taking during satellite-based video conferences. It may be difficult to interpret just where a breakdown occurred, as the breakdown may take some time to come to light, and be apparent at a different level from which it began. Alison and Brian are enjoying a day out at a country park:

Alison: Isn't that beautiful?
She points at a stag standing beside a large tree; Brian sees the tree.
Brian: The symmetry of the branches.
Alison: How some people can dislike them I can't understand.
Brian: Yes, the rangers ought to cull those deer, they strip the bark terribly in winter.
Alison: (*Silence*)

The breakdown began with a confused gesture, but led to a divergence of dialog focus. Unfortunately, Brian's remark about the branching (of the tree) could be interpreted in terms of Alison's focus (the stag's antlers) and thus the breakdown did not become apparent until Brian had well and truly put his foot in it. Happily, most breakdowns are detected more quickly, but the deeper the breakdown, and the longer it lasts, the more difficult it is to recover.

Despite the frequency of breakdowns in normal speech, our communication is not usually significantly affected because we are so efficient at repair. (Although Brian may have some difficulty.) Redundancy, frequency of turn-taking and back channels, all contribute to the detection of breakdown and its rapid repair. Electronic communications often reduce redundancy (a single channel), reduce the frequency of turn-taking and reduce back channels. The problem is thus not so much breakdowns in communication, but a reduced ability to recover from them.

14.3.5 Constructing a shared understanding

We have seen that human conversation is in itself inherently ambiguous, relying on context and shared understanding between the parties to disambiguate the utterances. In some spheres, such as legal contracts, the precise meaning out of context becomes very important and thus highly stylized language is used to reduce ambiguity.[3] However, even the legal profession depends on a large body of shared knowledge and understanding about legal terms, case law, etc. Similarly, a book, such as this, attempts to use less ambiguous language and only commonly available knowledge.

The major difference between a book and conversation is that the latter is interactive. The shared knowledge used in a book is static, whereas that used during a conversation is dynamic, as the participants increase their understanding of one another and as they shift their focus from topic to topic.

When participants come to a conversation, they may come from different backgrounds and bring different knowledge. Even close colleagues will have different recent experiences, and as we have seen in previous examples, have different foci. The participants do not try to unify their knowledge and background – indeed, they could not fully do so without living one another's lives. Instead, they seek to obtain a *common ground*, a shared understanding sufficient for the task in hand. Establishing this common ground will involve negotiating the meanings of words and constructing shared interpretations of the world. Clark and Schaefer [72] refer to this process as *grounding*.

A consequence of this model of conversation is that the participants are aware, at various levels both conscious and subconscious, that their common ground is incomplete. Their conversation is not then just an exchange of information about their task, but involves continual testing and cross-checking of the other party's understanding. Consider again a fragment from Alison's conversation about the way to the cinema:

> **Alison**: So, you turn right beside the river.
> **Brian**: Past the pub.
> **Alison**: Yeah...

Alison makes an utterance concerning the way to the cinema. Brian interprets this utterance given his current understanding of the conversation and the world. However, in order to check this understanding he makes the statement 'past the pub'. Now this is not a question of clarification like his earlier question about the bridge; instead it merely echoes back some evidence that he has correctly interpreted Alison's utterance. Alison is happy with this and so confirms it 'yeah'.

Such exchanges can be more protracted: for instance, if Brian's reply does not satisfy Alison she may reflect Brian's evidence back to him: 'you mean the Black Bull', or attempt to re-present her original utterance: 'along the road on this side of the river'. Alternatively, the exchange may be much shorter: rather than explicitly presenting evidence, Brian could have simply continued the conversation, making

---

3 Or left deliberately ambiguous.

his understanding implicit in his future utterances. If these utterances were not compatible with Alison's original utterance, she could then initiate repair. This was the course adopted in their conversation in the country park, although, in that case, with unfortunate results. Finally, the evidence of understanding may often be presented via back channels, little 'yes'es, or simply a continued look of comprehension.

Common ground is always partial, and thus any utterance will have a different meaning for the speaker and the listener. The aim of grounding is to construct a meaning *in the conversation* which is sufficient for the task. For example, Brian's understanding of the Black Bull may be of pleasant evenings sitting on its river terrace. Alison may never have visited the pub, but has seen its distinctive sign hanging over the road. These different understandings are not important: for the purpose of finding directions the pub is merely a way of identifying the road they are to follow.

In a conversation, we know that our partner does not share our knowledge of the world. In addition, we know that our partner will attempt to interpret our utterances. We thus frame our utterances based on this knowledge. Two guiding principles for our utterances are that they should be *relevant* and *helpful*.

To be *relevant* an utterance should further the current topic. This is because our partner is expecting an utterance in this context and any sudden shift in our topic focus will make it more difficult for our partner to make sense of the utterance. Such shifts happen in a conversation, but require less ambiguous utterances (as the common ground for that particular utterance is lower).

To be *helpful*, an utterance should be understandable to the listener and be sufficiently unambiguous given the listener's understanding. This requires the speaker to have a model of the listener's understanding and vice versa. So assuming he is being helpful, in saying 'past the pub', Brian implicitly assumes that there is a particular pub, which Alison will recognize as being significant. It is no good the pub being significant to Brian alone; he must know that it will carry its intended significance to Alison.

The ability to build such models is part of our social maturing. One of the key developmental steps for a child is from an egocentric world view, where things are interpreted in relation to the child, to a social one where the child recognizes others' viewpoints. At the age of $2\frac{1}{2}$, one of the authors' children was interviewed by a linguistics researcher. At one stage the conversation proceeded:

Child: We went to the doctor.
Researcher: Where was the doctor?
Child: Up the steps.

The researcher was clearly (in the context and to an adult) wanting to know whether the doctor was in a hospital or not. The child's answer would have been instantly meaningful to any local parent as the steps to the local doctor were a constant problem for people with prams. However, the child was at that stage unable to phrase the utterance in a way suited to her listener's understanding. At a certain age children assume you know everything they know.[4]

---

4 To be fair, adults often make the same assumption of children!

So, we see that conversation is an inherently social activity, based on a constructed shared understanding, and relying on the participants' models of one another. In addition, it depends on continuous interaction to correct misinterpretations and to confirm understanding.

14.3.6 Speech act theory

A particular form of conversational analysis, *speech act theory*, has been both influential and controversial in CSCW. Not only is it an analytic technique, but it has been used as the guiding force behind the design of a commercial system, Coordinator. Speech act theory has origins going back over 25 years, but was popularized by Winograd and Flores in the design of Coordinator [381].

The basic premise of speech act theory is that utterances can be characterized by what they *do*. If you say 'I'm hungry', this has a certain *propositional meaning* – that you are feeling hungry. However, depending on who is talking and to whom, this may also carry the meaning 'get me some food' – the intent of the statement is to evoke an action on the part of the hearer. Speech act theory concerns itself with the way utterances interact with the actions of the participants.

Some speech acts actually cause a significant effect by the act of being said. The classic example is when a minister says 'I pronounce you husband and wife'. This is not simply a statement that the minister is making about the couple. The act of saying the words changes the state of the couple. Other acts include promises by the speaker to do something and requests that the hearer do something. These basic acts are called *illocutionary points*.

Individual speech acts can contribute to a conversation. The basic structure of conversations can then be seen as instances of generic conversations. One example of such a generic structure is a *conversation for action* (*CfA*). This is shown as a state diagram in Figure 14.1. It represents the stages two participants go through in

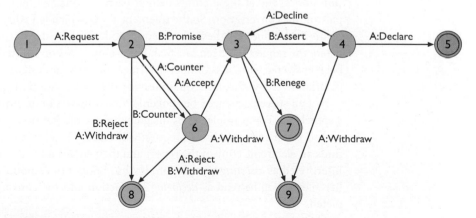

Figure 14.1 Conversation for action. Source: *Understanding Computers and Cognition: A New Foundation for Design* by Terry Winograd/Fernando Flores, © 1986. Reprinted by permission of Pearson Education, Inc., Upper Saddle River, NJ

initiating an external action that one of them should perform. There are two variants, the one shown representing a conversation where the first speaker (A) is requesting that the other participant (B) does something. The other, similar, variant is where the first speaker begins with an offer.

The numbered circles in Figure 14.1 are 'states' of the conversation, and the labeled arcs represent the speech acts, which move the conversation from state to state. Note that the speech acts are named slightly differently in different sources (by the same author even!), but the structure of a CfA is the same. The simplest route through the diagram is through states 1–5.

> **Alison**: Have you got the market survey on chocolate mousse?
> **Brian**: Sure.
> *Rummages in filing cabinet and hands it to Alison*
> **Brian**: There you are.
> **Alison**: Thanks.

Alison makes a *request* for the survey (although it is phrased as a question). Brian *promises* to fulfill the request ('sure'). After he feels he has done so (by handing it to Alison), Brian *asserts* that the request has been fulfilled ('there you are') and Alison *declares* her satisfaction that Brian has completed her request ('thanks').

More complex routes may involve some negotiating between the parties. For example, the conversation might have begun:

> **Alison**: Have you got the market survey on chocolate mousse?
> **Brian**: I've only got the summary figures.
> **Alison**: That'll do.

In this Alison's *request* is met by a *counter* from Brian, that is Brian attempts to modify Alison's request. This brings us to state 6 in the diagram. Alison then *accepts* Brian's counter, bringing the conversation back to state 3.

The network has some nodes marked with a double circle. These are the completion nodes, and at these points neither party expects any more acts by the other as part of this conversation. So the fragment above which left Alison and Brian in state 3 must continue. Of these completion nodes only state 5 represents conclusions where the request has been satisfied. For example, Alison's initial request could have been answered with 'it's confidential' (meaning 'you can't have it'). This is the action of Brian *rejecting* Alison's request, leaving the conversation in state 8 and complete.

Not all speech acts need be spoken! Often a silence or an unspoken action forms a speech act. For example, let us imagine that the market survey had not been handy and so Brian answers Alison's request with 'sure, I'll get it later'. Later in the day he finds an electronic copy of the report and then emails it to Alison. His action will be interpreted as *asserting* completion. If Alison does not respond within a short time, her silence will be read as *declaring* satisfaction and the conversation will be completed.

There are other generic conversation forms as well as CfA. These include:

conversation for clarification usually embedded within a CfA to clarify the required action (different from countering a request);

conversation for possibilities looking toward future actions;

conversation for orientation building up a shared understanding.

In addition, the participants may indulge in meta-conversation, discussing the acts themselves, perhaps questioning the legitimacy of an act: 'I'm hungry' . . . 'well I'm not your skivvy, get your own food'. Also CfA is the most extensive and well developed of the conversational forms. For example, the 'creative' conversation for possibilities will have a much less structured form.

The importance of CfA is that actions are central to organizational administration. In the words of Terry Winograd [380]:

> Conversations for action are the central coordinating structure for human organizations.

This belief in the importance of CfA, together with the assumption that making speech acts explicit will aid communication, prompted the design of the tool *Coordinator*. Coordinator is a form of structured email system. When sending a message, the participants must say what kind of illocutionary act they are performing and what part it plays in a conversation. The tool knows about CfA and a few other conversational forms. In addition, it allows time limits to be put on messages. Together these facilities allow the participants to keep track of their own commitments and those of others.

As an example, imagine Alison wishes to use Coordinator to request the market survey from Brian. She selects a menu option saying that she wants to initiate a CfA. The system then offers her two possibilities, a request or an offer. She chooses to make a request and from now on the system knows that a CfA is in progress. She then types 'have you got the market survey on chocolate mousse' into the text area of the message. Note that the system does not try to structure or interpret the natural language *content* of the utterance, but only demands that the sender declares the illocutionary point of it. Brian receives Alison's message and is told by the system that it is a request. He is then offered the various conversational moves that can follow: promise, counter-offer or decline (*reject*), plus a few more not on Figure 14.1. If he chooses promise, the system fills the message area with the default words 'I promise to do as you request', which can be altered (to 'sure') if Brian desires, or sent as it is. The intention is that many simple acts can be completed by the defaults.

Coordinator, being one of the earlier CSCW systems, has had plenty of criticism. Indeed, 'Coordinator bashing' has become so common in CSCW circles that it (the bashing) is coming under criticism itself. There are three main problems: reservations about speech act theory itself and CfA in particular, that people dislike using Coordinator, and whether the whole concept of making intentions explicit is a good idea.

The first criticism is that speech acts do not adequately describe conversations. For example, Alison walks into Brian's office while he is on the phone, he picks a report from the table and gives it to her, she walks out. Speech act theory would regard this as a conversation for action. The request is implicit; presumably Brian knows what Alison wants from some previous context. Then when Brian hands over the report, he is, by complying with her request, both implicitly *promising* to fulfill and *asserting* completion of the request. Finally, by going out of the office Alison implicitly declares completion. There seems to be an awful lot of squeezing to get the interchange to fit the CfA! Indeed, this is recognized in part within Coordinator as a valid response to a request is a report of completion (*assert*), that is taking the *promise* as read.

There have been mixed responses as to the usefulness of Coordinator, but most (certainly the most vocal) have been negative. The conversational forms basically do not do what people want. Those users who continued to use it ended up using 'free-form' messages – a non-interpreted action. Effectively, they used Coordinator as a standard email. It has been claimed that the only organizations that have used Coordinator successfully are those with strong authoritarian managerial structures where the employees have been ordered to use it. Coordinator has even been dubbed 'the world's first fascist computer system'[5] – which was certainly *not* the intention of the designers. As you can see, emotions tend to run high when discussing Coordinator!

The fundamental approach of Coordinator is different from any previous system, and from most since. Rather than starting with technology – build it and play with it – Coordinator started with a theory of communication and then used this to drive design. Such theory-led design is a thoroughly proper design approach. The debatable issue is the way in which the theory was incorporated into the tool.

Coordinator expects its users to make explicit what is normally implicit in our utterances. We hope the reader will have realized by now just how rich human conversation is, and how effective people are at communication. However, one of the fundamental lessons learnt by the expert systems community is that experts *do* things, they do not know *how* they do them. Forcing expert communicators (people) to think about their communication is rather like asking a centipede to think about walking. This all suggests that theory should be used to guide the design, but should not be embedded explicitly within it.

There is a counter-argument, however. First of all, there is some evidence to suggest that teaching managers to recognize their speech acts improves their communication. The extrapolation is that making the acts explicit improves communication, but that is a major extrapolation. A more measured claim would be that explicit representation is *at least* a good tool for training communication skills. The second argument concerns the nature of electronic communication. Although we are all experts at face-to-face communication with all its subtleties, our expertise is sorely challenged when faced with a blank screen. We lack the facilities to make our intentions implicit in our communications and thus explicit means will help.

Whatever the rights and wrongs of Coordinator's design, the evidence is that its users have largely voted with their feet. More recent systems have included a much greater level of user control, allowing users to build conversational structures of their own. Possibly, the structures they build are merely special cases of CfA and other speech act structures, but users clearly prefer to feel that they have the power over the system.

---

5 Even if one agreed with the sentiment, it would certainly not be the first.

14.4   TEXT-BASED COMMUNICATION

For *asynchronous* groupware (and even some synchronous systems), the major form of direct communication is text based. There are exceptions to this, for instance voice messaging systems and answerphones, and other media may be used in addition to text such as graphics, voice annotation or even video clips. But despite these, text is still the dominant medium.

Text-based communication is familiar to most people, in that they will have written and received letters. However, the style of letter writing and that of face-to-face communication are very different. The text-based communication in groupware systems is acting as a speech substitute, and, thus, there are some problems adapting between the two media.

There are four types of textual communication in current groupware:

discrete – directed message as in email. There is no explicit connection between different messages, except in so far as the text of the message refers to a previous one.

linear – participants' messages are added in (usually temporal) order to the end of a single transcript.

non-linear – when messages are linked to one another in a hypertext fashion.

spatial – where messages are arranged on a two-dimensional surface.

In addition, the communication may be connected to other shared computer artefacts, which will be described further in Chapter 19 (Section 19.6). In the case where the communication is an annotation, the annotation itself may be structured in any of the ways listed above.

A special case of a linear transcript is structured message systems such as Coordinator, where not only the order but also the function of each message is determined. The other extreme is where the transcript is presented as a single stream, with no special fields except the name of the contributor. Figure 14.2 shows a screen shot of the York Conferencer system showing such a transcript on the left of the screen. On the right is an electronic pin-board, an example of spatially organized text.

In this section, we will discuss some of the differences between face-to-face conversation and text-based communications. We will use several of the concepts introduced during our discussion of face-to-face communication and conversational structure in Sections 14.2 and 14.3.

14.4.1 Back channels and affective state

One of the most profound differences between face-to-face and text-based communication is the lack of fine-grained channels. Much of the coordination of face-to-face conversation depends on back channels and interpretation of the listener's expressions. Text-based communication loses these back channels completely. Consider the effect of this on even a two-party conversation. Where the

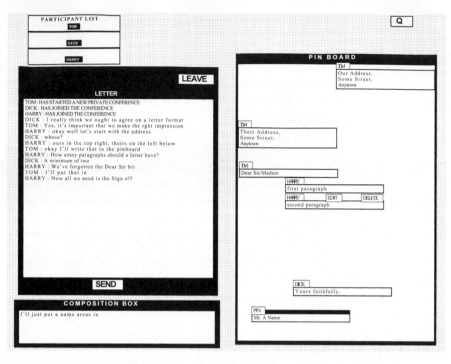

Figure 14.2 Conferencer screen shot showing text transcript and pin-board

speaker would pause to seek back channel confirmation or to offer the floor, the text 'speaker' must either continue regardless, or finish the message, effectively passing the turn. One consequence of the lack of interruptions and more measured pace of interaction is that the utterances are more grammatical than speech – but still *not* Queen's English!

In addition to this loss of back channels, the speaker's tone of voice and body language are of course absent. These normally convey the *affective state* of the speaker (happy, sad, angry, humorous) and the *illocutionary force* of the message (an important and urgent demand or a deferential request). Email users have developed explicit tokens of their affective state by the use of 'flaming' and 'smilies', using punctuation and acronyms; for example:

    :-)   – smiling face, happy
    :-(– sad face, upset or angry
    ;-)   – winking face, humorous
    LOL – laughing out loud.

People tend to use stronger language in email than in face-to-face conversation, for example they are more likely to be highly and emotively critical. On the other hand, they are less likely to get emotionally charged themselves. These apparently contradictory findings make sense when you take into account the lack of implicit affective communication. The participants have to put this explicitly into their messages – thus accounting for their stronger language. At the same time, they are emotionally 'distanced' by the text from their conversants and have the conversation spread out over time. In addition, they do not have to express their affective state by *acting* emotionally. Together these factors contribute to a more heated conversation by calmer conversants!

The culture of electronic mail

We use or receive many different kinds of paper messages: formal letters, memos, handwritten notes, pre-printed letters and postcards. In addition, we communicate by voice: in meetings and lectures, by telephone and as we pass in the corridor. The same message delivered by different media has a different meaning for us. Someone asks us to do something as we pass them in the corridor, but we forget. We don't feel too guilty. But if the same request came by formal letter we would be expected to respond.

These communication mechanisms have been around a long time and we largely understand the social force of different media. That is, we have a shared culture for paper and voice media. The situation for electronic media is far less clear.

In the past, email used to be very unreliable. So, if someone sent you a mail and you were slow to respond or didn't respond at all, you didn't feel too guilty. After all, for all the sender knew, you might never have received the message! That is, the unreliable nature of the medium built up a culture where the social force of email was weak – rather like the comment while passing in the corridor.

However, increasingly email is used within organizations for passing critical information or making important decisions. The expectation is that email will be treated with the same force as a formal letter or memo.

Imagine what happens when the two cultures meet . . . Sending a message to someone asking them to come to a meeting in half an hour will obviously only have its intended effect if the sender and recipient have a shared culture of use.

Often you cannot know when you send a message what the email culture of the recipient is. It varies between organizations and even between groups and individuals within an organization. The medium itself gives few clues. Even more frightening, many people do not even *realize* that there are such cultural differences.

14.4.2 Grounding constraints

In Section 14.3.5, we discussed the process by which conversants obtain common ground. This grounding process is linked strongly with the types of channels through which the conversants communicate. Clark and Brennan [71] describe the properties of these channels in terms of *grounding constraints*. These include:

cotemporality – an utterance is heard as soon as it is said (or typed);

simultaneity – the participants can send and receive at the same time;

sequence – the utterances are ordered.

These are all constraints which are weaker in text-based compared with face-to-face interaction. For example, simultaneity in face-to-face conversation allows back channel responses. Even where, say, two participants can see each other's typed messages as they are produced, the nature of typing makes it all but impossible to type your message whilst looking for your colleague's 'back channel' response.

In a text-based system, different participants can compose simultaneously, but they lack cotemporality. As we saw, even if the messages appear as they are produced, they will not be read in real time. In addition, the messages may only be delivered when complete and even then may be delayed by slow communications networks.

Linear transcripts obviously have some idea of sequence, but this is confused by the overlap and interleaving caused by the lack of cotemporality and simultaneity. Consider this typical interchange during the use of the York Conferencer system:

1.	**Bethan**:	How many should be in the group?
2.	**Rowena**:	Maybe this could be one of the four strongest reasons?
3.	**Rowena**:	Please clarify what you mean.
4.	**Bethan**:	I agree.
5.	**Rowena**:	Hang on.
6.	**Rowena**:	Bethan what did you mean?

Rowena and Bethan composed their first utterances simultaneously. When Rowena looks up to the transcript area, she sees Bethan's message and does not understand it, so she enters the canned phrase 'Please clarify what you mean' which is generated by a button marked 'Clarify'. Simultaneously, Bethan reads Rowena's message (2) and hits her canned phrase button 'Agree'. Rowena is then confused about what Bethan means by 'I agree' as the preceding message was her request for clarification.

In a spoken conversation, Rowena and Bethan would have quickly corrected themselves if they began to speak at once, and the linearity would have reflected a *common* experience. The trouble is that the participants in the text-based conference each experienced the messages in a different order:

Rowena: 2 1 3 4 5 6
Bethan: 1 2 4 3 5 6

We will discuss these problems of interleaving and overlapped messages further in the following sections.

Altogether, the lack of grounding constraints in text-based communication makes it more difficult to obtain a common ground. It has also been found that email and text-based meetings are less effective at resolving conflicts than a face-to-face meeting.

14.4.3 Turn-taking

We saw that one of the fundamental structures of conversation was *turn-taking* (Section 14.2.5). The last transcript was an example of a breakdown in turn-taking. In fact, such breakdowns are quite rare in two-party electronic conversations and are quickly corrected. What is more surprising is that such breakdowns so rarely occur during letter writing, which is in some ways similar. However, when conversing by letter, one has an objective timescale with which to work out whether one's fellow conversant ought to have replied. One therefore does not send a second letter unless the conversant is very remiss in replying to the first missive. However, in synchronous text-based conversation, the time taken to compose a message (from 30 seconds to several minutes) is far greater than the few seconds which feel 'immediate' on a computer system, but is too short to be able to reason about rationally. The replies always seem a long time coming and hence one is tempted to send a 'follow-on' message.

Despite the occasional breakdown, most observers of two-party text-based inter-action report an overall turn-taking protocol, which exhibits many of the structures of normal conversation including *adjacency pairs*. However, when we look at three or more participants, turn-taking and adjacency pair structure begin to break down completely.

In a pair of participants, turn-taking is simple; first one person says something, then the other. The only problem is deciding exactly *when* the exchange should happen. With three or more participants, turn-taking is more complex. They must decide *who* should have the next turn. This is resolved by face-to-face groups in a number of ways. First, the conversation may, for a period, be focused on two of the parties, in which case normal two-party turn-taking holds. Secondly, the speaker may specifically address another participant as the utterance is finished, either implicitly by body position, or explicitly: 'what do you think Alison?' Finally, the next speaker may be left open, but the cotemporality of the audio channel allows the other participants to negotiate the turn. Basically, whoever speaks first, or most strongly, gets in.

These mechanisms are aided by back channels, as one of the listeners may make it clear that she wants to speak. In this case, either the speaker will explicitly pass the turn (the second option above), or at least the other listeners are expecting her to speak. In addition, the movement between effective two-party conversation (the first option) and open discussion will be mediated by back channel messages from the other participants.

In an unstructured text-based conversation the third option is not available, nor, of course, are the back channels. Paired conversation is quite common and the second option, explicitly naming the next speaker, is possible. However, this naming is not particularly natural unless a direct question is being asked. In both options, the absence of back channels makes it difficult for another listener to interrupt the conversation. Some systems use more structured mechanisms to get round these problems, perhaps having a round-robin protocol (each participant 'speaks' in turn) or having a queue of turn-requests. Whether the strictures of such mechanisms are worse than the problems of occasional breakdown depends very much on the context and is a matter of opinion.

14.4.4 Context and deixis

We have seen how important context is in ordinary speech. Utterances are highly ambiguous and are only meaningful with respect to *external context*, the state of the world, and *internal context*, the state of the conversation. Both of these are problems in text-based communication.

The very fact that the participants are not co-present makes it more difficult to use external context to disambiguate utterances. This is why many groupware systems strive so hard to make the participants' views the same; that is, to maintain WYSIWIS ('what you see is what I see'). In Chapter 19 we will look at an example that shows that this is an issue even when the participants have audio/video communications or are in the same room!

Whatever the means of direct communication, remote participants have difficulty in using deictic reference. They cannot simply say 'that one', but must usually describe the referrant: 'the big circle in the corner'. If their displays are not WYSIWIS then they must also ensure that their colleague's display includes the object referred to and that the description is unambiguous. Asynchronous participants have even more problems with deixis as there is no opportunity for their colleagues to clarify a reference (without extremely lengthy exchanges). Furthermore, the objects referred to by a message may have changed by the time someone comes to read it! Similarly, group pointers are not really an option, but one can use methods of linking the conversation to its context, either by embedding it within the objects as annotations or by having hypertext links between the conversation and the object.

The trouble does not end with external context; there are also problems with deictic reference to internal context. In speech, the context is intimately connected to linear sequence and adjacency. As we have seen, even in linear text transcripts, overlap breaks the strict sequentiality of the conversation, and thus causes problems with indexicals and with context in general.

1. **Alison**: Brian's got some lovely roses.
2. **Brian**: I'm afraid they're covered in greenfly.
3. **Clarise**: I've seen them, they're beautiful.

Brian and Clarise both reply to Alison's message at the same time. However, in the transcript, where Clarise says 'they' this appears, at first, to refer to the greenfly. Brian is expecting a consoling reply like 'I've seen them. Have you tried companion planting?' Of course, the breakdown quickly becomes apparent in this case. The problem is not so much that people cannot recover from such breakdowns, as in the extra burden the recovery puts on the participants. If these messages are being sent, say, between continents, network delays and time differences may limit exchanges to once a day. Even one or two messages recovering from breakdown are then a major disaster.

Most email systems and some bulletin boards lack any implied sequentiality and thus any context to the messages. The users (ever inventive) get round this by including copies of previous messages in their replies. This is only partially effective and, of course, incredibly clumsy.

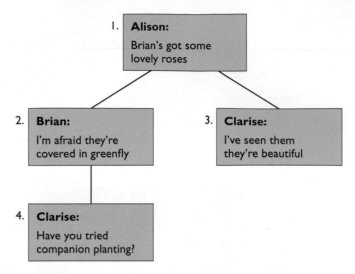

Figure 14.3 Hypertext conversation structure

Hypertext-based systems avoid the implied sequentiality of a linear transcript. In the above example, both Brian and Clarise replied to Alison's message at the same time. In a hypertext these would form parallel conversations. This is shown in Figure 14.3, where in addition Clarise has sent a second message offering advice on Brian's greenfly. The use of 'they' in Clarise's message (3) is now perfectly clear.

14.4.5 Pace and granularity

In a spoken conversation, the turns are often only a few tens of seconds long. If we take into account minor confirmations and back channels, the pace is still faster, perhaps a turn or back channel response every few seconds. Compared with this, the pace of email is very slow: messages can take from a few seconds to hours to deliver. Even synchronous text-based conversations are limited by the participants' typing speed and have a pace of at most one turn every minute or so.

The term *pace* is being used in a precise sense above. Imagine a message being composed and sent, the recipient reading (or hearing) the message and then composing and sending a reply. The pace of the conversation is the rate of such a sequence of connected messages and replies. Clearly, as the pace of a conversation reduces, there is a tendency for the *granularity* to increase. To get the same information across, you must send more per message. However, it is not as easy as that. We have seen the importance of feedback from listener to speaker in clarifying meaning and negotiating common ground. Even most monologs are interactive in the sense that the speaker is constantly looking for cues of comprehension in the listener. Reducing the pace of a conversation reduces its *interactivity*.

As well as at the small scale of clarifying individual utterances, interactivity is important in determining the direction of a conversation. Imagine that the conversation

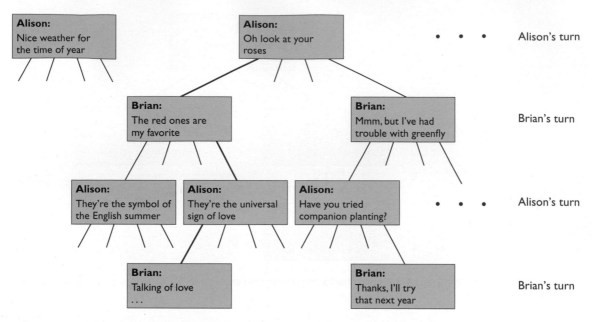

Figure 14.4 The conversation 'game'

is a little like a game, where the participants can make moves. In Figure 14.4, we can see some of the moves Alison and Brian can make whilst talking in the garden (Clarise has gone home). At each turn of the conversation, Alison or Brian can choose to say one thing which continues the discussion. That is, they gradually work out a path from the top of the tree downwards. A particularly promising conversation path is shown with bold lines.

In a hypertext-based system one can expand several branches of a conversation tree, but in speech or in a linear text transcript the conversation follows one branch. Whatever medium is used, you cannot normally progress down the tree faster than the pace of the conversation. To overcome these limitations, people adopt several *coping strategies*.

The simplest strategy is just to avoid conversation. This can be done by delegating parts of a task to the different participants. Each participant can then perform much of the task without communication. They must still communicate for large-scale strategic decisions, but have significantly reduced the normal communications. Of course, this approach reduces *communication* by reducing *collaboration*.

More interesting in a cooperative work setting are two coping strategies which increase the chunk size of messages in order to reduce the number of interactions required to complete a task. These strategies are frequently seen in both text-based conferences and in letter writing.

The first of these coping strategies is *multiplexing*. Basically, the conversants hold several conversations in parallel, each message referring to several topics. In terms of the conversation tree, this corresponds to going down several branches at once. For an example, consider the transcript in Figure 14.5 taken during a computer-mediated

E: I don't like the other three being in
cahoots – shall I form an alliance with
one to stitch them up? I'll move to
Holland first.

Figure 14.5   Excerpt of transcript from Hewitt et al. [171]. Source: Courtesy of
Professor Nigel Gilbert

game of Diplomacy as part of the TMPI (theories of multi-party interaction) project
[171]. The turn by England (E) introduces two topics: the forming of an alliance (for
subversive purposes), and a particular line of attack (through Holland).

The second coping strategy for increasing the size of message chunks is *eagerness*.
The participants can foresee the possible course of the interaction and frame communications which encompass many of the possibilities: for example, 'If you don't
pay within seven days we will take you to court'. Thinking of the conversation tree,
eagerness is a sort of depth-first strategy. The participant explores a branch of the
tree guessing the other participant's responses.

If we compare spoken with written communication we find that letters are far
more eager than speech. When writing a letter, one takes more care that the points
are stated clearly, and one may even consider alternative responses of the recipient
and state one's position on each. For instance, a letter may say 'if you marry me I will
be happy for ever, but if not, life will lie like bitter herbs upon my tongue' (lovers
have a tradition of being overeager). In extremis one frames a communication which
describes one's reaction in all possible situations.

One can find similar incidents of eagerness in electronic conversations, for example the messages in Figure 14.6 from Severinson Eklundh's corpus [317], quoted
by Bowers and Churcher [42], both exhibit eagerness, the contingent part of each
message being introduced by the key phrase 'In that case'.

Eagerness is less likely to lead to breakdown, except where the message tries to
foresee too great a breadth of possibilities and becomes confusing. However, there
are various circumstances: for instance, in many process control tasks, where the
number of possibilities at each stage of the tree is large. In this case eagerness cannot
solve the communication problems.

A: Subject: Report C 123660
The above mentioned report is out of stock.
The remaining ones are C 12366 + C 123660.
What to do? Reprint? In that case, do you have
any changes to suggest?
. . .   . . .

A: Subject: SIGSIM meeting
Are you going to Linkoping tomorrow?
In that case when are you leaving?
Does SIGSIM pay for the trip or what?

Figure 14.6   Excerpt from Severinson Eklundh's corpus [317]. Source: Courtesy of
Kerstin Severinson Eklundh

A potential problem of eagerness is that by following a particular branch of the conversation, other branches, which your colleague would have liked to explore, are missed. In spoken conversations it is quite difficult to return to a previous point. It is possible to say 'going back to . . .', but this can form a potentially rude break in the conversation. In text-based communications, the *reviewability* of the medium reduces this effect. It is easier to return to a missed point as both participants can refer to the conversation up to that point. In addition, the break in the line of conversation is less rude as both participants know that the current topic can itself be picked up again. Finally, there is even the option of multiplexing the current topic with the lost point.

Reviewability is another grounding constraint of communication, but this time one where text-based communication has the advantage over speech. You can of course tape speech, but it is far from easy to use this as a review mechanism.

14.4.6 Linear text vs. hypertext

Considerations of potential overlap suggest that hypertext-based communications may be better suited as a text-based communication medium. Similarly, the problems of pace may be partially solved in a hypertext. Multiplexed messages can be represented as updates to several parts of the hypertext, thus reducing the likelihood of breakdown and lost topics. In addition, if the messages themselves can be mini-hypertexts, then eager messages listing several possible courses of action can be explicitly represented by the message.

On the other hand, hypertext has its disadvantages. Even static hypertexts, which have been carefully crafted by their authors, can be difficult to navigate. A hypertext that is created 'on the fly' is unlikely to be comprehensible to any but those involved in its creation. Conklin and Begeman, themselves associated with the hypertext-based argumentation tool gIBIS, conclude that 'traditional linear text provides a continuous, unwinding thread of context as ideas are proposed and discussed' [76]. For the asynchronous reader trying to catch up with a conversation, a linear transcript is clearly easier, but it is precisely in more asynchronous settings where overlap in linear text is most likely to cause confusion.

We can see that there is no best solution, with possibly the best course in many situations being linear transcripts arranged by topic, with some automatically generated indication of overlap.

14.5   GROUP WORKING

So far we have been principally looking at the properties of direct communication, and largely two-party conversations. Group behavior is more complex still as we have to take into account the dynamic social relationships during group working. We will begin by looking at several factors which affect group working, and then discuss the problems of studying group working. This section deals with groups that are actively working together, rather than the organizational issues considered in the previous chapter, which are primarily concerned with the long-term structures within which people work.

14.5.1 Group dynamics

Whereas organizational relationships such as supervisor/supervisee are relatively stable, the roles and relationships within a group may change dramatically within the lifetime of a task and even within a single work session. For example, studies of joint authoring have found that roles such as author, co-author and commentator change throughout the lifetime of a document [254, 295]. This means that systems, such as co-authoring systems, which use a formal concept of *role*, must allow these roles to change together with the socially defined roles.

Even the naming of roles can cause problems. A person may be an author of a book or paper, but never write the words in it, acting instead as a source of ideas and comments. A particular case of this is the biographical story where the individual concerned and a professional writer co-author the book, but only the professional author writes. A co-authoring system such as Quilt would call the non-writing author a 'commentator' or a 'reviewer', but *not* an 'author'. One can imagine some of the social friction such naming will cause.

Within the microcosm of group interaction, authority roles can be entirely inverted. For example, if the managing director of a coal mining company visits the coal face, he should act under the authority of the supervisor at the face, for his own safety and that of the mine. These inversions can cause problems even in computer-free situations – it is hard for the supervisor to say 'No' to the MD. But, if a system demands an explicit controlling role, it is even harder for the manager to relinquish this explicit role, even if in the context the subordinate should be in control.

Not only do the social relationships *within* the group change, but the group membership and structure can change in time. A member leaving or a new member joining can cause dramatic changes in the behavior of the group. For example, if a very dominant member leaves, the group may change from a leader–follower to a democratic structure. New members have special problems adapting to the particular group subculture, which can develop very quickly among close colleagues. In addition to this social adaptation, the new member must 'catch up' with the substantive work of the group. Groupware systems, for example *argumentation tools*, can help in that they record the history of the group. Groupware designers should in general be aware that new members can and will enter the group and should design their software accordingly. For example, a latecomer to a synchronous conference should be able to review all past contributions, not just the new ones.

The group may also divide into subgroups for detailed discussion and then reform. Tools must be able to support this. For example, early versions of *CoLab's* software only catered for a single WYSIWIS screen – that is, they only supported a single group. Later versions were forced to allow subgroups to work independently and then share results. Note that the CoLab meeting room only has room for six persons; in larger meeting rooms subgroup working is the norm.

14.5.2 Physical layout

In Section 14.2, we discussed the importance of eyegaze and gesture in face-to-face communication and how these help to mediate turn-taking. In particular, we noted in Section 14.2.3 that we must ensure that monitors do not block the participants' views of one another. In general, the physical layout of a room has a profound effect upon the working relationship of those in it. This is particularly obvious for meeting rooms, but should be considered in any group-working environment.

As well as being unobtrusive, the orientation of computing equipment can affect group working. If we wish to encourage conversation, as we do in a meeting room, the participants must be encouraged to look toward one another. Meeting rooms have a natural focus toward the screen at the front of the room, but inward-facing terminals can counteract this focus and thus encourage eye contact [226].

The designers of Capture Lab, an eight-person meeting room, considered all these features and many other subtle effects. However, the users still had some difficulty in adapting to the *power positions* in the electronic meeting room. At first sight, the electronic meeting room is not unlike a normal conference room. If the shared screen is a whiteboard or an overhead projector, then the most powerful position is toward the front of the room (seats 1 or 6 in Figure 14.7). Managers would normally take this seat as they can then easily move to the whiteboard or overhead projector to point out some item and draw the group's attention.

Unless primed beforehand, managers of groups using Capture Lab took one of these seats, but quickly became uncomfortable and moved. In the electronic meeting room, there is no advantage to being at the front, because the screen can be controlled from any terminal. Instead, the power seat is at the back of the room (seats 3 or 4), as from here the manager can observe other people whilst still seeing the screen. Also, the other participants have to turn round when the manager speaks, adding to the manager's authority over the meeting.

14.5.3 Distributed cognition

In Chapter 1, we discussed human cognition, but the emphasis was, as in all traditional psychology, upon the activity *within* the person's head. A school of thinking has recently developed which regards thinking as happening not just within the head, but in the external relationships with things in the world and with other people. This viewpoint is called *distributed cognition* [208, 185].

In fact, this viewpoint is not as radical as it first appears. Traditional views talk about the movement of information between *working memory* and *long-term memory*: it is not so difficult then to regard bits of paper, books and computer systems as extensions to these internal memory systems. Similarly, many models of human cognition regard the mind as a set of interacting subsystems (see Chapter 12): the step to regarding several people as involved in joint thinking is not difficult.

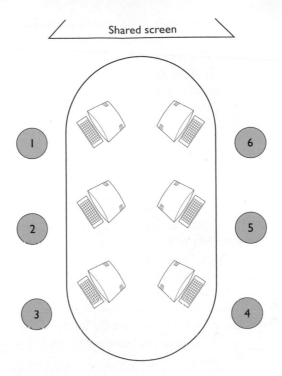

Figure 14.7 Meeting room layout

Remember that this is a view of cognition, that is thinking; it says nothing about awareness, personality or individuality.

Distributed cognition has profound effects on the way we look at group working and even individual work. It emphasizes the importance of *mediating representations*, for example the drawings on a whiteboard. These are no longer just a means of communicating between the parties, but can be a concrete embodiment of group knowledge. Furthermore, it constantly reminds us that communication is not just about getting knowledge from one person's head to another, but about the creation of new group knowledge, not necessarily grasped in totality by any single member.

The emphasis on external forms is encouraging for a designer. It is not necessary to understand completely the individual's cognitive processing in order to design effective groupware. That is an impossible task. Instead, we can focus our analysis of existing group situations and design of groupware on the external representations used by the participants.

14.6 SUMMARY

Face-to-face communication is extremely complex. People maintain precise distances, which can be disrupted through video links. Each utterance is mediated by subtle back channel responses signifying agreement, or on attempting to interrupt.

Body movement, facial expression, eye contact and eyegaze are all used for these back channels and also to establish context.

At a higher level, the structure of conversation can be seen as a sequence of turns, usually alternating between the participants. Context is important in disambiguating utterances, especially when deictic reference is also used. This also depends on the participants establishing a common understanding during the conversation. Breakdowns do occur in conversation, but conversational repair is very effective. Speech act theory, a detailed analysis of conversational structure, has been used to drive the design of Coordinator, a highly controversial, commercial, structured messaging system.

Text-based communication loses most of the low-level feedback of face-to-face conversation. This, and the possibility of overlapping turns, makes it more difficult to establish the context of a textual utterance, and therefore to disambiguate deixis. The reduced pace of text-based conversation means that participants are forced to increase the granularity of their messages. They may achieve this by multiplexing messages or by being eager, predicting their colleagues' responses.

Group dynamics make it very difficult to predict how a particular group will behave. In particular, small things, such as the layout of chairs in a room, can have a major effect. We can see the thinking in a group as being distributed, not locked in any individual, but being within the whole group and the physical representations they use.

EXERCISES

14.1 In Section 14.3.2, we discussed the highly contextual nature of the spoken word, including the use of deictic reference and indexicals, and the (officially) ungrammatical and fragmentary use of sentences. Try listening to social chat over cups of tea – collect examples of different forms of contextual utterance.

14.2 Go into an office or other place where several people are working together. Try to note down in as much detail as possible what they are doing and when. Do this with different foci: focus on the direct interpersonal communications, focus on the shared objects such as a calendar or document, or focus on one worker at a time. Whilst collecting data and when ordering your notes, look for breakdowns and misunderstandings, and for implicit communication through objects. Look also at a particular task over a period of time, and note the number of interruptions as a worker performs the task, or the way a single task is contributed to by several workers.

14.3 What is speech act theory? Describe positive and negative issues that have arisen when it has been embodied in a specific system.

14.4 Compare turn-taking, round-robin and free-for-all as floor control mechanisms. When might each be effective?

RECOMMENDED READING

J. Carroll, editor, *HCI Models, Theories, and Frameworks: Toward an Interdisciplinary Science*, Morgan Kaufmann, 2003.
See chapters by Perry on distributed cognition, Monk on common ground and Kraut on social psychology.

L. A. Suchman, *Plans and Situated Actions: The Problem of Human–Machine Communication*, Cambridge University Press, 1987.
This book popularized ethnography within HCI. It puts forward the viewpoint that most actions are not pre-planned, but situated within the context in which they occur. The principal domain of the book is the design of help for a photocopier. This is itself a single-user task, but the methodology applied is based on both ethnographic and conversational analysis. The book includes several chapters discussing the contextual nature of language and analysis of conversation transcripts.

T. Winograd and F. Flores, *Understanding Computers and Cognition: A New Foundation for Design*, Addison-Wesley, 1986.
Like Suchman, this book emphasizes the contextual nature of language and the weakness of traditional artificial intelligence research. It includes an account of speech act theory as applied to Coordinator. Many people disagree with the authors' use of speech act theory, but, whether by application or reaction, this work has been highly influential.

S. Greenberg, editor, *Computer-supported Cooperative Work and Groupware*, Academic Press, 1991.
The contents of this collection originally made up two special issues of the *International Journal of Man–Machine Studies*. In addition, the book contains Greenberg's extensive annotated bibliography of CSCW, a major entry point for any research into the field. Updated versions of the bibliography can be obtained from the Department of Computer Science, University of Calgary, Calgary, Alberta, Canada.

Communications of the ACM, Vol. 34, No. 12, special issue on 'collaborative computing', December 1991.

Several issues of the journal *Interacting with Computers* from late 1992 through early 1993 have a special emphasis on CSCW.

Computer-Supported Cooperative Work is a journal dedicated to CSCW. See also back issues of the journal *Collaborative Computing*. This ran independently for a while, but has now merged with *Computer-Supported Cooperative Work*.

See also the recommended reading list for Chapter 19, especially the conference proceedings.

15 TASK ANALYSIS

OVERVIEW

Task analysis is the study of the way people perform tasks with existing systems.

- Techniques for task analysis:
  - decomposition of tasks into subtasks
  - taxonomic classification of task knowledge
  - listing things used and actions performed.

- Sources of information:
  - existing documentation
  - observation
  - interviews.

- Using task analysis to design:
  - manuals and documentation
  - new systems.

15.1   INTRODUCTION

Task analysis is the process of analyzing the way people perform their jobs: the things they do, the things they act on and the things they need to know. For example, if we were considering the job of housekeeping, we would want to say things like:

in order to clean the house
> get the vacuum cleaner out
> fix the appropriate attachment
> clean the rooms
> when the dust bag gets full, empty it
> put the vacuum cleaner and tools away

To perform such a task, we need to know about vacuum cleaners, their attachments, dust bags (if used), cupboards (in which the vacuum cleaner is kept), rooms (to be cleaned) and so on.

We will consider three different approaches to task analysis, which overlap but which lay their emphases on slightly different areas. These are as follows:

Task decomposition which looks at the way a task is split into subtasks, and the order in which these are performed.

Knowledge-based techniques which look at what users need to know about the objects and actions involved in a task, and how that knowledge is organized.

Entity–relation-based analysis which is an object-based approach where the emphasis is on identifying the actors and objects, the relationships between them and the actions they perform.

Task analysis is about existing systems and procedures; its main tools are those of observation in various forms. We will discuss these sources of information later. One of the purposes of task analysis is to help in the production of training materials and documentation. For this purpose, analysis of existing systems is sufficient.

However, where a new computer system is required, the task analysis also contributes to the statement of requirements of this system. We will see how it can be applied in a fairly straightforward way to menu design. The process of designing a new system based on an analysis of an existing system will involve a considerable amount of professional insight and the contribution of task analysis to this is principally one of clarifying and organizing one's knowledge about the current situation.

15.2   DIFFERENCES BETWEEN TASK ANALYSIS AND OTHER TECHNIQUES

The scope of task analysis is quite wide. In addition to those tasks which directly involve a computer, the task analyst will typically model aspects of the world that are not, and are not expected to be, part of a computer system. So a task analysis of word processing would include activities such as fetching documents from the filing cabinet, changing the printer ribbon and putting floppy disks in and out of the computer as well as the more obvious interaction with the machine.

So, like traditional systems analysis, task analysis is not limited to activities including a computer, although (again like systems analysis) the intention is usually that a computer system will be installed. In fact, it is often hard to differentiate many modern task analysis techniques from their older cousins. The main difference is one of emphasis; task analysis is there specifically to recognize the importance of the user.

Some aspects of task analysis will look very like the goal-oriented cognitive models discussed in Chapter 12. Indeed, there would be little to prevent one using a GOMS-like notation to represent a task decomposition such as the vacuum cleaning above. The difference between the two lies in the intention of the models. The purpose of the goal-oriented models is to understand the internal cognitive processes as a person performs a task – the granularity is thus usually rather small. The emphasis of task analysis is more one of observing the user from the outside and will include actions, such as retrieval of a document from a filing cabinet, which would never be included in a GOMS analysis.

Task analysis therefore tends to look more at the observable behavior of users than their internal mental state. Some practitioners would say that task analysis should be restricted to precisely this objective observable behavior – you should be interested in what, not why. However, even the most objective analysis will include some inferences about the user's internal goals, and this will often be evident in the names used in task decomposition. Furthermore, other practitioners explicitly state that their intention is to build a *conceptual model* – the way the user views the system and the task. This latter approach will be particularly evident in the knowledge-based approaches.

Sometimes task analysis will produce quite low-level task decompositions which are identical to those one would expect from a goal-oriented analysis. However, for task analysis this would tend to be the end of the process, to be used, for instance, by the interface designer in structuring the dialog. For goal-oriented cognitive models, such a goal hierarchy is the central feature, to be further analyzed for complexity, learnability and the like.

In terms of the design life cycle (Chapter 6), task analysis belongs at the beginning in requirements capture, whereas the cognitive models are normally used toward the end of the process during evaluation.

15.3   TASK DECOMPOSITION

The example above of vacuum cleaning showed how a task, 'clean the house', was decomposed into several subtasks: 'get the vacuum cleaner out' and so on. Most task analysis techniques involve some form of task decomposition to express this sort of

```
0.    in order to clean the house
      1.    get the vacuum cleaner out
      2.    fix the appropriate attachment
      3.    clean the rooms
            3.1.    clean the hall
            3.2.    clean the living rooms
            3.3.    clean the bedrooms
      4.    empty the dust bag
      5.    put the vacuum cleaner and attachments away

Plan 0:    do 1 – 2 – 3 – 5 in that order.
           when the dust bag gets full do 4


Plan 3:    do any of 3.1, 3.2 or 3.3 in any order
           depending on which rooms need cleaning
```

Figure 15.1   How to clean a house

behavior. *Hierarchical task analysis (HTA)* is typical of such an approach [15, 318]. The outputs of HTA are a *hierarchy* of tasks and subtasks and also *plans* describing in what order and under what conditions subtasks are performed.

For example, we could express the house-cleaning example as in Figure 15.1, further decomposing the subtask 'clean rooms'. Indentation is used to denote the levels in the task hierarchy, and the tasks are also numbered to emphasize this hierarchy. The plans are labeled by the task to which they correspond. So plan 0 refers to the way in which we perform the subtasks 1–5 of task 0. Similarly plan 3 refers to the way in which we perform 3.1–3.3. There are no plans for subtasks 1, 2, 4 and 5 as these have not been decomposed.

Reading the plans, we see that not all the subtasks need be performed, and not necessarily in the order presented. Looking first at plan 0, subtask 4 'empty the dust bag' need only be performed when the dust bag is found to be full. As this is put in plan 0, we assume that we may empty the dust bag at any stage including when we first get the vacuum cleaner out or when we put it away. If we know that we only ever notice the bag is full when we are actively using the machine, we might choose to put this subtask within 3 'clean the rooms'. This sort of restructuring, finding the appropriate and meaningful hierarchy, is part of the process of HTA.

Looking now at plan 3, how to clean the rooms, we see that we are allowed to clean the rooms in any order. If the task had been varnishing the floors rather than cleaning them, we would presumably do the hall after the rest of the rooms! Furthermore, we only clean those rooms which need vacuuming. The bedrooms will not get dirty as fast as the hall, so we need not clean them so often. If we wanted to be more precise about when the rooms are cleaned, we could produce a more specific plan:

```
Plan 3:    do 3.1 every day
           3.2 once a week
           when visitors are due 3.3
```

How does one produce such a hierarchy with attendant rules? The process is iterative. Assume for the moment that we have some overall task in mind, such as house cleaning. We then ask, what subtasks must be accomplished in order to perform the main task? To answer this question we refer to various sources: direct observation, expert opinion, documentation and so on. These sources will be discussed later in Section 15.6. We then look at each subtask and seek to subdivide it, and so on.

One could go on with this process indefinitely, so one applies some form of *stopping rule* in order to decide when the tasks are basic enough. The level at which we do this will, of course, depend on the purpose of the task analysis. For example, imagine we were looking at a chemical plant and had produced a first-level decomposition of what to do in an emergency:

0.   in an emergency
   1.   read the alarms
   2.   work out appropriate corrective action
   3.   perform corrective action

If our ultimate aim is to install computer monitoring of the plant, we would be interested in expanding tasks 1 and 3. On the other hand, if the aim is to produce online operations manuals, then it is task 2 which would require expansion. In fact, at this high level of task description the analyst would probably expand all the subtasks as she ought to take a somewhat larger view. However, one would obviously put more effort into those subtasks which are directly relevant to the intended purpose.

A rule, which is particularly appropriate when the aim is to design training materials, is the $P \times C$ rule. This says that if the probability of making a mistake in the task (P) multiplied by the cost of the mistake (C) is below a threshold, then stop expanding. That is, simple tasks need not be expanded (because no one needs training), unless they are critical.

Another obvious stopping point is where the task contains complex motor responses (like mouse movement) or where it involves internal decision making. In the first case, decomposition would not be productive; explaining how such actions are performed is unlikely to be either accurate or useful. In the second case, we would expand if the decision making were related to external actions, such as looking up documentation or reading instruments, but not where the activity is purely cognitive. A possible exception to this would be if we were planning to build a decision support system, in which case we may want to understand the way someone thought about a problem in order to build tools to help. However, it is debatable whether HTA is the appropriate technique in this case.

The task hierarchy can be represented diagrammatically as well as textually. Figure 15.2 shows a task hierarchy for making a cup of tea. The main task, 'make a cup of tea', is decomposed into six subtasks. Of these only the first, 'boil water', is expanded further. The remaining tasks 2–6 and the subtasks of 1.1–1.4 are underlined showing that the analysis has been deliberately stopped at that point. This obviously denotes the same information as the textual form, but may be more accessible at a glance.

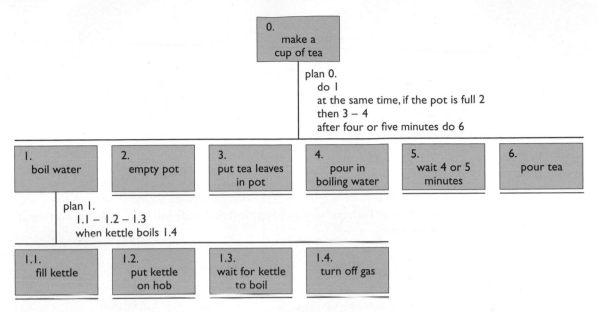

Figure 15.2   Hierarchical task analysis: making a cup of tea

Having produced a first stab at a task hierarchy, one would examine it for errors or omissions. One way of approaching this would be to describe the steps in the task hierarchy to a domain expert. This would quickly show that the plan for making tea has a significant error – it forgets to warm the pot. This has to be added between tasks 2 and 3.

It is the nature of expert knowledge that obvious things get missed for a task description. One way the analyst can search for such omissions is by examining the form of the subtasks. For example, 1.4 says 'turn off gas', but nowhere does it say to turn the gas on! Probably, this was implicit in 'put kettle on hob', but it should be added between tasks 1.2 and 1.3. At this point we might notice that the task hierarchy is a little unbalanced. This might be right, but we may have included too many detailed tasks at the highest level. We choose to add a new top-level node 'make pot' which would encompass the tasks 3 and 4 and also the new 'warm pot' task.

The top-level tasks would now be

0.   make a cup of tea
   1.   boil water
   2.   empty pot
   3.   make pot
   4.   wait 4 or 5 minutes
   5.   pour tea

Plan 0.   do 1
at the same time, if the pot is full 2
then 3 – 4
after four or five minutes 5

This is almost there: the actions 'empty pot' and 'wait 4 or 5 minutes' are pretty basic and clearly do not need expansion. Neither do they need to be included within one of the other tasks. We might think that 'empty pot' should be in with 'make pot', but we can empty the pot whilst the kettle is boiling whereas we have to wait for the kettle to boil to do any of the other tea-making tasks. Similarly, the 'wait' node belongs at the top as the pouring of the tea depends on it.

The 'pour tea' node is a little anomalous. Is it really so much simpler than, say, making the pot? Perhaps we should expand this node too. We could decompose it into three parts:

5.   pour tea
   5.1.   put milk in cup
   5.2.   fill cup with tea
   5.3.   add sugar to taste
Plan 5.   5.1 – 5.2
if desired 5.3

However, the mention of cups makes us wonder: do we really only want to describe the making of a single cup of tea? Perhaps we ought to allow several cups of tea to be made. To do this we modify the plan to allow repetitions of steps 1–3 for each cup. We could describe this plan in words, or use a simple diagram as in Figure 15.3.

The analyst can choose to use a more formal method of describing the plans, such as one of the dialog notations described in Chapter 16, a simple self-explanatory diagram, or plain text. The choice is very much a matter of taste, except that it would be unwise to use too formal a representation until late in the process.

The modified HTA after all this analysis is given in Figure 15.4. In addition, adding the sugar has been expanded to include asking the guests whether or not sugar is required. Also note that the main goal has been altered from 'make *a* cup of tea' to 'make cup*s* of tea'.

Plan 5.

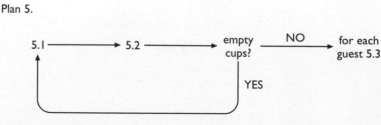

Figure 15.3   Plan for pouring tea

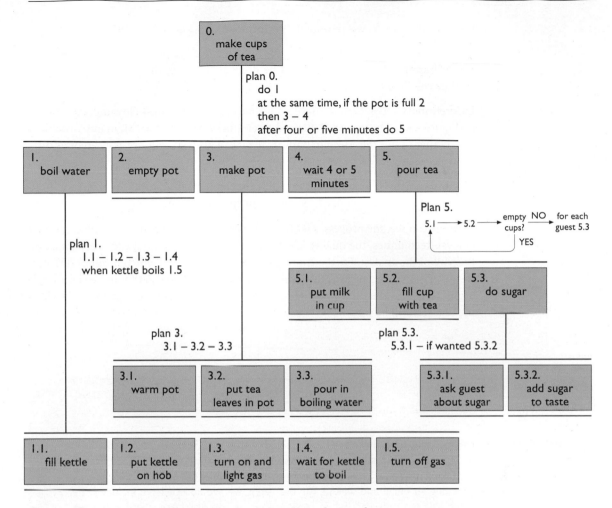

Figure 15.4 Modified task hierarchy for making lots of cups of tea

We have now seen all the types of plan that are commonly found, most of them in Figure 15.4:

Fixed sequence In plan 3, we always do the same sequence of subtasks.

Optional tasks In plan 0 'empty pot' and in plan 5.3 'add sugar' may or may not be performed depending on circumstances. Sometimes, there will be a choice between several options.

Waiting for events In plan 1, we had to wait for the kettle to boil, and in plan 0 we waited 4 or 5 minutes. The latter, waiting a certain time, is probably more common in real-world tasks, such as process control or office procedures, than in the use of computer software.

Cycles   In plan 5, we repeatedly perform tasks 5.1 and 5.2 until a condition is reached (no more empty cups).

Time sharing   Tasks 1 and 2 could be done at the same time (or at the very least they can be intermingled).

Discretionary   For this we have to go back to the vacuum-cleaning example in Figure 15.1. The person is allowed to clean the rooms (plan 3), in any order and whether or not they need it. Basically, you can keep your house as clean or as dirty as you like!

Mixtures   Most plans are a mixture of these elements. For instance, plan 1 for 'boiling water' is largely a fixed sequence but split by a wait.

As we can see, the process is far from straightforward. In common with other task analysis techniques, the quality and form of the final output depends very much on the skill of the analyst. Furthermore, different analysts are likely to produce different results, especially as regards the level of detail. Remember also that there is no single 'right' answer – the output of the task analysis should reflect the purpose to which the analysis will be put.

Waiting . . .

In the HTAs in Figures 15.2 and 15.4, there are tasks labeled 'wait 4 or 5 minutes', but also in the plan 'after 4 or 5 minutes'. This is clearly repetitive. The explicit subtask was added because the waiting during tea making is often a 'busy wait', perhaps chatting while the tea brews. If the task had been more like sending an email and waiting for the reply, we would not have included the waiting as an explict subtask and only had 'when reply arrives' in the plan. Arguably for the tea making we could have left the 'wait 4 or 5 minutes' out of the plan. However, the issue of the timing seems critical for the task sequence, hence belonged also in the plan – task analysis is not an exact science! The fact that tasks often have gaps in them is something we will return to in Chapter 19.

Worked exercise   *Produce a high-level hierarchical task analysis showing how you would find information on a website. Assume the site has a search facility as well as normal links.*

Answer   This HTA just shows the main stages. Subtask 1.1 only works if the page needed is one level below the top page. Really, one would like to add a task 1.1.3 to say something like 'if the information required is not on the new page found through the link then repeat the steps of 1.1 on the current page'.

Can you fix this? See our solution on the web at /e3/exercises/ch15/

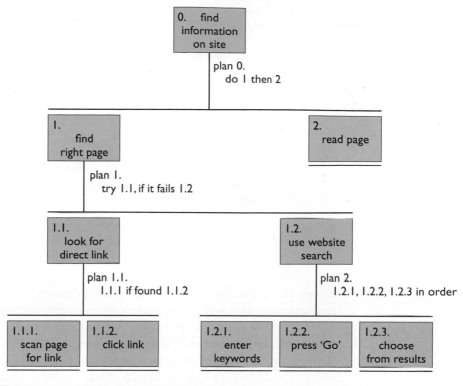

15.4 KNOWLEDGE-BASED ANALYSIS

Knowledge-based task analysis begins by listing all the objects and actions involved in the task, and then building taxonomies of them. Taxonomies are similar to the sort of hierarchical descriptions we often find in biology: animals are invertebrates or vertebrates, vertebrates are fish, birds, reptiles, amphibians or mammals, etc. The aim is to understand the knowledge needed to perform a task and thus to help in the production of teaching materials and in assessing the amount of common knowledge between different tasks.

We will begin by looking at simple hierarchies of objects. Consider first the controls in a (non-automatic) motor car. An example taxonomic structure is given in Figure 15.5; every control has exactly one place in the hierarchy.

Look at the figure for a moment: do you think it is a good one? We will discuss this shortly. Consider how we might have produced such a hierarchy, and how to use it. The car controls are particularly simple, as we can simply get in and look for them all. If we extended our analysis to driving a car in general, we would have to consider more objects: the instruments (speedometer, etc.), the car keys, seat-belts, road signs,

```
motor controls
      steering      steering wheel, indicators
      engine/speed
             direct        ignition, accelerator, foot brake
             gearing       clutch, gear stick
      lights
             external      headlights, hazard lights
             internal      courtesy light
      wash/wipe
             wipers        front wipers, rear wipers
             washers       front washers, rear washers
      heating       temperature control, air direction, fan, rear screen heater
      parking       hand brake, door lock
      radio
             numerous!
```

Figure 15.5   First attempt at taxonomy of car controls

other cars, etc. Just as with HTA it can be hard to know when to stop. However, with any such procedure it is best to start by listing everything you can, later removing items which are felt to be unnecessary. Other sources for forming a list of objects include manuals, transcripts and observation, and will be discussed in Section 15.6.

Having got an exhaustive list of objects, how do we go about forming the taxonomy? The analyst could ask a domain expert directly – often a classification may already exist for some of the domain objects. Another approach is to use a sorting task. Give a user cards with the objects listed on them and ask the user to sort the cards into piles of 'similar' objects. The user can then be asked to name the piles, or further sort the piles. This kind of sorting gives you the user's view of the structure.

Depending on the expected use of the task analysis, we may require different structures. If we were aiming to produce a car repair manual, we would almost certainly use a radically different taxonomy. For example, from a driver's viewpoint the accelerator and the brake perform related functions, but they have no connection mechanically.

Let us assume that our purpose is to produce an owner's manual for the car. It is likely that having produced a first attempt at an object taxonomy, we will examine it and find faults. Let us look again at Figure 15.5. The hand brake has been put with the door locks as an aspect of parking, but it should also be used as part of ordinary driving. Perhaps it would be better to put it in a separate 'braking' category with the foot brake. This shift might suggest a whole new superordinate classification into those controls needed for driving, namely steering, speed, brakes, most lights, as against those purely for comfort and security. With this classification, the courtesy lamp would get separated from the rest of the external lighting.

These decisions could be justified based on particular purposes, but others are purely arbitrary. We could just have easily classified the washers/wipers into front and rear first:

wash/wipe
    front
        front wipers, front washers
    rear
        rear wipers, rear washers

This better reflects the way they are positioned on most cars, but has no more logic to it than the classification in Figure 15.5. Really, there are two attributes: 'function' (wash or wipe) and 'position' (front or rear). One technique, *task analysis for knowledge description (TAKD)*, uses a special form of taxonomy called *task descriptive hierarchy (TDH)*. TAKD is discussed in detail by Diaper [92] in the recommended reading list at the end of this chapter. The branches in the simple taxonomy are either/or branches – a car control is either a steering control or an engine/speed control or a lighting control. As well as these XOR branches TDH also uses AND and OR branches. The AND branches are used where an object must have a place in several categories. For instance, the washer/wiper example could be shown as

wash/wipe **AND**
    function **XOR**
        wipe
            front wipers, rear wipers
        wash
            front washers, rear washers
    position **XOR**
        front
            front wipers, front washers
        rear
            rear wipers, rear washers

Notice that each control in the category 'wash/wipe' is mentioned both under 'function' and under 'position'.

    The OR branches arise where the object could fall into more than one of the categories, but not necessarily all. For example, if we were considering kitchen objects, we might want to say that they were for preparing food, cooking or dining. However, a plate may be used both for eating off (dining) and for chopping food on (preparation). Thus we have an OR branch:

kitchen item **OR**
    preparation
        mixing bowl, plate, chopping board
    cooking
        frying pan, casserole, saucepan
    dining
        plate, soup bowl, casserole, glass

Note that plate occurs under preparation and dining, but not under cooking (although one may cook a pie on a plate). The casserole is under cooking and under dining as a stew is often served in the casserole in which it was cooked.

TAKD has a uniqueness rule, which demands that a completed TDH can distinguish any two specific objects. The kitchen hierarchy above fails this test. We can distinguish, say, the plate from the soup bowl, because the plate is in categories preparation and dining, whereas the bowl is only under dining. However, we cannot distinguish the soup bowl from the glass. TAKD would demand that we further refine this hierarchy until all pairs can be distinguished from one another:

```
kitchen item AND
/___ shape XOR
/    |___ dished
/    |         mixing bowl, casserole, saucepan, soup bowl, glass
/    |___ flat
/              plate, chopping board, frying pan
/___ function OR
     {___ preparation
     {         mixing bowl, plate, chopping board
     {___ cooking
     {         frying pan, casserole, saucepan
     {___ dining XOR
          |___ for food
          |         plate, soup bowl, casserole
          |___ for drink
                    glass
```

Notice that the tree has been drawn using the characters: '/|{'. These are a characteristic of TDH and represent AND, XOR and OR branches respectively. The explicit labels AND, etc., are not used in a normal TDH as these are implied by the way the tree is drawn.

At this point, each object can be represented by a unique path(s) in the hierarchy and thus by a term in the *knowledge representation grammar* (*KRG*). The KRG term is built up using '/' for AND branches, '()' for XOR branches and '{}' for OR branches, similar to the diagram. For example, we could refer to the plate as

kitchen item/shape(flat)/function{preparation,dining(for food)}/

Translating, this says: a kitchen item whose shape is flat AND its function is preparation OR dining for food.

Strict application of the uniqueness rule is not always necessary. Other similar techniques cope quite happily without it, but they normally adopt simple hierarchies, rather than the more complex AND/OR/XOR TDH trees.

The test is perhaps most important when a tree has a lot of AND or OR branches rather than for simple hierarchies. In these cases, it is often difficult to see whether the classification scheme is suitably precise. Finding two simple objects which are not differentiated can be a good way of generating new classifiers. The lack of distinction between glasses and soup bowls in the original kitchen item classification is a case in point. These are so clearly different, and one can ask the question 'how can I tell the difference between a soup bowl and a glass?' yielding the obvious food/drink distinction.

However, there are other examples where attempting to follow the rule is less useful. In a more extensive list of items, with a more complex classification tree, it was found that a corkscrew and a tin opener were not distinguished. Although it is possible to distinguish these, the categories introduced were not of 'general' use, that is they did not help one to differentiate anything else. In general, then, the uniqueness rule is perhaps best viewed as an informative check, rather than adopted slavishly.

The production of a simple taxonomy, or a TDH, for actions is similar to that for objects. Imagine we have a list of specific actions which may occur in a kitchen: beating, mixing, pouring, frying, boiling, baking, eating and drinking. We may look at these and start to build a hierarchy. For example, we may use the same classes: preparation, cooking and dining as we did for the objects:

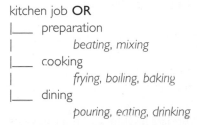

```
kitchen job OR
|___ preparation
|        beating, mixing
|___ cooking
|        frying, boiling, baking
|___ dining
         pouring, eating, drinking
```

We may subject this to the same analysis that we used for objects. For example, pouring has been put under dining, for instance pouring wine. However, we might also pour milk into a bowl to beat with eggs for an omelette. This would mean putting pouring into both categories, or possibly a second look at the specific actions called pouring. Perhaps we should distinguish those of pouring drinks and pouring ingredients?

Note the difference between this taxonomy of actions and that in HTA. The hierarchy above is one of genericity, whereas that in HTA was a 'how to do it' decomposition. HTA is about the sequencing of simple tasks to perform a single high-level task, whereas a taxonomy is about the similarity of simple tasks to one another. However, there will often be a relationship between the taxonomy of actions and the HTA descriptions of tasks. For example, having an omelette would consist of beating, frying and then eating, or having a cake would consist of mixing, baking and eating. In general, these tasks consist of one or more preparation and/or cooking actions followed by dining actions. It is precisely when we can begin to make these general task statements that the power and usefulness of object and action taxonomies becomes apparent.

Looking back and forth between the objects and the actions will suggest omissions or restructuring on one side or another: What action do we do with a chopping board? Clearly we should add chopping as an action. The action of baking may suggest that we include baking trays and bread tins under the objects. This cross-checking is particularly important for capturing all actions as it is often easier to see what people are *using* for their job than to work out what they are *doing*. Furthermore objects are often grouped naturally under their function, so the object groupings may suggest action groupings and vice versa. In addition, we can apply the TAKD uniqueness rule to the action TDH, which would mean performing some more subdivisions, perhaps adding distinctions between those actions concerned with liquids and those with solids.

Having produced object and action taxonomies, we can use these in order to produce generic descriptions of simple tasks. For an example, we are considering particular kitchen tasks, and we shall assume that we have extended the object taxonomy to include foods. Consider the task of eating a fried egg off a plate. This can be regarded as doing a 'kitchen job(dining)' using a 'kitchen item/shape(flat)/function{dining,preparation}/' to a 'food(dairy)'. If we observed a kitchen for a day, we could describe each simple task as it is performed using similar terms. In TAKD this is called a sentence in KRG.

Notice that the KRG terms do not use the complete KRG description of each action and object, but instead opt for a generic description. Choosing the appropriate generic description is an art, but there are guidelines to help. One way is to take the TDH tree and to annotate it with the number of times each object or action is mentioned by an expert, or used or performed during our day's observation. If the number of occurrences of objects below a node is small then one does not bother to use the lower-level distinctions. So, for example, in the above we have not bothered with the 'for food/for drink' distinction among dining items. This process is called *generification*.

The choice of an appropriate level to 'cut' the tree is also influenced by the number of different KRG sentences we get for simple tasks. If there are an unmanageable number of different sentences, then it suggests that more generification is required. If, on the other hand, we found that all the observed tasks were represented by only two or three sentences, then this would suggest that the level of abstraction is too great. Of course, what constitutes an appropriate number of different sentences depends on the circumstances, the complexity of the job we are analyzing and (again) the purpose of the analysis.

In addition, the appropriate generic categories chosen for actions and objects are linked. If we consider the task of beating an egg in a mixing bowl (to make an omelette?), we could describe it as

> kitchen job(preparation)
>   *using* a kitchen item/shape(dished)/function{preparation}/

However, the levels of detail of the action and object are not well matched. The detail about the mixing bowl – that it is dished – is needed for beating, but not for preparation in general. We should either be more specific about the action

> kitchen job(preparation(beating))
>   *using* a kitchen item/shape(dished)/function{preparation}/

or more generic in the description of the object:

> kitchen job(preparation)
>   *using* a kitchen item/function{preparation}/

Possibly, if we observe the cook beating eggs in a soup bowl, we might generalize in a different direction to

kitchen job(preparation(beating))
　　using a kitchen item/shape(dished)/

It is possible to go further, looking at *generic task sequences*; that is, looking at frequently occurring sequences of simple tasks and their representation in KRG sentences. The sequences may be derived from independent observations or from an HTA type of analysis. We have already had an example of this when we described a general kitchen task as consisting of one or more preparation and/or cooking actions followed by a dining action.

The utility of both KRG sentences and sequences is not proven, but they add to our tools for analysis. However, even when the more complex parts of TAKD are inappropriate, the process of producing taxonomies and generification can be employed. In particular, they are especially useful for teaching purposes, where the taxonomy can be used to structure the presentation and description of the objects and actions to the student.

15.5　ENTITY–RELATIONSHIP-BASED TECHNIQUES

Entity–relationship modeling is an analysis technique usually associated with database design and more recently object-oriented programming. When adopted for task analysis the major differences are in the kinds of entities modeled. In database and object-oriented design, the entities chosen for analysis will be those which are expected to be represented in the resulting computer system. However, in task analysis, we are interested in a wide range of non-computer entities including physical objects, the actions performed on them and the people who perform them.

Like knowledge-based approaches, the cataloging and examination of *objects* and *actions* is central to the analysis, but the emphasis is on the relationships between actions and objects, rather than on the similarity between different objects and the resulting taxonomic structure. For example, we might look at the three objects 'gardener', 'soil' and 'spade', and the action 'dig' and see how they are related. We would record that it is the gardener who *performs* the digging *acting upon* the soil *using* the spade. Particular importance is attached to the linking of actions with the objects which perform them, and thus the technique can rightly be seen as an *object-based methodology*.

As an example, we will consider a task analysis of the market gardening firm 'Vera's Veggies'. Imagine we have talked to Vera Bradshaw, the owner/manager of Vera's Veggies, and have walked around the premises.

We begin by listing all the objects in the domain of interest. In the tool shed, we see a spade, a garden fork, a hoe and a small Ferguson tractor (called 'Fergie') with implements, plough and spring-tine harrow. There are two employees, Sam Gummage and Tony Peagreen, and Vera herself works the land as well as acting as manager. From our conversation with her, we have found that there are two main growing fields, 'One Hundred Acre' and 'Parker's Patch', and also a large glasshouse. She also, rather proudly, demonstrated the new computer-controlled irrigation system she has just had installed; this has pumps for each field and the glasshouse, and, in addition, has a humidity sensor in the glasshouse. During the interview, we notice that Vera often refers to 'the kit', meaning all contents of the tool shed, and 'the men', meaning Sam and Tony. However, Vera has recently been on a management training course and so (when she remembers) she also uses the term 'the team' referring to the complete staff including herself.

We can classify the objects into three basic types: *concrete objects*, *actors* and *composite objects*. First of all there are simple concrete objects such as the spade, plough and glasshouse, that is all the 'things'. The human actors are obvious, Vera, Sam and Tony, but we may need to exercise some caution where things, such as Fergie, have been given names. One frequently finds that computers, cars and vegetable varieties are named after people. On the other hand, human actors may be named impersonally, indirectly or not at all, for example 'the seed merchant', 'the contractor's digger' or 'we sell a lot at the farm shop' (to whom?).

We may also want to discuss non-human actors, concrete objects which in some sense act autonomously, which can 'do' something. In the case of Vera's Veggies, we would place the irrigation computer in this category. It may not be clear whether or not to regard an object as an actor; we will see that consideration of the actions (below) helps to make this distinction clear.

Finally, we have composite objects such as 'the team', which consists of three other objects (Sam, Tony and Vera), and 'the kit'. These are both examples of a '*set*' composite object; we may also come across '*tuple*' composite objects. For example, during the interview, we may notice that a lot of times when 'the tractor' is mentioned Vera does not mean Fergie alone, but Fergie together with one or other implement, that is <Fergie, plough> or <Fergie, harrow>.

Composite objects need not always be named; for example, Vera may often say simply 'Sam and Tony' rather than 'the men'. Furthermore, it may sometimes be useful to regard an entity such as 'the team' as an abstract object in its own right, and link it to the (unnamed) composite object {Vera, Sam, Tony} by a relationship such as *consists_of* ('the team', {Vera, Sam, Tony}).

We may wish to list some of the *attributes* of each object, for instance

Object Pump3 **simple** – *irrigation pump*
    Attributes:
        status: on/off/faulty
        capacity: 100 litres/minute

We need not strive to be as complete in the listing of attributes as we would for object-oriented programming. Remember, the intention is not to produce machine representations of the objects, but to describe their participation in human and computer tasks. For example, it is likely we will want to discuss the turning on and off of irrigation pumps, so it is natural to record the status as an attribute. The relevance of the pump's capacity is less obvious, and we may decide to drop it as we proceed with the analysis. As with all the task analysis techniques, it is often best to be slightly overinclusive during early phases, as it is easier to drop unwanted items than to add them later.

We now move on to *actions*. Typically actions change the state of something, called the *patient*, and are performed by someone or something, the *agent*, for example 'Sam (*agent*) planted (*action*) the leeks (*patient*)'. There may be other attributes associated with an action, for example if there is an *instrument* used to perform the action, as in our earlier example: 'the gardener dug the soil *with* the spade'. Frequently, accounts of activities are written in an impersonal manner: 'Parker's Patch was ploughed' which really means 'Sam ploughed Parker's Patch'. Taking such an account and uncovering the agent responsible is an important job for the analyst as one of the goals of this analysis is to produce, for each object, a comprehensive list of the actions it can perform.

Tracing the agent performing an action is a good way of classifying the actors. Normally, the agent will be an actor. For example, consider 'the glasshouse irrigation is turned on when humidity drops below 25%'. The agent doing this action is the irrigation controller. This verifies our original statement that the controller is a non-human agent. Sometimes the agency is indirect. For instance, it is often better to water at night to reduce evaporation, so Vera may program the irrigation controller to come on at midnight. Is the controller an agent turning on the water, or an instrument being used by Vera to turn it on (although she is asleep when it happens!)? There is an element of judgment here, but the condition is not that much different from Vera telling Sam to dig the carrots. In the latter case, we would definitely regard Sam as the agent of the digging.

One special sort of action is a message. The last example is better thought of as two actions: the first a message, Vera tells Sam (to dig), the second the digging itself (assuming Sam complies). In any situation involving several people, messages and communication will be a major part of their jobs. This communication is of particular interest in the field of computer-supported cooperative work which was discussed in detail in Chapter 14.

As we analyze the actions people (or even non-human actors) perform, we will often find that they can be listed under several *roles*. For example, when Vera plants marrow seed, she is acting as *worker*, but when she tells Sam to dig the carrots, she is acting as *manager*. Identifying roles can be very important in a large organization as the result of introducing new systems may be to shift whole roles (not just specific tasks) between individuals or from humans to the computer.

At this stage of analysis, having identified the principal objects and actions, we can begin to build object/action descriptions of the form

> **Object** Sam **human actor**
> > **Actions:**
> > > S1:   drive tractor
> > > S2:   dig the carrots
>
> **Object** Vera **human actor** – the proprietor
> > **Actions:** as worker
> > > V1:   plant marrow seed
> > > V2:   program irrigation controller
> > **Actions:** as manager
> > > V3:   tell Sam to dig the carrots

Object the men **composite**
    Comprises: {Sam, Tony}
Object glasshouse **simple**
    Attribute:
        humidity: 0–100%
Object Irrigation Controller **non-human actor**
    Actions:
        IC1:   turn on Pump1
        IC2:   turn on Pump2
        IC3:   turn on Pump3

Closely allied to actions is the idea of an *event*. Events are anything which *happens*. The performing of an action is an event, but we may also encounter spontaneous events such as the germination of a marrow seed. There is no agent performing the germination and it should be listed as a spontaneous action of the marrow itself, but not implying that the marrow is in any sense an actor. Some spontaneous events, such as 'the humidity drops below 25%', have no associated object at all. A third type of event is timed, such as 'at midnight'.

Finally, we consider the *relationships* between objects, actions and events. The simplest relationships are object–object ones, such as the fact that Sam is subordinate to Vera, or that irrigation pump 3 is situated in the glasshouse. There are also action–object relationships. The relationship between the *agent* performing an action and the action itself is implicit, as the actions are listed under the object responsible. However, we may want to record explicitly the *patient* and *instrument* of an action. In addition, we may want to record relationships between actions and events, such as temporal order and causality:

Object Marrow **simple**
    Actions:
        M1:   germinate
        M2:   grow
Events
        Ev1:   humidity drops below 25%
        Ev2:   midnight
Relations: object–object
    location (Pump3, glasshouse)
    location (Pump1, Parker's Patch)
Relations: action–object
    patient (V3, Sam)
           –   Vera tells *Sam* to dig
    patient (S2, the carrots)
           –   Sam digs the *carrots*…
    instrument (S2, spade)
           –   …*with* the spade
Relations: action–event
    before (V1, M1)
           –   the marrow must be sown before it can germinate

before (M1, M2)
  – the marrow must germinate before it can grow
triggers (Ev1, IC3)
  – *when* humidity drops below 25%,
  the controller turns on pump 3
triggers (Ev2, IC1)
  – *when* it is midnight, the controller turns on pump 1
causes (V2, IC1)
  – the controller turns on the pump
  because Vera programmed it
causes (V3, S2)
  – Sam digs the carrots *because* Vera told him to

Rather than express all the ordering of events and actions using relationships, this form of analysis would normally be combined with some representation of the sequence between actions. For example, the *ATOM* method (*Analysis for Task Object Modeling* method) [360], upon which much of the above description is based, uses JSD diagrams to represent this (JSD diagrams are described in Chapter 16). Alternatively, one might use HTA diagrams, or one of the other dialog notations in Chapter 16.

This form of analysis can be applied in two ways. For a specific task, say growing marrows, we may analyze the order of subtasks and actions annotated by the objects involved. Using HTA we might have

0. in order to grow marrows
    1. Vera sows the marrow seed
    2. marrow germinates
    3. Vera programs controller
    4. controller waters field
    5. marrow grows
    6. Sam hoes
    7. Tony harvests marrows
Plan 0:   1 – 2 – 5 – when crop is mature 7
          when rainfall is low 3 – 4
          when weeds grow 6

Notice that even though this task is centered on the marrow, there are several actions (for example, 3) which do not include the marrow, in any capacity.

Alternatively, we can produce for any particular object a 'life cycle' diagram representing all the actions in which it participates. Typically, this would cross over several tasks. For example, the irrigation controller would water the fields and glasshouse in any order determined by its program and humidity. This is obviously more in keeping with an object-based approach, but both types of action sequence are important. Figure 15.6 shows an HTA diagram for the actions in which the tractor is involved. One is perhaps typically more interested in the life cycles of the agents, but in this example they are rather unstructured.

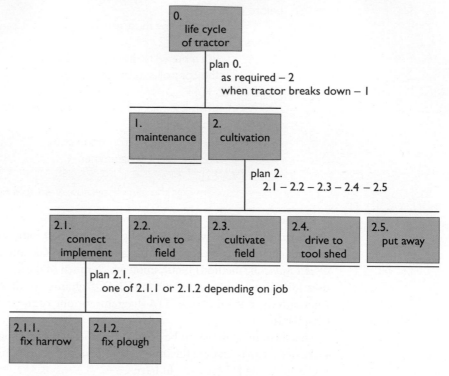

Figure 15.6   Life cycle of tractor

This form of analysis also fits very well with the sort of taxonomic analysis discussed previously – object-oriented methods usually include some notion of *class* or *inheritance* hierarchy. Indeed, looking at the commonality of actions and relationships can help us to find useful generic categories. For example, we may see that the two fields are treated very similarly, or that Sam, Tony and Vera perform many tasks in common.

Worked exercise   *Consider the activity of making a telephone call. Record the actions in an HTA diagram or textually. Start off simply, assuming you know the number to dial, but then add more complicated situations: finding the number in an address book, or what to do when the number is engaged.*

Answer   As with most of these exercises, this is an open-ended question. Here is a simple version with some expansion, but one can look at alternatives such as public payphones.

    0. make phone call
        1. pick up receiver
        2. dial number
        3. wait for reply
        4. talk
        5. replace receiver

Plan 0:   1 – 2 – 3
                when answered – 4
                when finished – 5

We now add looking up the number. The form this takes depends on whether we find the number in an address book or a telephone directory. If both fail, say if the call is long distance to someone not in a local directory, the telephone operator must be consulted. Note that contacting the telephone operator involves making a phone call, but the steps for this are not repeated in full!

0.   make phone call
    1.   find number
        1.1.   look in address book
        1.2.   look in phone directory
        1.3.   ask operator
                1.3.1. pick up receiver
                . . .

    2.   actually call
        2.1.   pick up receiver
        2.2.   dial number
        2.3.   wait for reply
        2.4.   talk
        2.5.   replace receiver

Plan 0:   if number unknown – 1
              when number found – 2
Plan 1:   if phoning friend – 1.1
              if local call – 1.2
              if 1.1 or 1.2 fail – 1.3
Plan 2:   2.1 – 2.2 – 2.3
              when answered – 2.4
              when finished – 2.5

Finally, we add the case when the phone is engaged. The simplest way to do this is simply to change Plan 2.

Plan 2:   2.1 – 2.2 – 2.3
              if answered – 2.4 then when finished 2.5
              if engaged – 2.5

However, looking at the second line it might suggest that we modify 2.4 to have two parts:

0.   make phone call
            . . .
    2.   actually call
            . . .
        2.4.   successful call
        2.4.1.   talk
        2.4.2.   replace receiver

2.5.   failed call
    2.5.1.   replace receiver

Plan 2:   2.1 – 2.2 – 2.3
    if answered – 2.4
    if engaged – 2.5

Plan 2.4:   2.4 then when finished 2.5

15.6   SOURCES OF INFORMATION AND DATA COLLECTION

The different task analysis methods allow you to structure data about tasks. However, the resulting task analysis can only be as good as the original data.

The process of task analysis is not a simple one of collect data, analyze and organize and present results. Instead, the process of analysis will often throw you back to your original sources with new questions and insights. Ideally, the process then should be iterative with periods of data collection interspersed with analysis. In practice, limitations of time and cost will cut this short, so the skill of the analyst lies in foreseeing possible problems in analysis and obtaining relevant data as quickly and economically as possible. The extreme cost of direct observation suggests that, where possible, the analyst ought to make maximum use of cheap sources of information such as manuals or pilot studies before embarking on more costly collection exercises.

15.6.1 Documentation

The easiest source of data for the analyst is the existing manuals, instruction booklets, training materials, etc., for the task. These are most likely to be focussed on specific items of equipment or computer software, but this is often the focus anyway. Furthermore, there may be corporate rule books and job descriptions which may be used to obtain information about tasks in a wider context. It should be remembered that these sources typically tell you how people are *supposed* to perform tasks, not what they actually do. In addition, equipment-specific manuals are likely to tell you about the *functions* of the device rather than the way it is used to perform a specific task. For example, a word processor may describe a centering menu option, but this would be used as part of specific tasks such as writing a chapter title or producing a figure caption.

Although the *structure* of material in these sources may be misleading, they are useful for providing basic actions and objects involved in a task. These lists may be incomplete, as they will often ignore non-device actions. For example, the word-processor manual may not mention the use of physical filing cabinets. However, manuals form a starting point for future analysis, and may be used to structure experimental studies, or interviews; one can ask questions such as 'when do you use the centering option?' Also the lists obtained from manuals may be compared with those of direct observation – unused facilities or objects may indicate either that the facility is redundant, or that it is part of a rare procedure. It is, of course, just these rare procedures which may be missed entirely by direct observation.

Rule books and job descriptions can be used as part of an interviewing process – 'your job description says . . . is that right?', or may be compared against observation and then reflected back to the subject – 'according to the instructions you do . . . but actually you did . . .'. Of course, for such questions to be useful it is essential that the subjects are not put on the defensive or believe that their bending of the rules will be reported back to management. This sort of issue is central to analyses for computer-supported cooperative work as we saw in Chapter 14.

15.6.2 Observation

Some form of direct observation, whether formal or informal, is essential if the analyst is to get an understanding of the task situation. At the simplest level, the analyst can simply spend time watching people and chatting, just to get the 'feel' of the task. Together with the reading of existing documentation, this can form a good first stage before going on to more extensive and formal observation.

Formal observation can occur in the field or in the laboratory. The advantages and disadvantages of each approach were discussed in detail in Chapter 9. Arguably, observation in the field is the ideal as this is the 'real' task. However, there may be better recording facilities in the laboratory (video, two-way mirrors, and so on) and we may want more control of the environment. Our observation can be passive (simply listening and watching) or active (asking questions). Especially where the observation is passive, we may want to perform a *post-task walkthrough*; that is, discuss the observations with the subject. This allows us to find out the reasons why the subject performed certain actions. We discussed different recording methods and post-task walkthroughs in Chapter 9.

Worked exercise   *The act of searching is quite complicated. Look up a person in an address book or telephone directory. Get several friends to look up words in a dictionary. Observe their methods closely. You will probably have to develop shorthand notations to keep track of what pages they visit. Compare the strategies used by the different people. If they differ, try to abstract out the common parts of the task and the variable parts. If you have a computing background, try to classify their methods in relation to known search algorithms: binary chop, linear search, etc.*

Answer   In order to see the range of possible search strategies, the authors asked two subjects to look up words in a dictionary. One was a literate, but young, child and the other an erudite English graduate.

To obtain any sort of useful record, the subjects had to be asked to work slowly and even then keeping track of the search was difficult. We noted down the page numbers they paused at, but often searches included thumbing through a sequence of pages, at which point some form of specific notation would be useful. As an alternative to noting down the page numbers, noting the words at the top of the page could be used.

The English graduate was also asked to talk aloud through the exercise. We discussed in Chapter 9 the possible effects this might have on the user's performance, but it is extremely difficult to keep track of the reader's focus on the page otherwise. The notes in the tables have been tidied up considerably from our original handwritten scrawl and the notes in italics were added afterwards. Unfortunately, in typesetting the notes, some of the spatial layout is lost. They do, however, retain the scrappiness of the original observations. Use of video can of course allow one to replay tasks at a slower rate and thus improve the detail of note taking.

The English graduate was asked to find unfamiliar words: 'daltonism' (Table 15.1) and 'parclose' (Table 15.2). The child was asked to look up simpler words: 'dig' (Table 15.3) and 'orange' (Table 15.4). The transcripts do not include timings – the whole process took no more than 30 seconds. To give an idea of relative timings: whereas the English graduate homed quickly onto the correct page, this took the child somewhat longer, but, once they were on the right page, both were so quick that it is hard to give judgment on relative speed.

Table 15.1 Adult looking up the word 'daltonism'

????	*note illegible, intended to convey that she turned the dictionary on its side and then opened it*
283 dog	*said that first cut was based on the position of 'd' in the alphabet*
flick backward	
overshoot to 'C'	
forward one page to beginning of 'D'	*'daltonism' on this page*
quick skim over page	
places finger on word	

Table 15.2 Adult looking up the word 'parclose'

right of center	*comment by subject on position of 'p' in dictionary*
729 O	*gets to page in the middle of 'O' section*
turn over forward	
741	*page begins with 'para' words*
? C or K	*subject says unsure whether spelt with c or k*
	says she'll look for 'c' first
scan with finger	
sequential	*she explains that the presence of the 'para' words made the task confusing*

Table 15.3 Child looking up the word 'dig'

525	*near middle of book*
429	*these first pages were quite rapid*
297	*page headed 'dualism'*
266	*correct page – luck!*
scan down and up	*sequential search item by item*

Table 15.4   Child looking up the word 'orange'

236	*last page of 'c'*
266	
flick forward	*too fast to note pages*
800	*overshoot*
flick back	
700, 690, 699	*start of 'O'*
sequential pages	
703	
flick forward page by page	
717	*right page*
sequential search through page	

From this evidence, about the best general description we could have is

    0.   look up word in dictionary
        1.   find right page
        2.   find word on page
   Plan 0:   1 – 2

The performance of subtask 1 was far more efficient for the adult as she used a heuristic to find the approximate position based on her knowledge of the alphabet. The child knew the relative position of words in the alphabet, but not enough to be able to say 'o' is just after the middle, in the way the adult did with 'p'. The difference in subtask 2 was less marked, but mainly because it was too rapid to annotate. There was some evidence that the adult used a more direct method than the child who simply (but quickly) scanned the page entry by entry.

If you carry out this observation with more subjects, or pool observations and compare notes, you may be able to abstract more specific, but still general, search strategies. For example, you may see something akin to binary chop. You should not look for a single strategy used by all people, but instead look for a small set of strategies, and then look for ways of telling how people choose one strategy or another.

Really, two observations, as described above, are only sufficient for a pilot study in order to sharpen up thinking. Looking at the notes may suggest shorthands, for instance arrows to represent different kinds of scanning. It also prompts one to ask questions. What happens if, when they scan the page at step 2, the subjects discover that they are still on the wrong page? Presumably this leads to a new 'find the right page' step. However, this subtask, essentially a fine correction, will be very different from the original search.

    0.   look up word in dictionary
        1.   find right page
        2.   find word on page
        3.   adjust page
   Plan 0:   1 – 2
           if still wrong page 3 – 2

Unlike the first HTA, this one is not based on *observation*, but on the authors' *imagination*, however. Given such refined expectations, you must return to observation in order to explore further. Perhaps you could deliberately choose words close to page boundaries in order to confuse the subjects. Alternatively, you could ask your subjects 'What would you do if you'd got the wrong page?' Note that there is a difference between a psychological experiment in problem solving and a task analysis observation. For the former, we would be simply trying to verify our guess/theory. For the latter, we might have an idea, but our observations should be open ended as we want to find out what really happens, whether or not it agrees with our theories.

Although the question is clearly oriented toward procedural analysis, one could also do some form of knowledge-based analysis. Clearly concepts such as 'position in the alphabet' and 'word at the top of the page' are important. Indeed, if we were designing an electronic dictionary such concepts may be more useful than emulating paper.

Indeed, one could extend this question into a design exercise – how to design the electronic dictionary. Assuming that we are not interested in totally automatic lookup, how would we design the interaction? Whereas in a book, one's normal action is to turn over one page backwards or forwards, in dictionary lookup one jumps into the middle, turns over several pages at a time and flicks through pages at high speed. This can emphasize that a question like 'how do we design an electronic book?' cannot be answered until we know for what purposes that book is to be used.

15.6.3 Interviews

Questioning domain experts is often a direct and quick way to get information about a task. Remember that the expert is not necessarily the manager or supervisor who knows *about* the job, but the worker who actually does it – although there may be advantages to interviewing both sorts of expert, as the views of the manager or professional instructor are based on years of experience even if they are likely to be 'idealized' versions of the task.

It may be particularly appropriate to interview the 'professional' experts after doing some formal or informal direct observation. It is then possible to ask them to reflect on the various expected and unexpected behaviors; this can become a form of third-party walkthrough.

More normally, one would begin with a general set of questions, possibly asking the expert to describe a typical day, or task. This can then be followed with more leading questions such as 'Why do you do that?' or 'What if this develops a fault?' The aim is both to uncover detail and to increase the range of behavior discussed.

Where appropriate, the expert can be asked to produce lists of objects/actions associated with the task, although it may be unwise to demand too structured information during a first interview, as this may limit the range of material discussed. The exception to this would be HTA where one often starts with a top-down decomposition. In this case one can begin by asking the expert 'What do you do to make a cup of tea?' and then successively expand the explanation.

15.6.4 Initial analysis

We assume we have got some sort of written transcript, whether from manuals, observation or interviews. The detailed analysis, of course, depends on the analysis method employed, but most start by trying to build up lists of elementary objects and actions. A simple device is to go through the transcript highlighting the nouns (which will be objects) and the verbs (which will be associated with actions). If the transcript is online this process can even be automated with the help of an online dictionary.

However, this simple association is rarely enough on its own. Some words may be either a verb or a noun, for instance in chess 'castle' is both a noun (the piece) and also a verb (a particular move). Technical language is often full of 'verbed' nouns and even 'nouned' verbs, although the latter are often names for processes, so are not as great a problem. In addition, the objects or actions may be implicit. This problem may be better dealt with by checking consistency between lists, within the particular task analysis method employed.

Context is often important in interpreting words. For instance, we may have the two verb phrases

'beat the eggs in the *bowl*'
'ate the porridge from the *bowl*'

It is only by looking at the context that we see the former is a mixing bowl and the latter is a soup bowl. Similar problems arise with verbs:

'the rain *poured*'
'she *poured* the mixture into the pan'
'I *poured* the tea'

The first is clearly a different sort of pouring from the rest. Also, the second sort of pouring may well be considered different from the last, as the pouring of the mixture is an action during the preparation of food. Clearly, this second distinction is somewhat debatable and hence one should attempt to leave such decisions till later in the analysis process. To do this the object and action lists can be annotated, for example 'pour (the tea)'.

15.6.5 Sorting and classification

Several of the techniques include the production of hierarchies and sorting of entries by various attributes. Some of this is carried out by the analyst, but some requires subjective assessments by domain experts.

Several techniques can be used to obtain the relevant information. This has been discussed briefly before in Section 15.4.

One way is to take the list of, say, task objects, and write each one on a slip of paper or card. The expert is then asked to sort them into piles of similar objects. Depending on the size of the piles the expert can be asked to subdivide the piles further, or to group the piles into larger ones. If desired, the piles and groups of piles can be tied together with elastic bands or put in envelopes and labeled by the expert by the common characteristic. This process can be repeated several times, each time asking the expert to perform a different grouping. Also, different experts can be asked and their groupings compared.

Alternatively, one can ask the expert to arrange the cards on a tabletop. This allows the expert to cluster the cards (showing similarity) and to use the spatial arrangement in order to give a classification by two attributes. Again, the expert can be questioned after the event as to why the particular arrangement was used.

A range of similar techniques can be used to elicit the user's or expert's knowledge about a task. Each object/action can be ranked against each task depending on how important the expert thinks they are for that task. Perhaps on a scale 0 (never used) to 10 (essential). So, for example, if the task were 'making an omelette' eggs would be scored 10, but the fork to beat the eggs may only be scored 5. Alternatively, the expert can simply be asked to rank the objects, as this may be easier than an absolute judgment.

However the classification and production of hierarchies is performed, the job of producing possibly large taxonomies and hierarchy diagrams is not trivial. This can be done by hand on paper or using a standard word processor, but is easier if an outliner is used. There are several commercial outlining tools, and most word processors and many spreadsheets have outlining facilities. These outliners make it easy to shift partially sorted groups as we refine the classification. They also allow us to hide unwanted information, say when we want to look at the top levels of decomposition of a task hierarchy, or if we want to 'cut' a TDH taxonomy to look at generic objects or actions.

15.7 USES OF TASK ANALYSIS

The output of task analysis is some breakdown of the tasks people perform and, depending on the techniques chosen, the things that are employed and the plans and sequences of actions used to perform the tasks. The way this information is utilized depends very much on the use to which it is put. Three such uses will be described briefly: the production of manuals and tuition material; requirements capture and high-level systems design; and detailed interface design. Of these uses, only the first is aimed at the actual system analyzed; the latter two use the analysis of the existing system in order to suggest the design of a new one.

15.7.1 Manuals and tuition

Some of the earliest techniques in task analysis were aimed at teaching novices how to perform a task. In particular, this was important for military training, for example how to disassemble and clean a rifle. Training had to be quick and efficient as conscripts in peacetime may only serve a few years before returning to civilian life, or in wartime may only survive a few months.

To make cups of tea

boil water – *see page 2*
empty pot
make pot – *see page 3*
wait 4 or 5 minutes
pour tea – *see page 4*

– page 1 –

Make pot of tea
once water has boiled

warm pot
put tea leaves in pot
pour in boiling water

– page 3 –

Figure 15.7   Instruction manual for tea making

The use of task analysis as part of the discipline of HCI is somewhat different, but training is still an important application. The hierarchical structure of HTA can be used to structure manuals or course material. For example, we want to write a beginner's manual on tea making based on the hierarchical task analysis in Figure 15.4. We base each page on one level of task decomposition and its associated plan (Figure 15.7).

This kind of 'how to do it' manual is often useful for initial training, but for structuring a course, or for more advanced training material, a more conceptual structure is better. This is precisely where the knowledge-based techniques are strong. The taxonomic structure can be used directly; for example, our course on cars may start with a lecture on steering controls, then have a lecture on controlling the engine speed and gears, etc. This is most likely to be useful when the taxonomy is a strict either/or tree. More generally, we can produce the shortened list of generic objects and actions by 'cutting' the taxonomic tree, and use these as the structuring principle. Given such a 'cut' of the taxonomy of kitchen tools and jobs in Section 15.4, we may structure a cookery course as follows:

Cookery in eight easy lessons
lecture 1.   preparation – dished utensils
lecture 2.   preparation – flat utensils
lecture 3.   jobs for food preparation
lecture 4.   cooking – dished utensils
               . . .
lecture 8.   dining – graceful eating and drinking
               (followed by four course dinner)

In addition to teaching totally new material, task analysis can be used to help a user transfer from one system to another. Assuming we have performed a task analysis of both systems, a comparison of these will highlight areas for training. A simple comparison of functionality is *not* sufficient as the crucial differences may be in procedures. On the other hand, two systems may seem completely different in terms of detailed commands and presentation, but have similar high-level concepts or similar patterns of use. These common features should be brought out and can be used to help the user transfer knowledge from one system to another.

15.7.2 Requirements capture and systems design

Task analysis can be used to guide the design of new (although possibly not novel) systems. Recall (from Chapter 6) that requirements capture is the process of eliciting what a new system should do. Task analysis in itself is not a form of requirements capture as it refers to the existing system, not the planned system, and it includes many elements which are not part of the system. However, it makes a strong contribution toward the complete statement of requirements. Typically, the original statement of requirements given by a client will mention the new elements required and possibly refer to the existing *system* and its functionality. Further information elicited by a system developer may well concentrate on what the system should *do* but may forget how it will be *used*.

The task analysis of an existing system can help in two ways. First, the analyst can ask 'Which of the existing objects, tasks, etc., should be in the new system?'. Secondly, the formalized presentation of the existing state of affairs may help the client to clarify what the novel features are to be. It may be decided to automate whole tasks or roles, or simply specific subtasks.

As the high-level design of the system progresses, task analysis continues to play a role. The structuring provided by, for instance, TDH taxonomies can help the designer to choose an internal model for the system which matches the existing expectations of the users. This may, of course, be modified to accommodate novel features, but gives a reasonable first structure.

We may also make some predictions about the use of the new system. Given the parts that are to be included and the planned behavior of the system, we may see how this will interact with existing procedures, including how information will move in and out of the new system. Some of the procedures may be able to continue as before, especially if the system has been designed to mimic the old, possibly nonautomated, system, but some may need to be retaught completely.

15.7.3 Detailed interface design

In a similar manner to the manual design, taxonomies of tasks or objects may be used in the design of menus. The TDH trees are obviously most useful in this respect. Top-level menus can be labeled after the top-level decomposition, and submenus after the next level, etc. For this, the tree may be first reduced to a simple either/or tree, thus guaranteeing that each object/action is under exactly one menu. Alternatively, more complex trees allowing AND and OR as well as XOR branches can be used. In this case, an object/action may be found by several paths through the menus.

An alternative menu layout could be based around roles and then tasks in roles. Again, for such a layout, it is likely that a particular action is found under several roles/tasks. There is a tendency for users to find new tasks to perform with new systems, and, for such a new task, the required actions on the system may be difficult to find and be widely dispersed. So this sort of layout is only sensible if the possible set of tasks is very well defined, but where this is true, such a layout and system design can be highly efficient.

If an object-oriented paradigm is being used in the interface, then the association of objects with actions may be particularly useful. For each object, a menu of possible actions, based on those for which it is the agent or patient, can be displayed. Default actions for each object may be chosen based on the frequency of actions (for efficiency) but informed by the generic classification scheme (for learnability). In most systems, the generic action associated with a double click is to 'open' the object for editing. However, in specialist domains a different choice may be more appropriate.

Task sequences obtained from a task decomposition can be used when designing the system's dialog (see Chapter 16). The order in which subtasks are performed in the system can be made to mirror that of the original job. Even where the interface style is more user directed, and hence the dialog sequence is not defined by the designer, the task decomposition and plans are useful. If we know that a certain task is frequently performed, then we want it to be easy for the user to perform the subtasks in the appropriate order. If, for example, it involves constantly swapping modes, or moving between widely different parts of a menu-based interface, this would be unacceptable.

Task analysis is never complete and hence it should not be the sole arbiter of the style and structure of an interface. However, the insights from a well-executed task analysis can make an interface that easily supports the way people want to work.

15.8 SUMMARY

We have seen several task analysis methods. Hierarchical task analysis decomposes a task into subtasks. These can be recorded either in a textual outline format or in a tree diagram. Knowledge-based techniques build taxonomies of the objects used during a task and the actions performed upon them. Cutting the taxonomy at some level gives us a set of generic objects and actions. Finally, we can again look at objects and actions, but concentrate on different kinds of object: passive object and active human and non-human agents, and the relationships between the objects and actions.

Information for task analysis can be drawn from existing documentation, observation of workers doing the tasks, or from interviews with workers and domain experts. Observations can be recorded in a variety of forms, from handwritten notes to video recording and computer logging. The early analysis may involve the subjects, asking them to 'relive' the task in a post-task walkthrough, or sort lists of task objects and actions for knowledge elicitation.

Analysis can be used to structure manuals and training courses. In this case, the system studied will be the 'target' system for the documentation. Alternatively, an existing system (or systems) can be studied and the task analysis used to structure a new design. This can guide the choice of functionality and the objects and actions implemented within the system. It can also be used to guide the detailed design of dialog so that frequent tasks are easy to perform.

EXERCISES

15.1   The following is a list of objects found in one of the authors' kitchens:

teapot, mug, soup bowl, plate, spoon, table knife, cook's knife, fork, saucepan, frying pan, kettle, casserole, fish slice, tin opener, baking tray, scales, mixing bowl, glasses, jugs, corkscrew, rolling pin, ladle, egg cup, chopping board

Produce a taxonomy using the TDH notation of these objects. Does it obey the TAKD uniqueness rule? Compare your answer with someone else's. (Note: the authors had great difficulty with items like the corkscrew, which did not fit easily into any generic category – perhaps you did better.)

15.2   Complete the tea-making manual in Figure 15.7. Do you think it would be useful? Think of situations where such a manual would be helpful and where a more conceptual manual would be better.

15.3   Figure 15.1 shows a textual representation of an HTA description of vacuum cleaning. Present the same information in a diagrammatic form.

15.4   (Converse to above) Figure 15.6 uses an HTA diagram to show the actions in which a tractor is involved; show the same information textually.

15.5   Observe an office, note the actions performed and the objects used depending on the available equipment; use different recording techniques as described in Chapter 9. Then use the different task analysis techniques to structure your findings. (Note: this could be a group project.)

15.6   This exercise is based on the mobile phone scenario on the book website at: /e3/scenario/phone/

A user interface designer analyzes Andy's behavior with his original phone and realizes that both scenarios A and B are part of a general pattern, as shown in the hierarchical task analysis (HTA) in Figure 15.8.

(i)   Complete the HTA for phoning using the original phone taking into account scenarios A and B only and briefly describe your solution.

(ii)   Do a complete HTA for phoning using the new phone based on scenario C only.

You will find that scenario C (and hence your solution to part (ii)) does not quite fit into the general pattern in Figure 15.8. Discuss whether the solutions to (i) and (ii) can be modified to emphasize their common features and whether this would clarify the overall task description.

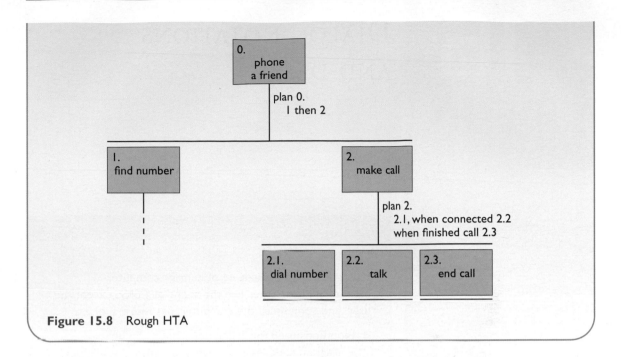

Figure 15.8   Rough HTA

RECOMMENDED READING

D. Diaper and N. Stanton, editors, *The Handbook of Task Analysis for Human–Computer Interaction*, Lawrence Erlbaum, 2003.
This long-awaited collection fills the gap left for many years since Diaper's previous collection (below) went out of print. It has chapters by experts in a wide variety of methods and case studies of real applications.

D. Diaper, editor, *Task Analysis for Human–Computer Interaction*, Ellis Horwood, 1989.
If you can find a copy, a classic collection.

P. Johnson, *Human–Computer Interaction: Psychology, Task Analysis and Software Engineering*, McGraw-Hill, 1992.
This is a short introductory HCI text, oriented toward task analysis and in particular Johnson's own KAT (knowledge analysis for tasks) methodology.

J. T. Hackos and J. C. Redish, *User and Task Analysis for Interface Design*, John Wiley, 1998.
Very detailed discussion of the processes and techniques for conducting a task analysis and applying it to interface design.

A. Shepherd, *Hierarchical Task Analysis*, Taylor and Francis, 2000.
A detailed exposition of HTA and its uses.

16 DIALOG NOTATIONS AND DESIGN

OVERVIEW

Dialog is the syntactic level of human–computer interaction; it is rather like the script of a play, except the user, and sometimes the computer, has more choices.

- Notations used for dialog description can be:
  - diagrammatic: easy to read at a glance
  - textual: easier for formal analysis.

- The dialog is linked:
  - to the semantics of the system, what it does
  - to the presentation of the system, how it looks.

- Formal descriptions can be analyzed:
  - for inconsistent actions
  - for difficult to reverse actions
  - for missing items
  - for potential miskeying errors.

16.1 WHAT IS DIALOG?

Dialog, as opposed to a monolog, is a conversation between two or more parties. It has also come to imply a level of cooperation or at least intent to resolve conflict. In the design of user interfaces, the *dialog* has a more specific meaning, namely the *structure* of the conversation between the user and the computer system.

We can look at computer language at three levels:

Lexical The lowest level: the shape of icons on the screen and the actual keys pressed. In human language, the sounds and spellings of words.

Syntactic The order and structure of inputs and outputs. In human language, the grammar of sentence construction.

Semantic The meaning of the conversation in terms of its effect on the computer's internal data structures and/or the external world. In human language, the meaning ascribed by the different participants to the conversation.

In user interfaces, the term dialog is often taken to be almost synonymous with the syntactic level. However, the lexical/syntactic barrier is somewhat fuzzy and actual use of dialog description often includes some lexical features.

In Sections 16.2–16.4 we will see why specific notations are required for dialog design, and review a range of diagrammatic and textual dialog notations. Having got a formal representation of the dialog, what do we do with it? Section 16.5 discusses the links between these dialog notations acting at the syntactic level and the detailed semantics of the system. Finally, in Section 16.6, we will see how a description of the dialog can be analyzed to discover potential faults and problems.

In the rest of this section, we will look at structured human–human dialogs which will demonstrate several features which we will later see in human–computer dialog.

16.1.1 Structured human dialogs

In contrast to most human conversation, dialog with computers is relatively structured and constrained. It is only on *Star Trek* that one can freely chat to the computer and expect a response (although not as far from the truth as all that, see Chapter 10). So, whereas in human conversation the grammar rules often stop once we get to the level of a sentence (and allow a lot of latitude even in sentence construction), those for computer dialogs may encompass the whole of the interaction.

There are, of course, more structured forms of human conversation. Consider the following fragment from a marriage service:

Minister:	Do you *man's name*, take this woman…
Man:	I do.
Minister:	Do you *woman's name*, take this man…
Woman:	I do.
Man:	With this ring, I thee wed… (*places ring on woman's finger*)

| Woman: | With this ring, I thee wed... (*places ring on man's finger*) |
| Minister: | I now pronounce you husband and wife. |

This is a sort of script for the three participants to follow. It demonstrates several important features which we will see in computer dialogs. The participants must say certain things in a specific order. Some of their contributions are entirely predetermined, for instance the phrase 'I do'. However, the minister must vary some words, substituting in the names of the husband- and wife-to-be. The instructions concerning the ring can be regarded as an annotation to the dialog, or part of the dialog. Different notations for describing computer dialog will similarly differ on precisely what actions are considered part of the dialog. Assuming the placing of the ring is included, we note that this happens at the same time as the marriage partners speak the words 'with this ring'. That is, parts of the dialog are performed *concurrently*. Again we shall see later that different notations differ in their ability to handle concurrent dialog.

Although the minister must substitute the man's name and the woman's name, this has no effect on the rest of the service. This dialog description makes no provision for alternative responses – 'I don't'!

However, typically, the future course of a dialog does depend on the responses of the participants, for example in a criminal trial:

| Judge: | How do you plead, guilty or not guilty? |
| Defendant: | *either* Guilty *or* Not guilty. |

If the defendant pleads not guilty then the trial will proceed with evidence and cross-examination. If, on the other hand, the defendant pleads guilty, the trial will move directly to the sentencing. Because of the formalized nature of judicial processes, we could develop these court scripts further. But they would still be normative; there is always the chance that the judge may address the court with a chorus of 'Somewhere over the rainbow', or, like the Queen of Hearts, 'Off with her head!'. The verdict of such an improper trial is likely to be overturned by a higher court, but is not ruled out because the human participants do not always behave as expected. Similarly, descriptions of computer dialogs may not cover all eventualities. Hitting the save option on a word processor's menu is expected to save the file and then give control back to the user. Occasionally, the computer may instead respond with a 'core dumped' or 'unrecoverable application error' message. Should the dialog description include such improper system responses? The answer is unclear and depends very much on the intended use.

Returning to the marriage service, the script given refers only to the words spoken. It does not directly address the *meaning* of those words: the legal nature of the ceremony, the fidelity of the partners or even whether the minister gets the partners' names right! We have noted that computer dialog descriptions are usually aimed at the syntactic level of language, not the semantics (meaning). Similarly, the marriage ceremony does not directly address the semantics of marriage; for instance, the marriage may be acted out as part of a television program, and the actor and actress would not expect to be really married at the end of it. However, an important issue for computer dialogs is how the syntax links into the semantics of the application. For instance, if I type 'print fred', I expect the file fred to be printed, not deleted.

16.2 DIALOG DESIGN NOTATIONS

In this section we shall look at some of the notations which have been used for describing human–computer dialogs. Some may be familiar to the computer scientist as they have their roots in other branches of computing and have been 'appropriated' by the user interface developer.

But why bother to use a special notation? We already have programming languages, why not use them? Let us look at a simple financial advice program to calculate mortgage repayments. (This is *not* supposed to be an example of good dialog design.)

```
rate = 10
term = 25
print "Our current interest rate is 10%"
print "What is your annual salary?"
input salary
max_loan = 3 * salary
print "How much do you want to borrow?"
input amount
if amount > max_loan
then  print "That is too much money"
      print "Please consult our financial advisor"
      goto finish
end if
repeat forever
      print "Our standard term is 25 years."
      print "Do you want this (yes/no)?"
      input answer
      if answer == "yes" goto calc
      if answer == "no"  goto rd_trm
      print "You must answer yes or no"
   end repeat
rd_trm: print "What term do you require (years)?"
      input term
calc:   r = ( 100 + rate ) / 100
        payment = r^term  * ( r - 1 )
                      * amount / ( r^(term-1) - 1 )
        print "Monthly repayment is ", payment
finish: stop
```

Notice how the dialog with the user is mixed up with the rest of the program; calculations are interspersed with input–output. Some of the if then statements represent the system's choices (amount > max_loan), others represent choices of the user (answer == "yes"). If you are a programmer, you will also have noticed the poor program structure and the use of goto. This is not because the authors are bad programmers. It would be possible to rewrite the program using only structured programming constructs. However, the resulting program would be equally obtuse, and, in general, programs which have to parse are full of nasty structures. In this program, the biggest complication is the check that the answer is either 'yes' or 'no'. Error checking and correction often dominate interactive programs.

Imagine now you have been asked to analyze the dialog in some way: for instance, to list all the possible sequences of user inputs and system responses, or to tell the user how to get the repayments on a 15-year loan. The mixing of user and system choices and the convoluted nature of the program structure make this surprisingly difficult.

Alternatively, you may be asked to change the interface style or fit the program with a mouse- and window-based interface – is this difficult? Remember, this is a short program which is almost all interaction with the user and should be relatively easy. Imagine a program of 10,000 or 100,000 lines. Various commercial applications began their life on traditional text-based terminals, but are now available on Windows or Macintosh platforms. The ancestry of such programs is often all too obvious – not really surprising.

This gives us two reasons for using a separate dialog description notation: ease of analysis and separation of the interface elements of the program from the actual calculations (semantics). These reasons both presuppose the program exists already – a third reason for using a special notation is to write down the dialog *before* a program is written. This allows the designer to analyze the proposed structure, or perhaps use a prototyping tool to execute the dialog. A dialog notation is also a way for members of a design team to talk about the design and eventually for the designer to pass on the intended dialog to the programmer of the actual application. Thus dialog notations often form an integral part of *prototyping* methodologies and tools (which were discussed in Chapter 6).

16.3 DIAGRAMMATIC NOTATIONS

Diagrammatic notations are heavily used in dialog design. At their best they allow the designer to see at a glance the structure of the dialog. However, they often have trouble coping with more extensive or complex dialog structures. Sections 16.3.1–16.3.4 describe variants of state transition networks, which are the most heavily used diagrammatic notation. As part of this description, several issues will be discussed which are shared by other diagrammatic and textual notations, in particular the treatment of concurrent dialogs and pre-emptive features. Sections 16.3.5–16.3.8 describe other diagrammatic notations: Petri nets, Harel's state charts, traditional flow diagrams and JSD diagrams.

16.3.1 State transition networks

State transition networks (*STNs*) have long been used for dialog description, the first uses for specification dating back to the late 1960s [258, 279] with executable tools developed from the late 1970s on [366, 367].

Consider a simple mouse-based drawing tool. It has a menu with two options, 'circle' and 'line', and a drawing surface. If you select circle you are allowed to click on two further points on the drawing surface. The first of these is the circle's center and the second any point on the circumference. After the first point is selected, the system draws a 'rubber band' line between the center and the current mouse position. After the second point is chosen, the circle is drawn.

The 'line' option in the menu is to draw a polyline. That is, the user can select any number of points on the drawing surface which the system connects with straight lines. The last point is denoted by a double click on the mouse. Again the system 'rubber bands' between successive mouse positions.

Figure 16.1 shows an STN describing the tool. Each circle denotes a 'state' the system can be in. For example, *Menu* is the state where the system is waiting for the user to select either 'circle' or 'line' from the menu, and *Circle 2* is the state after the user has entered the circle center and is waiting for the point on the circumference.

Between the states are arrows, the *transitions*. These are labeled with the user actions that triggered the particular transition and the response the system makes. For instance, state *Circle 1* is where the system is waiting for the user to select the circle's center. If the user clicks on a point, the system moves into state *Circle 2* and responds by drawing the rubber band between the point and the current mouse position. From this state, the user can click on another point, upon which the system draws the circle and then moves into the special *Finish* state. We can see from this that the STN is able to represent a *sequence* of user actions and system responses.

When in state *Circle 1*, the user has no other options: there is only one arc coming from it, corresponding to selecting a point. In other states, the user has several options. For example, from state *Menu* the user can select 'circle' from the menu, upon which the system moves into state *Circle 1* and highlights the 'circle' option on

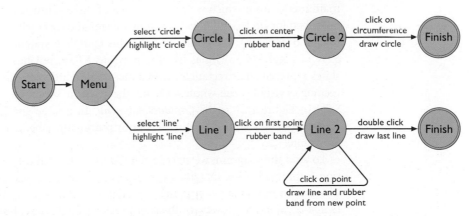

Figure 16.1 State transition network for menu-driven drawing tool

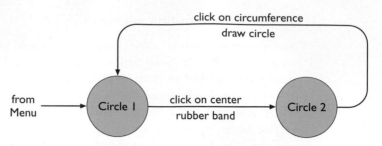

Figure 16.2 Portion of STN allowing multiple circles to be drawn

the menu, or alternatively, the user can select 'line' from where the system moves into state *Line 1*. That is, the STN is able to describe user *choice*.

There is a choice from state *Line 2* also: the user can double click on a point and finish the polyline, moving to the *Finish* state, or he can single click, which adds a new point to the polyline. In the latter case, the transition points back into state *Line 2*. This represents *iteration* – the system stays in state *Line 2* accepting any number of points on the polyline, until the user double clicks on a point.

Iterations need not involve just one state. The dialog as it stands only allows you to draw one circle. You presumably have to go through the menu selection again for each circle drawn. We could imagine altering the dialog to allow any number of circles to be drawn. To do this, we would make the arc from state *Circle 2* loop back to state *Circle 1*. This is shown in Figure 16.2. There are some problems with this arrangement as it stands which we will discuss later. However, note that already we are using the STN to discuss different dialog options.

16.3.2 Hierarchical state transition nets

The *Start* and *Finish* states are not real states, but are there merely to let us glue this bit of dialog into a bigger dialog. For example, the drawing tool may have a main menu, from which we can select one of three submenus: a graphics menu (as described for circles and lines), a text menu (for adding labels) and a paint menu (for freehand drawing). We could describe this complete system using the *hierarchical STN* in Figure 16.3. This is like the previous STNs, but has additional composite states represented as rectangles with a picture of a little STN in them. Each of these rectangles denotes the whole STN for the relevant submenu. We assume that the STN in Figure 16.1 is the *Graphics submenu*. In a large specification this may be represented by a caption for the STN or by putting the label *Graphics submenu* in the *Start* state.

To read this diagram, we start in state *Main menu* and follow the relevant transition from it as before. Imagine the user has selected 'graphics' from the main menu. The system responds by 'popping' the graphics submenu and then going into state *Graphics submenu*. However, this is not really a single state, but corresponds to the STN described in Figure 16.1. We therefore enter this subdialog at the state pointed to

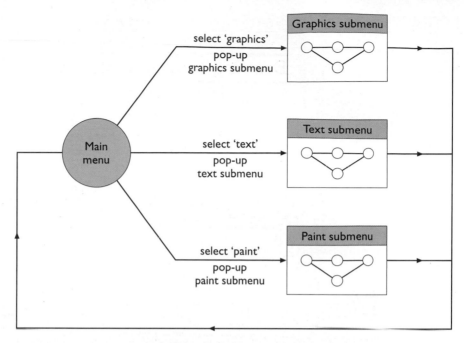

Figure 16.3 Hierarchical STN for complete drawing tool

by its special *Start* state, that is the *Menu* state. We then follow through the graphics menu STN, drawing either a circle or a polyline. When we get to a *Finish* state we revert to the main diagram in Figure 16.3 and follow the (single) arrow from the *Graphics submenu* state which leads us back to the *Main menu*.

The use of hierarchical elements does not change the power of the basic notation as one can simply imagine gluing the subdiagrams into the main diagram. However, it makes it far simpler to specify large systems; it would not be unreasonable to specify a whole system dialog in this fashion, from the highest level down to individual keystrokes and mouse clicks.

DESIGN FOCUS

Using STNs in prototyping

Producing a state transition network can be a good start for prototyping. In the simplest case you can use paper-based prototypes. For each state in the chart, draw *and label* a representative screen on paper, either by hand or printed from a computer drawing package. You can then run through example scenarios with a potential user or client. If the user asks what happens if a particular button or key is pressed, you can simply consult the STN, look up the current state on the chart, see what the next state ought to be and then show the relevant piece of paper.

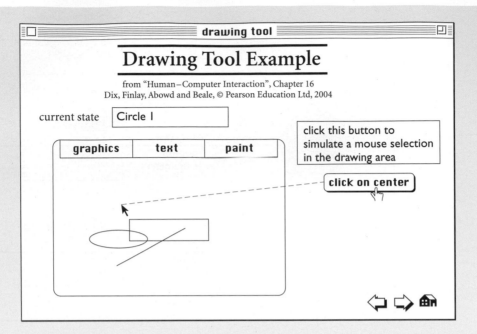

Figure 16.4   Prototyping using STNs – notice there are two mouse pointers: the hand is the real pointer, the arrow is a simulated one drawn onto the prototype

Alternatively, you can get the computer to do the work for you! Using a multimedia authoring tool or prototyping tool such as HyperCard or Macromedia Director draw each state as a separate screen, but leave a blank area for annotation and additional controls (see Figure 16.4). Name the screens using the same labels that you used in the STN. Now add buttons or active areas to each screen corresponding to the buttons on the intended final system and simply link them to the corresponding screen. (This is particularly easy to do in HyperCard.) Some user actions do not correspond to clicking areas of the screen. For these add extra buttons on the blank area and label them suitably, for example 'user types some text'.

Now you give this to your prospective users; they can click on buttons and see for themselves what will happen. Remember to warn them that this is a series of fixed screens not a functioning prototype. In particular, if you return to the same point in the dialog, the screen will be the same as the first time you were there.

Figure 16.4 shows an example of this sort of prototype based on the STN in Figure 16.1. It is built using HyperCard and can be downloaded from our website.

There are other ways of making STNs hierarchical. Each variant has its own rules for tying the high-level STN with the detailed STNs. In addition, the conditions which enable a transition and the system's responses may be attached to a low-level STN. *Generalized transition networks* are probably the most well known of such variants as they are used to describe the computer system's behavior in CCT (Chapter 12, Section 12.2.2).

16.3.3 Concurrent dialogs and combinatorial explosion of states

We have seen that STNs can be very good at representing the sequential, choice and iterative parts of a dialog. Where they fail, quite dismally, is in describing a dialog consisting of several *concurrent* parts. Take, for example, a simple dialog box for describing text style as one might find in a word processor (Figure 16.5). The box contains three toggles, one each for bold, italic and underline styles. A piece of text can be **emboldened**, *italicized*, <u>underlined</u> or any combination of these three. To select, say, emboldening, the user clicks over the bold toggle. To deselect it, the user simply clicks again.

If we look at each toggle individually, we have simple two-state STNs as in Figure 16.6. The arrows have been drawn with two heads, as the same user action moves you in either direction between the states. We have also omitted the system responses, which would be to invert the highlighting of the toggle, and possibly to change the style of any currently selected text in the document.

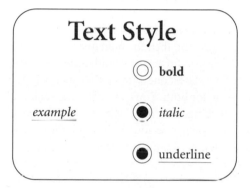

Figure 16.5 Simple dialog box with three toggles

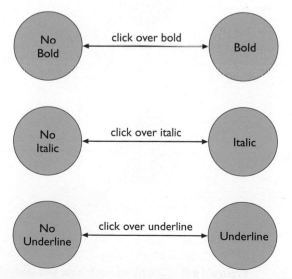

Figure 16.6 Individual bold, italic and underline state transition diagrams

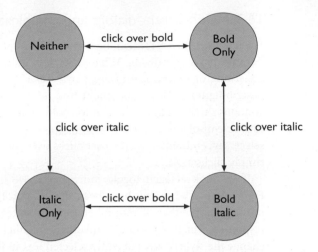

Figure 16.7 Combined bold and italic state transition diagram

However, this does not tell us what happens if, say, the user clicks over the italic toggle and then the bold one. To do this we need to combine the diagrams. We'll do this first for just the bold and italic options. This is shown in Figure 16.7. This has four states: one with neither style selected, one for bold only, one for italic only and one for both. You can verify that each user action performs as expected: for example, clicking over 'italic' whilst in *Bold Italic* would get you to the *Bold Only* state.

Finally, we add in the underline style in Figure 16.8. This time we have written the user actions simply as 'B' for 'click over "bold"', and so on, as the diagram has

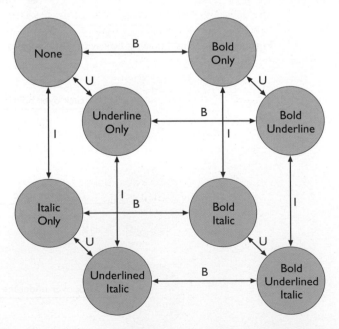

Figure 16.8 Combined bold, italic and underline state transition diagram

become cluttered enough as it is! Again, you can verify that the user actions perform as expected: for example, 'U' in state *Bold Italic* takes you to state *Underlined Bold Italic*.

The STN with two toggles had four states, the STN with three toggles had eight states and, in general, if we had had n toggles, we would have had a diagram with 2^n states in it – not particularly easy to read! The problem is that the user is effectively operating the toggles concurrently; he can perform an action on any of them, and the actions on one are independent of the actions on the others. If we have two STNs with m and n states respectively, then the STN representing the two acting concurrently will have $m \times n$ states. Furthermore, the resulting diagram would hide the regularity of the interface.

This inability of STNs to handle concurrent dialogs is particularly a problem with direct manipulation interfaces. These are often full of toggles, option switches, style sheets, etc., all of which can be operated independently of one another. This seriously calls into question their usefulness under these circumstances.

One suggestion, particularly associated with Jacob [191], is that STNs should be used to model the microdialog of direct manipulation systems. That is, each interface element (menu, toggle, dialog box) would have an associated STN. However, the way that these are put together would use some alternative notation. Thus, for example, the above dialog box would be represented as consisting of three STNs, as we originally had in Figure 16.6.

16.3.4 Escapes and help

Escapes and help systems pose problems that are similar to the combinatorial explosion from concurrent dialogs. Imagine that we have been observing the use of the drawing tool. We have noticed that users often find they have wrongly selected some option and want to get back to the menu. As the dialog is currently specified, once they select, say, the circle option, they must select two points before they are allowed to continue. As the current system does not have any deletion at present, this was found to be particularly irksome.

As a solution to this problem, we want to add an escape key, which, wherever you are, cancels what you are doing and returns you to the main menu. This seems quite a simple addition – it only took a sentence to say. However, to add it to the STN describing the system would require an arc from *every* state back to the main menu. Furthermore, this would make a complete mess of the hierarchical structure of the dialog description.

Some forms of hierarchical STN explicitly cater for this by saying that if a composite state has a labeled arc coming from it, then this acts as an escape from the subdialog. For example, we could redraw the overall system description as in Figure 16.9. Each submenu state now has two arcs coming from it. One arc is labeled 'normal Finish' and represents the path taken when the subdialog reaches its *Finish* state. This arc has a little state circle added to it in order to emphasize that it is tied to the *Finish* state within the subdialog. The other arc from the submenu state is

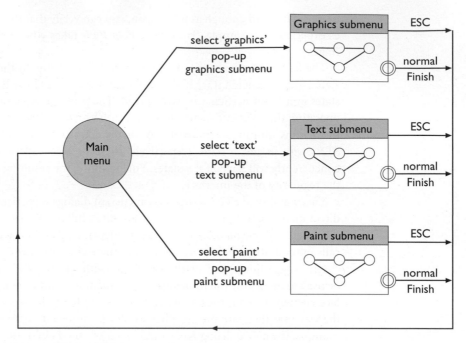

Figure 16.9 STN for drawing tool with escapes

labeled 'ESC' and this represents the user hitting the escape key. The difference is that this arc is 'active' at all times during the subdialog. Even when the user is in the middle of drawing a circle or a line, if the escape key is pressed, the subdialog is immediately aborted and the arc labeled 'ESC' is taken. In this case, both the 'ESC' and the 'normal Finish' arcs go to the same place. In general, this need not be so, and one may have several escapes activated by different user actions.

Help systems are similar to escapes in some ways, in that they may be invoked at any stage during the dialog. However, unlike escapes, when you have finished using the help system, you expect to return to the same point in the dialog that you left. That is, you can think of the help system as being a little subdialog hanging off every state in the network. Figure 16.10 shows this for two states of the dialog: as you can imagine, it would get a little tedious for the whole thing!

The case of a help system is very similar to concurrent dialogs (in fact, it is an embedded dialog), and the total number of states in the full diagram is again the product of the number of states in the help system times the number in the original system.

16.3.5 Petri nets

One of the oldest formalisms in computing science is the *Petri net*. It is a graphical formalism designed for reasoning about concurrent activities. In recent years it has been used by several researchers to specify aspects of single-user [276] and multi-user systems [277]. In an STN the system is always at exactly one state. Indeed, you

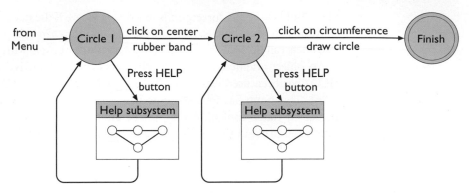

Figure 16.10   Portion of STN with help system

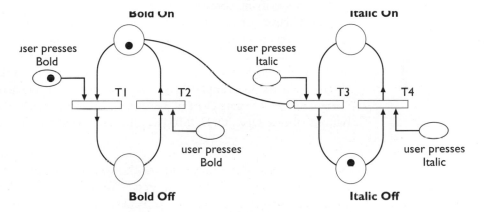

Figure 16.11   Petri net for Bold/Italic selection

can simulate the behavior of the system by moving a counter around the STN following arcs. A Petri net is similar except that the system has several 'states' at once. These are depicted as several black *counters* in Figure 16.11.

The figure shows a Petri net for a system having two near independent bold/italic toggles. The circles are called *places* (like states) and the thin rectangles are called *transitions*. There are three counters: one in the 'Bold On' place, showing that the bold toggle is currently on; one in the 'Italic Off' place showing that the italic toggle is currently off; and one in the slightly elliptic 'user presses Bold' place showing that the user has just pressed the bold toggle. The slightly elliptic places represent those where user input can occur. The rule is that if all the places with arcs going into a transition have a counter then the transition can *fire* and all the counters from the input places are removed and new counters placed on the outputs of the transition. So, in Figure 16.11, there are counters in both the input places of transition 'T1' which will therefore fire leaving a single counter in place 'Bold Off'.

The italic side is similar except it has an extra arc coming from the 'Bold On' place to the transition 'T3', but with a small circle rather than an arrowhead. This is an inhibition arc and means that the transition 'T3' cannot fire if there is a counter in place 'Bold On'. This corresponds to a dialog where if the italic toggle is on it cannot be turned off while bold is on. More useful conditions can be represented, for example Petri nets can be used to describe the interactions of users with web-based systems.

An object-oriented variant of Petri nets called Interactive Cooperative Objects (ICO) has been used extensively by the HCI Group at the University of Toulouse [276]. The group has focussed especially on safety critical applications and in particular air traffic control. A tool, the PetShop development environment, has been developed to aid in the verification and prototyping of ICO specifications [253].

16.3.6 State charts

Harel's *state charts* can be seen as a form of STN. They were developed as a way of visually specifying complex reactive systems and address many of the problems described above, for example concurrency and escapes, while still retaining a diagrammatic representation. They are characterized by a hierarchical structure, but not used as we have seen before to split a diagram up. The hierarchy in state charts is used within a single diagram to add structure, and to show which parts represent alternative states (like simple STNs) and which represent concurrent activity.

Figure 16.12 is a state chart of a television control panel. The controller has five buttons labeled 'ON', 'OFF', 'MUTE', 'SEL' and 'RESET'. The television can either

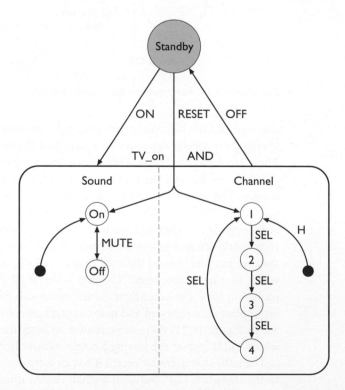

Figure 16.12 State chart for television control panel

be on, or in standby mode. Imagine we start at *Standby*. Pressing ON or RESET will turn the television on (TV_on); then when it is on, pressing OFF puts it back into standby mode. When the television is on, the user can control the sound with the MUTE button and the channel with the SEL button. Using MUTE turns the sound on or off, whereas SEL cycles between four channels (this is a rather cheap TV).

The *Sound* and *Channel* subdialogs each look somewhat like normal STNs. They are both part of the *TV_on* composite state – this is an example of hierarchical grouping. However, the dashed line between them, together with the AND keyword, says that the two subdialogs operate concurrently – that is, we can press MUTE or SEL in any order we like.

The *Sound* subdialog has a black blob with an arc going to the *On* state. This corresponds to the *Start* node in the earlier STNs and represents the default start state. Each time the TV is turned on, the sound will be on. The channel's selection is slightly different: its start arc is marked with an 'H', short for history. This says that the channel subdialog remembers where it last was – the first time you turn the TV on it will start in channel 1, but subsequently when you turn it on it will be set to the last channel you were watching. Unlike the ON arc the RESET arc overrides these default start states. Whereas ON is targeted at the *TV_on* box generally, RESET is directed to specific states within *TV_on*. Thus whenever the RESET button is pressed from standby mode, the television is turned on with the channel set to 1 and the sound on.

Notice also that the OFF button acts as an escape to the *TV_on* dialog. No matter where the *Sound* and *Channel* dialogs are, simply pressing OFF will put the TV in standby mode. A judicious use of the 'history' feature would allow one to specify a help system, but even with the expressiveness of state charts this would look clumsy.

16.3.7 Flow charts

Although somewhat out of fashion now, flow charts in various forms are perhaps the most widely used of any diagrammatic notation for programming. They can also be a simple, but useful, tool for dialog design. In expressive power, they differ little from STNs and share the problems of concurrency, escapes and so on. However, within the area of simple dialogs, they have the advantage of simplicity and the added benefit that most programmers will know what they mean.

The boxes in a flow chart represent processes or decisions and are thus not equivalent to the states of an STN. For example, in an STN, the act of accepting a user's input is attached to an arc (and is often difficult to read), whereas in a flow chart it is in one of the boxes.

Flow charts employ a wide range of box shapes to represent different activities, but these reflect a programmer-centered rather than a user-centered view: for example, the use of a parallelogram for input–output, whether this is interaction with the user or with a database or file. If you use flow charts for dialog specification, it is probably best to employ a set of box types which reflect user-oriented actions.

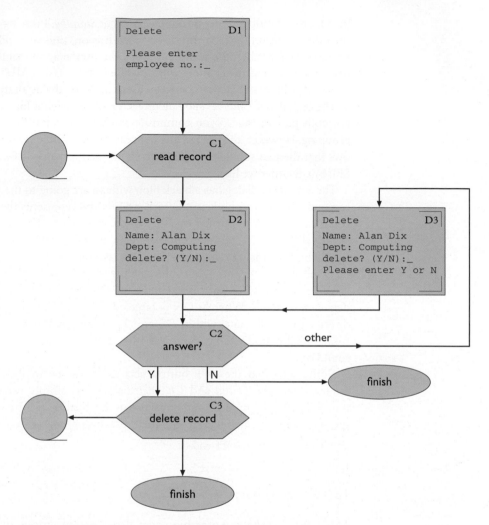

Figure 16.13   Flow chart of deletion subdialog

Figure 16.13 shows a flow chart as used by one of the authors, some years ago, for specifying dialogs for forms-based COBOL programs. The dialog shown is a portion of a personnel database update system and is the subdialog for deletion of records. The chart employs two main types of boxes: the rectangular boxes are 'screen images' of the forms used to communicate with the user. The angular boxes are the processes and decisions made by the system. In addition, there is an elliptical 'finish' box, where the user is returned to the main menu, and little 'tape' symbols which represent where the system reads or updates the database.

The dialog starts with a form D1, which asks the user for an employee number. When this has been given the system reads in the relevant record, and displays it to the user for confirmation (form D2). If the user responds 'Y' to the question 'delete? (Y/N)' the record is deleted. If the user does not answer 'Y' or 'N', the record is redisplayed (form D3) with the error message 'Please enter Y or N'. Of course, in a real system there would be a similar loop around form D1 if the user entered a non-existent employee number.

The big difference between using a flow chart for dialog design and using it for program design is the level of detail on the program side. If, for example, reading the employee record involved a sequential search through the file to find the relevant record, a program flow chart would include this loop. For the dialog, this would neither be necessary, nor appropriate. That is, the actual *program* flow chart would look nothing like this *dialog* flow chart.

It works!

Formal notations are often criticized for the amount of work required. However, the authors' own experience counters this. Flow diagrams such as in Figure 16.13 were used to specify dialogs within a *transaction-processing* environment. For various technical reasons the actual programs in such environments are very complex, being, like most windowing environments, event driven. Simple systems developed in this environment typically took many person-months to complete.

However, starting with these flow diagrams the same process could be completed in days, with changes accomplished within hours (no mean feat within such an environment!). This is because diagrams were converted by hand, but in a mechanical fashion, into COBOL programs. The complex structures needed to work under the transaction-processing environment were constructed automatically. Furthermore, the flow diagrams allowed systematic testing and also were a useful aid in talking through design alternatives with end-users.

The productivity improvement over ad hoc design in this context was well over 1000%. Although it might be nice to think this was due to the authors' superior programming skills(!), this could in no way account for an order of magnitude difference in productivity. That is, the adoption of a formal notation did not waste valuable time, but on the contrary made phenomenal time savings.

16.3.8 JSD diagrams

Of course, virtually any diagrammatic (or textual) notation employed in programming or system design can be recruited for dialog design. *Jackson structured design* (JSD), while not as old as flow charts, has been around for many years. During this time it has developed significantly; however, it is one of the older parts of this methodology, the *JSD diagram*, which has been used for various aspects of task analysis and dialog design. As with flow charts, there may be an advantage to using JSD diagrams if they are already familiar to the programmers who will implement the dialog.

Figure 16.14 shows a JSD diagram for the top-level structure of an employee personnel system. The system allows the user to update the personnel record in various

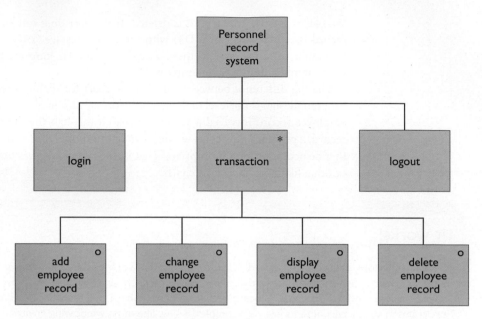

Figure 16.14 JSD diagram for personnel system

ways: adding new employees, displaying, altering and removing existing ones. The diagram looks rather like the hierarchical task analysis diagrams we saw in Section 15.3. However, the basic JSD diagram is somewhat more precise in its meaning. If we look at the top of the diagram, we see that the personnel system is decomposed into three parts: login, transactions and logout. These are implicitly in sequence left to right. That is, you are not allowed to do any transactions until you log in!

The login and logout are assumed to be quite simple, so the diagram only expands the transaction node. Under this are listed the various transaction types: add, change, display and delete.

Some of the boxes have a little asterisk or 'o' in their top right-hand corner. Without these decorations the diagram would represent a system which allowed you to log in, then add, change, display and delete once each in that order, and then log out. The decorations change this meaning. The asterisk represents iteration – any number of repetitions. That is, the dialog can consist of a login followed by any number of transactions before the logout. The little 'o' represents optional elements. That is, a transaction may be any one of the four options.

Taking the decorations into account, the diagram describes what we would expect of such a system: a login followed by any number of add, change, display or delete transactions, and finally a logout.

The class of dialogs which can be represented by simple JSD diagrams is rather limited, but includes many basic menu-driven information systems. Arguably, the simple form of such dialogs could be regarded as a positive asset, especially if the diagram sticks to the higher levels of dialog specification.

DESIGN FOCUS

Digital watch – documentation and analysis

Some diagrammatic notations may be clear enough to be used in user documentation as well as in design. Figure 16.15 shows a state transition diagram for the major modes of a digital watch, taken from the instruction booklet. The booklet goes on to use some similar diagrams and some tabular descriptions of each of the modes (using the other two buttons).

The watch has only three buttons, and only one of these, button A, is used to move between modes. As the diagram is being used in documentation, the states are denoted by representations of the watch in the appropriate mode. This is a useful approach for any stage in the design process, and is similar to the use of screen images in the flow diagram in Figure 16.13.

There are four modes, and pressing the button A moves between them. The most common modes are the time display and stop watch. So the dialog is designed to make it easy to switch between these modes and difficult to slip accidentally into the time- or alarm-setting modes. To achieve this aim, pressing 'A' usually toggles between the two main modes. However, the watch's owner will want to set the time eventually, and the designer does not want another button to be used (buttons cost money and the watch only costs £2). Therefore, the setting modes are achieved by holding the button down for two seconds or more. So, a quick press does one thing, whereas a long one does something else. The semi-formal nature of a state transition diagram makes this *real-time* behavior easy to denote. It is merely added as textual commentary.

But this documentation diagram does not have all the information one would require for design purposes. If you are in the time-setting mode and press 'A', what happens? Do you go to the time display or to the stop watch? Also, when going from time display to alarm setting, what do you see *during* the two seconds you hold down button A?

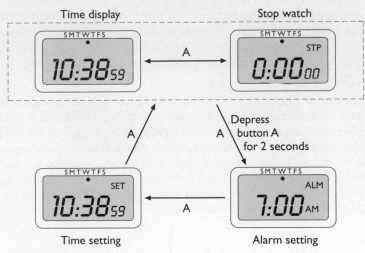

Figure 16.15   Instructions for digital watch

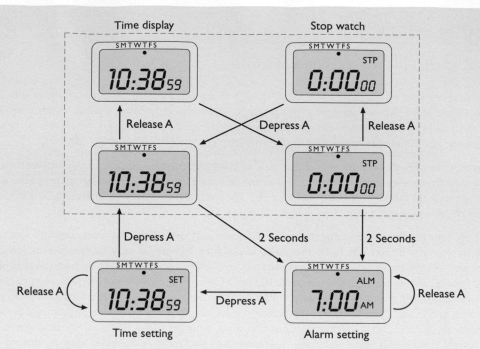

Figure 16.16 Design diagram for digital watch

After a little experimentation, one can generate the complete diagram, suitable for giving to the implementor of the watch electronics (Figure 16.16).

Notice that in order to deal adequately with the real-time behavior, it is necessary to separate the depress and release events on button A. This shows us that the toggle between time display and stop watch happens when the button is pressed down, but that each of these modes corresponds to two states, as the behavior differs depending on the state of the button. From the diagram you can see that if you are in the time-setting mode, then pressing 'A' will get you back to the time display, not to the stop watch. However, unexpectedly, if you do not release the button soon enough, you get back into the alarm-setting mode.

Is this getting a little complicated? In fact it only represents about 10% of the instructions. This kind of time-dependent behavior is rare in computer software, but common in interfaces to consumer goods (watches, video controllers, control panels on white goods). This is because the number of buttons tends to be small compared with the number of functions. As we can see, in the presence of real-time behavior even simple dialogs become complex. That is all the more reason for such dialogs to be *planned*. It is probably the case that the detailed design decisions above were taken as the watch was being programmed, not by the watch's designer. It is not surprising that many people cannot set the alarms or even change the time on their watches.

16.4 TEXTUAL DIALOG NOTATIONS

16.4.1 Grammars

As the images used for computer dialog are linguistic, it is not surprising that formal grammars have been used as a dialog notation.

BNF (*Backus–Naur Form*) is widely used to describe programming language syntax and we have already seen in Chapter 12 how descriptions of an interface can be used to measure its difficulty. The same description can be used to describe the dialog for other purposes. In particular, there are several parser generators based upon BNF, such as the UNIX 'yacc' tool, which are suitable for producing crude prototypes.

As the BNF notation has been described in detail in Chapter 12, we will not repeat the description here. But in order to compare it with other dialog description notations, we recall that BNF has two connectives to denote *sequence* and *choice*. Note that the use of '+' as a symbol for sequence in Chapter 12 is not standard – sequence is often simply represented by juxtaposition, and this convention will be followed in the examples below.

The definitions of named *non-terminals* gave a natural structure to the interface description. In addition, *recursive* definitions of non-terminals allowed the dialog to represent *iteration*. However, BNF has no way of representing concurrent dialogs, nor can it easily deal with pervasive commands like escapes or help systems. Note, however, that both BNF and *regular expressions* (described below) are focussed upon the user's actions, as opposed to the concentration upon the *state* in STNs.

Regular expressions are heavily used in editors to describe complex textual search criteria, and also in the *lexical analysis* of programming languages. They are similar to BNF but are slightly less powerful. However, their terseness and more easily computed behavior make them very suitable for the above purposes. Unfortunately, the notation used within regular expressions differs from that used for similar concepts in BNF, and, to make matters worse, there are many different types of regular expression with many different notations. For example, when using the tools supplied with the UNIX operating system, there are at least three different notations. This may be particularly confusing, if, say, you are used to a particular editor's regular expression syntax, and then find a different syntax.

In text editors and lexical analyzers, the basic unit is the character. Often choice is only available at this level (for example, `[+-*/]` represents any single arithmetic operator), and the whole notation is geared to rapid (for the expert), terse expression of relatively simple patterns. For example, '`Fred[.!?]`' finds the name Fred when used at the end of a sentence. However, where regular expressions have been used in dialog design, different criteria apply. The notation is less terse and tends to employ named subexpressions (like non-terminals in BNF) for clarity. Unfortunately, this notation is slightly different again from both BNF and from other regular expressions.

As an example, we consider again the polyline drawing from Figure 16.1. This can be represented by the regular expression

```
select-line click click* double-click
```

This says that you must select the line option from the menu, click somewhere with the mouse, then click as many times as you like on intermediate points, and finally double click. It is assumed that the low-level terms `select-line`, `click` and `double-click` either are primitives, or have been defined elsewhere. The only other two notational forms that are used are sequencing, denoted by juxtaposition, and iteration, denoted by the *Kleene star* operator '`*`'. The former is similar to sequencing in BNF; it is the Kleene star operator which is characteristic of regular expressions.

In general, a regular expression of the form 'thing*' means any number of *thing*, including none at all. To obtain the same effect in BNF, one would have to write

```
some-things ::= thing + some-things
```

That is, BNF obtains the effect of iteration by using recursion. In regular expressions, iteration is primitive. However, this is the only way it can be obtained; even where regular expression-based notations allow named non-terminals, these are not allowed to be recursively defined. This means that there are some forms of pattern which it is possible to represent in BNF, but not in regular expressions, for instance bracketing:

```
sentence ::= empty
           | word sentence
           | '(' sentence ')' sentence
```

No regular expression using Kleene star can express that the brackets must match. The best that you can do is say that the sentence is any number of words, open brackets or close brackets. In fact, regular expressions are as powerful in what they can express as STNs, it is just that BNF is more expressive. Whether that matters or not depends on whether the dialogs you want to represent include complex recursive elements such as bracket matching. Like STNs, neither BNF nor regular expressions can handle concurrent dialogs or escapes.

Where regular expressions have been used as a dialog notation, they are confined to low levels of the dialog, either the parsing of single lines of textual input, or the description of individual interface widgets. This is similar to the reflection that STNs are best used at this low level with different notation being used for high-level description.

One advantage of using BNF or regular expressions is that they are readily executed using existing tools. We have already mentioned the UNIX 'yacc' tool for BNF; there is also a tool 'lex' for compiling regular expressions. These tools are now also readily available on PCs. The tools are probably more suitable for parsing text commands than for graphical input. However, the execution techniques are so well understood that it is easy to write a prototyping tool if required.

16.4.2 Production rules

We have already encountered *production rules* as part of CCT in Chapter 12. They have also been used extensively to describe the dialog component of UIMS (see Chapter 8). Recall that production rules are of the general form if *condition* then *action*

These rules are represented in various forms, for instance

condition → *action*
condition: *action*

All rules are normally active and the system constantly matches the *condition* part of the rules against the user-initiated events which have occurred and its own memory. When the conditions of a rule become true, the rule is said to *fire* and the action part is executed. The action may take the form of a response to the user, or a change to the system's memory. Note especially that the order in which the rules are written is *not* important; any rule can fire at any time, so long as its condition part is true.

Production rule systems may be *event* or *state* oriented, or a mixture. We will consider first an event-oriented system, and describe again the polyline drawing part of Figure 16.1:

```
Sel-line              →   start-line <highlight 'line'>
C-point start-line    →   rest line <rubber band on>
C-point rest-line     →   rest-line <draw line>
D-point rest-line     →   <draw line> <rubber band off>
```

Notice that in this example the condition and action parts of the production rules take the simple form of a set of event names (again, the order of events does not matter). These events are of three types:

user events which begin in upper case. These are `Sel-line` (user selects the 'line' option from the menu), `C-point` and `D-point` which represent the user single and double clicking on the drawing surface.

internal events which begin in lower case. These are used by the dialog to keep track of the dialog state, for example `rest-line` is the state after the first point on the polyline has been selected.

system response events enclosed in angle brackets, such as `<draw line>`. These are the visible or audible effects of the system.

The dialog manager which executes this form of production rule has a memory consisting of a set of events. A rule fires if the events named in its condition are all present in the memory. All interaction with the user is mediated by this event memory: user events, such as a mouse click, are added to the memory, and system responses, such as `<draw line>`, are removed and acted upon by the display controller.

When a rule fires, all the events named in the condition are removed from the system's memory, and the events named in the action are added to it. For example, if the user has just selected the line option from the menu, the system's memory will contain `Sel-line`. This means that the first rule can fire. `Sel-line` is then removed from the memory and replaced by `start-line` and `<highlight 'line'>`. Finally, the display controller removes the `<highlight 'line'>` and performs the action. This leaves the system memory with only `start-line` in it, and so no more rules can fire until the user does something more.

The event-oriented nature of these production rules is evident in the way that events are removed from memory if they are used in the condition of a rule. The event has been 'dealt with' and can therefore be forgotten. This makes permanent status information difficult to represent. Notice in the third rule how the event `rest-line` is mentioned in both condition and action. It represents the state where additional points on the line are being selected after the first point. The rule is fired by a single click, which means that more points remain to be selected. The system must therefore continue in the same state. However, because the `rest-line` event has been mentioned in the condition it will be removed and therefore it must be re-established in the action part.

State-oriented production rules have a very different behavior. The system's memory is again a set of named values, but these are not removed by default when a rule is fired; instead they must be removed explicitly by the action part of a rule. The production rules in CCT operate in this fashion, as evidenced by actions such as (`DELETE-GOAL insert space`). A specific example of a state-oriented production system, slightly different from CCT rules, is Olsen's *propositional production system* (*PPS*) [272]. In PPS, the system's state is divided into a finite set of attributes, each of which can take one of a set of values. Some of the attributes are set as the result of user actions, and others have an effect on the system's display.

In the polyline drawing example we could have five attributes:

Mouse:	{ mouse-off, select-line, click-point, double-click }
Line-state:	{ menu, start-line, rest-line }
Rubber-band:	{ rubber-band-off, rubber-band-on }
Menu:	{ highlight-off, highlight-line, highlight-circle }
Draw:	{ draw-nothing, draw-line }

The first attribute, **Mouse**, is set automatically whenever the user performs the relevant action; the second attribute is used by the dialog to keep track of its state, and the last three are for controlling system responses. Again, we assume a display controller which acts appropriately upon these.

The PPS rules for polyline are somewhat similar to the previous event-based rules:

select-line	$\rightarrow$	mouse-off start-line highlight-line
click-point start-line	$\rightarrow$	mouse-off rest-line rubber-band-on
click-point rest-line	$\rightarrow$	mouse-off draw-line
double-click rest-line	$\rightarrow$	mouse-off menu draw-line rubber-band-off

The rules are executed again, when the condition matches the state, but, this time, the attributes are not changed by this alone. Only when a new value is set for a particular attribute is the old value lost. For example, in the second rule, the action 'rest-line' sets the **Line-state** attribute, thus removing the previous value of 'start-line'. Notice, that in the third rule, the value 'rest-line' of the attribute **Line-state** need not be mentioned in the action as it was in the event-based rules. This is because it persists by default.

The persistence of attributes has some rather odd effects on the user's input events. Each rule has to reset the **Mouse** attribute explicitly. Consider what would happen if this was not done. If the second rule fired, but did not have the 'mouse-off' action, then the system's memory would include the attribute binding **Mouse**=click-point (as it has not been reset) and **Line-state**=rest-line (set in the action of the second rule). This means that the third rule would be able to fire immediately, and, if it also did not reset **Mouse**, would continue to fire indefinitely without any further user actions whatsoever.

An appeal to formal simplicity would demand one used either purely event-oriented or purely state-oriented production rules, as it is always possible to get any effect with either. However, we can see from these two examples that some aspects of the dialog are best described using events and others are best described using attributes. Hence a mixed notation involving both events and state is to be preferred. Several variants of production rules (and some STNs) allow both, for example, allowing rules of the form

> *event: condition* → *action*

The event (or possibly events) triggers the rule, but the rule does not fire unless the condition, which checks the state part of the system's memory, is also true. The event is reset by default, but the state attributes are unchanged, unless they are explicitly set by the action. As well as changing the memory state, the action may itself generate new events, which may then trigger further rules.

Concurrent dialog elements may be represented easily using production systems as many rules may be active at the same time. For example, we can describe the bold/italic/underline dialog box of Figure 16.5, using mixed event/state production rules. We have three attributes:

> **Bold:**   { off, on }
> **Italic:**   { off, on }
> **Underline:** { off, on }

There are also three possible events, depending on which style the user clicks over: *select-bold*, *select-italic*, *select-under*. The six rules defining the dialog box are then

> *select-bold:*   **Bold**=off   →   **Bold**=on
> *select-bold:*   **Bold**=on   →   **Bold**=off
> *select-italic:* **Italic**=off   →   **Italic**=on
> *select-italic:* **Italic**=on   →   **Italic**=off
> *select-under:* **Underline**=off →   **Underline**=on
> *select-under:* **Underline**=on   →   **Underline**=off

These are (although somewhat uninteresting) exactly what one would expect, and, unlike STNs, the number of rules only increases linearly with the number of toggles. If there are n toggles, then there will be $2n$ rules – substantially better than networks with 2^n states!

Also, escapes can be handled by having a rule of the form

> *escape-key:*   →   *reset-action*

where 'reset-action' involves setting all state attributes to some standard value. Because of the continuous activity of each rule, this escape rule can fire at any stage of the dialog, whenever the user hits the escape key.

Although production rules are good at handling concurrency, they are not so good at sequential dialogs. The polyline drawing is a case in point. We want the user to perform actions in order: select 'line', click at first point, click at any number of intermediate points (including none) and then double click at the end point. However, to represent this simple sequence using a production system, we need to keep track of the current place in the sequence using some 'state' variable. In the examples this was the state attribute **Line-state** in the PPS description and the events `start-line` and `rest-line` in the event-oriented rules. This representation of sequence is both awkward to 'code' and difficult to analyze.

Where production rules are used as the dialog description within a UIMS or other prototyping tool, various extensions to the simple forms described are used. Variables are added to the state to describe numeric values such as the mouse position. We saw this in CCT with the 'binding' of the variables %LINE and %COL. Different precedence rules are used to decide which of several production rules, which could potentially fire, will fire first. This enables help systems and pre-emptive dialog boxes to be programmed. For example, in a word processor, we may give rules for the help system higher priority than those for the normal system. Hence an event, such as a cursor movement, which would normally refer to the movement of the cursor in the document, would instead be 'caught' by the rules for the help system.

16.4.3 CSP and event algebras

We have seen notations such as STNs which are very good at handling sequential dialog, but weak on concurrency, and production rules which are good at the opposite. The problem of dealing with both sequential and concurrent behavior is common to many other areas of computing, such as telecommunications protocols and concurrent programming. We have already seen how one notation, Harel's state charts, which was designed with such complex systems in mind, has been used in interface design. *Process algebras* are a class of formal notations which have been developed to handle similar situations. One of these, *CSP* (*Communicating Sequential Processes*), has been adopted for dialog specification as part of several formalisms, including Alexander's *SPI* [10] and Abowd's *Agents* [1].

The CSP notation is used because it is able to specify concurrency and sequence equally well, and because of its readability. We consider again the drawing tool from Figure 16.1, which demonstrates sequence and choice. The CSP description is as follows:

```
Draw-menu  = ( select-circle? → Do-circle
                    [] select-line? → Do-line )
Do-circle  = click? → set-center → click?
                    → draw-circle → skip
```

```
Do-line     = Start-line ; Rest-line
Start-line  = click? → first-point → skip
Rest-line   = ( click? → next-point → Rest-line
                [] double-click? → last-point → skip )
```

The events marked with a question mark are the user's mouse actions, the rest being internal system events. The description is built using four symbols '=' meaning definition, '→' event sequence (or guard), ';' process sequence and [] choice. The names in the dialog denote *events* (all lower case) or *processes* (initial upper case). The processes roughly correspond to non-terminals in a grammar and are used both for structuring the dialog description and also to give named points to go back to in recursion (for example, Rest-line).

The definition of Do-circle is a pure sequence. When the system executes Do-circle, it first takes a user mouse click, then does an internal event, set-centre, to record the mouse position, accepts a second click, draws the circle and is finished (shown by the special process symbol **skip**). Do-line is a sequence too, but has been written using the process sequencing symbol ';'. This is used between two processes, as opposed to '→' which is used after an event.

For an example of choice, look at the first line: Draw-menu is defined to be a choice of two options, a circle or a line. The choice is made by considering the events that start the sequences either side of the choice ([]), select-circle? and select-line?. The first event to happen determines the choice. If the user does select-circle?, that is selects the 'circle' option on the menu, then the Do-circle process is executed. Alternatively, if the user selects the line option (select-line?), the system executes Do-line.

The Do-line process begins by executing Start-line, which gets the initial point on the line, and then executes Rest-line getting one or more further points for the polyline. Rest-line is the only *recursive* definition. If we read through its definition, we have a choice. If the user double clicks, then the polyline is drawn and the process is finished. Alternatively, if the point is only single clicked, then it is processed (next-point) and the system repeats Rest-line.

So far this is pretty much like a BNF description but with slightly different operator symbols and names for things. The new operator is || indicating parallel composition. If we have two processes P and Q then P||Q is the *interleaving* of P and Q. To see the use of this operator, we consider again the dialog box example. We code the individual toggles:

```
Bold-toggle    = select-bold? → bold-on
                     → select-bold? → bold-off
                        → Bold-toggle
Italic-toggle  = select-italic? → italic-on
                     → select-italic? → italic-off
                        → Italic-toggle
Under-toggle   = select-under? → under-on
                     → select-under? → under-off
                        → Under-toggle
```

The event `select-bold?` represents the user selecting the bold toggle with a mouse. So, the process `Bold-toggle` then turns the bold style on and off with alternate selections. The italic and underline options behave similarly. The dialog box as a whole can then be represented as the parallel composition of the individual toggles:

```
Dialog-box
        = Bold-toggle || Italic-toggle || Under-toggle
```

Concurrent processes can also be used as a way of organizing the internal structure of the interface. For example, returning to the drawing tool, we may decide that we would like to allow keyboard shortcuts activated by the Alt key. As the line and circle options can be operated by the mouse or by the keyboard, we have a process for each. The mouse process simply waits for the user to select one or other menu option, and then performs an internal event depending on the choice. The keyboard process monitors the Alt key, and performs the same internal events depending on whether the user enters 'Alt-C' or 'Alt-L':

```
Mouse    = ( select-circle? → int-sel-circle → Mouse
             [] select-line? → int-sel-line → Mouse )
Keyboard = alt-key-down? → ( Alt ; Keyboard )
Alt      = ( alt-key-up? → skip
             [] c-key? → int-sel-circle → Alt
             [] l-key? → int-sel-line → Alt )
```

So an `int-sel-circle` event may occur either because the circle option is selected from the menu or because the user typed `Alt-C`. The existing definition of `Draw-menu` expects to be activated by the user's mouse selections directly, so this must be modified to accept these new internal events:

```
Draw-menu = ( int-sel-circle → Do-circle
              [] int-sel-line → Do-line )
```

The three processes can now be run in parallel:

```
Mouse || Keyboard || Draw-menu
```

Note that the events `int-sel-circle` and `int-sel-line` are used to *communicate*, sending messages from the `Mouse` and `Keyboard` processes to the `Draw-menu` process. However, although this direction of causality is obvious from the context, it is not immediately apparent from the notation. The only clue is that the events form the guards of the choice operator in the `Draw-menu` process, but that is not an infallible indication. The reason for this ambiguity is that CSP does not recognize causality; events are simply *synchronization* points. There are times when such an interpretation is useful, but in most dialog descriptions the causality is important. One way to avoid this problem is to match events in pairs, as is done in some other process algebras writing, for instance, `int-sel-line!` for the sending of an event and `int-sel-line?` for the receiving of it. This loses us the special decoration for direct user input, but these may be listed separately. Alternatively, if the notation is to be typeset rather than in straight ASCII, one can use other pairs, such as $x \uparrow$ and $x \downarrow$ for send and receive.

16.4.4 Parametrized and dynamic interleaved dialog structure

In many interfaces, the possible screen displays can be easily enumerated. The order in which such screens are produced and the detailed contents of fields may differ, but the basic screen designs are finite. Other systems are more anarchic, especially multi-windowed interfaces where user interaction may dynamically cause the creation of new windows. Thus there is a clear difference between static and dynamic screen presentations.

A similar and related issue arises at the level of the dialog structure. Some dialogs can be described by a finite set of dialog states between which the user may move, whereas others are far more complex. Clearly, multi-windowed systems will have a correspondingly dynamic dialog structure. Perhaps the dialogs within each window have a fairly static structure, but the number of such interleaved dialogs varies at run time.

The notations we have discussed can only address structurally static dialogs. Such notations would not (without modification) allow the expression of general multi-windowed dialogs. However, many WIMP-based systems do not require this level of generality. In addition, many run-time systems may only allow essentially static structures, for instance prototypes programmed in HyperCard (except for very complex scripts) or under most forms-based systems.

This issue of dynamic dialog structure is often linked with that of parametrization. An instantiation of a parametrized dialog often involves the creation of new screen resources. For example, we could imagine extending CSP to allow

```
Multi-window-editor
       = new-name(name)  →
               ( Edit-window(name) [] Multi-window-editor )
```

The instantiation of Edit_window(name) implies that a new window and dialog within that window would be initiated.

Both parametrization and dynamic dialog structures make it more difficult to analyze the dialog. A static notation has a sparser (and fundamentally less expressive) domain of application but allows a far greater degree of automatic or manual manipulation.

Thus, even where a notation allows parametrized or dynamic dialogs, they should be used sparingly. If there is a choice, the dialog should be encoded using the more static forms of representation.

16.5 DIALOG SEMANTICS

If the purpose of a dialog description is simply to communicate between designers, or as a 'tool for thought' early in design, it may be sufficient to annotate the formal dialog with the intended meaning of the actions, or to leave it to the reader to infer the semantics. However, if the dialog description is to serve as a formal specification, perhaps part of a contract, or for running as a prototype, there must be some way to describe formally the semantics of the dialog. The dialog notations we have seen more or less clearly describe the structure of the dialog. We must now move on to meaning.

There are two aspects to the dialog semantics, inward toward the application, and outward toward the presentation. The semantic part of the dialog should serve as a link between the two, performing as little as possible itself. Look back through the examples in this chapter and ask yourself how one knows that, for example, the lines drawn by the drawing tool are at the points indicated by the user's mouse location.

We will discuss three different approaches to linking dialog and semantics:

notation-specific semantics – special-purpose semantic forms designed as part of a dialog notation;

links to programming languages – attaching pieces of programming language code to the dialog;

links to specification notations – similar, but where a formal specification notation is used.

We will also discuss some issues which arise concerning the link between dialog and semantics.

16.5.1 Notation-specific semantics

Augmented transition networks (ATNs) are a form of state transition network (see Section 16.3.1). In the ATN, the system is assumed to hold a set of *registers*, storage locations which the transition network can set and test. Recall that the arcs in an STN may be labeled with the event that causes the transition and the system response. In an ATN this is extended. The arcs have a condition as well as the event; the condition can refer to the system's registers and the arc is only followed if the condition is true and the event occurs. The system response is augmented to include not only feedback and display, but also the setting of registers. These registers can be used simply to describe more complex dialogs, for example a cash dispenser which retains your card after three wrong numbers. They may also be used to communicate with the application and to hold values from the mouse.

Production rules come in many variants and the link to the semantics is equally varied. Often the system's memory contains variables which can be used by the system to store input values such as the mouse position, and can then be examined by the conditions and actions of the rules. These variables may also be used to communicate with the underlying application, or the functions of this may be invoked directly by special forms of action. For instance, the following is a production rule which, when the user clicks within a target region, puts a dot at the mouse location and invokes the application routine 'another_point':

click_at(x,y) → dot_at(x,y), **call** another_point(x,y)

16.5.2 Links to programming languages

Often dialog notations are 'attached' to a conventional programming language. For example, *input tools*, a regular expression-based notation, uses C to express the dialog semantics [355]. The input tool description consists of 'tool' definitions, including regular expressions intermingled with normal C code. For example, the tool to read a number (from Plasmeijer [292]) begins as follows:

```
tool number
{ char buf[80];
  int index;
  int positive;
  input { ( digit* + sign; digit; digit* ) ; return }
  tool digit
  { input { key:| key_c>='0' && key_c<='9' | }
    if ( index < 79 ) /* append character to string */
    { buf[index] = key_c;
      index = index + 1;
      echo(key_c);
    }
  }
  tool sign
  ...
  tool return
  { input { key:| key_c -= '\n' | }
    ...
  }
  ...

}
```

Input tools uses its own regular expression syntax and has additional operators. Sequencing is denoted by semi-colon ';' rather than simple juxtaposition, and the '+' symbol is used for choice (like '|' in BNF). The expression 'key: |*condition*|' is a postfix guard: the expression only matches if the condition is true.

The specific input tools' expressions are as follows. The keyword `tool` introduces a new tool, which is similar to a non-terminal in a BNF grammar, and the regular expression which it denotes is enclosed in the `input` statement. The tools are arranged in a scoped hierarchy, so that the `digit`, `sign` and `return` tools are private to the `number` tool. The call to `echo` simply echoes the character back to the user. Finally, `key` is a primitive tool which matches a single character read from the keyboard; the actual character read is stored in the global variable `key_c`.

Notice how the subtool `digit` communicates its results back to the main tool using shared variable `buf`. This and the way it accepts values from the `key` tool are rather untidy. Such messiness is not just an aspect of this particular notation: alternative regular expression-based notations are even worse!

16.5.3 Links to formal specification

Alexander's executable specification/prototyping language *SPI* (*Specifying and Prototyping Interaction*) is divided into two parts: *eventCSP*, a dialog notation based closely on CSP, and *eventISL*, which describes the dialog semantics. The CSP part is as described in Section 16.4.3, but for each event there is a corresponding event definition in eventISL. EventISL is partly standardized and partly dependent on the 'host' language chosen. The first host language was *me-too*, a formal specification notation based on VDM, but a C variant is also available. The part which is independent of the host language consists of several elements: a clause giving the global variables used and updated by the event, a precondition expressing when the event can occur, and output and input parts. The host language part simply describes the updates and the precise outputs.

Consider the following eventCSP description of a login sequence:

```
Login   = login-mess → get-name → Passwd
Passwd = passwd-mess → ( invalid → Login
                           [ ] valid → Session)
Session = ( logout → Login
          [ ] command → execute → Session )
```

A typical unsuccessful login sequence might be

```
login: fred
passwd: b9fGk              (invisible)
Sorry bad user-id/password
```

We will not consider the detailed semantics for the commands during the session, but will give the eventISL descriptions of the other events. The two events login-mess and get-name handle the first line of the above dialog:

```
event: login-mess =
     prompt: true
     out: "login:"
event: get-name =
uses: input
     set: user-id = input
```

The first event prints the prompt 'login:' (the **out:** clause) and says that user input is required (the **prompt:** clause). This user input is stored in a special variable called 'input'. The second event **uses** the input (which will be set to the name the user enters) and merely sets the variable 'user-id' to it. Note that 'user-id' is **set** to a new value by the event, but any previous value is not **used**.

The sequence for getting the password is similar except that there are two options depending on whether the user has typed a valid password or not:

```
event: passwd-mess =
     prompt: invis
     out: "passwd:"
```

      event: valid =
      uses: input, user-id, passwd-db
            when: passwd-id = passwd-db(user-id)
      event: invalid =
      uses: input, user-id, passwd-db
            when: passwd-id ≠ passwd-db(user-id)
            out: "Sorry bad user-id/password"

The password prompt is identical to the login prompt except that no echoing is required. However, the last two events demonstrate two additional features. As well as the user input variable, they also use the variable 'user-id', which was set by the get-name event, and the variable 'passwd-db'. This is assumed to be a database of passwords, so that 'passwd-db(user-id)' is the correct password for the user. The two events also have a '**when**' clause. This is a *precondition*, which specifies what must be true for the event to occur. So the 'valid' event can only occur when the user has typed a correct password and 'invalid' only occurs when it is incorrect.

    Notice that, like input tools, eventISL is heavily dependent on the use of global variables to pass information between events. This reliance on global variables in many dialog notations strikes against all good software engineering practice. At least in SPI the globals used and updated are made explicit and make tracing the effects of events somewhat easier, but still not straightforward. Dialog notations often include effective structuring mechanisms (hierarchical networks, non-terminals in grammars, processes in CSP); it is a pity that these are not mirrored in their semantic effects.

Worked exercise   *Using CSP, construct a dialog for one user with an application in one window of a multi-window system. Using this first general CSP description, provide a CSP description for a multi-window interaction using the parallel operator (||). How does this approach handle interference and information sharing between windows?*

Answer   The intention of this exercise is not so much to produce a clean description, but to show how complex the business of talking about multi-window applications is. Most interface designers and programmers do not have to worry about designing the windowing system itself. However, it does help one to appreciate why areas like cut–paste buffers can behave oddly.

First of all, we will give two simple applications, a calculator and a database, and then we will look at putting them together.

Calculator
In fact, calculator is a bit pretentious – this is really an adder! The user types in either 'quit' which exits the application, 'zero' which resets the adder to zero or a number which is added to the running total.

    Adder = add-prompt → (quit? → **skip**
                       [ ] zero? → show-sum → Adder
                       [ ] number? → show-sum → Adder)

The semantic description is given in eventISL (Section 16.5.3).

> **event:** add-prompt =
> >   **prompt:** true
> >   **out:** "next number"
>
> **event:** quit? =
> **uses:** input
> >   **when:** input = "quit"
>
> **event:** zero? =
> **uses:** input
> >   **when:** input = "zero"
> >   **set:** sum = 0
> >   **out:** "reset"
>
> **event:** number? =
> **uses:** input, sum
> >   **when:** is-number(input)
> >   **set:** sum = sum + input
>
> **event:** show-sum =
> **uses:** sum
> >   **out:** sum

Database

Another simple application could be a database, where the user actions are either 'quit', 'set *key value*', or 'find *key*'.

> Database = db-prompt → (quit? → **skip**
> >   [ ] set? → Get-key; Get-val
> >   [ ] get? → Get-key; print-val)
>
> Get-key   = set-key-prompt → get-key?
> Get-val   = set-val-prompt → get-val?

We will not bother with the semantic descriptions of the prompt events, or quit which is the same as for the adder. The descriptions of 'set?' and 'get?' are also similar to those for 'quit?', so are omitted.

> **event:** get-key? =
> **uses:** input
> >   **set:** key = input
>
> **event:** get-val? =
> **uses:** input, dbase, key
> >   **set:** dbase = db-update(dbase,key,input)
>
> **event:** print-val =
> **uses:** dbase, key
> >   **out:** db-lookup(dbase,key)

The functions 'db-update' and 'db-lookup' are assumed to add a new key-value pair and to look up the value associated with a particular key, respectively.

Multiple windows

Having got these two descriptions, putting them together is quite simple:

> Window-system = Adder || Database

However, it would be considerably more complex if we wanted two adders. Although this sounds a bit odd, if it were two text-editing windows or two spreadsheet windows, this would be quite reasonable. We might attempt to do it simply as

Window-system = Adder || Adder

But this would not work as the event names and the variables in the semantic description are global. The windows would both add to the same sum and it would be random as to which window responded to particular user events. This is an example of unintentional interference. The only way around this is to copy completely the description of Adder with new names for most of the events and variables.

You might also look for ways of addressing deliberate sharing. For example, a common cut–paste buffer can be achieved using shared variables, and explicit dependencies between dialogs can use internal events, as described in Section 16.4.3.

The modified dialog below has an extra command 'copy' in the database, which is like 'get' except it also puts the value from the database into a shared buffer and invokes the 'buffer-ready' event, which tells the adder to add the value in the buffer to its running total.

Database = db-prompt → (quit? → skip
                          [ ] set? → Get-key; Get-val
                          [ ] get? → Get-key; print-val
                          [ ] copy? → Get-key; Send-val)
Get-key = set-key-prompt → get-key?
Get-val = set-val-prompt → get-val?
Send-val = set-buffer → buffer-ready

The event 'copy?' is again a simple test of the input and 'buffer-ready' is described below with the modified adder.

event: set-buffer =
uses: dbase, key
        set: val-buffer = db-lookup(dbase,key)
        out: db-lookup(dbase,key)

The adder is modified to respond to the event from the database window.

Adder = add-prompt →
         (quit? → skip
         [ ] zero? → show-sum → Adder
         [ ] number? → show-sum → Adder)
         [ ] buffer-ready → show-sum → Adder)
event: buffer-ready =
uses: val-buffer, sum
        set: sum = sum + val-buffer

If you are working in a group, you could discuss further issues, such as how to represent the changes in keyboard focus. (This would probably require an extra keyboard multiplexer process.)

16.5.4 Distributed and centralized dialog description

If the dialog is described by a pure grammar, with no semantic element, then it is easy to look at the dialog syntax in isolation, and understand and evaluate it. At the other extreme, if we take a typical interactive program, aspects of the dialog will be distributed throughout the code, making it difficult to trace the course of a typical interaction.

A notation that wishes to describe the semantics of dialog as well as its syntax can try to retain the advantages of a simple syntactic description, by separating the semantic and syntactic parts, allowing the dialog designer to examine the dialog syntax in isolation. This is a *centralized dialog description*. Alexander's SPI is exemplary of this approach to the extent that it has separate sublanguages for the two parts. This also demonstrates another advantage of this approach. The same form of the syntactic dialog description may often be suitable both for high-level analysis and automatic coding (or run-time interpretation). The semantic description, on the other hand, is likely to have a different form when generated for specification or prototyping than for inclusion in a production system. Separating the two allows reuse of the dialog description with different semantic parts, reflecting differing uses of the specification.

Alternatively, the notation can choose to put associated parts of the syntax and semantics together, as in input-tools. This has the advantage that parts of the interaction can be examined in detail, allowing the evaluation of the syntax and semantics in tandem. It also has advantages of abstraction: associated semantics and syntax can be packaged together. Its disadvantage is that, like the typical program, it has a *distributed dialog description*. One has to examine diverse pieces of the specification in order to obtain an understanding of the large-scale flow of the interaction.

The two approaches are not fundamentally incompatible. Given a notation of the former type, it would be quite easy to separate parts of the dialog syntax and present them with the associated parts of the semantic description. Similarly, with some distributed notations it is possible to go through extracting the parts specifying the dialog syntax and look at these together. For instance, with input-tools one could extract all the `input` clauses which contain the regular expression subtool syntax. These would then form the centralized dialog for analysis.

16.5.5 Maximizing syntactic description

Extracting the dialog structure is only possible with some notations. The reason why it is not always possible, and is not usually possible for general interactive programs, is itself an important issue. Usually it is possible to isolate the parts that are responsible for input and output (identifiable by `print`, `read`, etc.). However, how these fit together into a dialog is masked by the surrounding code. In particular, what would be syntactic in a dedicated dialog grammar description may be coded semantically. For instance, in eventCSP, one could write

```
Text-editor = mouse-press → set-selection
            [] key-press → add-char-to-text
```

In a programming language one might have

```
ev = read_event();
if ( ev.type == EV_mouse_press )
            set_selection(ev.pos);
else        add_char_to_text(ev.char);
```

In the second version an analyzer would have to recognize that the boolean expression `ev.type == EV_mouse_press` corresponded to a simple dialog decision rather than a deep semantic decision in the application.

Even more problems may arise in production systems, window managers or UIMS with *external control*, that is where the application is invoked on each event from the user (see Chapter 8). In these systems, the most obvious form of dialog is completely user controlled. If the designer wishes to provide any control over the input syntax then a 'program counter' must be explicitly coded. So, for instance, if we were operating under a window manager that calls a user routine `process_event`, we might have the following code for text editor selection (written in C):

```
enum { normal, selected } mode;
process_event( event ev )
{
  switch ( ev.type ) {
    case button_down:
      ...
      if ( in_text ( ev.pos ) ) {
        mode = selecting;
        mark_selection_start(ev.pos);
      }
      ...
    case button_up:
      ...
      if ( in_text ( ev.pos ) && mode == selecting ) {
        mode = normal;
        mark_selection_end(ev.pos);
      }
      ...
    case mouse_move:
      ...
      if ( mode == selecting ) {
        extend_selection(ev.pos);
      }
      ...
  } /* end of switch */
} /* end of process_event */
```

The dialog for the selection is distributed widely over the event loop, and further it is only by keeping track of the `mode` variable that we can see that they are linked at all. The code is for a mythical but quite typical window manager.

In each case, the problem is that elements of the dialog can be given either a syntactic or a semantic form. Obviously, more complex elements of the dialog will require complex computed decisions, but where possible, the more syntactic the dialog description, the easier it will be to analyze. This concept underlies much of database normalization procedures which try to move the decision as to whether an update is acceptable from the semantic realm to the syntactic.

16.6   DIALOG ANALYSIS AND DESIGN

In this section, we will look at several ways in which dialogs can be analyzed in order to discover potential usability problems, considering principles such as those described in Chapter 7. We will discuss these dialog properties under three headings. The first focusses on user actions and whether they are adequately specified and consistent. The second concerns the dialog states, including those you want to get to and those you do not. Finally, we will look at presentation and lexical issues, what things look like and what keys do what. Some of these properties have equivalents in Chapters 17 and 18, where we discuss models of interactive systems that include semantics.

16.6.1 Action properties

Look back to the STNs describing a graphics program (Figures 16.1–16.3) at the beginning of Section 16.3. There are four types of user action in these diagrams: selecting from the main menu (graphics, text or paint), selecting a pop-up menu choice (circle or line), clicking on a point on the drawing surface and double clicking a point on the drawing surface.

If we look at the different dialog states, we see that for any state only one or two actions are mentioned. Sometimes this is because some actions are impossible. For example, the pop-up menu choices can only happen while a pop-up menu is displayed. So, we do not need to worry about the user doing 'select "line"' from the *Main menu* or while in state *Line 1*. But what happens if we click on the drawing surface whilst at the *Main menu*, or try to select something from the main menu whilst in the middle of the drawing a circle, say in state *Circle 2*? The dialog description is not *complete*.

If you take an actual system and try such odd combinations it is likely that the dialog description starts to explode in complexity, just as in the example of the digital watch. It was reasonable to have a partial description for the purposes of instruction, and for discussing the general dialog structure. But we need to make sure that these odd chains of events do not have disastrous consequences. Unfortunately, in practice, it is at best the implementor and, at worst, the user who discovers such behavior. This is wrong. It is the responsibility of the designer to foresee just how the system behaves in unforeseen circumstances.

Surely it is a contradiction in terms to design for behavior under *unforeseen* circumstances? Yes, but the presence of a dialog description can make previously unforeseen events become apparent. Just as with the graphics STNs, we can, in general, list all the possible actions and then at each dialog state look for 'forgotten events'. This can be done with any notation, but some are easier than others. In particular, it may be extremely difficult to perform such an analysis of a production rule system without automatic help. Furthermore, the structure of production rules may mean that you accidentally specify behavior – what you say may not be what you mean.

For each unforeseen state/action pair, the designer ought to decide (or at least check during testing) what the behavior will be. The simplest rule is to decide that all unspecified behavior will have no effect (except possibly a warning) – 'when in doubt do nowt'. If this rule is not followed, more care is required. Imagine the user is drawing a polyline, but, before double clicking on the last point, selects a new option from the main menu. One option is to discard the partially completed line. If the user had clicked on only one point, this would be the only sensible option. However, if he had just carefully selected 20 points and simply forgotten to double click on the last one, tempers may get frayed. A better option would be to treat the new selection as confirming the partially completed shape whenever this is at all sensible.

As well as finding that some states have forgotten actions, we may discover that some states have several arcs labeled with the same action. That is, the specification is not *deterministic* for that action. This can happen in several ways. It may be an accident. For example, if we are using a hierarchical STN with escapes, as in Figure 16.9, we may find that we have used an action as an escape at a high level, and for some other purpose at a lower level. Similarly, when using production rules, one may accidentally find that two rules are active at the same time triggered by the same event. The formalism may have default rules to deal with such eventualities. For example, both production rules may fire, or there may be a precedence between rules, the one with the highest precedence being chosen. Similarly, the STN may take the innermost arc. However, this is precisely where you should check that this default behavior is what you want.

Sometimes, this non-determinism reflects semantic decisions in the system. For example, a grammar for a bank automated teller machine (ATM) might look like

```
atm        ::= put-in-card get-number
get-number ::= digit digit digit digit
                        get-money return-card atm
           | digit digit digit digit return-card atm
           | digit digit digit digit atm
digit      ::= 0 | 1 | 2 | 3 | 4 | 5 | 6 | 7 | 8 | 9
get-money  ::=  ...
```

The two different options depend on whether the digits entered are the correct PIN. In the first case they are and the user gets some money out. In the second, the number is wrong and the card is returned. In the last case, too many wrong numbers have been used and the card is retained. Deciding which of the branches to take is a *semantic* issue, not one of dialog structure.

Both *completeness* and *determinism* can be automatically checked in a dialog description. However, the designer must go through the warnings thrown up by such an analysis and decide whether they represent a problem or are deliberate.

A third property, which cannot be automatically checked as easily, is *consistency*. We expect the same action in different circumstances to do roughly the same thing. For example, a user may get used to the 'tab' key moving the cursor eight spaces to the right. However, in a text entry area of a dialog box, most text-editing keys may behave as normal, but 'tab' may move to the next dialog box entry. Such examples of inconsistency can cause obvious problems for the user. It is not possible to automate checks for consistency on a dialog description. First, this is because consistency also involves the semantics: similar actions should *do similar things*. Secondly, the interpretation of *similar* involves an understanding of what the user regards as similar.

However, by listing all dialog states and actions, a dialog description can help the analyst to go through the various combinations. In particular, the analyst can divide the states into major *modes* where actions may have different effects or be inactive. For example, in a word processor, the search/replace key may not be active in the 'print' dialog box.

16.6.2 State properties

The states in a dialog represent points where the user has obtained information or where the system has done something useful. So, the user wants at least to be able to get to a desired dialog state and ideally to be able to get there easily. In general, we can think of properties of this sort as *reachability*.

A basic check of any dialog is whether it is fully connected. That is, for any two states is there a sequence of actions which will take the user from the first state to the second? Looking once more at Figures 16.1 and 16.3, we can see that, in so far as it is defined, the dialog is connected. For example, suppose we were in state *Circle 1*, but wished we were back at the graphics submenu (state *Menu*). We can click and then double click anywhere on the drawing surface, taking us to the end of the graphics submenu STN and back to the *Main menu*. From here, we can select the 'graphics' option and get to where we want.

However, one suggested 'improvement' was to alter the circle drawing to allow multiple circles. The amendment was shown in Figure 16.2. Unfortunately, this destroys the connectivity of the dialog. There is no way out of the circle dialog; one can only fill up the screen with zillions of circles. This is a fairly obvious problem, but it is easy for more complex cases to slip through. For example, one of the authors was once shown a form-based financial planning system. Some inconsistent information was entered on one page of the form, which was allowed by the system. But, because of this, a later page was repeatedly rejected. There was no valid user input for that page, but the system would not allow you to return to the incorrectly filled page until the later one was accepted – *impasse*.

Reachability checking can be entirely automatic, but care must be taken to distinguish which choices are user controlled and which are system controlled. This is one reason why we emphasized the importance of maximizing syntactic description in a dialog notation. In general, we cannot assume that the system will take the paths that we wish. So, for example, given the ATM dialog, we cannot assume that the user can get from the `atm` state to the `get-money` state, as this depends on the system accepting the PIN. An automatic tool can show where such unreachable points are, but the designer must say whether or not these are acceptable.

A special case of reachability is *reversability*, a form of *undo*. That is, the user wants to get to the previous state. For various reasons, some evident in Chapter 17, a dedicated 'undo' button or command is probably best dealt with as a meta-dialog feature. However, we can analyze the existing commands to see how easy it is to recover one's position in the dialog using standard commands. In effect, this is what we described at the beginning of this subsection. We were on the *Circle 1* state of Figure 16.1, and wanted to get back to the graphics pop-up menu. Indeed, this was possible, but rather long winded. Any fully reachable dialog will be able to reverse actions, but it may not be easy to do so. One form of reversability analysis is to take each action and label it with the number of arcs that must be traversed in order to get back. Actions with large reversing costs are worthy of closer scrutiny: perhaps the dialog ought to be redesigned to allow easier return paths, or possibly we may rely on a generic undo mechanism.

Note that this dialog-level reversability is *not* a true undo. For example, when the user goes from the *Circle 1* state back to the graphics menu, this leaves a circle behind on the screen. Thus the dialog state has been undone, but the full system state has not. Reasoning about undo at this level requires a model of the system, and will be discussed in Chapter 17. There is also a corresponding more complete form of reachability in this setting.

So, there are some states that the user wants to be in, movement to which the dialog ought to make easy. But there are other states, such as that where the hard disk is being formatted, which should be deliberately difficult to reach. Again, knowing which states are 'dangerous' cannot be determined automatically; it depends on the system semantics and the designer's judgment. However, having labeled the dangerous states (colored them red), we can perform analyses on the dialog to determine how easy it is to get to these dangerous states. This labeling process may involve duplicating states which otherwise appear similar at the dialog level.

If we discover that a dangerous state is too easily reached, then we can attempt to prevent accidents. To do this, many systems initiate a dialog with the user when a lot of information may be lost, for example

```
C>del test\*.*
Are you sure (Y/N)?
```

This in itself is not enough to prevent mistakes as frequent requests for confirmation may make the user habitually type 'Y' after every command. The moves to dangerous

Automatic analysis

Checking dialog properties by hand is likely to be tedious and error prone. Although some properties require judgment, others can be verified using automatic analysis tools.

One such support tool is *HyperDoc* [344], shown in Figure 16.17. The screen shows part of the description for a JVC video recorder. The top half of the screen is a drawing of the interface. The buttons on the drawing are active – the simulation runs when they are pressed. On the bottom left, we can see part of the dialog description. This describes the transitions from the state 'playPause'. For example, if the user presses the 'Operate' button, the state will change to 'offTapeIn'.

The designer can simply use this as a prototyping tool, by constructing the dialog description and then experimenting by clicking buttons on the top part of the screen. In addition, the tool can construct a graph of states and transitions from the dialog descriptions of each state. This graph is then analyzed using standard graph algorithms for properties such as reachability.

One problem with HyperDoc is that it constructs the complete graph of all states. However, recall the way *combinatorial explosion* can occur, meaning that quite a simple interface can have enormous numbers of states. This can exceed not only our ability to draw the states on paper, but also the ability of a computer to compute properties of the states. To avoid this problem other researchers have worked with *symbolic verification* which checks properties based on descriptions of states and transitions, rather than enumerating every state [8].

A tool similar to HyperDoc is available on our website, so you can try it out for yourself.

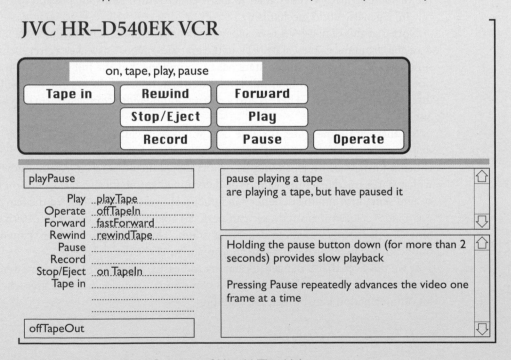

Figure 16.17 HyperDoc. Courtesy of Harold Thimbleby

states must be different from other sequences – that is, *not* consistent! The moves between safe states and dangerous states really need detailed examination by the analyst, as one must decide whether a particular path can easily be taken by accident or not. We will see in the remaining discussion that this is intimately connected to the presentation and lexical design of the system.

16.6.3 Presentation and lexical properties

It is often claimed that dialog design should be independent of the detailed design of the presentation and lexical details of the interface. That is, one begins by deciding on the functionality of the system, and then, possibly making use of cognitive models or task analysis, one designs the dialog to perform those functions. Finally, one designs the visual presentation of the system and the lexical bindings between keypresses and mouse movement and the more abstract dialog actions.

In fact, the dialogs described in this chapter have often involved detailed key bindings on their labels. For example, the STN for the graphics system in Figure 16.1 has arcs with labels such as 'click on point' or 'double click'. It could be argued that this is a fault in these descriptions. They should instead say things like 'enter a point', 'enter last point'. These actions could then be achieved with mouse clicks, or by typing coordinates.

For higher-level descriptions, such as the JSD diagram in Figure 16.14, this form of argument is valid; it would be inappropriate, at least in early design, to decide what keys or menu selections will move you to the 'add employee record' subdialog. However, later in design, and when we consider detailed dialog, such a position becomes less tenable.

In Section 16.6.1, we discussed the labeling of *modes* in which user actions may have different interpretations. It is generally regarded as good practice to minimize the number of modes. However, where modes are used they should be visually distinct. That is, one ought to be able to tell which mode one is in from the computer display. So, the visual presentation and the form of the dialog are intimately connected. As well as major modes, one can compare any two dialog states, and ask whether they can be distinguished from the display. If not, this may indicate a potential trouble-spot where the user can get confused. These are both *visibility* requirements, and similar issues of *observability* and *predictability* will arise in Chapter 17.

The visibility issues are, in principle, one way the dialog can be designed independently of the presentation, but can constrain the form of it. In practice, the two are more intermingled. However, there are further areas where the dialog is even more intimately tied to presentation.

Different types of interfaces have very different dialog styles. The normal dialog form of a command-based interface is verb–object, for example 'print fred'. However, mouse-based systems often have an object–verb syntax, for example select a file icon and then select 'print' from a menu. Although it is possible to mingle these styles, it is inadvisable as users expect to find a certain interface style with a particular medium. So, detailed dialog design must be dependent on the type of interface.

Furthermore, physical limitations may prohibit certain dialog structures. For example, the dialog for the digital watch (Figures 16.15 and 16.16) is designed with the restriction of only three buttons. A similar design for an on-screen alarm clock could make use of a full keyboard and thus have a completely different dialog. Similarly, the range of outputs, visual and aural, will restrict the dialog. If modes and states should be visually distinct, then the device's display must be able to distinguish these modes. Unfortunately, restricted input leads to a highly moded dialog. For example, for three buttons to control all the functions of a digital watch with alarm and stop watch requires many modes, of which the four major modes are only the beginning. But it is precisely those interfaces which have a limited input set which also have limited output, in particular consumer goods. It is thus no wonder that users often have trouble knowing what mode their video controller is in.

Dangerous states and key layout

The text editor being used for this passage has two main modes: an editing screen where you type and edit the document, and a menu screen, obtained by pressing the F1 function key. The STN for these modes is shown in Figure 16.18. The menu screen has several options including F2 to exit (and save), and F1 to return to the editing screen. Exiting will automatically save the text if it has been changed. However, this can be overridden by pressing the escape key in the main menu. This makes the system pretend that the text has not been changed until the next alteration.

Pressing the escape key in the main menu has *no* effect on the dialog, but the state of the system after this point can be thought of as dangerous. If the key has been pressed deliberately then all is well, but if there is any mistake, the user may lose the updated text. Figure 16.19 shows an STN with the dialog states duplicated to show the dangerous states (hatched). We want the dangerous states to be reachable, but they should be difficult to get to by accident. In fact, the really dangerous state is when we go to the hatched exit: if we return to the hatched edit state, then we are most likely to type a further editing command and the system becomes 'safe' again. Therefore we can see that the particularly dangerous sequence is 'F1–Esc–F2'. The question then is: can this be typed by accident? It is very similar to the standard exit and save sequence 'F1–F2', but users are unlikely to hit the escape key by accident – or are they?

Even knowing that you have a full keyboard and standard screen is not sufficient to design the dialog. The precise positioning can affect the usability of a particular dialog style. The text editor described above (Figures 16.18 and 16.19) was originally used on a computer with a separate

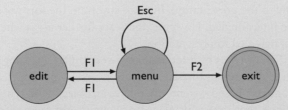

Figure 16.18 Main modes of text editor

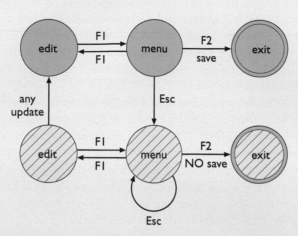

Figure 16.19 Revised STN with dangerous states

Figure 16.20 Dangerous function key layout

function keypad on the left of the keyboard. No problems were encountered with the 'dangerous' states of the system. However, the editor was later used on a system with a different keyboard layout. The function keys are set out in a line along the top of the keyboard, as in Figure 16.20, with the escape key right next to function keys F1 and F2! As we saw, the dangerous mistake is to hit the sequence 'F1–Esc–F2', which is similar to the exit and save sequence 'F1–F2'. With the original keyboard layout, this was an all but impossible mistake to make. However, on the new layout it is possible to hit the escape with the edge of your finger as you press down the function key F1. If this happens as you type the sequence 'F1–F2', then disaster. This scenario is easily predictable from the dialog structure and the physical layout – and it can happen, as the authors know!

16.7   SUMMARY

We saw, by example, how the dialog of a user interface can become unmanageable, and impossible to analyze, if we do not have a separate description. We have looked at two main classes of description: diagrammatic and textual. Diagrammatic notations included various forms of state transition network, Petri nets, Harel state charts, flow charts and JSD diagrams. Under textual notations, we considered grammars (regular expressions and BNF), production rules (event based and state based) and CSP.

We found that some very different notations were essentially equivalent: for example, JSD diagrams and regular expressions can describe exactly the same dialogs. However, we also saw that there were major differences in expressive power between different formalisms. For example, BNF grammars are able to deal with recursively nested dialogs and are thus more powerful than regular expressions or state transition networks.

One important difference in expressive power is whether or not the formalism can handle concurrent dialogs. We found that some notations favor sequential dialogs (for example, STNs) and some concurrent (for example, production rules), but few could handle both (the exceptions being Harel state charts and CSP). However, increased expressive power is not always desirable as it may mean a more complex and less easily understood description. The important point is to match the notation to the form of the desired dialog. Another important distinction was between state-oriented and event-oriented descriptions. This will be picked up in the next chapter.

Once we had a dialog description, we considered the connection between that dialog description and the description of the system semantics. We looked at examples where the dialog description is linked closely to a programming language and where it is linked to a more formal description. Two issues arose in this discussion. One was whether we want a centralized or a distributed dialog description; that is, should all the dialog be in one place and the semantics separate, or should the dialog be spread out with the associated semantics? The second issue concerned maximizing syntactic description. Where there is a choice, we should put things into the dialog description, where they can be analyzed automatically, rather than in the semantic description.

Finally, we looked at properties of dialogs. Action properties focus on user actions, and under this heading we considered completeness – are there any missing actions?; determinism – do any actions appear twice?; and consistency – do similar actions do similar things? The first two of these are amenable to partial automatic checking. State properties concern the ability of the user to move between dialog states. We considered reachability – whether we can reach any desired state – and reversability – a special case, whether we can get back to the last state. We noted that reversability at the dialog level is *not* undo as this involves the whole semantics of the system. Finally under state properties, we considered dangerous states, that is those we do not want to get into accidentally.

We found that presentation and lexical issues are *not* (as is commonly supposed) a separable issue from dialog design. We need to consider the visibility of modes and the style of interaction. Even the layout of keys and menu items can influence the likelihood of making serious errors.

EXERCISES

16.1 Complete the drawing tool STN in Figures 16.1 and 16.3 by writing dialog descriptions for the text and paint submenus. For the text submenu assume that there are three options: centered, left and right justified. The text is entered by clicking at a location in the drawing surface and then typing. You may initially assume that typing a line of text can be regarded as a single user action. But later try regarding each character typed as an action. The paint submenu has two options: a pencil for freehand drawing and a paint pot for flood filling. The former is performed by holding the mouse button down whilst moving the mouse about to draw the line. The paint pot is activated by simply clicking the mouse over the area to be filled.

16.2 Repeat the above exercise using different notations, grammars, production rules, JSD or CSP. You will need to specify the whole system from the main menu to the individual submenu selections such as circle drawing. Note the problems you have with each notation.

16.3 Develop the JSD diagram in Figure 16.14, expanding the various nodes until you get to basic operations such as 'prompt `"login"`' or 'user types in password'. Expand the 'delete employee' node using the dialog style as described in Figure 16.13, and use your imagination for the rest.

16.4 In the example of the digital watch in Section 16.3.8, what would be the dangerous states? Relate the lexical issues of the buttons for a digital watch to these dangerous states and provide some design advice. Does your own digital watch satisfy these criteria?

16.5 This exercise is based on the nuclear reactor scenario on the book website at: /e3/scenario/nuclear/

(a) Looking only at the STN diagrams in Figures 16.21 and 16.22 (that is, ignoring for now the meaning of the various actions), identify missing elements from the STNs. Taking into account the meaning of the actions, suggest possible corrections.

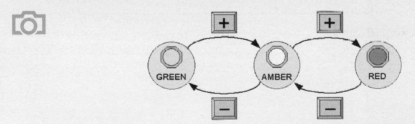

Figure 16.21   STN for alarm state

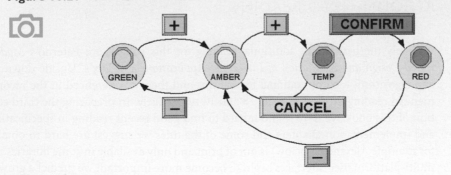

Figure 16.22   STN for revised alarm state

(b) Taking into account now the meaning of the various states and actions, explain why you believe the consultant suggested the change from the behavior in Figure 16.21 to that in Figure 16.22.

16.6 This exercise is based on the mobile phone scenario on the book website at: /e3/scenario/phone/

Figure 16.23 shows an STN for the simple mobile phone described in scenarios A and B on the web.

(a) Identify any missing transitions and suggest possible behavior that would be sensible for the user.

(b) Scenarios C and D demonstrate the additional behavior of the new phone. Update the STN in Figure 16.23 to add the new store and recall facilities of the new phone. Where there is not sufficient information in the scenarios choose suitable behavior. You can use ellipses (. . .) where you would expect major additional functionality (e.g. storing numbers); don't attempt to fully specify such additional functions. List and briefly describe and justify any such design decisions that are required or any other design issues that become apparent.

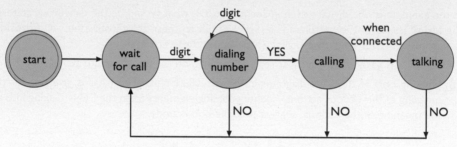

Figure 16.23   STN for original phone

RECOMMENDED READING

Probably the best recent additional reading for this subject are Paternó's *Model-Based Design and Evaluation of Interactive Applications* and Dix's 'Upside down As and algorithms – computational formalisms and theory', referenced in the recommended reading lists in Chapters 18 and 17 respectively. In preparing the third edition of this book, we have found it hard to find good recent reading in specification and implementation chapters and some of the titles we suggest are hard to obtain, for example Alexander (below) is out of print and only available in some libraries. As multi-platform user interfaces begin to become more important we predict a growth in this area, so we hope that by the time we are writing a fourth edition there will be a greater choice.

H. Alexander, *Formally-based Tools and Techniques for Human–Computer Dialogs*, Ellis Horwood, 1987.
This book is dedicated to the CSP-based notation, SPI (see Sections 16.4.3 and 16.5).

G. Cockton, Designing abstractions for communication control. In M. D. Harrison and H. W. Thimbleby, editors, *Formal Methods in Human–Computer Interaction*, Chapter 10, Cambridge University Press, 1990.
Describes generative transition networks, a form of state transition network which has many features of an event-based production system. In particular, it attempts to solve some of the problems that STNs have with concurrent dialogs.

D. R. Olsen, Propositional production systems for dialog description. In J. C. Chew and J. Whiteside, editors, *Empowering People – CHI'90 Conference Proceedings*, pp. 57–63, *Human Factors in Computing Systems*, ACM Press, 1990.
Original paper on propositional production systems, including examples and analysis.

H. R. Hartson, A. C. Siochi and D. Hix, The UAN: a user-oriented representation for direct manipulation, *ACM Transactions on Information Systems*, Vol. 8, No. 3, pp. 181–203, July 1990.
User Action Notation (UAN) is not a dialog notation as such, but operates at the dialog level. UAN is scenario based in the sense that it considers small snippets of user behavior, for example the deletion of a file. It describes the actions the user must perform *and* the system feedback.

See also the reading list for Chapter 8 since the greatest use of dialog description notations has been as the dialog control portion of user interface management systems.

17 MODELS OF THE SYSTEM

OVERVIEW

We need to know what a system does in order to assess its usability.

■ Standard software engineering formalisms can be used to specify an interactive system. These are of various types:
  – model based, such as Z, which describe the system's state and operations
  – algebraic formalisms, which describe the effects of sequences of actions
  – temporal and deontic logics, which describe when things happen and who is responsible.

■ Special interaction models are designed specifically to describe usability properties, including:
  – predictability and observability – what you can tell about the system from looking at it
  – reachability and undo – what you can do with it.

■ Most formal models and notations focus on events and changes that happen when they occur, but we need richer models to deal with:
  – interstitial behavior – the things that happen between events such as dragging an icon
  – physical objects in ubiquitous computing or virtual reality
  – the tension between precise time and more fuzzy human ideas of time.

17.1   INTRODUCTION

In the previous chapter we looked at the specification of dialog. In this chapter we will look at ways of modeling the semantics of an interactive system. The dialog just tells us about what user actions are legal at any point, but here we will be interested in what the user's actions *do* to the system.

There is some overlap. In the previous chapter we discussed some of the ways dialog is linked to semantics. Also, definitions of system semantics tend to define the acceptable dialog. However, a system-oriented description will not describe the dialog as well as a dedicated dialog notation, and a dialog notation may hardly define the system at all.

In Section 17.2, we will describe how standard formalisms can be used to specify interactive systems. Such formalisms are becoming part of software engineering practice and can be a way for interface designers to articulate their ideas and communicate them to system developers. These formal notations are used to specify the functionality and presentation of specific systems.

Section 17.3 looks at interaction models, formal models that describe general properties of systems. We will demonstrate how one such model, the PIE model, can be used to investigate generic principles such as WYSIWYG and undo.

Finally, in Section 17.4, we will discuss ways to model phenomena that involve more continuous interactions such as dragging an icon and also issues of time such as what we mean by 'let's meet this afternoon'.

Each modeling technique takes the view that it is not enough to design the 'interface' as a thin layer between the user and the system. Usability is affected by the whole system functionality: what is there, what can be done to it, and how it is presented at the interface.

17.2   STANDARD FORMALISMS

In this section we will discuss 'off-the-shelf' formalisms which can be used to specify interactive systems. The purpose of a formal specification is twofold: communication and analysis. Sections 17.2.1 and 17.2.2 will show how this influences their use for interface design.

We will then look at three brands of formalism. First we will look at model-oriented notations, Z in particular. We will use a graphics program as an example throughout this subsection and also Section 17.2.5 on algebraic specification. Finally, Section 17.2.6 looks at temporal and other logics. Another major brand of notation is the process algebras, such as CSP. However, these are most suited to dialog design and have been discussed in Chapter 16.

17.2.1 Formal notations for communication

A specification can be used as a common language within a design team, or between the designers and system developers. In the latter case it can also form a sort of contract between the parties. Ideas for screen layout can easily be visualized with the help of drawings or painting packages, but the dynamics and deeper behavior of the system are more difficult to communicate. It is easy to discuss ideas with other developers or with a programmer without ever being sure you are talking about the same thing.

The claim is frequently made that a formal specification gets rid of ambiguity completely and provides a precise unambiguous description of the system. However, this claim is false. The symbols used and the manipulations of them have defined meanings within the formal systems, but the *interpretation* of those symbols can still vary from person to person. For example, if a specification of a screen defines the color of pixels at any position (x,y), then one designer may think the coordinates have $(0,0)$ at the bottom left and another may think that they start at the top left. The internal geometry of the screen is unambiguous, but the interpretation of one designer is upside down! These ambiguities tend to be of a different kind from those of the spoken and written word (and are often as silly as the above). This is why it is crucial that any formal specification is accompanied by extensive commentary and a parallel written description.

In a small group, where a specification is developed in cooperation, the needs for extensive documentation are less strong. The group can build up a shared interpretation of the symbols used. In such a setting, formal statements can be a succinct and precise mode of communication. However familiar the formalisms become, the group must remember that they are using an esoteric language, which must be interpreted to outsiders.

17.2.2 Formal notations for analysis

Formal specifications can be analyzed in a variety of ways. First, they can be checked for internal consistency; that is, to see if any statement made in one part of it contradicts another. For example, we shall see in Section 17.3.3 that some of the requirements one might have for an undo command are, in fact, incompatible. It would, in theory and in practice, be impossible to build a system satisfying all the properties.

Secondly, a specification can be checked for external consistency with respect to the eventual program. This task of *verification*, previously discussed in Chapter 6, is one of the chief benefits of a formal specification, from a software engineering perspective. However, this is not the primary benefit for HCI.

Finally, a specification can be checked for external consistency with respect to requirements. Some of these requirements will be nothing to do with HCI (although still important), for example security properties. Other requirements will be about the particular system: for example, that any function can be accessed within no more than three keystrokes. In addition, there are generic usability requirements which cover a range of systems, for example the usability principles discussed in Chapter 7.

The model in Section 17.3 is aimed at defining this last sort of generic requirement. As the requirements are themselves formally stated, they can be checked for internal consistency among themselves.

17.2.3 Model-oriented notations

Model-oriented notations were developed in the late 1970s and 1980s to provide software engineers with the ability to describe and reason about software components using precisely defined mathematical constructs, which mirror the kinds of constructs used in real programming languages. These mathematical notations provide a means of describing the behavior of a software system in a way closely related to how they are programmed but in a more abstract language. This abstractness allows the designer to forget about machine or implementation bias at early stages of design and also allows the design, or specification, to be reasoned about rigorously.

The two major model-oriented specification notations in use today are *Z* and *VDM*. Both have been used for interface specifications. For example, Z has been used to specify editors [336], a window manager and a graphics toolkit called Presenter [347]. In the following description, we will follow the conventions defined in the Z notation. We do not assume any prior knowledge of Z; however, this chapter does not serve as a tutorial for the notation (interested readers should consult the Z reference manual for more details [328]).

Simple sets

Model-oriented notations are based on the use of sets and functions. The simplest sets correspond to standard types in programming languages, like reals $\mathbb{R}$, integers $\mathbb{Z}$ and the positive integers, or natural numbers $\mathbb{N}$. Non-standard types can be defined as new sets by explicitly listing the finite number of possible values in that set. For example, we can define a set that contains all possible types of geometric shapes used in a graphics package (line, ellipse and rectangle) and we can define another set of the possible keystrokes:

$Shape\_type == Line \mid Ellipse \mid Rectangle$
$Keystroke == a \mid b \mid \ldots \mid z \mid A \mid \ldots \mid 9 \mid Cursor\_left \mid \ldots$

In some instances, it is not necessary to give an exhaustive list of the members of a set; it simply suffices to know of the set's existence and worry about its detailed contents later. To signal the existence of such a set without providing a definition of its contents, we assert it as a *given set* and enclose it in square brackets. We could have introduced the set *Keystroke* in this manner:

$[Keystroke]$

From these base sets we can build more complex ones. These include ordered tuples, named and unordered tuples (like records in a programming language such as Pascal) called *schemas* in Z, sequences (or lists) and functions. For example, a point in space requires an *x* and a *y* coordinate. That is, it is a 2-tuple (or ordered pair) of real numbers, and we can define it using the cross-product-type constructor × as shown below:

Point $== \mathbb{R} \times \mathbb{R}$

A typical value of type *Point* would be written (1.2, −3.0). A geometric shape might be defined by its width and height, a point (*Point*) for its center and a tag describing what sort of shape it is (from *Shape_type*). This could be defined either as a 4-tuple *Shape_type* $\times \mathbb{R} \times \mathbb{R} \times$ *Point*, or using a Z schema, as we have done below. The schema type is named (*Shape*) and its constituent components are also identified by a name and their associated type.

```
┌─ Shape ──────────────────
│ type : Shape_type
│ wid : ℝ
│ ht : ℝ
│ center : Point
│
└──────────────────────────
```

If we use the schema declaration, then given a shape *s*, we can talk directly about the width or center of *s* by writing *s.wid* or *s.center*. The schema type corresponds to record types in Pascal or 'struct's in C.

A sequence type can be used to represent the history of a user's keystrokes:

History $==$ seq *Keystroke*

This says that an object of type *History* consists of any number (including zero) of *Keystroke*s. A sequence may have a fixed length, in which case it is rather like a Pascal array type. The mathematical sequence is more flexible than the Pascal array type as it may have a varying length. Two sequences *a* and *b* can be tied together end to end to give a new sequence, written *a* ⌢ *b*. When used like this a sequence is most like a list type as found in the LISP language.

Finally, we have *functions* that both play the role of standard calculation functions in a programming language, such as `sqrt` or `log`, and also act like a 'lookup dictionary'. Depending on the context of its use, a function in a specification may be implemented (if it is implemented at all) by a program-level function or a data structure. This is perhaps most strange to a programmer, but is an important abstraction.

We can demonstrate the use of a function in the graphics example. The schema type which defines any one shape does not allow us to single out any one shape or a collection of shapes, as we would need to do to represent the set of shapes that the user creates in any one session with the graphics editor. We can represent a group of identifiable shapes by naming a function that maps identifiers to particular shapes:

[*Id*]
Shape_dict $==$ *Id* $\nrightarrow$ *Shape*

The set *Id* is some set of identifiers which will be used to label the shape. We are not particularly interested in what the identifiers are – they could be natural numbers, for instance – so we just assert *Id* as a given set for the moment. An object *shapes* of type *Shape_dict* is a function mapping labels to shapes. If *id* were a particular label, then the shape dictionary *shapes* might map it to a rectangle with width 2.3, height 1.4 and center (1.2, −3). We could write this formally as

shapes(id).type = *Rectangle*
shapes(id).wid = 2.3
shapes(id).height = 1.4
shapes(id).center = (1.2, −3)

Shape_dict is only defined to be a set of *partial functions*. Functions map elements in one set to elements in another set. A partial function does not have to map every possible element in the source set to an element in the destination set. Therefore, not everything in *Id* is a valid argument for *shapes*. The set of values that are valid is called the *domain of shapes* and is written 'dom *shapes*'. For example, we might have

dom *shapes* = { 5, 1, 7, 4 }

So *shapes(5)*, *shapes(1)*, *shapes(7)* and *shapes(4)* would all be valid, but nothing else.

Zdraw – the state and invariants

Although it is not necessarily the case, model-oriented specifications tend to be written in an imperative fashion. One defines the *state* of the system, and then defines *operators* in terms of their effect on the state. In Z, this state and the operators are written using the schema notation. For example, the state of a simple graphics system, called Zdraw and depicted in Figure 17.1, would include a dictionary of shapes which have been created by the user and an indication of the currently selected shapes. The schema *State* below gives this definition:

```
┌─ State ──────────────────────────────
│ shapes : Shape_dict
│ selection : ℙ Id
├──────────────────────────────────────
│ selection ⊆ dom shapes
└──────────────────────────────────────
```

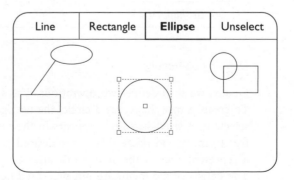

Figure 17.1   Zdraw – ellipse option has just been selected

The schema *State* is divided into two parts, above and below the middle line. Above the line we have the definition of components of the state of the graphics system. This part is similar to the component identification used to define the set *Shape*. Below the line is the state *invariant*, a condition which must always be satisfied by the components of the state. Predicates on separate lines are assumed to be joined by logical 'and' unless otherwise indicated. It says that the set of currently selected objects must always be contained in the set of created objects in the system. We will not allow a selected object to be one that has not been created by the user. Any operator which changes the state must ensure that it maintains this invariant.

What is the start state of the geometric modeling system? A reasonable assumption would be the state without any created or selected shapes. The initial state is defined by the schema *Init*:

```
┌─ Init ─────────────────────────────────
│ State
├────────────────────────────────────────
│ dom shapes = { }
│ selection = { }
│
└────────────────────────────────────────
```

Above the line we have included the previously defined schema *State*. Schema inclusion in Z is a mechanism to assist the gradual definition of a complex system in a series of simpler steps. Including the schema *State* above includes the declaration of all of its components (above the line in its original definition) and invariants (below the line). The additional invariants added in this initialization schema further restrict the initialized state, stipulating that the shape dictionary has no elements in its domain (there are no created shapes) and no currently selected shapes. The last predicate about the selected shapes was unnecessary, since it is already guaranteed by the invariant of *State*; that is, that the set of selected shapes is a subset of the created ones. So an equivalent definition of the start state would remove that predicate and leave it to the reader to deduce from the state invariant.

```
┌─ Init ─────────────────────────────────
│ State
├────────────────────────────────────────
│ dom shapes = { }
└────────────────────────────────────────
```

Defining operations

Finally, we shall define two operations. The system is going to operate as follows. To create a new shape, say a circle, the user goes to the menu option 'Ellipse' and selects it. A fixed-size circle appears in the middle of the screen. The user is then free to move and resize this to the desired position and shape. Figure 17.1 shows a representation of the screen just after the user has selected the ellipse option. The details of the menu are not presented here, but the basic functionality of the *NewEllipse* and *Unselect* operation is defined as schemas below.

To define an operation, we need to describe the state of the graphics system before and after the operation is invoked. To do this in the schema language, we include two copies of the state description, called *State* (the 'before' copy) and *State'* (the 'after' copy). If an operation requires input or provides output, these are marked with a question mark for input (?) and an exclamation point for output (!). The *NewEllipse* operation is defined next:

```
┌─ NewEllipse ──────────────────────────────────────────────
│  State
│  State'
│  newid? : Id
│  newshape? : Shape
├───────────────────────────────────────────────────────────
│          newid? ∉ dom shapes
│          newshape?.type = Ellipse
│          newshape?.wid = 1
│          newshape?.ht = 1
│          newshape?.center = (0,0)
│          shapes' = shapes ∪ { newid? → newshape? }
│          selection' = { newid? }
└───────────────────────────────────────────────────────────
```

This operation results in the creation of a new ellipse of a fixed size in the center of the coordinate space (assumed to be the point (0,0)). The result of the operation is that the shape dictionary is updated to include a mapping from some 'fresh' identifier (one that is not already used to point to an existing shape) to the new ellipse shape defined by *newshape?*. We do not indicate how this fresh identifier is provided to the operation – that is left as an issue for the implementor to settle. In addition, we have stipulated that the new object becomes the only selected object.

Note that the last part of the specification is quite an important interface choice and would *not* appear in a dialog specification. We could just as easily have left the selection as it was (*selection'* = *selection*). Possibly, we have made our choice because a (trivial) task analysis shows that users will normally want to move or resize a new object. This design decision may be wrong, but it is explicit and thus open to challenge. In an implementation such a decision would be deeply buried in the code.

The *Unselect* operation makes the set of currently selected objects empty. From this natural language description, we can derive an explicit formal description below:

```
┌─ Unselect ────────────────────────────────────────────────
│  State
│  State'
├───────────────────────────────────────────────────────────
│  selection' = { }
│  shapes' = shapes
└───────────────────────────────────────────────────────────
```

Notice that we chose to make explicit that the dictionary of shapes remained the same after the operation. This may seem obvious, but if the last predicate were removed from the definition of *Unselect*, then we would leave open the possibility that the shape dictionary could be anything at all after the operation, and that is certainly not intended. This becomes an even more important issue when the specification is used to judge the external consistency of the eventual program, as we discussed earlier.

17.2.4 Issues for model-oriented notations

The above is just a small sample of the method formally used to specify an interactive system with a model-oriented notation such as Z. But even this small example raises some important issues for interactive systems and formal specifications.

Recall in the definition *Init* of the initialized state that we did not have to mention explicitly that the set of selected shapes was empty. This fact is implied by the state invariant stipulating that the set of selected shapes is always a subset of the set of created shapes. However, in the definition of the *Unselect* operation, it was important that we explicitly state that the shape dictionary remains the same after the operation. This behavior, though probably understood by the person who provides the natural language description of the operation, is not implied by the state invariant. If we do not make it explicit, then we have defined an operation far different from the one intended.

This issue is called the *framing problem* and comes up in a variety of areas both in interface design and elsewhere. As readers, we are quite good at inferring what should happen when things are not stated explicitly, but it is hard to formalize. One general rule is that if something is not mentioned, we assume it is unchanged. However, this simple rule cannot be used when we are dealing with a state with invariants. Imagine we were defining a delete operation and said that the *shapes* component stayed the same except for the selected object which was removed. If we do not explicitly mention what happens to the set of selected objects after the operation, what can we infer? Does it remain unchanged? No, because that would break the invariant that *selection* was in the domain of *shapes*. Normally such design decisions get missed until the implementor either deliberately or accidentally chooses one option or another.

Another issue which is generally ignored in such model-oriented specifications is the *separation* between system functionality and presentation. In the above specification, we identified a dictionary of shapes which have been created, but we have said nothing about how those shapes are presented on the user's display. It is quite possible that the user will want to create an image larger than the display coordinate space, so not all of the created objects will be visible at once. Furthermore, how do we indicate which objects are selected? Adding this kind of information to the above specification would make it more complete, but also more complicated. The presentation information is not necessary to define how the system works internally, but it is necessary to be just as precise about presentation issues as we have been about system functionality.

To address this issue of separation formally, we will need to provide more structure to the formal specification than the model-oriented approach provides. We will discuss this additional structure in Section 17.3.

17.2.5 Algebraic notations

There are a wide number of algebraic specification notations including *OBJ*, *Larch* and *ACT-ONE*. In particular, ACT-ONE has been used as the functional part of the ISO standard language *LOTOS*.

In principle, an algebraic specification does not try to build up a picture of the components of an object, but merely describes what the object is like *from the outside*. For an interface specification this sounds like a good thing, as we want to talk about the behavior of a system from the user's viewpoint, not the way it is built. However, algebraic notations are more difficult to 'get into'. They have a specific mindset which, once understood, is very clear, but takes some getting used to.

An algebraic version of Zdraw

If we continue the graphics example, we could imagine in Z having gone on to define the actions of resizing an object, and deleting it. In addition, we have an operation *select* which, given a point, makes the nearest object to it the current selection, and an operation *unselect* which clears the current selection. We will instead define these operations algebraically. As we have mentioned, an algebraic specification does not provide an explicit representation (or model) of the system. Rather, the types of interest in the state are declared along with the set of operations which manipulate those types. A set of axioms then implicitly defines the system state. An algebraic specification for the graphics system is given below:

Algebraic–draw =
types
  State, Pt
operations
  init : $\rightarrow$ *State*
  new_ellipse, new_rectangle, new_line : *Pt* $\times$ *State* $\rightarrow$ *State*
  move, resize, select : *Pt* $\times$ *State* $\rightarrow$ *State*
  unselect : *State* $\rightarrow$ *State*
  delete : *State* $\rightarrow$ *State*
axioms
  for all *st* $\in$ *State*; *p, p'* $\in$ *Pt* $\cdot$
  1. *delete(new_ellipse(st))* = *unselect(st)*
  2. *delete(new_rectangle(st))* = *unselect(st)*
  3. *delete(new_line(st))* = *unselect(st)*
  4. *move(p, unselect(st))* = *unselect(st)*
  5. *resize(p, unselect(st))* = *unselect(st)*
  6. *move(p, move(p', st))* = *move(p, st)*
  7. *resize(p, resize(p', st))* = *resize(p, st)*
  8. *delete(delete(st))* = *delete(st)*

The specification is in a generic algebraic notation that captures the main features of most real notations. We first declare the types of interest in the specification – points, *Pt*, which will serve as arguments for some of the operations, and the overall graphics system state, *State*. No further information is provided about the construction of these types. The operations are then listed and are defined in terms of their input and output. For example, the operation *new_ellipse* is defined to take a point and the current state as arguments and returns a new state. The operation *init* takes no argument and produces a state. The types and operations together form the *signature* of the specification *Algebraic–draw*.

After the individual operations have been declared, the algebraic specification describes the relationships between the various operations by means of *axioms*. Axioms indicate how the operations interact with one another. The first three axioms tell us that creating any object and then immediately deleting it has no net effect other than unselecting the current object. This is an important *safety property* for the user saying that there are no unexpected side-effects.

The next two axioms say that attempts to move or resize when there is no selected object do nothing at all. Axioms 6 and 7 say that both move and resize are 'forgetful' in the sense that if you do two resizes in a row the second overrides the first as if the first had never happened. This forgetful behavior of the move operation is very different from the behavior defined in the model-oriented specification. In the model-oriented approach, it would be easier to specify that a move operation is cumulative – two successive moves are the same as doing one move equal to the sum of the two moves. Finally, the last axiom says that the action of *delete* is even more forgetful: it is *idempotent* – doing a second delete achieves nothing.

Reading time order in algebraic formulae

Note that the algebraic notation reads from the inside out. So the first thing done is in the middle of the expression. For example, if an axiom reads

$$resize(p, move\ (p', new\_rectangle(st)))$$

then this corresponds to doing first a *new_rectangle*, then a *move* and then a *resize*. This becomes more clear if we put in the temporary results:

$$st_1 = new\_rectangle(st)$$
$$st_2 = move(p', st_1)$$
$$st_3 = resize(p, st_2)$$

Some algebraic notations are more imperative having an implicit state. In such a notation, the first and fifth axioms of *Algebraic–draw* would be written

$$new\_ellipse\ ;\ delete\ = unselect$$
$$unselect\ ;\ resize(p)\ = unselect$$

Such a format is easier to read as 'time' goes from left to right, but is less flexible.

Completeness and observation

If we look back at the full set of axioms, we see that they are nowhere near enough to specify the behavior of *Algebraic–draw*. That is, they are not *complete*. As far as the axioms are concerned there is no difference between *move* and *resize*, or between *new_ellipse* and *new_rectangle*. Now we could add some more axioms, for instance adding an axiom to say that a move, resize or unselect after a delete has no effect.

There is a more fundamental problem, however. We are told nothing about the internal structure of *State* or *Point*. Presumably *Point* is generated from the mouse position, so we would really know something about it. We can put inputs into the system, but what do we get out? There are no *observation* operators. A system which cannot be observed can easily (and it is the simplest solution) do nothing at all. To be useful, this specification would have to be extended to include the presentation of a screen image or something similar. This screen image would be more concrete than the abstract internal state, and would be related to *State* by observation operators. This is a similar problem, concerning the relation between functionality and presentation, as was raised in the previous section with model-oriented notations.

17.2.6 Temporal and other logics

Many readers will be familiar with standard propositional logic, where letters are used to represent logical statements. For example, if one of the authors says

$(p \lor q) \land r$

where p = 'my nose is green'
     q = 'I've got ears like a donkey'
     r = 'I'm called Alan'

then you can conclude that either the author in question is Alan, or he or she will stand out in a crowd.

In fact propositional logic and predicate logic (which allows parametrized logical formulae such as $P(x) \lor Q(x)$) are used as part of many other formalisms, for instance in the model-oriented specification of the graphics drawing package.

However, propositional and predicate logic are only the simplest of vast families of logics developed as part of philosophy and mathematical logic. Of these specialized logics, several have been adopted and developed within computer science and have operators which are particularly useful for specifying properties of interactive systems.

Temporal logic

Temporal logics augment predicate logics with operators to reason about time. There are many different brands of temporal logic, but most share the basic symbols □ and , which are read as 'always' and 'eventually'. These are the temporal equivalents of the quantifiers ∀ (universal quantification, read 'for all') and ∃ (existential quantification, read 'there exists'). So the statement

□ (rains on Tuesday)

says that it 'always rains on Tuesday.' The statement $\square(\neg p)$ says that it is always *not* true that p. In other words, p never happens. So we can always read the combination $\square\neg$ as 'never':

$\square\neg$ (computer explodes)

We can see that temporal operators are useful at specifying *safety properties*. More complex properties can also be given, for example

$\square$ (user types 'print fred' $\Rightarrow$ the laser printer prints the file 'fred')

This statement says that at all times, if the user types the command 'print fred', then eventually the file 'fred' will be printed on the laser printer. Whereas it is easy with a model-oriented specification like Z to say what will happen immediately after a user action, this sort of delayed response property is very difficult indeed.

Further temporal operators

In fact, the above statement was quite weak; 'eventually' could mean in a thousand years' time. To cope with this, temporal logics introduce additional operators. These vary a bit more from logic to logic. Some reason over bounded time intervals, so that the meaning of 'eventually' becomes 'before the end of this interval'. A more popular approach is to use operators such as **until** and **before**.

p **until** q – p must remain true until q becomes true
p **before** q – p must be true at some time before q becomes true

We can think of **until** and **before** as bounded versions of $\square$ and   respectively, where the second argument q marks the end of the interval over which they act. Note that p **until** q is weaker than $\square p$ as the latter demands that p remain true for ever, whereas the former only until q becomes true. On the other hand, p **before** q is stronger than p as the former guarantees a timescale in which p must occur.

As well as being used to specify systems in abstract, temporal and similar logics have been used to prototype interactive systems. To do this, special executable forms have to be used, as in general a temporal logic formula can look arbitrarily far into the future. Consider, for example,

(user types 'print fred') $\Rightarrow$ the laser printer prints the file 'fred'

This formula says that if at any time in the future the user types 'print fred', then the system ought to print the file 'fred' *now*. Such clairvoyant systems are hard to produce, and thus the executable forms have to restrict the types of specification the user can enter.

Unfortunately, restricting oneself to executable formulae can also prevent the expression of useful requirements. Obviously all requirements should be consistent with being executed (we want to produce a system eventually), but they need not be sufficiently precise to be executable. This tension between executability and expressiveness is evident throughout the use of formal methods in computer science, but is especially pertinent to user interface design with its focus on a rapid prototyping cycle.

Real time

Temporal logics only deal with time in the sense that they represent the succession of events – one thing happens before another. They do not represent actual durations and times in hours, minutes and seconds. Clearly, there are important user interface aspects which require a real-time statement such as the following:

> When the ellipse option is selected it must be highlighted within 100 ms and the new object must appear on the screen within 1 second

Programming, specifying and reasoning about real-time behavior is a very active research area, and a variety of notations have been developed, such as *real-time logic* and timed versions of the process algebras (CSP and CCS). However, as yet, none has been extensively used within HCI. One barrier to effective use is that general properties are difficult to state exactly – we usually want a response time of 'around' 100 milliseconds. Also, the real-time notations have often been developed with time-critical applications in mind, whereas, for many human response time issues, there is a gradual degradation in performance as the time increases, rather than a critical time after which the system might as well not bother. On the other hand, there are some timing issues where critical bounds do occur: for example, in hand–eye coordination tasks, delays of even a few hundred milliseconds can destroy performance totally.

Whether or not we use a formalism to describe real-time properties of a design, we must always remember that these issues are important, and we are not using an 'infinitely fast machine' (see Chapter 2 and [93]).

Deontics – responsibility and freedom

Specifications say what the designer thinks should happen. Specifications of the system say what it should do, but real requirements are often about the world – 'the system should have a secure backup every week'. One could write a formal version of this statement using some form of temporal logic, but when we come to design a system to satisfy it we have trouble. We can design a 'backup' program which puts all the data onto tape, and which uses sophisticated error checking and redundancy to make sure the saved data are secure. We can even design a user interface which is resilient to mistakes on the operator's part, but which is so clear that such mistakes never happen. But all this is to no avail if the operator does not put the backup tape into the system! Traditional specifications say *what* happens, but do not mention *who* is responsible for making it happen.

Consider the following statements:

> *Hotel rules*: the guests are to be in the hotel by midnight
> *Prison rules*: the inmates are to be locked in their cells from 9pm to 6am

The two statements are similar in form, and their propositional meanings are almost identical. If we swap a few words they transform into one another. However, *from context* we know that the first statement expresses a requirement on the hotel guests, whereas the second expresses a requirement on the prison warders.

Deontic logics address these issues by including the concept of responsible agents (human, corporate and computer) and the mutual responsibilities between them. The most common deontic operators are *permission* (**per**) and *obligation* (**obl**). These both take two arguments: the first is who has the permission or obligation, and the second what it is they are permitted or obliged to make true. For example, we can refine the temporal logic statement about printing including these operators. The agents are the user 'Jane' and the laser printer 'lp3':

$$owns(\text{Jane, file 'fred'}) \Rightarrow \textbf{per}(\text{Jane}, request(\text{Jane, 'print fred'}))$$
$$request(\text{Jane, 'print fred'}) \Rightarrow \textbf{obl}(\text{lp3, prints the file 'fred'})$$

The first formula says that if Jane owns the file 'fred' then she is permitted to request the command 'print fred'. The second says that if she requests the command, then the printer is obliged to print 'fred'. The first statement is a little clumsy because it has to be phrased in terms of the proposition *request*(Jane, 'print fred'). If we also include the idea of actions, such as *request*('print fred'), which can be performed (**performs**) by agents, then the requirements can be rephrased using a modified obligation operator:

$$owns(\text{Jane, file 'fred'}) \Rightarrow \textbf{per}(\text{Jane}, request(\text{'print fred'}))$$
$$\textbf{performs}(\text{Jane}, request(\text{'print fred'})) \Rightarrow \textbf{obl}(\text{lp3}, print \text{ (the file 'fred')})$$

Such a statement is not far different from the statement of the requirements in English, and makes quite clear the balance of responsibility.

Deontic logics are becoming popular in requirements engineering. It is thus possible that as an interface designer, you may be asked to produce a system which satisfies some (suitably explained) deontic specification. Even if this is not the case, it is worth noting, formally or informally, exactly what expectations you have of your users. In practice, one ought to work with several levels of expectation. For example, if you are designing an automatic bank teller, it may be true that customers are obliged to use only their own cards, and to use them in a particular fashion. However, you do not want the system to crash too terribly if a customer does not behave in this fashion. As interactive systems begin to involve more than a single user (see Chapters 14 and 19), it becomes more important to keep track of these responsibilities and freedoms, who must do what and who can do what. If the user of a single-user system does not behave in the 'obliged' fashion then the impact is personal (although not necessarily acceptable). However, in a multi-user system, we want to restrict the bad effect on others – the system should still maintain its obligations to them and allow them to perform those things they are permitted to do.

17.3   INTERACTION MODELS

Interactive systems ought to be '*what you see is what you get*' (*WYSIWYG*), *consistent*, have a universal *undo* facility . . . the list goes on. But, if a supplier says that its word processor 'Sludge-Word' is WYSIWYG, how do we test this? The screen fonts look very impressive, but are they the same as on the page? Perhaps the system appears

WYSIWYG for simple jobs but this breaks down when things become more complex. What does WYSIWYG really mean?

It was to address these issues that the methodology described in this section was developed. Whereas the formal notations described in Section 17.2 describe specific systems, the aim in this section is to define *interaction models*, which are generic, formal models of interactive systems. Using such a generic model, one can define principles in a formal way which are then applicable to a range of systems. In particular, by regarding Sludge-Word as an instance of the general model we can verify (or refute) some of its supplier's claims.

The particular model we will describe, the *PIE model*, was designed to attack WYSIWYG-like properties. It would be nice to say that after reading this section, you will know exactly what WYSIWYG means. Unfortunately, it is too wide and varied a term to be formalized. However, we will describe several principles from Chapter 7, more limited in scope, which can be formalized. Of these some cover areas within the general area of WYSIWYG, namely *observability* – what you can tell about the current state of the system from the display – and *predictability* – what you can tell about its future behavior. In addition, we will define principles concerning the control of the system by the user, such as *reachability* – you can get anywhere from anywhere – and *undo* – the ability to perform backwards error recovery.

As we mentioned in Chapter 7, we certainly cannot define 'usability' totally; we cannot say that if a system obeys a set of formal principles then it will be usable. Nevertheless, some of the formal principles are necessary for usability: any system which breaks them is bound to have problems. The formal principles form a 'safety net' to prevent some of the worst mistakes in an interactive system, but do not ensure a good design. That depends on a good designer.

This 'safety net', although valuable, is not the principal benefit of using interaction models. Their chief value lies in the insights gained by considering properties of interaction, away from the surface clutter of real or imagined systems. These insights become part of the background with which you approach new areas, whether or not a formal approach is explicitly taken there. Furthermore, some of these insights can be abstracted into informal principles, which, though derived by formal analyses, can, once stated, be justified in their own right. It is a strange paradox that some of the informal concepts, which are obtained by such formal analysis, are not themselves fully formalizable.

17.3.1 The PIE model

The PIE model is a *black-box model*. It does not try to represent the internal architecture and construction of a computer system, but instead describes it purely in terms of its inputs from the user and outputs to the user. For a simple single-user system, typical inputs would be from the keyboard and mouse, and outputs would be the computer's display screen and the eventual printed output (Figure 17.2).

The difference between the ephemeral *display* of a system and the permanent *result* is central to the PIE model. We will call the set of possible displays D and the

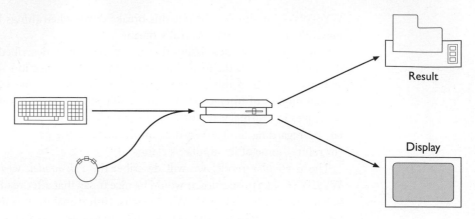

Figure 17.2 Inputs and outputs of a single-user system

set of possible results R. In order to express principles of observability, we will want to talk about the relation between display and result. Basically, can we determine the result (what you will get) from the display (what you see)?

For a formal statement of predictability it helps (but is not essential) to talk about the internal state of the system. This does not counter our claim to have a black-box model. First, the state we define will be opaque; we will not look at its structure, merely postulate it is there. Secondly, the state we will be discussing is not the actual state of the system, but an idealization of it. It will be the minimal state required to account for the future *external behavior*. We will call this the *effect* (E). Functions *display* and *result* obtain the current outputs from this minimal state:

$display : E \rightarrow D$
$result : E \rightarrow R$

The current display will be literally what is now visible. The current result is actually not what *is* available, but what the result would be if the interaction were finished. For example, with a word processor, it is the pages that would be obtained if one printed the current state of the document.

A single-user action we will call a *command* (from a set C). The history of all the user's commands is called the *program* ($P =$ seq C), and the current effect can be calculated from this history using an *interpretation function*:

$I : P \rightarrow E$

Arguably the input history would be better labeled H, but then the PIE model would lose its acronym! If we put together all the bits, we obtain a diagram of sets and functions (Figure 17.3), which looks rather like the original illustration.

In principle, one can express all the properties one wants in terms of the interpretation function, I. However, this often means expressing properties quantified over all possible past histories. To make some of the properties easier to express, we will also use a state transition function *doit*:

$doit : E \times P \rightarrow E$

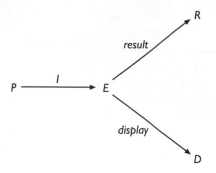

Figure 17.3 The PIE model

The function *doit* takes the present state *e* and some user commands *p*, and gives the new state after the user has entered the commands *doit(e, p)*. It is related to the interpretation function *I* by the following axioms:

$$doit(I(p), q) \quad = I(p \hat{\ } q)$$
$$doit(doit(e, p), q) = doit(e, p \hat{\ } q)$$

The PIE diagram can be read at different levels of abstraction. One can take a direct analogy with Figure 17.2. The commands set *C* is the keystrokes and mouse clicks, the display set *D* is the physical display, and the result *R* is the printed output:

$$C = \{ \text{'a'}, \text{'b'}, \ldots, \text{'0'}, \text{'1'}, \ldots, \text{'*'}, \text{'\&'}, \ldots \}$$
$$D = Pixel\_coord \rightarrow RGB\_value$$
$$R = \text{ink on paper}$$

This is a physical/lexical level of interpretation. One can produce a similar mapping for any system, in terms of the raw physical inputs and outputs. It is often more useful to apply the model at the logical level. Here, the user commands are higher-level actions such as 'select bold font', which may be invoked by several keystrokes and/or mouse actions. Similarly, we can describe the screen at a logical level in terms of windows, buttons, fields and so on. Also, for some purposes, rather than dealing with the final physical result, we may regard, say, the document on disk as the result.

The power of the PIE model is that it can be applied at many levels of abstraction. Some properties may only be valid at one level, but many should be true at all levels of system description. It is even possible to apply the PIE model just *within* the user, in the sense that the commands are the user's intended actions, and the display, the perceived response.

When applying the PIE model at different levels it is possible to map between the levels. This leads to *level conformance* properties, which say, for example, that the changes one sees at the interface level should correspond to similar changes at the level of application objects.

17.3.2 Predictability and observability

WYSIWYG is clearly related to what can be inferred from the display (what you see). Harold Thimbleby has pointed out that WYSIWYG can be given two interpretations

[342]. One is what you see is what you *will* get at the printer. This corresponds to how well you can determine the result from the display. The second interpretation is what you see is what you *have got* in the system. For this we will ask what the display can tell us about the effect. These can both be thought of as *observability* principles.

A related issue is *predictability*. Imagine you have been using a drawing package and in the middle you get thirsty and go to get a cup of tea. On returning, you are faced with the screen – do you know what to do next? If there are two shapes one on top of the other, the graphics package may interpret mouse clicks as operating on the 'top' shape. However, there may be no visual indication of which is topmost. The screen image does not tell you what the effect of your actions will be; you need to remember how you got there, your command history. This has been called the 'gone away for a cup of tea problem'. In fact, the state of the system determines the effects of any future commands, so if we have a system, which is observable in the sense that the display determines the state, it is also predictable. Predictability is a special case of observability.

We will attempt to formalize these properties. To say that we can determine the result from the display is to say that there exists a function *transparent$_R$* from displays to results:

$$\exists\ transparent_R : D \to R \bullet$$
$$\forall\ e \in E \bullet transparent_R(display(e)) = result(e)$$

It is no good having any old function from the display to the result; the second half of the above says that the function gives us exactly the result we would get from the system. We can call this property *result transparency*.

We can do a similar thing for the effect, that is the system state:

$$\exists\ transparent_E : D \to E \bullet$$
$$\forall\ e \in E \bullet transparent_E(display(e)) = (e)$$

We can call this property simply *transparency*.

What would it mean for a system to be transparent in one of these senses? If the system were result transparent, when we come back from our cup of tea, we can look at the display and then work out in our head (using *transparent$_R$*) exactly what the printed drawing would look like. Whether we could do this in our heads is another matter. For most drawing packages the function would be simply to ignore the menus and 'photocopy' the screen.

Simple transparency is stronger still. It would say that there is nothing in the state of the system that cannot be inferred from the display. If there are any modes, then these must have a visual indication; if there are any differences in behavior between the displayed shapes, then there must be some corresponding visual difference. Even forgetting the formal principles, this is a strong and useful design heuristic.

Unfortunately, these principles are both rather too strong. If we imagine a word processor rather than a drawing package, the contents of the display will be only a bit of the document. Clearly, we cannot infer the contents of the rest of the document (and hence the printed result) from the display. Similarly, to give a visual indication of, say, object grouping within a complex drawing package might be impossible (and this can cause the user problems).

When faced with a document on a word processor, the user can simply scroll the display up and down to find out what is there. You cannot see from the current display everything about the system, but you can find out. The process by which the user explores the current state of the system is called a *strategy*. The formalization of a strategy is quite complex, even ignoring cognitive limitations. These strategies will differ from user to user, but the documentation of a system should tell the user how to get at pertinent information. For example, how to tell what objects in the drawing tools are grouped. This will map out a set of effective strategies with which the user can work.

Ideally, a strategy for observing the system should not disrupt the state of the application objects, that is the strategy should be *passive*. For example, a strategy for looking at a document which involved deleting it would not be very useful. This seems almost too obvious, but consider again grouping in drawing tools. Often the only way to find out how a grouped object is composed is to ungroup it piece by piece. You then have to remember how to put it back together. The advantage of a passive strategy becomes apparent.

Using such a strategy then gives one a wider view of the system than the display. This is called the *observable effect* (O). In a word processor this would be the complete view of the document obtained by scrolling plus any current mode indicators and a quick peek at the state of the cut/paste buffer. The observable effect contains strictly more information than the display, and hence sits before it in a functional diagram (Figure 17.4).

We can now reformulate principles in terms of the observable effect. First of all the system is *result observable* if the result can be determined from the observable effect:

$$\exists\, predict_R : O \to R \bullet$$
$$\forall\, e \in E \bullet predict_R(observe(e)) = result(e)$$

This says that the observable effect contains at least as much information as the result. However, it will also contain additional information about the interactive state of the system. For example, you will observe the current cursor position, but this has no bearing on the printed document.

So you know what will happen if you hit the print button *now*. Refreshed from your cup of tea, you return to work. You press a function key which, unknown to you, is bound to a macro intended for an entirely different application. The screen rolls, the

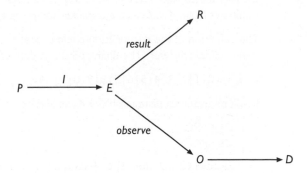

Figure 17.4 The observable effect

disk whirrs and, to your horror, your document and the entire disk contents are trashed. You leave the computer and go for another drink . . . not necessarily of tea.

A stronger condition is that the system be fully predictable:

$$\exists \; transparent_E: O \rightarrow E \; \bullet$$
$$\forall \; e \in E \bullet predict(observe(e)) = (e)$$

This says that you can observe the complete state of the system. You can then (in theory) predict anything the system will do. If the system were fully predictable, you would be able to tell what the bindings of the function keys were and hence (again in theory) would have been able to avoid your disaster.

This is as far as this bit of the formal story goes in this book. However, there are more sophisticated principles of observability and predictability which take into account aspects of user attention, and issues like keyboard buffers. Formalisms such as the PIE model have been used to portray other usability principles discussed in Chapter 7. Principles of predictability do not stand on their own; even if you had known what was bound to the function key, you might still have hit it by accident, or simply forgotten. Other protective principles like *commensurate effort* need to be applied. Also, although it is difficult to formalize completely, one prefers a system that behaves in most respects like the transparency principles, rather than requiring complicated searching to discover information. This is a sort of commensurate effort for observation.

Worked exercise

A two-function calculator has the following buttons: 0–9, +, − and =. These would comprise the command set (C) of a PIE model of the calculator. The state (E) would consist of three components: the two current numbers being entered, the last number (to be operated on) and the pending operation (+ or −). The display (D) is simply a signed number. For this example, ignore the result.

Write down (semi-formally) the doit *function updating the state for each user command and the* display *function relating the state (E) to the current display (D). To check your definitions: what does the display have on it after the user has entered '2 + 3 +'? Most calculators would show 5; does yours?*

Consider the displays after the sequences '2 + 2' and '2 +' and the effect on each of the additional user input of 3. Does the calculator satisfy the transparency property?

Answer

The definition of the *doit* function could proceed as follows. We will use the Z notation in this sample answer. The character set is defined as

$$C == 0 \mid 1 \mid 2 \mid 3 \mid 4 \mid 5 \mid 6 \mid 7 \mid 8 \mid 9 \mid 0 \mid + \mid - \mid =$$

It will be useful to distinguish the digits and operations (+ and −):

$Digit : \mathbb{P}C$
$Op : \mathbb{P}C$

$Digit = \{\, 0,\, 1,\, 2,\, 3,\, 4,\, 5,\, 6,\, 7,\, 8,\, 9,\, 0 \,\}$
$Op = \{\, +,\, - \,\}$

The state is defined as an ordered 4-tuple, consisting of the current number being entered, the last number (to be operated on) and the pending operation:

$$E == seq\ Digit \times seq\ Digit \times Op$$

The display is simply a projection of the current number being entered:

$D == seq\ Digit$

$display : E \rightarrow D$

$\forall\ (current, last, op) : E \bullet$
    $display(current, last, op) = current$

The *doit* function is defined below by case exhaustion. The notation $o(c, l)$ means to apply operation o to the arguments c and l, so that $2 + 3$ would be written $+ (2, 3)$, with $o = +$, $c = 2$ and $l = 3$.

$doit : E \times C \rightarrow E$

$\forall\ c, l : seq\ Digit; d, d' : Digit; o, o' : Op \bullet$
    $doit((c, l, o), =)\ \ = (o(c, l), 0, o)$
    $doit((c, l, o), d)\ \ = (d, c, o) \qquad\qquad if\ lastkey \in \{+, -, =\}$
                                  $\quad\quad\ (10c + d, l, o)\quad otherwise$
    $doit((c, l, o), o')\ = (o(c, l), c, o')$

The following table traces the execution of the calculator:

C	E	D
	(0,0,+)	0
2	(2,0,+)	2
+	(2,2,+)	2
3	(3,2,+)	3
+	(5,3,+)	5

Compare the trace tables for the 'programs' $2 + 3$ and $2 + 23$:

C	E	D	C	E	D
	(0,0,+)	0		(0,0,+)	0
2	(2,0,+)	2	2	(2,0,+)	2
+	(2,2,+)	2	+	(2,2,+)	2
3	(3,2,+)	3	2	(2,2,+)	2
			3	(23,2,+)	23

Notice that the display after the program $2 +$ is the same as it is after the program $2 + 3$, yet the behavior of the subsequent 3 command is different. Therefore, the calculator as defined does not satisfy the transparency property. Can you do better?

17.3.3 Reachability and undo

In Chapter 16, we discussed connectivity issues for dialogs. We could check a dialog description to see if there were any blind alleys, which once you had chosen them, would never let you back to the rest of the dialog. Systems can have similar problems at a semantic level.

In a commercial program debugger used by one of the authors, there is a window listing all the variables. If a variable is a complex structure, then hitting the 'insert' key while the cursor is over the variable will expand the variable showing all its fields. If you only want a few of the fields to be displayed, you can move the cursor over the unwanted fields and press the 'delete' key and the field is removed. These operations can be repeated over complex hierarchical structures. If you remove a field and then wish you had not, you can always press 'insert' again over the main variable and all the fields will be redisplayed. Even this breaks somewhat the principle of *commensurate effort*, but worse is to come. The 'delete' key also works for top-level variables, but once one of these is removed from the display there is *nothing* you can do to get it back, short of exiting the debugger and rerunning it from scratch.

A principle that stops this type of behavior is *reachability*. A system is reachable if from any state the system is in, you can get to any other state. The formal statement of this is as follows:

$$\forall e, e' \in E \cdot (\exists\, p \in P \cdot doit(e, p) = e')$$

Unlike the predictability principles, there are no awkward caveats. The only problem is that, if anything, it is too weak. For instance, a word processor could have a delete key, but no way to move the cursor about, so you always type at the end of the document. Now you can, of course, get from any document state to any other, you simply delete the whole text and retype what you want. However, if you had just typed in a whole letter and then noticed a mistake on the first line, you would not be pleased! So, ideally, one wants an independent idea of 'distance' between states and to make the difficulty of the path between them commensurate with the distance – small changes should be easy. Despite this, the principle on its own would have been strong enough to prevent the behavior of the debugger!

One special case of reachability is when the state you want to get to is the one you have just been in, that is *undo*. We expect undo to be easy, and ideally have a single undo button that will always undo the effect of the last command. We can state this requirement very easily:

$$\forall c \in C \cdot doit(e, c \,^\frown undo) = e$$

This says exactly what we wanted. We start in a state *e*. We then do any command *c* and follow it by the special command *undo*. The state is then the same as we began in.

Stop! Before patting ourselves on the back for so clearly defining undo, we should check that this requirement for undo is consistent. Indeed, it is consistent – so long as there are at most two states. That is, the above undo requirement is only possible for systems which *do* virtually nothing! The reason for this is that *undo* is itself a command and can undo itself. Take any state e and choose any command x. Let e_x be the state you get to after command x. That is $e_x = doit(e, x)$. Now we can apply the undo requirement to state e_x:

$$doit(e_x, undo) = doit(e, x \frown undo) = e$$

So, the *undo* command in state e_x gets us back to e. That is as expected. But what does *undo* do if we are in state e? Again we can employ the undo principle remembering that $e = doit(e_x, undo)$:

$$doit(e, undo) = doit(e_x, undo \frown undo) = e_x$$

This uses the undo principle when the command c is undo itself. However, our choice of command x was arbitrary, so if we had chosen another command, say y, we would have concluded that $doit(e, undo) = e_y$. This means that $e_x = e_y$, and in general anything we do from state e gets us to the same state. So at most we have two states, a toggle, with all the commands flipping back and forth between them. The only alternative is that the system does nothing.

We will not go on to describe the details of better undo requirements, the interested reader can find that elsewhere. The basis of most workable undo systems is that *undo* is not just any old command, but is treated differently. The simplest fix to the above undo principle is to restrict the commands to anything *except undo*!

The lesson from the above is clear. It is easy to say you want something which sounds quite reasonable. A formal description of the requirement may well reveal that, as in the case of undo, it is inconsistent – that is, *no* system could be built which satisfies the requirement.

17.3.4 Other interaction models

The PIE model was the inspiration for a wide variety of different models. Some of these are similar, but take a slightly different standpoint. For example, one model has results only available at some states. This actually corresponds to the intuition that a printed document is only available when you invoke the print function, or that an updated file is only available in the file system when you ask the editor to save. However, that model also only had the display available at some states – less intuitive.

There is also a range of models focussed at specific domain areas. The PIE model is a very general model of deterministic single-user systems. Other models address areas including:

Windowed systems This model describes the interference properties between windows. The distinctive feature is that the user is effectively regarded as having different personae when interacting with different windows. This reflects the observation that when swapping between tasks (associated with windows), the user should not have to keep track of dependencies and is therefore acting like several users.

Timing   What happens when the system is not fast enough and the user's actions get ahead of the system's responses? The formal model describes the relationship between the steady state behavior – what would happen if the machine was infinitely fast and there were no delays – and the actual temporal behavior. This analysis has highlighted deficiencies in the input–output model of window managers and operating systems.

Attention   This looks at ways of describing which parts of the display and result are used during any particular task. It uses *templates* for both, which model the selective attention during the task. The designer states what the expected templates are for any task, and then salience of the templates can be verified by experiment. These can then be tested using psychological experiments.

Non-determinism   If you are ignorant of certain information in a system, it may appear to behave non-deterministically. Many properties of different models, for example the predictability of PIEs, map onto problems of non-determinism. Methods of handling this non-determinism from one domain can then suggest similar methods in what would otherwise appear disparate areas. The fact that supposedly deterministic interfaces often appear random suggests that, where it is helpful for other purposes, the interface can be made deliberately non-deterministic.

Dynamic pointers   Interface objects often have special positions, such as the cursor or marked blocks. They may also have pointers into them, such as hypertext links. Dynamic pointers are a formalism that describes such positional information in a uniform manner. In particular, they help to manage the changes in pointers as the underlying object is updated. They also describe the mapping between positional information at different levels, for example when mapping mouse positions on the screen to their appropriate positions in application objects.

These are all principally single-user models. However, there has been some work in applying these formal models to group systems (such as those in Chapter 19). In particular, this has led to significant new insight into the meaning of undo in a group context.

17.4   CONTINUOUS BEHAVIOR

Although many of the systems and interfaces studied in rich media and in novel interfaces embody continuous real-time interaction, there are few models of this in the HCI literature. Possibly this is because of the conceptual dominance of discrete models. At a low level, computer systems are clearly discrete with step-by-step programs and users' actions being converted into streams of events. Even apparently smooth actions like dragging a mouse are treated as a series of individual 'mouse has moved' events.

There are two types of continuity:

continuous values – for example, the measurement of a weight;

continuous time – for example, a switch that could be sampled at any time.

Many sensors have both these properties: for example, the temperature of a room is both a continuous value and can be sampled at any time. It is the latter of these that we will consider in this section, as many standard notations such as Z deal with continuous values, whereas continuous time is less common.

In this section we will first look again at the PIE model and see how it can be extended to deal with mouse location.

17.4.1 Dealing with the mouse

The PIE model is very asymmetric between input and output. Some sorts of output are difficult to deal with, for example a beep used when something goes wrong. This is not clear in the formalism itself, but if we look at the principles, it is obvious that the display is expected to be persistent. If you go away and have a cup of tea, the display is still there when you get back. The beep is not. On the input side, mouse movement is not easy: one can regard each movement as being a command in C, but this is unnatural. Certainly, the user would not be conscious of each pixel movement!

A beep is similar to a keystroke: each is an *event*. The mouse's position is similar to the screen: they both have an observable value at any moment – we say each of them is a *status*. The PIE model is then an event-in/status-out model: the user does events (from C) and the system responds with a status (*display*). This suggests variations of the PIE model that have different combinations of event and status.

One version has events and status for its input, but still a purely status output (any-in/status-out). The (single command) state transition function then depends on both the command and the current mouse position (M):

$$doit : E \times C \times M \to E$$

The display function is now not just a function of the state, but it too depends on the mouse position:

$$display : E \times M \to D$$

This allows for the display to include the mouse cursor, which moves with the mouse (pretty obvious really) and also allows for the change in the display when the mouse drags an object.

This model only describes a special subclass of systems, those that are *trajectory independent*. The mouse position only has a permanent effect at the moment a command (keystroke or mouse button) happens; the intermediate positions are forgotten. For example, the model cannot describe freehand drawing. It is possible to extend the model to include more general systems; however, the subclass is interesting in itself. With the exception of drawing and similar tasks, such as 'air-brush' painting, most mouse-based systems are trajectory independent. Furthermore, the few that are not exhibit usability problems, suggesting that trajectory dependency is itself a general usability principle for all but exceptional situations.

17.4.2 Formal aspects of status–event analysis

Probably the earliest continuous time models in the formal uscr interface literature are the variants of status–event analysis [94,102] of which the variant of the PIE model above is a simple example. Status–event analysis (S–E) distinguishes events that occur at specific moments of time from status phenomena that have (typically changing) values over a period of time. Examples of events include keystrokes, beeps, and the stroke of midnight in the story of Cinderella. Examples of status phenomena include the current computer display, the location of the mouse pointer, the internal state of the computer and the weather. We will discuss status–event analysis in more detail in Chapter 18; here we will just look at the more formal aspects.

Perhaps one of the most significant features of S–E is its treatment of interstitial behavior. Whereas discrete models focus solely on what happens at the moments when events occur, S–E puts equal emphasis on the more fluid interaction between events. In many GUI systems this is what gives the 'feel' of interaction, for example, dragging, scrolling, etc., and in rich media this is likely to be the main purpose of interaction!

Status–event analysis is really a conceptual framework for viewing interaction, but does have several concrete models, both descriptive models (variants of the PIE) and specification notations. These all have the general form of a state-transition style description of events and a more continuous description of interstitial behavior:

action:
user-event × (current/history of) input-status × state
→ response-event × (new) state

interstitial behavior:
(current/history of) input-status × state → output-status

The treatment of the input status at events and during interstitial behavior distinguishes interactions of markedly different kinds, for example, the trajectory dependency described above (Section 17.4.1).

Another crucial aspect of S–E, which is not apparent in discrete systems, is status-change events. These occur when a status phenomenon crosses some form of trigger threshold. For example, when a temperature reaches some value, or the time (on the clock) is a certain time. The nature of these thresholds is application dependent and may be dynamic. Furthermore, there are a whole range of issues about how status-change events become system-level events: polling, active sensors, etc. Typically, at an abstract level of specification one would just say 'when this happens . . .', but as this becomes operationalized these issues of mechanism surface. We will see more of how these status-change events propagate in Chapter 18.

17.4.3 Making everything continuous

In engineering and physics, the idea of modeling continuous behavior being a special problem would seem strange. In those fields, and in real life, continuous phenomena are normal – discrete things are the exception. For example, you may recall, from high school physics, the equations of an object moving under gravity:

$$\frac{\mathrm{d}x}{\mathrm{d}t} = v \qquad \frac{\mathrm{d}v}{\mathrm{d}t} = -g \qquad x = vt - \frac{1}{2}gt^2$$

Objects in virtual worlds have to have similar behavior, and Wüthrich [384] has used general versions of this kind of equation from cybernetic systems theory to model virtual reality systems:

$$\text{state}_t = \phi \ (\ t,\ t_0,\ \text{state}_{t0},\ \text{inputs during } [t_0,t)\ )$$
$$\text{output}_t = \eta \ (\ \text{state}_t\ )$$

The difference between this and the S–E description is largely representational, although it should be noted that the state is different. In the S–E description the 'state' attempts to ignore the ephemeral changes during the interstices, whereas the systems theory model incorporates this (for example, that the mouse is at a particular position *now*). Both forms of state seem appropriate depending on the circumstances and can be incorporated as alternative views or levels of description.

Notice that the systems theory definition treats events on a par with status phenomena; both are merely part of an 'inputs at time *t*' and there is no equivalent of the action description when an event occurs. However, when viewed as functions of time, event phenomena have values only at a few points of time and for most of the time have some sort of special 'not happening now' value. There is a history of dealing with event phenomena in this way in applied mathematics where 'impulse' events, such as a voltage spike or collision, are modeled using Dirac delta functions, functions that are infinitely large for an infinitesimally short time.

This 'treat everything as continuous' leads to more complicated and less clear ways of expressing things, just as solely event-based formalisms do. The natural way of describing the world includes both status and event phenomena. In fact, when applying systems theory to a real example Wüthrich finds it more convenient to describe event phenomena as timestamped values – that is, even if the model has no events you are forced to invent them to deal with real examples!

17.4.4 Hybrid models

This problem of merging event-based and continuous status behavior arises in other areas of computing where control systems interact with real physical systems such as industrial controllers or fly-by-wire aircraft. There is a whole range

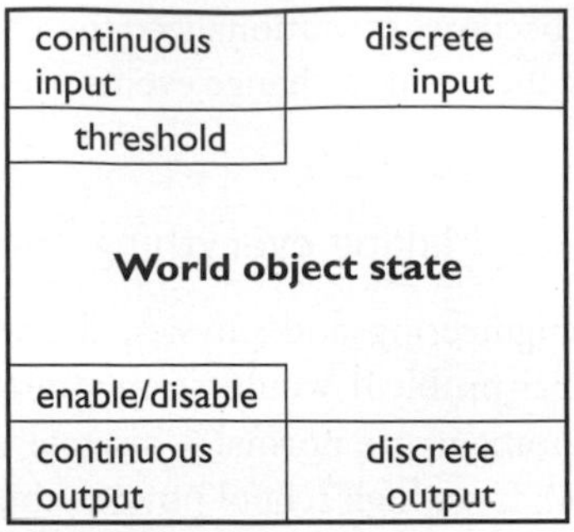

continuous input	discrete input
threshold	
World object state	
enable/disable	
continuous output	discrete output

Figure 17.5 Continuous interactor from [379]. Source: © Springer-Verlag Berlin Heidelberg 2001

of notations and methods for dealing with these 'hybrid systems' [158]. On the whole, this community has a largely dualist model of the world, with discrete computer systems interfacing with a continuous environment defined by differential equations.

This sort of model has been adopted by a few researchers in HCI. For example, the TACIT project [339] studied a variety of continuous-time interactive systems and also considered modeling using hybrid high-level Petri nets [229]. As we saw in Chapter 16, Petri nets allow us to express concurrent behavior, but have discrete behavior with tokens moving between places at transitions (event points). The hybrid Petri nets include 'continuous transitions', which are effectively a form of interstitial behavior.

A similar variant of hybrid Petri nets has been used to develop component/interactor models (see Figure 17.5) intended to model objects in virtual environments [379]. These interactors have both discrete and continuous output and input and a threshold on discrete input, which produces status-change events. Less clear from the figure, but evident in the Petri net specifications, is that there can be direct continuous connections between continuous input and output (status–status relations) controlled by the enable/disable switch.

17.4.5 Broad issues: granularity and Gestalt

It is clear that time can be divided almost arbitrarily (at least to the Planck time of about 10^{-43} of a second). However, we constantly divide it into discrete units: Monday, Tuesday, July, yesterday, today, next year. We talk about things happening at a particular time (the clock struck at noon), but, of course, nothing happens instantaneously (how long do the chimes last?). In day-to-day speech we manage these ambiguities, but as we formalize time, whether in computer tools or in formal notations, we have to try to make these precise.

Studies of the use of electronic calendar systems highlight this problem [283]. Although users think in terms of 'let's meet in the afternoon', the system forces you to give meetings precise start and end times '3pm–4:30pm'. In addition, many calendar systems regard time as being made of discrete days with continuous times within. Try creating an agenda item for an overnight plane flight! There has been some work on formalizing times like 'I'll do this today' (in the next 24 hours, before midnight), but it is still in its infancy [204].

The issue of things happening at precise times means that we have to be constantly careful when we talk about an interval of time such as 3pm to 4pm; do we mean to include both 3pm and 4pm, or do we mean from 3pm up to but not including 4pm? In mathematics these are called closed (when the end point is included) or open (when the end point is not included) intervals. Note that in the systems theory equations in Section 17.4.3 the formulae included 'inputs during $[t_0, t)$'. The square and round brackets are conventionally used to distinguish these boundaries where square brackets mean 'including the end' and round brackets mean 'excluding the end'. So the interval '$[t_0, t)$' means 'all times including t_0 and up to, but not including, t'.

This precision is needed to ensure that when we describe things we do not accidentally 'leave out' the moment of time between two intervals, or accidentally have intervals overlap by one moment when we mean them to be disjoint. For example, in Section 17.4.3, if the definition had been 'inputs during $[t_0, t]$' it would have meant that the state and output of a system at a particular moment depended on the inputs at that precise moment. This would have allowed a causal cycle if two such systems were interacting where the output of one depended on the current output of the other and vice versa. The definition given cuts this potential knot by saying that the state depends only on past inputs, but can take into account those arbitrarily recently in the past.

The ambiguity of end points is also problematic if we need to 'parse' continuous media, for example in speech interfaces, gesture recognition, or determination of context in ubiquitous computing. In all these cases, we find that continuous media exhibit temporal Gestalt phenomena: the higher-level units such as words, or contexts, only have meaning over time and do not have clear boundaries. Consider gesture recognition – the movement only has meaning once complete; music – the melody is only a melody whilst being played; even graphics get meaning through movement [19]. This is rather like the fact that the typed characters 'd', 'i', 'r', 'carriage-return' only mean 'list directory' when considered as a whole. The main difference is that the boundaries are clearer in the case of discrete phenomena – the gesture has no definitive start or end, although an end point would be made concrete by actual recognition software.

One final thing to note about the notations and models for continuous interaction is how similar they are. This is perhaps because the physical world is largely continuous and so there are fewer 'choices' to be made in modeling it. However, at another level human discourse and language is discrete: we use a finite lexicon of words and sentences. So at some level the sorts of difficulties discussed above merely reflect the tension between the world of physical actions and the fundamental nature of human language.

17.5 SUMMARY

This chapter has focussed on modeling the deeper semantic behavior of an interactive system. To design a usable system one needs to know what it *does*!

We began by looking at different kinds of software engineering formalisms that can be used to specify the behavior of specific systems. These specifications can be used for communication between designer and implementor, and for analysis. Model-based specifications define the state of the system, the invariants, which must always be true, and the operations that change the state (usually as the result of user actions). Algebraic specifications describe the system in terms of the relationships between operations. Both can suffer from incompleteness, where one has not specified enough to determine the behavior. In particular, it is as important to say what does *not* change as what does – the framing problem. Both of these concentrate on step-by-step changes that the user can perform on the system. Temporal logics allow you to specify properties such as 'it is *always* possible to quit', and deontic logics allow you to talk about permitted actions and other issues of responsibility.

In Section 17.3 we considered interaction models, in particular the PIE model. This type of model addresses classes of system rather than specific designs, allowing us to describe general properties such as predictability (the 'gone away for a cup of tea problem'), observability (what can we tell about the state of the system from its display?) and reachability (whether there are any dead ends from which we can never return). We looked at the issue of undo and how the PIE model allowed us to discover that the apparently obvious meaning of undo was, in fact, inconsistent. As well as the very general PIE model, more specific interaction models address issues such as timing properties and user attention.

Finally, we looked at continuous time phenomena. This included a variant of the PIE model for dealing with dragging and similar mouse-based interactions. At a more general level, the formal concepts of status–event analysis show that *both* major changes at events *and* the more continuous interstitial behavior between events are important. Other models based on systems theory and hybrid systems either have similar constructs, or are forced to create them when dealing with real problems. We need to deal with the relationship between the 'soft' ideas of time in day-to-day life ('let's meet this afternoon') and the hard-edged formal ideas of time ('starting at 3pm and continuing until, but not including, 4:30pm'), but this is still largely an open problem.

EXERCISES

17.1   Using the model-oriented approach with the example graphics program described in Section 17.2.3, specify the move operation as a schema which acts on the currently selected objects. Is the operation you have defined cumulative (two successive moves can be done as one move which is the sum of the other two) or is it 'forgetful'? Discuss the implications of the framing problem in your definition.

17.2   Write a similar schema for *Resize*. It should have the following informal semantics. The width and height attributes are of the shapes bounding box. The resize operation should make one corner of the bounding box be at the current mouse position (supplied as the argument *current_pos?*).

   Hint: The width of a box is twice the difference between the *x* coordinate of the center and the *x* coordinate of any corner:

$$wid = 2 \times |\, center.x - corner.x \,|$$

17.3   In Section 17.2.5, we said that the specification *Algebraic–draw* could be extended to say that a move, resize or unselect after a delete has no effect. The axiom for *unselect* looks like this:

   (9) $unselect(delete(g)) = delete(g)$

   Write two more axioms (10) and (11) which say the same about move and resize. Now use axioms (4) and (5) to show that (9) implies both your new axioms.

17.4   Imagine a normal calculator except that it displays A for 0, B for 1, up to J for 9. So the number 372 would appear as DHC. Does this affect the formal transparency of the calculator? Should it?

17.5   To some extent undo is similar to the 'back' command or button found in many web browsers, help systems and hypertext systems. Is the 'back' button on a browser just like undo?

   Hint: Consider scenarios where the pages are web forms updating a database.

17.6   Experiment with the 'back' button on different browsers, help systems, etc. Record systematically the behavior as you visit pages and use the 'back' button, and try to build a model (informal or formal) of the system. Pay particular attention to what happens if you revisit the same page during the same 'drill down' and the behavior in systems with multiple windows/frames. (Note that this behavior does differ dramatically even between different versions of the same web browser.)

17.7   Sections 17.2.1 and 17.2.2 give two reasons for using formal methods in HCI: communication and analysis. These are focussed on the sort of mathematical models found in this chapter. However, there are other sorts of 'formal' modeling in HCI: dialog notations are formal models of the syntax of the human–computer conversation, hierarchical task analysis is a formalization of the task structure, some cognitive models are effectively formal models of the user's mind.

   (a)   Are communication and analysis reasons for using these other sorts of formalism?
   (b)   Can you think of other reasons why you would or would not use formalisms?
   (c)   Try to use these pros and cons to formulate issues in the choice of appropriate forms of formal model and analysis.

17.8   This exercise is based on the mobile phone scenario on the book website at: /e3/scenario/phone/

   List the main elements of the state of the phone (you can use programming language variable declarations for this) and then write down a step-by-step walkthrough of the state as the user accesses a shortcut at position '3' as in steps C.1–C.10 of scenario C.

17.9 This exercise is based on the nuclear reactor scenario on the book website at: /e3/scenario/nuclear/ You will need to refer to this while completing the exercise.

The exercise is in four parts, but you will probably find it easier to work on them in parallel. As you try to define actions you will find state elements you have missed, and as you work through the scenarios you will probably find problems that you need to go back and change in the state and actions.

(a) Complete the following partial description of the state of the nuclear control panel.

```
Alarm_State:          {Green, Amber, TempRed, Red}
Confirm_Needed:       Boolean  [ that is true or false]
Target_Pressure:      Nat      [ that is { 0, 1, 2, ... } ]
Target_Temp:          Nat
Target_Flow:          Nat
Manual_Override_Value:  Nat
...
```

(b) Here is a description of the state change for two actions: when a digit is pressed on the keypad and when the '–' key is pressed. Note we have not written it in 'proper' Z, but in a form of pseudo code.

keypad_digit(d)

```
add d to the right-hand end of Manual_Override_Value
```

alarm_lower [minus key is pressed]

```
if ( Alarm_State is Red or Alarm State is TempRed )
then set Alarm_State to Amber
if ( Alarm_State is Amber or Alarm_State is Green)
then set Alarm_State to Green
```

Using these to guide you, complete the following two partial descriptions of the state changes for the CONFIRM and CANCEL buttons on the Emergency Confirm control panel.

confirm

```
set Confirm_Needed to false
if ( Alarm_State is TempRed )
then set Alarm_State to Red
... something about emergency shutdown too
...
```

cancel

```
set Confirm_Needed to false
if ( Alarm_State is TempRed )
then set Alarm_State to Amber
... something about emergency shutdown too
...
```

(c) Produce descriptions of the state change for the following actions:

(i) `alarm_higher` – the '+' key is pressed on the Alarm Control panel;

(ii) `shutdown` – the IMMEDIATE SHUTDOWN COMMENCE button has been pressed on the Emergency Shutdown panel;

(iii) `select_target(targ)` – the target pulldown has been used on the Manual Override panel. `targ` is one of {`Pressure, Temp, Flow`};

(iv) `set_target_value` – the SET button has been pressed on the Manual Override panel.

(d) Check your state and actions by running through the scenario and showing annotating each action with the current state. Use the following example of the first few steps as a guide to the appropriate level of detail.

```
Initial state:   Alarm_State is Green
                 Confirm_Needed is false
                 etc.  ...
Steps 1, 2       no system actions
Step 3           press '+' twice
                 alarm_higher:
                         Alarm_State = Amber
                 alarm_higher:
                         Alarm_State = TempRed
                         Confirm_Needed = True
Step 4           button glows because Confirm_Needed = True
Step 5           no system action
etc.
```

RECOMMENDED READING

A. Dix, Upside down As and algorithms – computational formalisms and theory. In J. Carroll, editor, *HCI Models, Theories, and Frameworks: Toward an Interdisciplinary Science*, Morgan Kaufmann, 2003.

Both an introduction to formalism in HCI and an apologetic for why more formal techniques are both useful and ultimately unavoidable. Contains material motivating the underlying concepts of formalism in both this chapter and Chapter 16, and a historical view of the development of formalism from Aristotle to the present day. Watch out, too, for a whole page about counting cockroaches.

M. D. Harrison and H. W. Thimbleby, editors, *Formal Methods in Human–Computer Interaction*, Cambridge University Press, 1990.

A collected works with chapters covering a range of approaches: formal cognitive modeling, PIE-like models of interaction and formal aspects of dialog description. Various notations are used: TAG (see Chapter 12), Z, functional programming and standard mathematical set theory. The chapters on dialog description include both eventCSP and generative transition networks, a cross between a production system and a state transition network (see Chapter 16). There are also chapters concerning the software engineering issues of moving from formal descriptions through to running programs.

A. J. Dix, *Formal Methods for Interactive Systems*, Academic Press, 1991.
The PIE model is described in detail, together with other, more domain-specific formal models. Issues covered in this formal framework include windowing systems, real-time response, pointing devices and direct manipulation. A chapter on models of status and events is the theoretical background for status–event analysis. In addition, the problems of refining a formal interface description into a running system are discussed.

P. Palanque and F. Paternó, editors, *Formal Methods in Human–Computer Interaction*, Springer-Verlag, 1997.
A more recent collection, which has its roots in a CHI'96 workshop. The chapters in this book address the specification of a world wide web browser using a variety of different notations and formal techniques. As each technique is wielded by an expert, it is an excellent comparative account. Perhaps most interesting to note is the way in which different techniques are suited for tackling specific parts of the general problem.

H. W. Thimbleby, *User Interface Design*, ACM Press, Addison-Wesley, 1990.
This is a general interface design book, but contains significant sections concerning formal aspects and models. As well as the explicitly mathematical parts, a formal approach to problems is often evident in the informal parts of the book.

J. M. Spivey, *The Z Reference Manual*, Prentice Hall International, 1989.
This book provides the standard definition of the Z language and a tutorial introduction to Z specification for the interested reader. There are also many other reference books and tutorials for the Z and the VDM notation.

A. F. Monk and N. Gilbert, editors, *Perspectives on HCI: Diverse Approaches*, Academic Press, 1995.
A collection of articles introducing key areas of HCI, including formal models (Chapter 2) and formal specification (Chapter 3). Readable introductions for newcomers to these topics.

C. Roast and J. Siddiqi, editors, *FAHCI – Formal Aspects of the Human–Computer Interface*, Springer-Verlag, 1996.
Report of a workshop of the same name held in 1996, principally containing articles on formal specification and modeling, but also includes some cognitive modeling.

There are several conferences that include more formal materials, most notably the annual conference on 'Design, Specification and Verification of Interactive Systems' held under the auspices of Eurographics since 1994, and published by Springer-Verlag, and the short-lived *FAHCI* (*Formal Aspects of the Human Computer Interface*) series, also published by Springer. The triennial IFIP WG 2.7/13.4 working conference *Engineering Human–Computer Interaction* is published by North-Holland (to *EHCI'92*), Chapman and Hall (*EHCI'95*) and Kluwer (*EHCI'98* and *EHCI'01*).

MODELING RICH INTERACTION

OVERVIEW

We operate within an ecology of people, physical artifacts and electronic systems, and this rich ecology has recently become more complex as electronic devices invade the workplace and our day-to-day lives. We need methods to deal with these rich interactions.

- Status–event analysis is a semi-formal, easy to apply technique that:
  - classifies phenomena as event or status
  - embodies naïve psychology
  - highlights feedback problems in interfaces.

- Aspects of rich environments can be incorporated into methods such as task analysis:
  - other people
  - information requirements
  - triggers for tasks
  - modeling artifacts
  - placeholders in task sequences.

- New sensor-based systems do not require explicit interaction; this means:
  - new cognitive and interaction models
  - new design methods
  - new system architectures.

INTRODUCTION

The majority of more detailed models and theories in HCI are focussed on the 'normal' situation of a single user interacting with traditional applications using a keyboard and screen. The models focus predominantly on the effects of individual planned user actions. In fact, this 'normal' situation is increasingly looking like the exception. As we noted in the last chapter (Section 17.4), much of interaction is about more continuous phenomena both in the computer (e.g. mouse movement) and in more ubiquitous computing environments, such as smart homes, that sense movement, temperature, etc. Even traditional computer systems are used not in isolation, but in office and other work settings that involve different people and physical objects. Normal human–computer interaction usually includes looking at pieces of paper, walking around rooms, talking to people. Finally, the more ubiquitous environments deeply challenge the idea of intention behind human–computer interaction: increasingly things simply happen to us.

In this chapter we look at several ways in which this 'normal' situation can be modeled either by new methods or by adapting existing ones.

In Section 18.2, we will demonstrate how a semi-formal technique, *status–event analysis*, can be used to understand the interplay between more instantaneous events and more continuous status phenomena. The examples in this section will be mainly focussed on more traditional computer systems, but unlike the models in previous chapters, status–event analysis is used to describe a 'slice' of the system at all levels of abstraction, rather than the whole system at a specific level. Also, by dealing with both more 'computer-ish' events and more 'world-ish' status phenomena it lays the ground for thinking about these increasingly rich interactions as the chapter progresses.

Section 18.3 is still focussed on traditional computer systems, but where the emphasis is on the physical and social environment in which they are based. We will be considering how aspects of the rich workplace ecology can be captured in more formal techniques, in particular task analysis. We will look at representing collaboration – who is doing what; information requirements – what do we need to know when; triggers – what makes things happen when they do; artifacts – how to model their behavior; and placeholders – how we keep track of where we are in a task.

Finally, Section 18.4 will explode the traditional model completely! The types of systems discussed in ubiquitous computing, and now beginning to be deployed, often do not require explicit interaction. There is a range of levels of intention, from fully intentional systems to those where the system observes and responds to actions of the user performed possibly for some completely different purposes. We will find that these incidental interactions require new ways of thinking about interaction, new ways to design systems and new ways to construct them.

The latter parts of this chapter, especially, involve areas where theory is struggling to keep up with technology and where there is still little idea of where eventually the technology will be used in practice.

18.2   STATUS–EVENT ANALYSIS

In Chapter 16 we saw that some dialog notations were state oriented, whereas others were event oriented. Each type of notation had trouble describing some phenomena, but was good with others. Similarly, in Section 17.4 we found that formal models of interactive systems need to be able to deal with both *status* and *event* input and output.

Note that the word 'status' is chosen rather than 'state', as the term will be used to refer to any phenomenon with a persistent value. This includes the position of a mouse on a table and the current screen contents, as well as the internal state of the system. The word 'state' has connotations of the complete state of the system, rather than the selective particular views meant here by status.

Note on pronunciation

Note that the plural of status is not statuses or even stati. Like salmon and sheep, the plural of status is simply status. However, according to the *Oxford English Dictionary* these are pronounced differently: the 'u' in the singular is as the 'u' in datum, whereas the plural has an 'u' as in tune.

The distinction between status and event is between being and doing. Status phenomena always have a value one could consult. For example, you can ask the question 'what was the position of the mouse on the tabletop at 3:27pm?'. An event, on the other hand, happens at a particular moment. Here the relevant question is 'at what time did the user press the mouse button?'.

This section describes *status–event analysis*, an 'engineering'-level technique which makes use of the status–event distinction. The label 'engineering' is used in a similar way to the way it is applied to the keystroke-level model (Chapter 12, Section 12.5.1). An engineering approach is built upon theoretical principles, but does not require a deep theoretical background on the part of the designer. Status–event analysis is built upon two theoretical foundations. On the one side, it is derived from work on formal models of interaction (as described briefly in Section 17.3.4). However, a designer using the method does not need to use, or even know about, these foundations. On the other side, status–event analysis makes use of fairly naïve psychological knowledge, to predict how particular interface features affect the user.

The strength of the method is that a single descriptive framework can be applied at a range of levels from the application, through the interface, to the user's perception. Indeed, the same descriptive framework can describe even the low-level electrical signals and logic in the microseconds from when a user hits a key to that key being 'noticed' by the system.

We will first consider an example of clocks and calendars, which demonstrates some of the important properties of events and status and how they interrelate. The design implications of this are discussed in Section 18.2.2. In particular, we will see that events generated by applications have an associated timescale which tells us when we *want* them to be perceived by the user. Section 18.2.3 discusses a few simple psychological facts which help us to predict when interface events become salient for the user.

Status–event analysis looks at different layers of the system, such as user, screen (presentation), dialog and application. It looks for the events perceived at each level and the status changes at each level. This, combined with the naïve psychological analysis of the presentation/user boundary, allows the designer to predict failures and more importantly suggest improvements. This approach is demonstrated in two examples: the 'mail has arrived' interface to an email system and the behavior of an on-screen button.

18.2.1 Properties of events: clocks and calendars

Brian is due to meet Alison to go to the cinema at 20 to 8. He decides he will stop work at 25 to, and keeps an eye on his watch. Every few minutes he looks at it, increasingly frequently as the time draws nigh. Eventually, he looks and it is 24 minutes to, so he quickly puts his coat on and leaves.

In fact Brian had an alarm on his watch. He could have set it for 7:35, and waited for it to ring. Unfortunately, he has never worked out how to set the alarm (nor how to stop it beeping every hour).

A few days later Alison is sitting in her office. In an idle moment she consults her calendar to see what is happening tomorrow. She sees that it is Brian's birthday, so decides to buy him the soundtrack of the film they recently saw.

From these scenarios, we can abstract many of the important properties of status and events:

Status Brian's watch is a status – it always tells the time – so is Alison's calendar. Moreover, assuming Brian's watch is analog, this demonstrates that status phenomena may be both discrete (the calendar) or continuous (the watch face).

Events The passing of the time 7:35, when Brian wanted to stop work, was an event. A different, but related, event was when Brian got up to go. The alarm on Brian's watch (if he could use it) would have caused an event, showing that Brian's watch is capable of both status and event outputs. Alison also experienced an event when she noticed it was Brian's birthday the next day, and of course, his birthday will also be an event.

Polling Given Brian only had a status – the watch face – and he wanted an event – 7:35 – he looked periodically at his watch. In computing terms, Brian *polled* his watch. Polling is a normal activity that *people* do as well as machines. It is a standard way to turn a status into an event.

Actual vs. perceived The event Brian was awaiting was when the watch said 7:35. This event happened, but Brian obviously did not look at his watch at just the right moment. Instead, this *actual event* became a *perceived event* for Brian a minute later when he next looked at his watch. If one looks at a fine enough timescale there are almost always gaps between actual and perceived events. Of course, there can be similar lags between actual and perceived status too.

Granularity   The watch showing 7:35 and Brian's birthday are both events, but they operate at completely different timescales. The interpretation of events and status may differ depending on the timescale one uses. In particular, the idea of immediacy changes.

These same properties all emerge during the analysis of interactive systems.

18.2.2 Design implications

Applications want to cause events for users and use various presentation techniques to do this. However, these techniques must be matched to the *timescale* of the desired event. For example, if a stock of 6 mm bolts is running low, this requires reordering within days or weeks. On the other hand, a coolant failure in a nuclear power plant may require action within seconds.

The presented form of the event for the user must match these timescales – both causing events too fast or too slow is wrong. It is fairly obvious that too slow an event is wrong. An email message to the power plant operator would be ineffectual; the operator and the computer would both be so much radioactive waste. However, the opposite fault can be equally damaging. Red flashing lights and alarm bells when the last box of 6 mm bolts is opened would be annoying, and could also distract the operator from more important tasks, such as dealing with that coolant.

A less extreme example would be an electronic alarm and calendar. Imagine we have an online alarm function, which can be set to sound a buzzer and put a message in the middle of the screen at any time we like. This would obviously have been useful for Brian who could have set it to say 'cinema with Alison' at 7:35. However, if Alison wanted to remind herself of Brian's birthday, she would be forced to set an alarm for a specific time, say noon on the day before. This would have been disruptive when it rang, and not in keeping with the timescale of birthdays.

In order to cause a perceived event for the user at the appropriate timescale, we must be able to predict the event timescale of various interface techniques. Simply presenting information on the screen, or causing an event at the interface, is no guarantee that that event will become a perceived event for the user.

18.2.3 Naïve psychology

In order to predict the effect of interface techniques, we need to employ some naïve psychology. This can tell us what sort of stimuli are salient and where the user's attention will be focussed.

First, we can sometimes predict *where* the user will be looking:

Mouse   When the user is positioning the mouse pointer over a target, his attention will be focussed on that target. This is guaranteed in all but a few situations by the feedback requirements of hand–eye coordination. However, this attention may not stay long after the target has been successfully 'hit'.

Text insertion point   While typing text, the user will intermittently look at the text just typed and hence the current insertion point. However, because of touch-typing, this is less certain than the mouse except when moving the insertion point over large distances using cursor keys – another positioning task.

Screen   It is reasonably safe to assume that the user will look at the screen intermittently. However, there is no guarantee that any particular message or icon on the screen will be noticed, only that very large messages spread across a large part of the screen will probably be noticed.

If we know where the user is looking, then we can put information there (not in a status line at the top where no one ever looks). Also, changes at the user's visual focus will be salient and become a perceived event for the user. An example, where the mouse pointer itself is used for information, is the egg-timer or ticking watch icon used when a system is busy.

Secondly, immediate events can be caused even when we do not know where the user is looking. The most common are *audible events*: beeps, buzzers, bells and whistles. These cause perceived events even when the user is not looking at the screen. In addition, our *peripheral vision* is good at detecting *movement* (see Chapter 1). Whereas we might not notice a small *change* unless it is in our visual focus, we will notice something moving out of the corner of our eye. We will see an interesting example of this in the next section, but a common example of *large* change (rather than movement) is the use of a screen flash as a silent bell. Not only does this cause an event when you are looking anywhere on the screen, but even if you are looking at the keyboard or at a document beside the screen. The only proviso is that the duration of the flash must be timed suitably to avoid it being mistaken for normal screen flicker.

Finally, recall from Chapter 1 that when people complete some goal, they experience *closure*. This means that they have a feeling of completeness and go on to the next thing. Closure has implications both on perception and actions. It is why in the mouse positioning task, the user's eye may stray from the target as soon as the target is perceived as 'hit'. In addition, the user may begin some of the actions for the next task, while certain automatic actions terminating the last task are still going on. For example, it is easy to knock a glass from the table by beginning to turn round before fully letting go of the glass.

We will see examples of each of these three effects in the succeeding subsections.

18.2.4 Example – email interface

Brian wants to thank Alison for his birthday present, which she left on his desk. He sends her a message by email. Consider the stages the message goes through, from when the message first arrives in Alison's system until Alison realizes it is there.

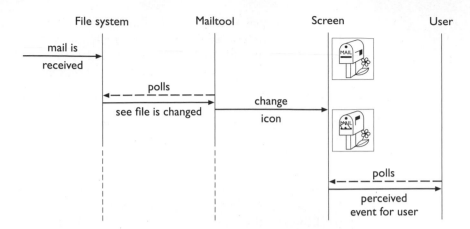

Figure 18.1 Inputs and outputs of a single-user system

To make life easy we will assume that Brian is on the same network as Alison. When he hits the 'SEND' button on his machine, the message is sent – this is an event. The way that many systems handle internal mail is simply to append it to the recipient's mailbox file, for example '/usr/spool/mail/Alison'. The *event* of receiving mail is therefore reflected in a change of *status* in the file system. You can see this event depicted as the first arrow in Figure 18.1. This figure shows timelines for various components in the interface, where time flows downwards. Events are denoted by arrows between the components' timelines.

On Alison's workstation runs a mailtool. When not in use, the mailtool is depicted by an 'empty mailbox' icon. The mailtool does not notice the change in the mailbox file immediately, but periodically it checks the file to see if it has changed – that is, it *polls*. So, after a while, the mailtool polls the file and sees that it has indeed changed. At this point the change in *status* of the file system has become a *perceived event* for the mailtool. Notice that we are using the term perceived event of computer agents as well as of the user. Obviously, the final perceived event for the user is what is important, but we are also interested in similar phenomena at different levels.

Having noticed the event, the mailtool now knows that mail has arrived, and must try to make this event a perceived event for the user. To do this it changes its icon to denote a mailbox with a letter sticking out. That is, we again see an *event* giving rise to a change in *status*, this time on the screen.

Finally, we come to the user, Alison. She is sitting at her workstation busy on a report she must finish. She gets to the end of a difficult section and breaks in her typing for a moment. During such breaks, her eyes wander over the screen, and in particular she occasionally glances at the mailtool's icon to see if any mail has arrived – she *polls* it. This time when she looks up, she sees that mail has indeed arrived – the mail arrival has at last become a *perceived event* for Alison.

If we look at Figure 18.1, we see that a number of active agents (Brian, the mailtool and Alison) cause events for one another mediated by status elements (the filestore and screen). This is a very common scenario, especially if you look at fine details of interaction. However, it is also possible to have direct event-based connections (which we will see in the next example), or even status–status connections. An example of the latter is the linkage between the mouse on the table and the mouse pointer on the screen. Even this is mediated by events in its implementation, but this is not apparent to the user.

Having analyzed the event–status dynamics of the system, we can ask whether it is functioning as it should. In fact, for this particular message and context it functioned well enough, but let us consider a few alternative scenarios.

If the message had been 'Fire! Get out quick' Alison might now be dead. Forgetting the interface design, the mailtool probably does not poll the file system often enough to respond within the timescale of such a message. If the system were required to support messages of such urgency, we would need to redesign the mail arrival mechanism so that the mailtool would receive a direct event, rather than wait to poll. Assuming this were done, would it have saved Alison? Probably not, because she would not have looked at the mailtool icon sufficiently often to see the crucial message.

On the other hand, the message may have been information about a forthcoming conference. Alison need not have read this message when she did. The perceived event is now at too fine a timescale, and it is an unwanted interruption.

Finally, if at 12:30 Brian sent the message 'Thanks for the gift, see you for lunch at 1 o'clock?', then the timescale may be appropriate, but the guarantee of delivery of the current system is too weak. Alison usually glances at the icon every few minutes, but occasionally, when engrossed in a task, she may miss it for hours. Alison has at least survived, but is getting hungry.

Split-second requests are not normally sent by email and so the last form of message is the most urgent encountered in typical email traffic. The timescale required is of the order of a few minutes. But we saw that the current interface, although of the appropriate timescale, does not carry sufficient guarantees. There are other interfaces available, so we shall see how they fare:

Explicit examination The traditional email interface required the user to examine the mailbox explicitly, say in the morning and evening. This was a form of polling, but at a much reduced timescale. This would obviously be useless for Brian's message, but would have been much more appropriate for the conference announcement.

Audible bell The existing mailtool can be set to sound a bell when mail arrives. This would cause an instant perceived event for Alison – if she was there. To avoid being missed entirely when Alison is out of the room, the bell has to be combined with a *status* indicator, such as the icon. However, even if Alison were there, the interruption caused to her work would not merit the normal timescales of email messages – unless it said 'Fire!', that is.

Moving faces Finally, there is a second mail-watcher available, which when mail arrives sees who it is from and slowly moves a bitmap picture of the sender into a sort of 'hall of fame' at the bottom of the screen. Whereas normally the mailtool icon is not noticed as it *suddenly* changes, this *movement* is noticed at once as it is in Alison's peripheral vision. Furthermore, it leaves a status indicator behind (the sender's face). It thus does the job of the buzzer and icon combined. However, the guaranteed event is still too quick.

What is really wanted is a guaranteed event at a timescale of minutes. None of the available options supplies this. However, knowing what is wanted one can suggest designs to supply the need. For example, we could automatically notice gaps in typing, and notify the user (aurally or visually) during a gap on the assumption that this will be less obtrusive. Alternatively, we can use a non-guaranteed technique of the appropriate timescale, such as the existing mailtool icon, but if the mail is not examined within a certain time we can use a more salient alarm.

Ideally, such mechanisms should be tuned to the particular timescale of the application and, if anything, email is one of the most difficult examples as the timescale depends on the message. Other applications, particularly command and control tasks, will have more well-defined timescales making the matching job easier.

18.2.5 Example – screen button feedback

The last example used status–event analysis to suggest an improved interface to email. However, email is, as we admitted, a complex example, so it is not surprising that improvements can be found. In the following example, we find that status–event analysis is even able to suggest improvements in something as simple and heavily used as an on-screen button.

Screen buttons activated by clicking the mouse over them are a standard widget in any interface toolkit and are found in most modern application interfaces. The application developer has little control over the detailed user interaction as this is fixed by the toolkit. So, the specific results of this example are most relevant to the toolkit designer, but the general techniques are more widely applicable.

A common problem with many on-screen buttons is that the user thinks the button has been pressed, but in fact it has not been. As an example, imagine Alison at work again on her word processor. The report is too long and so when she notices a superfluous paragraph, she selects it and then moves her button up to the 'delete' button. She clicks over the button and thinks it has had an effect, but actually as she lifted her finger from the button, the mouse slipped from the button and the click was ignored (the button is activated by the mouse *up* event). Unfortunately, she does not notice until having, with difficulty, pared the report down to 1000 words, she notices that the unwanted paragraph remains.

We have two questions: why is this mistake so frequent, and why didn't she notice? To answer these we use status–event analysis to look at two scenarios, the first where she successfully selects 'delete', and the one where she does not. There are four elements in the analysis: the application (word processor), the button's dialog (in the toolkit), the screen image and the user (Alison). Figures 18.2 and 18.3 depict the two scenarios, the first when successful – a hit – and the second when not – a miss.

Consider first the successful case in Figure 18.2, the hit. The first significant event is Alison's depression of the mouse button over the on-screen 'delete' button. This

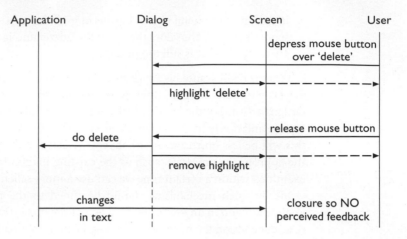

Figure 18.2 Screen button – hit

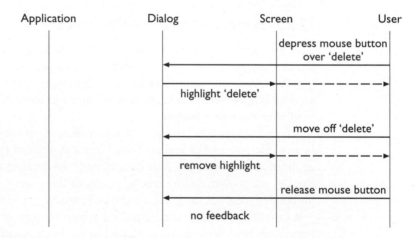

Figure 18.3 Screen button – miss

event goes directly to the toolkit dialog, which responds by highlighting the 'delete' button. The next event is as Alison lifts her finger from the button. Again this is received by the dialog which this time does two things: it removes the highlight from the 'delete' button, and also causes an event 'delete' for the application. The application then performs the action, deleting the paragraph. The effects of this change in the text are reflected in the screen content.

The unsuccessful case (Figure 18.3, the miss) starts similarly. Alison depresses the mouse button and receives feedback. However, this time, before releasing the mouse button, she accidentally moves the mouse off the button. The toolkit dialog responds to this by removing the highlight from 'delete' – the same feedback as in the first scenario. Alison's release of the mouse button has no further effect.

The two scenarios are very different in their effect: in one the application deletes some text, in the other it does not. However, Alison does not notice the difference.

Her feedback from the toolkit dialog is *identical*. In theory, she could have seen that the text did not change as she expected. However, after hitting the 'delete' button, she reaches *closure* on that operation and moves on to the next task. Her attention is not focussed on the text to be deleted and so there is *no perceived event* for the user corresponding to the application event of the text being deleted.

Furthermore, this closure makes the mistake not just a possibility, but highly likely. Consider the moment when Alison has just pressed down the mouse button and the on-screen 'delete' button has been highlighted. She has done what she wanted and attains closure, and the remaining release of the mouse button is initiated. She now starts to look for the next action and begins to move the mouse to the location of next interaction. However, the two actions, releasing the mouse and moving it, are not synchronized with one another. There is no particular reason why one should happen before the other. It is, of course, a particularly dangerous point in a dialog where the order of two unsynchronized user actions makes a crucial difference to behavior.

It is quite difficult to see how to avoid the problem occurring. It is not that the current feedback is not salient; it is at the focus of the pointing task. However, all the feedback concerns events at the dialog level. The most important event, the 'delete' to the application, has *no* corresponding perceived event. The toolkit assumes that the user will see some feedback from the application and therefore does not supply any feedback of its own. But, as we saw, the application's feedback is very likely to be missed.

The solution is fairly obvious: the dialog should itself supply an event, which will be perceived by the user, corresponding to the application-level event. This could be visual, but would have to be very salient as the user's eyes are beginning to move toward the next task. Alternatively, it could be aural, either with a keyboard-like 'click' as the button is successfully pressed, or with a beep if the mouse slips off. This improved feedback could be combined with some dynamic mechanism, such as making the screen button 'magnetic' and difficult to move out of.

It is interesting to note that, if Alison were a novice user, she would be more likely to check her actions and thus notice the mistake – an unnoticed button miss is an *expert slip*. As all but the most extensive user testing of a new device must, by definition, be with novices, there is no way this would be detected – which is perhaps why most on-screen buttons have this problem. We hope this demonstrates how, on occasions, semi-formal hand analysis may even be more effective than real user testing.

18.3   RICH CONTEXTS

Formalized methods such as task analysis adopt a systemized, almost Taylorist view of the workplace – people working to achieve well-defined goals following regular procedures.

However, even the earliest systems analysis texts took into account the richness of the work environment. One text, written in the late 1960s, described a printshop where productivity was lower than predicted after the installation of new machinery. The analyst was asked to advise on automating the equipment. After observing the workplace he asked for a small budget of a few hundred pounds and the productivity dramatically rose. What did he do? He bought white overalls. The equipment was oily and the operators, mostly young women, were reluctant to work too quickly for fear of damaging their own clothes. The overalls protected their clothes and obviated the need for a computer.

This is not a unique story. Again and again those studying real workplaces find that they have a rich ecology involving different people, the structure of the spaces they work in and the physical artifacts in the workplace. Observations of real photocopier use led to the ideas of situated action (see also Chapter 13, Section 13.3.5) challenging simplistic models of pre-planned human action and proposing instead that real interaction is not pre-planned, but rather acted out in response to the actual work situation [334]. Numerous ethnographic studies emphasize the incredible richness of human interaction and, often, the inability of formalized processes to incorporate it. For example, in a study of a printshop (yes, another) Bowers et al. [41] found that the operators constantly had to work around the job management software as it assumed linear patterns of work that did not reflect the contingent and dynamic re-planning necessary on the shopfloor.

In a philosophically different strand of work, the *distributed cognition* literature has challenged the model of cognition 'in the head' and instead suggests that real cognition happens in interaction with the environment and with each other (see Chapter 14, Section 14.5.3). One classic study showed how Polynesian sailors were able to navigate without formal charts and without the requisite experience in any one individual's head [185].

One could say that the lessons of situated action and of distributed cognition are about the parity in relationship between the 'actor' and the world. We do not just *act on* the world, but *act with* the world. We are driven by what we see and hear from other people, from automated systems and from the physical objects in the world. In response, our actions, words and sometimes gestures and demeanour speak back into that rich world.

In day-to-day life we understand about dialog with other people. In HCI we are used to thinking about dialog between users and the computer system. However, in a full ecological analysis we must also accept that users are in dialog with the physical environment. We use the information stored in artifacts and their physical disposition to trigger and guide our actions, and the physical properties of the world limit and constrain our actions on it.

In the rest of this section we will look at several phenomena of this dialog with the environment and see how they can be grafted onto more traditional methods.

18.3.1 Collaboration – doing it together

In Chapter 14, we discussed issues of communication and collaboration. However, you may notice that this is rarely mentioned in the other models in Part 3.

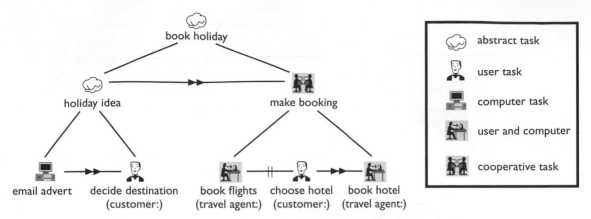

Figure 18.4 ConcurTaskTree [280]. Source: Icons reproduced courtesy of Fabio Paternò

In fact, several notations and methods do handle collaboration explicitly. There are two ways in which this can be done. One is where the process as a whole is mapped out and parts assigned to each person (common in function allocation, workflow and process methods). The other is where several role-oriented models interact. These are complementary representations and can be handled together with suitable tool support.

One example is *ConcurTaskTrees* (*CTT*) which are a form of hierarchical task analysis (HTA) [280]. CTT adds to HTA in two main ways. The first is that instead of the loosely described plans of HTA it includes a much more formal way of specifying the temporal relationships between subtasks using operators based on the LOTOS formal notation. A CTT task tree can be produced for each person involved in the task. It is, however, the second difference from HTA that is significant here. Where several people collaborate on a task, a larger task tree is produced where each subtask can be labeled as belonging to a specific individual, being automated, or being collaborative (see Figure 18.4).

It is interesting to note that the roles identified in CTT include both humans and automated systems, but not aspects of the physical environment. However, it is only a small step to imagine treating the environment or parts of it as dialog partners alongside the human and computer.

Another method that takes collaboration seriously is *GroupWare Task Analysis* (GTA), which includes a broad-ranging conceptual framework, elicitation techniques and toolset [357]. GTA has a rich taxonomy including agents and roles for modeling collaboration and objects both physical and electronic (see Figure 18.5). It aims to build a rich model of the situation in which tasks are performed.

18.3.2 Information – what you need to know and when you need to know it

When writing the first edition of this book, we bemoaned the fact that cognitive models took a view of human cognition that was almost totally dominated by output

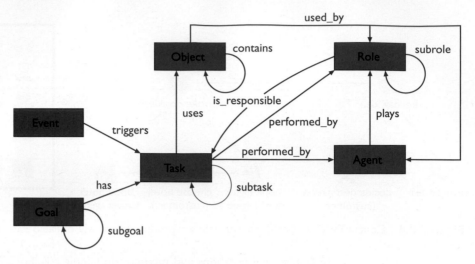

Figure 18.5   GTA ontology

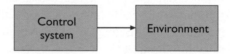

Figure 18.6   Open-loop control

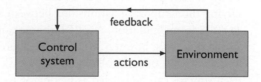

Figure 18.7   Closed-loop control

and action (see Section 12.4). We have goals, which translate into subgoals, and so on, until we perform actions – an entirely head-outward flow of control. In a similar vein, Lucy Suchman's theories of *situated action* were particularly critical of the artificial intelligence inspired views of human planning. These models of planning are largely based on creating internal plans based on internal models of the world, which are then 'blindly' executed. We use the word 'blindly' here quite carefully, as these are models of human action which ignore the human senses entirely. In control engineering, these output-only models would be described as open-loop control (Figure 18.6) as opposed to closed-loop control (Figure 18.7), which constantly monitors the effects of its outputs on the environment and uses these to modify future behavior.

In general, closed-loop control is more robust and it is not surprising that both internal physiological processes and external human behavior are typically closed-loop systems. Indeed, the user interface literature is full of the importance of

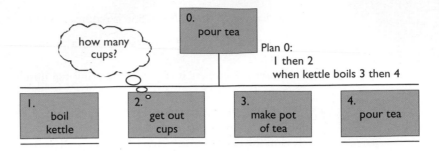

Figure 18.8 Tea-making task

feedback and effective information display; it is just that the early formal models have often left this out.

There are several examples of cognitive models that do take this feedback loop seriously. As noted in Chapter 12 (Section 12.4), there is a display-based version of task action grammar [180], and there have been several other variants of display-based models. Also, interacting cognitive subsystems (ICS) (Section 12.6.2) is focussed strongly on the transformations of representation during the perception-to-action cognitive cycle [26]. The earliest papers on cognitive complexity theory (CCT) included perceptual operators on the production-rule-based cognitive model component, but strangely it was the actions only that were matched against the system dialog model (Section 12.2.2).

It is not uncommon to see references to information seeking in the names of tasks in task models, but this is normally where the information-seeking activity is regarded as a substantive task. In practice, information is used throughout task execution. For example, in the simple tea-making task (Figure 18.8), the 'boil kettle' subtask does not require any information, but the 'get out cups' task requires the actor to know how many are required. Does he remember, or does it need to be written down?

Information is central to several task analysis methods, such as TAKD (Chapter 15, Section 15.4); however, these are focussed on what kinds of things the user needs to know in general – ontology and domain modeling – not on what the user needs to know at a particular moment.

It is a simple matter to add an information analysis stage to any task analysis method or notation. Note that some tasks have no information requirements – other than the fact that they are to happen. For example, the 'make pot of tea' subtask requires no information other than the fact that the kettle has boiled. However, information is required whenever:

(a) a subtask involves inputting (or outputting) information
(b) there is some kind of choice
(c) a subtask is repeated a number of times that is not prespecified.

Note that (c) is a special case of (b). To detect (a) one needs to look at the kind of task, whereas (b) and (c) are evident from the temporal structure of the task (for example, in the case of HTA, this would be in the plan).

Having discovered that information is required it may come from several sources:

(i) It is part of the task (e.g., in the case of a phone call, whom one is going to phone).

(ii) The user remembers it (e.g. remembering the number after ringing directory enquiries).

(iii) It is on a computer/device display (e.g. using a PDA address book and then dialing the number).

(iv) It is in the environment: either pre-existing (e.g. number in phone directory), or created as part of the task (e.g. number written on piece of paper).

Reducing memory load is part of standard usability guidelines. Knowing what information is required during a task allows us to design or redesign the task so that information is available when required. An infamous example of this is those all too common modal dialog boxes that ask you some question but hide the window containing the information you need to answer the question!

In most multi-windowed GUIs it has been possible for user interface designers to be quite careless about information requirements. One can make so much information available and let the user arrange different windows to perform the task. In contrast industrial control design is far more careful about knowing what is required, as there are often very many possible values to display. Industrial operators may have very little time to respond to an alarm and so cannot browse complex menu systems to find information. As user interaction moves away from the computer screen to dedicated devices, WAP phones, interactive television screens and smart appliances, these issues of careful information requirements analysis will become significant for all applications.

18.3.3 Triggers – why things happen when they happen

Workflows and process diagrams decompose processes into smaller activities and then give the order between them. Similarly, plans in HTA give some specification of the order of subtasks and, as noted earlier, in CTT these temporal orders are made more specific using operators derived from LOTOS.

Figure 18.9 shows a simple example, perhaps the normal pattern of activity for an office worker dealing with daily post. Notice the simple dependency that the post must be collected from the pigeonhole before it can be brought to the desk and before it can be opened. However, look again at the activity 'open post' – when does it actually happen? The work process says it doesn't happen before the 'bring post to desk' activity is complete, but does it happen straightaway after this or some time later?

Figure 18.9 Simple work process

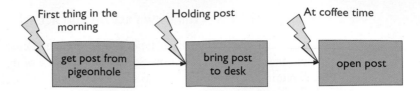

Figure 18.10 Triggers for activities

Trigger analysis [108] looks in detail at the triggers that cause activities to happen when they happen. In the case of opening post, this could easily be something like 'at coffee time' rather than straightaway. It identifies a number of common triggers:

immediate – straight after previous task;

temporal – at a particular time or after a particular delay;

sporadic – when someone thinks about it;

external event – some event occurs, such as a phone call;

environmental cue – something in the environment prompts action.

We can augment the work process with triggers for each activity (Figure 18.10). Notice how we have examples of different types of trigger: two temporal and one environmental (letters in the office worker's hand prompting her to carry them to her desk).

Triggers are important not only for understanding the temporal behavior of the task, but also because they tell us about potential failure modes. If two environmental triggers are similar, one might do parts of the task out of sequence; if a trigger may not occur, or may be missed (likely for sporadic triggers), activities may be omitted entirely. Triggers also help us assess the likelihood of problems caused by interruptions – for example, immediate 'just after' sequences are disrupted badly, whereas environmental cues tend to be robust (because they are still there).

Sometimes triggers are seen in the plans of HTAs, and sometimes 'waiting' sub-tasks are included for external events, but these are both exceptions; the normal assumption is that tasks are uninterrupted. However, it is straightforward to add a trigger analysis stage to most task analysis methods.

In addition, you may have noticed that the ontology of GTA in Figure 18.5 includes events and triggers. However, the word 'trigger' in GTA is usually used only for events that originally set a task in motion (e.g. a customer making an order) and events that make major changes (e.g. the customer ringing to cancel the order).

In terms of the ecology of interaction, triggers remind us that tasks are not typically performed uninterrupted and continuously from start to finish. In practice, tasks are interleaved with other unrelated tasks or, potentially more confusingly, with different instances of the same tasks, and may be interrupted and disrupted by other activities and events. Furthermore, the performance of the tasks is dependent both on a host of interactions with the environment – and these may be fragile – and on apparently unconnected events.

18.3.4 Artifacts – things we act on and act with

Notice that one of the trigger types is environmental cues – things in the environment that prompt us to action. Some years ago one of the authors got a telephone call reminding him to respond to a letter. He couldn't recall having received it at all, but searching through a pile on his desk he found it, and several other letters from a period of several weeks unopened and unread. What had happened? His practice was to bring the post upstairs to his desk, but not always to read it straightaway. Not being a coffee drinker, it was not coffee time that prompted him to open the post but just the fact that there was unopened post lying on his desk. This process had worked perfectly well until there was a new office cleaner. The new cleaner didn't move things around on his desk, but did 'tidy': straightening up higgledy-piggledy piles of paper. However, he had unconsciously been using the fact that the bundle of unopened post was not straight as a reminder that it needed dealing with. But since the arrival of the new cleaner post that for some reason was not opened one day would look the next morning as if it was tidily 'filed' in a pile on his desk.

This story is not unique. The ethnographic literature is full of accounts of artifacts being used to manage personal work and mediating collaborative work. Some of that purpose is to do with the content of the artifacts – what is written on the paper – but much of it uses the physical disposition: by orienting a piece of paper toward a colleague you say 'please read it'. In the case of the author's desk, the cue that said 'post needs to be opened' was purely in the physical orientation (not even the position).

Of course, artifacts also carry information, and are often the inputs or products of intellectual work. Furthermore, in physical processes the transformation of artifacts is the purpose of work.

One example that has been studied in detail in the ethnographic literature is air traffic control, in which all these uses of artifacts are apparent [183]. Flight strips are central (Figure 18.11) – small slips of card for each aircraft recording information about the aircraft (flight number, current height, heading, etc.). This information is important both for the controller managing the aircraft, and also as an at-a-glance representation of the state of the airspace for other controllers. However, the controllers also slightly pull out those strips corresponding to aircraft that have some issue or problem. This acts partly as a reminder and partly as an implicit communication with nearby controllers. Finally, the strips in some way represent the aircraft for the controllers, but, of course, the real purpose of the process is the movement of the aircraft themselves.

Figure 18.11   Air traffic control flight strip

Task models often talk about objects, either implicitly in the description of subtasks or explicitly in the task model. However, the objects are always 'second class' – users act on them, but they are not 'part of' the task. CTT and most work process notations do talk about automated tasks, but not about the artifacts, whether electronic or physical, included within the interaction.

In object-oriented design methods it is common to give life-cycle descriptions of 'objects'; however, this is usually because we are intending to store and automate the object electronically. And though workflow analysts do study document life cycles, this again is largely because of the intention to automate.

The entity–relationship style task analysis in Chapter 15 (Section 15.5), based largely on the ATOM method [360], does treat physical objects as 'first class', but this type of method has not gained widespread acceptance.

There is no reason why most task analysis methods should not adopt some form of artifact tracking. This may be as simple as recording which artifacts are triggers for, used by, modified by, or produced by any particular subtask. For tasks where artifacts are particularly central, more sophisticated artifact life cycles could sit alongside the task description. These life cycles may be mundane (letter closed – letter open), but this is the point; users recruit their everyday knowledge and physical properties of the world to coordinate their activity.

18.3.5 Placeholders – knowing what happens next

It is half past five in the evening. The busy office building is beginning to quiet as people pack up to go home. One or two work late in their offices, but as the evening wears on they too go home. Soon there is only the hum of vacuum cleaners and the clatter of wastebins as the office cleaners do their work, until eventually, the last light goes out and the building sleeps. A few have taken papers and laptops home and continue to work, but eventually they too put aside their work and sleep.

It is three o'clock in the morning. In the darkness and silence of the office and the deep sleep of all the employees, where is the memory of the organization? The next morning at nine o'clock the office is a flurry of activity; it has not forgotten and has restarted its activities, but how?

We have already discussed two aspects of this memory: information required to perform tasks, and triggers that remind us that something needs to happen. However, there is one last piece of this puzzle that we have hinted at several times already. As well as knowing *that* we need to do something, we need to know *what* to do next. In the complex web of tasks and subtasks that comprise our job – *where* are we?

In fact, in looking at triggers we have already seen examples of this. The untidy post on the author's desk said 'something needs to happen', but the fact that it was also unopened said, 'it needs to be opened'. We already noted that similar triggers may cause subtasks to be performed out of sequence. If we have only a small number of dissimilar tasks this is unlikely to happen, since we can remember where we are in each task. However, as the number of tasks increases, especially if we are

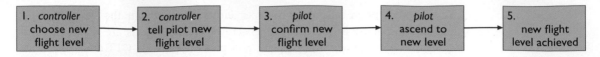

Figure 18.12   Flight level management task

performing the same task on different things, it becomes harder to remember where we are.

Let's look again at air traffic control. One of the controller's tasks is to manage the flight level of aircraft. A much-simplified model of this activity is shown in Figure 18.12. Because this is a shared task between the controller and the pilot, each box is labeled with the main actor (although tasks 2 and 3 are both communications). Recalling earlier parts of this section, we might ask what information is required at each stage; for example, task 1 would depend on radar, locations of other planes, planned take-off and landings, and new planes expected to enter the airspace.

Note that box 5 is not really a task, more a 'state of the world' that signifies task completion; however, it is important, as the controller will need to take alternative actions if it doesn't happen. Of course, without appropriate placeholders the controller might forget that a plane has not achieved its target level, causing problems later because the old level is still occupied and allowing potential conflicts between aircraft.

In fact, the flight strips encode just such a placeholder (see Figure 18.13). When the controller informs the pilot of the new height he writes the new level on the flight strip (i). When the pilot confirms she has understood the request the controller

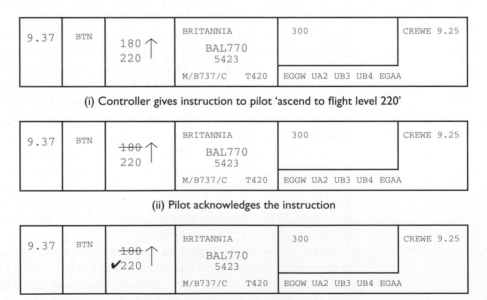

(i) Controller gives instruction to pilot 'ascend to flight level 220'

(ii) Pilot acknowledges the instruction

(iii) New height is attained

Figure 18.13   Flight strip annotated during task

crosses out the old level (ii). Finally when the new level has actually been reached the new level is ticked (iii).

Virtually all task-modeling notations treat the placeholder as implicit. The sequence of actions is recorded, but not why the user should do things in the way proposed. Of course, one purpose of task analysis has been to produce training – that is, to help people learn what the appropriate processes are, but this doesn't help them actually to remember where they are in the process.

Just like other forms of information, placeholders may be stored in different ways:

(a) in people's heads – remembering what to do next
(b) explicitly in the environment – to-do lists, planning charts, flight strips, workflow systems
(c) implicitly in the environment – is the letter open yet?

Although often forgotten, placeholders are crucial in ensuring that tasks are carried out effectively and in full. At a fine scale it is rare to find explicit records because the overhead would be too high. Instead (a) and (c) predominate. As users' memories may be unreliable when faced with multiple tasks and interruptions, it is not surprising to find that various forms of environmental cue are common in the workplace. However, electronic environments do not have the same affordances to allow informal annotations or fine 'tweaking' of the disposition of artifacts.

18.4 LOW INTENTION AND SENSOR-BASED INTERACTION

In traditional computer applications a user was expected to approach the system with a clear intention to perform some activity or achieve some goal. The actions were purposeful and direct and the results were explicitly attended to and evaluated. The design emphasis is on making the affordances of interaction unambiguous and available and ensuring that system feedback and state are clearly visible.

However, in many areas of human–computer interaction we have seen a growing number of systems and interaction paradigms where user attention and intention is lower. In CSCW the concept of awareness has been central for many years, and, similarly, ambient interfaces emphasize low salience displays of background information. A number of terms have been used to refer to interfaces that include less explicit interactions: calm interfaces, tacit and implicit interaction. All emphasize output that is non-intrusive, and ecologically natural forms of input/control.

Whereas the traditional interface was based around controls and input devices, these low attention and natural input paradigms are more closely related to sensing technologies and contextual interpretations. Furthermore, human physiology may be sensed to influence interaction; for example the 2002 Commonwealth Games baton had an electronic 'flame' that flashed depending on the bearer's heart rate.

At the extreme end of the spectrum are *incidental interactions*, where an actor (user) performs an action for some purpose (say opening a door to enter a room), and the system senses this and *incidentally* uses it for some purpose of which the actor is unaware (perhaps adjusting the air conditioning), but which affects their future interactions with the environment or system.

In this section we'll look at some examples of incidental interaction and see how it fits within a spectrum of different levels of intention. We'll then see how this challenges major areas of traditional interaction design: the fundamental execution–evaluation cycle implicit in much of HCI, and the limits of our innate cognitive abilities. Finally, we'll consider how to design and implement this sort of system, although these are still areas with no established best practice or standards.

18.4.1 Examples

Car courtesy lights operate differently depending on the model of car. They may turn on when the doors are unlocked or when the doors are opened. They may turn off after some fixed time, or when the doors are closed or the engine is started. Underlying this is some designer's model of the task of getting into a car – perhaps sorting out belongings in the car, looking at a map, etc., before setting off. The sensors are unreliable means of detecting the user's intentions, but the incidental interactions with the lights are designed to support the task. Note that the driver's *purpose* is to get into the car and *incidentally* the lights come on.

In the *Pepys* project at Xerox EuroPARC, all staff wore an 'active badge' that detected their location in the building using infrared sensors [361]. At the end of each day, the Pepys system analyzed the logs of people's location and used these to produce a personal diary for each person [259]. Because Pepys knew about the layout of the offices, and who was where when, it was able to detect when two or more people were in the same location and create a diary entry for all of them, e.g. for Brian – 'had meeting with Alison and Clarise'. Again, Alison and Clarise's *purpose* is to visit Brian's office and *incidentally* a diary entry is created for each of them.

The *MediaCup* [148, 33] also facilitates incidental interaction. It is a base unit that can be attached to an ordinary coffee mug and detects movement (when drinking, walking around, etc.), pressure (for fullness), temperature (fresh coffee versus old) and location. The information gathered by this gives some indication of the drinker's current activity and location, which can then be used for community awareness. Brian's *purpose* in filling the mug is to have a drink of coffee and *incidentally* his colleagues become aware he is taking a break.

Courtesy of Michael Beigl, University of Karlsruhe

Incidental interactions can also take place entirely within the electronic domain. In many electronic shopping sites, the system keeps track of the items you have purchased or examined and then suggests additional products based on your inferred tastes. Your *purpose* is to buy product X and *incidentally* the system infers your tastes and suggests product Y.

One system some of the authors have worked on personally is *onCue*. This is an 'intelligent' toolbar that sits on the side of the user's screen. When the user cuts or copies any text, onCue examines the clipboard. It analyzes the content and, depending on the type of material, changes the tool items to reflect it. If the copied text is a postcode, onCue suggests internet mapping services; if it looks like a name (initial capitals, etc.), onCue suggests internet directory services; if the text is a list or table of numbers, onCue suggests spreadsheet or graphing applications. As well as the triggering event being implicit, the 'suggestion' is deliberately low salience; the currently suggested services slowly fade in as small icons in the toolbar. Note again, the user's *purpose* is to copy the text somewhere else and *incidentally* potential useful services are offered. (See the onCue case study at /e3/casestudy/onCue/)

18.4.2 The intentional spectrum

If we look back at these examples and think of related ones, we can see that they differ in just how 'incidental' the results are. If you get into the car and the courtesy light does not come on you may notice. Even though you didn't explicitly ask for the lights to turn on, you still *expect* them to do so.

In fact, there is a continuum of intentionality (Figure 18.14). At one extreme are 'normal' intentional interactions such as pressing the computer key or pressing a light switch and expecting the light to come on. This would also include, for example, a gesture recognition system. Imagine a complex image recognition system that watches your hand movements so that you can point at a particular light bulb and say 'light on' or 'light off'. Although this would be far from a traditional computer system, it is clearly intentional – the user wants the light on and deliberately does something that will have the desired effect.

The automatic lights that are found in some public toilets fit somewhere in between. They are based on infrared or ultrasonic sensors that detect movement. If there is movement they come on; if not they turn off. These are more like the car courtesy light. When you walk in you expect the light to go on and would be unhappy if, as the door closed behind you, you found yourself in darkness.

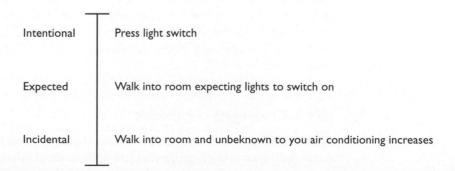

Figure 18.14 The continuum of intentionality

The automatic central heating controller that detects who is in the room and adjusts the temperature accordingly is at the extreme end of incidental interaction. Unless the users consult the manuals in detail they may have no idea that this is happening behind the scenes. Certainly, when they walk into the room it is no part of their model of what the act of entering means.

The automatic room lights are quite interesting as a small design change can turn them from an expected interaction to an incidental one. Imagine a house that has real light switches, but (for energy saving) always switches off the lights in rooms that no one is in. When you approach the room the lights automatically turn on, so that you are never aware that they switch off. Fridge lights and doors that automatically unlock when an active badge is near are another example.

In addition, there may be changes between these caused by the user's understanding of the system. The continuum from intentional, through expected, to incidental interaction is largely about purpose – what the user thinks – not the actual system itself. Of course, certain types of system will suggest more or less strongly one mode of interaction, but there is some fluidity depending on the user's experience, awareness, etc. As users become more aware of the interactions happening around them, they may move through the continuum toward more purposeful interaction.

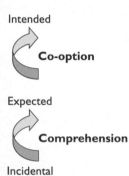

Comprehension: incidental → expected   If users notice, consciously or unconsciously, that incidental interactions are taking place they may come to expect or rely upon them. For example, if you realize that the courtesy lights come on when you get into the car you may leave checking your route until you get in, knowing that the car will be lit then.

Co-option: expected → intended   When users know that something will happen when they perform an action, they may deliberately perform the action to cause the effect. For example, you may deliberately open and close the car door to trigger the courtesy light mechanism.

The opposite can happen as well. Imagine you use a gesture recognition system to open the door. Placing your palm open in front of you when you approach the door means 'open the door now'. After a while this action becomes proceduralized and you may no longer be conscious that you do it. For you, it is as if the door always opens when you approach it. One day you approach the door, but you are carrying a box . . .

18.4.3 Challenging our models

As well as being an interesting interaction paradigm in its own right, incidental interaction really pushes our fundamental assumptions about interaction and our ways of modeling it. This will require a rethinking of HCI theory and practice more fundamental than that of the 1980s when GUI interfaces replaced character terminals.

Interaction models

The explicit or implicit model behind nearly all interaction is some form of intentional cycle such as the Norman execution–evaluation loop [266]. The user has some goal (intention), formulates some action that he believes will act toward that goal, performs the action and then reformulates future actions based on the feedback.

In traditional cognitive modeling, this is seen as very plan-driven, with goal stacks, hierarchies, etc. In these accounts, the intentional cycle is seen as starting with the user, even to the point that the effects of feedback are often ignored. In more contextual accounts of interaction, such as situated action [334] or distributed cognition [185], the goals or intentions are more at the level of overall motivations or end-state aspirations. The focus tends to shift to a cycle of activity starting with the state of the world and recent system 'responses', with the user acting on the world in response to the current state. However, this is still clearly purposeful activity.

Incidental interaction and, to a lesser extent, expected interactions do not fit this picture. The user and system share the experience of the user's actions, but the purposeful activity of the user is distinct from the intended outcomes of the system.

This is not just a theoretical issue: it is an underlying assumption that cuts through nearly every usability guideline, principle and method. For example, the importance of rapid and visible feedback is based on the assumption that users need to understand fully the effect of their actions. In incidental interaction and low awareness applications the opposite is often true; feedback may be unobtrusive (and not explicitly noticed) or delayed (e.g. the heating level slowly changing). Even expected interactions are more likely to be noticed when they don't happen than when they do.

Cognition

Natural *inanimate* physical things have a set of properties intrinsic to their physicality:

Directness of effect   You push something a little and it moves a little, you push hard and it moves a lot.

Locality of effect   Effects are here and now. If you pushed a rock and then two seconds later it moved you would be disturbed.

Visibility of state   Solid objects have a small number of relevant parameters that define their dynamic state: location, orientation. We have some difficulty with invisible properties such as velocity and even more when physical things have hidden states, for example the joke balls that have a ball bearing inside and so do not move in a straight line. Of course, this example is not natural but constructed.

We have evolved as creatures to cope with physical things and other creatures, not technological devices. Although we have higher-level reasoning that enables us to cope – the same reasoning that enables us to create technology – this is only significant when we 'think about' things; our more innate cognitive abilities are shaped by the natural.

Computer systems (and other complex technology such as electrical and pneumatic systems) break these intrinsic properties of physical objects. Computation creates complexity of effect, networks introduce non-locality in space, memory non-locality in time, and a computer has a vast number of invisible variables in its hidden internal state.

We cope (just) with this, because either we rationalize and use higher-level thinking to make sense and to make models of these complex non-physical interactions, or we treat the computer as animate. In addition, one of the reasons for the development of the GUI interface style is that it makes the electronic world more like real (inanimate) things.

In incidental, expected and low awareness interactions the design is such that the user is not paying attention to, or is unaware of, the system's activities. That is, we are not able to bring our higher cognitive abilities to bear and are dependent on our more innate intelligences, which are, of course, ill prepared for unphysicality. To make matters worse, the system activities are often triggered by physical actions and movements of the user and are manifest in the physical world. In a computer system we are able to re-frame ourselves to expect odd or apparently magical actions to occur. In the real world these are deeply disturbing.

18.4.4 Designing for incidental interaction

Traditional task analysis is also highly purposeful, although debatably less wedded to this than cognitive models. Certainly, to cope with more contextual interactions task analysis methods need to evolve to include or link to representations that are more about the physical world and the rich ecology of lived work or domestic life. In the previous section we examined some of the potential issues and extensions that may be necessary for this.

However, incidental interaction poses a more fundamental question – what task do we need to model? In incidental interaction, we have two 'tasks' that are occurring:

1. The user's primary task – their purposeful activity.
2. The task that the incidental interaction is attempting to support or achieve.

Often, as in the case of the courtesy light, the two are the same task, but it is used in different ways. The user's purposeful activity is assumed to occur, to a large extent, independently of the system's actions. We need to model it in order to computationally interpret the user's actions as activity. In contrast, we need to model (2) in order to understand how to facilitate or progress it.

In addition, low intention and sensor-based systems often include uncertain inferences. In traditional interfaces there is intended to be no ambiguity – the user presses the 'x' key and an 'x' appears in the document. Of course, the user may have mistyped, or may not realize the system is in a mode where 'x' means 'exit', but these are 'errors' or misdesigns; if all is going well there is no ambiguity. In contrast, a sensor-based system may 'think' that you are resting because you are not moving about much and turn down the music volume, but you may simply be sitting still listening to the strident sounds of Beethoven's *Fifth Symphony*. Happily, the things controlled or intended to be controlled by these interactions are often less critical. You might like the heating a little warmer or colder, but it is not absolutely essential whether the system gets it right.

At the time of writing, there are no developed methods for dealing with these low intention interactions, although there are some proposals [111, 319]. However, we can begin to see how more traditional methods may change to accommodate these new interaction styles.

Clearly any design for low attention must identify two things:

input – what is going to be sensed (e.g. body heat, pressure pad)

output – what is going to be controlled (e.g. light, heating).

Once we know these we can look at scenarios or task models and label them to see what we would like to happen at each step. In some cases there will be a definite requirement (e.g., the car courtesy lights must not be on when the car is moving), in

---

DESIGN FOCUS

Designing a car courtesy light

The first step in designing a sensor-based system is to work out what you would like to control. In this case the car's interior light. Next we look through some scenarios and label the steps. At each stage we note whether the lights should be on (more pluses) or off (more minuses). Here is one such scenario:

1. deactivate alarm	0	
2. walk up to car	●	is this safe?, advertises presence
3. key in door	−	
4. open door and remove key	+	
5. get in	+ +	
6. close door	0	
7. adjust seat	+	
8. find road atlas	+ +	
9. look up route	+ + +	
10. find right key	+	
11. key in ignition	−	
12. start car	0	
13. seat belt light flashes	0	
14. fasten seat belt	+	
15. drive off	− − − −	illegal !

Step 2 is interesting, if you ask different people you get different responses. Some like to see the lights go on when the alarm is disarmed. However, others fear it advertises their presence and leaves them vulnerable to attack.

Note, too, that we have assumed the alarm remote control does not actually unlock the car. This was partly so that we could have step 3 where the lighted interior makes it slightly more difficult to put the key in the car door.

At this stage, we can either work a full task analysis and mark this up similarly so that each task and subtask has a desired lighting attached. Alternatively we could move forward to a more detailed design.

See the book website for the full case study: /e3/casestudy/car-lights/

others there may be simply a desire (e.g., it would be good for the light to be on to put the key in the ignition). Of course, the steps in the task or scenario may involve user intentions or other aspects of context not immediately available to the computer system – that is why we need to be able to infer this context. To do this, we can look at the available sensors and see how certain we can be of the current context based on their data. This can then be used both to verify whether we can be certain of the context at points at which there is a definite requirement (and add explicit controls if not), and also to be able to control the output at other times so that the users usually (but not always) get what they want.

18.4.5 Implementing sensor-based systems

In incidental interactions it is very likely that sensors are not used solely for their original purpose. This suggests the need for quite open architectures. For example, onCue uses a very open blackboard-style architecture for exchanging information between self-discovering and self-configuring components [106]. Unfortunately, at the level of individual applications it is far harder to get contextual information without writing special code for each potential application. This is one of the reasons for using copy/cut to the clipboard as the main trigger – it is one of the few cross-application standards.

Furthermore, many of the contextual interactions envisaged in this area occur in domestic or other private environments. If we are not careful, architectural openness could violate privacy – imagine if the can of beans (with intelligent food label) you just bought communicated back to the manufacturer the contents of your food cupboard.

Highly contextual interactions must also take on board the fact that many of the most important phenomena are not events (things that happen at specific moments), but status (things that always have some measurable value). Status–event analysis highlights common phenomena that can be used to understand such systems, but this also impacts on the underlying system architectures [94, 102].

Although there are many research and commercial systems being produced using sensors, there are no clear 'standard' architectures like the Seeheim model or MVC (see Section 8.5.1) developed for traditional interfaces. However, there are some features that are likely to be present in many systems (see Figure 18.15).

Some sensor-based systems may employ quite simple sensors, for example the door open/closed sensor for car courtesy lights. However, where the raw sensors are capturing richer data it may well be that there is too much data to process fully. In these cases, the sensors may have to somehow filter or pre-process their outputs before passing on their data. For example, the MediaCup senses the temperature of the cup and pressure on the bottom of the cup, and has ball bearing sensors to give approximate tip in two x–y directions, all of which could be sensed many times per second and at high resolution. However, only a small bit-mask with indicators such as hot/cold, moving/still is sent via the infrared link to the network.

Often the results from several sensors may need to be processed together to give a usable output. For example, several heat sensors may be averaged. This is a form of *data fusion* – bringing together multiple data sources to build a more accurate

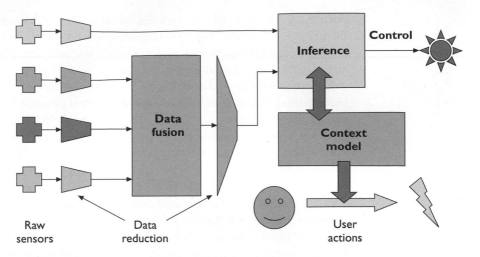

Figure 18.15 Potential architecture of sensor-based system

picture. This data fusion stage may also reduce the information; for example, the single average from 10 individual temperature readings.

These processed sensor readings are then used to drive some form of inference. This may be a few hand-coded rules: 'when Alison's MediaCup is moving she is in the office'; more sophisticated rule-based systems; or some form of neural network. This inference will typically interact with some form of model of the users' context built up over time. For example, if in the past the ultrasound sensors have detected movement in a room and the pressure sensors under the doormat have not been triggered, then the system 'knows' there is likely to be someone there, even though the ultrasound sensors currently detect no movement.

Finally, this contextual information has to be used. It may be used directly to drive some controlled output, for example, the lights in the car or room heater. Alternatively, it may be used to modify the effects of users' actions based on the inferred context. For example, depending on who is believed to be in the house and the time of day, the TV may default to different channels when it is turned on.

18.5 SUMMARY

Real interaction is not simply pressing a button and seeing something happen on screen. In this chapter we have looked at some of the ways to model and understand rich aspects of interaction.

We looked at status–event analysis, an 'engineering'-level technique that encompasses formal methods, semi-formal analysis and naïve psychology, allowing us to consider issues that bridge system and user behavior. Whereas most formal notations focus on the state changes occurring at particular moments (events), status–event analysis puts equal weight on status phenomena, such as computer screens, which always have a value. Important properties of status–event descriptions include the difference between actual and perceived events, polling to discover status change and the granularity of time. Timeline diagrams showing events and status in human–computer interaction allowed us to examine the delays in notification of email arrival and errors using on-screen buttons.

In Section 18.3 we looked at the way existing task models could be extended to encompass rich contexts including other people and physical artifacts. Several existing techniques including CTT and GTA already include ways to allocate subtasks for different human and machine roles. In contrast, few methods deal well with the information required at each stage, although this is not difficult to add. In order to keep tasks operating in the right order at the right time, we saw that physical artifacts as well as other external events act as triggers that make things happen when they happen, and placeholders implicitly record where people are in a process.

Finally, we looked at the way that some recent ubiquitous computing applications have radically new modes of interaction. We considered a continuum based on the level of intentionality. At one extreme were traditional intentional acts. At the other extreme was incidental interaction where the user acts for one purpose and incidentally the system interprets the action to aid or help the user. In between is behavior that the user does not explicitly request, but which is expected to occur. These low intention interactions cannot easily be understood within standard models of interaction. As yet there are no established design techniques or implementation architectures, but we saw that there are promising early methods.

EXERCISES

18.1 Can you suggest any improvements to the screen button feedback problem discussed in Section 18.2.5 that would distinguish at the interface between the two cases of hitting or missing the button? Is there any guarantee with your solution that the user will notice the distinction?

18.2 Brian wants to make a dinner date with Alison. He knows she will not be able to read email, as she is away for a few days, and he doesn't have her hotel number. He types and prints a letter, which he puts in her pigeonhole. Alison's secretary always checks the pigeonhole several times a day, and when she finds the letter she reads it and rings Alison and tells her.

Analyze this story using a status–event description.

18.3 Look again at the tea-making task analysis in Chapter 15 (Figure 15.4). Go through this and look for triggers and placeholders. You will need to make assumptions (e.g. is the kettle the kind that whistles when it boils?) so document these.

18.4 Rank the following in terms of levels of intention or consciousness:

automatic doors into hotel, automatic water taps in washbasin, reversing lights in a car, ultrasonic burglar alarm, auto-numbering lists in a word processor, web page counter, font menu in word processor that shows recent fonts at the top of the list

If you are working in a group, you could each rank them separately and then discuss your answers.

Why are some more consciously considered than others?

Think of more examples.

RECOMMENDED READING

P. Dourish, *Where the Action Is: The Foundations of Embodied Interaction*, MIT Press, 2001.
Philosophical and practical discussion of what Dourish calls 'embodied interaction', that is interaction taking place in a real physical and social context.

F. Paternó, *Model-Based Design and Evaluation of Interactive Applications*, Springer-Verlag, 2000.
A full design methodology and approach focussed on the use of ConcurTaskTrees. Note that the collaborative aspects of CTT were developed after this book.

A. Dix, D. Ramduny-Ellis, J. Wilkinson, Trigger analysis – understanding broken tasks. In D. Diaper and N. Stanton, editors, *The Handbook of Task Analysis for Human–Computer Interaction*, Lawrence Erlbaum, 2003 (in press).
Detailed treatment of the triggers and placeholders discussed in Section 18.3.

B. Nardi and V. O'Day, *Information Ecologies – Using Technology with Heart*, MIT Press, 1999.
A beautiful book probing the rich interactions between people and technology. It seeks to find a middle way between those who abhor technology and those who adore it. The majority of the material in the book is structured around real case studies of systems in different settings from schools to hospitals, libraries to offices. It is full of vignettes like the researcher who, failing to make conversation with a group of schoolchildren, sits down at a terminal near them and instantly becomes accepted within their online community.

OUTSIDE THE BOX

In this part, we look in more detail at interactive applications that go beyond a single user with a desk-based computer. In Chapter 19 we revisit group interaction, this time focussing on groupware technology itself: what it can support, how it can be classified, and what particular implementation challenges it presents. In Chapter 20 we look at systems that link the real world with electronic worlds, examining ubiquitous and context-aware computing and virtual reality, including its use in information visualization. Chapter 21 looks at the design and use of hypertext and multimedia systems. In particular, it examines the role of the world wide web in popularizing hypertext and examines some specific design issues for the web.

19

GROUPWARE

OVERVIEW

Groupware is a term for applications written to support the collaboration of several users.

■ Groupware can support different activities:
  – direct interpersonal communication
  – ideas generation and decision making
  – sharing computer objects.

■ It can be classified in several ways:
  – by where and when it happens
  – by the sort of information shared
  – by the aspects of cooperations supported.

■ Implementing groupware is more difficult than single-user applications:
  – because of network delays
  – because there are so many components to go wrong
  – because graphical toolkits assume a single user.

19.1 INTRODUCTION

Much of the discussion in this book concerns a single user with a computer. However, in Chapter 14 we met computer-supported cooperative work (*CSCW*), which is about groups of users – how to design systems to support their work *as a group* and how to understand the effect of technology on their work patterns. Both HCI and CSCW draw on knowledge from a wide range of disciplines, but whereas the principal axis in HCI is psychology–computing, the equivalent axis in CSCW is sociology–computing. If we allow the *human* in HCI to be plural, we can regard CSCW to be within the general sphere of HCI, which is why it is present in this book and in conferences and journals on HCI. However, CSCW is now a field in itself, and would require a book of its own to do it justice. We looked at models of collaboration in Chapter 14; here we turn our attention to the technology that supports group working.

One major area within CSCW is the provision of computer systems to support group working. These products are often called *groupware*. As the reader may not have come across any but the most common of such systems, this chapter describes the range of such groupware systems and the associated architectural and implementation issues. In addition, we shall discuss frameworks that classify groupware systems and that describe how they fit into the wider area of cooperative working. Many of these applications are research systems; however, the number of commercial systems with a groupware component has risen significantly over recent years.

Any computer system, whether or not it is specifically groupware, will have an effect on the work-groups within an organization and upon the organization as a whole. It is not possible to cover the full sociological and anthropological background that is being brought to bear on these issues, but it is important that the reader is aware of these knock-on effects of even individual computer systems. In Chapter 14, we described some of the theory of human communication and the group and organizational factors that influence the design of groupware.

19.2 GROUPWARE SYSTEMS

In this chapter, Sections 19.3–19.5 describe a range of groupware systems, from email and video conferencing to shared editors and co-authoring systems. Section 19.6 uses several frameworks that help us to analyze groupware systems, and which will give some structure to the issues that arise during the previous three sections. Section 19.7 discusses some of the implementation problems facing a groupware developer.

Groupware can be classified in several ways. One of these is by *where* and *when* the participants are performing the cooperative work. This is summarized in a *time/space matrix*. Another classification is by the *function* of the system, for example meeting

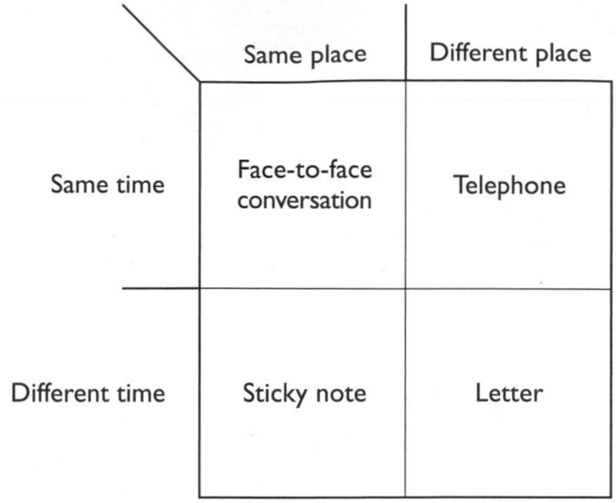

	Same place	Different place
Same time	Face-to-face conversation	Telephone
Different time	Sticky note	Letter

Figure 19.1   Time/space matrix

support or group authoring. The subsections on specific areas of groupware follow this functional classification. However, there are at least 10 such categories here and the list could extend as fast as one could think up new application areas. To give a broader categorization for the sections, we follow a framework that classifies groupware by the aspect of cooperative work which it supports.

The rest of this section describes briefly the time/space matrix and cooperative work framework, both in terms of non-computerized 'real-world' examples. We will return to these and other frameworks in Section 19.6, once the reader is familiar with the range of groupware systems currently available. As with analysis techniques for single-user systems, these frameworks can help to structure the design of new systems, or to suggest possible application areas.

The time/space matrix is a very useful shorthand to refer to the particular circumstances a groupware system aims to address. Basically, we look at the participants and ask whether they are in the same place or not, and whether they are operating at the same time or not. Figure 19.1 shows how various non-computer communication technologies fit into the time/space matrix.

The axes are given different names by different authors. The space dimension is also called the geographical dimension and is divided into *co-located* (same place) and *remote* (different place). Many of the earliest groupware systems were aimed at overcoming the barriers of distance, for example email and video conferencing. More recently, systems have arisen which aim to augment face-to-face meetings and other co-located cooperation.

The time axis is often divided into *synchronous* and *asynchronous* systems; so we would refer to a telephone as a synchronous remote communication mechanism, whereas sticky notes are asynchronous co-located. These terms are used heavily in the CSCW literature; often the intended geographical location is obvious from context, or the application domain, and thus synchronous/asynchronous becomes the principal distinction. However, there are some problems with this simple

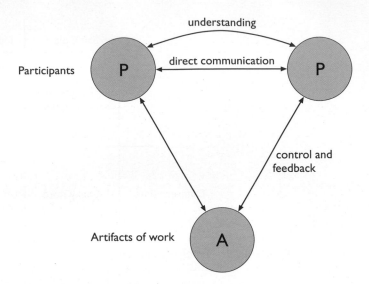

Figure 19.2 Cooperative work framework

distinction, which we will return to in Section 19.6.1. As we discuss each groupware system, it will be placed in its appropriate time/space category.

The framework used to organize Sections 19.3–19.5 is based on the entities involved in cooperative work, that is the participants themselves and the things upon which they work. Figure 19.2 summarizes these relationships. Implicit in the term 'cooperative work' is that there are two or more participants. These are denoted by the circles labeled 'P'. They are engaged in some common work, and to do so interact with various tools and products. Some of these are physically shared (for example, two builders holding the ends of a measuring tape), but all are shared in the sense that they contribute to the cooperative purpose. These tools and other objects are denoted by the circle labeled 'A' – the *artifacts of work*.

The participants communicate with one another as they work, denoted by the arrow between them. In real life this may be by speech (the builders with the tape), or letter (a lawyer and client); in fact, this *direct communication* may be in any of the categories of the time/space matrix. Part of the purpose of communication is to establish a common understanding of the task the participants are engaged in. This understanding may be implicit in the conversation, or may be made explicit in diagrams or text.

For some jobs, such as research and aspects of management, the development of understanding and ideas constitutes the primary task. Where this is not the case, the participants will interact with the tools and work objects to perform their job. This is shown by the arrows between the participants and the artifacts of work. This arrow represents a two-way flow of information: of *control* from the participants to the artifacts, and *feedback* from the artifacts to the participants. In real-world tasks, these two hardly seem distinct: as you wield a hammer, you feel the weight of it. However, as should be evident from the previous discussion of single-user interfaces, this will not necessarily be the case for computer systems.

We will classify groupware systems by the function in this framework which they primarily support:

computer-mediated communication supporting the direct communication between participants;

meeting and decision support systems capturing common understanding;

shared applications and artifacts supporting the participants' interaction with shared work objects – the *artifacts of work*.

Of course, many systems may support more than one of these functions, and indeed this can be seen as a sign of good groupware. Furthermore, there are some further relationships between these functions. Both these aspects will be developed in Section 19.6.3.

19.3 COMPUTER-MEDIATED COMMUNICATION

Implicit in the terms groupware and CSCW is that we have two or more participants and that they are communicating with one another. We begin by looking at systems which support this direct communication. This is called *computer-mediated communication (CMC)*, and is an important part of CSCW. However, good communication is not sufficient – the participants must be able to cooperate about their work. Improving communications may help this, but not necessarily.

Under the heading of computer-mediated communication we will look at email and bulletin boards, well-established, largely text-based means of *asynchronous remote* communication, structured message systems, developed from simple email, instant messaging and SMS, and various video-based systems, which support *synchronous remote* communication.

19.3.1 Email and bulletin boards

Most readers of this book will have used some form of email system. Many will also have used some form of bulletin board or electronic conferencing system such as Usenet News or Yahoo! Groups. Although among the simplest groupware systems, they are most certainly the most popular and successful.

Consider the stages during the sending of a simple email message:

1. **Preparation** You type a message at your computer, possibly adding a subject header.
2. **Dispatch** You then instruct the email program to send it to the recipient.
3. **Delivery** At some time later, anything from a few seconds (for LAN-based email) to hours (for some international email via slow gateways) it will arrive at the recipient's computer.

4. **Notification** If the recipient is using the computer a message may be displayed, saying that mail has arrived, or the terminal may beep.
5. **Receipt** The recipient reads the message using an email program, possibly different from that of the sender.

These stages differ slightly from tool to tool, but are essentially similar. For example, preparation may take place within the mail tool itself, or the tool may import an externally prepared document. Although email systems are so well known and simple, they have been the springboard for several more advanced groupware applications.

In theory, from the user's perspective we need not worry about the exact delivery mechanism – it should be hidden – just as we do not worry about the details of telephone exchanges. However, with email these mechanisms become only too apparent, most obviously in the varying delays we may experience and in the reliability of different channels. These factors are not always predictable as they may depend on faults and loadings of computers used to relay the message. Furthermore, error messages and even the forms of addressing relate directly to the path from computer to computer which the message takes.

In the simple email example, there was just one recipient. However, most email systems also allow a set of recipients to be named, all of whom receive the message (see Figure 19.3). Like letters, these recipients may be divided into the direct recipients (often denoted by a To: field) and those who receive copies (Cc:). These two types of recipient are treated no *differently* by the computer systems – the distinction serves a social purpose for the participants. This is a frequent observation about any groupware system – the system should support *people* in their cooperation.

Often users will be able to set up *distribution lists*, named groups of other users to whom mail is often sent. There is only a small difference between the use of such lists and fully fledged bulletin boards or electronic conferencing systems. In these systems you address your message (or contribution) to a particular conference or newsgroup, and then anyone who has subscribed to that newsgroup receives the message.

It is to be expected that the differences between email and electronic conferencing, especially within the interface, will blur over time. However, there are important differences for the participants. First, they vary in terms of who controls the

```
To: janet, abowd
From: alan
Subject: HCI book
Cc: R.Beale@cs.brum.ac.uk

How are your chapters getting on?
Could one of you meet me over lunch?
I'm having trouble using the minipage
environment doing illustrations of email messages.
```

Figure 19.3 Simple email message

distribution list. Some email distribution lists are private to the sender, that is the *sender* can vary the list at will, and knows exactly who is on it. Alternatively, a distribution list may be shared, in which case it is often added to and updated by the *system administrator*. Finally, in a bulletin board or news systems, it is the *recipient* who decides which newsgroups to subscribe to. For example, Usenet News sends *all* news items to *all* connected computers. Users may well read contributions posted before they subscribed, and certainly the sender will have no idea as to who will read the contribution. We can see this progression in two ways. One is control which moves from the sender, to the administrator and then to the recipient. The second is the nature of the recipient, from specific individuals in email, through organizational or social groups, to topic areas. Again these different emphases have important social implications – communication is about people, not systems.

Although email between sites takes from several minutes to hours to arrive, LAN-based email within a single site will often arrive within seconds. It is thus possible to have email 'conversations'. Typically email interfaces are not designed to deal with this form of exchange, but it is relatively easy to have a sequence of exchanges, say every minute or so. Many computer systems also allow a form of *synchronous* text-based communication, whereby two (or more) participants can instantly see each other's contributions. Examples of this are the UNIX 'talk' program or VAX 'phone'. In these, the participants' screens are divided into two and while your typing goes to the bottom half, your colleague's goes into the top. The typing is usually echoed character by character, so you can see your colleague's half-typed phrases, deletions, etc. A variant of this concept, used as part of several groupware systems, is to have a single transcript. The participants have a separate composition area and when they hit the return key (or click on a special button), their contribution is added to the end of the transcript. Notice the difference in *granularity*: the 'talk' program works with a grain size of characters, whereas the transcript acts on contributions (often a single line, or at most a short paragraph). The granularity of standard email and bulletin boards tends to be greater again, as people may send quite large messages (although some interfaces discourage this).

The ether never sleeps

One advantage of asynchronous messages is that they do not interrupt your work and allow you to pursue tasks in your own way, giving you greater autonomy and personal control.

Because of the ubiquity of internet mail and personal access via modems, it is increasingly the case that people (especially in the US) assume that you read email every day, either at the office or at home – including weekends and when you are on holiday! You may arrive back after a weekend or week away at a conference and find messages which *expect* you to have done something yesterday . . . autonomy and personal control?

19.3.2 Structured message systems

A common problem with email and electronic conferencing systems is *overload* for the recipient. As distribution lists become longer, the number of email messages received begins to explode. This is obvious: if each message you send goes to, on average, 10 people, then everyone will receive, on average, 10 messages for each one sent. The problem is similar to that caused for paper mail by photocopiers and mail merge programs. If we consider that newsgroups may have hundreds of subscribers, the problem becomes extreme. Happily, most newsgroups have only a few active contributors and many passive readers, but still the piles of unread electronic mail grow. Various forms of *structured message system* have been developed to help deal with this overload, perhaps the most well known being the *Information Lens* [225]. This adopts some form of *filtering* in order to sort items into different categories, either by importance or by subject matter. As well as a text message, normal email has several named fields: To, From, Subject. Structured message systems have far more, domain-specific, fields. The sender of the message chooses the appropriate message type, say a notification of a seminar. The system then presents a *template* which includes blank fields pertinent to the message type, for example Time, Place, Speaker and Title. Figure 19.4 shows a typical structured message similar to those in Lens.

The named fields make the message more like a typical database record than a normal email message. Thus the recipient can filter incoming mail using database-like queries. This can be used during normal reading – 'show me all messages From "abowd" or with Status "urgent"'. Alternatively, users may set up filtering agents to act on their behalf. Such an agent is a sort of electronic secretary; it is programmed with rules based on the field contents and can perform actions such as moving the message into a specific mailbox, deleting the message or informing the user.

The problem with such systems is that they put a great burden on the sender to fill in the fields accurately, but it is the recipient who benefits. This problem of

```
Type: Seminar announcement
To: all
From: Alan Dix
Subject: departmental seminar

Time: 2:15 Wednesday
Place: D014
Speaker: W.T. Pooh
Title: The Honey Pot
Text: Recent research on socially constructed
       meaning has focussed on the image of the
       Honey Pot and its dialectic interpretation
       within an encultured hermeneutic.
       This talk ...
```

Figure 19.4 Structured message

disproportionate benefit recurs throughout CSCW. In order to make the job of the sender as easy as possible, message types will often be created with easy defaults for fields, and perhaps menus of alternatives. Also, in order to make finding appropriate message templates easier, they may be arranged in a type hierarchy.

Until recently these structured message systems were only found in academic and research centers, but simpler forms are now available in commercial PC-based email products.

More complex structured message systems are based on models of conversation. So, for example, if I am sent a message of type 'request for information', I am obliged to return either a message of type 'informative reply' or of type 'don't know'. There is a variety of such systems differing in the models used and the rigidity with which they are applied. In the most rigid, you are only allowed one of the pre-programmed replies, whereas more flexible systems merely suggest possibilities. We discussed one such system, *Coordinator*, in Chapter 14 (Section 14.3.6), in the context of models of conversation.

There is, in fact, considerable debate between those who feel that messaging systems should impose conversational structures and constraints, and those who believe they should supply systems within which the participants can develop their own structures. It is argued that such user-defined structures are more likely to meet users' needs, and the systems will be more flexible to accommodate changes in group working. The message systems based upon conversational models are the most constrained. Those offering structured messages, as we have described above, are toward the middle of the spectrum. The original email and bulletin board systems were at the other, unstructured, extreme, but lack sufficient features for the users to define their own structure. More modern systems from the 'user-structured' arena are developed from the bulletin board concept, but are more like a shared hypertext. The structure allowed by links and cross-references allows users to have subconferences and digressions, to annotate each other's messages and to post follow-on messages. An example of such a system is the *Amsterdam Conversation Environment* [113].

This conflict between *global structuring* by the designers and *local structuring* by the participants in their own situation arises within many areas of CSCW and has similarities to issues of user control in HCI in general (see Chapter 7).

19.3.3 txt is gr8

While groupware developers produce more and more complex structured message systems, in the wider world people have voted with their fingers and adopted unstructured informal text messaging systems: instant messaging while online and SMS or paging through mobile phones.

In November 1996 a small Israeli start-up company, Mirabilis, launched a program, ICQ, that allowed registered users to send short text messages to one another. By 2003 this had grown to over 100 million users. Other large internet companies soon noticed this rapidly growing phenomenon, including AOL and Yahoo! who launched their own, incompatible, messaging systems based on their existing user groups.

Many readers will have accounts with one or more of the instant messaging (IM) clients. Compared with email, messaging is more lightweight and instant. Users can send a message, usually a single line of text, to any other registered user of the system. If the other user is currently logged into the system they receive an instant notification of the message and can start a chat-style session. If the other user is not logged in, the central system remembers the messages and when the user next logs on they receive any messages stored for them. So IM systems are unusual in that they allow a fluid movement between asynchronous and synchronous use.

Whereas email is more like an exchange of letters, IM is more like conversation with short exchanges, often not even complete sentences.

Hi, u there
yeh, had a good night last night?
uhu
want to meet later

Because of the conversational style there is extensive use of *emoticons* or smilies (see Section 14.4.1). Whereas in traditional email these were simply a text convention such as ':-)', messaging systems (and now many email systems too) substitute small icons (like the face above) and allow easy insertions of faces using drop-down lists.

SMS stands for Short Message Systems, but few users know this or care – they simply send an 'SMS' or 'text' a friend. The SMS phenomenon is a salutary lesson to any of us who believe we can design the future. It was originally an 'extra' service, making use of a technical fix that allowed mobile phone companies to send messages to mobile phones to inform of voicemail or update internal settings. However, in many countries SMS has overtaken voice calls in its use of airtime.

Like IM, SMS messages are short plain text messages – limited to 160 characters in the original system. However, the potential recipient is anyone with a mobile phone. SMS was able to break the critical mass problem (see Chapter 13) because even when only a few phones were able to send SMS messages, many existing phones were able to receive them. The real surprise of SMS was not just that it grew, but that the group who adopted it as their own were not business people wanting the latest stock update, or sales representatives sending an order, but teenagers. From being an add-on service, text messaging became *the* reason people bought mobile phones and pricing plans are often focussed on the number of free text messages per month.

Perhaps the defining feature of SMS text messages is the fact that they are entered via a telephone keypad. To type 'hello' you typically need to type '4433555*pause*555666' using multiple number keys to produce the letters. SMS users soon 'lrnt 2 txt usng shrt wds', both to reduce the effort of typing so many letters and also to allow longer messages within the same 160 character limit. Belatedly, technology caught up and text entry was made easier using the T9 algorithm (T9 is a trademark of Tegic Communications), which matches single number strokes against a dictionary: so '43556' becomes 'hello', as other matches to the digits such as 'gfjkn' are not proper words. Paradoxically, many experienced txt-ers turn this off as it makes the messages longer (and so fits less into 160 characters) and also looks less cool!

Another paradox of SMS is that it is an area where the United States lags behind due to the fragmented nature of its mobile telecoms industry. Dedicated devices such as pagers with small keyboards are used, but not with the same penetration that SMS has achieved elsewhere.

Both IM and SMS have gradually become more 'functional', adding features such as file sharing with IM and links between IM, email and SMS services. Also there are IM clients for PDAs allowing users to keep messaging even when away from their computers. As countries adopt higher bandwidth mobile phone networks, the potential for new services has increased. Japan has led the world here with several (incompatible) services. This was partly a technical issue and partly demand driven due to long commute times and high fixed-line telephone costs. Some of the services are likely to be closer to traditional broadcast media, but messaging is becoming multi-media with voice and image messages based on the MMS (Multimedia Messaging Service) standard. Many phones now include a digital camera so that it is possible to take a photograph whilst at a party and instantly send it to all your friends.

DESIGN FOCUS

SMS in action

SMS is not just for teenagers to hear the latest gossip or arrange to meet at the local night club. In the north of England the Croftlands Charitable Trust is using an SMS-based system called SPAM to coordinate the activities of its staff in a hostel and associated semi-independent living accommodation for former psychiatric patients [70]. Staff and patients can send SMS messages to a central number which are then displayed on touchscreens in the staff offices. As staff spend a considerable amount of time off site this is used extensively, for example when meetings over-run or people encounter traffic delays. Also, they can leave messages without tying up the phone during busy times of the day.

See the book website for a full case study: /e3/casestudy/spam/

One of the SPAM displays showing messages received. Source: Courtesy of Mark Rouncefield

In contrast with email, IM grew as an informal communication medium. There has been some concern in the business community that it would add to internet surfing and private email as a drain on employees' time. However, several studies seem to indicate that the opposite is true and that IM is being used to facilitate group working and business contacts. SMS, too, is being used for 'serious' uses, from paying for goods at vending machines to coordinating staff activity in a residential facility for former psychiatric patients.

19.3.4 Video conferences and communication

The idea of *video phones* has been around for a long time, from Flash Gordon's days onwards, and early video phones have been available for at least 20 years. Until recently, pervasive person-to-person video has been impossible without special and very expensive cabling. However, the introduction of *ISDN* changes this dramatically. ISDN (integrated services digital network) is a form of moderately high-bandwidth (64 kbaud) digital telephone connection. It is available in major cities across the world and enables, amongst other things, LAN-type connections between computers and real-time video connections. The need for this becomes apparent if you calculate the bandwidth required for a typical video image. If we consider an 8 bit 600×400 pixel image being sent at 25 frames a second, this amounts to 24 million bits per second. This is not high video quality and yet requires a vast bandwidth far in excess of a normal telephone line. It is also far greater than the capacity of ISDN lines. However, recent (and expensive) *video compression* techniques can reduce the required capacity to a level within the range of ISDN. Pervasive video communication is clearly a technology coming of age.

As these hardware developments are quite recent, most experimental and commercial video systems use existing technology and *lots* of wire. There are three broad uses of video: *video conferences*, pervasive video for enhancing social communication and video integrated with another shared application. These are all *synchronous remote* facilities.

Video conferences sit rather oddly in CSCW in that they typically do not use computers at all! However, computers and telecommunications are becoming so interlinked that it is widely considered an appropriate area of CSCW. Video conference facilities are readily available commercially using dedicated telecommunications lines and satellites for transcontinental conferences. The quality of a video conference compared with a face-to-face meeting is appalling, but, when faced with the costs of, say, flying executives across an ocean or even across the American continent, the inconveniences are often accepted.

One set of problems is connected with the small field of view of a television camera, and the size and quality of the resulting images. Even with a one-to-one video conversation, we need to decide whether to take a simple head and shoulders shot, the whole torso, or head to foot. If there is a group at either end, even just two or three people, the problems magnify enormously. If you view all three people at once, then the image of the speaker may become so small that it is hard to see the body

CuSeeMe

Special-purpose video conferencing is still relatively expensive, but low-fidelity desktop video conferencing is now within the reach of many users of desktop computers. Digital video cameras are now inexpensive and easily obtainable. They often come with pre-packaged video phone or video conferencing software. However, the system which has really popularized video conferencing is a web-based tool. CuSeeMe works over the internet allowing participants across the world owning only a basic digital video camera to see and talk to one another. The software is usually public domain (although there are commercial versions) and the services allowing connection are often free. The limited bandwidth available over long-distance internet links means that video quality and frame rates are low and periodic image break-up may occur. In fact, it is sound break-up which is more problematic. After all, we can talk to one another quite easily without seeing one another, but find it very difficult over a noisy phone line. Often participants may see one another's video image, but actually discuss using a synchronous text-based 'talk' program.

Devina

.5 fps   88 Kbps(103 cap)

Geoffrey

.8 fps   49 Kbps

Chat Window

Geoffrey: Hello. Did you receive my vrml world in the email this morning?
Devina: yes thanks. I really like the colour scheme in your office
Geoffrey: Did you find your way onto the roof garden?

I did not go in there because it was raining :-)

Filter | Reset | Config

CuSeeMe – video conferencing on the internet. Source: Courtesy of Geoff Ellis gestures. These gestures are one of the big advantages of video conferences over the much cheaper telephone conference. However, you need a skilled camera technician to follow the speaker, zooming in and out as necessary. Furthermore, zooming in to the speaker runs the risk of losing the sense of presence. The participants at the far end do not know whether the speaker's colleagues are nodding in agreement or falling asleep!

Video conferences support specific planned meetings. However, one of the losses of working in a different site from a colleague is the chance meetings whilst walking down a corridor or drinking tea. Several experimental systems aim to counter this, giving a sense of *social presence* at a distance. One solution is the *video window* or *video wall*, a very large television screen set into the wall of common rooms at different sites [134]. The idea is that as people wander about the common room at one site they can see and talk to people at the other site – the video wall is almost like a window or doorway between the sites.

The problems of camera positioning and focussing are, if anything, worse for the video wall than for the simple video conference. At least in a video conference the participants stay relatively still, probably seated at a table, whereas in a common room the participants are likely to wander about. It is quite easy to move out of the range of the camera, whilst still being able to see your colleague. That is, there is a lack of *reciprocity* compared with normal face-to-face conversation. In addition, positioning the camera is a nightmare. To give the 'window' illusion, the camera must be positioned very close to the video wall and must be focussed to get a full-depth shot of the conversants. Even then, because of the camera's restricted field of view, you must not stand too close or your colleague will get a 6 foot (1.8 m) high view of your navel!

A stereo audio channel for the video wall, and indeed for any video connection, can help the participants orient to the speaker and also filter out unwanted noises (see Chapter 1 for a discussion of selective attention to sound). However, a problem with communicating using loudspeakers in a common room is a lack of privacy. Normally, people just move closer and lower their voice, but this is not effective with the video wall.

Similar facilities have been made available within individual offices at several research sites. For example, at Xerox EuroParc in Cambridge, UK, every office is wired up with video cameras and monitors. Typically, one has a camera strapped to the top of one's monitor, or on an angle-poise-like arm, and an image on a separate monitor, or even in a window on the computer screen. Participants may have two-way or multi-way video conversations, or set up virtual rooms – a constant video connection.

Even with the camera strapped just above a monitor, it is very difficult for the participants to get *eye contact*. In normal face-to-face conversation, participants periodically look one another straight in the eye. If the camera is just above the monitor, your partner will always see you looking slightly downwards, and vice versa. For strictly one-to-one conversation, a technique called the *video tunnel* can be used (Figure 19.5). A half-silvered mirror is used so that the camera can view the user as if it were in the middle of the screen. The feeling of engagement between the participants is reported to be far greater than more standard video arrangements

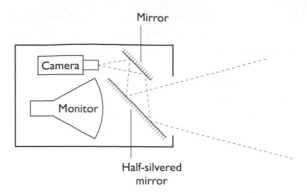

Figure 19.5 Video tunnel

[326]. Unfortunately, the sheer bulk of the video tunnel means that it is not really practical for large-scale use. However, frequent users of less optimal camera/monitor configurations eventually get used to the rather odd visual angles involved.

19.3.5 Virtual collaborative environments

Virtual reality techniques are now being used to allow participants to meet within a virtual world. Each participant views a virtual world using desktop or immersive VR. Within the virtual worlds the other participants appear, often rendered as a simple cube-based figure perhaps with a fixed or even video image texture mapped onto it. The representation of a participant in *virtual space* is called an *embodiment*.

As participants move around in virtual space then their embodiments move correspondingly. Thus one can approach another within the virtual environment, initiate discussion and focus on common objects within the virtual environment. These systems attempt to mimic as much as possible of the real world in order to allow the participants to use their existing real-world social skills within the virtual world. For example, when other people speak, the volume may be adjusted so that those a long way away or behind you (in virtual space) are quieter than those close and in front. This is clearly very important in a heavily populated virtual environment.

Given the virtual environment is within a computer, it makes sense to allow participants to bring other computer-based artifacts into the virtual environment. However, many of these are not themselves 3D objects, but simple text or diagrams. It is possible to map these onto flat virtual surfaces within the 3D virtual world (or even have virtual computer screens!). Text is especially difficult to read when rendered in perspective and so some environments take advantage of the fact that this is a *virtual* world to present such surfaces face on to all participants. But now we have a world the appearance of which is participant dependent.

Imagine you and a colleague are facing each other and looking at the same text object. It will be rather like having a piece of paper held up between you with the same text printed on both sides. Your colleague points at the left-hand side of the text and refers to it. What should you see – a virtual finger pointing at the wrong side of the text, a disembodied hand tear off from your colleague's arm and point at the correct place on your side of the paper? This is similar to the problems of shared focus which we shall discuss in the next section, but perhaps worse in this context as the users are lulled into a false sense that the world they are dealing with is truly like the normal real world.

Although collaborative virtual environments are still mainly research systems, it is possible to sample some of the features by visiting 'virtual places' on the web [84], also known as *MUDs (Multi-User Domains)*. When you visit the page, you are allowed to specify an icon or image which becomes your embodiment or *avatar* within the pages. Your own avatar and those of other visitors appear within the page. Although these are 2D worlds, many of the same possibilities arise. You can bump into people within the virtual world, who, as they are visiting the same place as you, may share common interests and you can also usually initiate text-based or even audio conversations.

Real and virtual worlds meet

The *video wall* allows people from remote locations to meet. In a sense it extends the normal physical space of the participants as they can see the remote room, but the image rendered is a real physical space, albeit on a video screen.

Virtual collaborative environments also allow remote participants to meet one another, this time within a purely virtual space.

The *Nottingham Internet Foyer* merges these two worlds. In a real physical foyer at Nottingham University there is a large video screen. However, what you see when you look at it is not a room in a remote building (as with a video wall), but a fixed view of a virtual space. The virtual space that is seen is itself a collaborative virtual environment, a sort of virtual foyer, which participants can enter over the internet using either desktop or immersive VR systems. The embodiments of the electronic participants are visible to those at the real foyer. In addition, the video image of the real foyer is also projected onto a surface in the virtual foyer. Thus the physical foyer and the virtual foyer are linked by a virtual video wall!

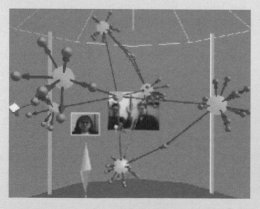

The real foyer and the electronic foyer. Source: Courtesy of Steve Benford, The Mixed Reality Laboratory, The University of Nottingham

19.4   MEETING AND DECISION SUPPORT SYSTEMS

In any conversation, the participants must establish a common understanding about the task they are to perform, and generate ideas. In some areas this is a secondary activity: you are discussing the job you are doing, the ideas support that job. However, there is a class of activities where the job is itself generating ideas and understanding. This is typically the case in a research environment, in design tasks, in management meetings and brainstorming sessions.

We will discuss three types of system where the generation and recording of ideas and decisions is the primary focus.

Argumentation tools which record the arguments used to arrive at a decision and support principally *asynchronous co-located* design teams.

Meeting rooms which support face-to-face groups (*synchronous co-located*) in brainstorming and management meetings.

Shared drawing surfaces which can be used for *synchronous remote* design meetings.

19.4.1 Argumentation tools

In Chapter 6, we discussed *design rationale*, methods of recording decisions and the arguments that lead to those decisions. We saw that design rationale could fulfill two roles: recording design decisions for future references and clarifying the available options during design. Both of these have a potential CSCW impact. One reason to record your design decisions is so that a future designer can understand why you made the decisions you did and hence be in a better position to modify or learn from your design. That is, you are communicating with someone possibly years in advance. However, the one-way nature of the communication makes it information passing rather than collaboration.

More important from a CSCW viewpoint is when the design argument is used to communicate decisions between a group of designers. Here the communication is two way – the designers may both add to the design argument and look at each other's contributions. Argumentation support tools often have a hypertext-like structure, and may easily be used to support design teams as well as individuals. At the simplest level, the designers can use the tool one at a time, rather like writing a co-authored document by taking turns to use the word processor. As the detailed design of, say, a piece of software may take many months it is unlikely that two people will want to use the tool at exactly the same moment, and if they do . . . well it is a chance for an impromptu design meeting!

Sophisticated tools also have facilities to allow several designers to use the system simultaneously. To allow this, the tool must have mechanisms to stop the different designers' work interfering with that of another. This problem is called *concurrency control*. Happily, this is particularly easy with hypertext – so long as people work on different nodes, there is no conflict. To ensure this, a node must be *locked*; that is, when one participant starts to edit the node, no other participant is allowed to edit or update the same node. Given that there are typically hundreds of nodes in a design rationale, with only a short text description in each, the chances of two participants wanting to work on the same node are small. However, if they do, the system will refuse permission to one or the other. In addition to these locking mechanisms, the systems have *notification mechanisms* to let the participants know which nodes have been edited. For example, changed nodes may be highlighted until the participant has examined them or marked them as read. This highlighting must, of course, be on a per user basis – if Jane edits a node and Sam marks it as read, then when Mary comes to the system she should still see the node highlighted.

A good example of argumentation tools is the family of tools developed to support the argumentation model called *issue-based information system* (*IBIS*), the best known being gIBIS [76] (which we met in Chapter 6). This system has node types including 'issues', 'positions' and 'arguments', and these are linked together by relationships such as 'argument *supports* position'.

Notice that argumentation tools may allow a range of interaction styles from asynchronous, when the designers use it one at a time, to fully synchronous, when several use it at once. Although there is no reason why the systems should not be used for distant collaboration they are typically used by groups within the same office, and in the case of one-at-a-time use, on one machine. They are thus largely, but not solely, *asynchronous co-located* groupware systems.

19.4.2 Meeting rooms

The advantages of email, bulletin boards and video conferences are obvious – if you are a long way apart, you cannot have a face-to-face meeting. Similarly, it is obvious why one should want to record decisions during a long-lived design process. The need for *meeting rooms* is less obvious. These are specially constructed rooms, with extensive computer equipment designed to support face-to-face meetings. Given face-to-face meetings work reasonably well to start with, such rooms must be very well designed if the equipment is to enhance rather than disrupt the meeting.

Early examples of such rooms, catering for groups of between four and 30 participants, included Xerox PARC's CoLab [329], Project Nick [32] and Capture Lab [226]. The general layout consists of a large screen, regarded as an electronic whiteboard, at one end of the room, with chairs and tables arranged so that all the participants can see the screen. This leads to a U- or C-shaped arrangement around the screen, and in the biggest room even several tiers of seating. In addition, all the participants have their own terminals, which may be recessed into the tabletop to reduce their visual effect. Figure 19.6 shows a computer-supported meeting using NLS, a very early groupware system [125]. Obviously, changes in display technology have made the displays less obtrusive, but the basic principle remains.

Such systems will support various forms of working, including private use of the terminals and subgroup working on a teleconferencing or email basis. However, the characteristic mode of operation is where all the participants' screens and the central screen show the same image. This is termed *WYSIWIS* ('*what you see is what I see*').

Figure 19.6   A computer-supported meeting. Photograph courtesy of Douglas Engelbart and Bootstrap Institute

The screen then takes the form of an electronic whiteboard, similar to a simple graphics drawing package, on which the participants can all write. One advantage of such an arrangement over a normal whiteboard is the ease with which data can be moved to and from the participants' normal computer files. As more work is prepared online this will increase in importance. Also, the electronic whiteboard has some advantages over the real thing. Whereas on a real whiteboard you can only write and rub out, on the electronic version you can move items around just as you would with a drawing tool, and, of course, you can get a printout of the results rather than just hoping the cleaners do not wipe it all off.

There are potential problems if several participants decide to write at the same time, so different systems adopt different *floor control policies* to determine which participant can write at any moment.

The simplest policy to implement is to use *locking*, similar to that described previously. When a participant, say Jane, wants to write to the screen she presses a key, or clicks on an on-screen button to request the floor. If no one else has the floor, she may go ahead and type on the screen, or if it supports graphics draw a diagram. When she has finished, she relinquishes the floor, using some other key or mouse selection. However, if some other participant, say Sam, already has the floor when Jane requests it, she must wait until Sam relinquishes the floor. There will be some sort of status indicator to say who has the floor at any moment, so Jane can ask Sam to relinquish, just as you might ask for the pen to write on a whiteboard.

In practice, such meetings tend to be punctuated with far too many requests such as 'Sam have you finished yet?', as often a participant will forget to relinquish the floor after writing. Also, it can be a pain to request the floor explicitly from the system – with a whiteboard you simply pick up your pen and write. Various more lenient locking mechanisms are used to reduce these problems. A lock may be *implicitly* requested when you begin to type or draw. If no one else has the floor, then the floor is implicitly granted. If someone else has the floor, then your writing will be blocked. There is also implicit relinquishing: the lock may be automatically released after several seconds of inactivity. This may, of course, happen during a pause, rather than when the floor holder has finished, but the ease with which the floor can be regained does not make it a nuisance.

A conceptually simpler idea is to let everyone write to the screen at the same time – just as people may use several pens to write on a whiteboard at the same time. This sounds like a recipe for chaos, with people forever writing on top of one another. However, with reasonably small groups there is little problem. Try going to the whiteboard as someone is writing on it, and writing on top of what they write. It is possible, but it does not make you many friends. Similarly in the electronic version, as soon as two people begin to write on the same part of the screen they say 'oops!' and start to write elsewhere.

The various forms of locking constitute a software protocol for floor control. The way that people negotiate for screen space in the free-for-all situation is a *social protocol*. The reason that this is possible is because the participants are in the same room and are able to talk to one another.

If there is only one floor holder, then the screens can all show the floor holder's cursor. However, as soon as several participants are active at once, it is less clear what to do. One option is to display all the users' cursors. These may be accompanied by the user's name so that you can tell who is entering what. With large numbers of participants this can become distracting, and it is costly in terms of network traffic. The alternative is to show none of the cursors. If the participants are talking as they write, it is usually obvious who is writing what. In addition, during brainstorming phases, anonymity is an advantage – people are more likely to put up an 'off-the-wall' suggestion, thus stimulating more ideas and discussion.

If you are using a real whiteboard, you may go up to a diagram on the board and say 'I think *that* should go *there*'. As you say the words '*that*' and '*there*', you point at the relevant parts of the diagram. This is called *deictic reference* or simply *deixis*. If the participants' cursors are invisible to one another, then this form of pointing is impossible. Indeed, in such a meeting, even where the cursors are visible, the participants may momentarily forget and point at their own screen. Obviously, the participant can get up and point at the shared screen as you would at a whiteboard, but that is rather intrusive and precludes writing at the same time. To allow this deictic reference a *group pointer* may be supplied. This is an icon visible on all the screens, perhaps in the form of a pointing finger. Any participant can pick it up with his own mouse and use it to gesture on the screen. The control of the group pointer poses similar problems to those of floor control. However, the most lenient locking policies work well since the use of the pointer is usually synchronized with speaking, and thus it is easy to avoid and resolve conflicts.

The design and building of meeting rooms is both expensive and time consuming, but less sophisticated facilities are more widely available. The simplest is the hardcopy whiteboard, which has some of the advantages of an electronic whiteboard

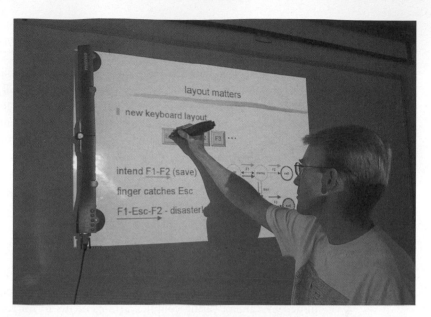

Figure 19.7   Meeting capture at the whiteboard

(and with greater resolution). If these were more closely coupled to a computer system, they would have even more scope. LCD projectors or transparent LCD screens for putting on top of an overhead projector can give any computer a vast screen image. In the simplest case this can just be manipulated by one person, but if several computers are networked together and use commercial shared screen software (see below in Section 19.5.1), one can obtain a similar effect to that of the more expensive conferencing facilities (Figure 19.7). However, experience of the various meeting room projects has shown that the social dynamics are very fragile and the difference between a successful meeting environment and a complete disaster is narrow.

These lower cost and more readily available technologies have made it possible to *capture* the results of ordinary meetings (see also Chapter 20). A number of devices are available commercially to turn an ordinary whiteboard into an electronic surface. Ordinary pens are placed in some sort of holder so that fixed detectors around the board can track the location of the pen on the whiteboard. This can then be used to record the strokes produced on the whiteboard and so keep an electronic copy. If instead an LCD projector is used to project a computer screen onto the whiteboard, then inkless pens can be used to act as a mouse pointer and so allow interaction with applications. Both of these can be combined with audio recording to allow rich capture of meetings for future review, aiding minute making and so on.

19.4.3 Shared work surfaces

The idea of a shared screen forming an electronic whiteboard is not confined to face-to-face meetings. One can easily imagine using the same software which runs in a meeting room, working between several sites. That is, we can take the *synchronous co-located* meeting room software and use it for *synchronous remote* meetings. As before, each participant's screen shows the same image, and the participants can write on the screen with the same sort of floor control policies as discussed earlier. There are additional problems. First, the participants will also require at least an audio link to one another and quite likely video as well. Remember that the social protocols used during lenient floor control, not to mention the discussion one has during a meeting, are difficult or impossible without additional channels of communication. As well as the person-to-person communications, the computer networks may have trouble handling the information. If there are delays between one person writing something on the board and another seeing it, the second participant may write to the same location. A situation which is easily avoided in the co-located meeting could become a major problem when remote. Many researchers in the area blithely assume that such problems will be solved by cheaper high-bandwidth telecommunications, such as ISDN.

In order to make the whiteboard effect more realistic, several systems are arranged so that participants write by hand directly onto large screens. The writing is either filmed by camera (using complex arrangements of mirrors), or captured digitally using a sensitive screen. The image of one participant's writing is then displayed on the others' screens. The effect is very like all being able to write at once on the same screen, except that the other participants' writing will be slightly less distinct than your own because of the resolution of the TV image. You may also experience problems of *parallax* as your own writing is on the outer surface of the screen and the projected image on the inside.

One system, VideoWhiteboard [340], arranges its lighting and cameras such that you can see not only the other participants' writing, but also shadowy images of their hands and bodies, getting gradually dimmer and more out of focus as they move away from the screen. For two participants, it is rather as if your colleague is writing on the other side of a smoked glass panel. When used by more than two participants, your ghostly colleagues can appear to occupy the same space and move through one another! This sounds rather disconcerting, but the users soon get used to the effect and are able to interpret one another's body language, even as a soft-focus shadow.

A third variation of the shared work surface is where the participants write on a sheet of paper on their desktop, which is then filmed from above. The images from each participant are then mixed and displayed on a screen in each participant's work area. By looking at the screen while they point and write, the participants can refer to one another's work. The advantage of such a system is that the participants' individual paperwork is easily integrated into their shared environment. The desktop images can also be mixed with a shared computer screen, so that paper and computer work can be mixed. One such system, the *TeamWorkStation* [188], has been used for the remote teaching of Japanese calligraphy. The student is able to paint letters on paper or on the computer screen and see these strokes overlaid with the teacher's strokes. In this system, the participants also have a face-to-face video link.

The things that were being shared in the previous section were ephemera; they were there to support the meeting or design process, but were not the end purpose. In this section we will look at systems where the focus of sharing is the participants' work domain itself. These include the computers people are using, applications on those computers, and the documents they are working with. Some of these systems are similar in technology to the various shared work surfaces above, but the focus in this section is on *work*.

19.5.1 Shared PCs and shared window systems

Most of the groupware tools we have discussed require special *collaboration-aware* applications to be written. However, *shared PCs* and *shared window systems* allow ordinary applications to be the focus of cooperative work. Of course, you can co-operate simply by sitting together at the same computer, passing the keyboard and mouse between you and your colleague. The idea of a shared PC is that you have two (or more) computers which function as if they were one. What is typed on one appears on all the rest. This sounds at first just like a meeting room without the large shared screen. The difference is that the meeting rooms have special shared drawing tools, but the shared PC is just running your ordinary program. The sharing software monitors your keystrokes and mouse movements and sends them to all the other computers, so that their systems behave exactly like yours. Their keystrokes and movements are similarly relayed to you. As far as the application is concerned there is one keyboard and one mouse.

Imagine two users type at once. As the application does not know about the multiple users it will merely interleave the keystrokes, or should we say '*inkeyterslt reaokevetshe*'? Interleaved mouse movements are, if anything, more meaningless. The sharing software therefore imposes some form of lenient locking. For the mouse, this will be an automatic lock while the mouse is being moved, with the lock being relinquished after a very short period of inactivity. The keyboard lock will have a longer period as natural gaps in typing are greater than gaps in mousing. Alternatively, the keyboard may have no lock, the users being left to sort out the control with their own *social protocol*.

A shared window system is similar except, rather than the whole screen, it is individual windows which are shared. While the user works with unshared windows, the system behaves as normal, but when the user selects a shared window the shared windowing system intervenes. As with the shared PC, all the user's keystrokes and mouse movements within the window are broadcast to the other computers sharing the window.

These facilities may be used within the same room, as originally suggested, in which case we have a *synchronous co-located* system. Alternatively, they may be used in conjunction with telephone or video connections at a distance, that is *synchronous remote.* The extra audio or video channel is necessary when used remotely as the systems in themselves offer no direct communication. It is just possible to use such systems, without additional channels, by writing messages in the application's workspace (document, drawing surface, etc.). However, the social protocols needed to mediate the mouse and keyboard cannot be achieved by this channel.

Shared PCs and window systems have two main uses. One is where the focus is on the documents being processed, for example if the participants are using a spreadsheet together to solve a financial problem. The other is technical support: if you have a problem with an application, you can ring up your local (or even remote) technical guru, who will connect to your computer, examine where you are and offer advice. Compare this scenario with trying to explain over the phone why your column is not formatting as you want.

19.5.2 Shared editors

A *shared editor* is an editor (for text or graphics) which is *collaboration aware*, that is it knows that it is being shared. It can thus provide several insertion points or locking protocols more tuned to the editor's behavior. The software used in meeting rooms can be thought of as a form of shared editor and many of the issues are the same, but the purpose of a shared editor is to collaborate over normal documents. Just as with shared PCs and windows, the users are expected to have some additional means of communication, such as face-to-face (co-located), audio or video channels, or at the very least textual communications.

Shared editors may be text based or include graphics. For simplicity, we shall just consider text. Even so, there are a wide range of design options. Should you have a single insertion point with some form of *floor control* to avoid interleaving, or should you have one insertion point per participant? Assuming you have several insertion points, do you just see your own, or do you see your colleagues' insertion points as well, and if you can see them should they be identified by the user's name or be anonymous? In addition to the insertion point options, there is the issue about what you should see. Do all the participants see the same part of the screen, so if one participant scrolls, so do all the rest? Or do we allow different views on the document so that one participant can edit the beginning of the document while another edits the end?

There is not a right answer to these questions; different policies are useful for different purposes – close cooperation on a single sentence, or writing separate sections. Even within a single editing session the appropriate policy will vary. Unfortunately, in the past, these policy decisions were usually enshrined in the various shared editors, rather than being configured by the users. However, there is a growing recognition that more adaptable systems are needed to allow for the wide variation between groups, and within the same group over time. We will look at some of the options and how they affect the style of cooperation.

Thinking about the shared view versus different view options, it at first seems obvious that we should allow people to edit different parts of a document. This is

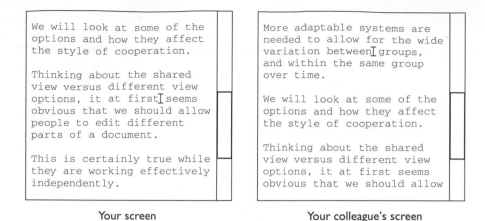

Figure 19.8 Shared editor with separate insertion points and different views

certainly true while they are working effectively independently. However, as soon as they begin to discuss the text together – that is, really *collaborate* synchronously – problems arise: 'I don't really like that line at the top' you say; 'I just wrote that, I think it's really good' your colleague replies. Possibly the end of your good working relationship, and, sadly, unnecessary. Your screens show different parts of the document and so the line at the top of your screen (which you disliked) is not the one your colleague has just written (Figure 19.8). Of course, the participants know they do not necessarily see the same screen, but you naturally use terms which relate to the context you can see, called *indexical expressions*. One reason given for the Charge of the Light Brigade is that the commander gave the order 'take the position on the hill'. Unfortunately the hill the commander could see was not the one in front of the Light Brigade. Paradoxically, the better the impression of a shared environment, the more likely it is that participants will accidentally use indexical expressions.

These problems are precisely why the principle of WYSIWIS – what you see is what I see – is used in meeting rooms. Even minor differences between displays, such as lags between the appearance of one participant's typing on the others' screens, can cause severe problems – no wonder different views cause trouble. Of course, WYSIWIS is not always appropriate, for example if we want to edit different parts of a document. Neither is it a solution to all problems. For example, if two people try to scroll the shared view at the same time, we have scroll wars. People find this conflict harder to resolve than typing clashes. This is probably because scrolling is a less direct and less predictable action anyway, and thus it is more difficult to diagnose what is going wrong. This suggests that better locking of scrollbars and visual clues are required. As we will discuss later (Section 19.7) graphics toolkits do not make such modifications easy.

Separate views, of course, demand separate insertion points. Even with shared views, it is not obvious why one should want a single insertion point with the attendant floor control problems. However, a shared cursor offers a point of focus for close cooperation, and should perhaps be an option. Of course, a shared view with shared cursor is almost identical to a single-user editor in a shared window. Where there is no shared cursor, a *group pointer* can be used to focus discussion. Indeed, one could imagine using a group pointer with different views, but there are no extant systems which allow this.

As we have indicated, the differences between groups mean that some configuration by the group is essential. That is, shared editors require some form of *local structuring*. However, that does not mean that there will be no problems. Participants will point at the screen with their fingers when in different rooms, and use indexical expressions when they are in separate screen mode. The more their sense of *engagement*, that is the more they feel as if they are working together, the more likely they are to revert to natural forms of expression. We cannot prevent this entirely; as we saw, mistakes can happen in 'real life' too.

19.5.3 Co-authoring systems

Shared text editing is a short-term activity, occurring over a timescale of, at most, a few hours. Co-authoring is much longer term, taking weeks or months. Whereas shared editing is synchronous, co-authoring is largely *asynchronous*, with occasional periods of synchronous work. This may involve shared editing, but even if it does this is only one of the activities. Authors may work out some sort of plan together, apportion work between them, and then exchange drafts commenting on one another's work. In fact, this is only one scenario and if there is one consistent result from numerous studies of individual and collaborative writing, it is this: everyone and every group is different.

Fortunately, even though the details of writing differ, especially in the process, there are enough similarities to produce systems which support co-authoring. The majority of these are built around a hypertext model. The text itself is the basis and comments and discussion of these comments are linked into this basic structure. Although a general-purpose shared hypertext can be used, specific co-authoring systems are tuned to the writing task. The shape of the hypertext may be limited to a tree rather than the arbitrary graph of a hypertext. The document itself may be flat, a linear list of sections or may be grouped into a hierarchical section–subsection tree. Comment nodes are then attached to the document nodes, and other follow-on remarks attached to the comments. These are intended to emulate the scribblings on paper drafts during normal collaborative writing. Special facilities may be added to inform one writer of another's comments or additions.

As in previous systems, co-authoring systems must have some sort of *concurrency control* to cater for times when two participants attempt to edit the same text at the same time. This may take the form of locking, as described previously, or the system may allow the users to enter into periods of synchronous activity. That is, the node editor acts as a shared editor. However, this is not the dominant form of working and most often co-authors will have divided up the work amongst themselves, so that a section will have only one principal author, and thus *social protocols* ensure that writing clashes do not occur.

These social protocols may be supported or enforced by the co-authoring system. For example, in one system, *Quilt* [210], users are assigned *roles*, such as author, commentator, reader, with respect to each document node. An author is allowed to edit the text and add comments, a commentator is only allowed to add comments, and a reader cannot alter it at all. These roles resemble access rights in a normal filestore or database. However, both their naming and their particular semantics are aimed at supporting the types of role which occur in co-authoring situations. Of course, we are again into the territory of local versus global structuring. Who decides on the roles and the associated access rights, and can they be changed during use? These questions are not too much of a problem for Quilt, where the roles are on a per node basis, but some systems have roles which apply to the whole document. It is often the case that a person who gives extensive constructive comments is asked to co-author a paper, or someone who originally was to be an author cannot find sufficient time. Roles in real life have a degree of flexibility; those in groupware must try to keep suit.

19.5.4 Shared diaries

We want to find a time for a meeting to discuss the book we are writing: when should it be? Four diaries come out and we search for a mutually acceptable slot. We eventually find a free slot, but decide we had better double check with our desk diaries and the departmental seminar program. This sort of scenario is repeated time and again in offices across the world. The idea of a *shared diary* or *shared calendar* is simple. Each person uses a shared electronic diary, similar to that often found on PCs and pocket organizers. When you want to arrange a meeting, the system searches everyone's diaries for one or more free slots.

There are technical problems, such as what to do if no slots are free (often the norm). The system can return a set of slots with the least other arrangements, which can then form a basis for negotiation. Alternatively, the participants can mark their appointments with levels of importance. The system can then assign costs to breaking the appointments, and find slots with least cost. Mind you, someone may regard all their appointments as critical.

This reminds us that whatever the technical sophistication, it is people who use these systems and people who must cooperate. There are varying reports of success and failure with shared diaries. Where they have failed it is invariably because they have ignored the social needs and behavior of their users.

One such area is privacy. Are people allowed to look at your diary to find free slots? If so, do they just see 'busy' or can they see exactly what you are doing? You would be extremely annoyed if someone looked in your personal paper diary; is the electronic one any different? There is a trade-off between privacy and cooperation. In an office situation, one has a succession of diaries and calendars for specific purposes: a private diary with personal information, a desk diary and possibly a parallel desk diary with your secretary, and various forms of wall calendar showing periods on vacation and similar major meetings. These vary in their visibility to other members of the organization: your secretary can consult her copy of your diary but not your personal diary; anyone can look at the wall calendar. You choose your level of privacy by where you put information. Of course, the problems of keeping such diaries up to date with one another is one reason why electronic diaries are produced, but they must supply similar forms of privacy control or people will simply not use them. This is precisely what happens.

There are similar problems with the update of diaries. If someone wants to book a meeting with you, can they fill in a slot, or must they ask you? Again you may want to vary these rights according to who it is and the sort of appointment. Many systems allow other users to 'pencil in' appointments, but require them to be confirmed by the diary's owner.

Many people use private electronic diaries and time management software. It is reasonable to expect that groupware versions of these will become commonly available in the near future. The extent to which they work will be largely the extent to which the design takes note of personal and social factors.

19.5.5 Communication through the artifact

In each of the last four systems – shared PCs and windows, shared editors, co-authoring systems and shared diaries – the focus has been upon the artifacts on which the participants are working. They act *upon* the artifacts and communicate with one another *about* the artifacts. However, as well as observing their own actions on the artifacts, the participants are aware of one another's actions. This awareness of one another's actions is a form of communication *through* the artifact.

This can happen even where the shared artifact is not 'real' groupware. For instance, shared files and databases can be a locus for cooperation. Sales figures may be entered into the company database by a person in one department and then used as part of a query by another employee. At a loose level, the two are cooperating in jobs, but the database, and the information in it, may be their only means of communication. Such communication is one-way, and is thus a weak form of collaboration, but often important. For example, casework files are a central mechanism for communication and cooperation in many areas from taxation to social work. However, the facilities for cooperation in a typical shared file store or database are limited to locking, and even that may be rudimentary.

People may also explicitly pass documents, produced by single-user systems, between themselves. For example, the cooperative use of spreadsheets has been studied. Some of this involves close working between the participants, but some users simply pass the spreadsheet data between them with little, if any, comment. If you change a formula, then the intent is obvious – you thought it was wrong.

Of course, in most situations, direct communication is necessary as well, especially where there is some conflict (your colleague thinks the original formula was right). The lesson from these more extreme examples is that cooperation does not necessarily involve direct communication and, even where it does, the indirect channel through the artifact may be central to effective working.

One shared database which is explicitly designed to promote cooperation is *Liveware* [383]. This is a card-index-type database implemented over HyperCard, designed to be updated by users at many sites, and spreading the information by floppy disk as people meet during normal social contact. When different versions of the Liveware database 'meet', they choose the newest version of each record. Each record has a single owner, so problems of conflicting updates are avoided.

Lotus Notes

The most widely used groupware application, excepting email, is Lotus Notes. Notes has aspects of a structured message system, a bulletin board and a shared database. At its simplest a Notes database consists of a collection of items. Each item belongs to a particular type and depending on the type has different named fields – just like a structured message system. In addition, each item may have responses and responses to responses, very like a bulletin board. The distinguishing feature, however, is its ability to replicate and reconcile replicas. There may be several copies of a single Notes database lodged on different servers. Users may connect to different servers and add or edit items and responses. Later, when the servers connect via network or modem, they update each other taking the most up-to-date version of each item just like *Liveware*. This has made it particularly popular with users of portable computers working away from their central office.

Although Lotus Notes has been very successful, much of its use has been simply for email. However, it is also customizable and programmable so many bespoke applications have been produced using it as a base platform. In particular, it can be used to implement or support *workflow* systems.

Notes' key market is in corporate information and messaging systems. However, it is being challenged in this market by web-based *intranet* solutions, where the web's cross-platform and cross-vendor compatibility makes it an ideal candidate. Clearly aware of this threat, Lotus (now part of IBM) has added web publishing features to Notes.

19.6   FRAMEWORKS FOR GROUPWARE

In this section we will discuss several frameworks for understanding the role of groupware. One use for these is as a classification mechanism, which can help us discuss groupware issues. In addition, they both suggest new application areas and can help structure the design of new systems.

19.6.1 Time/space matrix and asynchronous working

First of all we will look again at the time/space matrix. At the beginning of Section 19.2, we placed familiar technologies in the matrix. Figure 19.9 shows the same matrix, but populated with the groupware systems we have discussed.

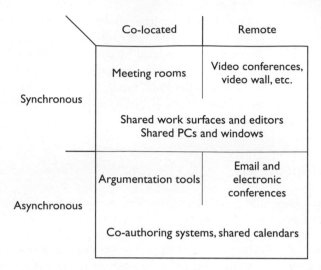

	Co-located	Remote
Synchronous	Meeting rooms	Video conferences, video wall, etc.
	Shared work surfaces and editors Shared PCs and windows	
Asynchronous	Argumentation tools	Email and electronic conferences
	Co-authoring systems, shared calendars	

Figure 19.9 Groupware in the time/space matrix

This matrix has become a common language amongst the CSCW community. It can also be useful during design as one of the earliest decisions is what sort of interaction you are planning. The design space for *synchronous* interaction is entirely different from that for *asynchronous*.

However, the synchronous/asynchronous distinction is not as simple as it at first seems. In Section 19.2 we simply said 'whether [the participants] are operating at the same time or not'. However, for an email system, it makes no difference whether or not people are operating at the same time. Indeed, even in Figure 19.1, when we classified letter writing as different time/different place, a similar objection could be brought.

The difference between email systems and (most) co-authoring systems is that the latter have a single shared database. Thus when people work together, they know they are working together, and, depending on the locking regime used, can see each other's changes. An email system, on the other hand, may take some time to propagate changes. Perhaps, a better distinction is to look at the data store and classify systems as *synchronized* when there is a real-time computer connection, or *unsynchronized* when there is none.

For unsynchronized systems it makes little difference whether or not the participants are operating at the same time. Also location is not very significant. (A co-located unsynchronized system is possible; imagine two computers in the same room with no network, which are periodically brought up to date with one another by floppy disk transfer.)

If we consider synchronized systems, then the actual time of use becomes more important. If the participants are operating at the same time (*concurrent access*), we have real-time interaction as seen in meeting rooms (co-located) or video conferences (remote).

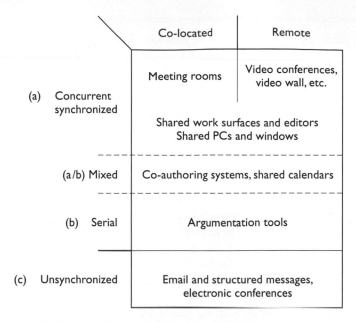

Figure 19.10   Refined time/space matrix

Alternatively, the system may prevent users working at the same time, by large-scale locks, leading to non-concurrent synchronized working. Earlier argumentation tools fall into this category. Because the participants are forced to use the system one after another, we can call this *serial access*.

Finally, co-authoring systems like Quilt [210] allow fine-grained locking so that participants can use the system at the same time or not. Therefore, they allow both serial and concurrent synchronized access.

Figure 19.10 places the groupware systems into this refined matrix. This matrix is not widely used, but is far more accurate for placing a prospective design. This is particularly obvious when one considers systems designed for users of mobile computers or home computers. These may be totally unconnected to central computers, except by occasional direct connection, floppy disk transfer or dial-up modem. The only existing groupware systems which could support such users are email and message systems, and *Liveware*. However, even email systems are rarely available except when connected via a modem. Liveware is the only groupware system *designed* for unsynchronized cooperation.

Systems, principally co-authoring tools, which describe themselves as operating in both synchronous and asynchronous modes are normally in class (a/b) in the diagram. That is, they have centralized data and allow users to operate in closely coupled modes like a group editor, or one at a time. No current system allows fluid access across the synchronized/unsynchronized divide. The authors of this book are operating from different sites and different continents and all often work at home. So we can vouch for the need for such systems.

Worked exercise   *Find out how many different forms of direct computer-mediated communication are available on your system (start with email). Are they heavily used, and if so, where do they fit in the time/space matrix (Figure 19.9) and its refinement (Figure 19.10)?*

Answer   Obviously the answer to this depends on your own particular facilities, but here are some suggestions based on the authors' sites.

The question says 'start with email'. In fact, on many systems several email interfaces are available. On one of the authors' systems there are two command line interfaces as well as various GUIs for different window managers (under X, on the Macintosh, etc.). Although email is just one communication mechanism, it is used in a wide variety of ways. Its 'normal' use is essentially asynchronous/remote, or in terms of the refined matrix, unsynchronized. However, delivery over a LAN is often virtually instantaneous and you can observe users engaging in effectively synchronous communication. The possibility of these modes of use is often determined by the style of the interface, as was shown in Section 18.2.4. Clearly, the way in which new mail is notified and the speed with which mail can be read both determine the pace at which the conversation can proceed. A further complication in some sites is that internal and external email have entirely different interfaces: sending mail off site may involve remotely logging into a gateway machine and then using some obscure mailer there, rather than the familiar workstation-based tools.

In addition to email, you may have one or more text-based synchronous communication tools. For example, many UNIX machines have two tools, 'write' and 'talk'. The command 'write Alison' followed by some text prints that text on Alison's screen. She can respond by doing a 'write' back to the sender. The 'talk' command establishes a more continuous conversation, as described in Section 19.3.1, where both participants' screens are split in two, each half displaying one of the participants' contributions. Although both can be seen as synchronous/remote, they operate at different *levels of sharing* (Section 19.6.2). Whereas 'write' only sends the text after the contribution is completed, 'talk' sends each user's contributions character by character as they are typed. That is, 'talk' sits further down toward the bottom left of the diagram in Figure 19.11. Note also that 'write' can be used in a semi-asynchronous mode. If the other user is logged in, but not at his terminal, the message waits there until his return.

Another asynchronous communication tool commonly available is bulletin boards, such as Usenet News. As discussed in Section 19.3.1, these have different properties from email, being rather less personal.

In addition to these standard tools, some of the authors' colleagues have permanent video connections between their offices. You may have similar facilities, or other computer-augmented communications, perhaps video in a window on your workstation, or possibly CUSeeMe. Don't forget apparently low-tech things such as computers which automatically dial telephone calls.

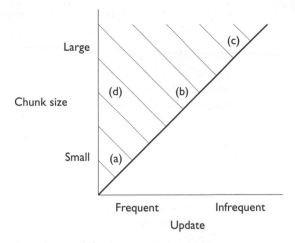

Figure 19.11   Granularity of sharing

19.6.2 Shared information

Electronic conferences and shared workspaces share information primarily for communication, whereas a document is shared for the purpose of working. Both raise similar issues concerning the degree of sharing required.

Granularity

The groupware systems we have seen differ as to the *granularity* of sharing they allow, in terms of both object chunk size and frequency of update.

Looking first at object chunk size, some systems operate at a very fine grain, allowing participants to edit the same sentence, or even the same word in a sentence. At the other extreme, shared file systems may often have locks so that only one user can edit a file at the same time. The granularity here is the document. The majority of groupware systems, in particular argumentation and co-authoring tools, operate somewhere between these extremes. They have some idea of a node or a section, which only one person can update at once, but which is significantly smaller than a whole document.

In the time dimension, systems may show participants' updates to one another immediately, within seconds, or when the user has finished editing the chunk. It is usually the case that a fine-grained chunk size requires fine-grained updates. For example, if you are allowed to edit the same word, it is not helpful if it takes a minute to see your colleague's typing! However, the converse is not necessarily true. Some systems operate locks on largish chunks but show other participants the updates immediately. Examples of this are some meeting rooms which have long-lived floor holders. This means that groupware systems all reside in the hatched region of Figure 19.11.

In the figure, four points are plotted representing different grain size choices, as typified by the examples we have discussed:

(a) shared editors
(b) co-authoring systems like Quilt
(c) network file systems with locking
(d) meeting system with floor holder.

Levels of sharing

As well as varying in terms of how much is shared, systems vary as to what is shared. At one extreme are WYSIWIS systems, such as shared window systems and many meeting rooms. In these, the participants all see exactly the same presentation of the data. However, in other shared editors, such as *Grove* [121, 122], the participants can edit different parts of the document at once. That is, they share the object, but not the presentation.

There is an interesting middle ground which is rare in explicit groupware, but common in the use of shared databases. That is, sharing a view, but not the presentation of that view. For example, two people may be viewing the same part of a database, but one person sees it presented as a graph, and the other in tabular form. We thus have three levels, as depicted in Figure 19.12.

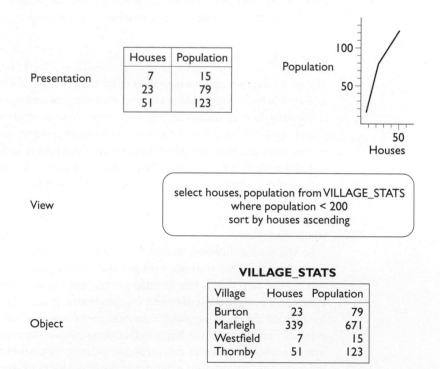

Figure 19.12   Levels of sharing

In addition to this output-oriented sharing, we can also look at input. On the one hand there are those systems which have a single shared virtual keyboard, for example the shared window systems. On the other, we have the majority where the participants can input at different places. This can be characterized as single versus multiple insertion points. There is no real middle ground here, but for those with separate insertion points we have the issue of visibility: whether or not the participants can see each other's insertion points or mouse pointers. Furthermore, if the other participants' cursors are not visible, we may have a *group pointer*, as discussed in Section 19.4.2. This gives us four levels of input sharing:

single insertion point   ■ shared virtual keyboard
multiple insertion points   ■ other participants visible
                                                       ■ group pointer
                                                       ■ no visibility

Again, there are loose connections between the two levels of sharing. For example, it makes little sense to have a single insertion point but different views. However, one document annotation system has separate insertion points but a shared view. Any user can choose to scroll the view of the document, but it then scrolls for all users. To make matters worse, the other users' insertion points stay at the same point on the *screen* as the document moves. So if they are typing when the screen is scrolled, their characters appear all over the document! It is a testimony to the power of *social protocols* that this system is not only used successfully, but also enjoyed.

Types of object

The kind of object or data we are cooperating over obviously affects the way we share them. This is particularly important in the *unsynchronized* case or where there is a danger of *race conditions*. That is, where two participants perform updates simultaneously and there is confusion as to which comes first.

Consider first the text of a shared editor. Participants can add, edit or delete text anywhere in the document. We thus have to worry about them interfering with one another, for example one participant deleting the text that another participant is in the middle of editing. Contrast this with a linear text transcript, as produced by some electronic conferencing systems. The transcript is *monotonic,* that is one can only add to it, never take away, and *appending* contributions are always added to the end. This makes the job of handling updates much easier. Every time a participant completes a contribution, it is simply added to the end.

However, the text transcript is inherently *sequenced*. This makes it best suited to *synchronized* groupware. If we imagine two distant sites, with no fast communications, it is difficult to keep the transcripts similar. If each site adds any new items to the end, the sites will show different transcripts. Imagine we have a user, Alison, at site A, and a user, Brian, at site B. The transcript has two contributions 'a1 b1'. Alison and Brian both make a contribution at the same time, say 'a2' and 'b2' respectively. So site A sees 'a2' first and site B sees 'b2' first. After a while the contributions are transmitted from site to site, leaving at site A the transcript 'a1 b1 a2 b2' and at site B the transcript 'a1 b1 b2 a2'. The alternative is for the contributions to be timestamped, and to be ordered by time. However, this would mean that when a site received a contribution before the current time, it would have to *insert* it into the conversation. That is, the transcript ceases to be appending. We saw in Chapter 14 some of the effects this has on the participants' conversation.

Now, consider a shared hypertext, with no editing and deleting, just adding new nodes. It is not only monotonic, but also *unsequenced*: the order in which contributions are added does not matter. They are structured explicitly by the links between nodes, not by the order in which they occurred. It has a weaker appending property in that all new contributions are toward the leaves of the hypertext, but there are of course many leaves. A monotonic unsequenced data structure is ideally suited to unsynchronized groupware; indeed several electronic conferencing systems adopt just such a structure.

A shared whiteboard, again without an eraser, is also monotonic and unsequenced, but the limited size of the display does not make it feasible for large-scale conferencing. However, the properties are useful when implementing such a system. Basically, one only needs to worry about synchronizing the participants' systems when one of them is using an eraser. Another advantage of such spatially organized data is that the participants can use proximity to denote relationships and set aside areas for different purposes. The participants can create their own structure, rather than use predefined structures.

Finally, imagine a complex structured object, such as a hypertext, or a shared file system. What happens if someone moves a portion of the hypertext tree while you are editing a node in it? This is similar to the problems of shared text, but the nature of text makes it easier for social protocols to operate. Furthermore, it is even harder to make sense of multiple structural updates than textual ones.

19.6.3 Integrating communication and work

In Section 19.2, we described the framework for cooperative work used to structure Sections 19.3–19.5. Figure 19.13 shows the framework diagram, but with two extra arcs added. Recall first the arcs that were in the original diagram in Section 19.2. Each of the sections dealt with the computer support of one of these arcs:

direct communication supported by email, electronic conferences and video connections;

common understanding supported by argumentation tools, meeting rooms and shared work surfaces;

control and feedback from shared artifacts supported by shared PCs and windows, shared editors, co-authoring systems and shared diaries.

The first new arc represents *deixis*. Recall that we encountered deictic reference in the context of meeting room software (Section 19.4.2). The participants needed to refer to items on the shared screen, but could not use their fingers to point. In general, direct communication about a task will refer to the artifacts used as part of that task.

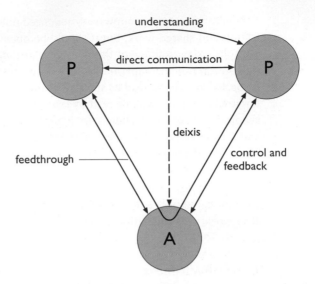

Figure 19.13 Cooperative work framework

The other new arc runs between the participants, but through the artifact. This reflects the *feedthrough* where one participant's manipulation of shared objects can be observed by the other participants. As we discussed in Section 19.5.5, this *communication through the artifact* can be as important as direct communication between the participants.

Although systems have been classified by the arc which they most directly support, many support several of these aspects of cooperative work. In particular, if the participants are not co-located, many systems will supply some alternative means of direct communication. For example, shared window systems are often used in conjunction with audio or video communications. However, these channels are very obviously separate, compared with, say, the *TeamWorkStation* where the shared work surface video images of hands are overlaid (see Section 19.4.3). In particular, this close association of direct communication with the artifacts makes deixis more fluid – the participants can simply point and gesture as normal.

In general, a test of a groupware product is how well it supports the whole of cooperative work. Another example of a system which does closely integrate direct communication and shared artifacts is the co-authoring system Quilt. In Section 19.5.3, we emphasized the structure of the artifact, but this is integrated with communication in two ways. First of all (and common to many similar systems), the comments which are attached to the text are themselves a form of direct communication – *embedded* within the *context* of work. This embedding makes deixis particularly easy. The comment itself may be attached to a particular point in the text, and also indexical terms like 'the last sentence' are easily interpreted. In addition, directed messages can contain references to Quilt objects, aiding deictic reference in that medium also.

Finally, note that a groupware system need not automate every aspect of communication and shared work, but it should be open to supporting cooperative work as a whole. As an example of this consider *bar codes*. A can of beans may be baked in Boston and sold in a supermarket in Solihull, but the bar code printed on the can and its packaging can be read by the staff at the supermarket. The bar code can be used for stocktaking and can be read by laser at the checkout, both pricing the item and keeping track of sales. These sales figures can then be used as part of stock control and for marketing. This is possible because of international standards of bar coding. The code identifies the manufacturer, factory, product and package size, and can thus be used to identify the product at many stages in its journey from production to consumption. That is, the bar code is a computerized form of deixis. However, even though it only automates one aspect it aids very diffuse but large-scale cooperative work, crossing national and organizational boundaries.

19.6.4 Awareness

An important issue in groupware and CSCW is awareness – generally having some feeling for what other people are doing or have been doing. Awareness is usually used to refer to systems that demand little conscious effort or attention as opposed to, say, something that allows you to explicitly find out what others are doing.

There are a number of different kinds of awareness, summarized in Figure 19.14. First we may want to know who is there (a) – are they available, at their desk, in the building or busy? For example, instant messaging systems often have some form of buddy list (Figure 19.15). Your friends are listed there and the messenger window shows whether they are logged into the system, if they appear to be idle (not typed for a while), or whether they have left some sort of status message (e.g. 'gone for

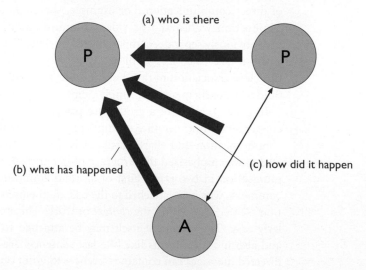

Figure 19.14   Forms of awareness

Figure 19.15 Awareness in Yahoo! Messenger

lunch'). Always-on video or audio connections also give a sense of being 'around' your remote colleagues and effortlessly having a feeling for what they are doing, whether they are busy or in a meeting.

You may also want to be aware of what is happening to shared objects (b). For example, you might request that the system informs you when shared objects are updated. Although knowing *what* has changed is important, ideally we would like to know *why* it has changed. Of course we could ask, but if we know how the change happened (c), then we may be in a better position to infer the reasons for the change. Actually, very few systems do this except in so far as they allow users to add annotations to explain changes. These two together (b and c) are called workplace awareness.

DESIGN FOCUS

TOWER – workspace awareness

Alison is sitting at her desk working on a spreadsheet. She has just finished a complicated formula and as she sits back for a moment her eye drifts down the screen to a small window. It shows an electronic landscape in which there are small avatars. She reaches for the phone. 'Hi Brian', she says. 'Didn't realize you were in', 'Just noticed you were looking at the year-end report. Don't be alarmed if it looks a little rough, still finalizing it'.

Alison and Brian are using TOWER (Theatre of Work Enabling Relationships), an architecture and set of components that allow workspace awareness. The system has a number of sensor modules for detecting events, including watching for file system accesses, which can be linked to generic visualization components such as a simulated world or treemap representations. These use different means to show the structure of files/folders or other structures in the workspace and also to show activity on the workspace: the virtual landscape shows avatars where people are working, the treemap highlights changed areas in red (see the illustration).

One of the partners which developed TOWER is the Bonn Fraunhofer FIT Institute (previously GMD), which also developed BSCW (Basic Support for Cooperative Work), one of the most widely used tools for remote document sharing [34].

As well as graphical interfaces, various ambient interfaces (see Chapter 20) have been designed including a fan that spins faster when there is activity on a website. New sensors and visualizations are easy to add because of the generic event notification infrastructure (ENI) underlying TOWER. Getting the right implementation architecture is very important.

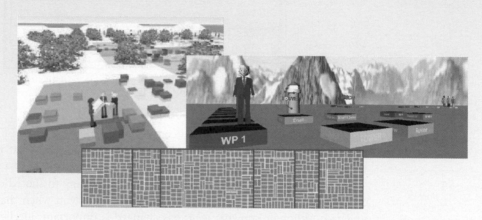

See: http://tower.gmd.de/ Images courtesy of Wolfgang Prinz

19.7 IMPLEMENTING SYNCHRONOUS GROUPWARE

We have discussed a wide range of groupware systems, but there are formidable problems with implementing such systems, particularly *synchronous* groupware. Groupware systems are intrinsically more complicated than single-user systems. Issues like handling updates from several users whilst not getting internal data structures or the users' screens in a mess are just plain difficult. These are made more complicated by the limited bandwidth and delays of the networks used to connect the computers, and by the single-user assumptions built into graphics toolkits.

19.7.1 Feedback and network delays

When editing text, a delay of more than a fraction of a second between typing and the appearance of characters is unacceptable. For text entry, a slightly greater delay is acceptable as you are able to type ahead without feedback from the screen. Drawing, on the other hand, demands even faster feedback than text editing. Groupware systems usually involve several computers connected by a network. If the feedback loop includes transmission over the network, it may be hard to achieve acceptable response times. To see why, consider what happens when the user types a character:

1. The user's application gets an event from the window manager.
2. It calls the operating system . . .
3. which sends a message over the network, often through several levels of protocol.
4. The message is received by the operating system at the remote machine,
5. which gives it to the remote application to process.
6–8. the reply returns (as steps 2–4)
9. and the feedback is given on the user's screen.

This process requires two network messages and four context switches between operating system and application programs in addition to the normal communication between window manager and application. However, even this is just a minimum time and other factors can make the eventual figure far worse. Network protocols with handshaking can increase the number of network messages to at least four (two messages plus handshakes). If the application is running on a multi-tasking machine, it may need to wait for a time slice or even be swapped out! Furthermore, the network traffic is unlikely to be just between two computers: in meeting rooms we may have dozens of workstations. Clearly, any architectural design for cooperative systems must take the potential for network delays very seriously.

19.7.2 Architectures for groupware

There are two major architectural alternatives for groupware, *centralized* and *replicated*, with variations upon them both. In a centralized or *client–server architecture* each participant's workstation has a minimal program (the client) which handles the screen and accepts the participant's inputs. The real work of the application is performed by the server, which runs on a central computer and holds all the application's data (Figure 19.16). Client–server architectures are probably the simplest to implement as we have essentially one program, with several front ends. Furthermore, if you use X Windows then there are standard facilities for one program to access several screens[1] (see also Chapter 8).

As a special case, the server may run on one of the users' workstations and subsume the client there. Typically, this would be the user who first invoked the shared application. This arrangement is a *master–slave architecture*, the master being the merged server–client and the slaves the remainder of the clients. The user of the master will have a particularly fast response compared with the other users.

---

1 But beware, X uses the terms client and server in the opposite sense. The X server is on the workstation and the X client is the application program.

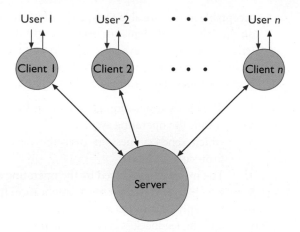

Figure 19.16 Client–server architecture

The second major architecture is *replicated*. Each user's workstation runs its own copy of the application. These copies communicate with one another and attempt to keep their data structures consistent with one another. Each replicate handles its own user's feedback, and must also update the screen in response to messages from other replicates. The intention is often to give the impression of a centralized application, but to obtain the performance advantages of distribution.

Compared with a client–server architecture, the replicated architecture is difficult to program. In the last paragraph we deliberately wrote '*attempt* to keep their data structures consistent' as this is a major problem. If two users, say Jane and Sam, hit a key almost simultaneously, then Jane's workstation will process Jane's keystroke first, and Sam's second, but Sam's workstation will process them the other way round, and yet they must give the same result – help!

This race condition is a common problem in distributed computing. A standard solution there is to *roll back* one or other replicate and re-execute the commands. However, if the results have already been displayed on the user's screen this is not acceptable – standard computing algorithms often fail for groupware. Happily, many of the *concurrency control* mechanisms, such as locking or floor holders, mean that such races do not occur, or at worst occur only when users obtain locks or other large-scale events. So, when rapid feedback is not required, standard mechanisms may be applied, but, for real synchronous update, special-purpose algorithms are required.

The main advantage of a replicated architecture over the client–server is in the local feedback. However, the clients are often not completely dumb and are able to handle a certain amount of feedback themselves. Indeed, the server often becomes merely a central repository for shared data with the clients having most of the application's functionality. On the other hand, a replicated architecture will rarely treat all the replicates identically. If a user tries to load or save a document, that action does not want to be replicated. Either one of the replicates is special, or there is a minimal server handling movement of data in and out of the system. So we see that there is a continuum between the client–server and the replicated architecture.

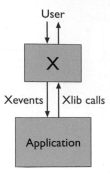

Figure 19.17   Single-user application

19.7.3 Shared window architectures

Shared window systems have some similarities with general groupware architectures, but also some special features. Recall that there is a single-user application which is being shared by several participants on different workstations. The single-user application normally interacts with the user via a window manager, say X (Figure 19.17). The shared window manager works by intercepting the calls between the application and X.

Where the application would normally send graphics calls to X, these are instead routed to a special application stub. This then passes the graphics calls from the X library (Xlib) on to a user stub on each participant's workstation. A copy of X is running on each workstation and the user stub passes the graphics calls to the local copy of X. Similarly the users' keystrokes and other actions cause X events which are passed to the user stub and thence through the application stub to the application (Figure 19.18). In fact, the nature of X's own client–server approach can make the user stub unnecessary, the application stub talking directly to an X 'server' on each workstation.

The input side has to include some form of floor control, especially for the mouse. This can be handled by the application stub which determines how the users' separate event streams are merged. For example, it can ignore any events other than those of the floor holder, or can simply allow users' keystrokes to intermingle. If key combinations are used to request and relinquish the floor, then the application stub can simply monitor the event streams for the appropriate sequences. Alternatively, the user stub may add its own elements to the interface: a floor request button and an indication of other participants' activities, including the current floor holder.

The problem with a client–server-based shared window system is that graphics calls may involve very large data structures and corresponding network delays. One can have replicated versions where a copy of the application sits on each workstation and stubs communicate between one another. But, because the application is not *collaboration aware*, problems such as race conditions and reading and saving files become virtually intractable. For this reason, most shared window systems take a master–slave approach where the application runs on the first user's workstation and

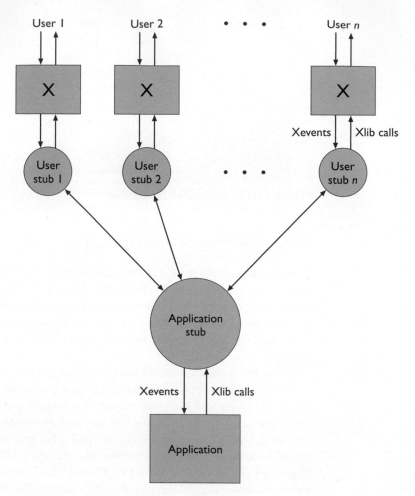

Figure 19.18   Shared window architecture

subsequent users get slave processes. The delays for other users are most noticeable when starting up the application.

19.7.4 Feedthrough and network traffic

We have discussed the necessity of rapid *feedback* to the user who performs an action, and we have seen how replication or partial replication can solve this. However, we must also worry about *feedthrough*, the reflection of one user's actions on the other users' screens. The requirements for feedthrough are not quite so stringent as for feedback, and this can be used to reduce the amount of network traffic. There is little difference in this respect between client–server and replicated architectures, so, for the sake of argument, we will assume a client–server architecture.

Imagine a user has just typed a character. The character appears on the user's screen, either through local feedback or after an exchange with the server. However, all the other clients need to be informed also. That is, with n participants, each user action causes a minimum of $n - 1$ network messages. If this is repeated for each character, the network will grind to a halt with the number of messages. Just think of the effect if we wanted to send out updates for each mouse movement!

There are several ways out of this, the common thread being to reduce the number of messages. In principle, one could send a single *broadcast message* to all the other clients, as the information is the same for all of them. Unfortunately, in practice, many network protocols only support point-to-point messages. A more successful approach is to increase the *granularity* of the messages. The rapid feedback to the user who initiated an action is necessary, but the feedthrough to other users may be able to cope with less frequent updates. The server can save up several characters' worth of updates and send a single message. We thus only need to send the $n - 1$ messages to the clients on each chunk.

The choice of this chunk size can be crucial to the success of the system. If the participants can talk to each other (either co-located or with audio/video channels) they will refer to the contents of their screens. In such cases, lags of more than a few seconds can be disastrous. However, even if the computer is the only communications medium, the chunk size has an effect as the gradual appearance of text is an indication of other people's activity.

19.7.5 Graphical toolkits

We discussed in Chapter 8 some of the *widgets* one finds in a typical graphics toolkit or window manager, such as menus, buttons, dialog boxes and text and graphics regions. These are useful for creating single-user interfaces, and one would like to use the same components to build a groupware system. Unfortunately, the single-user assumptions built into such toolkits can make this very difficult.

Some widgets may take control away from the application. For instance, a pop-up menu may be invoked by a call such as

```
sel = do_pop_up("new","open","save","exit",0);
```

The call to `do_pop_up_menu` constructs the pop-up menu, waits for the user to enter a selection, and then returns a code indicating which choice the user made (1 for 'new', 2 for 'open', etc.). Of course, during this time the application cannot monitor the network. This can be got round, by careful programming, but is awkward.

More fundamentally, the functionality of toolkit widgets may be insufficient for groupware. This is particularly obvious for text areas. The toolkit often takes over a lot of the tedium of handling an editable text region: the user can type and delete, do cursor movement and even cut and paste, all without the application's intervention. However, the groupware developer may want to have multiple cursors, or to ensure that all the participants can see the same portion of a document. Unfortunately, even information such as what portion of the document is in view, or where a particular logical character is displayed on the screen is difficult to come by, as is control over a scrollbar if this is to be shared. One is often forced to design the application round the limited capabilities of the text widget, or to use bitmap operations to paint the text oneself.

Despite the difficulties of toolkits, some have facilities which are a positive help. For example, the SunView toolkit and its X version, XView, are both *notification based* (see Chapter 8). As well as notifications of user events, they can be asked to tell you when a network channel is ready for reading or writing. Thus, the interface and the network can be programmed in a similar style.

19.7.6 Robustness and scaleability

If you are producing a shared application to test an idea, or for use in an experiment, then you can make a wide range of assumptions, for instance a fixed number of participants. Also, the occasional crash, although annoying, is not disastrous. However, if you expect a system to be used for protracted tests or for commercial production then the standards of engineering must be correspondingly higher. Four potential sources of problems are:

1. Failures in the network, workstations or operating systems.
2. Errors in programming the shared application.
3. Unforeseen sequences of events, such as race conditions.
4. The system does not scale as the number of users or rate of activity increases.

A full description of these problems and their solutions is, of course, beyond this book. For this, the reader should turn to texts on software engineering, real-time and distributed programming. Furthermore, the details will differ between networking software, operating systems and other software support. However, there are a few general remarks and specific issues which we will discuss.

To some extent, the above problems are common to single-user systems: hardware problems, bad programming and the like. Indeed, most commercial software the authors have used suffers the occasional (or frequent) crash. However, there are factors which make multi-user systems more fragile. The large number of different hardware and software components of a multi-user system means that a fault of type 1 is more likely to occur. Also, the complexity of the algorithms used in groupware makes a fault of type 2 more likely. In both cases there is a danger that the consequences of the failure will propagate throughout the system. If a single failure crashes the whole system, it probably will not be used twice! Interleaving of different users' actions and the unpredictable effects of network delays increases the chance of errors of type 3. Finally, system development and testing may involve only two or three people, and thus hidden assumptions about the number and activity of users may not become apparent until the system 'goes live'. So, faults are more likely and the effects are far worse – instead of losing one user's document or datafile (sad though that might be), a groupware crash can destroy the work of a whole team of people.

Server faults

The most obviously disastrous problem in a client–server-based system is a server crash, whether hardware or software. Fortunately, this is most amenable to standard solutions. Most large commercial databases have facilities (such as transaction logging) to recover all but the most recent changes. If the groupware system is not built using such a system then similar solutions can be applied; for example, you can periodically save the current state using two or three files in rotation. The *last* entry[2] in each file is the date of writing and the system uses the most recent file when it restarts, ignoring any partially written file. Remember, though, that this might mean your server going 'silent' for a few seconds each time it saves the file – can your clients handle this? In really critical situations one can have multiple servers and copies of the data, so that a backup server can take over after a crash of the primary server.

Workstation faults

More often, individual workstations, or the programs running on them, will crash. This is partly because there are more of them, and partly because their code is more complex. In particular, these programs are handling all the user's interactions and are built upon complex (and frequently flaky) graphical toolkits. Of course, one tries to program carefully and avoid these errors, but experience shows that they will continue to occur. The aim is to confine the fault to the particular user concerned and to recover from the fault as quickly as possible. When thinking about a client–server architecture, there are three 'R's for the server:

Robust A client failure should not destroy or 'hang' the server. In particular, *never* have the server wait for a response from the client – it may never come. The server should either be *event driven* or *poll* the clients using non-blocking network operations.

Reconfigure The server must detect that the client has failed and reconfigure the rest of the system accordingly. The client's failure can be detected by standard network failure codes, or by timing out the client if it is silent for too long. Reconfiguring will involve resetting internal data structures, and informing other participants that one of them is unavailable and why. Do not let them think their colleague is just being rude and not replying!

Resynchronize When the workstation/client recovers, the server must send sufficient information for it to catch up. A server may normally broadcast incremental information (new messages, etc.), so make sure that the server keeps track of all the information needed to send to the recovered client. This is very similar to the case of a new participant joining the groupware session.

---

2 A crash might happen in the middle of the save.

Replicated architectures have similar issues. Imagine we have three replicates A, B and C. Replicate A has crashed, so both B and C must detect this and correct their internal data structures accordingly. An additional problem is that one replicate, say B, may detect the failure before the other. So, C may send B a message which refers to A in some way – B must deal with this situation gracefully.

Algorithm faults

Some application failures do not crash the application and may therefore be more difficult to detect. For instance, data structures between replicates or between client and server may become inconsistent. Obviously this *should not* happen, if the algorithms are correct. Indeed, such critical algorithms should be given the closest scrutiny and perhaps proved correct using formal methods (see Chapter 17). However, one should be prepared for errors and, where possible, include sufficient redundancy and sanity checks in the code so that inconsistencies are at least detected and, ideally, corrected.

Such defensive programming mechanisms, against hardware and software errors, may be very expensive in programming effort and execution time. For experimental systems they may be excessive. A minimum requirement for all but toy systems is some form of reset, which forces the system to resynchronize all its data structures between clients and server or between replicates; hopefully, losing none but the most recent updates in the process.

Unforeseen sequences of events

Distributed programming has many problems of which possibly the most well known is *deadlock*. This is when two (or more) processes are each waiting for the other to do something. A common scenario is where process A is trying to send a message to B and B is trying to send one to A. Because A is busy trying to send, it does not want to receive a message from B, and vice versa. The possibility of deadlock can often go undetected during testing because of operating system and network buffers. A's message to B is stored in the operating system's buffer, so A can then read B's message. Unfortunately, as load increases, one day the buffer is full and deadlock can no longer be avoided – this may only happen *after* the system has been released.

The first rule to avoid deadlock is *never* to use blocking input or output. That is, always use network calls which time out, or return immediately if the operation cannot continue. Use of an event-driven programming style can also help, as does the use of constructs such as the UNIX 'select' system call, which monitors several communication channels simultaneously.

At a higher level, one should also avoid making assumptions about the ordering of incoming events. This is also important to avoid problems with race conditions. For example, if a client process has sent a message to a server requesting information, it should *not* assume that the next message from the server will answer the query.

A common assumption in groupware programs is that messages sent from one computer arrive in the same form at another. This depends very much on the particular protocols used. Consider UNIX stream-based sockets, commonly used in experimental groupware applications. The communication paradigm is not packet based, but of a character stream. Imagine a client sends two messages to the server. The first is 26 characters long, 'abcd . . . xyz', the second is 10 characters long, '0123456789'. When testing such a system it is very likely that the server will read two messages of 26 and 10 characters, exactly as sent, but this is not guaranteed. It is perfectly possible to get one message of 36 characters, 'abc . . . xyz01 . . . 89', or even one of 10 and one of 26, 'abcdefghij' and 'klm . . . xyz01 . . . 89'. The solution is easy: one always uses fixed-length messages, or alternatively you code the message length into the message header. The recipient can then reconstruct the messages from the byte stream. The difficulty is that the problem can go undetected for a long time and then cause a major disaster. Read your network manual *very* carefully and assume nothing.

Scaling up

In general, the most certain way to avoid algorithmic errors is to use simple algorithms: tables rather than complicated data structures, fixed-length fields for names and messages. These all go toward reducing the likelihood of some of the faults described earlier, and are the recommended techniques for prototyping an application. Unfortunately, these are precisely the programming techniques which frustrate the scaling up of the system to larger numbers of users, or greater loads.

As the system develops, the initial algorithms and data structures will need to evolve. This will be easier if the future scaling of the system is taken into account at the beginning. Good software engineering practice helps. For example, if the message passing is in a separate module then an initial design can use fixed-length and textually coded messages (for ease of debugging). But, when the throughput of the system increases, the message passing can be easily changed to variable length messages, perhaps buffering several messages together (to reduce network traffic) and binary coding of the messages (for efficiency).

Where fixed-size assumptions are made in early versions, these should be documented: 'the present design only caters for up to six users'. Even more important, the system ought to detect when these bounds are broken and behave sensibly. In programming terms, this tends to mean checking array bounds, rather than scribbling randomly over memory! Sometimes these bounds are known in advance, but always try to encapsulate these decisions so that if the bounds do need to change you know where in the code to find them.

A particular problem for the server is that the operating system may limit the number of open files/network connections at any time. For example, let us suppose the limit is 16 files and suppose the server is using one for the application datafile and one for logging. This means that at most 14 clients can be connected at once. Even worse, say the server periodically opens the datafile to save data, but closes it between times. Unless the server itself keeps the number of clients below 14, it may be that 15 clients get connected, which, including the logging file, saturates the server's allowable files. Now, when the server comes to save the data, it cannot open the datafile. Obviously, the groupware writer must at least be aware of these limits in order to prevent such a disaster.

There are a few solutions to this problem. The operating system limit can be altered; for example, in MS-DOS this involves changing the 'FILES=' line in the file 'CONFIG.SYS'. However, this is more difficult under UNIX, and in general the limits and how to alter them are very system dependent. The server can avoid the use of permanent network connections and instead use *datagram protocols*, where the client and the server are only connected while a message is being exchanged. Finally, there may be more system-dependent 'tricks', for example forking extra servers under UNIX.

Testing for robustness

Often the functionality of an application is tested by having several windows on the same workstation, each acting as a different 'user'. Unfortunately, this is unlikely to catch the sort of problems discussed above as it is impossible to type simultaneously into two windows. A more violent approach is required; in fact, the general rule is . . . mistreat it.

Crashes and major faults can be simulated. Try rebooting a workstation or pulling out a network connector.[3] To be slightly more gentle, you could simply kill a client process and see the effect on the server (or on replicates).

Similarly, you can simulate race conditions and odd sequences by running the system between two workstations and then hitting keys on them simultaneously. A little bit of knowledge of the system will suggest the best combination.

Random input may crash your system. Push it hard at several levels. Have a group of colleagues on different workstations type and hit mouse buttons as fast as they can – but log the keystrokes as you may want to recreate the resulting situations for later debugging. Create a rogue client/replicate, which sends random, but correctly formed, messages to the server or other replicates. Alternatively, this can be arranged without network communications by building a test harness round a single process. A similar, possibly less fair, approach is to send random data down the network at a process.

Finally, the real acid test. Offer a group of computer science undergraduates a drink each if they can break the system – you will lose your money, of course.

Unfortunately, discovering you have a fault is only the first step – correcting it is more difficult still. Modular and defensive programming and logging of communications so that errors can be recreated are a good beginning, but experience and hard work are the final answer.

---

3 But beware, check with other users and your system administrator first – this may crash some operating systems.

19.8 SUMMARY

We discussed groupware under three headings: computer-mediated communication, meeting and decision support systems, and shared applications and artifacts. Computer-mediated communication supports direct interpersonal contact. Some CMC systems are asynchronous, including traditional email and structured messaging systems. Various forms of video communication support synchronous communication, such as video conferences, direct person-to-person video or social contact.

Meeting and decision support systems are aimed at helping users to generate and record new ideas and reach decisions. Meeting rooms use large shared screens to support synchronous co-located collaboration. Participants' own terminals are often WYSIWIS and they may use group pointers to support deictic reference. When the participants are remote, various forms of work surface can be used instead. Finally, for asynchronous working, systems like gIBIS help designers to record their decisions and why they came by them.

Shared window systems and PCs allow non-collaboration-aware applications to be used by a group. However, collaboration-aware applications such as shared editors, diaries and co-authoring systems can better support the use of shared objects. Shared objects may even be the sole means of communication. Whether or not there is additional direct communication, we must always recall the importance of communication through the artifact.

Several frameworks for classifying groupware were discussed. The time/space matrix classifies systems by where and when the participants are working. However, we saw that the term 'asynchronous' is rather ambiguous. Shared information may be shared at different granularities, and at different levels of detail. Also, different data structures are better suited to different situations. Finally, we discussed the framework used to structure the discussion in this chapter. This looks at the different paths of communication between the participants and the artifacts of work and at which aspects are automated: direct communication, shared understanding, deictic reference, control of and feedback from the object. A good groupware system will not just automate one path, but do so in a way which supports the whole process of cooperation. As an example, bar codes merely automate deixis, but are important in facilitating transnational collaboration.

Groupware systems are more complex than single-user ones. We considered architectures for synchronous groupware, client–server and replicated, and for shared windowed systems. The choice of architecture combined with network delays influences the sort of feedback participants receive of their own actions. As important, it also influences the feedthrough they experience of other participants' actions. The widgets supplied by graphical toolkits are designed with single-user applications in mind, and so the groupware designer must either fit around these limitations or program group widgets from scratch. Finally, it is very important that groupware is robust. Problems are more likely to occur owing to the increased complexity, but are more damaging, because of the large number of people affected.

EXERCISES

19.1 We discussed the use of a group pointer in a shared editor with a shared view. Consider the advantages and problems of using a group pointer when participants have different views. How do you show the pointer if it is outside part of the document you are working on? Think also about the issues when the system is a hypertext-based co-authoring system. Is there any use for a group pointer in this case?

19.2 Repeat the worked exercise in Section 19.6.1, but this time look for shared data on your system. Is the data updated by one person and viewed by many, or have you got files or databases which are updated by several people? If the latter, find out what methods are used to prevent two users changing the same data at the same time. There may be no mechanism at all, a computerized one (for example, locking) or a social protocol (for example, a floppy disk is passed around).

19.3 (a) Consider the widespread use of email. What explanations are there for its success and what lessons can be learned from its development to assist the design of other computer-mediated communication systems?
 (b) What are the main issues that need to be addressed to ensure the success of email in an organization?

19.4 How do you think groupware is likely to affect our lives in the future? Justify your answer with examples.

19.5 (a) Low bandwidths and single media groupware systems reduce the transmission of back channels. How does this affect communication?
 (b) Emoticons are used in text-based communication to provide information about the mood of the sender. Is there any need for such augmentation in audio or video conferencing? Justify your answer.

19.6 How effective is the time/space matrix as a tool for classifying and analyzing groupware?

19.7 What is meant by the terms *control and feedback* and *feedthrough* in the classification by function framework?

19.8 Distinguish between direct and indirect communication. How can each be supported in groupware?

19.9 Identify three types of shared application. What are the main issues that need to be addressed in the design of these applications?

19.10 How far do technological factors limit what groupware can achieve at present? Suggest an example of groupware that is limited by factors other than technology.

19.11 What are the two main architectures used for groupware systems? Identify the strengths and limitations of each and suggest how they can be resolved.

19.12 A company has offices in New York and London. They are considering using some form of video to supplement their existing email, fax and telephone communications.

 (a) Discuss the options available and potential advantages and problems they may encounter.
 (b) How would your advice be changed if the two offices were in London and Sydney Australia?
 (c) Email and video are 'just' electronic substitutes for face-to-face conversation. What radically different forms of groupware might the company consider? Justify your answer using examples and appropriate theoretical frameworks.

RECOMMENDED READING

G. Olson and J. Olson, Groupware and computer supported cooperative work. In J. J. Jacko and A. Sears, editors, *Handbook of Human–Computer Interaction*, pp. 583–95, Lawrence Erlbaum, 2003.
A detailed overview of different kinds of groupware.

T. Rodden, A survey of CSCW systems, *Interacting with Computers*, Vol. 3, No. 3, 1991.

J. S. Olson, G. M. Olson, L. A. Mack and P. Wellner, Concurrent editing: the group's interface. In *Human–Computer Interaction* – INTERACT'90, pp. 835–9, North-Holland, 1990.

C. Ellis, S. J. Gibbs and G. L. Rein, Groupware: some issues and experience, *Communications of the ACM*, Vol. 34, No. 1, pp. 38–58, January 1991.
Overview and survey articles on groupware systems. The last article also includes a description of the Grove system.

Tutorials on building groupware. In previous editions we have suggested reading tutorial notes and attending tutorials on building groupware. The ones we used in the past are looking rather dated, but it is much harder now to find places to find out about groupware construction. This is perhaps partly because a lot of experimental groupware is built over web platforms (see also Chapter 21 for this). We will include what links and information we can on the book web pages for this chapter: /e3/chaps/ch19/

A. Schill, *Cooperative Office Systems*, Prentice Hall, 1995.
Describes international standards in distributed computing, databases and document description. Aimed principally, but not solely, at asynchronous groupware.

The ACM *CSCW* conference has run biennially in even years from 1986. The proceedings from *CSCW'86* on are all ACM publications. It is now hard to get hold of earlier proceedings, but more recent proceedings are available.

The European *CSCW* conference runs in the odd years, since 1989, and proceedings are available. The proceedings of the first conference *ECSCW'89* are also available as a book (see below).

J. M. Bowers and S. D. Benford, editors, *Studies in Computer-supported Cooperative Work*: *Theory, Practice and Design*, North-Holland, 1991.
Selected papers from *ECSCW'89*.

See also references in the text to papers describing particular groupware systems.

20

UBIQUITOUS COMPUTING AND AUGMENTED REALITIES

OVERVIEW

- The traditional computer is a glass box – all you can do is press buttons and see the effect.

- Ubiquitous computing and augmented reality systems break this glass box by linking the real world with the electronic worlds.

- Applications include:
  - ubiquitous computing
  - virtual reality
  - augmented reality
  - information visualization.

This chapter is based on 'The human experience' by Gregory Abowd, Elizabeth Mynatt and Tom Rodden, which appeared in *IEEE Pervasive Computing Magazine*, Special Inaugural Issue on Reaching for Weiser's Vision, Vol. 1, Issue 1, pp. 48–58, Jan–March 2002, © 2002 IEEE.

20.1 INTRODUCTION

There are several ways in which the earliest assumptions of HCI are challenged. For example, we no longer assume there is a single user; rather, we consider groups and larger organizational concerns when discussing interactions. In this chapter, we challenge another assumption concerning the form factor of the computing device. Traditionally, we think of computers as a glass box, a workstation with keyboard, mouse and monitor sitting on a desk that we seek out when we want to do some work. Since the late 1980s, this traditional form factor has been expanded to include a variety of more mobile devices and computing services that are distributed throughout the physical world and more tightly integrated with it. The trend is towards a ubiquitous or pervasive computing experience, in which computing devices become so commonplace that we do not distinguish them from the 'normal' physical surroundings. Improved display technologies give us the ability to augment the physical world with electronic information through head-mounted displays or steerable projection surfaces. We have also seen display technologies that provide complete virtual replacements of the physical world, creating a so-called virtual reality.

In this chapter, we will review the progress and challenges in the areas of ubiquitous computing, augmented reality, virtual reality and visualization.

20.2 UBIQUITOUS COMPUTING APPLICATIONS RESEARCH

We first introduced the notion of *ubiquitous computing* (or *pervasive computing*) in Chapter 4. The interest in ubiquitous computing has surged over the past few years, thanks to some influential writings and plenty of experimental work. The defining characteristic of ubiquitous computing is the attempt to break away from the traditional desktop interaction paradigm and move computational power into the environment that surrounds the user. Rather than force the user to search out and find the computer's interface, ubiquitous computing suggests that the interface itself can take on the responsibility of locating and serving the user.

Mark Weiser is credited with coining the phrase ubiquitous computing (or ubicomp) when he put forth a vision of people and environments augmented with computational resources that provide information and services when and where desired [369]. Though his vision has excited many technologists, it is important to realize that the main motivation behind Weiser's vision was centered on the impact ubicomp would have on the human experience:

> Machines that fit the human environment instead of forcing humans to enter theirs will make using a computer as refreshing as a walk in the woods.
>
> (Weiser, 1991)

> We wanted to put computing back in its place, to reposition it into the environmental background, to concentrate on human-to-human interfaces and less on human-to-computer ones.
>
> (Weiser et al., 1999)

> Inspired by the social scientists, philosophers, and anthropologists at PARC, we have been trying to take a radical look at what computing and networking ought to be like. We believe that people live through their practices and tacit knowledge so that the most powerful things are those that are effectively invisible in use. This is a challenge that affects all of computer science. Our preliminary approach: Activate the world. Provide hundreds of wireless computing devices per person per office, of all scales (from 1″ displays to wall sized). This has required new work in operating systems, user interfaces, networks, wireless, displays, and many other areas. We call our work 'ubiquitous computing'. This is different from PDAs, dynabooks, or information at your fingertips. It is invisible, everywhere computing that does not live on a personal device of any sort, but is in the woodwork everywhere.
>
> (Weiser, 1994)

What is ubiquitous computing technology? Our general working definition is any computing technology that permits human interaction away from a single workstation. This includes pen-based technology, handheld or portable devices, large-scale interactive screens, wireless networking infrastructure, and voice or vision technology. Realizing the human-centered vision of ubicomp with these technologies presents many challenges. Here we will focus on three:

■ defining the appropriate physical interaction experience;
■ discovering general application features;
■ theories for designing and evaluating the human experience within ubicomp.

20.2.1 Defining the appropriate physical interaction experience

Ubiquitous computing inspires application development that is 'off the desktop'. In addition to suggesting a freedom from a small number of well-defined interaction locales (the desktop), this vision assumes that physical interaction between humans and computation will be less like the current desktop keyboard/mouse/display paradigm and more like the way humans interact with the physical world. Humans speak, gesture and use writing implements to communicate with other humans and alter physical artifacts. The drive for a ubiquitous computing experience has resulted in a variety of important changes to the input, output and interactions that define the human experience with computing. We describe three of those changes in this section.

Toward implicit input

Input has moved beyond the explicit nature of textual input from keyboards and selection from pointing devices to a greater variety of data types. As we will show, this has resulted in not only a greater variety of input technologies, but also a shift from explicit means of human input to more *implicit* forms of input [315]. By implicit input we mean that our natural interactions with the physical environment provide sufficient input to a variety of attendant services, without any further user intervention. Recall the discussion of levels of intention in Chapter 18 (Section 18.4), some implicit interaction is intentional, for example tipping a PDA to move between pages. However, implicit interaction is most radical when it allows low intention and incidental interaction. For example, walking into a space is enough to announce one's presence and identity in that location.

Computer interfaces that support more natural human forms of communication (e.g. handwriting, speech and gestures) are beginning to supplement or replace elements of the graphical user interface interaction paradigm. The emerging area of perceptual interfaces is being driven by long-standing research communities in computer vision and multi-modal recognition technologies (mainly handwriting and speech). Pen-based interaction, unsuccessfully rushed to the market in the early 1990s, is also experiencing resurgence. Large-scale touch-interactive surfaces, using technologies such as capacitive coupling have made it possible to create multi-person interactive surfaces on tables and walls (see Figure 20.1). Recognition of free-hand writing is improving, but more significantly, mass adoption has followed the introduction of less sophisticated and more robust recognition technologies, such as Grafiti. We have even seen compelling examples of how voice and pen input can be used effectively in applications without requiring any recognition at all (e.g. [174]).

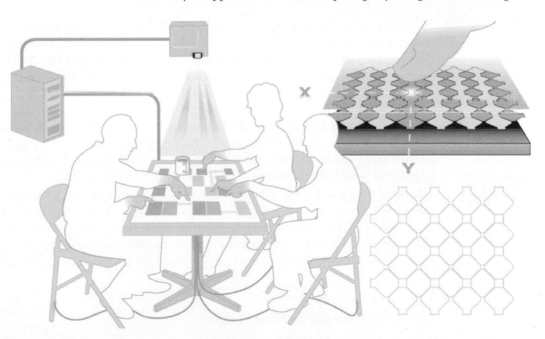

Figure 20.1   The DiamondTouch input technology from Mitsubishi Electric Research Lab (MERL) uses capacitive coupling through humans to provide a large-scale input surface for multiple simultaneous users. See www.merl.com/projects/DiamondTouch/ for more details. Source: Courtesy of Mitsubishi Electric Research Laboratories, Inc.

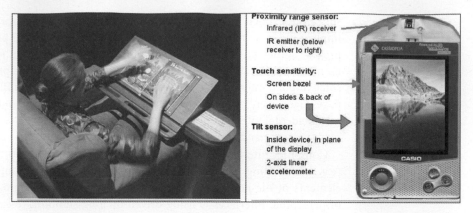

Figure 20.2 Two examples of simple sensing embedded into devices. On the left, the Listen Reader from Palo Alto Research Center [20] uses electric field sensors located in the book binding to sense the proximity of the reader's hands and control audio parameters, while RFID tags embedded in each page allow fast, robust page identification. Picture courtesy Palo Alto Research Center. On the right, is an experimental PDA platform used at Microsoft Research to investigate how a variety of simple sensors can improve the interaction between a user and various handheld applications [173]. Picture courtesy Ken Hinckley

These recognition technologies are some examples of interpreting meaning from sensed signals of human activity. There are many other ways to infer information about people and environments by sensing a variety of other physical signals. There have been many recent advances in sensing the physical world; the significance here is that sensing and interpretation of human activity provides a more implicit notion of input to an interactive system. For example, many researchers have investigated how simple sensors such as RFID (the technology behind the security tags used on library books, clothes in shops, etc.), accelerometers, tilt sensors, capacitive coupling, infrared range finders and others can be incorporated into artifacts to increase the language of input from the user to control that artifact (see Figure 20.2).

Invisibility of computing, from the human perspective, can start when we are able to determine an individual's identity, location, affect or activity through her mere presence and natural interactions within an environment. The union of explicit and implicit input defines the *context* of interaction between the human and the environment, a theme we will return to in the next section on emergent application features.

Toward multi-scale and distributed output

The integration of ubiquitous computing capabilities into everyday life also requires novel output technologies and techniques. Designers of targeted information appliances, such as personal digital assistants and future home technologies, must address the form of the technology, including its aesthetic appeal. Output is no longer exclusively in the form of self-contained desktop/laptop visual displays that demand our attention. A variety of sizes or scales of visual displays, both smaller and larger than the desktop, are being distributed throughout our environments. More importantly, we are seeing multiple modalities of information sources that lie more at the periphery of our senses and provide qualitative, ambient forms of communication.

Weiser described the form factor ubicomp technology in three scales – the inch, the foot and the yard. The middle (foot) scale is similar to the standard laptop and desktop displays. Many of us have one or a small number of these devices and we largely use them in stationary settings. A new generation of tablet-like portable pen-based computers, devices that rival the experimental MPAD prototypes developed at Xerox PARC, hit the market in 2002. Pagers, cellular phones and PDAs, handheld displays with relatively low resolution today represent the small end of the scale (inch). We carry around an increasing number of these display devices at all times. The large end of the scale (yard) is now represented by high-resolution wall-sized displays that are created by effectively stitching together multiple low-resolution projected displays, such as the Stanford Interactive Mural [184], see Figure 20.3, or the Princeton Display Wall [67].

As these displays continue to proliferate in number and variety, two important trends have emerged. First, we want to move information between separate displays easily and coordinate the interactions between multiple displays. This was initially

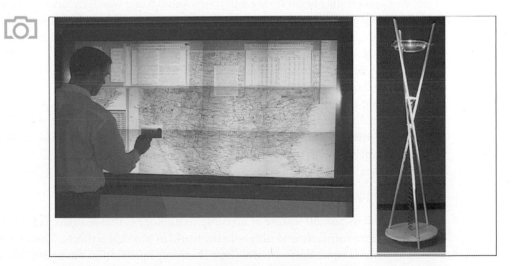

Figure 20.3 The figure on the left is the Stanford Interactive Mural, an example of a large-scale interactive display surface created by tiling multiple lower-resolution projectors. Picture courtesy François Guimbretière. The figure on the right is an example of an ambient display, the Water Lamp from Ishii's Tangible Media Group at the MIT Media Lab. Light shines upwards through a pan of water, which is actuated by digitally controlled solenoids that can tap the water and cause ripples. External information can be used to drive the tapping of the solenoids. Source: Courtesy of Hiroshi Ishii, MIT Media Lab. Photograph by Andrew Daly

explored by Rekimoto's 'pick-and-drop' demonstration [302], and further developed in the Stanford Interactive Room [139]. Secondly, as displays proliferate, we desire them to be less demanding of our attention. Weiserian invisibility comes through design of output that provides for peripheral awareness of information out of the foreground of our conscious attention.

The trend toward peripheral output has been explored for a particular class of displays, called *ambient*. Ambient displays require minimal attention and cognitive effort, and are thus more easily integrated into a persistent physical space. One of the first ambient displays, the Dangling String [372], was invented at Xerox PARC by the artist Natalie Jeremijenko. Using analog sensing of network traffic from the cabling in the ceiling, a motor drove the spin of a long string. The more traffic, the faster the rotation. During high traffic periods, the whir of the string was faintly audible as well.

The Dangling String shares many features with subsequent efforts in ambient displays. A data source drives the abstract representation such that the output can be monitored by the user's peripheral perception. The data source is generally information that is of medium to low priority, but beneficial for the user to be aware of, perhaps for some opportunistic action. As these displays are meant to be persistently available in the environment, they are often designed to be aesthetically appealing and novel (for example, the Water Lamp in Figure 20.3). Other examples of ambient displays include ambientROOM, which projects information about colleagues as pinpoints of light on the wall [190], Audio Aura, which encodes the arrival of incoming email as auditory cues in a mobile device [249], and Kandinsky, which assembles images triggered from keywords in information bulletins into an aesthetically pleasing and intriguing collage [138].

Though our experience with computing output is dominated by the use of the visual channel, examples such as Audio Aura demonstrate how other modes of output can be effective at communicating ambient information. Other forms of output include actuation of small devices. With the introduction of simple programming tools for dealing with motors and other actuators, such as Phidgets [156], mechanical actuation to drive distributed output devices will increase.

Seamless integration of physical and virtual worlds

An important feature of ubicomp technology is that it attempts to merge computational artifacts smoothly with the world of physical artifacts. There have been plenty of examples demonstrating how electronic information can be overlaid upon the real world, thus producing an augmented reality [130]. An example of such augmented reality is NaviCam, a portable camera/TV that recognizes 2D glyphs placed on objects and can then superimpose relevant information over the object for display on the TV screen (Figure 20.4 shows a shot of what the portable TV shows the user). This form of augmented reality only affects the output. When both input and output between are intermixed, as with the DigitalDesk [374], see Figure 20.4, we begin to approach the seamless integration of the physical and virtual worlds. Researchers have suggested techniques for using objects in the physical world to

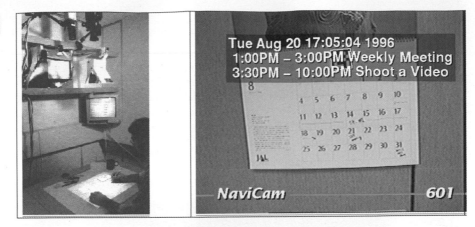

Figure 20.4 On the left, the DigitalDesk prototype integrating physical and virtual desktop environments with the aid of projection and vision technology [374]. Source: © 1993 ACM, Inc. Reprinted by permission. On the right, the NaviCam system which recognized 2D glyphs on objects and then superimposed additional information over that object [303]. Source: Courtesy of Sony Computer Science Laboratories, Inc.

manipulate electronic artifacts, creating so-called graspable [136] or tangible [189] user interfaces. Sensors attached to devices themselves provide ways for physical manipulations of those devices to be interpreted appropriately by the applications running on those devices [164, 173], see Figure 20.2.

DESIGN FOCUS

Ambient Wood – augmenting the physical

Birds sing and dappled light breaks through the leaves. In a high tree branch a half-open laptop computer is wedged and a surreal structure of thin steel stands near a clearing. Then over the bird song comes the sound of children's laughter.

Jenny and Caroline run excitedly into the clearing. A field trip is always better than a day in school! Jenny is holding a small device. It is like a PDA, but at one end is a long probe (and yes the teacher did tell them *not* to run with it!). They push the device into the ground in the center of the clearing. It tells them the moisture level and light level. 'Let's try sticking it in the tree bark' says Caroline. 'OK', says Jenny, 'but I want to try it at the edge of the trees first'.

'What's this?,' says Caroline when she sees the steel contraption. Tree-like itself it has 'branches' with small glass Petri dishes. There are various things to put in the Petri dishes. One is a sample of moss. She puts this in and looks into the black hooded box at eye level. It is a bit like one of those old hooded cameras. Under the hood is a small screen, just big enough for two or three people to see it. Because she has put the moss in the Petri dish it shows a small clip about the growth of moss.

As they wander further into the wood, they suddenly hear a strange, otherworldly sound and the screen on their PDA shows a picture of a butterfly feeding on a flower head. The sound they are hearing is an amplified recording of nectar being sucked through the butterfly's proboscis – like a giant drinking straw!

This rich educational experience is supported by technology. The laptop wedged in the tree is acting as a wireless network repeater carrying the moisture and temperature readings to the resource tent where they will discuss their findings as a class later. The location of each reading is captured using a GPS receiver on each PDA. The steel contraption, the 'periscope', knows which images to show the children as each object is RFID tagged and the butterfly sound is triggered when their PDA comes close enough to a small beacon buried in the leaves.

The Ambient Wood is an experience project of the Equator project.

See the book website for an extended case study: /e3/casestudy/ambient-wood/

Photographs courtesy of Yvonne Rogers

20.2.2 Application themes for ubicomp

Many applications-focussed researchers in HCI seek the holy grail of ubicomp, the killer app that will cause significant investment in the infrastructure that will then enable a wide variety of ubicomp applications to flourish. It could be argued that person–person communication is such a killer app for ubicomp, as it has caused a large investment in environmental and personal infrastructure that has moved us close (though not entirely) to a completely connected existence. Whether or not personal communication is the killer app, the vision of ubicomp from the human perspective is much more holistic. It is not the value of any single service that will make computing a disappearing technology. Rather, it is the combination of a large range of services, all of which are available when and as needed and all of which work as desired without extraordinary human intervention. A major challenge for applications research is discovering an evolutionary path toward this idyllic interactive experience.

The brief history of ubicomp demonstrates some emergent features that appear across many applications. One feature is the ability to use implicitly sensed context from the physical and electronic environment to determine the correct behavior of any given service. Context-aware computing demonstrates promise for making our interactions with services more seamless and less distracting from our everyday activities. Applications can be made to just work right when they are informed about the context of their use. Another feature of many ubicomp applications is the ability to easily capture and store memories of live experiences and serve them up for later use. The trajectory of these two applications themes coupled with the increasing exploration of ubiquitous computing into novel, non-work environments, points to the changing relationship between people and computing, and thus the changing purpose of ubicomp applications. We describe this newer trajectory, coined *everyday computing*, following a discussion of the two more established themes.

Context-aware computing

Two compelling early demonstrations of ubicomp were the Olivetti Research Lab's Active Badge [361] and the Xerox PARCTab [362], both location-aware appliances. These devices leverage a simple piece of context, user location, and provide valuable services (automatic call forwarding for a phone system, automatically updated maps of user locations in an office). This technology was also the basis for the Pepys automatic diary system described in Chapter 18 (Section 18.4.1). These simple location-aware appliances are perhaps the first demonstration of linking implicit human activity with computational services that serve to augment general human activity.

Location of identifiable entities (usually people) is a very common piece of context used in ubicomp application development. The most widespread applications have been GPS-based car navigation systems and handheld 'tour guide' systems that vary the content displayed (video or audio) by a handheld unit given the user's physical location in an exhibit area [6, 68]. For example, The Sentient Computing Project uses a 3-D ultrasonic indoor location system to track each worker in a building and so maintain a map of office worker locations that helps coworkers find each other and talk by phone.

Of course, there is more to context than position (where) and identity (who). Although a complete definition of context remains an elusive research challenge, it is clear that in addition to who and where, context awareness involves:

When   With the exception of using time as an index into a captured record or summarizing how long a person has been at a particular location, most context-driven applications are unaware of the passage of time. Of particular interest are the relative changes in time as an aid for interpreting human activity. For example, brief visits at an exhibit could be indicative of a general lack of interest. Additionally, when a baseline of behavior can be established, action that violates a perceived pattern would be of particular interest. For example, a context-aware home might notice when an elderly person deviated from a typically active morning routine.

What   The interaction in current systems either assumes what the user is doing or leaves the question open. Perceiving and interpreting human activity is a difficult problem. Nevertheless, interaction with continuously worn, context-driven devices will probably need to incorporate interpretations of human activity to be able to provide useful information. One strategy is to incorporate information

DESIGN FOCUS

Exploring intimate computing in the arts

Ubiquitous and related technologies push the boundaries of 'normal' interaction. Some experiments (such as Classroom 2000 opposite) are both informative about future interactions and also clearly useful now, but most struggle between the two – artefacts designed apparently for utilitarian purposes, but clearly not what any-one would really want to use. We simply understand too little about the way the future will be, but can't know unless we experiment more radically!

One way through this impasse is through performance and installation arts. Freed of the constraint of being 'useful' it is possible to experiment with radically new modes of interaction. One group, thePooch, have explored various limits of inter-action including what Jenn Sheridan calls 'computing intimacies' – technologies such as wearable and personal environments which are not just physically but emotionally felt as 'close' to you. The schizophrenic cyborg is one performance that breaks the normal boundaries of self.

See /e3/casestudy/arts/ and www.thepooch.com/

Photograph courtesy
of Peter Phillips

---

about what a user is doing in the virtual realm. What application is he using? What information is he accessing? 'Cookies', which describe people's activity on the world wide web, are an example that has both positive and negative uses. Another way of interpreting the 'what' of context is to view it as the focus of attention of one or more people during a live event. Knowledge of the focus of attention at a live event can inform a better capture of that event, the topic of the next subsection.

Why Even more challenging than perceiving 'what' a person is doing is under-standing 'why' they are doing it. Sensing other forms of contextual information that could give an indication of a person's affective state, such as body temper-ature, heart rate and galvanic skin response, may be a useful place to start.

An obvious challenge of context-aware computing is making it truly ubiquitous. Having certain context, in particular positioning information, has been shown useful. However, there are few truly ubiquitous, single-source context services. Positioning is a good example. GPS does not work indoors, and is even suspect in some urban regions. There are a variety of indoor positioning schemes as well, with differing characteristics in terms of cost, range, granularity and requirements for tagging, and no single solution is likely to ever meet all requirements.

Automated capture and access

Much of our life in business and academia is spent listening to and recording, more or less accurately, the events that surround us, and then trying to remember the important pieces of information from those events. There is clear value, and potential danger, in using computational resources to augment the inefficiency of human record taking, especially when there are multiple streams of related information that are virtually impossible to capture as a whole manually. Tools to support automated capture of and access to live experiences can remove the burden of doing something humans are not good at (i.e. recording) so that they can focus attention

DESIGN FOCUS

Classroom 2000/eClass – deploying and evaluating ubicomp

An influential case study in deployment and evaluation of a ubicomp application is the Classroom 2000 system, developed at Georgia Tech [2]. The project began in July 1995 with the intent of producing a system that would capture as much of the classroom experience as possible to facilitate later review by both students and teachers. In many lectures, students have their heads down, furiously writing down what they hear and see as a future reference. While some of this writing activity is useful as a processing cue for the student, it was desirable from the student and teacher perspective to afford the opportunity for students to lift their heads occasionally and engage in the lecture experience. The capture system was seen as a way to relieve some of the note-taking burden. (See also Figures 21.5 and 21.6 and a description of the e-learning issues of Classroom 2000/eClass in Chapter 21.)

To test the feasibility of this hypothesis quickly, an environment for capture was implemented within six months and used to support the capture of an entire course to observe whether the initial hypothesis was worth testing more vigorously. Some very valuable lessons were learned during this first extended experience. The initial experiments included student note-taking devices that were clear distractions to the students. Support for private student note taking was abandoned, only to be resumed two years later when the technology had caught up.

To understand the impact of this capture system on teaching and learning, it would have to be used by many more students and teachers in a wider variety of courses. This required significant engineering effort to create a robust and reliable capture system that by early 1997 was able to support multiple classes simultaneously. During a three-year experimental period ending in mid-2000, over 100 courses were supported for 30 different instructors.

This extended deployment made possible an extensive quantitative analysis that revealed how such an automated capture and access system impacts the educational experience *once it has been incorporated into the everyday experience* [48]. As a direct result of these deeper evaluations, we know that the system encourages 60% of its users to modify their in-class note-taking behavior. We also know that not all of this modified behavior is for the better. Taking no notes, for example, is not a good learning practice to reinforce. We know that it is time to reintroduce student note-taking units that can personalize the capture experience and also encourage better note-taking practices. We also know to facilitate more content-based retrieval and synchronized playback of the lecture experience. These insights have motivated further research efforts and established a long-term research project, eClass.

The Classroom 2000/eClass experience demonstrates the importance of substantial deployment in order to be able to evaluate ubicomp systems effectively. It is only when these systems become part of everyday life that we see the ways in which they are really used.

on activities they are good at (i.e. indicating relationships, summarizing and interpreting).

We define capture and access as the task of preserving a record of some live experience that is then reviewed at some point in the future. Vannevar Bush was perhaps the first to write about the benefits of a generalized capture and access system when he introduced the concept of the memex [51]. The memex was intended to store the artifacts that we come in contact with in our everyday lives and the associations that we create between them. Over the years, many researchers have worked toward this vision. As a result, many systems have been built to capture and access experiences in classrooms, meetings and other live experiences.

The earliest work on automated capture was explored at Xerox PARC to support meeting capture, building on their experience in collaborative meeting support systems (see Chapter 19, Section 19.4.2). Since then a number of capture applications have been explored in a variety of environments including education and project management in support of individuals or groups [349].

Toward continuous interaction

Providing continuous interaction moves computing from a localized tool to a constant presence. A new thread of ubicomp research, *everyday computing*, promotes informal and unstructured activities typical of much of our everyday lives. Familiar examples are orchestrating daily routines, communicating with family and friends, and managing information.

The focus on activities as opposed to tasks is a crucial departure from traditional HCI design. The majority of computer applications support well-defined tasks that have a marked beginning and end with multiple subtasks in-between. Take word processing as an example. Word processing features are tuned for starting with a blank document (or a template), entering text, formatting, printing and saving. These applications are not well suited to the more general activity of writing, encompassing multiple versions of documents where text is reused and content evolves over time.

The emphasis on designing for continuously available interaction requires addressing these features of informal, daily activities:

- They rarely have a clear beginning or end so the design cannot assume a common starting point or closure requiring greater flexibility and simplicity.
- Interruption is expected as users switch attention between competing concerns.
- Multiple activities operate concurrently and may need to be loosely coordinated.
- Time is an important discriminator in characterizing the ongoing relationship between people and computers.
- Associative models of information are needed, as information is reused from multiple perspectives.

Of course, activities and tasks are not unrelated to each other. Often an activity will consist of a number of tasks, but the activity itself is more than these component parts for the reasons listed above. For example, communication activities contain well-defined tasks such as reading a message or composing a reply. The interaction falters when the task refers to the larger activity: how does this new message relate to previous messages from this person? What other issues should be included in the reply? The challenge in designing for activities is encompassing these tasks in an environment that supports continuous interaction.

20.2.3 Understanding interaction in ubicomp

The shift in focus inherent within ubicomp from the desktop to the surrounding environment mirrors previous work in HCI and CSCW. As the computer has increasingly 'reached out' in the organization, researchers have needed to shift their focus from a single machine engaging with an individual to a broader set of organizational and social arrangements and the cooperative interaction inherent in these arrangements.

We have seen aspects of this change in Chapters 13 and 14 looking at organizational, social and collaborative aspects, and also in Chapter 18 where we have already considered aspects of the physical environment and in particular the extreme end of low-intention, incidental interaction.

Many of these models and methods are applicable to ubicomp with its emphasis on integrating numerous devices in one setting.

Knowledge in the world

Traditionally, research and evaluation efforts in HCI have been informed by the Model Human Processor theory of human cognition and behavior [56]. This model focusses on internal cognition driven by the cooperation of three independent units of sensory, cognitive and motor activity where each unit maintains its own working store of information. As the application of computers has broadened, designers have turned to models that consider the nature of the relationship between the internal cognitive processes and the outside world. Designing for a balance between 'knowledge in the world' versus 'knowledge in the head' is now a common maxim in the design community [186, 266].

Three main theories that focus on the 'in the world' nature of knowledge are being explored within the ubicomp community as guides for future design and evaluation: activity theory, situated action and distributed cognition.

Activity theory

Activity theory is the oldest of the three, building on work by Vygotsky [358]. The closest to traditional theories, activity theory recognizes concepts such as goals ('objects'), actions and operations. However, both goals and actions are fluid based on the changing physical state of the world instead of more fixed, a priori plans. Additionally, although operations require little to no explicit attention, such as an expert driver motoring home, the operation can shift to an action based on changing circumstances such as difficult traffic and weather conditions. Activity theory also emphasizes the transformational properties of artifacts that implicitly carry knowledge and traditions, such as musical instruments, cars and other tools. The behavior of the user is shaped by the capabilities implicit in the tool itself [252]. Ubiquitous computing efforts informed by activity theory, therefore, focus on the transformational properties of artifacts and the fluid execution of actions and operations.

Situated action and distributed cognition

Theories of situated action have already featured several times in Chapters 13 and 14, and distributed cognition is discussed in detail in Section 14.5.3. Recall that both reject the 'pre-planned goals giving rise to actions' model inherent in MHP.

Situated action [334] emphasizes the improvisational aspects of human behavior and de-emphasizes a priori plans that are simply executed by the person. In this model, knowledge in the world continually shapes the ongoing interpretation and execution of a task. Ubiquitous computing efforts informed by situated action also emphasize improvisational behavior and would not require, nor anticipate, the user to follow a predefined script. The system would aim to add knowledge to the world that could effectively assist in shaping the user's action, hence an emphasis on continuously updated peripheral displays. Additionally, evaluation of this system would require watching authentic human behavior and would discount post-task interviews as rationalizations of behavior that is not necessarily rational.

Distributed cognition also de-emphasizes internal human cognition, but in this case, it turns to a systems perspective where humans are just part of a larger system. Of all three theories, distributed cognition plays the greatest attention to knowledge in the world, as much of the information needed to accomplish a system's goal is encoded in the individual objects. For example, in Chapter 18 (Section 18.3), we saw how objects act as triggers prompting users to do things and also how they act as placeholders keeping track of where they are in a task. Ubiquitous computing efforts informed by distributed cognition, focus on designing for a larger system goal, in contrast to the use of an individual appliance and emphasize how information is encoded in objects and how that information is translated, and perhaps transmitted, by different users.

Understanding human practice: ethnography and cultural probes

Any form of model or theory by its nature is limited and the above theories all emphasize the very rich interactions between people and their environments that are hard to capture in neat formulae and frameworks. Office procedures and more formal work domains can be modeled using more rigid methods such as traditional task analysis, but as we saw in Chapter 18, even these have rich aspects that need additional modeling. When one looks more closely at how people actually work there is a great complexity in everyday practices that depends finely on particular settings and contexts.

Weiser also emphasized the importance of understanding these everyday practices to inform ubicomp research:

> We believe that *people live through their practices* and tacit knowledge so that the most powerful things are those that are *effectively invisible in use.* [our emphasis]
>
> (Weiser, 1994)

The challenge for ubicomp designers is to uncover the very practices through which people live, and to make these invisible practices visible and available to the developers of ubiquitous computing environments. Ethnography (see Chapter 13, Section 13.3.4) has emerged as a primary approach to address the need to gain rich understandings of a particular setting and the everyday practices that encompass these settings.

In the context of ubicomp, the goal of an ethnographic investigation is to provide these descriptions and analysis of everyday life to the IT designers and developers so that ubicomp environments seamlessly mesh with the everyday practices that enscapsulate the goals, attitudes, social relationships, knowledge and language of the intended setting. These techniques have been applied to inform design of social communications devices for the home [175] and to enhance the social connection between older people and their extended families [251].

Perhaps a more intriguing method of conveying the nature of settings to developers of future technologies has emerged from an art and design tradition. The work of Gaver et al. [144] has explored the use of cultural probes (see Design Focus in Chapter 5, Section 5.4) to collect information from settings in order to *inspire* the development of new digital devices. Unlike ethnography which focusses on the everyday and routine nature of the setting, cultural probes seek to uncover the emotional, the unusual and even the spiritual in order to inspire designers.

20.2.4 Evaluation challenges for ubicomp

We must also assess the utility of ubicomp solutions. Researchers have only recently begun to address the development of assessment and evaluation techniques that meet the demands of ubicomp. One reason for the relatively slow development of these techniques is the gradual evolution of the vision of ubiquitous use of technology. In order to understand the impact of ubicomp on everyday life, we navigate a delicate balance between prediction of how novel technologies will serve a real human need and observation of authentic use and subsequent co-evolution of human activities and novel technologies.

Formative and summative evaluation of ubicomp systems is difficult and represents a real challenge for the ubicomp community. With the notable exception of the work at Xerox PARC on the use of the Tivoli capture system and at Georgia Tech with the Classroom 2000/eClass system (see Design Focus earlier in the chapter), there has been surprisingly little research published from an evaluation or end-user perspective in the ubicomp community. A number of significant challenges need to be addressed in order to develop appropriate assessment methods and techniques.

The shift away from the desktop inherent within the ubicomp vision also represents a shift away from the office and the managed structuring of work inherent within these environments. Much of our understanding of work has developed from Fordist and Taylorist principles on the structuring of activities and tasks. Evaluation within HCI reflects these roots and is often predicated on notions of task and the measurement of performance and efficiency in meeting these goals and tasks.

However, it is not clear that these measures can apply universally across activities when we move away from structured and paid work to other activities. For example,

DESIGN FOCUS

Shared experience

You are in the Mackintosh Interpretation Centre in an arts center in Glasgow, Scotland. You notice a man wearing black wandering around looking at the exhibits and then occasionally at a small PDA he is holding. As you get closer he appears to be talking to himself, but then you realize he is simply talking into a head-mounted microphone. 'Some people can never stop using their mobile phone', you think. As you are looking at one exhibit, he comes across and suddenly cranes forward to look more closely, getting right in front of you. 'How rude', you think.

The visitor is taking part in the City project – a mixed-reality experience. He is talking to two other people at remote sites, one who has a desktop VR view of the exhibition and the other just a website. However, they can all see representations of each other. The visitor is being tracked by ultrasound and he appears in the VR world. Also, the web user's current page locates her in a particular part of the virtual exhibition. All of the users see a map of the exhibition showing where they all are.

You might think that in such an experiment the person actually in the museum would take the lead, but in fact real groups using this system seemed to have equal roles and really had a sense of shared experience despite their very different means of seeing the exhibition.

See the book website for a full case study: /e3/casestudy/city/

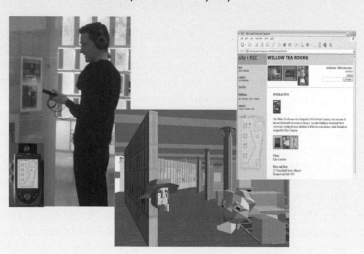

City project: physical presence, VR interfaces and web interface. Source: Courtesy of Matthew Chalmers. Note: City is an Equator project

it is unclear how we may assess the domestic devices suggested by the Royal College of Art [143] or the broad range of devices to emerge from Philips' Vision of the Future [286]. This shift away from the world of work means that there is still the question of how to apply qualitative or quantitative evaluation methods. Answering this question requires researchers to consider new representations of human activity and to consider how to undertake assessment that broadens from existing task-oriented approaches. Although many researchers have investigated the use of observational, and semi-structured interviews, the lack of deployment of ubiquitous environments has hampered many of these activities.

The technology used to create ubicomp systems is often on the cutting edge and it is difficult to create reliable and robust systems that support some activity on a continuous basis. Consequently, a good portion of reported ubicomp applications work remains at this level of demonstrational prototypes that are not designed to be robust, although there are notable exceptions, for example the SPAM system described in Chapter 19 (Section 19.3.3). Deeper empirical evaluation results cannot be obtained through controlled studies in a traditional, contained usability laboratory. Rather, the requirement is for real use of a system, deployed in an authentic setting. A number of researchers are seeking to roll out ubiquitous devices into a range of settings, such as museums, outdoor city centers and the home. These researchers are creating 'living laboratories' for ubicomp research by creating testbeds that support advanced research and development as well as use by a targeted user.

20.3 VIRTUAL AND AUGMENTED REALITY

Virtual reality (VR) refers to the computer-generated simulation of a world, or a subset of it, in which the user is immersed. It represents the state of the art in multimedia systems, but concentrates on the visual senses. VR allows the user to experience situations that are too dangerous or expensive to enter 'in the flesh'. Users may explore the real world at a different scale and with hidden features made visible. Alternatively, the virtual worlds that are generated may be entirely synthesized: realistic within themselves, but purely a manifestation of electronic structures.

The term 'virtual reality' conjures up an image of a user weighed down with a helmet or goggles, grasping, apparently blindly, into empty space. The user, isolated within his virtual environment, moves through a simulated landscape, picking up objects on the way. This is fully *immersive VR*. However, it is only one part of the spectrum of VR, which also includes desktop VR, command and control situations, and augmented reality, where virtuality and reality meet.

20.3.1 VR technology

The technology involved in VR is quite elaborate. The individual devices have been discussed in Chapter 2, but now we shall see how they work together.

Since the user has to 'see' a new environment, a headset is usually used in a VR setup. With independent screens for each eye, in order to give a 3D image, the headset is often a large, relatively cumbersome piece of head-mounted gear. However, smaller, lighter VR goggles are now available and may soon become only slightly oversized spectacles.

Having to produce and render realistic images in real time requires vast amounts of computing power, and the resources for full realism are rarely available; they may not even exist as yet. This means that the world inhabited by the user tends to be 'blocky', with little variation in texture, and flat lighting. This makes the calculations much simpler and more achievable. As far as input to VR systems is concerned, a dataglove that captures gestural information is often used. Feedback can be incorporated into the glove, so that resistance is felt when grasping a virtual object. Speech recognition systems can also be incorporated, and, in general, audio feedback is utilized in some form or another. Stereo headphones are a simple piece of VR kit, but at the other extreme a full-body version of the dataglove is available too!

20.3.2 Immersive VR

Virtual reality can be used to produce environments that mimic our everyday world. Architects have always used models and sketches to show clients how a building will appear. Now they can use VR to take clients through a virtual tour of the building, fly over it from above, look at it from the streets outside, enter the doors and walk through the corridors. Similar techniques are used to plan kitchens and even gardens.

However, there are also many things that we cannot see, either because they are invisible to the naked eye (heat, magnetism, gravity) or because they are too small or too large. Scientific and data visualization systems make use of VR technology to expose and explore these features. In Section 20.4 we will see one example of this in the virtual wind tunnel, which makes the airflows around an aircraft wing visible using virtual bubble trails (see Figure 20.6). Another example is in the field of protein chemistry, where individual molecules are, of course, too small to see except by electron microscope.

Proteins are complex chemicals, made up of convoluted folded chains of simpler components known as amino acids. The particular acids involved, their order in the chain and the nature of the folding all contribute to the particular behavior and function of the protein. In trying to understand the behavior of particular proteins, scientists have turned to VR techniques to help them probe the secrets of these vital components of life. Work by Hubbard [181] has produced a VR system using a headset and dataglove. The user dons the headset, and is immersed in a 3D world where atomic dimensions become tangible distances and the protein exists like a ball of hairy twine. Using the dataglove, the user can reach out into the space and grab hold of the molecule, twisting it this way and that to appreciate its complex structure better. The chain of amino acids can be followed from one end to the other, winding around and almost back on itself as the complex chemistry is created. A better knowledge of the structure has allowed the scientists to understand how some very complex proteins work; one particular protein reacts with specific enzymes but the reactive site is hidden deep inside the coiled structure. Data obtained during reactions and used in the system have shown that the protein opens up what is effectively a molecular trapdoor when the enzyme approaches, allowing it to dock with the reactive site. Once seen in animated form the nature of the reaction is obvious, but without this technique to visualize things, the situation is much less clear. In the VR setup, color and shading are used in a primitive form to give dimension and depth to the images, but work is continuing on developing efficient algorithms on dedicated machines to allow more detailed imaging.

20.3.3 VR on the desktop and in the home

Virtual reality has been made possible by the advent of very fast high-performance computers. Despite the exponential rise in processor speeds, high-resolution immersive VR is still not available for mass-market applications, and many systems are primarily research projects. Desktop VR is a lower-cost alternative. In desktop VR, 3D images are presented on a normal computer screen and manipulated using mouse and keyboard, rather than using goggles and datagloves. Many readers may have used such systems on personal computers or games consoles: flight simulators, or interactive games such as DOOM or MYST.

This form of VR is available to many through *VRML (Virtual Reality Markup Language)*, which allows virtual worlds to be distributed over the web and integrated with other web-based materials (Figure 20.5). VRML worlds can include static 3D objects, which the user can navigate around looking at different aspects, and dynamic objects that move about and react when 'touched' by the mouse cursor. In addition, VRML is integrated with the rest of the web by link objects, which, when clicked, take you to another web page or VRML world. Other internet-based VR systems are also available that allow greater interactivity and collaboration with other remote users (see also Chapter 19). However, despite many available systems and technologies, web-based VR has not, as yet, 'taken off' except for some multi-player games.

```
#VRML V1.0 ascii
Separator {
  Separator {    # for sphere
    Material  {
      emmissiveColor  0  0  1    # blue
    }
    Sphere  { radius 1 }
  }
  Transform { translation 4 2 0 }
  Separator {    # for cone
    Texture2 { filename "big_alan.jpg" }
    Cone  {
      radius 1  #  N.B. width = 2*radius
      height 3
} } }
```

Figure 20.5 VRML – virtual reality on the web

20.3.4 Command and control

In many command and control situations, real users are at one remove from the physical world, seeing it through windows, or cameras. The windows or video screens can be replaced by synthesized pictures. The user operates within an immediate physical environment, with real controls and instruments, but the world outside is virtual.

One such interactive VR application in widespread use is the flight simulator. A full cockpit system is placed in a hydraulically supported container, with large screens replacing the cockpit windows. Images are generated and projected onto the screens, whilst the box can be moved rapidly in any direction by the hydraulic rams. The visual information and physical motion simulate accurately the conditions encountered by aircraft. Flight simulators are used extensively in pilot training programs. Landings can be practiced, with the system responding to the commands of the pilot; descending too fast and off to one side, the pilot will have to correct the situation if she wishes to avoid a crash. Emergency situations can also be created, in which aircraft system malfunctions can be artificially created in order to train the pilot to take the correct course of corrective or life-preserving action. With VR, entertainment is never far behind and this kind of system can also be found in many fun fairs!

The military is heavily involved in VR, allowing war scenarios to be fought out with great realism, or training to be given about particular territories that are to be infiltrated. The increased realism at this stage is designed to save lives later on, when, by being better prepared, people are more able to cope with whatever arises. It is in such application areas that VR has been most used since the cost of the necessary equipment is negligible compared with the savings that can be made in terms of human life and expensive military hardware.

20.3.5 Augmented reality

In *augmented reality systems* electronic images are projected over the real world – virtuality and reality meet. The head-up displays in many aircraft and even some automobiles can be regarded as an example of this, but the data in such displays are not typically connected to the objects seen through them and, hence, the blend between virtuality and reality is quite weak.

A stronger sense of connection can be obtained using semi-transparent goggles. Users can move around in the real world and see real objects, but computer images are reflected off the inside of the glass and overlay the physical objects. Again, this can be used to show unrelated information; for example, some *wearable computers* allow users to read their email whilst walking around. However, the real sense of two worlds meeting comes when the projected image in some way links or refers to the object it overlays. For example, one experimental system has virtual balls, which can be picked up and thrown by the user [11]. When the virtual ball 'hits' the real wall it bounces off. The balls can even bounce down a real staircase.

The great difficulty with such systems is in ensuring that the physical and virtual world are correctly aligned, a problem called *registration*. If not properly registered, the virtual ball would either bounce short of the real wall or else appear to go through the wall and then bounce back from the other side! Most experiments have been in very controlled environments where the positions of real objects are known and the user's position and direction of gaze are detected. To be useful in practice, image-processing techniques will often be needed. A digital camera monitors what the user is seeing, uses image recognition to determine what each object is, and then uses this to generate the appropriate electronic image to overlay.

One class of augmented reality system finesses this problem by projecting images onto the real world itself. For example, video images may be projected onto a paper desktop. So long as the desktop and camera are fixed, the system can be calibrated and, thereafter, registration guaranteed (see Figure 20.4, left).

20.3.6 Current and future applications of VR

To date, the most extensive use of VR has been for military simulations and militaristic games. More esoteric and less violent uses of VR have been proposed; the imagination is the limit! Since worlds with arbitrary physics and behaviors can be created, anything is possible within VR. One interesting suggestion is the idea of VR holidays – by walking into a VR environment, you can go on holiday to the tropical rainforest, go on safari, walk on the moon, fly over the cities of the world, sunbathe on a beach or ski in the mountains, all without moving from the room!

DESIGN FOCUS

Applications of augmented reality

Augmented reality techniques hold great promise, and have been investigated especially in situations involving the maintenance or assembly of complex equipment. One example is the maintenance of photocopiers. There are many different photocopier models, and field engineers have to look up service details in large manuals and then attempt to relate the photographs and diagrams to the actual equipment before them. With augmented reality, instructions can be shown in front of their eyes including labeling of all parts. Another example is in the electronics of large aircraft. The wiring looms that run from end to end may include dozens of colored wires, each of which has to be routed to the right place. With augmented reality, the schematic wiring diagrams can be overlaid onto the physical wiring, helping the engineer to correctly identify and route each wire.

Note that, in both cases, accurate registration between the real and electronic data is essential. However, in both cases the degree of image analysis needed is limited. In the case of the photocopier, the system can be told what photocopier is being repaired and then all it needs to do is work out where the copier is and what its orientation is (and possibly also whether doors are open, etc.). Given that the system can hold schematics and photographs, this is not beyond current image-processing capabilities. The case of the wiring loom is more difficult, as the individual wires may be too small for the resolution of digital cameras. In this case, it may be better simply to color-code the schematic accurately and rely on the engineer's eyesight – the best interfaces make *appropriate* use of human and computer capabilities.

A more serious application is a medical one, in which a virtual operation can be carried out on the actual patient: the patient's scans provide data for a computer model of the body, which can then be operated on by a surgeon until he perfects the technique for that particular person. Once correct, the actual operation can be performed. The best such simulations include *force feedback* where the surgeon can feel resistance as the scalpel is drawn through the virtual body.

VR is also being used in experimental treatments for phobias [178]. Vivid imagery is often used as part of the treatment for conditions such as arachnophobia, agoraphobia or acrophobia. For example, a patient afraid of heights can ascend in a virtual glass lift. Knowing that the experience is simulated does not remove the fear. However, the anxiety is reduced by the combination of unrealness and the ability to control and, if necessary, quickly escape the virtual environment. By increasing the height and duration of the lift journey, patients can gradually conquer their fears in readiness for real-world experiences.

20.4   INFORMATION AND DATA VISUALIZATION

Virtual reality and 3D displays can be used to visualize scientific data and other complex information. Whether or not 3D representations are used, animation techniques, especially when under interactive user control, can give a sense of engagement with data, and encourage discovery and pattern formation.

20.4.1 Scientific and technical data

Three-dimensional representations of scientific and technical data can be classified by the number of dimensions in the virtual world that correspond to physical spatial dimensions, as opposed to those that correspond to more abstract parameters.

Perhaps the most engaging images are where all three dimensions have some physical validity. An example of this is the virtual wind tunnel [50]. In a physical wind tunnel, an accurate model of an aircraft is constructed and then subjected to winds that, when appropriately scaled, correspond to realistic situations. The intention is to investigate patterns of air movement and pressure, for example to discover those places where turbulence forms. Of course, air is invisible, so small pieces of ribbon may be attached to the aircraft surface, small bubbles released into the chamber or polarized light used to expose the hidden airflows. In the virtual wind tunnel, air movements are calculated using the equations of fluid dynamics. An engineer can then see the simulated aircraft using VR goggles and can move around a (virtual) baton from which stream (virtual) bubbles (Figure 20.6). By moving the baton to different parts of the aircraft, areas of interest can be investigated.

Model making can be very expensive and time consuming, so the virtual wind tunnel can save money and increase the rate at which changes can be made and

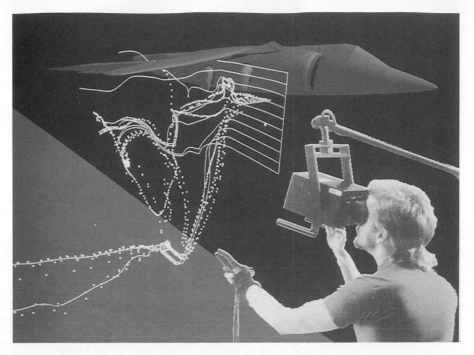

Figure 20.6   Virtual wind tunnel. Reprinted from *Animation and Scientific Visualisation*, R. A. Earnshaw and D. Watson (eds), 1993

evaluated. However, there are also ways in which the virtual wind tunnel is more effective than a real wind tunnel. In the virtual wind tunnel, engineers can get as close as they like to the simulated aircraft in order to investigate particular details. In the real tunnel this would involve stepping inside the tunnel, which would disrupt the airflow, making any measurements valueless.

The next step away for 3D reality is when two of the dimensions represent a physical plane and the third is used to represent some data for each point. For example, a relief map can be drawn where the height at any point represents average annual rainfall (as opposed to the height of the terrain). In any such representation it is hard to choose a viewing point, as it is likely that tall structures in the foreground will hide important features in the background. This is probably why such representations are quite rare in static paper publications.

Finally, we have the case where only one or none of the dimensions represents a spatial dimension. For example, most spreadsheet packages support a range of 3D graph options that allow you to regard two columns as x and y coordinates, while a third column is used as the height. In this case, none of the 2D or 3D patterns in the image corresponds to real-world features. However, we can use our ability to discern 3D features to help us understand and appreciate this more abstract data.

DESIGN FOCUS

Getting the size right

When faced with a 2D histogram it is the area that we perceive as being the size of a bar, not the height. Survey data of family groups at a fun fair have shown that 25% had only one child, 50% had two children, 10% had three children and the remaining 15% of families had between four and six children.

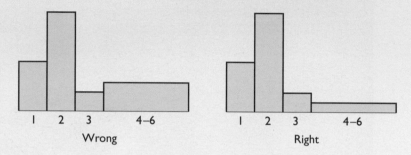

If we display the height of the 4–6 group proportional to the percentage of families it makes it look as if this is much more than 15% of the data. This is because the column is three times wider than the rest. We actually perceive the data to be in the ratio 25:50:10:45. The right thing to do is to draw the area of the columns proportional to the number of families, which makes the data look right.

Similar problems arise in 3D representations. If we draw a map with 3D columns proportional to the population rising from each country, we will probably not be able to see anything except a single enormous block for China! We should display the heights of the blocks proportional to the population density. Of course, if we start with density data, we can simply use height to start with.

If data ranges are extremely large, we may use non-linear (for example, logarithmic) scales. Users clearly need to be aware of this, but at least if density data are used, bigger areas/volumes represent bigger data.

20.4.2 Structured information

Scientific data are typically numeric, so can easily be mapped onto a dimension in virtual space. In contrast, the data sets that arise in information systems typically have many discrete attributes and structures: hierarchies, networks and, most complex of all, free text. Examples of hierarchies include file trees and organization charts. Examples of networks include program flow charts and hypertext structures.

One common approach is to convert the discrete structure into some measure of similarity. For a hypertext network this might be the number of links that need to be traversed between two nodes; for free text the similarity of two documents may be the proportion of words they have in common. A range of techniques can then be applied to map the data points into two or three dimensions, preserving as well as possible the similarity measures (similar points are closer). These techniques include

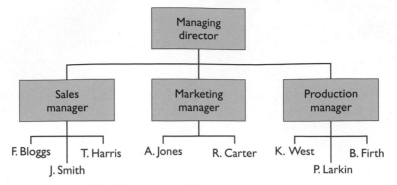

Figure 20.7 Two-dimensional organization chart

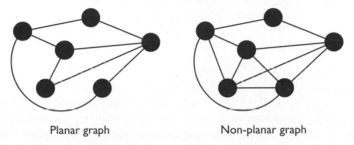

Figure 20.8 Two-dimensional network layout

statistical multi-dimensional scaling, some kinds of self-organizing neural networks, and simulated gravity. Although the dimensions that arise from these techniques are arbitrary, the visual mapping allows users to see clusters and other structures within the data set.

There are standard ways of representing networks and hierarchies in two dimensions. Figure 20.7 shows a typical organization chart. Notice that even with such a small chart the names have been staggered slightly to make more space available. In fact, very large wall displays are usually needed even for quite small organizations.

Space problems are also evident with flow charts and network diagrams, with charts frequently split over several pages. Furthermore, it is only possible to lay out certain sorts of network (called planar graphs) in two dimensions without lines crossing (Figure 20.8).

The third dimension can be used to help with both network and hierarchy layout. In the case of a network, nodes can be laid out in three dimensions, both reducing clutter and meaning that lines no longer cross, but simply pass by one another. Of course, this has the disadvantage that nodes and lines may obscure one another, but so long as the user can rotate the network or fly around it, these hidden nodes can be seen. Similar techniques can be used for hierarchies. Figure 20.9 shows the Camtree, part of the Xerox PARC Information Visualizer [310]. The Camtree displays a hierarchy from left to right, with the subordinate nodes arranged in a circle about the base of a cone with their parent as apex. Although the tree grows from left

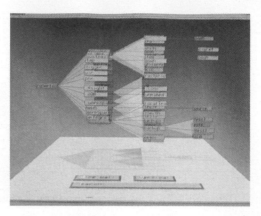

Figure 20.9   Camtree – visualizing hierarchies [310]. Copyright © 1991 ACM, Inc. Reprinted by permission

to right, this growth is far less than the corresponding 2D representation. When a node is selected within the tree, the system rotates the cones so that the node and its parents are closest to you. Thus, although some nodes are hidden at any particular moment, it is possible to view the entire tree. Also notice how the shadows both enhance the impression of three-dimensionality and give additional information about the hidden parts of the tree. A second hierarchy visualization, the Conetree, is similar to the Camtree but displays the hierarchy from top to bottom as in the organization chart. Although these two representations are very similar, it is far easier to display names for each node in the Camtree. This is because most hierarchies are relatively broader than they are deep. Hierarchies with up to 10,000 nodes have been visualized with the Camtree and Conetree.

20.4.3 Time and interactivity

We can consider time and visualization from two sides. On the one hand, many data sets include temporal values (dates, periods, etc.) that we wish to visualize. On the other hand, the passage of time can itself be used in order to visualize other types of data. In 2D graphs, time is often mapped onto one spatial dimension; for example, showing the monthly sales figures of a company. Where the time-varying data are themselves 2D images, multiple snapshots can be used. Both comic books and technical manuals use successive images to show movement and changes, often augmented by arrows, streamlines or blurring to give an impression of direction and speed. Another type of temporal data is where events occur at irregular intervals. Timelines are often used for this sort of data, where one dimension is used to represent time and the second axis is used to represent the type of activity. Events and periods are marked as icons or bars on the time axis along the line of their respective type. One of the most common examples of this is the Gantt chart for representing activity on tasks within a project. This sort of technique can also be used in computer

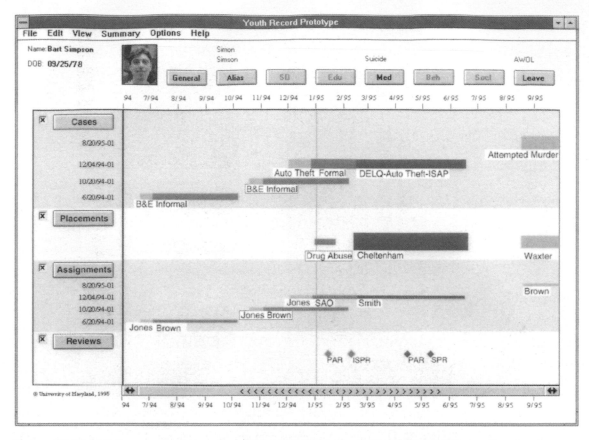

Figure 20.10   Lifelines – visualizing personal histories [291]. Copyright © 1996 ACM, Inc. Reprinted by permission

visualization; for example, Lifelines [291] uses a Gantt-chart-like representation to visualize medical and court records (Figure 20.10).

The passage of time can also be used to aid visualization. The simplest case is where time in the data is mapped directly onto time at the interface. That is, the time-varying data are simply replayed. The rate of replay need not be in real time: a year's worth of weekly sales figures could be replayed in less than a minute at a week per second. Standard video controls can be used in the interface to such a visualization. Alternatively, a spatial dimension (or other parameter) may be mapped onto the passage of time at the interface. Consider a static but solid 3D object. Looking at a few 3D rendered images, one can gain a good understanding of the outside of the object. However, it is very hard to see what it is like inside. Several slices of the object can be displayed simultaneously, but obviously the number of these and the size of each are limited. One solution to this is to show successive cross-sections as an animation, gradually moving the 'cutting' plane, mapping distance through the object onto time. An example of this is the Visible Human Project. It is only possible

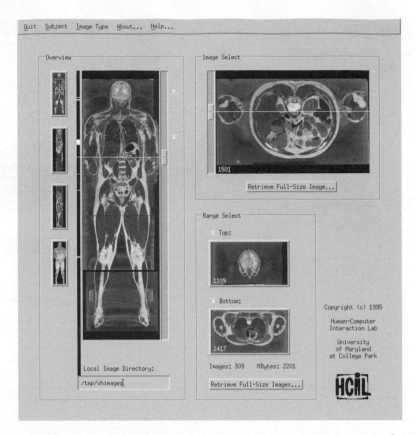

Figure 20.11 Interactive browser for the Visible Human. [271]. Copyright © 1996 ACM, Inc. Reprinted by permission

to see a few slices simultaneously (even at low resolution), but one can watch a movie showing slices from the head down through the torso to the feet. From the movie one can clearly see the bones and internal organs (artificially colored).

Perhaps the most powerful use of time is when changes are under user control – interactivity. This is central even to our perception of three dimensions. Stereo vision, shadows and lighting all give an impression of depth, but it is the ability to move around an object, to view it at different angles, which gives a true sense of a real 3D object. Interactivity is also a key factor in the virtual wind tunnel. A movie of the wind tunnel would be useful, but the real power comes because the engineer can move about inside the tunnel, using bubble tracers to investigate particular areas of interest. Another example of the use of interaction is the interface in Figure 20.11 for viewing the Visible Human [271]. A slider is used to control the position of the viewed slice in the body. In this case the slider corresponds to spatial dimension. In other systems sliders are used to select values or ranges for parameters. One system, Homefinder, uses max–min sliders to select price ranges, number of rooms, etc., while in real time a map shows the locations of all houses satisfying the criteria. Even more complex data are visualized using the Influence Explorer [353], which

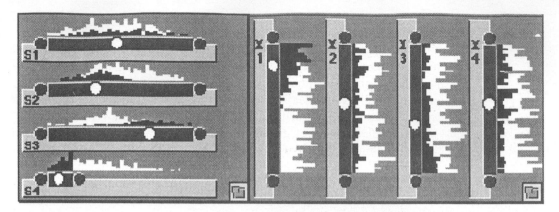

Figure 20.12 The Influence Explorer. [353]. Copyright © 1996 ACM, Inc. Reprinted by permission

shows the results of a multi-parameter/multiple result mathematical model. The user selects parameter/performance ranges and in real time a histogram displays the number of simulations that satisfy all or most of the criteria (Figure 20.12). Color is used to represent full versus partial matches.

20.5   SUMMARY

Moving our focus of interaction away from the traditional two-dimensional graphical user interface on the desktop presents many exciting and new challenges to the field of HCI. Weiser's vision of ubiquitous computing was human-centered, and many years later, it still presents a grand challenge for those who wish to address this new interaction paradigm. These challenges cover three main areas. First, the physical interface between humans and a computationally enhanced environment requires a shift in emphasis for both input and output. Secondly, while a 'killer app' for ubicomp has arrived in the form of person–person communication, the more interesting challenge is to understand what general features of ubicomp applications matter. The past decade has seen two emergent features – context awareness and automated capture. The next decade should see an increased focus on continuous services that support everyday activities. Thirdly, different theories of human cognition inform the design of ubicomp applications, as 'knowledge in the world' becomes even more important. The design process must better incorporate an understanding of the invisible meaning of everyday activities. Evaluation of the utility of ubicomp applications is harder to do in controlled usability laboratories, so we must build a new form of laboratory that facilitates observation and measurement as well as everyday activity.

The technologies of virtual and augmented reality are no longer reserved for laboratories with multi-million-dollar equipment, but can be experienced on ordinary machines and over the internet. Early applications of virtual and augmented reality were often for military training, and for ubicomp it was the office place. Now, much of this technology is showing its promise in the entertainment and leisure domains. Many advances of VR and other forms of 3D graphics are an important resource in the visualization of scientific data and other complex information. In particular, by interacting with the visualization, the user may obtain a deeper understanding of the data and discover features that would be impossible with static representations.

Since the first edition of this book, virtual reality and interactive visualization have moved from being interesting blue-skies research areas to accepted commercial technologies. We expect that in future editions we will see ubicomp move from being an exciting, but not yet practical, research area into being simply part of day-to-day life.

EXERCISES

20.1 Many researchers are beginning to explore the potential of ubiquitous computing technologies and applications in the home environment. Discuss how the application themes of context awareness, automated capture and the continuous interaction of everyday computing are relevant to domestic life. Focus your answer on the challenges of family life or life for an aging population.

20.2 Virtual reality has found a number of applications in the games market. Is this a suitable use of such technology? Discuss the possible benefits and disadvantages of exploiting leading edge technology in a leisure market.

20.3 Data visualization techniques have often increased our comprehension of phenomena: consider the effect that 3D graphics has had on looking at complex models such as those of the atmosphere or the ocean, or in understanding the structure of molecules. What do you consider to be the areas that may benefit most from virtual reality visualization techniques?

RECOMMENDED READING

G. D. Abowd, E. D. Mynatt, Charting past, present and future research in ubiquitous computing, *ACM Transactions in Human–Computer Interaction*, special issue on HCI research in the new millennium, Vol. 7, No. 1, pp. 29–58, March 2000.

This paper provides an excellent overview of the advances of ubiquitous computing from an HCI perspective and expands on many of the ubicomp issues introduced in this chapter. Another version of this work, by Abowd, Mynatt and Rodden, appeared in the inaugural issue of *IEEE Pervasive Computing*.

R. Pausch, Virtual reality on five dollars a day. In *Proceedings of ACM CHI'91*, pp. 265–70, ACM Press, 1991.

A classic paper which not only showed that virtual reality could be available at a much lower cost than previously assumed, but also exposed the critical factors for a sense of engagement.

R. A. Earnshaw and D. Watson, editors, *Animation and Scientific Visualisation*, Academic Press, 1993.
A collection with examples of applications, techniques and theory of scientific visualization and containing over 100 color plates of various kinds of visualization.

S. K. Card, J. D. Mackinlay and B. Shneiderman, editors, *Readings in Information Visualization. Using Vision to Think*. Morgan Kaufmann, 1999.
A wonderful resource, 47 key papers on all aspects of information visualization.

R. Spence, *Information Visualization*. ACM Press/Addison-Wesley, 2001.
A more personal overview and introduction to information visualization, including a structured view of the subject and detailed analysis of selected techniques.

21 HYPERTEXT, MULTIMEDIA AND THE WORLD WIDE WEB

OVERVIEW

- Hypertext allows documents to be linked in a non-linear fashion.

- Multimedia incorporates different media: sound, images, video.

- The world wide web is a global hypermedia system.

- Animation and video can show information that is difficult to convey statically.

- Applications of hypermedia include online help, education and e-commerce.

- Design for the world wide web illustrates general hypermedia design, but also has its own special problems.

- Dynamic web content can be used for simple online demonstration or for complete web-based business applications.

21.1   INTRODUCTION

Increases in desktop computing power have enabled the rapid growth of the multi-media industry. CD-ROMs, stereo sound and often video input/output are now part of the specification of standard personal computers. Furthermore, the dreams of Vannevar Bush and Ted Nelson (see Chapter 4) have now become reality in the world wide web, which links computers, information and ultimately people across the world.

In this chapter we look at the distinctive features of hypertext and multimedia, where they are used and their potential problems. The world wide web is just one example, albeit an important one, of a hypertext system. We will first consider some of the common features of hypermedia including different types of content and application areas. Diagrams and photographs can enliven text, but some of the most exciting effects are seen when the computational power of the computer is used to allow animation, video and interactive features. We will also consider in Section 21.3 the 'lost in hyperspace' problem, how to design hypertext that is easy to understand and to navigate and how features such as bookmarks, the back button and search can make hypertext and the web accessible. The chapter then focusses on the web. We will look at the technology that underlies the web and how issues of networking influence usability. We will then consider static web content including graphics and streamed media. Finally, we will review ways in which web pages can be made dynamic through interactive content and through server-side generation of web pages from databases.

21.2   UNDERSTANDING HYPERTEXT

21.2.1 Hypertext definition – text, hypertext and multimedia

Although pictures and sculpture came first, it is text – the written word – that is commonly seen as the defining point of civilization; pre-literate and oral societies are often regarded as pre-history simply because they have no extant story. Hiero-glyphics, Babylonian mud tablets, the Book of Kells, the Caxton press: these are the stepping-stones toward our current information-centric society.

All these traditional texts share a common linear nature. Aristotle in his *Poetics* said that a story must have a beginning, a middle and an end, and even postmodern non-linear narrative is actually written in a linear fashion even though the events may not be causally connected.

This linearity is partly because of the nature of the media used – papyrus scroll, painted frieze or paper book – but perhaps more significantly because we are crea-tures in linear time. We are natural story-tellers and natural story-hearers. This is why, in Chapter 5, we found that scenarios were so powerful. The skill of the author is in producing an experience for the reader that introduces new events and new concepts so that they fit meaningfully into what has gone before.

However, there are classes of activities where the reader needs to establish their own path through a text. For example, in the online documentation or help systems discussed in Chapter 11, the user wants to know the right thing for him at that moment, not a full description of the system (although of course tutorials are typically linear). During some forms of exploratory learning the learners may want to follow their own paths through material: each one delving into details in different parts. Experts in a subject, too, may well want to remind themselves of some particular issue or fact.

For such purposes the linear form of a traditional text is a hindrance. For example, when using manuals, the user may not understand all the terms used in the text, and will have to keep going back to a different series of pages to look up the definitions, returning to the original pages and trying to pick up the thread of discussion afterwards. Paper books include tables of contents or indexes and encyclopedias and dictionaries are designed for non-linear reading. However, still the reader is left physically skipping back and forth.

Hypertext attempts to get around these limitations of text by structuring it into a mesh rather than a line. This allows a number of different pages to be accessed from the current one, and, if the hypertext is well designed, the user should find it easier to follow his own particular idea through the mesh rather than being forced down one route. Typically, hypertext systems incorporate diagrams, photographs and other media as well as text. Such systems are often known as *multimedia* or *hypermedia* systems, although the three terms are often used interchangeably.

A hypertext system comprises a number of pages and a set of *links* that are used to connect pages together. The links can join any page to any other page, and there can be more than one link per page. Thus a hypertext document does not simply start a linear progression and follow it to an end, but goes in lots of different directions, some of which terminate, while others link back into different parts of the document (see Figure 21.1, which illustrates the difference between linear text and hypertext).

There are many different ways of traversing the network, and so there are many different ways of reading a hypertext document – the intention is that the user is able

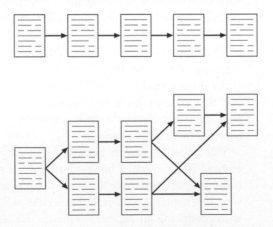

Figure 21.1   Typical structures of linear text and hypertext

to read it in the way that suits him best. Links can exist at the end of pages, with the user choosing which one to follow, or can be embedded within the document itself. For example, in an online manual, all the technical words may be linked directly to their definitions in the glossary. Simply clicking on an unknown word takes the user to the relevant place in the glossary. Another unknown word encountered there can also be traced back to its definition and then the user can easily return to his original place in the manual. The positions of these links are known as *hot-spots* since they respond to mouse clicks. Hot-spots can also be embedded within diagrams, pictures or maps, allowing the user to focus his attention on aspects that interest him.

21.2.2 Rich content

As well as static material – text and static diagrams and photographs – hypertext systems may also include more dynamic material such as animation, video and audio clips, and even full computer applications.

Animation

Animation is the term given to the addition of motion to images, making them move, alter and change in time. A simple example of animation in an interface is in the form of a clock. Digital clocks can flick by the seconds, whilst others imitate Salvador Dali and bend and warp one numeral into the next. Analog clocks have moving hour and minute hands, with an optional second hand sweeping round the clock face. Such a desktop accessory is found in a lot of interface setups, and the additional processing time required to produce such effects is no longer a major factor.

Another common use for animation in current windowing systems is to animate the cursor. Instead of simply having a basic pointer always on the screen, many interfaces now use the typical 16×16 bitmap that makes up the cursor to indicate more complex information. We saw in Chapter 3 that there are a number of different static cursors in use, but animation takes this one stage further by adding motion to the images. This is usually done to indicate that some process is in progress, to confirm to the user that something is actually happening. Animating the cursor means that messages do not need to be printed out to a window, making it a neat and concise way of presenting the desired information. On the Macintosh, work in progress is indicated by a watch icon, with the hands moving round and round, or by a spinning disk. One system uses a stick person, apparently doing weightlifting, to show that heavy work is in progress, whilst another has an hourglass trickling down.

Non-cursor process indicators often take the form of a pop-up box with a moving slider, or a stick person walking backwards and forwards. These are important to give the user a sense of progress and to prevent inactivity being interpreted as an indication of a system fault. In addition, *animated icons* may be used to show system state; for example, Netscape Navigator has shooting stars to indicate that it is downloading information. Animated icons can also be used to make the meaning of the icon clearer. This is especially useful for icons representing actions that are not well represented by static images. However, such animation must be used sparingly to avoid distraction!

Animation can be used to great effect to show changes in data sets, where slow fluctuations can be visualized with the help of rippling three-dimensional colored surfaces, or abrupt changes shown by sudden discontinuities in an otherwise regular motion.

Animation is also used in a cartoon-like way, where animated objects are used to perform particular functions for the user. For example, in an animated help system, a character can appear on the screen and interact with the user, guiding him through a number of stages of help before being dismissed. Such a guide can be endowed with a certain character, making the interaction less impersonal and more interesting for the user, who becomes more involved with the system and is happy to learn more about it.

Talking heads

One use of animation is to produce *talking heads* [359]. These are images of human faces either completely computer generated or derived from photographs of real people. They are based on models of human anatomy so that realistic lip movement can be synchronized with generated speech. Surprisingly, this is not just a fun activity but is actually useful! One important use is for deaf or partially deaf users who can lip read the image. Another application is to synchronize the lips with telephone speech allowing a form of video phone over low-bandwidth telephone lines.

These faces can also express emotion. Users have imputed personality to computers since they only had flashing lights. By simulating human expressions the designer can express intended affective states rather than leaving this to the user. For example, this could be useful in a learning environment where the students might naturally view the computer as a harsh, unforgiving teacher, but by means of a suitable face and expressions could be induced to regard it as a colleague or facilitator in learning.

Video and audio

In a media dominated world, there are strong arguments for using video or audio material as part of hypertext systems whether for education, entertainment or reference. Both audio and video material are expensive and time consuming to produce, but increasingly even home-PC systems include video and audio editing as standard. For example, the iMac includes a suite for editing video and burning DVDs. Combined with digital video cameras these bring the production of audio/video material into the reach of many. Furthermore, standard formats such as QuickTime allow this material to be embedded in web pages for easy distribution. Of course, quality video production requires extensive experience, but then so does text!

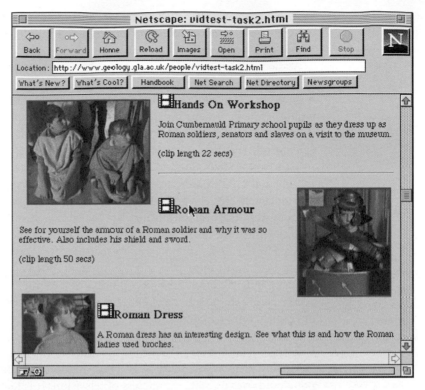

Figure 21.2 Hunterian Museum – learning about the Romans. Source [194a] reprinted with permission of Springer-Verlag; Netscape browser window © 2002 Netscape Communications Corporation, used by permission

Perhaps the biggest problem with audio and video is still the memory requirements. As we saw in Chapter 2, this is becoming more manageable as memory capacities increase, but it will probably continue to be a major problem, especially for web-based material, for some time to come.

The most common use of video is as a clip to be embedded within a text or graphical document or web page. For example, Figure 21.2 shows an example of a prototype website produced by Glasgow University for the Hunterian Museum [194] including video clips. (Notice, too, the use of the still picture for each video clip and the indication of the length of the clip.)

Longer video sequences are, of course, more linear than plain text. This may be acceptable if the hypertext is acting effectively as an index for video material. For example, one might have a collection of silent movies online and access them through a website. However, if the video is regarded as an integrated part of the hyper-media experience it needs to be active in some way as well. It is possible to have hot-spots in video images just as in graphics; however, clicking on a gymnastics star to get information on her recent performance may be difficult if she is in the middle of an exercise on the asymmetric bars. Interactive television manages this by having a smaller number of context sensitive options, or images may be frozen to enable exploration.

Perhaps gaming stations best manage this interaction between video and other material, as clips of live action or pre-recorded high-quality generated images are interspersed seamlessly with game playing.

Audio material can be used in the same way as 'clips' within a document; for example, in an interactive guide to Beethoven's music. Because most hypertext material is visual, audio can also be used for background music or sound effects to establish mood, or to provide 'voice-over' for static graphics or animations.

Audio material may be stored as sound samples, that is digital recordings, which can include instruments, voice or other sounds. As we are often more sensitive to poor sound than poor video images, and sounds are, by definition, constantly changing, it can be harder to *compress* sound than video. MP3, used for much web downloadable music, recruits knowledge of the auditory system to achieve its high compression. For example, if there are two simultaneous sounds, one a lot louder than the other, the quieter one can be played with less fidelity because its details are masked by the louder sound. For pure instrumental music, MIDI files simply record which instrument must play and the duration, pitch and loudness of each note – basically a digital form of the sheet music.

Any sound in the interface can, of course, be potentially annoying, especially in open-plan working environments, and so audio should be used with care and it should be easy to mute. As these words are being written, the current author's wife is struggling to turn off an annoying musical backing to a web page she is viewing!

Moving pictures are excellent at conveying information, and exert a quite hypnotic hold over us; note the success of television. It is fair to say that many design practices will have to be updated to make the most of the possibilities that these techniques offer; moreover, it is also the case that people are unsure how to get the most out of such technology. The techniques required to gain maximum benefit from moving images are very different from those that are used for static or minimal motion displays, and designers do not have enough experience to start applying the relevant technology at the relevant time. It may well be that computer interface designers will have to study the techniques of the film makers and cartoonists before they start to discover the real benefits that these techniques can provide. Indeed, partly due to Brenda Laurel's influential book *Computers as Theatre* [207], drama theory is now a respectable and popular topic in HCI.

Computation, intelligence and interaction

Of course the good thing about a computer is that not only can it *show* things that have previously been prepared, it can also *do* things. This book has an index, but it does not contain every word in the text (it may also refer to parts of the text that do not have a particular word). However, the web search can look through all the chapters and find any words you want.

More interactive hypermedia may contain embedded games or applications. For example, Figure 21.3 shows a puzzle from the website of one of the authors (Alan), a sort of 2D Rubik's cube that you can play online. Hypermedia running on the user's own computer may interact closely with other applications; for example, on a

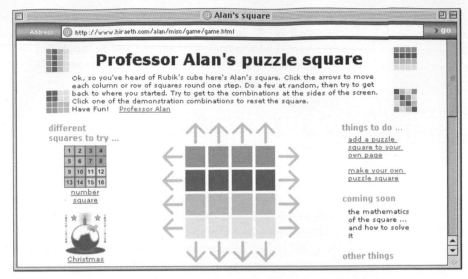

Figure 21.3   Interacting with hypertext – Professor Alan's puzzle square.
Screen shot frame reprinted by permission from Microsoft Corporation

Macintosh HyperCard stacks can control applications using AppleEvents, or on a Windows platform hypermedia can include ActiveX components.

Whilst the 'text' in hypertext suggests passive content under the user's control, some hypermedia may contain more intelligent components or agents actively working to shape the experience for the user. For example, some educational hypertexts adapt their content depending on a model of the learner. Similarly e-commerce sites may suggest additional products to buy depending on your previous purchasing and browsing behavior.

21.2.3 Delivery technology

On the computer

Some hypertexts, in particular help systems, are downloaded or installed permanently on a computer. This has the advantage of instant access and such applications need not use a standard viewer but may include their own bespoke browsing software. However, with media-rich hypertexts containing substantial graphics, video and audio clips it may be impractical to store everything on hard disk. Also, for copyright protection, some systems will deliberately not allow themselves to be copied from their original distribution media.

Many hypermedia systems are supplied on CD-ROM. This has the advantage of reasonably large capacity (650–700 Mbytes), but access is slower than with installed systems. For highly dynamic material, such as educational media, a special player is installed; alternatively, material such as software documentation may use a standard format such as web pages.

DVD delivered material is interesting as it is not text enriched with video, but instead a movie that has been 'made interactive'. As older computers tend to have only CD-ROM drives, it is not possible yet to supply, for example, tutorial material on DVD and know that it could be used on any machine.

On the web

Of course, the *world wide web* is the best-known multimedia hypertext system of all. The world wide web offers a rich environment for the presentation of information. Documents can be constructed that are very different from paper versions; basic text can be augmented through the use of hypertext links to other documents, while graphics can easily be incorporated as pictures, photographs, icons, page dividing bars, or backgrounds. Pages can also have hypertext links embedded into different regions, which take the user to a different page or graphic if they are clicked on; these are known as active image maps. These features allow web pages to become interactive, acting as the interface to the information as well as its holder. Dynamic material in the form of movies and sounds is also available to the designer; all these features push web page design well away from the conventional paper-based kind.

However, the fact that the web has many more technological features than a book doesn't mean that web pages are necessarily better than their paper counterparts. Also, the fact that a web page is packed full of features doesn't imply that it gets its message across effectively. Designing web pages is a developing art, and should be viewed in much the same way as designing any other interactive system. Good pages have been developed with the reader as the focus, and act as effective interaction tools or presentation tools to allow the user to obtain the information he is looking for most effectively.

The web is an example of the usability of the medium being paramount rather than the technological supremacy of certain aspects of it. For any single aspect of the web, there are custom multimedia systems that are far superior in terms of quality, usability, speed and so on. However, the common availability of web browsers on multiple platforms and the low-tech and usable nature of the system have ensured the web's popularity and made it ubiquitous.

The web allows the user to browse documents and follow links transparently, with the underlying system taking care of the details of fetching the data from different parts of the world. Theoretically, as far as the user is concerned, any page can be reached as easily as any other; geographical location ceases to become important, whereas linking by content is crucial. The ability for anyone to publish information on the web is one factor in its success as a multimedia system, but the fact that anyone can create a page and, by linking it to others already in existence, immediately integrate their opinions seamlessly into the information space is another.

On the move

Mobile phones, PDAs (personal digital assistants), and notebook computers have all increased the demand to have hypermedia available on the move. Furthermore, across many countries governments have sold franchises for high-bandwidth mobile services. After spending billions on these franchises the telecommunications giants *really* want people to use new mobile services!

Notebook computers can use just the same mechanisms as desktop computers, using CD-ROM or DVD for standalone material, or connecting to the web through wireless access points or through modems linked to mobile phone networks. However, the fact that the computer is mobile means that location can be used as a key into context-aware hypermedia showing different content depending on location. The 'stick e note' system developed by the University of Kent uses a sticky note metaphor with notes stuck to particular locations [49]. Only when you visit the location does the note become visible. This is a bit like an image map on a web page, but rather than clicking a mouse over an image to link to information, here you need to physically move to a location! Another example is the GUIDE system, which uses various means to detect location (closest network access point or GPS) and then delivers appropriate tourist information [69].

PDA access poses different problems. They often have standard web browsers, but of course on a substantially smaller screen. This may mean designing special pages or being especially careful to design ones that resize well. Because PDAs are often not network connected there are also systems to allow access to information when disconnected. For example, AvantGo (www.avantgo.com) allows users to select 'channels' of interest and then, when the PDA is docked, downloads any pages that have changed, so that users always have the most up-to-date information possible.

By nature, mobile phones are (nearly) always connected to a network. However, memory and screen size are even more constrained. Some phones allow download-able applets so that small dynamic applications can be used. More web-like content can be accessed via WAP (wireless application protocol), which, like HTTP (hypertext transfer protocol) for the web, gives access to remote servers. WAP content can be produced as static or dynamic content using a mark-up language called WML, which is a simplified version of HTML (hypertext markup language). This allows hyperlinks like the web and even simple images, but due to the small screen size most pages consist mainly of small amounts of information or simple lists of links. See the book WAP site at /e3/wap.wml

21.2.4 Application areas

There are many applications of hypermedia, too many to describe in detail here. However, it is worth noting the type of domains in which hypermedia systems have proved successful, looking briefly at some example systems.

Rapid prototyping

Although now lacking the wealth of features expected of a hypermedia system, HyperCard on Macintosh computers has been very influential as a basis for experimental hypertext systems. HyperCard uses the metaphor of a card index, around which the user can navigate. Each card can hold text, diagrams, photographs, bitmaps and so on, and hot-spots on the cards allow movement between cards. Cards may also contain forward and backward buttons and a home icon, to allow the user to move sequentially and start from scratch respectively. HyperCard can be used for a range of applications including information management and teaching.

However, HyperCard's simple scripting language and easy to produce graphical interfaces meant it was also used extensively as a *rapid prototyping tool* for generating interactive systems. In fact, HyperCard stacks for both single-user and networked applications are available from the book website.

For similar reasons, other hypermedia tools such as Macromedia Flash and Director are often used to produce dynamic interface mock-ups or even fully functioning systems. The web, too, is used like this, both to deliver applications and also as a way of mocking up an application interface as a series of storyboard web pages.

Help and documentation

Hypermedia systems are ideally suited to online manuals and other help system applications (see Chapter 10). They allow user-oriented access to the information, and support browsing. In addition the information can be organized hierarchically, with successive selections providing more detailed information. This supports the varying needs that users have, such as quick reference, usage information, full details and so on. Many commercial help systems use hypermedia-style help. Good examples are the Sun Guide system, HyperCard help and Microsoft Windows help (used by many Windows applications).

Educational systems are another common application. Hypermedia provides an environment for the learner to explore, in her own time and at her own pace. The inclusion of animation and graphics can allow the user to see things happen as well as read about them. So, for example, animation can be used to simulate an experiment. Educational applications are discussed in more detail in Section 21.6.

Education and e-learning

Hypertext and hypermedia are used extensively in educational settings, as they allow varied subjects to be related to each other in numerous ways so that the learner can investigate the links between different areas. In contrast to *computer-aided learning* (*CAL*) packages, hypermedia allows a student-controlled learning process.

An early example of a hypermedia learning environment that inspired many subsequent systems was Intermedia [385]. This is a hypermedia system built and used at Brown University to support teaching in subjects as varied as English literature and biology. The system includes text, diagrams, photos and so on. Both learners and teachers can add information and links, giving students access to each other's opinions as well as those of their tutors. A map provides an overall view of the information for direct access and navigation, with links providing browsing facilities in the normal way. Intermedia has been successfully used for university-level teaching, and can be seen as a forerunner of the educational resources now facilitated by the web.

Microcosm is an open hypermedia system, developed in the Electronics and Computer Science Department at the University of Southampton and shown in

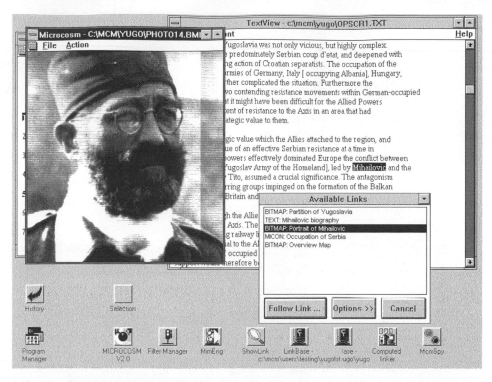

Figure 21.4 Microcosm: an open hypermedia environment shown running a teaching application entitled 'The civil war in Yugoslavia 1941–45' (developed by the Departments of Electronics and Computer Science and History at the University of Southampton and used by permission)

Figure 21.4; it allows users to browse through large amounts of multimedia information by following links. Microcosm does not contain links explicitly hardwired into its structure, but instead holds a database of link sources and destinations. Not only does this allow processes to examine the links divorced from their surrounding information, but it allows links to be made to read-only media such as CD-ROM, video discs and external web pages. Microcosm is able to integrate many different types of media, including other applications, and provides a set of viewing tools to look at text, bitmaps, video, audio and other component information media.

Outside organized educational settings, the increasing availability of multimedia PCs has made the home an attractive marketplace for CD-ROM-based educational software. One example of this is Dorling Kindersley's series of CD-ROMs based on their popular large-format book series.

As in other areas, the web has come to dominate most educational uses of technology. The term e-learning is sometimes used to refer to all forms of electronic learning, but is most often used for learning delivered via the web. This may be distance learning or it may be augmenting classroom teaching using the web.

The eClass project (previously called Classroom 2000) is an example of the latter [4]. It records pen strokes on an electronic whiteboard during a lesson (Figure 21.5) along with audio and video, and then allows students to review the material later

Figure 21.5 eClass – recording a lecture

Figure 21.6 eClass – indexed playback on student's web browser.
Source: Netscape browser window © 2002 Netscape Communications
Corporation, used by permission

using a web interface (Figure 21.6). Each slide presentation and pen stroke is time-stamped so that students can click on a particular pen mark on the web interface and the audio or video is replayed from that point in the lecture.

Collaboration and community

Although strictly not hypertext, the web has become a central platform for collaborative applications and community. These use the hypertext structure of the web to structure and access shared resources and message areas. For example Yahoo! Groups (groups.yahoo.com) allows mailing lists, shared images (such as family photo albums), web archives of the mailing list and chat, all accessed through a web interface.

Establishing a sense of community can be very important on websites as it is one way to ensure loyalty and get visitors to return. This may involve explicit community features such as chat areas, or may simply be a matter of using a design, language and image that suggests a site which is open and listening to 'readers' [214].

E-commerce

For some companies the web is simply another sales opportunity. Many readers will have used online stores such as Amazon or bought from an auction site such as eBay. Hypertext's use of hierarchies, links, images and so on, makes it ideal for displaying certain kinds of product. Actual buying and selling requires not only security at the level of the networks, websites, etc., but also trust. When you walk into a shop you can see the person you are dealing with, and the fact that it is physically there today gives you confidence that it will be there tomorrow if anything goes wrong. How to build and ensure this trust is an active area in HCI research (see, for example [307]).

21.3   FINDING THINGS

21.3.1 Lost in hyperspace

Although the non-linear structure of hypertext is very powerful, it can also be confusing. It is easy to lose track of where you are, a problem that has been called 'lost in hyperspace'. There are two elements to this feeling of 'lostness'.

The first is cognitive and related to content. In a linear text, when a topic is being described, the writer knows what the reader has already seen. In a hypertext, the reader can browse the text in any order. Each page or node has to be written virtually independently, but, of course, in reality it cannot be written entirely without any assumption of prior knowledge. As the reader encounters fragmentary information, it cannot be properly integrated, leading to confusion about the topic.

The second is related to navigation and structure. Although the hypertext may have a hierarchical or other structure, the user may navigate by hyperlinks that move across this main structure. It is easy to lose track of where you are and where you have been.

The solution to the former issue is to design the information better. The solution to the latter is to give users better ways of understanding where they are and of navigating in the hypertext. To say 'the solution' is disingenuous – there is no simple 'solution'. If we want to provide information that allows complex, unplanned, non-linear access, there will probably always be problems. However, good design can help!

21.3.2 Designing structure

We discussed the importance of good structural design in Chapter 5. Some of the task analysis techniques presented in Chapter 15 may be useful in giving a task-oriented or knowledge-orientated breakdown of a hypertext. In some areas there may be pre-existing understood structures to mirror; for example, the faculty and departmental structure of a university, or the main disciplines (circulatory, neurological, etc.) within medicine.

In a paper format one is stuck with a single structure, which can lead to tensions: for example, the fact that in this book structural design is discussed in several places. As another example, imagine a car mechanic using a manual. She might want to use the classical breakdown into transmission, fuel system, etc., while fault finding, but if she were dismantling the engine it might be more useful to look at the car components in terms of physical location.

If multiple structures are used, you have to consider what to do about the common material. For example, if we examine a car hypermedia text under 'engine compartment' and get to the fuel pump, this would also appear in the functional view under 'fuel system'. Such common elements may be replicated. This has the advantage that the material can be presented in ways that make sense given their context, but it can also lead to inconsistencies.

Alternatively we may make links across the hierarchy at some level; for example, the engine compartment may have a diagram of the engine with a labeled arrow saying 'fuel pump (fuel system)', which takes you to the description of the pump in the fuel system part of the hypertext. Notice, too, the importance of making links that go to different parts of the hypertext very clear, following the 'knowing where you are going' principle from Chapter 5 (Section 5.6.1).

An in-between solution would be to have a small dedicated description of the fuel pump in the context of the engine compartment: perhaps describing how it is physically connected to the engine block and how the piping is routed. This could then be linked to a more extensive explanation of its function in the fuel system section, using a 'see also' link.

In all cases it is important that the structure and the naming of parts is meaningful for the user. In a more detailed and theoretical approach to the 'knowing where you are going' principle, Pirolli and others have developed information foraging theory [289]. This uses an analogy with foraging animals searching for patches of food and trying to make decisions about when to move to a different area or stay with the food available, and, if they move, where to go. This is likened to the way an information seeker browses, making decisions about whether to stick with the information available or spend time looking for more, and, if more is needed, deciding where to seek it. For animals, the scent of food is very important in deciding where to go, and information foraging theory suggests that it is crucial that our structures, access methods and detailed page designs give users some sort of scent – hints about what they may find – to allow them to make good browsing decisions.

21.3.3 Making navigation easier

No matter how well designed the site structure is, there will still be problems: because the user does not understand the structure; or because the user has individual needs that the designer has not foreseen; or because even a good structure is not perfect. However, there are various things that can make it easier for users.

One solution is to provide a map of the hypertext document, identifying the current position of the reader within it. Links to home or end points can then be identified and the user is less likely to get lost. This may be a separate part of the hypertext; for example, some websites have a site map link leading to a special page, and many help systems have a table of contents view. Alternatively, the site map can be woven into the layout of the document; for example, some sites have an outliner-style sidebar listing the main sections and drilling down to the current location. This acts both as an indication of where you are in the site (like the breadcrumbs discussed in Chapter 5) and as a constant reminder of the overall site structure.

One way to deal with the differing uses that are envisaged for a hypertext is to provide the user with 'recommended routes' through hypertext documents. If these are too strongly defined they defeat the objectives of the system. However, successful applications have been developed that have a guided tour or bus tour metaphor [13]. Users can follow the tour, which takes them through one or more selected routes, but can deviate from it at interesting points whenever they wish. Users can then return to the 'bus stop' to continue the tour when they have satisfied their interest.

Another type of hypertext takes the form of 'levels of access' to a document. Different levels of access privilege 'see' different amounts of information. A document structured in this way may provide one level of access that gives only a brief overview of the topic. The next level of access presents a fuller description of the system, while the next level may also include information regarding the precise meaning of technical terms used in the system. The final level of access may add historical information and suchlike. The user can choose at which level he wants to read the document, cutting out irrelevant information while obtaining all the necessary details. Such a document tends to be linear in nature, which makes navigating and printing it easier, but removes the user's choice in structuring his progress through it.

Once information has been retrieved, a paper version is often needed. Printing a document requires the pages to be in a particular order, but hypertext does not support the concept of one single order. This is against the ethos of hypertext, which intends the user to structure the information in the way that suits him best. It can therefore be difficult to get a hard copy of the information that is required.

Although there is no simple way to linearize a hypertext, one can at least make it possible to print individual linear parts, whether single pages or groups of linearly linked pages. In general, you should not rely on the print facility of a browser as this is printing a page designed for on-screen viewing. You may notice websites offering printer friendly pages. These may be in a different format such as PDF, or may simply be web pages without sidebar navigation aids, etc.

For both web and non-web hypertext, remember that once the page is printed someone who hasn't seen the full hypertext may read it. If they like what they read, can they find the source? If a web page is likely to be printed, do include the full URL on the page, perhaps in the footer. On pages from a CD-ROM or similar hypertext, include perhaps a copyright notice with details of the original.

21.3.4 History, bookmarks and external links

Hypertext viewers and web browsers usually have some sort of history mechanism to allow you to see where you have been, and a more stack-based system using the 'back' button that allows you to backtrack through previously visited pages. The back button may be used where a user has followed a hyperlink and then decided it was to the wrong place, or alternatively, when browsing back and forth from a central page that contains lots of links. The latter is called *hub and spoke* browsing. In fact, in studies of web browsing the back button accounted for 30% of all navigation actions [63]. Other studies have shown frequent revisiting of pages during a single browsing session [341].

Although the back button is used extensively, it is used relatively little to go back more then one step. For error correction this makes sense, but for general revisiting one might think that moving back several steps would be common. Possibly, one reason for this is confusion about the meaning of the back button; indeed a formal comparison of back and history mechanisms in four different hypertext and web browsers found that the operation of back and history were subtly different in each [104].

For longer-term revisiting, browsers typically support some form of bookmarking of favorite pages. Both this and, on the web, external links from other people's sites mean that users may enter your hypertext at locations other than the top level or home page. On the web this is called *deep linking*. Many websites rely on the user remembering where they have come from to make sense of a page. If a page does not adequately show where it fits, then a user coming to it from outside may have no idea what site it is from, or why they are reading the material. Furthermore, if the original site depended on the user pressing 'back' to return to higher levels of the site hierarchy it may be impossible for a visitor to find the rest of your site at all!

All pages should therefore make clear where they belong and have links into the full site structure. For example, the breadcrumbs along the top of a web page function both to make the context clear and, if they are 'live', as navigation back into the site hierarchy (see Chapter 5, Section 5.6.1).

Framed websites are particularly difficult. The material you want to bookmark or link to may be one of the frame content pages, but the URL you can see or bookmark is that of the overall frameset. This may either discourage linking to the site or, if circumvented, it may mean linking directly to the content of one of the frames, which is then very likely to lack sufficient context, being designed to be seen within the frameset. Search engines, too, may generate links to individual frames in a frameset. Many web style guides heavily discourage the use of frames for this reason. If the site is designed using a development tool that supports page templates, or is being dynamically generated, there is rarely any need for frames as most of the effects can be obtained using other page formatting.

Very occasionally you may want to discourage deep linking; for example, if the framed page is more of an interactive application or you know the inner structure is unlikely to stay constant. In such cases you can include a small piece of script in the inner framed pages that makes them redirect to the outer frame if they are ever opened 'bare' in a window. This means that if a site or a search engine does link into the inner frames, following the link takes the user to the full, framed site.

For more on usability issues of frames see /e3/online/frames/

21.3.5 Indices, directories and search

As well as a hierarchical table of contents structure, many help systems, hypertexts, and for that matter paper books, have some kind of index. Note that an index is not a complete list of all words in a document. If this were the case then the index for this book would be as big as the rest of the book! The words in an index are chosen because they are significant key phrases or words with a domain meaning, and not every occurrence of a word is indexed, only those deemed in some way important. The main difference between an electronic index and a paper one is that with the paper index you have to physically look up the page after finding the word in the index, whereas in an electronic index the links are 'live' so you can simply click to the content.

On the web an index would be very big (!); however, directory services such as Yahoo! (www.yahoo.com) or the Open Directory Project (ODP) (www.dmoz.org) can be seen as a form of index. The main difference is that while an index is simply an alphabetical list of keywords, web directories give a hierarchical categorization to sites. The categorization is done either by self-submission, or, in the case of quality directories such as ODP or Yahoo!, by experts in the relevant field.

For exhaustive searching by keywords, some kind of automated search is required. In the case of a standalone hypertext, the viewer application may do this either by using a pre-computed electronic index of all word occurrences used by the hypertext, or by scanning it on demand. The latter will take longer for each search, but may be more effective if the hypertext is not too big or the material is rapidly changing. Where the hypertext is generated from a database, the search may be performed on the underlying data rather than the generated pages.

In the case of the web the content is dynamically changing, but it would be imposs-ible to scan the whole web every time you wanted to find anything! Search engines such as Google or AltaVista use web crawling. Starting from an initial collection of pages they look for all links from these pages. These links are followed and the new pages reached are scanned, and so on. As pages are visited, an index is built of which words occur in which pages. The search engines typically do not keep a copy of every page visited, but may just keep the title and the first hundred or so words on each page. Even the index is vast and so the most common words are usually not indexed; these are called *stop words*. When you do a search, the search engine uses the index and the summary information to construct the results page with links to the actual pages. Because it is using the page summaries and not looking at the pages themselves, it is possible that a page may have been removed or changed since the index was constructed.

The web is enormous and so the number of pages containing a given word is enormous. Web search engines allow you to search for several words at once or for exact phrases, or, with Boolean searches, to specify using logical and/or options what is required: for example, 'engine AND NOT car'.

Even when looking for multiple words or Boolean queries, the number of results may be in the tens or hundreds of thousands. So search engines need some way to rank pages. Some use simple, content-based measures such as the number of times the requested words occur, whether they occur in the title or body, whether they occur near the beginning or end of the page. Some search engines keep track of how many times users click through for specific pages and so can build up a model of popularity. In addition, some search engines sell the right to be top, based on keywords, or have a special advertisers or sponsors links section.

Google gained its reputation for quality based on the way it ranks pages, and seems almost magically to get just what you want in the first page or so of results, and often as the very top ranked result. It does this by using the structure of links. It uses heuristics such as: if a page is linked from lots of places it is likely to be good, especially if the pages linking to it are already known to be good; and also the opposite: if a page links to lots of good pages then it is a good page.

Some specialist searches, for example for video, books, etc., and even some more general-purpose search engines, allow you to rate pages you have visited. Ratings are then used to rank the more popular pages for future visitors. These are called recommender systems [304]. As well as explicit recommendations, e-commerce sites often track your browsing on the site and use this to build a profile of which users are similar to you. The books or goods they purchased may then be suggested to you.

When designing web pages, it is possible to make them more 'search engine friendly' by adding 'META' tags in the head section of the web page, in particular keywords and description, as well as a relevant 'TITLE' tag. In the early days, people tried to fool search engines by including invisible lines with lots of popular keywords at the top of their document. Now most search engines are able to detect such sub-terfuge and discard such pages – so be honest! However, it is worth making sure that something near the top of your page says what it is about!

Search engines have trouble scanning sites with many generated pages, especially if they are accessed through a search box only, for example a dictionary or thesaurus. There are many large data sets available on the web, often public domain or freely accessible, which contain high-quality information – often better quality than any old web page – but are not easy to find unless you know the site. This has been called the hidden web and some estimates say that it is an order of magnitude larger than the visible web. Currently, there are no accepted ways to link such material into broader web searches although some products, such as onCue described in Chapter 18 (Section 18.4.1) attempt to link into these publicly accessible data sources.

Searching for research literature

When you are asked to do a project or a literature review you will probably reach straight for Google! You will get many pages that are not relevant and many that appear to be, but how do you know which are worth reading? Unless, of course, you just assume that Google knows best!

Part of the process by which papers are accepted into a conference or journal is peer review – the papers are read and judged by other workers in the field. On the web, it is hard to judge the quality of information you find.

There are some heuristics you can use. Is the online page an electronic version of an article published in a refereed paper publication? Where is the page: in a major corporation or university, or a free home page? This doesn't mean that you can't find good pages by unknown people, but existing position is a heuristic. If the author has a publications page, are other articles published in good venues? Do other pages that you have judged to be of good quality reference an online article? And, of course, not to be forgotten . . . does it make sense? No matter who wrote it, if it is not well argued then don't believe it!

If you are looking for articles in computing you can also use *citeseer* (citeseer.jn.nec.com). This is a search engine for online copies of papers, hosted by NEC Corporation. Unlike standard web search engines, this only searches for articles, and in particular is able to scan PDF, PostScript and other electronic formats. Not only does citeseer search by title, author, etc., it is also a citation index. For each paper, it scans it to find the bibliography at the end. When you look at the entry for a paper, it shows you what other papers it references (looking back in time) and also which further papers have cited it (looking forward), as the diagram shows.

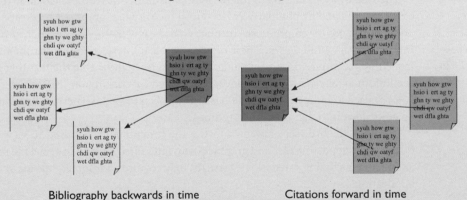

Bibliography backwards in time   Citations forward in time

21.4   WEB TECHNOLOGY AND ISSUES

The web has featured strongly already in this chapter and for the remainder of the chapter we will focus exclusively on it.

21.4.1 Basics

The web consists of a set of protocols built on top of the *internet* that, in theory, allow multimedia documents to be created and read from any connected computer in the world. The web supports hypertext, graphics, sound and movies, and, to structure and describe the information, uses a language called *HTML* (hypertext markup language) or in some cases, XML (extensible markup language). HTML is a markup language that allows hypertext links, images, sounds and movies to be embedded into text, and it provides some facilities for describing how these components are laid out. HTML documents are interpreted by a viewer, known as a *browser*; there are many browsers, and each can interpret HTML in subtly different ways, or support different levels of functionality, which means that a web page viewed through one browser can look very different from the same page viewed through another. The web requires no particular multimedia capabilities from the machines that run the browsers; for example, if sound is unavailable on a particular machine, then obviously no sound is heard but the browser still displays the text happily.

The web owes its success to many factors, including the robustness and (relative) ease of use offered by popular browsers from the very first graphical browser *Mosaic*, and continued in commercial browsers such as *Netscape Navigator*, *Microsoft Internet Explorer* and *Opera*. These offer a graphical interface to the document, controlled by the mouse. Hypertext links are shown by highlighting the text that acts as the link in an alternative color, and are activated by clicking on the link. A further color is used to indicate a link that has already been visited. Hypertext links can also be embedded into regions within an image.

Although the browser contains most of the functionality required to view a web document, supporting text and graphics in an integrated package, special file formats and media, including some movie formats, may require additional plug-ins or helper applications.

As well as publishing personal, corporate and governmental information, the web is used as a source of entertainment, an advertising medium, a communication environment, and more. The vast and ever-increasing quantity of information available on the web certainly exacerbates the user's 'lost in hyperspace' problems (Section 21.3.1). But increased familiarity with hypertext, and better web page design, are aiding the situation at least as much as technological efforts to create maps and indexes of the data. Another problem is that of information overload: multimedia images, gigabytes of graphics and mountains of text swamp the reader in a glitzy but unmoderated world, in which the fact that almost anyone can make anything available leads to the gemstones often being lost amongst the slag.

As well as static web content such as text and images, many pages are *dynamic*: for example, they may be generated from data held in databases, respond to individual information entered into forms, or include dynamic elements such as Java applets. We will discuss this dynamic content further in Section 21.6.

21.4.2 Web servers and web clients

Whereas a conventional PC program runs and is displayed on one computer, the web is *distributed*. Different parts of it run on different computers, often in different countries of the world. They are linked, of course, by the internet, an enormous global computer network (see also Chapter 2, Section 2.9.3).

The pages are stored on web servers that may be on a company's own premises or in special data centers. Because they are networked, the webmaster for a site can upload pages to the server from wherever she is. For example, the web pages for www.hcibook.com are stored in a data center several thousand miles from where any of the authors live!

Your machine, the PC running the web browser, is called a *client* because it wants the pages from the servers. When you click on a link your web browser works out the full URL of the page it needs: say 'http://www.hcibook.com/e3/authors.html'. It splits this into parts. The first part is the protocol 'http' which says how it talks to the server (other alternatives include 'ftp'). The second part 'www.hcibook.com' is the host name, that is the name of the web server containing the requested page. The last part '/e3/authors.html' gives the particular file on the site. The browser then establishes a connection to the required web server (in this case 'www.hcibook.com'), and sends a message, formatted using the HTTP protocol, to the web server, which then finds the requested html file (or image, or other file type) and returns it to the browser, which then displays it to you.

If the page contains images the same process is repeated for each image, and if the page is a framed one for each frame within the page.

21.4.3 Network issues

The fact that the web is networked raises a series of issues that can impact on usability.

Network capacity is called *bandwidth*. This is a measure of the amount of information that can pass down the channel in a given time. For example, a typical modem speed is 56 kbs – that is 56 kilobits per second. This equates to about 6000 characters per second. This sounds fine until you realize that images may take many tens or hundreds of characters (bytes) to encode . . . this is why many have renamed the web the 'world wide wait'!

However, bandwidth is not the only important measure. There is also the time it takes for a message to get across the network from your machine to the web server and back. This delay is called *latency*. Latency is caused by several factors – the finite speed of electrical or optical signals (no faster than the speed of light), and delays

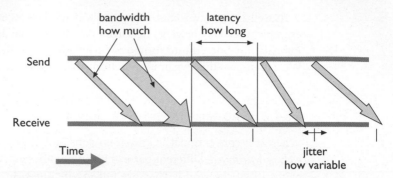

Figure 21.7 Bandwidth, latency and jitter

at routers along the way that take messages from one computer network and pass them on. This latency may not always be the same, varying with the exact route through the network traveled by a message, the current load on the different routers, etc. Variability in the latency is called *jitter* (see Figure 21.7).

As well as the underlying latency and jitter of the network, each layer of network software adds its own. The underlying internet protocols are *lossy*, that is messages can be lost. When this happens, higher level software (the TCP – transmission control protocol – layer) notices and resends messages to give reliable communication. These losses mean that the average delays increase, but also that the jitter increases – a lost and resent message takes more time than one that gets there first time.

There may also be an appreciable amount of time setting up a new connection, which may outweigh the time taken to actually send data. This is particularly a problem with sites containing many small images.

Web usability guides will give plenty of advice on ways to minimize web page size, but one recommendation, which sadly we promulgated too in earlier editions of this book, should be taken with a pinch of salt. Virtually every guide suggests keeping pages short – enough to fit within a single screen of a typical web browser. Now there are arguments for this – some users may not realize there is more content off the bottom of the screen, the material lower down may be ignored, search engines are better able to index multiple small pages. However, the reason that is often given, namely download time, is not a good one. Of course, an enormous page takes a long time to load, but on the whole interaction is faster if a larger page is downloaded and then scrolled through than if the user has to click links on many small pages and wait for each.

This latter point is an example of a broader issue. In general, if you want rapid *feedback*, try to make the interaction happen at the web browser end. Feedback that involves a cycle to the web server and back, except for intranets on fast networks, will take several seconds, which is too slow for fluid interaction. Unfortunately, for collaborative applications there is no way to prevent at least some network delays for *feedthrough* (see Chapter 19, Section 19.6.3), but even then it is important to prevent too many cycles of network messages.

Delivering WAP content – balancing usability and feedback

Because of the tiny screens on phones it is difficult to scroll through a long WAP page. However, if every link involved going back to the WAP server the feedback would be very slow. For this reason WML divides WAP content into *stacks* of *notes*. For the user browsing the content, the note is the parallel of the normal web page. A link may be to a note in the same stack or one in a different stack; the user is largely unaware of which it is. However, when you request a note in a stack the whole stack is downloaded to the WAP browser on your phone. This means that links to notes in the same stack have much faster feedback. By carefully arranging content within stacks and notes, the overall user experience can be improved.

21.5   STATIC WEB CONTENT

21.5.1 The message and the medium

One thing is often forgotten when web pages are created. It is of vital importance, and hence will be discussed first.

It is content.

Many people assume that because they can make information available on the web, they should. Unfortunately, because it is very easy to publish information, much less care is taken with the actual content. Material may be nonsense, it may be incorrect, it may not read well, or be incomplete, or inane.

Excellent page design can make useless material look attractive, but it still remains useless material. On the other hand, poor design can mean that excellent material is never seen by potential readers, as they have become bored, or intolerant of the medium, or confused, or for a host of other reasons have aborted their attempts to download and view the information. Pages do have to look immediately interesting and attractive if people are to spend time, effort and, because of the communication costs, money, in viewing them; the user-centered nature of the medium makes this imperative. This is in marked contrast to television or cinema or other dynamic media, which are not under any direct user control, where information is presented to a passive audience. With web documents, people have actually to want to see the information, and make an effort to retrieve it, which clearly must have an influence on design.

Whatever is being presented, underlying all the comments made on good and bad design, the fundamental message is that, for the user group or groups who are targeted, the content should be worth reading.

When it is likely that a user will require a paper copy of the information made available over the web, ideally they should be able to download it in one go as a single complete file, with the same information content but possibly a different layout. Paper does not have the same inbuilt hypertextual and active capabilities as the web page, and will be accessed in a predominantly linear fashion.

21.5.2 Text

Because web pages are displayed on many different machines, there are only a small set of fonts that can be guaranteed to be available: a standard font and a typewriter font (e.g. `courier`) with bold and italic versions in different sizes. However, it is possible to specify preferred fonts and many of these such as Arial, Verdana or Comic Sans are available on most web platforms. The difficult thing is to balance fine tuning the appearance of the text on one platform with making it readable on all.

The various structured styles such as headings allow the web designer to create material that will lay out passably on all platforms. But these offer a fairly coarse level of control. The size and boldness of the heading should be chosen carefully; for example, huge dark fonts on a page can look loud and brash.

There is an increasing desire to have fine control. Cascading style sheets (CSS) allow you to specify fonts, line spacing, size, etc., in a similar way to styles in a word processor or DTP package. However, care must be taken. For example, many pages specify fixed point sizes that may not display well on different platforms and can cause problems for people with visual impairments.

The use of color is of great importance for web pages, but it is often abused. First, it should be remembered that a significant proportion of the potential viewers of the page will have problems with color, either because they are using older machines with a limited color palette, or because they have some form of color blindness. Color, when used, should not be the only cue available. Users also bring a deep-rooted emotional interpretation to colors; as we have seen, in some cultures, red is associated with danger and anger, whilst green is regarded as go, or safe. Blue can be a cool color, orange a warm one, and so on.

Links usually change color once they have been accessed, providing cues to the user about what material they have already explored. This means that two distinct but still suitable colors need to be associated with each link, so that the system is acceptable whether or not the links have been activated. Note, too, that consistent use of color can help the user understand the role of particular elements more intuitively, whereas color used for no clear purpose is often distracting.

One common mistake is to put colored text onto a similar colored background so that it becomes nearly invisible. One of the authors had a student who designed a beautifully laid out page of text, and decided to add a background to the page just before demonstrating it to the rest of the group. It was only at the demonstration that he realized that the cool black background he had added made the black text impossible to see!

There are only a limited number of text-placing options: text can be left or right justified, or centered. There are a few predefined formatting styles such as ordered and unordered lists that have additional structure, in the form of indentation from the left margin, with numbering in the case of ordered lists. Vertical positioning is even more limited, but tables and (cautious use of) frames allow a greater degree of horizontal and vertical placement. More precise positioning still can be obtained using 'dynamic HTML' (DHTML), which allows parts of an HTML document (called layers or 'div' sections) to be positioned as if they were separate mini-pages within the browser window. The word 'dynamic' is used because these can then be controlled using JavaScript to produce various animated effects (those pages where little stars follow your mouse!).

Remember that monitors are different sizes and that some people use full-screen windows and others smaller ones. To prevent very long lines, many designers lay out pages within tables that put maximum widths (in pixels) for columns based on typical minimum expected monitor sizes (perhaps 800×600 or even 640×480). If fixed layouts or large graphics are used then they may either display strangely on smaller windows or force the user to scroll horizontally, which many users find confusing. And don't forget people viewing the page on PDAs!

The lack of explicit textual positioning makes it very difficult to produce complex mathematical equations, and the font set available is not rich enough to provide a suitable approximation. Developments in the specification are addressing this, though the intrinsic complexity of typesetting mathematics suggests that it may be a while before a simple, usable solution is found that is acceptable to readers, page designers, and implementors of web browsers alike.

21.5.3 Graphics

Obtaining graphics

There are a number of sites on the web that contain archives of graphical images, icons, backgrounds and so on. There are also paint and image manipulation packages available on almost all computer systems, and scanners and digital cameras, where available, enable the input of photographs and diagrams.

Using graphics

While graphics and icons tend to play a significant role in web page design, their use should be carefully thought out. Graphical images take longer to load than text, and this may become a problem. Text uses 8 bits to represent a character: some rough calculations show that approximately 2000 characters represent about a screenful of information, and so 16,000 bits (2 K) are required. For graphics, one pixel may use 8 bits to represent its color: a page-sized image will be at least 600 by 400 pixels, which will take 1,920,000 bits (240 K), or 120 times as long to load. Put another way, while a picture may tell a thousand words, it takes approximately 50 times as long to appear! Users become bored with operations that take a long time to complete, and are unlikely to wait for ages while a page appears.

Complex backgrounds are the worst offenders in this area; they offer little in the way of added value to the information presented on the page, and cause great frustration for the poor reader. They tend to be designed and tested only on local machines, with high-bandwidth connections between them, which means that the time factor is negligible for the designer/user. However, this disregards the fact that many people accessing the page will be using congested, slow networks, with a transfer rate sometimes down to a few kilobits per second, rather than fast megabit links. Fussy backgrounds also have the unfortunate ability to obscure text, making it very difficult or impossible to read.

Different browsers support different types of functionality, with more recent versions having features that try to alleviate the usability problems introduced by the delay involved in downloading graphics. Most browsers support caching, in which graphics are downloaded once and temporarily stored on the user's local machine. If the same image is reused, it is fetched from the local store far more rapidly than if it were retrieved from the remote site. This clearly has implications for page design: if graphics are to be used, then their reuse wherever possible speeds up the whole process of drawing the page. Complex graphics can sometimes be broken down into a set of items, many of which can be reused and assembled in different ways to add visual impact to the page without causing large delays. Most browsers also offer the option of turning off automatic image loading, so that only the text is downloaded. If a page then appears to be of interest, the graphics can be explicitly requested. It is sometimes possible to set out a page so that it still looks attractive even without the graphics, which is necessary if the user has turned off image loading. There are other browsers that are purely text based and do not support graphics of any sort, and for these HTML offers an additional image attribute that allows a textual description of the image to be used as an alternative. The need to support these different user preferences and browser capabilities provides a great challenge in designing pages that are acceptable to all.

Some browsers have additional features related to image handling as a technological response to the problem of page usability. If the designer specifies the size of the image in advance, the browser can lay out the text on the page first, leaving spaces for the images. This allows the user to continue to read the page contents whilst the images are being downloaded into their respective slots. This capability improves the usability of the page, and so should be supported by the page designer whenever possible, by incorporating the necessary information into the image reference.

Both GIF (graphics interchange format) and JPEG (Joint Photographic Experts Group), the most widely used web graphic image formats, can be saved in forms that allow them to be progressively transmitted. This means that images appear as a whole, but very blurred, version that becomes gradually sharper, rather than appearing in perfect resolution a line at a time. An overall impression of the page and the graphic information appearing is thus given to the user, who is then better informed about whether or not to continue the download.

The JPEG format is optimized for photographic images and makes use of their properties to offer a higher compression ratio and hence faster loading. However, its compression is *lossy*, that is the image reproduced is slightly different from the original, losing certain kinds of visually indistinguishable colors and, more importantly, losing high-frequency change. The latter is because photographs tend to have slowly varying changes with few sharp edges. If sharp-edged images such as diagrams or text labels are stored as JPEGs, small *artifacts* are produced such as ripples appearing around letters and lines. In contrast GIF uses a *lossless* compression so that the image appears exactly as it started. Although GIFs can be used for photographic images, the compression is very poor.

The GIF format also allows *animated GIFs*. These are a sort of mini-slide show or movie where several images are stored in the same file and play one after another. These can be used to produce simple and effective animations, but when overused can lead to very 'noisy' pages.

Active image maps are pictures with defined 'hot' areas, which, when clicked, execute a particular script, usually calling another web page or graphic. The careful use of such maps can transform an interface, but there is an overhead to pay in loading the map and calling and running the script, and this should be considered carefully by a page designer. Another characteristic of image maps is that there is rarely any indication of which areas are active and which are not, and it can be difficult for users to ensure that they have visited all the active regions. For accessing spatially organized information, image maps are very suitable (for example, in a tourist information system, the area about which information is available can be represented well), but for information that does not have any clear spatial analog, their use is more questionable.

Icons

Icons often appear on web pages, and while there are many available to choose from, they should be used with care. On web pages, icons are typically used in one of two ways. They are either visual cues, associating some small picture with different parts of the text (for example, some pages have icon-sized characters that appear next to instructions). Alternatively, they are used in much the same way as in a standard WIMP interface to represent aspects of the functionality of the underlying pages. In this latter case, they must represent their associated functionality in either a concrete or an abstract form. This means that the design of the individual icon has to be carefully thought out, as a lot of information may have to be represented in a small area of screen estate. However, icons are rarely seen on their own, and when placed next to their neighbors, the whole effect has to be pleasing rather than disruptive and garish. Therefore, the group of icons has to be designed together, with a coherent and recognizable style. The picture is broader than this, however: other applications also use icons, which has its advantages and disadvantages. One advantage is that certain icons are already associated with specific functionality (for example, a picture of a floppy disk to represent 'save'). Disadvantages are that it restricts the individuality and style icon sets can show, and may mean that icons designed for one purpose are misunderstood by users because they have seen something similar in another context. It is therefore vital that time is spent in examining the way icons are used in other systems, before importing them into web pages or designing new ones.

Icons sometimes appear for no apparent reason at all, when the page creator has decided that as graphics are supported, a few should be used. One interesting example is the icon that is a copy of the roadworks sign, used in conjunction with text saying something like 'This page still under construction!'.

This is an interesting social effect brought on by the ease of web publishing – incomplete (sometimes even non-existent!) information can be made immediately available. It's like buying a map of the world nowadays and finding 'here be dragons' around the edges because the geographer could not be bothered to draw all the countries in. Most pages can be designed properly before they are made available, structured and presented in a complete and coherent way, allowing for extensions and updates from the beginning.

There are times when the disclaimer 'under construction' has its uses: when critically important information becomes available, publishing it may well be more important than presenting it (much like older maps with their dragons – if maps had only been printed once the whole world had been explored, civilization would be very different today). There is, too, a sense in which web pages can be continually 'under construction', changing, evolving and growing, because of their dynamic nature and the ease with which they can be updated, but this does not obviate the designer's responsibility to create pages that have both form and content.

Graphics and color

Using many different colors within graphics may well result in the browsers for older machines running out of entries in the colormap, with unpredictable consequences. This is often problematical as the browser may be running in tandem with other color applications, and only has a restricted range of colors to begin with.

For many consumer markets, for example in the UK and the US, this is unlikely to be a problem as home machines are often relatively recent. However, many businesses continue to use older PCs so long as they 'do the job' and PDAs may not have a full color palette. Furthermore, in economically deprived areas, where there is computer access it may well be through older or second-hand machines.

If universal access is required it is therefore still wise, where possible, to restrict images to a limited number of colors, taken from the standard 216 color web palette, and to reduce complex color images to simpler approximations. Reducing the number of colors used also allows the depth of the images to be reduced; a change from a default of 8 bits to, say, 4 bits will produce a twofold speedup in image loading. The earlier comments on the use of color obviously apply as much to graphics as they do to text.

One further point should be made about graphics: computer screens are typically limited to a resolution of around 72 dpi (dots per inch), and so either high-resolution images will have to be displayed much larger than actual size, or the increased resolution will be forfeited.

21.5.4 Movies and sound

Movies and sound are both available to users of the web, and hence to page designers. One problem associated with them is actually obtaining appropriate sound and video clips, as they usually require some sort of multimedia capability on behalf of the host machine in order to be able to digitize sound and capture and digitize video. Video suffers from the same problems as graphics, magnified by an order of magnitude or two; it can take extremely large amounts of time for a video segment to download. Video is also not well integrated into the web, requiring the creation of a process to run it that is separate from the page from whence it came. Not all receiving machines have the capability to play video, or sound, and so it is unwise for a designer to rely on these dynamic media to convey information without replicating it elsewhere.

The use of sound and video moves page design further away from the typesetter and toward the sound engineer and cinematographer; the integration of these cinematic media with the enhanced textual capabilities offered by the web is a new domain, in which the techniques that work and those that fail have not yet been fully explored, let alone understood.

The need to download movies and sound (see Figure 21.8) puts sharp limits on the length of clip that can be shown. Streaming media over the internet, such as RealVideo, RealAudio and CuSeeMe, allow potentially unlimited sources. As well as longer prepared clips, these techniques allow live transmission (e.g. live radio broadcasts over RealAudio) and long recorded sequences for asynchronous communication. An excellent use of the latter is the eClass project, introduced in Section 20.2.2, which links recordings of audio and video during a lecture with pen strokes on an electronic whiteboard, so that students can replay the part of a lecture associated with any slide or annotation.

Acceptable streaming video and audio is achieved by a combination of high compression and large client-end buffers. The former leads to loss of quality including blurring and ghosting after rapid changes in screen content. The latter leads to delays, often of several seconds, which makes it impossible to support video conferencing. The challenges of achieving high quality transmissions (e.g. for video on demand) and low latency (e.g. for video conferencing) are active research topics in multimedia technology.

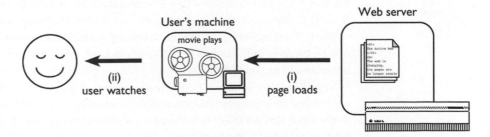

Figure 21.8   Animated GIF or movie needs to download completely

Stepping back a bit to look again at this, note that it is often not raw bandwidth which is the problem on the internet, but packet losses and jitter. Buffering effectively solves this by trading off quality against delay, which is okay for fixed content, or low pace change (as in eClass), but is problematic when we require a *high pace* of interaction (as in video conferencing). CuSeeMe uses little buffering and hence is more likely to suffer break-up of video and audio (see box in Chapter 19, Section 19.3.4, page 675).

21.6 DYNAMIC WEB CONTENT

21.6.1 The active web

In the early days, the web was simply a collection of (largely text) pages linked together. The material was static or slowly changing and much of it authored and updated by hand. Some pages were generated on the fly, in particular the gateways into ftp servers and to gophers, which were so important in adding 'free' content to the web [97]. However, even here the user's model was still of a static repository of information. Web surfers may not have always known where they were, but they had a pretty good idea of what they were seeing and that if they came back it would be the same.

It was a pleasant, if somewhat boring world, but from a usability viewpoint it was wonderful – a consistent interface to terabytes of information. Who could ask for more? Indeed, this is one of the key arguments Nielsen brings against frames-rich sites in his famous alertbox, *Why frames suck (most of the time)* [263] – frames break this simple user model and hence cause trouble. Nielsen calls for a new richer model for the web, which preserves the simplicity of the old model, but which can accommodate and guide the development of new features.

Well, if frames cause trouble, what about applets, timed refreshing pages, rollovers, dynamic content creation? What are we interacting with – is it information, is it computer systems? In fact, this was a problem with hypertext interfaces well before the web existed. Back in 1989, two of the authors, Janet and Alan, wrote about the potential problems of these shifts between passive and active paradigms within an interface. Our solution was to accept these differences, but to make them evident to the user through the design of an effective medium of interaction [103]. Of course it's easy to say . . .

As HCI researchers and designers, we can neither ignore nor uncritically accept new technology in the web. The active web is here, our job is to understand it and to learn how to use it appropriately.

In previous sections, we have already looked at the simplest form of active web page, those with movies, animated gifs or streaming audio. These are simplest, not in the sense that no effort is required – a short video clip may require many days of production effort – but in the sense that they have least user interaction. In this section we'll look at more complex forms of interaction. First, where the actual content is fixed, but the user can change the form of presentation; secondly, at the generation of pages from database content; and finally at the update of database information through the web.

21.6.2 What happens where

When considering dynamic material on the web we need to take the external, user's viewpoint and ask *what* is changing: media, presentation or actual data; by *whom*: by the computer automatically, by the author, by the end-user or by another user; and *how often*, the *pace* of change: seconds, days or months? From a technical standpoint, we also need to know *where* 'computation' is happening: in the user's web-browsing client, in the server, in some other machine or in the human system surrounding it? The 'what happens where' question is the heart of architectural design. It has a major impact on the pace of interaction, both *feedback*, how fast users see the effects of their own actions, and *feedthrough*, how fast they see the effects of others' actions. Also, where the computation happens influences where data has to be moved to with corresponding effects on download times and on the security of the data.

The user view

One set of issues is based on what the end-user sees, the end-user here being the web viewer.

What changes?   This may be a media stream (video, audio or animation) which is changing simply because it is the fundamental nature of the medium. It may be the presentation or view the user has of the underlying content; for example, sorting by different categories or choosing text-only views for blind users. A special form of presentation change is when only a selection of the full data set is shown, and that selection changes. The deepest form of change is when the actual content changes.

By whom?   Who effects the changes? In the case of a media stream or animation, the changes are largely automatic – made by the computer. The other principal sources of change are the site author and the user. However, in complex sites users may see each other's changes – feedthrough.

How often?   Finally, what is the pace of change? Months, days, or while you watch?

We'll use the 'what changes?' categories as we examine alternatives and trade-offs in more detail below. But first we also need to look at the technological constraints.

Technology and security

The fundamental question here is where 'computation' is happening. If pages are changing, there must be some form of 'computation' of those changes. Where does it happen?

Client   One answer is in the user's web-browsing client enabled by Java applets, various plug-ins such as Flash, scripting using JavaScript or VBScript with dynamic HTML layers, CSS and DOM (Domain Object Model).

Server   A second possibility is at the web server using CGI scripts (written in Perl, C, UNIX shell, Java or whatever you like!), Java Servlets, Active Server Pages or one of the other server-specific scripting languages such as PHP. In addition, client-side Java applets are only allowed to connect to networked resources on the same machine as they came from. This means that databases accessed from client-side JDBC (Java database connectivity) must run on the web server (see below).

Another machine   Although the pages are *delivered* from the web server, they may be *constructed* elsewhere. For hand-produced pages, this will usually be on the page author's desktop PC. For generated pages, this may be a PC or a central database server.

People   Of course, as noted earlier, the process of production and update may even involve people!

It is easy to roll out maxims such as 'users first', but, in reality, the choice between these options is not solely a matter of matching the end-user requirements. The best choice also depends on the expertise of the web developer and external limitations. If the server runs on a UNIX machine, you can't expect to use Microsoft Active Server Pages. On the other hand, if you are designing for an intranet you may even get to influence the choice of client software and so make it easier to use more complex client-end solutions.

The choice of technological solution is also heavily influenced by issues of security. When we do any computation on data the computation and the data must be in the same place [299]. This apparently simple factor means that if we want to keep data secure (read 'on well-protected servers') then we must also perform the critical computation on the same servers. For example, imagine a password check. It would be foolish to send the correct password to a Java applet to check!

21.6.3 Fixed content – local interaction and changing views

Probably the most hyped aspect of the web in recent years has been Java. In fact, Java can be used to write server-end software and platform independent standalone programs (not to mention the embedded systems for which it was originally designed!), but the aspect that most people think of is Java applets.

Applets are just one of the techniques that can be added to give client-end interaction (and about the least well integrated into the rest of the page). The most common alternatives are JavaScript, Flash and if you are prepared to limit yourself to Windows platforms, ActiveX plug-ins. These techniques share the characteristic that they are downloaded to the user's own machine (see Figure 21.9) and thereafter all interaction happens on the PC, not across the network (with caveats – see below).

The simplest use of this is to add interaction widgets such as roll-over buttons (usually using JavaScript). More complex pages may add the equivalent of an

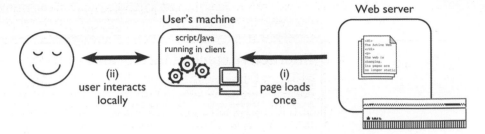

Figure 21.9 Java applet or JavaScript running locally

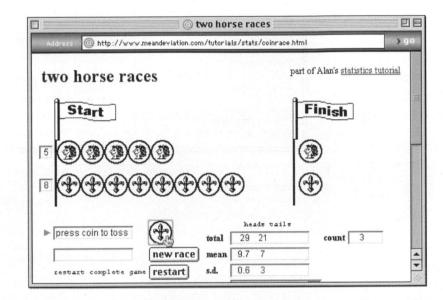

Figure 21.10 Simulated coin tossing using JavaScript. Screen shot frame reprinted by permission from Microsoft Corporation

interactive application on the page. For examples, see Alan's pages on coin tossing experiments (Figure 21.10), which use JavaScript to emulate real and biased coins, and dancing histograms (Figure 21.11), which use a Java applet. See Sun and JavaSoft's own sites for many more examples. The addition of DHTML gives even more opportunities for dynamic pages where parts of the page can move, change size, or change content all without any interaction with the web server.

Notice how this local interaction confuses the static model of the web. What should happen when you go back to a previously visited page, or reload it? Do you get the original state or the last state of your interaction? What happens if you launch a second window on the same page? The actual behavior tends to be browser specific and not always what you would expect! In particular, some browsers do not re-initialize applets on a reload and so if you edit the applet's parameters and then reload you may not see the effects of your changes. More of a problem for web developers than end-users, but very confusing.

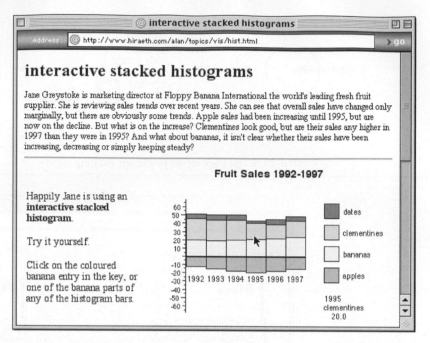

Figure 21.11 Dancing histograms using Java applet. Screen shot frame reprinted by permission from Microsoft Corporation

21.6.4 Search

Some user-driven interaction can be accommodated at the client end, but not all. Consider search engines. It would be foolish to download several megabytes of information so that a Java applet can search it online! Instead, all common web search pages work by submitting forms to the server where CGI programs perform the searches and return results. An additional reason for this approach is that most browsers support forms, but some still do not support Java or scripting in a consistent manner. The web search engine for this book works in this way. The user's keywords are submitted to the server using an HTML form, they are compared against pre-prepared indexes at the server and all matching paragraphs in the book are returned (Figure 21.12). This also reminds us of another reason for not down-loading all the text to the user's machine – security; we don't want to distribute the full electronic text for free!

Notice that, in all the above, the underlying content does not change; the variable factor is the user's input. The computation (working out what to show) needs both the data supplied by the web author (pages, databases, indexes, etc.) and the user's input. The result must end up on the user's screen. Either the data must come to the user's machine (as in Alan's dancing histograms where the histogram data are in applet parameters); or the user's input must go to the server (as with the search). We can see from the examples that the choice between these depends on the required pace of interaction, the size of the data set required, security and available technology.

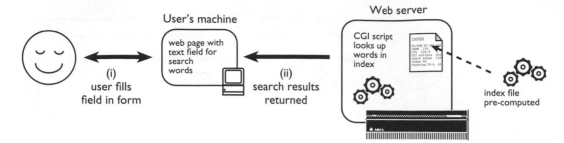

Figure 21.12 HCI book search

21.6.5 Automatic generation

It was evident in the earliest days of the web that a key problem for the future would be maintenance. In the first rush of enthusiasm, individuals and organizations produced extensive and fascinating sites built largely of hand-crafted HTML. Not surprisingly, vast areas of the web are not just static but in perpetual stasis. Web surfing sometimes seems not so much a watersport, but an exercise in archaeology.

From the beginning it was clear that websites would eventually need to be created from databases of content combined with some form of templates or layout description. However, at that stage there were no tools available and those who saw the database future used a variety of ad hoc methods.

Happily, there are now a (sometimes bewildering) array of products for automating web production from existing and bespoke databases. These include vendor-specific products such as Oracle Web Server and Domino (for publishing Lotus Notes), and also more general techniques such as using SQL (structured query language) or JDBC to access databases from CGI scripts or even from running Java applets.

Database-generated websites have many advantages. They make use of existing data sources. They guarantee consistency of different views of the data within the site and between the site and the corporate data. They allow easy generation of tables of contents, indices, and inter-page links. They separate content and layout.

The most dynamic way to get database content on the web is by accessing a database directly from a running applet. The interface can then have any look-and-feel that can be programmed in Java and can allow very rapid interaction with the user. The Java applet can establish an internet connection back to the web server to access data files using HTTP (as if they were web pages), it can connect to a bespoke server (e.g. for chat type applications) or it can use standard database access methods. The latter would normally use JDBC, the Java database access package. Using JDBC the applet can issue complex SQL queries back to the database meaning that some of the most complex work happens there (Figure 21.13).

In all cases, the Java security model built into most web browsers means that the applet can only connect back to the machine from which it came. This means that the database server must run on the *same* machine as the web server. Think about

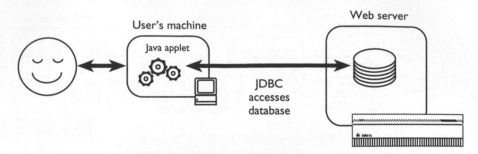

Figure 21.13 Java applet accesses database using JDBC

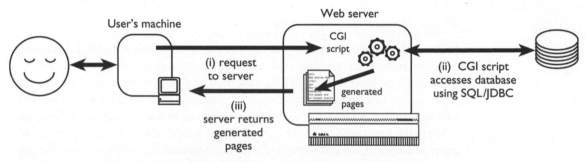

Figure 21.14 CGI script accesses database

this. The most insecure part of any system is usually the web server, both because it is easy to leave loopholes in the many file access permissions and also because it often sits outside the most secure part of a corporate firewall.

The more common solution is where the user uses a web forms interface (or special URL) and then a CGI script runs at the server end accessing the database (Figure 21.14). The CGI script generates a web page, which is then returned to the user. Some of the vendor-specific solutions use essentially this approach but bypass the web-server/CGI step by having their own special web server which accesses the database directly using their own scripting language or templates.

The user interface of such systems is limited to standard HTML features. This is a limitation, but is at least consistent and means that it will work with virtually any browser. Java applets can offer more rapid surface interaction, but both have to wait for the actual data to move between server and client. Of course, the pages generated by a CGI script can themselves contain JavaScript or Java applets for local inter-action, so the difference between the two solutions is not so radical as first appears.

From a security angle, the database accessed from the CGI script can run on a sep-arate machine (using standard database remote access methods or even a Java/JDBC CGI program), thus making the system more secure. However, the database cannot be entirely secure – if the web-server machine is compromised the CGI scripts can be altered to corrupt or modify the database! The special vendor-specific web servers are probably more secure as they don't require a standard web server to be running.

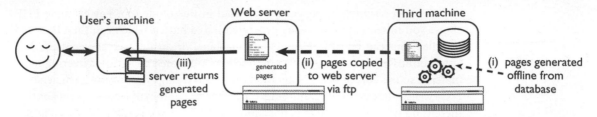

Figure 21.15   Batch pre-generation of web pages

21.6.6 Batch generation

A low-tech but very secure solution is to generate pages offline from a database and then upload them to the web server (Figure 21.15). Many of Alan's earliest web pages were generated in this way from HyperCard stacks.

This is certainly a simple solution as it separates out the task of page generation from that of page delivery. Pages can be generated directly using many standard database packages such as Access or HyperCard. Alternatively, standalone programs in languages such as Visual Basic, Java or C can access a database and output HTML pages. These programs can run on a central computer, or on your own PC. The generating program simply produces a set of HTML pages on your own disk that can be checked locally and then copied onto the web server using ftp or shared network disks. Many people think that this will be difficult, but in reality it is remarkably easy, as you can use the tools you are used to – if you can create a text file you can create HTML. In fact, the snippet of Visual Basic in Figure 21.16 is a trivial but fully functioning HTML generator!

```
Set db = openDatabase("C:\test.mdb");
sql = "select Name, Address from
Personnel;"
Set query = db.OpenRecordset(sql)
Open "out.html" For Output As #1

Print #1, "<h1>Address List</h1>"
query.MoveFirst
While Not query.EOF
  Print #1, "<p>" & query("Name") & " ";
query("Address")
  query.MoveNext
Wend

Close #1
query.Close
```

Figure 21.16   Visual Basic code to generate a web page

Some web scripting languages can be used in this mode too. For example PHP allows you to send the page being generated into a buffer, which can then be saved to a file. This can be run on a separate machine, or on the web server itself. The latter sounds unnecessary; however, web servers are more efficient at delivering static material so this sort of batch generation can be used simply to improve efficiency.

As well as the ease of programming, the offline generation of web pages means that there is no need for an online connection between the web server and the database, so a breach in the security of the web server doesn't compromise your database. In addition, it may mean that the web server can be configured without CGI scripting enabled at all, which considerably increases its security.

The downside is that you can only show the indices and pages that you can pre-compute. So, you could use a product database to produce a pro-forma page for each stock item, plus alphabetic and categorized lists, but you could not produce a special list based on a user's own search criteria.

This low-tech solution is appropriate in many circumstances – whenever the pace of change is low (e.g. overnight or when periodic updates are acceptable), the volume of data is not too large and no online searching is required. Even when some of these conditions don't hold, it is possible to use the general approach. For example, searching can often be arranged by having a much cut-down database or index on the web server with most pages pre-computed.

21.6.7 Dynamic content

The mechanisms we have been discussing manage the feedthrough when the database is updated by some non-web means. Perhaps the most 'active' web pages are those where the content of the pages reacts to and is updateable by the web user.

If pages are generated from database content using either the Java-applet/JDBC method or the CGI method, the same mechanisms can as easily be used to update as to access the database. The feedback of changes to the user is thus effectively instantaneous – you check for seat availability on the theatre web page, select a seat, enter your credit card details and not only is the seat booked, but you can see it change from free to booked on the web page.

This sort of web application opens up many additional problems. You may need to add some form of login or authentication. If credit card numbers are supplied you need to ensure that the web server is secure. Also, without care it is easy to design solutions that accidentally book multiple seats if the user presses the back button and ends up on what appears to be a simple confirmation screen.

If we consider an estate agent's web page, with houses for sale and potential buyers, the situation is rather different. The pace of change is slow; house purchases take place over days, weeks and months. A solution that automatically marked a house as sold would neither be necessary nor desirable! In this case a socio-technical solution using low-tech database generation would probably be sufficient. The web page can have a contact telephone number, email address or message form. Queries via these channels (as well as non-web-based queries) come to the estate agent who

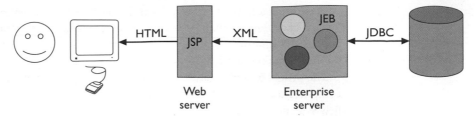

Figure 21.17 *n*-tier architecture

is responsible for deciding when to mark the house 'sold'. There is a continuous loop between web user and the database, but it involves human as well as automatic processes.

Going in the direction of greater complexity, many business applications operate an *n*-tier web architecture. This involves multiple layers of software where the outer layers are concerned more with the user interface and the inner layers more with business functionality. Figure 21.17 shows this using several web standards. The user interacts through a web browser with a web server. The pages are generated using Java Servlet Pages (JSP). To generate the page the servlets connect to Java Enterprise Beans (JEB) on an enterprise server. These are components that encapsulate 'business logic'. For example, in a banking system this could include rules on whether a particular transaction is allowed. These Java Enterprise Beans draw their data from the corporate database using JDBC connections.

21.7 SUMMARY

The non-linear nature of hypertext, in conjunction with the use of different media, can be a powerful combination for education, documentation and marketing. Furthermore, the world wide web has made it possible to publish such material globally at very little cost. However, we saw that users can become confused and disoriented if the structure of a hypertext document is not clear, becoming 'lost in hyperspace'. These problems may become more severe on the web where links cross between sites, and across national borders. Furthermore, web pages are often developed incrementally rather than being pre-planned.

Animation can be used within traditional windowing systems, to aid visualization within special-purpose applications or as part of multimedia systems. The large storage and performance requirements of digital video are still a problem, but one that is gradually being overcome by technological progress. However, the problem of effective use of such technology, beyond the short video clip, may take somewhat longer to resolve.

Dynamic web content can include interactive pages running on the browser or pages generated at the web server from a database. They make use of the same web interface as normal web pages, so in principle they are easy to use. However, they pose additional usability challenges as the user has to understand what is static and what is changing content. Also, it is important to choose carefully where change is happening, whether at the client PC or the web server, as this has a major impact on the nature of interaction, especially the pace of feedback.

The production of multimedia in the form of web pages is now feasible for most computer users and is a good way of making demonstrations and prototypes publicly available. Have a go!

EXERCISES

21.1 Experiment with HyperCard or another hypertext system if you have access to one. As you work through the system, draw a map of the links and connections. Is it clear where you are and where you can get to at any point? If not, how could this be improved?

21.2 Do the same for this book's website and tell us what you think!

21.3 What factors are likely to delay the widespread use of video in interfaces? What applications could benefit most from its use?

21.4 Using a graphics package such as Adobe Photoshop or Macromedia Fireworks save different types of image (photographs, line drawings, text) in different formats (GIF, JPEG, PNG). Compare the file sizes of the different formats, experimenting with different compression ratios (where applicable), numbers of colors, etc.

RECOMMENDED READING

E. J. Conklin, Hypertext: an introduction and survey, *IEEE Computer*, Vol. 20, No. 9, pp. 17–41, September 1987.
A classic review of hypertext.

R. Bentley, U. Busbach, D. Kerr and K. Sikkel, editors, *Groupware and the World Wide Web*, Kluwer, 1997.
The web has become perhaps the most common platform for groupware systems. This collection includes seminal work in this area and covers most of the issues that are still current.

T. Boyle, *Design for Multimedia Learning*, Prentice Hall, 1997.
Covers both educational aspects and multimedia design.

P. Greenspun, *Philip and Alex's Guide to Web Publishing*, Morgan Kaufmann, 1999.
Lovely photos and a strong focus on database-driven web publishing. (Alex probably does his web searching using Lycos.)

J. Niederst, *Learning Web Design: A Beginner's Guide to HTML, Graphics, and Beyond*, O'Reilly, 2001.

J. Niederst, *Web Design in a Nutshell*, O'Reilly, 1998.
    Technically oriented introduction and reference guide for web page design.

A. Badre, *Shaping Web Usability: Interaction Design in Context*, Addison-Wesley, 2002.

J. Nielsen, *Designing Web Usability: The Practice of Simplicity*, New Riders, 2000.

J. Spool, T. Scanlon, W. Schroeder, C. Snyder and T. DeAngelo, *Web Site Usability: A Designer's Guide*, Morgan Kaufmann, 1999.
    Three different approaches to web usability. Badre takes a more traditional HCI and interaction design focus. Nielsen also comes from this angle, but with a more utilitarian view. Spool is the 'other' web usability guru, but doesn't like being called one.

Recommendations for web design are rapidly changing, reflecting developing technology and growing experience. This book's web pages contain links to up-to-date online web style guides.

References

[1]   G. Abowd. Agents: recognition and interaction models. In D. Diaper, D. Gilmore, G. Cockton and B. Shackel, editors, *Human–Computer Interaction – Proceedings INTERACT'90*, pages 143–6. North-Holland, Amsterdam, 1990.

[2]   G. D. Abowd. Classroom 2000: an experiment with the instrumentation of a living educational environment. *IBM Systems Journal*, 38(4):508–30, Special issue on Human–Computer Interaction: a focus on pervasive computing, 1999.

[3]   G. D. Abowd and R. Beale. Users, systems and interfaces: a unifying framework for interaction. In D. Diaper and N. Hammond, editors, *HCI'91: People and Computers VI*, pages 73–87. Cambridge University Press, Cambridge, 1991.

[4]   G. D. Abowd, C. G. Atkeson, J. Brotherton, T. Enqvist, P. Gulley and J. LeMon. Investigating the capture, integration and access problem of ubiquitous computing in an educational setting. *CHI'98 Conference Proceedings*, pages 440–7, Los Angeles, ACM Press, 1998.

[5]   G. D. Abowd, C. G. Atkeson, A. Feinstein, C. Hmelo, R. Kooper, S. Long, N. Sawhney and M. Tan. Teaching and learning as multimedia authoring: the classroom 2000 project. In *Proceedings of the ACM Conference on Multimedia – Multimedia'96*, 1996.

[6]   G. D. Abowd, C. G. Atkeson, J. Hong, S. Long, R. Kooper and M. Pinkerton. Cyberguide: a mobile context aware tour guide. *ACM Wireless Networks*, 3:421–33, 1997.

[7]   G. D. Abowd, A. Dey, R. Orr and J. Brotherton. Context-awareness in wearable and ubiquitous computing. Technical Report GIT-GVU-97-11, GVU Center, Georgia Institute of Technology, June 1997.

[8]   G. Abowd, H. Wang and A. Monk. A formal technique for automated dialogue development. In *Proceedings of Designing Interactive Systems – DIS'95*, pages 219–26. ACM Press, New York, 1995.

[9]   ACM Special Interest Group on Computer–Human Interaction Curriculum Development Group. ACM SIGCHI curricula for human–computer interaction. Technical report, ACM, New York, 1992.

[9a]   C. Alexander, S. Ishikawa and M. Silverstein. *A Pattern Language*. OUP, New York, 1977.

[10]   H. Alexander. *Formally-based Tools and Techniques for Human–Computer Dialogues*. Ellis Horwood, Chichester, 1987.

[11]   D. G. Aliaga. Virtual objects in the real world. *Communications of the ACM*, 40(3):49–54, 1997.

[12]   J. Allanson. Electrophysiological interactive computer systems. *IEEE Computer*, pages 60–5, March 2002.

[13]   L. Allinson and N. Hammond. A learning support environment: the hitch-hiker's guide. In R. McAleese, editor, *Hypertext: Theory into Practice*. Intellect, 1993.

[14]   J. R. Anderson. *The Architecture of Cognition*. Harvard University Press, Cambridge, MA, 1983.

[15]   J. Annett and K. D. Duncan. Task analysis and training design. *Occupational Psychology*, 41:211–21, 1967.

[16]   Apple Research Laboratories. Apple data detectors homepage. Available at http://www.research.apple.com/research/tech/AppleData Detectors/, 1997.

[17]   A. Asthana, M. Cravatts and P. Krzyzanouski. An indoor wireless system for personalized shopping assistance. In L. Cabrera and M. Sattyanarayanan, editors, *Workshop on Mobile Computing Systems and Applications*, pages 69–74. IEEE Computer Society Press, December 1994.

[18]   AT&T Laboratories. Sentient Computing Project Home Page, Cambridge, 2002. http://www.uk.research.att.com/spirit/

[19]   M. Bacigalupi. Designing movement in interactive multimedia: making it meaningful. *Interfaces*, 44:12–15, autumn 2000.

[20]   M. Back, J. Cohen, R. Gold, S. Harrison and S. Minneman. Listen reader: an electronically augmented paper-based book. In *Proceedings of the 2001 ACM Conference on Human Factors in Computing Systems – CHI 2001*, pages 23–9, 2001.

[21]   A. D. Baddeley. *Human Memory: Theory and Practice*, p. 68ff. Lawrence Erlbaum Associates, Hove, 1990.

[22]   A. D. Baddeley and D. J. A. Longman. The influence of length and frequency of training sessions on rate of learning to type. *Ergonomics*, 21:627–35, 1978.

[23]   R. W. Bailey. *Human Performance Engineering: A Guide for System Designers*. Prentice Hall, Englewood Cliffs, NJ, 1982.

[24]   P. Barnard. Interacting cognitive subsystems: a psycholinguistic approach to short-term memory. In A. Ellis, editor, *Progress in the Psychology of Language*, volume 2, chapter 6. Lawrence Erlbaum Associates, Hove, 1985.

[25]   P. Barnard. Cognitive resources and the learning of human–computer dialogs. In J. M. Carroll, editor, *Interfacing Thought: Cognitive Aspects of Human–Computer Interaction*, pages 112–58. MIT Press, Cambridge, MA, 1987.

[26]   P. Barnard and J. May. Interactions with advanced graphical interfaces and the deployment of latent human knowledge. In F. Paternó, editor, *Proc. of Design, Specification and Verification of Interactive Systems, DSVIS'94*. Springer-Verlag, 1995.

[27]   P. Barnard, M. Wilson and A. MacLean. Approximate modelling of cognitive activity with an expert system: a theory-based strategy for developing an interactive design tool. *The Computer Journal*, 31(5):445–56, 1988.

[28]   F. C. Bartlett. *Remembering*. Cambridge University Press, Cambridge, 1932.

[29]   L. Bass and J. Coutaz. *Developing Software for the User Interface*. Addison-Wesley, New York, 1991.

[30]   D. Bauer and C. R. Cavonius. Improving the legibility of visual display units through contrast reversal. In E. Grandjean and E. Vigliani, editors, *Ergonomic Aspects of Visual Display Units*. Taylor and Francis, London, 1980.

[31]   R. Beale and J. Finlay, editors, *Neural Networks and Pattern Recognition in Human–Computer Interaction*. Ellis Horwood, Chichester, 1992.

[32]   M. Begeman, P. Cook, C. Ellis, M. Graf, G. Rein and T. Smith. Project Nick: meetings augmentation and analysis. In D. Peterson, editor, *CSCW'86: Conference on Computer Supported Cooperative Work*, MCC Software Technology Program, Austin, Texas, 1986. ACM Press, New York.

[33]   M. Beigl, H.-W. Gellersen and A. Schmidt. MediaCups: experience with design and use of computer-augmented everyday objects. *Computer Networks*, 35(4):401–9, Special issue on Pervasive Computing, Elsevier, March 2001.

[34]   R. Bentley, W. Appelt, U. Busbach, E. Hinrichs, D. Kerr, S. Sikkel, J. Trevor and G. Woetzel. Basic support for cooperative work on the world wide web. *International Journal of Human–Computer Studies*, 46(6):827–46, Special issue on Innovative Applications of the World Wide Web, Academic Press, June 1997.

[35]   H. Beyer and K. Holtzblatt. *Contextual Design: Defining Customer Centered Systems*, Morgan Kaufmann, 1998.

[36]   M. Blattner, D. Sumikawa and R. Greenberg. Earcons and icons: their structure and common design principles. *Human–Computer Interaction*, 4(1):11–44, 1989.

[36a]   B. W. Boehm. Verifying and validating software requirements and design specifications. *IEEE Software*, January: 75–88, 1984.

[37]   J. Borchers. *A Pattern Approach to Interaction Design*. John Wiley, Chichester, 2001.

[38]   W. A. Bousfield. The occurrence of clustering in recall of randomly arranged associates. *Journal of General Psychology*, 49:229–40, 1953.

[39]   S. Bovair, D. E. Kieras and P. G. Polson. The acquisition and performance of text-editing skill: a cognitive complexity analysis. *Human–Computer Interaction*, 5(1):1–48, 1990.

[40]   J. M. Bowers and S. D. Benford, editors, *Studies in Computer Supported Cooperative Work*. North-Holland, Amsterdam, 1991.

[41]   J. Bowers, G. Button and W. Sharrock. Workflow from within and without: technology and cooperative work on the print industry shop floor. In *Proc. of ECSCW'95*, pages 51–66, Kluwer, 1995.

[42]   J. Bowers and J. Churcher. Local and global structuring of computer mediated communication: developing linguistic perspectives on CSCW in COSMOS. In *CSCW'88: Proceedings of the Conference on Computer-Supported Cooperative Work*, pages 125–39, Portland, OR, 26–28 September 1988. ACM SIGCHI and SIGOIS, ACM, New York.

[43]   T. Boyle. *Design for Multimedia Learning*. Prentice Hall, 1997.

[44]   J. Breuker. *EUROHELP*. CEC, Brussels, 1991.

[45]   S. A. Brewster. Non-speech auditory output. In J. Jacko and A. Sears, editors, *The Human–Computer Interaction Handbook*, chapter 12, pages 220–39. Lawrence Erlbaum Associates, USA, 2002.

[46]   S. Brewster and M. Zajicek. A new research agenda for older adults. Workshop held at HCI2002, South Bank University. 2002. Papers available at: http://www.dcs.gla.ac.uk/~stephen/workshops/utopia/index.shtml (last accessed March 2003).

[47]   S. A. Brewster, P. C. Wright and A. D. N. Edwards. A detailed investigation into the effectiveness of earcons. In G. Kramer, editor, *Auditory Display, Sonification, Audification and Auditory Interfaces. Proceedings of the First International Conference on Auditory Display*, pages 471–98. Santa Fe Institute, Santa Fe, NM, Addison-Wesley, 1992.

[48]   J. A. Brotherton. eClass – Building, observing, and understanding the impact of capture and access in an educational domain. PhD thesis. College of Computing and GVU Center, Georgia Institute of Technology. 2001. Available at: http://www.jasonbrotherton.com/brothert/thesis/Thesis.pdf

[49]   P. J. Brown. Triggering information by context. *Personal Technologies*, 2(1):1–9, 1998.

[50]   S. Bryson. Virtual environments in scientific visualisation. In R. A. Earnshaw and D. Watson, editors, *Animation and Scientific Visualisation*, pages 113–22. Academic Press, London, 1993.

[51]   V. Bush. As we may think. *Atlantic Monthly*, 176(1):101–8, 1945.

[52]   W. Buxton. There's more to interaction than meets the eye: some issues in manual input. In R. M. Baecker and W. A. S. Buxton, editors, *Readings in Human–Computer Interaction: A Multidisciplinary Approach*. Morgan Kaufmann, San Francisco, 1987.

[53]   W. Buxton. A three-state model of graphical input. In D. Diaper, D. Gilmore, G. Cockton and B. Shackel, editors, *Human–Computer Interaction – INTERACT'90*, pages 449–56. North-Holland, Amsterdam, 1990.

[54]   J. Callahan, D. Hopkins, M. Weiser and B. Shneiderman. An empirical comparison of pie vs. linear menus. In *Proceedings of CHI'88*, pages 95–100. ACM Press, New York, 1988.

[54a]   W. B. Cannon. The James–Lange theory of emotions: A critical examination and an alternative theory. *American Journal of Psychology*, 39: 106–24, 1927.

[55]   S. K. Card, T. P. Moran and A. Newell. The keystroke-level model for user performance with interactive systems. *Communications of the ACM*, 23:396–410, 1980.

[56]   S. K. Card, T. P. Moran and A. Newell. *The Psychology of Human–Computer Interaction*. Lawrence Erlbaum Associates, Hillsdale, NJ, 1983.

[57]   S. K. Card, G. G. Robertson and W. York. The WebBook and the Web Forager: an information workspace for the world-wide web. In *Proceedings of CHI'96*, pages 111–17. ACM Press, New York, 1996.

[58]   J. M. Carroll. Minimalist design for active users. In B. Shackel, editor, *Proceedings of IFIP Conference, Interact'84*, pages 39–45. North-Holland, Amsterdam, 1984.

[59]   J. M. Carroll. Infinite detail and emulation in an ontologically minimized HCI. In J. C. Chew and J. Whiteside, editors, *Empowering People – CHI'90 Conference Proceedings*, pages 321–7. ACM Press, New York, 1990.

[60]   J. M. Carroll and C. Carrithers. Blocking learner errors in a training wheels system. *Human Factors*, 26:377–89, 1984.

[61]   J. M. Carroll and T. P. Moran, editors, *Human–Computer Interaction*, 6(3 & 4) 1991. Special journal double issue on design rationale.

[62]   J. M. Carroll and M. B. Rosson. Deliberated evolution: stalking the view matcher in design space. *Human–Computer Interaction*, 6(3 & 4):281–318, 1991.

[63]   L. Catledge and J. Pitkow. Characterising browsing strategies in the world-wide web. In *Proceedings of the 3rd International World Wide Web Conference*, Darmstadt, Germany. Published in *Computer Networks and ISDN*, 27, 1065–1073, Elsevier Science, 1995. Available at: http://www.igd.fhg.de/www/www95/papers/

[64]   W. G. Chase and H. A. Simon. The mind's eye in chess. In W. G. Chase, editor, *Visual Information Processing*. Academic Press, New York, 1973.

[65]   W. G. Chase and H. A. Simon. Perception in chess. *Cognitive Psychology*, 4:55–81, 1973.

[66]   P. B. Checkland. *Systems Thinking, Systems Practice*. John Wiley, Chichester, 1981.

[67]   Y. Chen, D. W. Clark, P. Cook, S. Damianakis, G. Essl, A. Finkelstein, T. Funkhouser, A. Klein, Z. Liu, E. Praun, R. Samanta, B. Shedd, J. P. Singh, G. Tzanetakis, K. Li, H. Chen and J. Zheng. Early experiences and challenges in building and using a scalable display wall system. *IEEE Computer Graphics and Applications*, 20(4):671–80, 2000.

[68]   K. Cheverst, K. Mitchell and N. Davies. Design of an object model for a context sensitive tourist guide. In *Proceedings of Interactive Applications of Mobile Computing – IMC'98*, Rostock, Germany, November 1998. Available at: http://www.egd.igd.fhg.de/~imc98/proceedings.html

[69]   K. Cheverst, N. Davies and K. Mitchell. The role of adaptive hypermedia within a context-aware tourist guide. *Communications of the ACM*, Special issue on adaptive web-based systems and adaptive hypermedia, May 2002.

[70]   K. Cheverst, D. Fitton and A. Dix. Exploring the evolution of office door displays. In K. O'Hara, M. Perry, E. Churchill and D. Russell, editors, *Public and Situated Displays: Social and Interactional Aspects of Shared Display Technologies*, Kluwer, 2004.

[71]   H. H. Clark and S. E. Brennan. Grounding in communication. In L. B. Resnick, J. Levine and S. D. Behreno, editors, *Socially Shared Cognition*. American Psychological Association, Washington DC, 1991.

[72]   H. H. Clark and E. F. Schaefer. Contributing to discourse. *Cognitive Science*, 13:259–94, 1989.

[73]   G. Cockton. Designing abstractions for communication control. In M. Harrison and H. Thimbleby, editors, *Formal Methods in Human–Computer Interaction*, chapter 10. Cambridge University Press, Cambridge, 1990.

[74]   A. M. Collins and M. R. Quillian. Retrieval time from semantic memory. *Journal of Verbal Learning and Verbal Behaviour*, 8:240–7, 1969.

[75]   J. Conklin. Hypertext: an introduction and survey. *Computer*, pages 17–41, September, 1987.

[76]   J. Conklin and M. L. Begeman. gIBIS: A tool for all reasons. *Journal of the American Society for Information Science*, March, 1989.

[77]   J. E. Conklin and K. C. Burgess Yakemovic. A process-oriented approach to design rationale. *Human–Computer Interaction*, 6(3 & 4):357–91, 1991.

[78]   G. F. Coulouris and H. W. Thimbleby. *HyperProgramming*. Addison-Wesley, Wokingham, 1993.

[79]   J. Coutaz. Pac, an object oriented model for dialog design. In H. J. Bullinger and B. Shackel, editors, *Human–Computer Interaction – INTERACT'87*, pages 431–6. North-Holland, Amsterdam, 1987.

[80]   J. Coutaz. Architectural design for user interfaces. In *Proceedings of the 3rd European Conference of Software Engineering, ESEC'91*, 1991.

[81]   L. Cowen, L. J. Ball and J. Delin. An eye-movement analysis of web-page usability. In X. Faulkner, J. Finlay and F. Détienne, editors, *People and Computers XVI – Memorable Yet Invisible: Proceedings of HCI 2002*. Springer-Verlag, London, 2002.

[82]   Csikszentimihalyi. *Flow: The Psychology of Optimal Experience*. Harper and Row, New York, 1990.

[83]   A. Cypher. Eager: Programming repetitive tasks by example. In *Reaching through Technology – CHI'91 Conference Proceedings*, pages 33–9. ACM Press, New York, 1991.

[84]   B. Damer, C. Kekenes and T. Hoffman. Inhabited digital spaces. In *Common Ground – CHI'96 Conference Companion*, pages 9–10. ACM Press, New York, 1996.

[85]   C. Davenport and G. Weir. Plan recognition for intelligent advice and monitoring. In M. D. Harrison and A. F. Monk, editors, *HCI'86: People and Computers II*, pages 296–315. Cambridge University Press, Cambridge, 1986.

[86]   A. Dearden, M. Harrison and P. Wright. Allocation of function: scenarios, context and the economics of effort. *Int. J. of Human–Computer Studies*, 52(2):289–318, 2000.

[87]   L. Degen, R. Mander and G. Salomon. Working with audio: integrating personal tape recorders and desktop computers. In *Proceedings of ACM CHI'92 Conference*, pages 413–18, May 1992.

[88]   A. D. DeGroot. *Thought and Choice in Chess*. Mouton, The Hague, 1965.

[89]   A. D. DeGroot. Perception and memory versus thought. In B. Kleinmuntz, editor, *Problem Solving*. John Wiley, New York, 1966.

[90]   A. Dey, G. D. Abowd, M. Pinkerton and A. Wood. Cyberdesk: a framework for providing self-integrating ubiquitous software services. Technical Report GIT-GVU-97-10, GVU Center, Georgia Institute of Technology, June 1997.

[91]   D. Diaper, editor, *Task Analysis for Human–Computer Interaction*. Ellis Horwood, Chichester, 1989.

[92]   D. Diaper. Task Analysis for Knowledge Descriptions (TAKD): the method and an example. In D. Diaper, editor, *Task Analysis for Human–Computer Interaction*, chapter 4, pages 108–59. Ellis Horwood, Chichester, 1989.

[93]   A. J. Dix. *Formal Methods for Interactive Systems*, chapter 10. Academic Press, London, 1991.

[94]   A. J. Dix. Status and events: static and dynamic properties of interactive systems. In D. A. Duce, editor, *Proceedings of the Eurographics Seminar: Formal Methods in Computer Graphics*, Marina di Carrara, Italy, 1991.

[95]   A. Dix. Accelerators and toolbars: learning from the menu. In *Adjunct Proceedings of HCI'95*, 1995.

[96]   A. J. Dix. Closing the loop: modelling action, perception and information. In T. Catarci, M. F. Costabile, S. Levialdi and G. Santucci, editors, *AVI'96 – Advanced Visual Interfaces*, pages 20–8. ACM Press, New York, 1996.

[97]   A. Dix. Challenges for cooperative work on the web: an analytical approach. *Computer-Supported Cooperative Work: The Journal of Collaborative Computing*, 6:135–56, 1997. Reprinted in R. Bentley, U. Busbach, D. Kerr and K. Sikkel, editors, *Groupware and the World Wide Web*. Kluwer, 1997.

[98]   A. Dix. Welsh mathematician walks in cyberspace (the cartography of cyberspace). (keynote). *Proceedings of the Third International Conference on Collaborative Virtual Environments – CVE2000*, pages 3–7, ACM Press. http://www.hcibook.com/alan/papers/CVE2000/

[99]   A. Dix. Incidental interaction. 2002. Available online: http://www.hcibook.com/alan/topics/incidental/

[100]   A. Dix. Managing the ecology of interaction. *Proceedings of Tamodia 2002 – First International Workshop on Task Models and User Interface Design*, Bucharest, Romania, 18–19 July 2002.

[101]   A. Dix. Deconstructing experience – pulling crackers apart. In M. Blythe, A. Monk, K. Overbeeke and P. Wright, editors, *Funology: From Usability to Enjoyment*. Kluwer, 2003.

[102]   A. Dix and G. Abowd. Modelling status and event behaviour of interactive systems. *Software Engineering Journal*, 11(6):334–46, 1996.

[103]   A. J. Dix and J. E. Finlay. AMO – the interface as medium. *Poster sessions, HCI International'89*, page 22, Boston, 1989. Available at: http://www.hcibook.com/alan/papers/amo89/

[104]   A. Dix and R. Mancini. Specifying history and backtracking mechanisms. In P. Palanque and F. Paternó, editors, *Formal Methods in Human–Computer Interaction*, pages 1–24. Springer-Verlag, London, 1997. Available at: http://www.hcibook.com/alan/papers/histchap97/

[105]   A. Dix and D. Ramduny. Building and prototyping groupware. *HCI'95 Tutorial Notes*, 1995.

[106]   A. Dix, R. Beale and A. Wood. Architectures to make simple visualisations using simple systems. *Proceedings of Advanced Visual Interfaces – AVI2000*, pages 51–60, ACM Press, 2000.

[107]   A. Dix, J. Finlay and J. Hassell. Environments for cooperating agents: Designing the interface as medium. In J. Connolly and E. Edmonds, editors, *CSCW and Artificial Intelligence*, pages 23–37. Springer-Verlag, London, 1994.

[108]   A. Dix, D. Ramduny-Ellis and J. Wilkinson. Trigger analysis – understanding broken tasks. In D. Diaper and N. Stanton, editors, *The Handbook of Task Analysis for Human–Computer Interaction*. Lawrence Erlbaum Associates, 2003 (in press).

[109]   P. Dourish. *Where the Action Is: The Foundations of Embodied Interaction*. MIT Press, 2001.

[110]   A. Druin. Cooperative inquiry: developing new technologies for children with children. *Proceedings of CHI'99*, pages 592–9, Pittsburgh, PA, 15–20 May, ACM, New York, 1999.

[111]   E. Dubois, P. Gray and L. Nigay. ASUR++: a design notation for mobile mixed systems. In F. Paternó, editor, *Proceedings of the 4th International Symposium, Mobile HCI 2002*, pages 123–39, LNCS 2411, Springer-Verlag, 2002.

[112]   A. T. Duchowski. *Eye Tracking Methodology: Theory and Practice*, Springer-Verlag, London, 2003.

[113]   E. A. Dykstra and R. P. Carasik. Structure and support in cooperative environments: the Amsterdam conversation environment. *International Journal of Man-Machine Studies*, 34:419–34, 1991.

[114]   R. A. Earnshaw and D. Watson, editors, *Animation and Scientific Visualisation*. Academic Press, London, 1993.

[115]   K. D. Eason. *Information Technology and Organizational Change*. Taylor and Francis, London, 1988.

[116]   K. D. Eason and S. Harker. An open systems approach to task analysis. Internal report, HUSAT Research Centre, Loughborough University of Technology, 1989.

[117]   H. Ebbinghaus. *Uber das Gedactnis*. Dunker, 1885. Translated by H. Ruyer and C. E. Bussenius, 1913, Memory, Teacher's College, Columbia University.

[118]   A. Edwards. Soundtrack: an auditory interface for blind users. *Human–Computer Interaction*, 4(1):45–66, 1989.

[119]   A. D. N. Edwards, editor, *Extra-ordinary Human–Computer Interaction*. Cambridge University Press, Cambridge, 1993.

[120]   A. D. N. Edwards and S. Holland, editors, *Multimedia Interface Design in Education*. Springer-Verlag, Berlin, 1993.

[121]   C. A. Ellis, S. J. Gibbs and G. L. Rein. Design and use of a group editor. In G. Cockton, editor, *Proceedings of the IFIP Engineering for Human–Computer Interaction Conference*, pages 13–25. North-Holland, Amsterdam, 1990.

[122]   C. A. Ellis, S. J. Gibbs and G. L. Rein. Groupware: some issues and experiences. *Communications of the ACM*, 34(1):38–58, January 1991.

[123]   S. Elrod, R. Bruce, R. Gold, D. Goldberg, F. Halasz, W. Janssen, D. Lee, K. McCall, E. Pedersen, K. Pier, J. Tang and B. Welch. Liveboard: a large interactive display supporting group meetings, presentations and remote collaboration. In *Proceedings of ACM CHI'92 Conference*, pages 599–607, May 1992.

[124]   D. C. Engelbart. A conceptual framework for the augmentation of man's intellect. In P. W. Howerton and D. C. Weeks, editors, *Vistas in Information Handling*, volume 1, pages 1–29. Spartan Books, Washington, DC, 1963.

[125]   D. C. Engelbart and W. K. English. A research centre for augmenting human intellect. In *Proceedings Fall Joint Computing Conference*, pages 395–410. Thompson, Washington, DC, December, 1968.

[126]   J. Erlandson and J. Holm. Intelligent help systems. *Information and Software Technology*, 29(3):115–21, 1987.

[127]   I. Essa and A. Pentland. A vision system for observing and extracting facial action parameters, pages 76–83. IEEE Computer Society, 1994.

[128]   I. Essa and A. Pentland. Facial expression recognition using a dynamic model and motion energy, pages 360–7. IEEE Computer Society, Cambridge, MA, 1995.

[129]   M. W. Eysenck and M. T. Keane. *Cognitive Psychology: A Student's Handbook*. Lawrence Erlbaum Associates, Hillsdale, NJ, 1990.

[130]   S. Feiner, B. MacIntyre and D. Seligmann. Knowledge-based augmented reality. In *Communications of the ACM*, 36(7): 53–62, 1993.

[131]   S. S. Fels and G. E. Hinton. Building adaptive interfaces with neural networks: the glove-talk pilot study. In D. Diaper, D. Gilmore, G. Cockton and B. Shackel, editors, *Proceedings of Interact'90*, pages 683–7. North-Holland, Amsterdam, 1990.

[132]   S. A. Fincher. The Pattern Gallery. 2000. Available at: http://www.cs.ukc.ac.uk/people/staff/saf/patterns/gallery.html (last accessed March 2003)

[133]   G. Fischer, A. Lemke and T. Schwab. Knowledge-based help systems. In *Human Factors in Computing Systems CHI'85 Proceedings*, pages 161–7, 1985.

[134]   R. S. Fish, R. E. Kraut and B. L. Chalfonte. The VideoWindow system in informal communications. In *CSCW'90: Proceedings of the Conference on Computer-Supported Cooperative Work*, pages 1–11, Los Angeles, October, 1990. ACM SIGCHI and SIGOIS, ACM Press, New York.

[135]   P. M. Fitts and M. I. Posner. *Human Performance*. Wadsworth, Wokingham, 1967.

[136]   G. W. Fitzmaurice, H. Ishii and W. Buxton. Bricks: laying the foundations for graspable user interfaces. In *Proceedings of the 1995 ACM Conference on Human Factors in Computing Systems – CHI'95*, pages 442–9, 1995.

[137]   G. W. Fitzmaurice, S. Zhai and S. H. Chignell. Virtual reality for palmtop computers, Special issue on virtual worlds. *ACM Transactions on Information Systems*, 11(3):197, 1993.

[138]   J. Fogarty, J. Forlizzi and S. E. Hudson. Aesthetic information collages: generating decorative displays that contain information. In *Proceedings of the 14th Annual ACM Symposium on User Interface Software and Technology – UIST 2001*, 2001.

[139]   A. Fox, B. Johanson, P. Hanrahan and T. Winograd. Integrating information appliances into an interactive workspace. *IEEE Computer Graphics and Applications*, 20(3), 2000.

[140]   M. M. Gardiner and B. Christie, editors, *Applying Cognitive Psychology to User–Interface Design*. John Wiley, Chichester, 1987.

[141]   W. Gaver. Auditory icons: using sound in computer interfaces. *Human–Computer Interaction*, 2(2):167–77, 1986.

[142]   W. Gaver. The sonicfinder: an interface that uses auditory icons. *Human–Computer Interaction*, 4(1):67–94, 1989.

[143]   W. Gaver and A. Dunne. Projected realities: conceptual design for cultural effect. In *Proceedings of the 1999 ACM Conference on Human Factors in Computing Systems – CHI'99*, pages 600–7, Pittsburgh, PA, 1999.

[144]   W. Gaver, A. Dunne and E. Pacenti. Design: cultural probes. In *Interactions: New Visions of Human–Computer Interaction*. ACM Inc., Danvers, MA, 1999.

[145]   W. Gaver and R. Smith. Auditory icons in large-scale collaborative environments. In D. Diaper, D. Gilmore, G. Cockton and B. Shackel, editors, *Proceedings of Interact'90*, pages 735–40. North-Holland, Amsterdam, 1990.

[146]   B. Gaver, T. Dunne and E. Pacenti. Design: cultural probes. *Interactions*, 6(1):21–9, ACM Press, 1999.

[147]   W. W. Gaver, R. B. Smith and T. O'Shea. Effective sounds in complex situations: the ARKola simulation. In S. P. Robertson, G. M. Olson and J. S. Olson, editors, *Reaching Through Technology – CHI'91 Conference Proceedings*, pages 85–90. Human Factors in Computing Systems, ACM Press, New York, April, 1991.

[148]   H.-W. Gellersen, M. Beigl and H. Krull. The MediaCup: awareness technology embedded in an everyday object. *Int. Sym. Handheld and Ubiquitous Computing – HUC99*, Karlsruhe, Germany, 1999.

[149]   M. L. Gick and K. J. Holyoak. Analogical problem solving. *Cognitive Psychology*, 12:306–55, 1980.

[150]   J. H. Goldberg and X. P. Kotval. Computer interface evaluation using eye movements: methods and constructs. *International Journal of Industrial Ergonomics*, 24:631–45, 1999.

[151]   E. B. Goldstein. *Sensation and Perception*, 3rd edition. Wadsworth, Wokingham, 1989.

[152]   J. D. Gould, S. J. Boies, S. Levy, J. T. Richards and J. Schoonard. The 1984 Olympic message system: a test of behavioural principles of system design. In J. Preece and L. Keller, editors, *Human–Computer Interaction*, chapter 12. Prentice Hall, Hemel Hempstead, 1990.

[153]   C. Gram and G. Cockton, editors, *Design Principles for Interactive Software*. Chapman and Hall, London, 1996.

[154]   W. D. Gray, B. E. John and M. E. Atwood. The precis of Project Ernestine or an overview of a validation of GOMS. In P. Bauersfeld, J. Bennett and G. Lynch, editors, *Striking a Balance, Proceedings of the CHI'92 Conference on Human Factors in Computing Systems*, pages 307–12. ACM Press, 1992.

[155]   S. Greenberg, editor, *Computer-Supported Cooperative Work and Groupware*. Academic Press, New York, 1991.

[156]   S. Greenberg and C. Fitchett. Phidgets: easy development of physical interfaces through physical widgets. *Proceedings of the 14th Annual ACM Symposium on*

User Interface Software and Technology – UIST'01, pages 209–18, ACM Press, New York, 2001.

[157]   S. Greenberg, J. Darragh, D. Maulsby and I. H. Witten. Predictive interfaces: What will they think of next? In A. D. N. Edwards, editor, *Extra-ordinary Human–Computer Interaction*. Cambridge University Press, Cambridge, 1993.

[158]   R. L. Grossman, et al., editors, *Hybrid Systems*. LNCS 736, Springer-Verlag, 1993.

[159]   J. Grudin. Why CSCW application fail: problems in the design and evaluation of organizational interfaces. In *CSCW'88: Proceedings of the Conference on Computer Supported Cooperative Work*, pages 85–94, Portland, OR, 26–28 September 1988. ACM SIGCHI and SIGOIS, ACM, New York.

[160]   J. Grudin. The case against user interface consistency. *Communications of the ACM*, 4(3):245–64, 1989.

[161]   K. Hamnes. Smelly interfaces. A brief review of the application of smell in user interfaces. Internal report, Future Media Group, Telenor R&D, Fornebu, Norway, 20 February 2002. www.telenor.no/fou/KH_olfactory_displays_200202.pdf

[162]   W. J. Hansen. User engineering principles for interactive systems. In *AFIPS Conference Proceedings 39*, pages 523–32, AFIPS Press, 1971. Reprinted in W. J. Hansen. User engineering principles for interactive systems. In D. R. Barstow, H. E. Shrobe and E. Sandewall, editors, *Interactive Programming Environments*, pages 217–31. McGraw-Hill, New York, 1984.

[163]   M. Harrison and H. Thimbleby, editors, *Formal Methods in Human–Computer Interaction*. Cambridge University Press, Cambridge, 1990.

[164]   B. J. Harrison, K. P. Fishkin, A. Gujar, C. Mochon and R. Want. Squeeze me, hold me, tilt me! An exploration of manipulative user interfaces. *Proceedings of the 1998 ACM Conference on Human Factors in Computing Systems – CHI'98*, pages 17–24, May 1998.

[165]   H. R. Hartson, A. C. Siochi and D. Hix. The UAN: a user-oriented representation for direct manipulation. *ACM Transactions on Information Systems*, 8(3):181–203, July 1990.

[166]   The HCI Service, Department of Trade and Industry, UK. *HCI Tools & Methods Handbook*, 1991.

[167]   M. Helander, editor, *Handbook of Human–Computer Interaction. Part II: User Interface Design*. North-Holland, Amsterdam, 1988.

[168]   M. Helander, editor, *Handbook of Human–Computer Interaction. Part V: Tools for Design and Evaluation*. North-Holland, Amsterdam, 1988.

[169]   D. Heller. *XView Programming Manual*, volume 7 of *The X Window System*. O'Reilly and Associates, Inc., Sebastopol, CA, 1990.

[170]   T. Hemmings, A. Crabtree, T. Rodden, K. Clarke and M. Rouncefield. Domestic probes and the design process. *Proceedings of the 11th European Conference on Cognitive Ergonomics*, pages 187–93, Catania, Italy, European Association of Cognitive Ergonomics, 2002.

[171]   B. Hewitt, N. Gilbert, M. Jirotka and S. Wilbur. Theories of multi-party interaction. Technical report, Social and Computer Sciences Research Group,

University of Surrey and Queen Mary and Westfield Colleges, University of London, 1990.

[172] R. D. Hill, T. Brinck, S. L. Rohall, J. F. Patterson and W. Wilner. The rendezvous architecture and language for constructing multi-user applications. *ACM Transactions on Computer–Human Interaction*, 1(2):81–125, 1994.

[173] K. Hinckley, J. Pierce, M. Sinclair and E. Horvitz. Sensing techniques for mobile interaction. In *Proceedings of the 13th Annual ACM Symposium on User Interface Software and Technology – UIST 2000*, pages 91–100, 2000.

[174] D. Hindus and C. Schmandt. Ubiquitous audio: capturing spontaneous collaboration. In *Proceedings of ACM CSCW'92 Conference*, pages 210–17, 1992.

[175] D. Hindus, S. D. Mainwaring, A. E. Hagstrom, N. Leduc and O. Bayley. Casablanca: designing social communications devices for the home. In *Proceedings of the 2001 ACM Conference on Human Factors in Computing Systems – CHI 2001*, pages 325–32, April 2001.

[176] D. Hix. Generations of user-interface management systems. *IEEE Software*, 7(5):77–87, September 1990.

[177] D. Hobbs and D. Moore. *Human–Computer Interaction*, Pitman, 1998.

[178] L. F. Hodges, B. O. Rothbaum, R. Kooper, D. Opdyke, T. Meyer, M. North, J. J. de Graaff and J. Williford. Virtual environments for treating the fear of heights. *IEEE Computer*, 28(7):27–34, 1995.

[179] R. C. Houghton. On-line help systems: a conspectus. *Communications of the ACM*, 27, 2, 1984.

[180] A. Howes and S. Payne. Display-based competence: towards user models for menu-driven interfaces. *Int. J. of Man–Machine Studies*, 33:637–55, 1990.

[181] R. E. Hubbard. Molecular graphics: from pen plotter to virtual reality. In A. Monk, D. Diaper and M. D. Harrison, editors, *HCI'92: People and Computers VII*, pages 21–7. Cambridge University Press, Cambridge, 1992.

[182] D. A. Huffman. A method for the construction of minimum-redundancy codes. *Proceedings of the IRE*, 40, 1952.

[183] J. Hughes, J. O'Brien, M. Rouncefield, I. Sommerville and T. Rodden. Presenting ethnography in the requirements process. In *Proc. IEEE Conf. on Requirements Engineering, RE'95.* pages 27–34, IEEE Press, 1995.

[184] G. Humphreys and P. Hanrahan. A distributed graphics system for large tiled displays. In *Proceedings of IEEE Visualization*, 1999.

[185] E. Hutchins. The technology of team navigation. In J. Gallagher, R. Kraut and C. Egido, editors, *Intellectual Teamwork: Social and Technical Bases of Collaborative Work*. Lawrence Erlbaum Associates, Hillsdale, NJ, 1990.

[186] E. Hutchins. *Cognition in the Wild*. MIT Press, Cambridge, MA, 1995.

[187] E. L. Hutchins, J. D. Hollan and D. A. Norman. Direct manipulation interfaces. In D. A. Norman and S. W. Draper, editors, *User Centered System Design*, pages 87–124. Lawrence Erlbaum Associates, Hillsdale, NJ, January, 1986.

[188] H. Ishii and N. Miyake. Towards an open shared workspace: computer and video fusion approach of TeamWorkStation. *Communications of the ACM*, 34(12):37–50, December 1991.

[189] H. Ishii and B. Ullmer. Tangible bits: towards seamless interfaces between people, bits and atoms. In *Proceedings of CHI'97*, pages 234–41, May 1997.

[190] H. Ishii, C. Wisneski, S. Brave, A. Dahley, M. Gorbet, B. Ullmer and P. Yarin. ambientROOM: integrating ambient media with architectural space. Short paper. In *Proceedings of the 1998 ACM Conference on Human Factors in Computing Systems – CHI'98, Companion Proceedings*, pages 173–4, 1998.

[191] R. J. K. Jacob. Survey and examples of specification techniques for user–computer interfaces. Technical report, Naval Research Laboratory, Washington, DC, 1983.

[192] B. E. John. Extensions of GOMS analyses to expert performance requiring perception of dynamic visual and auditory information. In J. C. Chew and J. Whiteside, editors, *Empowering People – Proceedings of CHI'90 Human Factors in Computer Systems*, pages 107–15. ACM Press, 1990.

[193] P. Johnson. *Human–Computer Interaction: Psychology, Task Analysis and Software Engineering*. McGraw-Hill, London, 1992.

[194] C. W. Johnson. Ten golden rules for video over the web. In J. Ratner, E. Grosse and C. Forsythe, editors, *Human Factors for World Wide Web Development*, pages 207–24. Lawrence Erlbaum, 1997.

[194a] C. W. Johnson. The impact of utility and time on distributed information retrieval. In H. Thimbleby, B. O'Conaill and P. Thomas, editors, *People and Computers XII: Proceedings of HCI'97*, pages 191–204. Springer-Verlag, 1997.

[195] W. Johnson, H. Jellinek, L. Klotz Jr, R. Rao and S. Card. Bridging the paper and electronic worlds: the paper user interface. In S. Ashlund, K. Mullet, A. Henderson, E. Hollnegel and T. White, editors, *INTERCHI'93 Conference Proceedings*, pages 507–12. ACM Press, New York, 1993.

[196] P. W. Jordan, S. W. Draper, K. K. MacFarlane and S.-A. McNulty. Guessability, learnability and experienced user performance. In D. Diaper and N. Hammond, editors, *HCI'91: People and Computers VI*, pages 237–45. British Computer Society Special Interest Group on Human–Computer Interaction, Cambridge University Press, Cambridge, 1991.

[196a] D. J. Kasik. A user interface management system. *Computer Graphics*, 16(3), July, 1982.

[197] A. Kay and A. Goldberg. Personal dynamic media. *IEEE Computer*, 10(3):31–42, March 1977.

[198] J. N. Kaye. Symbolic olfactory display. Unpublished Master of Science thesis, Massachusetts Institute of Technology, Cambridge, Boston, MA. Available: http://web.media.mit.edu/~jofish/thesis/

[199] D. E. Kieras and P. G. Polson. An approach to the formal analysis of user complexity. *International Journal of Man-Machine Studies*, 22:365–94, 1985.

[200] M. Kirby. Custom manual. Technical Report DPO/STD/1.0, HCI Research Centre, University of Huddersfield, 1991.

[201] C. Knowles. Can cognitive complexity theory (CCT) produce an adequate measure of system usability? In D. M. Jones and R. Winder, editors, *HCI'88: People and Computers IV*, pages 291–307. Cambridge University Press, Cambridge, 1988.

[202] W. Kohler. *The Mentality of Apes*, 2nd edition. Harcourt Brace, New York, 1927.

[203]   G. E. Krasner and S. T. Pope. A cookbook for using the model-view-controller user interface paradigm in Smalltalk-80. *JOOP*, 1(3), August, 1988.

[204]   M. Kutar, C. Britton and C. Nehaniv. Specifiying multiple time granularities in interactive systems. In P. Palanque and F. Paternó, editors, *DSV-IS 2000 Interactive Systems: Design, Specification and Verification*. LNCS 1946, pages 169–90, Springer-Verlag, 2001.

[205]   J. E. Laird, A. Newell and P. Rosenbloom. Soar: an architecture for general intelligence. *Artificial Intelligence*, 33:1–64, 1987.

[206]   K. Larson and M. Czerwinski. Web page design: implications of memory, structure and scent for information retrieval. In *Proceedings of CHI 98, Human Factors in Computing Systems*, pages 25–32, Los Angeles, 21–23 April 1998, ACM Press.

[207]   B. Laurel. *Computers as Theatre*. Addison-Wesley, Reading, MA, 1991.

[208]   J. Lave. *Cognition in Practice: Mind, Mathematics and Culture in Everyday Life*. Cambridge University Press, Cambridge, 1988.

[209]   J. Lee and K.-Y. Lai. What's in a design rationale. *Human–Computer Interaction*, 6(3 & 4):251–80, 1991.

[210]   M. D. P. Leland, R. S. Fish and R. E. Kraut. Collaborative document production using Quilt. In *CSCW'88: Proceedings of the Conference on Computer Supported Cooperative Work*, pages 206–15, Portland, OR, 26–28 September 1988. ACM SIGCHI and SIGOIS, ACM, New York.

[211]   L. Lemay, J. M. Duff and J. C. Mohl. *Laura Lemay's Web Workshop: Graphics and Web Page Design*. Sams.net, 1997.

[212]   S. Lewis. *The Art and Science of Smalltalk*. Hewlett-Packard Professional Books, Prentice Hall, Hemel Hempstead, 1995.

[213]   C. Lewis and J. Rieman. *Task-centered User Interface Design: A Practical Introduction*. A shareware book published by the authors. Original files for the book are available by FTP from ftp.cs.colorado.edu, 1993.

[214]   A. Light. Interaction at the producer–user interface: an interdisciplinary analysis of communication and relationships through interactive components on websites for the purpose of improving design. PhD thesis, University of Sussex, UK, 2000.

[215]   Q. Limbourg, C. Pribeanu and J. Vanderdonckt. Towards uniformed task models in a model-based approach. In *Proc. DSV-IS 2001*, pages 164–82, Springer-Verlag, 2001.

[216]   S. Long, D. Aust, G. D. Abowd and C. G. Atkeson. Rapid prototyping of mobile context-aware applications: the cyberguide case study. In *Proceedings of the 1996 Conference on Human Factors in Computing Systems – CHI'96*, 1996. Short paper.

[217]   S. Long, R. Kooper, G. D. Abowd and C. G. Atkeson. Rapid prototyping of mobile context-aware applications: the cyberguide case study. In *Proceedings of the 2nd Annual International Conference on Mobile Computing and Networking*, November 1996.

[218]   A. C. Long, Jr, S. Narayanaswamy, A. Burstein, R. Han, K. Lutz, B. Richards, S. Sheng, R. W. Brodersen and J. Rabaey. A prototype user interface for a mobile

multimedia terminal. In *Proceedings of the 1995 Conference on Human Factors in Computing Systems – CHI'95*, 1995. Interactive experience demonstration.

[219]   L. MacCaulay, C. Fowler, M. Kirby and A. Hutt. USTM: a new approach to requirements specification. *Interacting with Computers*, 2(1):92–108, 1990.

[220]   W. E. Mackay. EVA: an experimental video annotator for symbolic analysis of video data. *SIGCHI Bulletin: Special issue on video as a research and design tool*, 21(1):68–71, 1989.

[221]   I. S. MacKenzie, A. Sellen and W. Buxton. A comparison of input devices in elemental pointing and dragging tasks. In S. P. Robertson, G. M. Olson and J. S. Olson, editors, *Reaching through Technology – CHI'91 Conference Proceedings*, pages 161–6. Human Factors in Computing Systems, ACM Press, New York, April 1991.

[222]   A. MacLean, R. M. Young, V. M. E. Bellotti and T. P. Moran. Questions, options, and criteria: elements of design space analysis. *Human–Computer Interaction*, 6(3 & 4):201–50, 1991.

[223]   M. Macleod and R. Rengger. The development of DRUM: a software tool for video assisted usability evaluation. In *People and Computers VIII Proceedings of HCI'93*. Cambridge University Press, Cambridge, 1993.

[224]   N. R. F. Maier. Reasoning in humans II: the solution of a problem and its appearance in consciousness. *Journal of Comparative Psychology*, 12:181–94, 1931.

[225]   T. W. Malone, K. R. Grant, K. Lai, R. Rao and D. Rosenblitt. Semistructured messages are surprisingly useful for computer supported coordination. *ACM Transactions on Office Information Systems*, 5(2):115–31, 1987.

[226]   M. Mantei. Capturing the capture lab concepts: a case study in the design of computer supported meeting environments. In *CSCW'88: Proceedings of the Conference on Computer-Supported Cooperative Work*, pages 257–70, Portland, OR, 26–28 September 1988. ACM SIGCHI and SIGOIS, ACM, New York.

[227]   A. Marcus. *Graphic Design for Electronic Documents and User Interfaces*. ACM Press Tutorial Series, New York, 1992.

[228]   M. V. Mason. Adaptive command prompting in an on-line documentation system. *International Journal of Man–Machine Studies*, 25(1):33–51, 1986.

[229]   M. Massink, D. Duke and S. Smith. Towards hybrid interface specification for virtual environments. In D. J. Duke and A. Puerta, editors, *DSV-IS 1999 Design, Specification and Verification of Interactive Systems*, pages 30–51, Springer-Verlag, 1999.

[230]   D. J. Mayhew. *Principles and Guidelines in Software and User Interface Design*. Prentice Hall, Englewood Cliffs, NJ, 1992.

[231]   R. J. McCall. PHI: A conceptual foundation for design hypermedia. *Design Studies*, 12(1):30–41, 1991.

[232]   J. A. McDermid, editor, *The Software Engineer's Reference Book*. Butterworth–Heinemann, Oxford, 1991.

[233]   A. Mével and T. Guéguen. *Smalltalk-80*. Macmillan Education, Basingstoke, 1987.

[234]   G. A. Miller. The magical number seven, plus or minus two: some limits on our capacity to process information. *Psychological Review*, 63(2):81–97, 1956.

[235]   S. Minneman, S. Harrison, B. Janseen, G. Kurtenbach, T. Moran, I. Smith and B. van Melle. A confederation of tools for capturing and accessing collaborative activity. In *Proceedings of the ACM Conference on Multimedia – Multimedia'95*, November 1995.

[236]   A. Monk, editor, *Fundamentals of Human–Computer Interaction*. Academic Press, London, 1985.

[237]   A. F. Monk. Mode errors: a user-centred analysis and some preventative measures using keying contingent sound. *International Journal of Man–Machine Studies*, 24, 1986.

[238]   A. F. Monk and N. Gilbert, editors, *Perspectives on HCI: Diverse Approaches*. Academic Press, London, 1995.

[239]   A. F. Monk and S. Howard. The rich picture: a tool for reasoning about work context. *ACM Interactions*, 5(2), 21–30, 1998.

[240]   A. Monk, P. Wright, J. Haber and L. Davenport. *Improving your Human–Computer Interface: A Practical Approach*. Prentice Hall International, Hemel Hempstead, 1993.

[241]   T. Moran, P. Chiu, S. Harrison, G. Kurtenbach, S. Minneman and W. van Melle. Evolutionary engagement in an ongoing collaborative work process: a case study. In *Proceedings of ACM CSCW'96 Conference*, November 1996.

[242]   M. J. Muller. PICTIVE: an exploration in participatory design. *Proceedings of the SIGCHI Conference on Human Factors in Computing Systems: Reaching through Technology*, pages 225–31, 27 April–2 May, New Orleans, LA, 1991.

[243]   E. Mumford. *Designing Participatively*. Manchester Business School Publications, Manchester, 1983.

[244]   P. Muter, S. A. Latremouille, W. C. Treurniet and P. Beam. Extended reading of continuous text on television screens. *Human Factors*, 24:501–8, 1982.

[245]   B. A. Myers. *Creating User Interfaces by Demonstration*. Academic Press, New York, 1988.

[246]   B. A. Myers. User-interface tools: Introduction and survey. *IEEE Software*, 6(1):47–61, January 1989.

[247]   B. A. Myers and M. B. Rosson. Survey on user interface programming. In P. Bauersfeld, J. Bennett and G. Lynch, editors, *CHI'92 Conference Proceedings on Human Factors in Computing Systems*, pages 195–202. ACM Press, New York, 1992.

[248]   E. D. Mynatt. The writing on the wall. In A. Sasse and C. Johnson, editors, *Human–Computer Interaction – INTERACT'99*, IFIP TC.13, IOS Press, 1999.

[249]   E. D. Mynatt, M. Back, R. Want, M. Baer and J. Ellis. Designing audio aura. In *Proceedings of the 1998 ACM Conference on Human Factors in Computing Systems – CHI'98*, pages 566–73, Los Angeles, CA, 1998.

[250]   E. D. Mynatt, T. Igarashi, W. K. Edwards and A. LaMarca. Flatland: new dimensions in office whiteboards. In *Proceedings of the 1999 ACM Conference on Human Factors in Computing Systems – CHI'99*, 1999.

[251]   E. D. Mynatt, J. Rowan, S. Craighill and A. Jacobs. Digital family portraits: providing peace of mind for extended family members. In *Proceedings of the 2001 ACM Conference on Human Factors in Computing Systems – CHI 2001*, pages 333–40, April 2001.

[252]   B. Nardi, editor, *Context and Consciousness: Activity Theory and Human–Computer Interaction*. MIT Press, Cambridge, MA, 1996.

[253]   D. Navarre, P. Palanque, F. Paternó, C. Santoro and R. Bastide. A tool suite for integrating task and system models through scenarios. In C. Johnson, editor, *DSV-IS 2001 Interactive Systems: Design, Specification and Verification*. LNCS 2220, pages 88–113, Springer-Verlag, 2001.

[254]   C. M. Neuwirth, D. S. Kaufer, R. Chandhok and J. H. Morris. Issues in the design of computer support for co-authoring and commenting. In *CSCW'90: Proceedings of the Conference on Computer-Supported Cooperative Work*, pages 183–95, Los Angeles, October, 1990. ACM SIGCHI and SIGOIS, ACM, New York.

[255]   A. Newell and H. Simon. *Human Problem Solving*. Prentice Hall, Englewood Cliffs, NJ, 1972.

[256]   A. F. Newell, J. L. Arnott, A. Y. Cairns, I. W. Ricketts and P. Gregor. Intelligent systems for speech and language impaired people: a portfolio of research. In A. D. N. Edwards, editor, *Extra-ordinary Human–Computer Interaction*. Cambridge University Press, Cambridge, 1993.

[257]   A. Newell, G. Yost, J. E. Laird, P. S. Rosenbloom and E. Altmann. Formulating the problem-space computational model. In R. F. Rashid, editor, *CMU Computer Science: a 25th Anniversary Commemorative*, chapter 11. ACM Press, New York, 1991.

[258]   W. M. Newman. A system for interactive graphical programming. In *Proceedings of the 1968 Spring Joint Computer Conference*, pages 47–54. American Federation of Information Processing Societies, 1969.

[259]   W. Newman, M. Eldridge and M. Lamming. Pepys: generating autobiographies by automatic tracking. In *Proceedings of the Second European Conference on Computer Supported Cooperative Work – ECSCW'91*, pages 175–88, 25–27 September, Kluwer Academic Publishers, Amsterdam, 1991.

[260]   J. Nielsen. *Usability Engineering*. Academic Press, New York, 1992.

[261]   J. Nielsen. The usability engineering life cycle. *IEEE Computer*, 25(3):12–22, March 1992.

[262]   J. Nielsen. Heuristic evaluation. In *Usability Inspection Methods*. John Wiley, New York, 1994.

[263]   J. Nielsen. Why frames suck (most of the time). 1996. Available at: http://www.useit.com/alertbox/9612.html

[264]   J. Nielsen and T. K. Landauer. A mathematical model of the finding of usability problems. *Proceedings of ACM INTERCHI'93 Conference*, pages 206–13, Amsterdam, The Netherlands, 24–29 April 1993.

[265]   D. A. Norman. *The Psychology of Everyday Things*. Basic Books, New York, 1988.

[266]   D. Norman. *The Design of Everyday Things*. Doubleday, New York, 1990.

[267]   D. A. Norman. *Turn Signals are the Facial Expressions of Automobiles*. Addison-Wesley, Reading, MA, 1992.

[268]   D. A. Norman. *Things That Make Us Smart*. Addison-Wesley, Reading, MA, 1993.

[269]   D. Norman. *The Invisible Computer*. MIT Press, Cambridge, MA, 1998.

[270]   D. A. Norman and S. W. Draper, editors, *User-Centered System Design: New Perspectives on Human–Computer Interaction*. Lawrence Erlbaum Associates, Hillsdale, NJ, 1986.

[271]   C. North and F. Korn. Browsing anatomical image databases: a case study of the Visible Human. In *CHI'96 Conference Companion*, pages 414–15. ACM Press, New York, 1996.

[272]   D. R. Olsen. Propositional Production Systems for Dialog description. In J. C. Chew and J. Whiteside, editors, *Empowering People – CHI'90 Conference Proceedings*, pages 57–63. Human Factors in Computing Systems, ACM Press, New York, 1990.

[273]   D. Olsen. *User Interface Management Systems: Models and Algorithms*. Morgan Kaufmann, San Francisco, 1991.

[274]   J. S. Olson, G. M. Olson, L. A. Mack and P. Wellner. Concurrent editing: the group's interface. In D. Diaper, D. Gilmore, G. Cockton and B. Shackel, editors, *Human–Computer Interaction – INTERACT'90*, pages 835–40. North-Holland, Amsterdam, 1990.

[275]   Open Software Foundation. *OSF/Motif Style Guide*. Prentice Hall, Hemel Hempstead, 1991.

[276]   P. Palanque and R. Bastide. Petri net based design of user-driven interfaces using the interactive cooperating objects formalism. In F. Paternó, editor, *Interactive Systems: Design, Specification and Verification (1st Eurographics Workshop, Bocca di Magra, Italy, June 1994)*, pages 215–28. Springer-Verlag, Berlin, 1995.

[277]   P. Palanque and R. Bastide. Formal specification and verification of CSCW. In M. A. R. Kirby, A. J. Dix and J. E. Finlay, editors, *People and Computers X – Proceedings of the HCI'95 Conference*, pages 213–31. Cambridge University Press, Cambridge, 1996.

[278]   M. Pandit and S. Kalbag. The selection recognition agent: instant access to relevant information and operations. In *Proceedings of Intelligent User Interfaces'97*. ACM Press, 1997.

[279]   D. L. Parnas. On the use of transition diagrams in the design of a user interface for an interactive computer system. In *Proceedings of the 1969 ACM National Conference*, pages 379–85, 1969.

[280]   F. Paternó. *Model-based Design and Evaluation of Interactive Applications*. Springer-Verlag, 1999.

[281]   F. Paternó and P. Palanque, editors, *Formal Methods in Human–Computer Interaction*. Springer-Verlag, Berlin, 1997.

[282]   R. Pausch. Virtual reality on five dollars a day. In *Reaching through Technology – CHI'91 Conference Proceedings*, pages 265–70. ACM Press, New York, 1991.

[283] S. J. Payne. Understanding calendar use. *Human–Computer Interaction*, 8(2):83–100, 1993.

[284] S. J. Payne and T. R. G. Green. Task-action grammars: a model of mental representation of task languages. *Human–Computer Interaction*, 2(2):93–133, 1986.

[285] G. Pfaff and P. J. W. ten Hagen, editors, *Seeheim Workshop on User Interface Management Systems*. Springer-Verlag, Berlin, 1985.

[286] Philips Corporate Design. Vision of the future. 1996. Available at: http://www.design.philips.com/vof/

[287] R. Picard. Affective computing. Technical Report 321, MIT Media Lab, Perceptual Computing, November 1995. Available as MIT Media Lab Perceptual Computing Techreport #362 from http://vismod.www.media.mit.edu/vismod/

[288] R. W. Picard. *Affective Computing*. MIT Press, Cambridge, MA, 1997.

[289] P. Pirolli and S. K. Card. Information foraging. *Psychological Review*, 106(4):643–75, 1999.

[290] I. Pitt and A. Edwards. Navigating the interface by sound for blind users. In D. Diaper and N. Hammond, editors, *HCI'91: People and Computers VI*, pages 373–83. British Computer Society Special Interest Group on Human–Computer Interaction, Cambridge University Press, Cambridge, 1991.

[291] C. Plaisant, B. Milash, A. Rose, S. Widoff and B. Shneiderman. Lifelines: visualising personal histories. In *Proceedings of CHI'96*, page 221–7. ACM Press, New York, 1996.

[292] M. J. Plasmeijer. Input tools – a language model for interaction and process communication. Technical report, Katholieke Universiteit Nijmegen, 1981.

[293] M. E. Pollack. Information sought and information provided: an empirical study of user/expert dialogues. In L. Borman and B. Curtis, editors, *Proceedings of CHI'85*, pages 155–60. ACM Press, New York, 1985.

[294] P. Polson, C. Lewis, J. Rieman and C. Wharton. Cognitive walkthroughs: A method for theory-based evaluation of user interfaces. *International Journal of Man–Machine Studies*, 36:741–73, 1992.

[295] L. R. Posner, R. M. Baecker and M. M. Mantei. How people write together. Technical report, Computer Systems Research Institute and Department of Computer Science, University of Toronto, 6 Kings College Road, Toronto, Ontario, M5S 1A1, Canada, 1991.

[296] L. Postman and L. W. Phillips. Short-term temporal changes in free recall. *Quarterly Journal of Experimental Psychology*, 17:132–8, 1965.

[297] C. Potts and G. Bruns. Recording the reasons for design decisions. In *Proceedings of 10th International Conference on Software Engineering*, pages 418–27, 1988.

[298] J. R. Quinlan. Discovering rules by induction from large collections of data. In D. Michie, editor, *Expert Systems in the Micro-Electronic Age*. Edinburgh University Press, Edinburgh, 1979.

[299] D. Ramduny and A. Dix. Why, what, where, when: architectures for co-operative work on the WWW. *Proceedings of HCI'97*, pages 283–301, Bristol,

UK, Springer-Verlag, 1997. Available at: http://www.hcibook.com/alan/papers/WWWW97/

[300]   J. C. Read, S. J. MacFarlane and C. Casey. Measuring the usability of text input methods for children. In *Proceedings of HCI2001*, pages 559–72, Lille, France, Springer-Verlag, 2001.

[301]   P. Reisner. Formal grammar and human factors design of an interactive graphics system. *IEEE Transactions on Software Engineering*, SE-7(2):229–40, 1981.

[302]   J. Rekimoto. Pick-and-drop: a direct manipulation technique for multiple computer environments. In *Proceedings of the ACM Symposium on User Interface Software and Technology – UIST'97*, pages 31–9, 1997.

[303]   J. Rekimoto and N. Katashi. The world through the computer: computer augmented interaction with real world environments. *Proceedings of the ACM Symposium on User Interface Software and Technology – UIST'95*, pages 29–36, 1995.

[304]   P. Resnick and H. R. Varian, guest editors, *CACM*, 40(3):56–89, Special issue on Recommender Systems, 1997.

[305]   H. Rheingold. *Tools for Thought*. Prentice Hall, Englewood Cliffs, NJ, 1985.

[306]   E. Rich and K. Knight. *Artificial Intelligence*, 2nd edition. McGraw-Hill, New York, 1991.

[307]   J. Riegelsberger and M. A. Sasse. Designing e-commerce applications for consumer trust. In O. Petrovic, editor, *Vertrauen in der vernetzten Wirtschaft/Trust in the Network Economy. Evolaris*, Vol. 2, Springer-Verlag, April 2003.

[308]   H. Rittel and W. Kunz. Issues as elements of information systems. Working paper #131, Institut für Grundlagen der Planung I.A., University of Stuttgart, 1970.

[309]   C. Roast and J. Siddiqi, editors, *FAHCI/Formal Aspects of the Human–Computer Interface*. Springer-Verlag, London, 1996.

[310]   G. G. Robertson, S. K. Card and J. D. Mackinlay. Cone trees: animated 3D visualisation of hierarchical information. In *Proceedings of CHI'91 Conference of Human Factors in Computing Systems*, pages 184–94. ACM Press, New York, 1991.

[311]   C. Robson. *Experiment, Design and Statistics in Psychology*, 2nd edition. Penguin, Harmondsworth, 1985.

[312]   T. Rodden. A survey of CSCW systems. *Interacting with Computers*, 3(3):319–53, 1991.

[312a]   S. Schacher and J. Singer. Cognitive, social and psychological determinants of emotional state. *Psychological Review*, 69: 379–99, 1962.

[313]   F. Schiele and T. Green. HCI formalisms and cognitive psychology: the case of task-action grammars. In M. Harrison and H. Thimbleby, editors, *Formal Methods in Human–Computer Interaction*, chapter 2. Cambridge University Press, Cambridge, 1990.

[314]   A. Schill. *Cooperative Office Systems*. Prentice Hall, 1995.

[315]   A. Schmidt. Implicit Human–Computer Interaction Through Context. *Personal Technologies*, 4(2 & 3):191–99, June 2000.

[316]   J. A. V. Serrano and U. Kirchhoff. A novel methodology for world-best teamwork in hospitals. In B. Standford-Smith and P. T. Kidd, editors, *E-business, Key Issues, Applications and Technologies*, IOS Press, ISBN 1 58603 089 2, 2000.

[317]   K. Severinson Eklundh. Dialog processes in computer-mediated communication: a study of letters in the com system. Technical report, Linkoping Studies in Arts and Science, 1986.

[318]   A. Shepherd. Analysis and training in information technology tasks. In D. Diaper, editor, *Task Analysis for Human–Computer Interaction*, chapter 1, pages 15–55. Ellis Horwood, Chichester, 1989.

[319]   J. G. Sheridan and J. Allanson. PICK – a scenario-based approach to sensor selection for interactive applications. *Proceedings of the 10th International Conference on Human–Computer Interaction*, 22–27 June, Crete, Greece, 2003.

[320]   B. Shneiderman. The future of interactive systems and the emergence of direct manipulation. *Behaviour and Information Technology*, 1(3):237–56, 1982.

[321]   B. Shneiderman. *Designing the User Interface: Strategies for Effective Human–Computer Interaction*. Addison-Wesley, New York, 1987.

[322]   *SIGCHI Bulletin*, Special issue on video as a research and design tool, 21(2), 1989.

[323]   T. Simon. Analysing the scope of cognitive models in human–computer interaction: a trade-off approach. In D. M. Jones and R. Winder, editors, *HCI'88: People and Computers IV*, pages 79–93. Cambridge University Press, Cambridge, 1988.

[324]   R. B. Smith. The alternate reality kit – an animated environment for creating interactive simulations. In *Proceedings of Workshop on Visual Languages*, pages 99–106, Dallas, TX, June, 1986. IEEE, New York.

[325]   S. L. Smith and J. N. Mosier. Guidelines for designing user interface software. Mitre Corporation Report MTR-9420, Mitre Corporation, 1986.

[326]   R. B. Smith, T. O'Shea, C. O'Malley, E. Scanlon and J. Taylor. Preliminary experiments with a distributed, multimedia, problem solving environment. In J. M. Bowers and S. D. Benford, editors, *Studies in Computer Supported Cooperative Work*, pages 31–48. North-Holland, Amsterdam, 1991.

[327]   I. Sommerville. *Software Engineering*, 4th edition. Addison-Wesley, Wokingham, 1992.

[328]   J. M. Spivey. *The Z Notation: A Reference Manual*. Prentice Hall International, Hemel Hempstead, 1988.

[329]   M. Stefik, D. G. Bobrow, G. Foster, S. Lanning and D. Tatar. WYSIWIS revisited: early experiences with multiuser interfaces. *ACM Transactions on Office Information Systems*, 5(2):147–67, 1987.

[330]   R. Stevens and A. Edwards. Analysis of audio approaches. MATHS project, Internal report number 6, Department of Computer Science, University of York, 1994.

[331]   L. J. Stifelman. Augmenting real-world objects: a paper-based audio notebook. In *Proceedings of ACM CHI'96 Conference*, pages 199–200, April 1996. Short paper.

[332] L. J. Stifelman, B. Arons and C. Schmandt. The audio notebook: paper and pen interaction with structured speech. *Proceedings of ACM CHI 2001 Conference on Human Factors in Computing Systems*, pages 182–9, 2001.

[333] M. F. Story, J. L. Mueller and R. L. Mace. The Universal Design File: designing for people of all ages and abilities. 1998. The Center for Universal Design, North Carolina State University. Available at: http://www.design.ncsu.edu/cud/pubs/center/books/ud_file/toc3b14.htm (last accessed March 2003).

[334] L. Suchman. *Plans and Situated Actions: The Problem of Human–Machine Interaction*. Cambridge University Press, Cambridge, 1987.

[335] L. A. Suchman and R. H. Trigg. A framework for studying research collaboration. In D. Peterson, editor, *CSCW'86: Conference on Computer Supported Cooperative Work*, pages 221–8, MCC Software Technology Program, Austin, TX, December 1986. ACM Press, New York.

[336] B. Sufrin. Formal specification of a display editor. *Science of Computer Programming*, 1:157–202, 1982.

[337] Sun Microsystems, Inc. *OpenLook Graphical User Interface Application Style Guidelines*. Addison-Wesley, New York, 1990.

[338] J. A. Sutton and Ralph H. Sprague Jr. A study of display generation and management in interactive business applications. Technical Report RJ2392, IBM, 1978.

[339] TACIT: Theory and Applications of Continuous Interaction Techniques, EU TMR Network ERB FMRX CT97 0133. Available at: http://kazan.cnuce.cnr.it/TACIT/TACIThome.html

[340] J. C. Tang and Scott L. Minneman. VideoWhiteboard: video shadows to support remote collaboration. In S. P. Robertson, G. M. Olson and J. S. Olson, editors, *Reaching Through Technology – CHI'91 Conference Proceedings*, pages 315–22. Human Factors in Computing Systems, ACM Press, New York, April, 1991.

[341] L. Tauscher and S. Greenberg. How people revisit web pages: empirical findings and implications for the design of history systems. *International Journal of Human Computer Studies*, 47(1):97–138, 1997.

[342] H. W. Thimbleby. *User Interface Design*. Addison-Wesley, New York, 1990.

[343] H. Thimbleby. Design of interactive systems. In J. A. McDermid, editor, *The Software Engineer's Reference Book*, chapter 57. Butterworth–Heinemann, Oxford, 1991.

[344] H. W. Thimbleby. HyperDoc: an interactive systems tool. In M. Kirby, J. Finlay and A. Dix, editors, *HCI'95: People and Computers X*, pages 95–106. Cambridge University Press, Cambridge, 1995.

[345] J. Tidwell. Common ground: a pattern language for human–computer interface design. 1999. Available at: http://www.mit.edu/~jtidwell/common_ground_onefile.html (last accessed March 2003).

[346] M. A. Tinker. *Bases for Effective Reading*. University of Minnesota Press, Milwaukee, 1965.

[347] R. Took. Surface interaction: a paradigm and model for separating application and interface. In J. C. Chew and J. Whiteside, editors, *Empowering People –*

CHI'90 Conference Proceedings, pages 35–42. Human Factors in Computing Systems, ACM Press, New York, 1990.

[348]   R. H. Trigg. Computer support for transcribing recorded activity. *SIGCHI Bulletin*, Special issue on video as a research and design tool, 21(1):72–74, 1989.

[349]   K. N. Truong, G. D. Abowd and J. A. Brotherton. Who, what, when, where, how: design issues of capture and access applications. In *Proceedings of Ubicomp 2001*, Atlanta, GA, pages 209–24, 2001.

[350]   W. Tsukahara and N. Ward. Responding to subtle, fleeting changes in the user's internal state. *Proceedings of CHI 2001*, pages 77–84, ACM Press.

[351]   E. R. Tufte. *Envisioning Information*. Graphics Press, Cheshire, CT, 1990.

[352]   C. Turk and J. Kirkham. *Effective Writing*, 2nd edition. E. and F. N. Spon, London, 1989.

[353]   L. Tweedie, R. Spence, H. Dawkes and H. Su. Externalising abstract mathematical models. In *Proceedings of CHI'96*, pages 406–12. ACM Press, New York, 1996.

[354]   The UIMS tool developers workshop: a metamodel for the runtime architecture of an interactive system. *SIGCHI Bulletin*, 24(1):32–7, 1992.

[355]   J. van de Bos and R. Plasmeijer. Input-output tools: a language facility for interactive and real time systems. *IEEE Transactions on Software Engineering*, SE-9(3):247–59, 1983.

[356]   D. K. Van Duyne, J. A. Landay and J. I. Hong. *The Design of Sites: Patterns, Principles and Processes for Crafting a Customer-Centred Web Experience*. Addison-Wesley, Boston, MA, 2003.

[357]   G. C. Van der Veer and M. Van Welie. Task based groupware design: putting theory into practice. In *Proceedings of DIS 2000*, New York, 2000.

[358]   L. Vygotsky. The instrumental method in psychology. In J. Wertsch, editor, *The Concept of Activity in Soviet Psychology*. Sharpe, Armonk, NY, 1981.

[359]   J. H. Walker, L. Sproull and R. Subramani. Using a human face in an interface. In *Celebrating Interdependence – CHI'94 Conference Proceedings*, pages 85–91. ACM Press, New York, 1994.

[360]   P. Walsh. Analysis for task object modelling (ATOM): towards a method of integrating task analysis with Jackson system development for user interface software design. In D. Diaper, editor, *Task Analysis for Human–Computer Interaction*, pages 186–209. Ellis Horwood, Chichester, 1989.

[361]   R. Want, A. Hopper, V. Falcao and J. Gibbons. The active badge location system. *ACM Transactions on Information Systems*, 10(1):91–102, January 1992.

[362]   R. Want, B. Schilit, N. Adams, R. Gold, K. Petersen, J. Ellis, D. Goldberg and M. Weiser. The PARCTab ubiquitous computing experiment. Xerox Palo Alto Research Center, Technical Report CSL-95-1, March 1995.

[363]   R. D. Ward and P. H. Marsden. Physiological responses to different web-page designs. To appear in *International Journal of Human–Computer Studies*, special issue on Applications of Affective Computing in Human–Computer Interaction, (in press).

[364]   W. H. Warren and R. R. Verbrugge. Auditory perception of breaking and bouncing events: a case study in ecological acoustics. *Journal of Experimental Psychology: Human Perception and Performance*, 10:704–12, 1984.

[365]   P. C. Wason. Reasoning. In B. M. Foss, editor, *New Horizons in Psychology*. Penguin, Harmondsworth, 1966.

[366]   A. I. Wasserman. Extending state transition diagrams for the specification of human–computer interaction. *IEEE Transactions on Software Engineering*, SE-11(8):699–713, 1985.

[367]   A. I. Wasserman, P. A. Pircher, D. T. Shewmake and M. L. Kersten. Developing interactive information systems with the user software engineering methodology. *IEEE Transactions on Software Engineering*, SE-12(2):326–45, 1986.

[368]   K. Weber and A. Poon. Marquee: a tool for real-time video logging. In *Proceedings of ACM CHI'94 Conference*, pages 58–64, April 1994.

[369]   M. Weiser. The computer of the 21st century. *Scientific American*, 265(3):66–75, September 1991.

[370]   M. Weiser. Some computer science issues in ubiquitous computing. *Communications of the ACM*, 36(7):75–84, July 1993.

[371]   M. Weiser. The world is not a desktop. *ACM Interactions*, pages 7–8, January 1994.

[372]   M. Weiser and J. S. Brown. Designing calm technology. In *PowerGrid Journal*, http://www.ubiq.com/hypertext/weiser/calmtech/calmtech.htm, 1995.

[373]   M. Weiser, R. Gold and J. S. Brown. The origins of ubiquitous computing research at PARC in the late 1980s. *IBM Systems Journal*, 38(4):693–6, Special issue on Human–Computer Interaction: a focus on pervasive computing, 1999.

[374]   P. Wellner. Interacting with paper on the digital desk. In *Communications of the ACM*, 36(7):87–96, 1993.

[375]   A. Wexelblat. Building collaborative interfaces. CHI'91 Tutorial No. 28, 1991.

[376]   C. Wharton, J. Rieman, C. Lewis and P. Polson. The cognitive walkthrough: a practitioner's guide. In *Usability Inspection Methods*. John Wiley, New York, 1994.

[377]   J. Whiteside, J. Bennett and K. Holtzblatt. Usability engineering: our experience and evolution. In M. Helander, editor, *Handbook of Human–Computer Interaction*. North-Holland, Amsterdam, 1988.

[378]   S. Whittaker, P. Hyland and M. Wiley. Filochat: Handwritten notes provide access to recorded conversations. In *Proceedings of ACM CHI'94 Conference*, pages 271–7, April 1994.

[379]   J. S. Willans and M. D. Harrison. Verifying the behaviour of virtual world objects. In P. Palanque and F. Paternó, editors, *DSV-IS 2000 Interactive Systems: Design, Specification and Verification*. LNCS 1946, pages 65–77, Springer-Verlag, 2001.

[380]   T. Winograd. A language/action perspective on the design of cooperative work. In I. Greif, editor, *Computer-Supported Cooperative Work: A Book of Readings*, pages 623–51. Morgan Kaufmann, San Mateo, CA, 1988.

[381]   T. Winograd and F. Flores. *Understanding Computers and Cognition: A New Foundation for Design.* Addison-Wesley, New York, 1986.

[382]   P. H. Winston and S. Narasimhan. *On to Java.* Addison-Wesley, Reading, MA, 1996.

[383]   I. H. Witten, H. W. Thimbleby, G. Coulouris and S. Greenberg. Liveware: a new approach to sharing data in social networks. *International Journal of Man–Machine Studies*, 34:337–48, 1991.

[384]   C. A. Wüthrich. An analysis and model of 3D interaction methods and devices for virtual reality. In D. J. Duke and A. Puerta, editors, *DSV-IS 1999 Design, Specification and Verification of Interactive Systems.* pages 18–29, Springer-Verlag, 1999.

[385]   N. Yankelovich, B. J. Haan, N. K. Meyrowitz and S. M. Drucker. Intermedia: the concept and construction of a seamless information environment. *IEEE Computer*, pages 81–96, January, 1988.

[386]   R. M. Young and T. R. G. Green. Programmable user models for predictive evaluation of interface designs. In K. Bice and C. Lewis, editors, *Proceedings of CHI'89: Human Factors in Computing Systems*, pages 15–19. ACM Press, New York, 1989.

Index

Note: **W/E** denotes a worked exercise.